D0386005

BULIMIA: PSYCHOANALYTIC TREATMENT AND THEORY

BULIMIA: PSYCHOANALYTIC TREATMENT AND THEORY

Edited by
Harvey J. Schwartz, M.D.

International Universities Press, Inc.
Madison   Connecticut

Library of Congress Cataloging-in-Publication Data

Bulimia: psychoanalytic treatment and theory/edited by Harvey J. Schwartz.
    p. cm.
    Includes bibliographies and index.
    ISBN 0-8236-0605-8:
    1. Bulemia. 2. Anorexia nervosa. 3. Psychoanalysis.
I. Schwartz, Harvey J.
    [DNLM: 1. Bulimia—therapy. 2. Psychoanalytic Theory.
3.Psychoanalytic Therapy. WM 175 B933]
RC552.B84B85 1988
616.85'2—dc19
DNLM/DLC
for Library of Congress   87-29756
                                                   CIP

Manufactured in the United States of America

To Jan

Contents

Contributors

Maria V. Bergmann
   Training and Supervising Analyst, Faculty Emeritus, New York Freudian Society, New York.

Harold N. Boris
   Assistant Professor of Psychology, Harvard University Medical School, Cambridge, Massachusetts.

Martin A. Ceaser, M.D.
   Associate Clinical Professor of Psychiatry, Georgetown University School of Medicine, Washington, DC. Teaching Analyst, Baltimore–D.C. Institute for Psychoanalysis.

Daniel B. Gesensway, M.D.
   Clinical Associate Professor of Psychiatry, Jefferson Medical College, Thomas Jefferson University, Philadelphia, Pennsylvania. Faculty, Institute of the Philadelphia Association for Psychoanalysis.

Remi G. Gonzalez, M.D.
   Clinical Professor of Psychiatry, Tulane Medical School, New Orleans, Louisiana. Training and Supervising Analyst (Adult and Child), New Orleans Psychoanalytic Institute.

David W. Krueger, M.D.
   Clinical Associate Professor of Psychiatry, Baylor College of Medicine, Houston, Texas. Graduate, Houston–Galveston Psychoanalytic Institute.

Ira L. Mintz, M.D.
Associate Clinical Professor of Psychiatry, New Jersey College of Medicine and Dentistry, Newark, New Jersey. Supervising Child Psychoanalyst, Columbia University Psychoanalytic Training Center, New York.

Marion Michel Oliner, Ph.D.
Faculty, Psychoanalytic Training Institute, New York Freudian Society, New York.

Kent Ravenscroft, M.D.
Clinical Associate Professor, Department of Psychiatry, and Associate Director and Director of Training, Division of Child and Adolescent Psychiatry, Georgetown University School of Medicine, Washington, DC. Member, Washington Psychoanalytic Society.

Lynn Whisnant Reiser, M.D., F.A.P.A.
Associate Clinical Professor and Director of Medical Studies, Department of Psychiatry, Yale University School of Medicine, New Haven, Connecticut. Member, Western New England Psychoanalytic Society.

Harvey J. Schwartz, M.D.
Clinical Associate Professor and Director of Residency Training, Department of Psychiatry and Human Behavior, Jefferson Medical College, Thomas Jefferson University, Philadelphia, Pennsylvania.

Marjorie P. Sprince (deceased)
Former Member, British Institute for Psychoanalysis, London.

Clifford J. Tabin, Ph.D.
Fellow, Harvard Medical School, Cambridge, Massachusetts. Faculty, Massachusetts General Hospital, Boston, Massachusetts.

Johanna Krout Tabin, Ph.D.
     Faculty, Chicago Center for Psychoanalytic Psychology.

C. Philip Wilson, M.D.
     Assistant Clinical Professor of Psychiatry, Columbia College of Physicians and Surgeons, New York. Faculty, Columbia and New York University Psychoanalytic Institutes.

H. U. Ziolko, M.D.
     Director, Psychotherapeutic Division of the Psychiatric and Neurologic Hospital of the Free University of Berlin. Faculty, Berlin Psychoanalytic Institute, Berlin.

Many neurotics suffer from abnormal feelings of hunger. Women in particular are affected with this symptom. Specialists in nervous diseases are very well acquainted with those female patients who are suddenly seized with hunger in the street or other places, and must therefore take care always to have something to eat with them. Such persons habitually wake up with a gnawing hunger, and they prepare for this before going to bed by putting some food beside them. Certain characteristics of this neurotic hunger are to be noted, namely, that it has no relation to whether the stomach is full or empty, that it comes on at irregular intervals, and that it sets in like an attack with accompaniments of a harassing nature which do not belong to the normal need for nourishment, the most important of which are feelings of anxiety.

The patients complain of their "attacks of ravenous hunger". They recognize the difference between normal hunger and this "ravenous hunger", but nevertheless are inclined to confuse the two conditions with one another. They show the most violent resistances when psychoanalysis discloses the connection of their neurotic ravenous hunger with repressed libido. . . . Strong libidinal impulses, against the undisguised appearance of which consciousness protects itself, can be unusually well masked by a feeling of hunger. For hunger is a sensation that can be admitted to oneself and to others, even if it is excessive. No one, not even the patient himself, suspects from what source the neurotic symptom obtains its power. In some cases this impulse can be so strong that the patient is forced to adapt and subordinate his whole way of life to his morbid craving for food. The power that such a neurotic hunger obtains over the patient enables us to estimate the enormous strength of the repressed impulses which gain expression by this means.

Karl Abraham, "The First Pregenital Stage of the Libido" (1916)

Introduction

HARVEY J. SCHWARTZ, M.D.

The method of treatment for bulimia detailed in this volume is psychoanalytic. It is the paradigm of mental functioning that recognizes the role that the unawareness of unconscious ideation has in the formation of symptoms. It is that which is unknown to the patient, which includes the mechanisms of the unknowing, that is understood as being responsible for the syndrome of bulimia. This simple truth dictates a technique of treatment whose form and content is necessarily directed to the study of resistance and transference. Toward this end, patients' titrated regression in thinking processes is facilitated to allow the emergence of previously unrecognized aspects of self, and is met by the clinician's uniquely psychoanalytic regression in service of the other. The resultant collaboration is intimate, allegorical, and affect laden. It is the vehicle through which the complex interplay of the variety of etiologic infantile elements in bulimia may be recognized, experienced, and left behind.

In contrast, recent years have seen patients with eating disorders from all characterologic levels being treated by a rigidly phenomenologic paradigm that artificially isolates one symptom from many and from the underlying personality matrix. Reminiscent of the treatment of hysteria in Freud's day, bulimic patients today are often subjected to a variety of formats that fail to recognize the symbolic and infantile basis of the irrational. Behavior is conceptually detached from the motivational origins that give it meaning with the result that organic,

1

nutritional, and social etiologies must be invoked in order to fill the void left by the unawareness of the unconscious. Manipulative and reassuring interventions limit themselves to the conscious realm and reflect an action orientation that colludes with the patient's defensive concreteness.

A contribution to this simplification of psychopathology has been the lack of adequately presented clinical data that demonstrates the true breadth and depth of the intrapsychic material that underlies these disorders, the understanding of which leads to effective treatment. In the relative absence of detailed case material, the literature has focused on statistical studies that of necessity highlight the superficial and ignore the latent. Exceeding the important need for accurate description, this exclusive emphasis on material reality has resulted in a static phenomenology drained of clinical immediacy. The identification and categorization of increasingly minute manifest behavioral and social aspects of eating disorders has led to a caricature of understanding that obscures the essential elements of fantasy, history, and transference. Patients' phobic avoidance of their inner psychical experience is reinforced by treatment approaches that are preoccupied with the surface and hence reify resistances.

The contributors to this book have documented in detail their psychoanalytic work with a wide range of bulimic patients. They all understand this condition to be an acting out on the body of the infantile struggles variously derived from the first five years of life and reanimated in the second decade. Uniformly, the treatment employed is intensive. Their demonstration of the clinical unfolding of layers of affective understanding reveals the power in a therapeutic method that appreciates the unconscious multiple determinants of symptoms, their intertwining with character, and their derivation from the intrapsychic images of the past. Their work reveals that the evocation and affective recognition of a previously warded off inner self enables patients to supplant the automatism of the repetition compulsion with the prerogative of voluntary control. Under this conceptual umbrella, the authors approach their patients from at times differing vantage points. Rather than presenting a monolithic theoretical foundation, the chapters throughout this volume reflect the range of perspectives within psychoanalytic thought today. Much of the recent dynamic literature on eating disorders has come from the object relations school which is well represented in these pages. In addition, the structural paradigm is presented in depth with attention to the contributions from all psychosexual stages.

The differences between these models of the mind as they apply to eating disorders are considerable, as I review from the vantage point of theory in the opening chapter, "Bulimia: Psychoanalytic Perspectives." This variety of views in part derives from the well-known characterologic variability of patients within whom bulimia appears. However, it is worth recognizing that for the most part these two models are all-inclusive and make absolute claims of explanation. The first sees eating dysfunction as arising from the patient's repeated attempts to master through the use of the body the failure of their evocative memory to sustain the nurturing aspects of the practicing subphase of separation–individuation. An uncohesive maternal introject is viewed as creating the vulnerability to the crises of undifferentiated aloneness and aggression. Autonomy, therefore, represents the acme of maturation. The structural model, in contrast, emphasizes the centrality of the repression barrier and intrapsychic conflicts over, including defensive regression from, arousing oedipal impregnation fantasies. Accordingly, the infantile catastrophes associated with the drive derived wishes of incestuous genitality are seen as the stimulus for anxiety on a signal level and the impetus for the construction of compromise symptoms.

Again, at the center of controversy is the role of the Oedipus and associated castration complex as being the shibboleths of depth psychology and symptom formation. A central differentiating question is whether or not an oedipal way of experiencing the self is seen as forming an intrapsychic structuring absence when dyadic conflicts appear ascendant. Unfortunately for scientific precision, the answer to this question depends to a considerable degree on the tools of investigation utilized. Not surprisingly, the different models of the mind maintain somewhat incompatible views on the technique of neutrality, as they do on the process of neurosogenesis, and the theory of cure.

As will be reviewed in this introduction and described in detail throughout the text, the breadth of clinical and theoretical issues that are raised in the evaluation and treatment of a patient with bulimia are considerable and call upon expertise from all facets of dynamic practice. The patient's initial presentation brings with it descriptions of dramatic lapses of impulse control that appear to represent a confluence of forces from all developmental levels. Decisions on treatment selection must also take into account the meaning of the frequently accompanying weakened ability to observe and verbalize feeling states, and the associated question of fixation and regression. The symptom onset in mid- to late adolescence poses issues of young adult individuation and gender consolidation as well as the role of intrapsychic and interpersonal impingements on psychosexual progression. Parental intrusiveness, both unconscious and behavioral, is common and requires a delicate boundary setting in order to focus the patient's habitual projective mutuality into the transference. Regression from heterosexual genital fantasy is regularly deep, acted out, and self-destructive, and poses technical questions regarding the location of the interpretive surface, as well as on occasion methods of management. The encoding of fantasy into somatic discharge leads to the challenging task of retranslating a symbolic conversion that for some is also derived from precurser psychosomatic processes. Efforts to define an analyzable transference often encounter it being resisted with all the concreteness of the somatic, or else serving as a resistance with the adhesiveness of the screened oral–genital cravings. The countertransference regularly requires rigorous scrutiny as it becomes the repository of patients' warded off aggression and excitement in their reenactment of their defensive tendency to experience themselves alloplastically.

In addition to these more or less routine challenges somewhat more esoteric questions have been raised by some regarding the issue of the biology of the mind, or ultimately, the neurochemistry of the infantile neurosis. Recent double-blind controlled studies have documented the efficacy of antide-pressants—heterocyclics and monoamine oxidase inhibitors (MAOIs)—in reducing the frequency of binge eating in some patients. This important research raises the issue of the theo-retical and clinical interface between the neurosciences and psychodynamics. The ability of these two treatment modalities to bring about symptomatically similar results—with no sug-gestion implied as to an equivalency of cure—leads to provoc-ative questions of synthesis that must at the same time recognize the fundamentally differing levels of abstraction that each par-adigm represents. Although based in unique and not inter-changeable systems of meaning, description, data gathering, and verification, it appears that synaptic neurochemical alter-ations relate to interpretively reorganized compromise forma-tions at least on the level of symptom alteration. The possibility that there ultimately exists a physical denominator common to and representative of both sciences is an intriguing possibility that is, however, not immediately relevant to the focus of this volume.

There are some investigators who suggest that pharma-cotherapy and psychotherapy, like cake ingredients, may simply be added to each other in the expectation that more is better and that the sum is greater than the parts. Examination of their research, however, reveals the interpersonal focus of their psy-chotherapy—a treatment model that for the most part could not be expected itself to resolve symptoms and character mal-formations that have intrapsychic origins. Accordingly, medi-cations would be called for in their work to address symptoms whose etiology is specifically avoided by their paradigm. The issue then remains if there is any place for the simultaneous use of biologic and interpretive interventions. This question as-sumes that the disguising elements of compromise that are cre-ating the symptom are in fact interpretively inaccessible in a field carefully cleared of obscuring counterresistances. Fine tuning this question entails discriminating between analysis and psychotherapy, differentiating between the transference object being the prescription giver or not, and fundamentally whether the giving of a medication is a parameter that may be analyzed out of contamination even if it continues to be administered.

These issues are not directly addressed in this book. They remain perhaps for the next generation of psychoanalytically informed studies on the eating disorders to explore. Here the role of unconscious fantasy in the neurosogenesis of bulimia is investigated independent of its neurochemical correlates. The wealth of data revealed by the psychoanalytic method of investigation itself remains a formidable storehouse of information the understanding of which is of inordinate value to those who work with these patients.

The absence of any awareness of emotionally derived inner cravings that is characteristic of many patients with eating disorders had led object relations investigators to conclude that these patients' concreteness is more real than apparent. The paradigm suggests that the advanced psychic circuitry of symbolization has not taken form in these patients with the result that symptoms are understood to be fantasyless semiliteral reenactments of the separation–individuation drama. The ubiquitous and grave body image distortions are seen as a direct toxic precipitate from the failed mother–infant mixture with unmetabolized remnants of the mother's own past being replayed in the new version of her own unsuccessful individuation. The mother's necessary access to a historically derived inner soothing symbiosis places at the foundation of this seemingly new relationship the artifacts from earlier generations' motherings.

Krueger presents the object relations perspective on eating disorders in "Body Self, Psychological Self, and Bulimia: Developmental and Clinical Considerations" and takes into account the recent research into the building blocks of later structure formation. The early unconscious reverberations between mother and infant are shown to have a lasting influence on future development with particular impact on the nascent body boundaries of the child. Transient blurring on the mother's part of the distinction between self and other is a usual and essential contribution to the symbiotic period where the infant exists psychically through her narcissistic mirroring. The mother's syntonic continuation of this state, however, leads to confusion between the distinctness of her own infantile urges and those of her now separating child, and portends later disturbances in self–other differentiation and the capacity for symbolization. It is the titrated absence of the empathic mother who separates from her child in a delicate parallel dance that allows the child to create an inner metaphorical realm freed from the malformations of unstructuralized rage.

Krueger finds that in eating disorder patients, it is the chronic struggle with a semisymbolic activity–passivity circularity that accounts for the defective as-if functioning. Access to verbalizable fantasies are accordingly limited, with action and somatic expression of affect predominating. The body is not imbued with a history that can be recollected; the past is always now, and food is equated with the failed mothering of infancy. Maturation of body image cannot take place for lack of a self that exists through time. Feeding oneself, therefore, never has the possibility of enriching the variety of moods and settings that give a satisfying complexity to life. Krueger concludes that bulimia is an addictive quest for a magical need-satisfying and aggression-stifling fullness which, by virtue of its counterfeit literalness, stands in the way of a genuinely soothing self-empathy.

Freud's recognition of the limitations of the hypnotic and cathartic techniques led to his discovery of the psychoanalytic method of treatment. Initially this was a procedure designed to overcome conscious suppression in an effort to free the newly recognized instincts from their transformation into anxiety. During this period, patients with anorexia nervosa, like others, were subjected to direct id interpretations of their impregnation wishes. Advances in analytic technique have long since led to a focus on the analytic surface and defense analysis which allows patients greater affective immediacy in their discovery of the infantile content of their transference wishes.

The advances in appreciating the side of the ego in intrapsychic conflict led to an understanding of signal anxiety and its ability to exert regression-inducing back pressure. In

recent years, attention has been focused by some on those patients for whom pregenital conflicts exert their own backward
pull and are not initially accessible affectively from the oedipal
side, positive or negative. Sprince describes the challenges of
working with these patients who also have eating disorders in
her chapter, "Experiencing and Recovering Transitional Space
in the Analytic Treatment of Anorexia Nervosa and Bulimia."

Sprince finds that for these patients the fantasied all-heal-
ing merger with the idealized nurturant mother is filled with
such desperation, with consequent danger of terrifying engulfment and abandonment, that they turn to the deadening
solution of ascetic self-sufficiency in order to deny an interpersonal vacuum that could be filled with desire. A grandiose
spirituality is invoked to safely express the now denuded aggression while the patient projects her own neediness onto the surrounding mortals. Parents, friends, analyst are stimulated to
want her to eat–live–love—she herself remains without such
desires. Sprince suggests that the binge–purge compulsion represents the negated longing to ingest that leads to a repetitively
failed encounter with the object neither as fully separate nor
safely internalized.

Sprince concludes that some patients, in a setting created
by some therapists, are able to approach, explore, and survive
the "crucial phase in the treatment of anorexic and overeating
patients . . . when they find themselves experiencing their analyst as if she were the part they feel to be missing in themselves,
the part that they can no longer replace by food or concentration on it, or their body image" (p. 72). Working through this
presumptively unsurvivable experience of transference creates
for the patient first an analytic and from that an intrapsychic
transitional space that ideally allows development to proceed,
the presence of father to be acknowledged, and further structuralized conflict involving whole and distinct inner objects to
be addressed. Until that point, one is often left for long periods
of time forced to tolerate in the countertransference patients'
disavowed and projected neediness and rage as they turn to
action in an effort to cope with the unnamed urges. With these

patients, enactment quite regularly precedes insight, for therapist and patient alike.

The therapist's availability as both the object and observer of patients' intrapsychic fantasies allows for joint study of these genetically charged paradigms that fuse the present with the past. For some, however, the distinctness of self that these object-directed concerns take for granted is lacking, with the result that separateness is associated with torment. Boundaries are drawn in such a way that frustration, and hence distinctiveness, is impossible. If necessary, objects qua objects are turned to in order to fill in when internal imagoes are psychically unavailable as reciprocators. Food, as a bridge between inside and outside, may be put in service to continue to blur an innerness whose definition would, among other anticipated catastrophes, leave mother on her own.

Boris, in "Torment of the Object: A Contribution to the Study of Bulimia," describes the necessity of reversing this process of desymbolization in the context of his early encounter with the family of a bulimic woman. The interpersonal treatment arena revealed the repository nature of the family's interactions, with each member both projecting and introjecting affects in a matrix forestalling autonomy and inner conflict. As a result of the insistence with which family members used each other to express their unconscious wishes, and the psychic impermeability that derived from the caricatured relatedness, the individual psychoanalytic treatment of the patient was undertaken.

In progressing from an interpersonal to an intrapsychic treatment setting, Boris found that a consequent change in his own inner frame was required. His prior actual encounter with the external attributes of his patient's inner objects necessitated in him an intentional decathexis of their outer characteristics in order to open himself to the potential mystery in his patient's associative experience. This expanding of his ego to permit him to take liberties with his perception of external objects introduced the same crucial task for the patient. This maturation of relatedness beyond the seductive literalness of physical representations revealed the patient's use of others as containers specifically for that which was without coherence in herself. Accordingly, free association in the context of an alliance was replaced by verbalization functioning as transferential acting in. Reflecting in part her family's unconscious communication pattern, self-awareness was experienced as an alloplastic process. Boris finds, therefore, that the translation of the inter-personalized affect, if it is to occur, takes place in the counter-transference. The therapeutic task then becomes to tolerate the boundless reciprocity which is demanded while intrapsychically metabolizing the projected poisonous rage into interpretations digestible to the patient. In time the patient's warded off in-nerness began to be experienced as the point of origin for that which had been responded to reactively. This set the stage for a future that contained the possibility of recognizing her own desires unprojected.

Patients' transferences to the therapist begin at the point that they first entertain the idea of entering treatment. In parallel, one's own study of and counterreactions to the patient are initiated with the call for an appointment. From that moment, the evaluation process begins with the employment of an increasingly microscopic lens focused on all facets of the patient's physical demeanor, form of interaction, associative linkages, and finally content of anamnesis. History taking reveals the past complexity of object relations, the extent of the ego's involvement in its defensive efforts, tolerance for frustration, and zealousness of superego injunctions, to name but a few of the many measurable indices of ego capacities. Of particular importance to the subject at hand is the gauging of the extent and quality of the urgency attached to the quick removal of presenting symptoms. While this diagnostic assessment is not entirely free from interpersonal subjectivity and is itself a poor relation to the ultimate determination based on the patient's ability to develop, sustain, and observe a regressive transference neurosis, it is an essential component of the determination of the treatment of choice—what has come to be known as differential therapeutics.

As Ceaser describes in "Anorexia Nervosa and Bulimia: An Integrated Approach to Understanding and Treatment," the ritualized monotony of the binge–purge symptom complex is in fact the final common pathway for a wide range of organic and psychological disorders. On the functional side, a careful dynamic diagnostic evaluation will distinguish between those patients for whom the eating disorder represents an ego defect and those in whom it is a compromise solution for intrapsychic conflict. This determination enables one to appropriately make available to the characterologically incapacitated patient a range of supportive measures—including antidepressants, suppression strengthening cognitive counseling, displacement reinforcing nutritional advice—with minimal risk of iatrogenic infantilization. Ceaser finds that for these patients their experience of fragility is not the product of conflicted fantasies and as such should be treated with auxiliary ego supports.

In contrast, there are patients in whom an apparent quality of as-if emptiness with mimicry of others for definition, in fact represents but another of the unconscious ego's compromise efforts to remain unaware of and unaccountable for underlying drive fantasies. Accordingly, a classically interpretive defense analysis is indicated with particular attention to phallic level conflicts. Building upon the child analytic work that describes an early phallic phase, Ceaser documents the latent meanings to be found underlying many of the manifest character and symptom configurations in higher functioning eating disorder patients. In the clinical material, he finds that the patient's acted out obsession with an asexually thin physique represented a behavioral elaboration of bisexual fantasies; that is, of her conflicted wish to be both phallic and pregnant. Similarly, passive fears of being violated derived from retroflexed castrating wishes and, through a self-punitive identification with the victim of her own aggression, abandonment concerns substituted for her hostility. Ceaser describes that the commonly encountered preoccupation in these patients with issues of seeing/being seen and of body comparisons and flaws represents the recrudescence of the infantile overevaluation of the phallus, typical of the young girl. He concludes that, unlike the sicker bulimic, these patients' vacillating conflicts over phallic aggressive and feminine receptive fantasies can be both elaborated in and contained by a transference neurosis, the working through of which frees from guilt-derived inhibition the creative potentials of the sexual and aggressive strivings.

Time defines the barrier that separates the child from the gratification of its longings. To wait is to give temporary credence to this boundary while maintaining the expectation that the future promises relief. The wait contains the insisted upon control over destiny where oral deprivation is to be sated, castration undone, and father finally won from mother. Sleeping Beauty waits passively forever to be sexually awakened by her hero. In contrast, waiting also serves as an expression of aggressive and destructive impulses; that is, killing time. Patients' time-consuming ruminations and doubts over eating manifest their violent ambivalence between activity and passivity, and suggest the magnitude of the satisfaction they are awaiting.

Some symptomatic patients turn to treatment when patience has all but been exhausted. The transference becomes the final hope for a reversal of fortune where to be made to wait any longer is felt to be unbearable. The lifelong problem of time is finally to be solved in the timelessness of the expected infantile gratification. In the opening phase of treatment where the peculiar conditions of evocative abstinence are first encountered, such patients are confounded to find that yet again they are to face the rageful frustrations of the past. Mintz details in "Self-Destructive Behavior in Anorexia and Bulimia" the many forms of defense that represent patients' sadism, and outlines technical approaches to their titrated introduction to consciousness. Passive defiance in the transference presents a formidable resistance that needs interpretation from both the side of the ego as well as the id, but most importantly from a consistent position of empathic neutrality. As a priority, unconscious guilt must be addressed before the defenses against aggression in an effort to forestall a negative therapeutic reaction. The syntonicity of patients' self-destructiveness is a reminder that the superego knows of the id while the ego does

not. As Mintz documents, interpretation of the multiple behavioral and psychic manifestations of patients' guilt-derived
self-punitiveness establishes an alliance capable of observing the
increasingly dystonic search for punishment. This leads the
patient to become curious about the meaning of the affects that
have been displaced onto eating.

The successful analysis of the guilt underlying binging
often leads to higher level compromise formations that now
express the aggression in more symbolic form; that is, phobias.
This projection of a rage that the patient cannot acknowledge
but can only suffer has always been present in the helplessness
and impotence imposed upon those around her. It may further
emerge in the transference in feelings of persecution which
may in part originate from the effect of the parents' failure to
adequately neutralize their own hostility. Careful identification
of the patient's prohibitive injunctions that lead to the turning
on the self of sadistic impulses allows for their undoing and
with it the opening to awareness of the additionally retroflexed
libidinal wishes. As Mintz demonstrates, the paradox of analytic
treatment with its open-ended format that is simultaneously
limited to carefully defined session times establishes in form
the therapeutic conditions for the affective evocation of infantile aggressive fantasies as well as their integration into a secondary process level of meaningful insight.

The concrete and ritualized food preoccupations of eating
disorder patients has a tendency to create a parallel process of
counterresistance that focuses one's attention to the manifest
level of observation. When a dynamic perspective is maintained,
patient's deadening of fantasy and frenzied self-stimulation are
understood as defensive attempts through action disguises to
solve seemingly insurmountable developmental tasks. The recognition that conflicted inner passions underly and are contained in these symptomatic outbursts is a crucial initial
conceptual and therapeutic step in discovering their meaning,
origin, and need for masking. As has been the case for close
to 100 years, while agreement is easily reached over the presence of the defensive mechanisms themselves, that which is

being warded off and is initiating such obfuscations remains less accessible, and, hence, the subject of greater debate. In eating disorder patients in particular, the at times confusing simultaneous presence of conflicts over separateness from mother and sexuality toward father has reinforced the theoretical dichotomization that emphasizes one or the other of these characteristics.

Tabin and Tabin, in "Bulimia and Anorexia: Understanding Their Gender Specificity and Their Complex of Symptoms," present a reformulation derived from clinical data, their own and others, that reflects an integrating theoretical position. They find that the conflicts of these patients fit parsimoniously neither in the usual separation–individuation models that minimize the importance of early sexual urges, nor in the classical oedipal paradigm that insists that defensive regression alone accounts for the common ego fragility one finds in otherwise triangularly engaged patients. They conclude that these patients are indeed struggling against the emergence of erotic fantasies but are doing so with a disabling desperateness uncharacteristic of most neurotics and indicative of deficiencies in their synthesizing capacity. They feel that this is due to the early age and ego consolidation from which these sexual urges are originating; that is, that they derive from the two- to three-year-old stage and not the more integrated four- to six-year-old period. Accordingly, for bulimics, sexuality is enmeshed with the vicissitudes of individuation and is imbued with the primitiveness, of drive and retaliation danger, of the barely structuralized omnipotent thinking of that phase.

Introducing the concept of triangular sexual urges at the toddler stage clarifies for Tabin and Tabin the origin of the gender specificity of eating disorders. This rivalrous dimension to the two-year-old's relationship with her mother complicates her already difficult phase specific struggles with her which involve, simultaneously, centrifugal surges toward separation and centripetal needs for closeness in service of gender identification and modeling. These tasks, unique to the development of the girl, put considerable strain on her dependency–self-actualization equilibration and add a far-reaching fragility to the integration of her early sexual feelings. Accordingly, the Hobson's choice she often faces is to remain aware of her developing autonomous erotism at the risk of perceived retaliatory abandonment or to maintain her intimacy with mother at the cost of her sexuality. This painful dilemma is one that is regularly encountered in the clinical work with adult eating disorder patients. Tabin and Tabin report that their reformulation adds precision to one's interpretive focus in the all-important technical effort to cope with and understand patients' terror motivated action resistances that are regularly invoked when these instinctual wishes come alive in the transference.

The toddler's discovery that she can obtain pleasure on and by herself is a cornerstone of development characteristic of the anal phase. As master of the fecal object, the child is now able to reverse the earlier physical helplessness, undifferentiated neediness, and object dependency of the oral period and proclaim autonomy and authority on her new throne. Sadistic and controlling impulses are in the ascendency during this time, the integration and neutralization of which are essential in order for the later genital phase in the girl to be one where receptivity is freed from its castrating analogue and romantic conquest can activate the cherishing of the object as opposed to endangering it.

The failure to overcome the anal sadistic urges and their reinforcement by the retreat from the consequently perceived sadomasochism of the genital period leads to an analization of object relations and an intensified blurring of the mouth–anus–vagina equation. As an orifice common to both sexes, analized conflicts are additionally turned to in order to relieve the turmoil associated with the inequalities of the phallic phase. Despite the appearance of oral factors in binge eating, Oliner describes in "Anal Components in Overeating" its essential anal elements, derived from both fixation and regression, reflecting its nonnurturant goals. Clinical data on a behavioral level reveals a preoccupation with food viewed as junk, expelling rituals focused on the toilet, laxative abuse, and compulsive collecting. Underlying these findings one discovers an inner world filled with bad fecalized objects, the aggressive devouring of which is in the service of establishing absolute control, separateness from mother, and protection against a penetrable emptiness. Compulsive eating, which abolishes the object and places it inside to be manipulated, functions to homogenize, as opposed to differentiate, the multiple meanings of that which is consumed in order to reduce it, like feces, to the lowest controllable denominator. Object-directed wishes for the phallus and baby are intentionally drained of value in the anal–sadistic incorporative process which regressively covets only mastery and self-sufficiency.

As Oliner notes, the position of anality midway between self and object love facilitates the bulimic's retreat to the safety of narcissistic nonrelatedness which serves to sidestep the aggression and erotism which accompany the recognition of the sexual and generational differences. Narcissistically, inner fullness passes for camaraderie. Anal–sadistic turned-on-self preoccupations with control and independence undo outer directed competitiveness with mother and libidinization of the vagina for father, and prevent the transformation of the consumed fecal object into a full-fledged inner phallus–baby. Object-directed genital fantasies and arousal are unavailable to energize a sublimated feminine exhibitionism as the vagina remains a castrating anal orifice regressively capable only of displaying ugliness and badness. The binge compulsion dirties the woman's potential cavity erotism as it turns the body into a receptacle for a devalued fecal object which in turn permeates the self-image with disgust.

The neurotic process entails the transfiguration of conflicted unconscious oedipal-derived fantasies into manifest level character and symptom compromise formations. The disguising process of passing through the metaphor creating repression barrier entails more or less equivalent participation by all three psychic structures and reveals the ubiquitous presence and functioning of the incest taboo. Both valences of the oedipal scenario emerge in the analytic field and demonstrate the unique organizing and symbolizing capacity of this phase in the creation and consolidation of neurotic conflicts and symptoms. Prephallic strivings may contribute by becoming regressively infused with oedipal intent all the while acting in search of relief from the anticipated catastrophes of the triangular scenario.

As I discuss in "Bulimia and the Mouth–Vagina Equation: The Phallic Compromise," for many patients the binge–purge symptom complex represents the final common pathway for the expression of the universal dilemmas of the phallic–oedipal period. Reactivated in the adolescent turmoil of intensified genitality, the unresolved unconscious questions of childhood sexuality—Where do babies come from? What is the difference between a girl and a boy? What do mommy and daddy do in bed at night?—lead to a failure to integrate a relatively conflict-free heterosexual body image and adaptation. For the young woman with bulimia, a defensive and defiant persistence of phallic bisexuality is revealed in the narcissism of body–phallus grandeur, the repudiation of receptivity through expulsive tendencies, and the displacement of vaginal cathexes via the mouth–vagina equation.

In the treatment situation, the dangers associated with the awareness of object-directed drive organized desires regularly activate superego and narcissistic resistances. In eating disorder patients, the body is turned to not only as a masturbatory displacement for transference wishes, but in the service of a retreat from genitality itself. Receptive erotic ideation is infiltrated with an overstimulating violence which interferes with the creation and definition of an inner genital nucleus that can tolerate both the excitement and disappointment of oedipal strivings. Accordingly, gender-polarized fantasy is drained of content and is instead narcissistically condensed on the body leading to an automated self-abuse that represents the defensively neutered identification with both sides of the sadomasochistic encounter. This inability to unconsciously compliment the phallic oedipal father with a partially neutralized expectant femininity leads to the defensive deflection of inner desire onto the periphery of the body with an emphasis on exteriorized beauty and motoric hyperactivity. Regressively, somatic perfection, not love, becomes the goal. The task of first enlarging the self-curiosity of the patient and then discovering with her the individual fantasy-based drive determinants of her symptomatic condensation is a challenging and not always completed process. The potential yield for her in uncovering and coming to take pleasure in a femininity that is able to remain unshaken by, and indeed is enriched through the encounter with its oedipal origins makes the task worth undertaking.

The continuous construction of intrapsychic compromise formations characterizes normal mental functioning throughout the lifespan. The creative synthesis of genetically derived instinctual wishes with their defensive counterweights leads to the complexity of character configuration that is the hallmark of adaptive psychic functioning. Within the limitless variety of potential fantasy paradigms, key developmental stages organize the child's perception of its relation with others and form a lasting unconscious nucleus around which adult functioning orbits. For the young girl, the fantasy-imbued meaning of her emergent concave erotism with its stimulating relativity to the oedipal father's phallus can serve as a source of a deeply pleasurable femininity or tragically as a lifelong stimulus for regressive self-punishment.

A measure of the success of the girl's syntonic integration of her genitality is her ability to transform her infantile impregnation wishes into an esteem enhancing feminine object seeking. As Gesensway describes in "A Psychoanalytic Study of Bulimia and Pregnancy," this maturation may come to include conscious wishes to be pregnant, the absence of which, however, comments not at all on the presence of underlying unconscious impregnation fantasies. Character shaping derivatives of instinctual wishes are not necessarily connected to their manifest proclamation, positive or negative. It is when the latent impregnation fantasies have failed to be assimilated into the ego and ego ideal that they make their appearance in disguised symptomatic form, often as bulimia. In that case, upward displacement, negation, and regression are turned to in a defensive effort to cope with the guilt-filled excitement of the chronically conflicted oedipal wishes for father's child. All the distortions of the childhood theories of sexuality are revealed unchanged in the otherwise rational adult, so long as a technique geared to their recognition is utilized.

Gesensway distinguishes between the analytic and nonanalytic conceptualizations of pathogenesis and stresses the essential metaphorical basis of eating, and for that matter, all other symptomatology. Accordingly, the supposed reality traumata of early deprivation, conscious attitudes toward dieting, and concerns over cultural imperatives to be thin, all, like food itself, have little to do with psychical reality and the elements of compromise of which bulimia is the outcome. As detailed in the clinical material, these manifest issues are screen representations of underlying fantasies that originate in the conflicted neurosogenic passions and prohibitions of oedipal sexuality. Gesensway concludes that unchanged since Freud's time, and before, and with the constancy of the dreamwork, conflicts over unconscious infantile fantasies of incestuous sexuality and impregnation remain at the core of much human suffering.

The creativity from which constructive labor is born is based on an aggressiveness relatively free from self-destructive mimicry or compensatory self-aggrandizement. For both male and female, the successful capacity to work relies on a neutralized phallic self-concept that primarily seeks neither rivalrous domination nor narcissistic self-sufficiency. The unconscious meaning of the product of one's labors associates with bisexual images of intake–output, activity–passivity, and autonomy –dependency. Learning represents the mastery of secondary process adaptation and, as with all ego functions, may itself become reinstinctualized and intertwined in conflict. All the components of effective study–work (i.e., seeing, thinking, producing, showing) represent the sublimated triumph of eros over aggression and as such are inherently liable to be reanimated with the gender specific meanings with which they were originally endowed.

For the woman, an active work self that is evolved beyond a defensive masculine identification is based, in part, on access to an internalized heterosexually distinct father whose phallic attributes are comfortably recognized as complimentary. An underlying tolerance for gratification delay is what allows for the transformation of initial insistent object demands into neutralized identifications that activate the potential for the subtle gratifications of gradual understanding, synthesis, and creation. This capacity depends, as Bergmann describes in "On Eating Disorders and Work Inhibition," on an early formative experience with mother where both parties come to transcend the use of the body to express frustration and aggression. In contrast, for the child in an environment marked by oscillating overindulgence and excessive denial, a special intimacy with mother is formed such that urgency contaminates curiosity, learning is distorted by perfectionism, and anticipation evokes abandonment. For the child, time fails to define a future where mastery promises joy. Productivity comes to be imitative and pseudoprecocious as it is in service of mother's narcissistic needs for display, while a creativity that is a harbinger of autonomy is linked with rage-filled emptiness.

Bergmann finds that the intrusion into the oedipal period of the earlier turned-on-self hostility intensifies the later triangular anxieties whose mastery is additionally essential for the development of pride in both one's body and body of work. The retreat to the acting out on the body of the externally concretized conflicts of the binge–purge syndrome quite regularly entails a parallel incapacity to consume and digest knowledge capable of enriching self-definition. Both symptoms entail the giving up of an aggressivized fragile independence and competence in deference to the rivalrous and abandoning mother. In the clinical material, the deformed child that the patient's aborted work represented was a product of the loathing and guilt of her frustrated oral and incestuous yearnings. The unresolved early surgical malformation of the patient's body image contributed to a defect in her ability to conceive of herself as a container and producer of that which is splendid. Her ambivalence toward her perceived unattuned mother and rage at father for his rejection of her, distorted her capacities for benevolent self-observation and led to a work inhibition that reflected a self-punitive rumination with repairing in herself that which she fantasied to be damaged. Bergmann finds that for many work-inhibited bulimics, early maternally evoked conflicts over intake and elimination persist, and link the patient addictively to the omnipotent phallic mother of childhood allowing for the development of only an imposter version of sublimated self-expression. She concludes that ideally the work of analysis itself becomes the new battleground so that through the progressive metabolization of the now abstracted transference neurosis, the patient can come to create and define the capacity for pleasure in the body and its sublimated products.

The changing cultural influences affecting women today have become a focus of study in an effort to understand the recent increases in eating disorder symptomatology. A limitation to this approach lies in the ambiguity and hence seductiveness of the social scene to act as a surface upon which is often projected investigators' own unconscious fantasies which are then discovered in the form of external reality. The defensive attractiveness of this opportunity to externalize one's unconscious past weakens the observational power of most culturally based models. The inevitable cross-fertilization between that which is outside oneself and the veil of inner fantasy through which it is perceived limits the arenas of productive study to those designed to recognize the screening function of sociologic findings.

A properly conducted treatment is able to produce data on those external forces that are discovered to exist independent of infantile motivational needs. The ability of these outside conditions to influence the form of contemporary intrapsychic compromise formations is determinable from a comparison of analytic data from previous generations with that of today. As Reiser documents in "Love, Work, and Bulimia," the intrapsychic present is more similar to the past than different. Her clinical findings from a high-functioning bulimic woman reveals the impact of puberty on the unconscious conflicts over heterosexual identity and gender consolidation that were well known to our forebears. This significant finding informs us that to the extent that changes in the outside world at all influence symptom expression—and the greater incidence of bulimia today supports the conclusion that they do—it appears that it is effected through the distorting overemphasis on particular developmental phases that otherwise participate in a relatively fluid psychosexual progression. The adult patient presented evidences an overvaluation of phallic attributes that more usually represents a transient preoccupation of the phallic level child and early to midadolescent. Reiser raises the possibility that it may be more than a coincidence that the current cultural ideal for women, as it was for the flappers of the 1920s, is the phallic superwoman.

This bisexual metaphor is demonstrated to be a crystallization of multiply determined progressive and regressive inner images that similarly inform and reflect cultural ambivalences toward the fully feminine woman. Its suspension between the intrapsychic and interpersonal realms derives from its noncommittal position between the two sexes. A gender specific self-concept that is no longer cued by external stereotyping can be empowered by the interpretive resolution of the infantile basis of the retreat from femininity. Links with one's unconscious infantile past break the dependency on outside cultural distortions and can be formed, as Reiser demonstrates, through the analysis of a patient's dreamlike use of seemingly simple childhood lyrics. The interpretive understanding of these bridges between past and present converges the latent with the manifest and thereby dispenses with the symptomatic amnesia of socially interactive acting out. The resultant distinctiveness of sexual identity is able to define a coherent personal self in relation to which social forces may then be observed undistorted.

Biological maturation at puberty reawakens the dormant drives of latency and begins a host of structural changes, physical and psychic. Genital development introduces the frightening new capability of consummating incestuous fantasies and is anxiously responded to by the uniquely irreversible turn toward external objects. This decathexis of infantile imagoes initially entails a midadolescent period of heightened narcissism that imbues the body with all the attentiveness that had been vested in the idealized parents. This phase of intensive self-involvement is characterized by hypochondriacal concerns, ascetic and intellectual grandiosity, and projections of one's idealized self onto interchangeable heroes. If a life rich in object relatedness is to be achieved, this period of incubating autonomy must progress in late adolescence to include an investment in others through the medium of a sexually distinct gender identity. Homoerotic attachments come to be relegated to the ego ideal allowing, with superego sanction, the acting out in reality of the gender-polarized impulses derived originally from the phallic–oedipal period.

The catastrophes associated with the realization of the necessarily incompletely neutralized oedipal wishes adds a poignant fragility to the late adolescent's object seeking and leads to frequent regressions to narcissistic pseudo self-sufficiency. Gonzalez reports in "Bulimia and Adolescence: Individual Psychoanalytic Treatment" on the centrality of these conflicted incestuous wishes in the etiology of adolescent eating disorders, and comments on the technical difficulties that arise from the ready availability of the earlier action modes of conflict resolution. Provocations to be managed instead of analyzed are common and reflect resistance to a transference that is feared as overstimulating. The not remembered past which is being relived in the symptomatic outbursts becomes enacted in the transference resistance and requires of the therapist a high degree of tolerance for impulsivity in order to avoid the temptation to strike back. Metabolizing analytically the out-of-control action storms, in favorable cases, yields a new investment in memory that can tentatively initiate an observing response to transference urges.

Gonzalez finds that the manifest oral aspects of eating symptomatology are not a dependable indicator of the level of regression or fixation. In some patients, the presence of intact constant inner objects and repetitive triangular engagements indicates latent phallic–oedipal conflicts, regression from which is achieved through initially syntonic defenses. The press of instinctual impulses in bulimia tends to reinforce the ego's inclination to not observe its own unconscious resistances, which are in themselves neither conflicted nor emergent. The persistent analysis though of the multiple methods by which anxiety is warded off can carve out a self-awareness of the otherwise automatic defensive maneuvers and can come to include a tolerance for the content that is exerting the back pressure. Gonzalez describes clinically that in many adolescents with eating disorders, it is the tension in the perceived forbidden genital and rivalrous fantasies that is the stimulus for the symptomatic regression. Their analysis, he concludes, can yield a character enriching capacity for drive gratification and neutralization, as well as a cure for bulimia.

The narcissistic investment in the physical changes of adolescence reawakens in some the shared digestive–body intimacies with mother from early childhood. The difficulty these patients have in using the new augmenting genital energies to carve out a progressive self-definition derives not only from regression-inducing oedipal rivalries, but also from parental inability to tolerate maturational affects in the child that invoke their own unresolved infantile conflicts. In years past, simultaneous analyses of parent and child revealed the pathogenic pull of parental unconscious fantasy in maintaining the child in a regressive libidinal position that she herself was only marginally in need of. The parents' recapitulation of their own oedipal and preoedipal aggressions now cast the child as either a devalued aspect of themselves or an ambivalent past object and leads to the empowering of hostile fantasy with an historical magicalness that demands a clingy connectedness to undo. The overstimulating reality of mother's own death wishes interferes with her ability to form for the child a subliminatory pathway for hostile impulses. This reifies for both partners the calamitous anticipation that if the daughter is strong enough to separate from her, she is strong enough to be her rival. The daughter's aggression becomes the stimulus for an upsurge in the mother's defenses against her own hatred, with the child then becoming special by virtue of the guilt felt in relation to her. In these cases where the child's symptoms are additionally held in place by powerful emotional forces in the parents, treatment of the parents is often essential in freeing the child to experience her conflicts autoplastically.

In recent years, this recognition of the role of unconscious parental gratification in maintaining children's psychopathology has led to the development of a psychoanalytic family therapy paradigm that maintains the appreciation of the essential infantile basis of current conflicts. As Ravenscroft describes in "Psychoanalytic Family Therapy Approaches to the Adolescent Bulimic," the recognition of the transferential basis of family distortions deepens the family systems notion of enmeshment to include an awareness of the content of the unconscious object-directed strivings that are being defensively disavowed in the pseudocohesiveness of the group. Ravenscroft maintains the centrality of the concept of primary gain as he documents the regressively spiraling family disequilibrium that results from the convergence of adolescent sexuality with parental overstimulating vicariousness. Clinically, it is demonstrated that the daughter's developmentally commonplace beating fantasies transcend ideation into action in proportion to the degree that parental oedipal excitement crosses the generational barrier. Ill-defined interpersonal boundaries produce and are a product of a simultaneously amorphous and overrigid repression barrier, as well as pathological projective identification.

The patient's projection of ideal aspects of herself onto her mother and the agreed upon internalization of both partners' badness led to breakthroughs of voracious binging on all the goodness that was kept outside of herself for safekeeping. Ravenscroft concludes that the absence of an early holding environment had led to a defective capacity to integrate an internally consistent and benevolent self-identity leaving her at the mercy of her split hostile inner objects. The inner spoiling of the consumed goodness by the guilt-filled hatefulness is seen as having led to an emergency purging-reprojection of the incompatible aspects of self, and mirrored the family's projection of their own badness onto the outside world. This paranoid avoidance of outsiders—a rigid family/nonfamily boundary in association with a blurred intrafamily generational boundary —encouraged the patient's midadolescent collapse back into the

increasingly sexualized family unit. Phase specific hatching into
a safe outside world was inhibited in part by the parental need
to possess the daughter for their own oedipal drama, as well
as to keep her as a repository for their intergenerationally transmitted hostile inner objects.

   The refusal by the ego to acknowledge an association with
presumptively dangerous drive fantasies leads to the construction of symptoms designed to strengthen that unawareness.
The success of a symptom is determined by its ability to sidestep
anxiety while coalescing in holographic form all the contributing elements from the underlying fantasies, countercathectic
mechanisms, and penitent rituals. An ever deepening defensive
investment by the ego is demanded by the persistence of the
anticipation of calamity despite the initial attempts at gratification displacement. This leads to a multiplication of symptoms
whose origin only appears to be further removed from the key
neurosogenic fantasies. Shifting patterns of somatic discharge,
acting out, and symbolized inhibitedness all are interchangeable
constructions by the ego in its dynamic efforts to contain that
which it keeps itself ignorant of. Accordingly, short of life-
threatening self-destructiveness, no one symptom warrants
greater analytic scrutiny than any of the alternating disguises,
and similarly the disappearance of any one compromise formation promises no greater adaptive capacity so long as underlying conflicts remain unaddressed and hence empowered
to disable.
   A properly conducted analysis of resistances evokes early
patterns of infantile fantasy and a deepening recognition of the
methods of defense. The consequent introduction of the transference object into the inner life of the patient creates the condition whereby the fantasies of that relationship can now
become the observable stimulus for the formation of symptoms.
Wilson, in "Bulimic Equivalents," describes the fluidity of displacements, from binging to weeping to wheezing, that reflect
the desperate disguises of genetic affects in forms that come to
serve as a resistance to the transference. Their function of turning object directed wishes onto the body derives from early

childhood channels of somatic compliance contributed to by parental preoccupations with an unmetaphorically endowed soma. Intrapsychically, the difficulty in maintaining these fantasies in a state of suspended observation, or readiness for transference, leads to their discharge in multiple and often sequential symptoms that indicate the superego's intolerance for the ego observing itself.

Wilson's work reveals that it is only in appearance that unpleasant affects arise secondary to symptoms. He demonstrates that the depression that follows a binge is but another of the ego's responses, not to the binge but to the inadequately solved catastrophes associated with the still latent neurosogenic fantasies. The eating disorder is usually unsuccessful in warding off anxiety; hence the necessity for further psychic shifts that institute increasingly incapacitating and alloplastic symptoms. The recognition and tolerance of the otherwise insistently avoided anxiety state that initiates these regressive patterns of defense allows observation to supplant action resistances, both behavioral and somatized. Wilson's clinical data show that the journey to voluntary control over the automatism of bulimia equivalents needs to pass through a phase of character analysis in order to bring under conscious scrutiny the elements of compromise that have been safely defused into the syntonic attitude toward the world. Progress in the process of symptoms becoming ego alien is noted by their transformation into dream manifest content. Wilson demonstrates that, as much as patients would like it to be otherwise, the disappearance of a symptom is but the first step in the overcoming of its dynamic genetic determinants.

The quest to avoid pain for pleasure is as human a desire as eros. Perhaps no experience is as intolerable as a chronic sense of acute defectiveness. Inner feelings of being flawed derive from environmental strain trauma, developmental distortion, and intrapsychic retaliatory guilt, and stimulate a host of adaptive, neurotic, and action responses. Their common goal is to disavow the childhood sensations of inferiority and helplessness, though the variety of the ego's coping compromises may initially mask the singularity of their narcissistic motivations.

The search to possess that which is outside oneself and is endowed with a magical perfection which can heal the inner wound represents a concretized intermediary solution to the unconscious fantasies of aggression and incest. Bulimia and kleptomania—the secret taking of forbidden things—are common collaborative attempts to solve these universal dilemmas. Ziolko's 1966 case report in German, "Bulimia and Kleptomania: Psychodynamics of Compulsive Eating and Stealing," describes the psychoanalytic treatment of a patient with these two symptom complexes and is presented here in an English translation. The relationship of these two manifest level disorders, as well as the more common compulsive clothes and shoes shopping, only begins to be revealed in noting the acquisitive quality common to both.

Ziolko describes an extensive overlap of latent conflicts that drive these alloplastic enactments. The need to revenge and reverse the inner experience associated with a sense of disappointing inferiority and guilt-filled passivity leads to the acting out of aggressive grasping, displaced stimulation, and self-punishment characteristic of binging and stealing. The infantile experiences of humiliating genital envy and perceived forbidden sexual desire are screened by their externalization onto contemporary objects and social prohibitions. The infuriating object-related boundary that defines both the sexual and generational differences is insistently denied in the narcissistic turn to a here-and-now material arena where everything can be possessed by anyone. Under superego pressure, incestuous masturbatory arousal is regressively transformed into the excitement of the binge–theft which additionally gratifies the masochistic strivings associated with the underlying wishes. The exhibitionistic solution for these quandaries of the castration complex is represented by its opposite secretiveness which derives its compensatory power from the model of the hidden illusions of early psychosexual life. The persistent self-concept of being damaged and guilty enervates the endless repetitiveness of these action symptoms, and the failure to neutralize their aggression subverts the development of less distorted, and hence esteem enhancing, instinctual as well as sublimated gratifications. The therapeutic task remains the translation of the bulimic-kleptomaniac's current cravings into the realm of infantile fantasy within which the screened original longings and objects can be affectively identified.

It is the hope that the tragically symbolic fate suffered by the patient described on the final page—a woman with bulimia and kleptomania who was killed by an automobile as she was crossing the street binging on a sausage she had just begged—can be averred through the application of the findings presented by the authors of this volume. This compilation of their clinical and theoretical work is intended as an organizer of current psychoanalytic perspectives on this topic. The goal is that this text will stimulate others' thinking in their clinical care of patients with eating disorders and will simultaneously inform and provoke further psychoanalytic research in this area.

Chapter 1

Bulimia: Psychoanalytic Perspectives

HARVEY J. SCHWARTZ, M.D.

Food, seen as the semisymbolic equivalent of the oral mother (Sperling, 1949, 1968), has led many analytic writers to view the binging–vomiting syndrome as a concrete expression of the introjection–projection struggles of early infancy. Using the prerepresentational imagery of pathological splitting, the adult patient is seen as longing for oral mothering yet compelled to expel the introjected mother as it becomes poisoned by the rage of frustration (Jessner and Abse, 1960). Rizzuto (1982), proposes "that the need to eat is the dissociated search for the oral maternal object and the need to vomit the urge to rid oneself of the monstrous creature who demands so much so frantically."

In a similar vein, Sugarman traces the bulimic problem to a developmental arrest of the practicing subphase of the separation–individuation period.

> Our working thesis is that bulimia reflects an arrest at the earliest stage of transitional object development. Specifically, the failure to adequately separate both physically and cognitively from the maternal object during the practicing subphase leads to a narcissistic fixation on one's own body at the expense of reaching out to other objects in the wider world, through the use of external transitional objects. This arrest in the area of transitional objects has profound con-

Reprinted from *Journal of the American Psychoanalytic Association*, 34/2:439–462 (1986).

sequences as regards self-other boundary differentiation, individuation, and the capacity for symbolization [Sugarman and Kurash, 1981, p. 58].

It is this failure to successfully traverse the period of differentiation from mother that is seen as leading to the fundamental incapacity to sustain a historical perspective on one's body. The evocative presence of early developmental nurturing sequences ordinarily yields a generalized ability to recognize the boundary between internal and external stimuli. The early use of the body as transitional object—"neither pure subject nor pure object" (Sugarman)—creates the later capacity for illusion.

When there is a defect in this function, when the neutralized energy is not available to sustain a metaphorical level of consciousness, symbols lose their transcendent potential and are replaced by "symbolic equations" (Segal, 1978). Enduring objects whose cathexis can be maintained in their absence give way to need-fulfilling objects "the fate of which is to lose [their] cathexis in the absence of internal need" (Parkin, 1983, p. 338). As the maternal object, more properly object relation, is not available symbolically and therefore has not infused the psychic apparatus with the potential for individuation, the bulimic patient repeatedly returns to her own body in a concrete sensorimotor fashion in a recreation of the struggle with the mother of the practicing subphase.

> Thus, the bulimic finds herself in a twofold dilemma. She lacks the cognitive capacity to symbolize the maternal object which would allow her to give up the use of her body as a transitional object. And her body as a transitional object is actually experienced as her mother, not like her mother's, because of the "symbolic equation" or preoperational nature of her thinking. She cannot go forward because of her complex cognitive and object relational limitations. To feed her body is to lose herself in the experience of being one with mother. Starving or controlling it serves the function of maintaining her tenuous self-other boundary [Sugarman and Kurash, 1981, p. 62].

In the clinical material presented (psychotherapy), Sugarman concludes, "Gorging became identified as an act of symbiotic reunion; vomiting as an act of separation from, if not annihilation of mother" (p. 65).

Sours (1974) similarly emphasizes in these patients the centrality of the ego regression that occurs secondary to "unresolved infantile object dependency and failure in achieving autonomy" (p. 572). He notes their struggle with longed-for passive submission to the overpowering maternal object which in turn evokes fears of regressive fusion and dedifferentiation. He sees the unconscious life of the actual external object and the relationship matrix created by that object as leading to the symptom picture in the child.

> These patients have been attached to a domineering and controlling mother who attempts to attain passive submission and perfection for the child as her own fulfillment. Power and control exerted by the omnipotent mother is overwhelming, remarkably interfering with separation and individuation in all phases of the child's development [p. 571].

It is this focus on the pathogenic role of the mother's unconscious psychic life that uniquely characterizes the psychoanalytic literature on the eating disorders. More than just a noxious stimulus around which the child's unconscious fantasies coalesce, the intrapsychic processes of the mother are seen by many as directly leading to eating conflicts in the child. As early as 1895 (Stephens), intense and destructive interactions between mother and psychosomatic child were noted and, in the reported case, viewed as responsible for the demise of the patient.

Early analytic researchers also noted unusual parental involvement in patients' eating conflicts, but studied it with a low resolution lens. This led to nonspecific findings such as "the peculiarities and characteristics of the older members of the family group will leave their impress on the personalities of the children" (Waller, Kaufman, and Deutsch, 1940, p. 4). Emphasis on the orally frustrating mother (Lorand, 1943) and the maternal overstrict superego (Leonard, 1944) were similarly valid but incomplete attempts to grasp the meaning of the psychosomatic dyad. More recently, Blitzer, Rollins, and Blackwell (1961) noted, "the anxiety-laden fantasies about food and eating, preoccupation with foods, fear of adult sexuality, and reluctance to give up the child's dependent status that were present in our [child] patients often paralleled identical fantasies and attitudes of their parents" (p. 382). In addition, fathers of these patients have been found to exhibit oral conflicts and eating peculiarities of their own, along with overstimulating seductiveness toward and covert rejection of their daughters' femininity (Blitzer et al., 1961; Sours, 1974; Sperling, 1983).

The mother and her experience of the child have received the most thorough analytic attention. Sperling has focused her investigations on the unconscious bond that exists within the mother and her psychosomatic child. From her simultaneous analyses of both partners, she found that "mother and child represented a psychologic unit in which the child reacted to the unconscious need of the mother with correspondingly unconscious obedience . . . it is as if one were to observe two parallel curves—the mother and child curve—where a specific change (elevation or decline) in the mother produces a specific reactive change in the child curve" (Sperling, 1949, p. 377).[1] In her reported cases the mother views the child as an unconsciously hated sibling or parent, or as a narcissistic projection of a part of her own self, in particular her wished-for penis.[2] Maternal

[1] This mother–child enmeshment has been documented physiologically by noting the synchronicity of alterations in serum-free fatty acids—a barometer of emotional arousal. An anxious mother's elevated free fatty acid level decreases to normal levels in response to the introduction of the ill child whose own free fatty acid level in turn increases to pathological and symptom-producing levels (Minuchin, Rosman, and Baker, 1978, p. 46).

[2] The body–phallus fantasy, as will be discussed, is a common constellation in patients with bulimia, and indeed was first described by Abraham (1924) in a patient with psychogenic vomiting. It originates as an intrapsychic compromise for narcissistic mortification, scoptophillic awe, and oral-incorporative wishes directed toward the paternal phallus. It also derives from the experience of "being the penis" of the mother. In these cases, mother views herself as castrated and conceives of the child as a compensatory extension of her self—a partial object, a thing—to narcissistically repair her own esteem. In the child this results in an intense dependency on the object she makes complete, with a reinforcement of alloplastic solutions; an identified-with diffuse over-

overcontrol, homosexual possessiveness, and intense ambivalence uniformly lead to submissiveness, drive regression, and
symptom formation in the psychosomatic child. As the child's
symptoms resolve, the "psychosomatogenic" mother often becomes depressed and develops an eating disorder of her own
(Sperling, 1973, 1978). Similarly, analytic treatment of the
mother leads to amelioration of the symptoms in the child (Sperling, 1949, 1978).

Briefly, three representative analytic investigators have
studied under high resolution the psychic mechanics of this
mother–child enmeshment. While their language differs, all
seem to be defining similar terrain. Otto Sperling (1943–1945)
finds that the mother of the psychosomatic child perceives the
child as a literal extension of her own ego. The mother does
not invest the child with object libido, which would create the
possibility of an empathic relationship, but through the process
of "appersonation" imbues the child with her own narcissistic
libido. As a result, the child is seen literally as her "right arm,"
without a psychic life of his own.

Bird (1957) notes that there is a failure of differentiation
between the ego of the child and that of the mother. There is
a prolongation of the normal infantile condition whereby the
child's rudimentary ego responds directly to the id of the
mother, with her ego in turn reacting to the id of the child. In
these cases, her ego continues to act for him and interferes with
his establishing structures that would allow conflicts to be
worked out between his own ego and his own id.

Zinner and Shapiro (1972) found that parental projective
identification leads to permanent structural change in the recipient of the projections. They conclude that the internal object
representation of the child that resides in the parental psychic
structure is communicated through "delineations." These acts
and statements become the raw material for the child's internalization and lead to an identification with the parent's defensively distorted images of him.

---

cathexis of the exhibitionistic-peripheral aspects of the body, without awareness of
inner individuating self- and object drive cathexes; and the intergenerational transmission of a defective feminine ego ideal.

In contrast to the above, the structural perspective on symptom formation emphasizes its symbolic and conflictual elements. Infantile impulses are seen to be transformed metaphorically by and around the ego's repression barrier. This semipermeable membrane derives from the internalization of the incest taboo and creates overdetermined compromise solutions from the drives and catastrophes associated with the oedipal situation. Structuralization sets in this repression barrier as well as signal anxiety, with the result that manifest symptomatology (i.e., oral binging), necessarily derives from latent-level fantasy, (i.e., castration). Symptoms are understood to be analyzable into components and layers of meaning, each of which expresses in disguise, impulse, defense, and punishment. Each facet of a symptom, like a piece of a hologram, contains in and of itself the entire neurosogenic fantasy and drive-defense configuration of the larger symptom and character structure. Manifest expression, as with a dream, is viewed as the end product of a complex developmental series of childhood wishes and fantasies, and defensive transfiguration and revision.

Unlike the previous literature which views bulimic disturbances as a fixation at presymbolic oral-separation levels, the structural view is that it represents a defensive regression and displacement from genital wishes. Thus Sandler and Dare (1970) note that "Simply because the disturbance involves oral function it should not be inferred that the psychopathology of the disturbance either represents the revival of infantile oral drive or originated in early infancy" (p. 215).

Brenner (1974) views manifest oral symptoms as developmentally representing the oral aspects of the genital phase, Masserman's (1941) "oral oedipus."

> Oral and, for that matter, anal wishes do not disappear at the onset of the oedipal period. Children between the ages of two and a half and six years have very active oral and anal wishes. Oedipal fantasies are often expressed in oral and anal terms, not necessarily as a result of regression. . . . The instinctual mode in which a wish or fantasy is ex-

pressed is not a sure guide to its time of origin in infantile development [Brenner, 1974, p. 10].

Similarly, Chasseguet-Smirgel (1984) states:

> Fertility is inseparable from internalization, the model for which is probably the penis which is retained to become a child, and not the nipple in the mouth . . . it is the primacy of the wish for the child, combined with the presence of the feminine receptacle, which produces the oral conception of coitus and pregnancy, and not the primacy of orality over genitality [p. 169].

Kestenberg approaches the issue developmentally from the viewpoint of function and, agreeing with Greenacre (1950, 1952), Fraiberg (1972), and Sperling (1973), notes the universality and symmetry in women of the mouth–vagina equation.

> The mouth . . . as the model opening becomes the symbol of all "holes" of the body. Thus the vaginal opening becomes endowed with oral representations stemming from a direct equation with the mouth as well as from an indirect one, which emerges from oral admixtures incorporated in the image of other openings with which the introitus is successively equated [Kestenberg, 1956a, p. 458].

> The difficulty in localization as well as the enigmatic quality and multilocality of fleeting vaginal sensations create a confusion in the young girl. . . . In one type of solution she fuses vaginal tensions with others coming from the inside of her body and projects their common bulk to orifices with which she has become familiar, such as mouth, anus and the urethral orifice [1956b, pp. 276–277].

This more traditional approach to the problem of binge eating, whether viewed as a specific component of the genital phase or as a symptom with endowment from successive developmental phases (Sterba, 1941), emphasizes the symbolic elements in the activity, sees it as a compromise product of conflict, and stresses the role of the genitalization of the oral cavity.

The early psychoanalytic writing on vomiting focused on psychogenic vomiting—without manual stimulation. As early as 1899, in his letters to Fliess, Freud described the underlying fantasy in this condition that would later be confirmed by numerous other analysts—oral pregnancy. In so doing, he also identified the presence of self-punishing trends in this symptom and delineated its function as a drive-defense compromise formation.

> Do you know, for instance, why X.Y. suffers from hysterical vomiting? Because in phantasy she is pregnant, because she is so insatiable that she cannot put up with not having a baby by her last phantasy-lover as well. But she must vomit too, because in that case she will be starved and emaciated, and will lose her beauty and no longer be attractive to anyone. Thus the sense of the symptom is a contradictory pair of wish-fulfilments [p. 278].

Later Freud (1908) identified the image in childhood thinking from which this symptom elaborates—that a baby is gotten through a kiss and through eating. The wish to eat and thereby conceive father's baby reflects the merging of recent oral incorporative mechanisms with active oedipal–genital wishes (Freud, 1905), and in males, of the negative oedipal constellation (Deutsch, 1930; Falstein, Feinstein, and Judas, 1956). Eating is erotized. "Since 'bed and board' constitute marriage, the latter often takes the place of the former in dreams and the sexual complex of ideas is . . . transposed on to the eating complex" (Freud, 1900, p. 355). To the child and the unconscious, food is the paternal phallus, ingestion of which undoes castration and conceives the oedipal baby (Waller et al., 1940; Lorand, 1943; Leonard, 1944; Sylvester, 1945; Blos, 1974). The incorporative act of eating–gorging contains the desire for abdominal distention and impregnation, the defense of upward displacement with oral submission to mother, and the punishment of physical revulsion. The expulsive act of vomiting de-sexualizes the receptive wish, symbolically rejects and restores the ingested phallus–baby, sadistically punishes the thwarting object, and masochistically relieves the guilt evoked by the desire to castrate and possess father (Masserman, 1941; Leonard, 1944; Kestenberg, 1968).[3] Through the masturbatory act of manually stimulating the throat, the original wish for fellatio and impregnation is gratified (Moulton, 1942; Sperling, 1983), with the vomiting revealing, through the body–phallus equation, the (partial) identification with the ejaculating–urinating organ (Lewin, 1933). The obsessive preoccupation with the idealized flat abdomen symbolizes the masked desire for pro-tuberation and impregnation, the defensive retreat to a cari-catured boy's physique, and the return of the repressed through living out the body–phallus fantasy (Sarnoff, 1983; Wilson, 1983).[4]

In addition to expressing the positive oedipal wish, a number of authors have reported on the function that oral castration of father has on the relation with mother. Masserman (1941) describes the wish to possess father's phallus in order to please mother and replace father in her bed, "to acquire their penises as a symbol of masculinity desired by her mother and thereby eliminate them as competitors and displace them homosexually in her mother's affections" (p. 221). Sperling (1983) disagrees with Masserman. In stressing oral-sadistic components in the conflict over eating, she finds that the wish to orally castrate father and possess his penis is in the service of having omni-potent control over mother as the powerful father of infancy had. Hogan (1983) agrees and finds, with others (Waller et al., 1940; Lorand, 1943), that in the eating disorders it is often the early oral struggles with mother (breast) that lead to heightened

[3] This physical expulsion is a somatic forerunner of "negation" (Freud, 1925) and reflects the generalized tendency for reversals (i.e., seeing–being seen, castrated–phallic, etc.) characteristic of binge–purge patients (see Thoma, 1967, pp. 264–276).

[4] Other compulsive extrusions—such as weeping and urinating—may similarly serve as an aggressive defense against receptive wishes and have been shown to be interchangeable with vomiting. They too represent a displacement of sexual excitement, with phallic identification and exhibitionism acting as compensation, specifically ma-sochistic, for intense penis envy (see van der Heide, 1941; Greenacre, 1945).

cannibalistic and castrating impulses that are then brought to father in the oedipal period, leading to an "oral cathexis of the penis" (Sperling, 1950; see also Chasseguet-Smirgel, 1970). [The downward migration of oral drive and object frustration has long been recognized and can lead to a "biting" rather than "sucking" vagina (Brierley, 1936).]

Alternately, in Sachs's view (1929) it is the frustration of the daughter's genital wishes toward father that leads to the regressed oral mode of relating to him. The *object*, however, remains distinctly the father in accordance with the normal positive Oedipus. He suggests that the maintenance of this oral engagement with father interferes with the optimal frustration, renunciation, and sublimation of the oedipal bond. This precludes the establishment of a fully autonomous superego and may contribute to the commonly noted tendencies in bulimic patients of both sadistic self-criticism and impulsive acting out. Sachs, in these cases, also finds a failure of maturation of the ego ideal, a condition noted in bulimic women (Thomä, 1967; Blos, 1974).

Early and frequent exposure to primal-scene stimuli occurs with great frequency in eating-disorder patients (Wilson, 1985, personal communication, see also Székács, 1985), and has been found to intensify the mouth–vagina equation (Greenacre, 1950). This displacement is central in bulimia (Schwartz, see chapter 9). The particularly visual overstimulating primal-scene experience is frequently responded to by a defensive turning away from genital fantasy to a secondary superimposed schema of nursing mother and child (Edelheit, 1974), as well as to a regressive desexualized "narcissistic condensation" (Gero and Rubinfine, 1955) of perceived violent copulation. Thus, the stereotyped ritual of gorging on food and forcing one's finger down the throat to induce regurgitation represents in part a simultaneous identification with both parents of the primal scene with an acting out on one's own body of the imagined role of the sadistic phallic father and castrated suffering mother. This defensive bisexual identification denies the humiliation of primal-scene exclusion, undoes "castration," and reverses passive (masochistic) oedipal impregnation wishes.

Withdrawing object libido from incestuous coital wishes— narcissistic desexualization—leads to, in disguise, doing to one's self what was wished for from father. Regressively, fantasy itself is replaced by the symptom. [This alternating identification with both partners of the sadomasochistic primal scene has also been reported in patients with asthma (Karol, 1980).]

A retreat to autoeroticism with the acting out of complementary sexual roles is also manifest in the masturbatory gratification in bulimia. In these patients masturbation itself may be either suppressed or compulsive; in either case it reflects intense anxiety over accompanying fantasies, and is in the service of self-punishment. The struggle against masturbation may be directed against the actual manipulation of a part of the body or the content of the fantasy. In the binge–purge syndrome, the act of phallic stimulation is displaced to the mouth, "while the phallic nature of the fantasy is preserved intact. Such an involvement of the oral zone with cathexes from phallic drives may be elaborated into symptoms which appear to be intensifications of oral demands but which are in actuality, at this level, derived from oedipal wishes. . . (Arlow, 1953, p. 49).

In bulimia, the symptomatic activity is an acting out of the unconscious masturbatory fantasy. It consists of punitive ruminations about eating as well as states of nameless agitation that lead to outbreaks of frenetic and secret gorging, often to the point of stupor. The masturbatory character of the symptom, while apparent to the listener, is not recognizable to the patient. Under superego pressure, the frequently masochistic (and exhibitionistic) fantasies have been defensively decathected with identification replacing an object relation. The symptomatic ritual reoccurs repeatedly as the unrealized libidinal fantasy reactivates the masturbatory urge. The defenses are overrun, though the renewed attempts to relieve erotic tension are only partially successful as the receptive vaginal cathexis remains displaced. The stereotyped form of the compulsive behavior is driven by and is a reenactment of the "endless monotony of the crude fantasies which accompany masturbatory acts; the compulsive and periodic character of the acting out corresponds to the periodic need for masturbation. . . ." (Freud,

1949, p. 203). The brutal guilt feelings and depressions that follow these outbreaks are testimony to their instinctual origins.

Food becomes the object of conflict by virtue of its role as the medium of mothering and boundary formation and its availability to accept displacements and transfer excitation from beneath the repression barrier (Sperling, 1978). Food and eating, in addition, function as one of the many semisymbols—"heirs of the transitional object"—that are used by the girl child to externalize and define new inner genital sensations. As a familiar and parallel experience, eating and oral sensations are available to localize and detoxify enigmatic and confusing vaginal sensations. This process of externalization transforms inside excitement into an outside object that can be mastered and controlled. The act of using an outside object and the objects themselves represent an attempt at secondary-process organization of primary-process visceral sensations and fantasies (Kestenberg, 1968). Food and its consumption, art work (Roiphe and Galenson, 1981), dolls (Kestenberg, 1956b; Bradley, 1961) and horses (Pearson, 1965; Fraiberg, 1967; Kestenberg, 1968) serve not only as the secret illusory female phallus and paternal penis–baby, but also as the externalizer and organizer of inside genital imagery and sensations. Their use as masturbatory equivalents reveals their function as synthesizer of depressive castration reactions, sadistic impulses toward mother, and masochistic incestuous wishes.

An intense devotion to horses has been frequently noted in women with eating disorders. As early as 1906, Janet reported on a twenty-two-year-old woman who suffered from "boulimia" and who "wished to run or to ride horseback the whole day." In the analytic literature, in a paper investigating the unconscious meaning of horses in a young woman (Schowalter, 1983) it was parenthetically noted that the patient also suffered from bulimia. In reports studying the eating disorders (Sours, 1980; Risen, 1982), it has similarly been noted in passing that the women patients have been "horse-crazy." There has not been a detailed study of the relation between these two entities, though they appear together with some frequency.

The unconscious meaning of the horse has been well studied. It has been discovered analytically [and historically (Frazer, 1922)] to often represent the ambivalently awed paternal phallus (Freud, 1965; Fraiberg, 1967). The mounting, controlling, and breeding of the phallic horse—simultaneously one's own to be displayed and father's to be beaten—undoes the shame, rage, and envy of the adolescent girl's self-perceived castration (Pearson, 1965; Schowalter, 1983). Body–phallus identification and identification with the phallic father are also lived out on the galloping horse through the displacement from the phallus-moving-through-space to that of the body-moving-through-space (Glover and Mendell, 1982).[5]

Most often the hypercathected horse successfully serves to ease the transition from a defective self-percept with idealization of the paternal organ (intelligence, values, etc.)—the phallic "prepubertal ego ideal" (Hendrick, 1964)—to the abstracted ideal of feminine identification and receptivity (Jacobson, 1954). In these cases it has succeeded in the task for which it was created and may then be desexualized and discarded as a remnant of adolescent development.

In future bulimic patients, however, the concrete horse–phallus remains the central focus of psychosexual life. There is a failure of neutralization of scoptophilic impulses, vengeful castrating wishes, and ego ideal precursors. As is characteristic of the phallic phase, an outside object—the idealized phallus—persists as the primary regulator of self-esteem (Thomä, 1967; Blos, 1974). Its continued nonabstracted and instinctualized nature reinforces regressive functioning and a turning away from approaching genital conflicts, and encourages re-

---

[5] It is not only the grandeur of the horse that serves as a reparative externalization for the pubertal castration complex in future bulimic women. Other objects and activities serve the same function. For one binging and vomiting woman, her early adolescence was marked by an intense devotion to the playing, mastering, and displaying of her father's trumpet. She proudly marched with it in her high school band, the only woman to do so, in order to "measure up" in her father's eyes and be as valued as his sons—"his stallions."

Intense and exhaustive exercise, including weight lifting, not only precedes, but may also emerge with the eating disorder. It, too, via libidinization of the body and its motor activity, is part of the effort to create a "perfect" phallic self and thereby undo "castration" via introjection-identification with the idealized paternal phallus.

treat, however contaminated, to the safety of phallic identification. Rather than the usual progression to receptive genital–oedipal wishes, strengthened by a dependable maternal identification, gorging and vomiting develop, often immediately after the cessation of riding, reflecting the continued quest for the introjection of and identification with the external source of self-regard—the paternal penis–baby. The self-punitive obsession with everything put in the mouth and the endless preoccupation with body configuration reveals the continuity of the infantile search for and idealization of phallic power, control, and beauty. [A further regression from an already masculine ego ideal to one that is "transcendent" and sexless is characteristic of severe anorexia nervosa and is not usually present in normal-weight bulimia (see Thomä, 1967, p. 253).]

A parallel manifestation of the orally driven wish to possess the paternal penis–baby is kleptomania. Phenomenologic observers have noted binges of stealing in 44 percent of patients with bulimia (Hudson, Pope, Jones, and Yurgelon-Todd, 1983). From analytic data, Hogan (1983) reports both phallic and oral greed to be the underlying mechanisms in this compulsion. The thievery most often involves clothing or food, and symbolizes the confluence of drives from multiple developmental levels. As Fenichel (1939) noted, "We know from the psychoanalysis of kleptomania that its object is often the penis (therefore it is more frequent in women than in men), but only if the penis envy was dealt with in a certain pregenitally determined way. For, to the kleptomanic, the stolen goods are basically always the external supplies that are necessary for his self-regard" (p. 149).

This amalgamation of oral and phallic concerns similarly expresses itself in many of the food idiosyncracies of these patients. The avoidance of red meat has been frequently documented in patients with eating conflicts. Analytic investigation finds both cannibalistic urges and fellatio-impregnation fantasies underlying the repugnance for eating meat (Bergler, 1935; Goldman, 1938; Risen, 1982; Mintz, 1983). Anthropologic studies support these findings. They reveal that throughout history it has been believed that swallowing any one of a number of fruit, fish, roots, and nuts led to pregnancy "without fleshly intercourse." Hartland (1909, p. 9) notes in particular that "flesh-meat" has been considered "a more fecundating substance."

Conflicts over coprophagic impulses also frequently contribute to the eating idiosyncracies and inhibitions of these patients. The common abuse of laxatives and the central role of the toilet in the regurgitation ritual highlight the importance of anal conflicts and specifically the "mouth-anus-vagina" equation (Jones, 1927). The young girl's diffuse "cavity erotism" includes anal sensations and leads to aggressive and receptive wishes to anally incorporate and control father's penis. This wish-to-be-retained inner fecal baby—a version of illusory phallus—suffers the same expulsive fate as the oral baby, as they are both plagued by the guilt of the genital impulses from which they are regressively derived (Oliner, 1982).[6]

Additionally, as Lewin (1930) has described, the wish to undo anal loss and castration may find expression not only in coprophagic wishes, but also in the incorporative act of smearing oneself. Both are suggestive of an incomplete renunciation of the oedipal bond with father. The compensatory urge to smear is often expressed symbolically through shopping sprees for expensive clothes—that is, through exhibitionist cutaneous smearing. Clinically one finds that food binging and compulsive clothes-shopping quite usually occur together, with the latter often replacing the former. As Lewin noted, "what is smeared, does not need to be eaten" (p. 25).

Some analytic writers (Levin, 1959–1961) view the symptom of eating dysfunction as in and of itself invariably representing the tip of an unanalyzable ego. Most agree though that the spectrum of character development within which eating disorders make their appearance is broad (Blitzer et al., 1961;

---

[6] Clinically this point was demonstrated by a patient of normal weight who secretly vomited her dinner nightly for nearly two decades while simultaneously suffering from chronic abdominal pain and intractable constipation. With the beginning working through of her oral castrating-incorporative wishes and guilt-filled fantasies of masochistic impregnation, her purging compulsion lessened significantly only to be followed immediately by the development of explosive diarrhea.

Sours, 1974), a conclusion shared by Anna Freud from her work with childhood eating disturbances (1946). Confusion results when hospitalized near-terminal anorexics are compared with analyzable normal-weight bulimics. Varying degrees of patient character dysfunction and differing data-gathering instruments, from initial evaluations to completed analyses, have yielded incompatible and contradictory findings.

These methodologic limitations aside, differences in emphasis remain on the degree to which, in the otherwise non-regressed patient, manifestly oral symptoms and fantasies are understood to be primary or defensive. As mentioned, some see the struggle over eating as representing the inevitable and aggression-laden precipitate from the failed mother–infant admixture (Meyer and Weinroth, 1957; Jessner and Abse, 1960) with specific reference to the process of individuation (Mushatt, 1982–1983). Others view the "bottomless depth of orality" as a regressive "hiding place for the oedipus complex, sometimes well concealed, sometimes only thinly veiled," but always being used to express oedipal elements (Friedman, 1953, p. 305). An arena for the study of this issue presents itself in the "oral dream."

As Jones revealed (1911), both dreams and neurotic symptoms are compromise formations expressing, in allegorical form, latent wishes and fantasies. "The two are merely different ways of obtaining an imaginary gratification of the same buried wishes. One may in fact describe dreams as the neuroses of the healthy, just as neurosis is a dream of the invalid" (p. 271). Indeed, it is well recognized that dreaming of any symptom represents progress toward its resolution (Wilson, 1983). Analysis of food dreams therefore can be expected to shed light on the meaning of symptomatic eating.

Hamburger (1958) studied the occurrence of dreams concerned with food and eating in his analysands, including those with eating symptomatology. He found that the patients' associations to their own dreams "always lead into nonnutritional areas . . . so, in a negative sense, the very representation of food and eating in a manifest dream makes us look for hidden (latent) wishes only symbolized by food and eating in the manifest content" (p. 13). He concluded:

> I have gained the distinct impression, from studying these dreams of food and eating, that such dreams often represent by displacement and symbolic substitution, the sexual drive. This finding in these four cases tends to coroborate what Coriat pointed out when he wrote [1921] ". . . the dreams (of eating) represent symbolically a means of utilization of another erotogenetic zone, one that is not repulsive to social conventions or to ethical ideas, as a means of harmlessly securing sexual gratification." In other words, by unconscious displacement and symbolization, the eating drive is substitute for the sexual drive. There is not only substitution at work but regression. My translation of this dream work would be: "My adult sexual urges are too threatening. Give me instead the (assumed) asexual gratifications of my childhood." In my opinion, this is the meaning of those food and eating dreams which represent regressive substitution of the hunger for the sexual drive [p. 13].

Hamburger also recognizes the patients for whom the eating dream symbolizes "an anaclitic type of object relation." He hypothesizes that repetitive dreams of *actively eating* reflect these stronger pregenital conflicts while a greater incidence of dreams of *feeding others* indicates an "oral retreat from genital sexuality." "The differing incidence and latent meaning of the food and eating dream appears to reflect these characterologic differences and may thus be of some aid in differential diagnosis" (p. 5). He suggests that the decreasing occurrence of food dreams throughout an analysis may be used as an index of progress as the conflict around genital sexuality is reduced and the need for regressive oral gratification is diminished.

The centrality of the wish for incestuous impregnation lies at the heart of the classical work on bulimia. The anxiety and guilt of sexual (masturbatory) fantasies leads to a defensive regression from genitality and from fantasy itself. Drive-organized wishes are defensively disowned and their energy projected onto others (i.e., parents) and into the now brutal superego (Boris, 1984). The emergence of libidinal (and aggressive) fantasy into consciousness (through analysis of resistances to the transference) heralds new outbreaks of symptom resistance, thereby confirming the neurosogenic power of the id–ego conflict. Empathically derived interpretations that cross the repression barrier and speak to the latent conflicts from which the patient is retreating enlarge the ego's capacity for self-observation, broaden the sources of drive energy available for the ego, and limit the back pressure from intense unconscious guilt. Focused superego analysis often makes up much of the early work of treatment.

This emphasis on motivational forces is not to suggest, as some misconstrue it (Bruch, 1978), the appropriateness of intrusive, poorly timed, or critical interpretations. Nor does it countenance early drive interpretation. As with all neurotic patients, the interpretive point of urgency varies from session to session and moment to moment. Drives, defenses, and object relations from all developmental levels need analytic attention as they approach affective-preconscious accessibility. For some, dependency on mother does represent a (bilateral) failure of separation. For most, however, an exclusive focus on the conflicts from below obfuscates the defensive elements in the negative oedipal constellation. Clinging to mother always includes the defensive function of retreating from competing with her. In deference to mother, genital libidinal cathexes are detoxified and displaced to submissive and self-destructive oral (and anal) conflicts. Father and his phallus are manifestly given up. The repressed returns through the oral rage at mother which contains the rivalrous matricidal wish in disguise. The quest for father's penis–baby remains paramount through the living out of the body-phallus fantasy and the obsession with abdominal distension-impregnation. The incorporative incestuous act itself is revealed through its condensed narcissistic version —gorging and violent self-stimulated regurgitation—of excitedly and secretly doing to oneself what was wished for from father.

The successful analysis of the elements of compromise in the binge–purge symptom yields the individually unique fantasies that emerge from the universal dilemmas of the oedipal situation. Individuation, autonomy, and gender satisfaction are accomplished analytically through the broadening of ego functioning to include mastery of drive fantasies and infantile prohibitions. These are the tasks of the oedipal child.

CONCLUSION

Eating disorders have been alternately understood as expressing the semisymbolic introjection–projection struggles of early infancy as well as the fully metaphorical compromise formation for oedipal impregnation fantasies. Negative oedipal intimacy with mother, in its oral version, is conceptualized as an effort to create a nurturing image that will help maintain a coherent self–other boundary and encourage mastery of the practicing subphase. In contrast, negative oedipal sexuality as an expression of the phallic–oedipal position is seen as a regressive retreat from the receptive incestuous wishes of the positive oedipal stage. This approach views fertilization as the model for internalization and emphasizes the centrality of the castration complex. The explanatory power for normal weight bulimia of the phallic–oedipal paradigm with its defensive structure of displacement, regression, and narcissistic condensation needs confirmation through detailed clinical data.

REFERENCES

Abraham, K. (1924), Development of the libido. In: *Selected Papers*. London: Hogarth Press.
Arlow, J. (1953), Masturbation and symptom formation. *J. Amer. Psychoanal. Assn.*, 1:45–58.
Bergler, E. (1935), Psychoanalysis of a case of agoraphobia. *Psychoanal. Rev.*, 22:392–408.
Bird, B. (1957), A specific peculiarity of acting out. *J. Amer. Psychoanal. Assn.*, 5:630–647.

Blitzer, J., Rollins, N., & Blackwell, A. (1961), Children who starve themselves: Anorexia nervosa. *Psychosom. Med.*, 23:369–383.

Blos, P. (1974), The genealogy of the ego ideal. *The Psychoanalytic Study of the Child*, 29:43–88. New Haven, CT: Yale University Press.

Boris, H. (1984), The problem of anorexia nervosa. *Internat. J. Psycho-Anal.*, 65:315–322.

Bradley, N. (1961), The doll: Some clinical, biological and linguistic notes on the toy-baby and its mother. *Internat. J. Psycho-Anal.*, 42:550–555.

Brenner, C. (1974), The concept of phenomenology of depression, with special reference to the aged. *J. Geriat. Psychiat.*, 7:6–20.

Brierley, M. (1936), Specific determinants in feminine development. *Internat. J. Psycho-Anal.*, 17:163–181.

Bruch, H. (1978), *The Golden Cage*. Cambridge, MA: Harvard University Press.

Chasseguet-Smirgel, J. (1970), Feminine guilt and the oedipus complex. In: *Feminine Sexuality*, ed. J. Chasseguet-Smirgel. Ann Arbor: University of Michigan Press, pp. 94–134.

——— (1984), The femininity of the analyst in professional practice. *Internat. J. Psycho-Anal.*, 65:169–178.

Coriat, I. (1921), Sex and hunger. *Psychoanal. Rev.*, 8:375–381.

Deutsch, H. (1930), Hysterical conversion symptoms: Paralysis, speech defects, gluttony. In: *Neuroses and Character Types*. New York: International Universities Press, 1965, pp. 43–73.

Edelheit, H. (1974), Crucifixion fantasies and their relation to the primal scene. *Internat. J. Psycho-Anal.*, 55:193–199.

Falstein, E., Feinstein, D., & Judas, I. (1956), Anorexia nervosa in the male child. *Amer. J. Orthopsychiat.*, 26:751–772.

Fenichel, O. (1939), Trophy and triumph. In: *Collected Papers*, Second Series. New York: Norton, 1954, pp. 141–162.

Fraiberg, S. (1967). The analysis of an eight-year-old girl with epilepsy. In: *The Child Analyst at Work*, ed. E. Geleerd. New York: International Universities Press, pp. 229–287.

——— (1972), Some characteristics of genital arousal and discharge in latency girls. *The Psychoanalytic Study of the Child*, 27:439–475. New Haven, CT: Yale University Press.

Frazer, J. G. (1922), *The Golden Bough*. New York: Macmillan.

Freud, A. (1946), The psychoanalytic study of infantile feeding disturbances. In: *Writings*, Vol. 4,. New York: International Universities Press, 1968. pp. 39–59.

——— (1949). Certain types and stages of social maladjustment. In: *Writings*, Vol. 4. New York: International Universities Press, 1968, pp. 75–94.

——— (1965), Normality and Pathology in Childhood. In: *Writings*, Vol. 6. New York: International Universities Press.

Freud, S. (1899), Extracts from the Fliess papers. *Standard Edition*, 1: 175–280. London: Hogarth Press, 1966.

——— (1900). The Interpretation of Dreams. *Standard Edition*, 4 & 5. London: Hogarth Press, 1953.

——— (1905). Three essays on the theory of sexuality. *Standard Edition*, 7:125–230. London: Hogarth Press, 1953.

——— (1908). On the sexual theories of children. *Standard Edition*, 9:205–226. London: Hogarth Press, 1959.

——— (1925). Negation. *Standard Edition*, 19:235–239. London: Hogarth Press, 1961.

Friedman, L. (1953), Defensive aspects of orality. *Internat. J. Psycho-Anal.*, 34:304–312.

Gero, G., & Rubinfine, D. (1955), On obsessive thoughts. *J. Amer. Psychoanal. Assn.*, 3:222–243.

Glover, L., & Mendell, D. (1982), A suggested developmental sequence for a preoedipal genital phase. In: *Early Female Development*, ed. D. Mendell. New York: SP Medical & Scientific Books, pp. 127–174.

Goldman, G. (1938), A case of compulsive handwashing. *Psychoanal. Quart.*, 7:96–121.

Greenacre, P. (1945), Pathological weeping. In: *Trauma, Growth and Personality*. New York: International Universities Press, 1971, pp. 120–131.

——— (1950), Special problems of early female sexual development. *The Psychoanalytic Study of the Child*, 5:122–138. New York: International Universities Press.

——— (1952), Anatomical structure and superego development. In: *Trauma, Growth and Personality*. New York: International Universities Press, 1971, pp. 149–164.

Hamburger, W. (1958), The occurrence and meaning of dreams of food and eating. *Psychosom. Med.*, 20:1–16.

Hartland, E. (1909), *Primitive Paternity: The Myth of Supernatural Birth in Relation to the History of the Family*. London: David Nutt.

Hendrick, I. (1964), Narcissism and the prepuberty ego ideal. *J. Amer. Psychoanal. Assn.*, 12:522–528.

Hogan, C. (1983), Technical problems in psychoanalytic treatment. In: *Fear of Being Fat*, ed. C. Wilson, C. Hogan, & I. Mintz. New York: Jason Aronson, pp. 197–215.

Hudson, J., Pope, H., Jonas, J., & Yurgelon-Todd, D. (1983), Phenomenologic relationships of eating disorders to major affective disorder. *Psychiat. Res.*, 9/4:345–354.

Jacobson, E. (1954), The self and the object world. *The Psychoanalytic Study of the Child*, 9:75–127. New York: International Universities Press.

Janet, P. (1906), On the pathogenesis of some impulsions. *J. Abnorm. Psychol.*, 1:1–17.

Jessner, L., & Abse, D. (1960), Regressive forces in anorexia nervosa. *Brit. J. Med. Psychol.*, 33:301–312.

Jones, E. (1911), The relationship between dreams and psychoneurotic symptoms. In: *Papers on Psycho-Analysis*, 5th ed. Baltimore: Williams & Wilkins, 1950, pp. 251–272.

——— (1927), Early development of female sexuality. In: *Papers on Psycho-Analysis*, 5th ed. Baltimore: Williams & Wilkins, 1950, pp. 438–451.

Karol, C. (1980), The role of primal scene and masochism in asthma. *Internat. J. Psychoanal. Psychother.*, 8:577–592.

Kestenberg, J. (1956a). Viscissitudes of female sexuality. *J. Amer. Psychoanal. Assn.*, 4:453–476.

——— (1956b), On the development of maternal feelings in early childhood.

The Psychoanalytic Study of the Child, 11:257–291. New York: International Universities Press.

——— (1968). Outside and inside, male and female. *J. Amer. Psychoanal. Assn.*, 16:457–520.

Leonard, C. (1944), An analysis of a case of functional vomiting and bulimia. *Psychoanal. Rev.*, 31:1–18.

Levin, S. (1959–1961). Problems in the evaluation of patients for psychoanalysis. *Bull. Phila. Assn. Psychoanal.*, 9 11:86–95.

Lewin, B. D. (1930), Smearing of feces, menstruation, and female superego. In: *Selected Writings of Bertram D. Lewin*, ed. J. A. Arlow. New York: Psychoanalytic Quarterly, 1973, pp. 12–25.

——— (1933), The body as phallus. *Psychoanal. Quart.*, 2:24–47.

Lorand, S. (1943), Anorexia nervosa. *Psychosom. Med.*, 5:282–292.

Masserman, J. (1941), Psychodynamics in anorexia nervosa and neurotic vomiting. *Psychoanal. Quart.*, 10:211–242.

Meyer, B., & Weinroth, L. (1957), Observations on psychological aspects of anorexia nervosa. *Psychosom. Med.*, 19:389–398.

Mintz, I. (1983), Anorexia nervosa and bulimia in males. In: *Fear of Being Fat*, ed. C. Wilson, C. Hogan, & I. Mintz. New York: Jason Aronson, pp. 25–60.

Minuchin, S., Rosman, B., & Baker, L. (1978), *Psychosomatic Families: Anorexia Nervosa in Context*. Cambridge, MA: Harvard University Press.

Moulton, R. (1942), A psychosomatic study of anorexia nervosa including the use of vaginal smears. *Psychosom. Med.*, 4:62–74.

Mushatt, C. (1982–1983), Anorexia nervosa: A psychoanalytic commentary. *Internat. J. Psychoanal. Psychother.*, 9:257–265.

Oliner, M. (1982). The anal phase. In: *Early Female Development*, ed. D. Mendell. New York: SP Medical & Scientific Press, pp. 25–60.

Parkin, A. (1983), On structure formation and the processes of alteration. *Internat. J. Psycho-Anal.*, 64:333–351.

Pearson, G. H. J. (1965), A young girl and her horse. *Bull. Phila. Assn. Psychoanal.*, 15:189–206.

Risen, S. (1982), The psychoanalytic treatment of an adolescent with anorexia nervosa. *The Psychoanalytic Study of the Child*, 37:433–459. New Haven, CT: Yale University Press.

Rizzuto, A. (1982), Eating and monsters. Presentation, Tufts University School of Medicine. April 1, 1982.

Roiphe, H., & Galenson, E. (1981), *Infantile Origins of Sexual Identity*. New York: International Universities Press.

Sachs, H. (1929), One of the motive factors in the formation on the superego in women. *Internat. J. Psycho-Anal.*, 10:39–50.

Sandler, J., & Dare, C. (1970), The psychoanalytic concept of orality. *J. Psychosom. Res.*, 14:211–222.

Sarnoff, C. (1983), Derivatives of latency. In: *Fear of Being Fat*, ed. C. Wilson, C. Hogan, & I. Mintz. New York: Jason Aronson, pp. 327–334.

Schowalter, J. (1983), Some meanings of being a horsewoman. *The Psychoanalytic Study of the Child*, 38:501–517. New Haven, CT: Yale University Press.

Segal, H. (1978), On symbolism. *Internat. J. Psycho-Anal.*, 59:315–319.

Sours, J. (1974), The anorexia nervosa syndrome. *Internat. J. Psycho-Anal.*, 55:567–576.

———— (1980), *Starving to Death in a Sea of Objects*. New York: Jason Aronson.

Sperling, M. (1949), The role of the mother in psychosomatic disorders in children. *Psychosom. Med.*, 11:377–385.

———— (1950), A contribution to the psychodynamics of depression in women. *Samiksa*, 4:86–101.

———— (1968). Trichotillomania, trichophagy and cyclic vomiting. *Internat. J. Psycho-Anal.*, 49:682–690.

———— (1973), Conversation hysteria and conversion symptoms: A revision of classification and concepts. *J. Amer. Psychoanal. Assn.*, 21:745–771.

———— (1978), Case histories of anorexia nervosa. In: *Psychosomatic Disorders in Childhood*. New York: Jason Aronson, pp. 139–173.

———— (1983), A reevaluation of classification, concepts and treatment. In: *Fear of Being Fat: The Treatment of Anorexia Nervosa and Bulimia*, ed. C. Wilson, C. Hogan, & I. Mintz. New York: Jason Aronson., pp. 51–82.

Sperling, O. (1943–1945), On appersonation. *Internat. J. Psycho-Anal.*, 24–26:128–132.

Stephens, L. (1895), Case of anorexia nervosa. *Lancet*, 1:31–32.

Sterba, E. (1941), An important factor in eating disturbances of childhood. *Psychoanal. Quart.*, 10:365–372.

Sugarman, A., & Kurash, C. (1981), The body as a transitional object in bulimia. *Internat. J. Eating Dis.*, 1/4:57–66.

Sylvester, E. (1945), Analysis of psychogenic anorexia and vomiting in a four-year-old child. *The Psychoanalytic Study of the Child*, 2:3–16. New York: International Universities Press.

Székács, J. (1985), Impaired spatial structures. *Internat. J. Psycho-Anal.*, 66:193–199.

Thomä, H. (1967), *Anorexia Nervosa*. New York: International Universities Press.

van der Heide, C. (1941), A case of pollakiuria nervosa. *Psychoanal. Quart.*, 10:267–284.

Waller, J., Kaufman, M., & Deutsch, F. (1940), Anorexia nervosa: A psycho-somatic entity. *Psychosom. Med.*, 2:3–16.

Wilson, C. P. (1983), The fear of being fat in female psychology. In: *Fear of Being Fat*, ed. C. P. Wilson, C. Hogan, & I. Mintz. New York: Jason Aronson, pp. 9–27.

Zinner, J., & Shapiro, R. (1972), Projective identification as a mode of perception and behavior in families of adolescents. *Internat. J. Psycho-Anal.*, 53:523–530.

Chapter 2

Body Self, Psychological Self, and Bulimia: Developmental and Clinical Considerations

DAVID W. KRUEGER, M.D.

DISRUPTIONS IN BODY–SELF DEVELOPMENT

Freud (1923) recognized the ego as "first and foremost a body ego": bodily experiences are the center around which the ego is developed. He defined body image as the aggregate deposit of internalized images which encompasses the self-representation and internalized representations of love objects. Since Freud's notion of the body ego, the consensus of most developmentalists is that the body self refers to the full range of kinesthetic experiences on the body's surface, in its interior, and its functions (Lichtenberg, 1978, 1985). The body and its evolving mental representation is the foundation of a sense of self.

Lichtenberg (1978, 1985) describes the concept of the body self as a combination of the psychic experience of body sensation, functioning, and image. He hypothesizes that reality testing occurs in a definite developmental sequence of increasing awareness and integration of body self.

The histories of patients with bulimia indicate that early preverbal developmental arrest results in a failure to develop a distinct and separate body self, boundaries, and an accurate body image (Krueger and Schofield, 1987; Krueger, in press).

55

A distorted or nonformed body image is a basic developmental deficit in people coming to treatment for eating disorders (Krueger, 1987). This nonintegration (rather than defensive splitting) of mind and body is related directly to the deficient self-regulation, pathological narcissism, and separation— individuation problems in eating disorder patients (Krueger and Schofield, 1987). The discussion following will, however, apply to bulimic individuals, although we have found many developmental similarities, including the sequence that every bulimic individual whom I have seen had an initial episode, however brief, of anorexic behavior.

Patients who suffer from bulimia have an inadequate internal regulation system, to the extent that they may be unable to recognize such basic body sensations as hunger (Krueger, in press; Bruch, 1973, 1978). The bulimic individual experiences a dreaded state of feeling that her body, indeed her self-organization, is easily invaded, influenced, exploited, and overwhelmed by external force. She has little or no recognition of an internal center of initiative or reference (Krueger, in press). She has struggled for her entire life to be perfect in the eyes of others, to please others, or to reconstitute herself to gain some sense of recognition, identity, effectiveness, and control.

The early developmental arrests which affect the sense of self seem to be based on the absence of a coherent, cohesive, organized body image. The afflicted individuals have a poor or absent sense of their body boundaries (Stroker, Goldberg, and Green, 1979; Garner and Garfinkel, 1981; Krueger and Schofield, 1987).

In the treatment of over 300 eating disorder patients in both inpatient and outpatient settings two findings are consistent.[1] First, the body image of each patient is developmentally

---

[1] The inpatient setting is a nine-person, multidisciplinary treatment team comprising the Eating Disorders Treatment Program which I direct. The treatment efforts are psychoanalytically informed and developmentally organized, integrating both verbal and nonverbal treatment modalities. The outpatient work is psychotherapy or psychoanalysis.

disrupted—blurred, distorted, indistinct, or incomplete.[2] It has been well demonstrated that patients with eating disorders have a sense of estrangement from their bodies, insensitivity to body sensations, and blurred body boundaries (Stroker et al., 1979). Second, they have an early preoedipal and even preverbal developmental arrest which includes a lack of internal body boundaries, distinct body image, and cohesive sense of self (Krueger and Schofield, 1987; Bruch, 1978). Additionally, each individual began definitive developmental improvement (i.e., more than just symptomatic improvement) when aspects of body self (including body image) were addressed and integrated in treatment along with aspects of the psychological self (Krueger and Schofield, 1987).

Lacking internal evocative images of a body self or a psychological self, they rely on external feedback and referents, such as the reactions of others to their appearance and actions, and mirrors. There is a distinct lack of object and internal image constancy.

Previous research indicates that the highest and earliest relapse rate in eating disorder patients occurs in individuals with the most distorted body image (Stroker et al., 1979).

Sugarman and Kurash (1982) postulate that an arrest occurs at the earliest stage of transitional object development in which there is a failure to adequately separate physically and cognitively from the maternal object. This thesis is based on the tenet that the infant's body is the first transitional object on the path to separation and individuation.

Bruch first described (1973) the crucial role of the body image in eating disorders. The association between body image distortion, specifically overestimation of body image, and anxiety, depression, physical anhedonia, and a sense of pervasive ineffectiveness has been demonstrated by other investigators (Garner and Garfinkel, 1981; Rizzuto, Peterson, and Reed,

---

[2] The body image assessment and clinical work is done by sensorimotor assessment and therapy, dance-movement developmental work including projective drawings and videotape (Krueger, 1987), biofeedback techniques developed to address body image and simulation of preverbal mirroring, and other body image work including clay sculpting of body image, and body image tracing.

1981). The severity of this distortion has been correlated with the poorest prognosis (Garfinkel, Moldofsky, and Garner, 1977).

Psychoanalytic explanations of eating disorders have been based in a limited way on a psychosexual model. This model emphasizes a regression from phallic, oedipal issues to oral or anal conflicts and the bodily emaciation is viewed as a secondary retreat to a prepubertal condition. Bruch (1973) stressed interpersonal, familial, and ego disturbances. Only most recently has an object relations model been proposed, in which patients with eating disorders are seen to have developmental difficulties in the separation–individuation process with disruptions and distortions of the underlying self and object representations (Masterson, 1977).

Bruch (1973) described the outstanding pathology as disturbances of body image and concept; defects in the accuracy, perception, and interpretation of stimuli from within the body; and a paralyzing and pervasive sense of ineffectiveness. The central feature of all three predominant symptoms is the experience, perception, and image *of the body*. Other clinicians traced the initial interruption to the state of separation –individuation crystallized during the third year of life (Garner and Garfinkel, 1981; Rizzuto et al., 1981).

These observations can be advanced to include the postulate that the failure to achieve autonomy and separation stems from an even earlier nucleus of arrested development, encountered when the nascent sense of self emerges from mirroring experiences with the mother in the first weeks and months of life. This process extends in changing forms throughout development. The preverbal experiences in the first year of life have failed to acknowledge and confirm a body self separate from the mother (Krueger and Schofield, 1987). It is as if the mother is incapable of accurate, consistent mirroring; of reflecting the child's aliveness, special distinctness, and body and psychic boundaries. In such cases the mother is unable to allow the child the opportunity for an autonomous, internally directed origin of experience and action.

Some very specific developmental functions have either not

occurred or have occurred without sufficient completeness to provide a consistent nucleus for further evolution. Specifically, we have seen evidence that some preverbal and early verbal experiences forming the beginning body self have not developed (Krueger and Schofield, 1987), as though these children's emotions and their bodies were not seen by the parents as separate entities. The parents are typically unable or unwilling to perceive the child as an independent person with a distinct body, feelings, and initiative.

Winnicott (1971) has speculated that the mother's face serves as a mirror for her baby. The sensitive mother is attuned to the feelings emanating from the infant and is able to reflect them in her expressions. The less successful mother recognizes only her own and not her baby's feelings.

The infant's first awareness of being is reflected in the mother's responses and the physical sensations and body presence represented by the mother's handling. Vocalizations and eye contact resonate with the affective state of the infant, and vice versa, so that the pair is in intimate communication. The mother's mirroring of the infant reinforces, affirms, and forms the baby's sense of itself. Empathic, consistent, and accurate mirroring encourages the development of a body self cohesiveness from the unorganized sensory experiences of the infant.

Sensorimotor events initiate the first self and object awareness and representations in the earliest developmental period (Garfinkel et al., 1977). Awareness of the self object is in effect a very tentative distinction between the infant and his interactions. The self object at this point of development is thus almost entirely embedded within the infant's action sequence (Sugarman and Kurash, 1982). The infant's body is his immediate experience of self through reflection, resonance, and internalization of the self object. One's body is the first object and tool of experience, the original substance which can be touched, smelled, and kinesthetically felt. The first external objects are the transitional items which evoke the illusion of the mother. The transitional object is simultaneously external and internal, a creation of the toddler representing both himself

and mother. It further represents development away from reliance on the mother's physical presence, and the capacity to
evoke a representation of her.

The ego and psychological sense of self emanate from this
early body self (Krueger and Schofield, 1987). This seems to
form the basis for an accurate representation of the self, individually fashioned. If the infant's sensations, movements, and
affects are not regularly and accurately acknowledged and af-
firmed, or if they are supplanted by the mother's own needs
and *her* internal state is projected onto the baby, the baby's
development of a sense of self will necessarily be affected. The
process of affirmation continues in varying degrees throughout
development. A false or distorted body image and the failure
to recognize an internal focus of sensation is the basis for some
forms of narcissistic pathology. The nucleus of this pathological
process occurs during the earliest formation of the sense of self,
in the autistic and symbiotic stages of life before separation–
individuation begins. The *preverbal experiences* in the first year
of life typically have failed to acknowledge and confirm a *separate body self* from the mother for individuals who present during early adulthood with eating disorders.

These individuals' nuclear sense of self has not been co-
hesively formed, and remains disorganized and primitive. They
have never integrated mind and body and are, therefore, unable to deny or defensively split them. The resulting maladaptive behaviors represent deficits rather than conflicts. The
individual may not be simply denying a painful affect, she may
have not developed an ability to recognize or distinguish different affects and bodily sensations. The narcissistic individual
may not have a consolidated body image to either deny or
achieve.

A variety of early development processes can go awry and
lead to the disruption or nonestablishment of body self, and
culminate in pathological narcissism. We have found three predominate patterns: empathic unavailability, overintrusiveness,
and inconsistency or selectivity of response (Krueger, in press).
These patterns have emerged from direct observation and from

reconstruction material seen in individual and family work, correlated with projective drawings and body image modalities.

The developmental task is the formation of a stable, integrated, cohesive mental representation of one's body—a core body image of what is inside, what is outside, and a distinct sense of boundaries between the two. The creation of an individual internal space and the evolution of a psychological self typically occur simultaneously.

Disturbances in differentiating self and other affect the ability to create symbols, to distinguish the symbol from the object symbolized, and in turn promotes an arrest at concrete thinking (Segal, 1957).

Lacking an ability to distinguish symbols from objects symbolized, the affected individual elicits a self representation from her own body. The representation of self must emerge from the body self experience, not from a symbolic representation of the self, because, for these individuals, a viable representational image of the self has never developed. The psychological distance required for developmental progress beyond a transitional object is unavailable at this concrete nonsymbolic operational level. *Symbolic equations* rather than *true symbols* predominate (Segal, 1978). Symbolic equations differ from true symbols because they are experienced as the actual object rather than as an emblem of it. With a symbolic equation, there is no as if quality. The individual must engage in body-oriented action or stimulation to regain the need-meeting object. Events which in some way stimulate the body (pain, gorging, starvation, overexertion) create a sensorimotor experience of the body-self. Food is the vehicle used to achieve an experience of a self within the body and re-create the feelings associated with the mother's presence.

These individuals, because of their concrete, nonsymbolic mode of operation, are not able to move to an external non-bodily transitional object. They seem instead to struggle to *create* a transitional object which *is* external, concrete, and specific. This transitional object becomes food, and it is temporarily able to regulate affective states. The effectiveness of the object is fleeting, however, and can remain no more fixed in emotional consciousness than the defective internal images of body, self, or other.

Food is the first transitional object—the bridge between mother and infant. It is not the mother, but it represents her, and is an extension of her body. Food is, however, more a symbolic equation than a true symbol.

These psychological deficits are most profoundly elaborated in bulimia. The pathological developmental course which leaves the young individual with a defective or absent body image, a defective sense of wholeness, and impaired function is the preverbal bedrock of missed experience that appropriate therapeutic efforts must address.

CASE EXAMPLE 1. CLINICAL SEQUENCE: AN ILLUSTRATION

The following case of Jennifer was chosen as representing the most typical symptom–dynamic composite. Jennifer, a college senior, had a four-year history of bulimia, worsening at the beginning of her senior year, two months prior to her presentation for treatment. As we examined a bulimic episode in detail, she described first being aware of a mixture of feeling empty and uncomfortable, and occasionally depressed. She turned immediately to food, with a desire to numb the emptiness. During the binge itself, she felt pleasure, sometimes euphoria. She experienced a magical omnipotence in which she could have, for a moment, whatever she wanted, entirely within her control. During the binge itself she often was frantic, rushed, or anxious. After the binge, she experienced a distended and painful stomach. This gave her a "bad" feeling both real and localized; additionally, it was something she created —both by the action sequenced of binging and by the "bad" food chosen: sweets or "junk" food. Her dysphoria was now an entity which had form, shape, and remedy. She could actively and immediately rid herself of the problem by purging. "Feeling fat" was deemed the cause of feeling bad. Various active maneuvers could then be directed at this malady: dieting, taking diuretics, giving enemas, taking laxatives, and especially incessant exercise. By taking one or more of these directives, she could achieve the illusion of control by controlling actions of her body—literally to get rid of what she had eaten (the bad feeling/object). Then followed a period of feeling guilty about one of these actions, interspersed with feeling tired and relieved at having managed these events. She tried desperately to control her overwhelming compulsion to exercise. She reported that, "I tried and tried not to give in and exercise, but the anxiety was overwhelming. I felt that if I didn't exercise I would lose it—that I would just fade into everyone else around me. Then I'd be like everyone else—not special."

She regressively attempted to vividly reestablish her body self experience and boundaries in order to feel real and distinct. Her stimulation and reintegration of her basic body self was, at the time, a primitive but effective effort at psychic reorganization. A tenuous equilibrium was established until the next precipitant.

The precipitant, important to reconstruct in therapeutic work, was typically a disruption in a self/self-object bond, with the impending or actual disconnectedness with an important person. A narcissistic hurt followed immediately, with resultant emptiness or rage.

Feeling "bad" was the result for Jennifer of feeling ineffective: particularly ineffective in either maintaining an empathic connectedness with an important other, or in maintaining a connectedness with the ideal self (which was unattainable as her goal was perfection). Her unattainable goals of perfection particularly centered on grades, weight, and other highly valued social referents.

Jennifer vividly described this process of attempting to find something external, concrete, and specific to be able to control, in order to feel effective when her internal state is unfocused.

When I felt empty and lonely as a girl, I would wish something really bad would happen to me. So then I would have a real reason for feeling bad, something concrete and real. It would have to be something really terrible, like an accident and bleeding, so others could see my hurting and

believe it; then I could believe it, too, and know what it
was. I didn't understand what was the matter. After I had
something bad that would happen to me in my fantasy,
then I'd feel better. When it's inside and no one sees it, you
just want people to know, to be able to see it. Maybe then
it would feel more real. I would also daydream about it
after I came to make something bad happen, then I would
have someone to comfort me. I would imagine, for example, being hit on the head and getting a bruise so that
someone could see it—so they could see I was hurt. I would
actually do that at times, but then I'd feel embarrassed and
hide it even though I wanted someone to care for me and
comfort me. Recently, when I binge and feel fat, and see
my distended stomach it is something for me to feel bad
about. I created it. I wished to get skinny so that people
could see how skinny I was and see me as sick. Sometimes
I wish they'd find something wrong with me physically so
they could see it and get rid of it.

The search for a focus for dysphoric affect is an attempted
mastery, of converting passivity to activity, and to be effective
in eliciting a specific response–validation from an important
self object.

Jennifer recognized more detail. "I feel helpless, worthless
that I can't control how someone responds to me. That's what
brings me back to my body—to be destructive at least—to binge.
It's a substitute for the things I can't get and want. I'm out of
control. I take in something to feel better, then I feel more in
control." As I commented that this must seem the only way at
the moment that she can feel effective, she responded, "Yes.
If it's not the way I want it to be, I can eat my way into feeling
better—at least for a little while. Then I'm back to where I was
before—miserable."

I indicated that at least, though, she determined this misery. Her response: "Yes. I brought that about. At least I'm in
control of something. It's also a substitute for the intimacy that
I can't seem to achieve with anyone. It makes me feel better.
It calms the anxiety. Binging and purging makes me feel slowed

down and tired. It makes me blank out, and I don't have to think, and for that moment I don't have to think about how bad I feel."

She further indicated one bite could initiate her binge, thinking of it as "all or nothing." I interpreted how it was as if she were not responsible at that point. She agreed that she readily abdicated responsibility, then added that it was probably her wish not to grow up, not to assume full responsibility for what she did.

"What I do to feel good hasn't worked. Feeling good is going to have to come from someone else. It's more important what someone else thinks. If you think about yourself, you'll end up not having anything. I think, 'so what' of what I think. My opinion is worthless." I pointed out how her active process of invalidation, and of not listening to herself from inside resulted in a feeling of worthlessness.

She felt ineffective at getting her parents to respond to her feeling and perceptions. Her conclusion, present from early childhood, was that she was not good enough, and needs to try harder. More achievement, more attractiveness, thinness, seemed to her to be the answer.

We reconstructed, from an adaptive context, the usefulness of her symptom. While the search has been for magical cure, her intent was to regulate her affect and sense of self during the pretreatment symptomatic time using food as the symbol of the nurturing self object.

PSYCHODYNAMIC ASPECTS

Particularly at times of major increments of separation–individuation, the body assumes a crucial importance. An emergence of sexuality occurs in pubescence; separation from the parental home in young adulthood necessitates independent functioning. At these major developmental junctures, as well as others such as marriage and pregnancy, many bulimic individuals become aware of their pervasive reliance on external cues to direct them, and of the absence of an internal center of initiative and regulation.

Their developmental arrest includes the arrest of the cognitive capacity to symbolize self objects without effective separation and individuation, with the result that self/self-object distinction is blurred and incomplete. Disengagement and symbolization of the self object are incomplete. The affected individuals have not objectified and symbolized their bodies: their bodies are still used as transitional objects, and they have failed to progress beyond preoperational *symbolic equations* to such complex cognitive and object-relational capacities as *symbolism* of self, body, and other.

Maintenance and control of self–other boundaries is a lifelong process. For this individual, the sense of the body remains a central focus, and can never be accepted and internalized as long as development is stalled at this level. The body as a transitional object fails to gradually lose meaning as it does (and as transitional objects do) in normal development.

The individual who has never completely integrated body self and psychological self has difficulty resolving an essential addiction to maternal part objects. The excessive reliance on self objects supplements functioning. This continuing need is alternately gratified or denied in the arena of the body. Symbols of autonomous selfhood are either lacking or totally confined to the context of bodily experience. The developmental arrest affects body self and schema, psychological self, and some cognitive capacities, particularly abstractions and objectification regarding one's self as a whole, and the permanence and completeness of body image.

These disorders manifest as deficiencies of self-regulation. Food is used as an external replacement for a deficient internal regulator and a deficient integration of mind and body. Relying on other people for their supply of affirmation, enhancement, function, and esteem, they attempt to find a way to internalize the source of these emotional goods. The frenetic pace of excruciating exercise, running, and swimming may appear to be for the purpose of losing weight, but is actually a desperate attempt to experience the reality of their bodies, for which they do not have an accurate or distinct mental representation. It is also an effort (as is controlling eating or vomiting) at countering the anguish of internal emptiness, boredom, and deadness. As a young bulimic woman explained, "I feel completely helpless and ineffective, and I don't know what's wrong or how to feel better. At least when I focus on food and feel fat, I have *something* I can control and do something about."

Many bulimics have experienced emotional deprivation imposed by others, and unconsciously choose to convert their role as passive victims to the role of active victim by imposing deprivation (of food) upon themselves, alternating with engorgement. The bulimic patient attempts to supply for herself what is missing via the symbolic equation of food and nurturance. This dynamic, incorporating symbolism with magical thinking, was summarized by a patient who said, "It's like I have anything and everything I've always wanted when I am in the middle of a binge. And by getting rid of it all immediately I don't even have to pay the price of getting fat."

The first words used are metaphors for the body, and its separateness from the mother. The infant who learns to say "no" states a distinctness from the parent. "No" says "I am not an extension of you. I am me, and I am in charge of me." This is also the attempt of the anorexic who says "no" to food proffered by her parents: "I don't need you or anything you give me."

In every one of the over 300 bulimics seen to date, the individual has first developed anorexic symptoms: They say "no" to food. This caricature of normal development is an attempted statement of *separation* ("I don't need you or anything you provide; this is where you end and I begin—me and my body are not an extension of you") and of *individuation* ("I am not you and I can control *one* thing in the world—what comes into my body").

As these attempts at separation–individuation inevitably fail, some individuals proceed from a passive to an active effort by binging and purging. Here both sides of the developmental dilemma are expressed. Binging or addictive overeating are attempts to create a need-satisfying person or function (e.g., self-soothing). The addictive eating is an effort to fill the emptiness of depression and the absence of self-regulation. There is a yearning for nurturing, characterized by consuming a "good" object (food), and expelling a "bad" object (acidic vomitus). The bulimic individual expresses her intense anger at those who fail to meet her needs by denying need. Her effort at self-regulation in a cycle of binging and purging metaphorically states that "I will take you in my own way and I will vomit you out and be without you, proving that I don't need you. She attempts to incorporate what is good, soothing, nurturing, and essential to life, to be independent of the need for others, and to anesthetize painful affects with food.

The binging briefly provides the illusion that all the emotional hunger of the past is being satisfied, as if a dream comes true. The "magic" of early childhood is incorporated in the binge and purge: hurts, rebuffs, and feelings of emptiness are soothed, and all sense of responsibility and consequences are subsequently expelled. This reenacts the nonseparation and nonindividuation of early childhood. The process is designed to avoid mourning the past and extract a feeling of nurturance. But, in the end, a symbol is only a symbol. Food is at best a disappointing counterfeit for a genuine emotional life.

Bulimic patients come to be aware that their interactions with food are representations of other interactions and feelings.

CASE EXAMPLE 2. SEPARATION–INDIVIDUATION ISSUES

Kari, at age nineteen, was in her first year of college when she presented for treatment with a six-year history of bulimia. She captured her dilemma in these words: "Binging was a dream come true—the one area in my whole life where I can have anything and everything I want. All my fantasies of having no limits or bounds are here, and I don't even have to worry about getting fat. Then I lost control of it a few months ago and can't stop."

Kari first began refusing food at age thirteen by imposing on herself a strict diet, as she felt "fat." At that time, her parents began having serious difficulties with their marriage. With a withdrawal of her parents into their own problems, a thinly veiled abandonment depression was crystallized in this already depleted young girl. She was on the brink of becoming symptomatic with the mounting tensions of pubescence, the associated bodily changes, and the increased social pressure at school, and her parents' emotional estrangement was the additional stressor that could not be tolerated. When Kari first refused food, pushing it back at the table, her restriction metaphor said, "I don't need food or anyone else" and "I'm pushing back the anger I am full of." Her food restriction lasted about three months and she lost 18 pounds, until she became scared and depressed, and interspersed binging episodes with her restriction. When she binged, she felt nurtured and provided for, and as if she could have anything and everything she wanted—like childhood restored. The binge focused her pain on her distended stomach, and she came to prefer the discomfort of a stomach engorged with food to the discomfort of a consciousness engorged with rage or the discomfort of emptiness.

She began to increasingly compensate for the loss of connectedness with her parents by binge eating. She could magically construct her parents in her mind as she ate and be completely in control of a source of nurturance. By displaying her behavior to her parents, she could elicit predictable (although negative) responses from them and force them to engage rather than withdraw from her.

When her parents did not respond immediately and exactly as she wanted—as an extension of her desire and interest—she became enraged. She was thus confronted with her separateness, distinctness, and disconnectedness from them and others.

During therapy she became aware that her focus during the binge was always on what she could have *next*, never what she had at the moment. What she could eat next kept the illusion of satisfaction seemingly only a bite away. She reflected, "It's like I'm looking for something, but never finding it. The food isn't it."

By "looking for the answer," she maintained the hope that perfect satisfaction (just the right food) would be only one step away. The food chosen was always "taboo" (sweets), which confirmed her feeling that she was bad for eating in the way she did.

Her purge was a symbolic release of the fullness of anger *and* of her need for anyone or anything external. She would then ask her parents for something which she knew would be refused, such as permission to stay out until 1:00 A.M. As planned, they refused, and she became angry, with two results: She had engineered a situation in which she controlled where, when, and how circumstances would unfold, and she had an opportunity to focus her anger at her parents, again becoming the victim, but predictably and by her own hand.

By reviewing this sequence to assess the internal as well as external scenarios, she came to recognize her own self-abandonment as she experienced the rupture of a self-object bond. The resultant emptiness, which she had attempted to fill with food, could be examined as an active process of her failed self-empathy.

These events, and the onset of her bulimia, appeared at the developmental juncture of the recognition of her parents as entities distinct from her, the objectification of parents as people with problems and human feelings. This traumatic disillusionment was complicated by her already fragile connectedness with her parents and her sense of self.

SUMMARY

Disturbances in differentiating self and other affect the individual's ability to create symbols of the body self and the affective self. Distinctions between the symbol and the object symbolized are incomplete; thinking is concrete, without the capacity for abstraction or representation of the body and its contents, including feelings.

The failure to achieve this subjectivity of body self and self experience relates to the difficulty for the individual to symbolize, fantasize, or integrate body self and psychological self. The enhanced subjectivity and objectivity of the self as a result of developmentally informed treatment is a reflection of the ability to differentiate the symbol, the object being symbolized, and the action creating the symbol (Segal, 1957).

An individual with a defective or incomplete body self (and thus psychological self) is motivated toward completion and restitution of that basic defect. The symptomatic act is an attempted adaptation of restitution of body self integrity and restoration of self/self-object bond. Evaluation of the symptom's adaptive function must consider the locus and nature of the symptom and its sequence, the nature of the restitutive attempt, and the state or condition which restitution seeks.

REFERENCES

Bruch, H. (1973), *Eating Disorders.* New York: Basic Books.
——— (1978), *The Golden Cage.* Cambridge, MA: Harvard University Press.
Freud, S. (1923), The ego and the id. *Standard Edition,* 19:12–60. London: Hogarth Press, 1961.
Garfinkel, P., Moldofsky, M., & Garner, D. (1977), Prognosis in anorexia nervosa as influenced by clinical features, treatment and self-perception. *Can. Med. Assn. J.,* 117:1041–1045.
Garner, D., & Garfinkel, P. (1981), Body image in anorexia nervosa: Measurement, theory and clinical implications. *Internat. J. Psychiat. Med.,* 11:263–184.
Krueger, D. (1987), The "parent loss" of empathic failures and the model symbolic restitution of eating disorders. In: *The Problem of Loss and Mourning: New Psychoanalytic Perspectives,* ed. D. Dietrich & P. Shabad. Madison, CT: International Universities Press.
Krueger, D. (in press), *Body Self and Psychological Self: Developmental and Clinical Aspects of Disorders of the Self,* New York: Brunner/Mazel.
Krueger, D., & Schofield, E. (1987), An integration of verbal and nonverbal therapies in disorders of the self. *J. Arts in Psychother.* 13:323–331
Lichtenberg, J. (1978), The testing of reality from the standpoint of the body self. *J. Amer. Psychoanal. Assn.,* 26:357–385.
——— (1985), *Psychoanalysis and Infant Research.* Hillside, NJ: Analytic Press.
Masterson, J. (1977), Primary anorexia nervosa in the borderline adolescent: An object-relations view. In: *Borderline Disorders,* ed. P. Hartocollis. New York: International Universities Press, pp. 475–494.
Rizzuto, A., Peterson, M., & Reed, M. (1981), The pathological sense of self in anorexia nervosa. *Psychiat. Clin. N. Amer.,* 4:471–487.
Segal, H. (1957), Notes on symbol formation. *Internat. J. Psycho-Anal.,* 38:391–397.
——— (1978), On symbolism. *Internat. J. Psycho-Anal.,* 59:315–319.
Stroker, M., Goldberg, I., Green, J., (1979), Body image disturbances in

anorexia nervosa during the acute and recuperation period. *Psychol. Med.*, 9:695–901.
Sugarman, A., & Kurash, C. (1982), The body as transitional object in bulimia. *Internat. J. Eat. Disord.*, 1:57–62.
Winnicott, D. (1971), *Playing and Reality.* New York: Basic Books.

Chapter 3

Experiencing and Recovering Transitional Space in the Analytic Treatment of Anorexia Nervosa and Bulimia

MARJORIE P. SPRINCE

In my previous communications on anorexic and bulimic patients (Sprince, 1978, 1981, 1984) I described my experience of the countertransference to demonstrate the unconscious impulsion felt by these patients to restore the lost union with the feeding mother. I emphasized that this fusion is both relentlessly sought and equally relentlessly defended against. I suggested that food is used unconsciously to represent and control intrapsychically, both the object and the affects belonging to that relationship, in such a way as to avoid terror, fusion, and/or dissolution of the self. I stressed that early interpretations of libidinal material is experienced as irrelevant and may bring about a state of despair and rage that sexuality rather than emptiness, loneliness, longing for union, and terror of closeness, was to be the area of analytic attention.

Since the time of writing other clinicians have been impressed by the anorexic's wish for and fear of fusion with the mother (Boris, 1984; Hughes et al., 1985; Birksted Breen, 1985). Hughes et al. (1985), suggest that fear of fusion with the mother by projection and reintrojection could lead to the necessity of finding a way of having a body different from the mother. In her view it is as if maturing into adulthood is experienced not as being like the mother, but as *becoming* the mother. Winnicott's paper, "Fear of Breakdown" (1974), emphasized that agonies of emptiness and nonexistence belonging to the past have to be lived through in the present. It is still my experience that the crucial phase in the treatment of anorexic and overeating patients is when they find themselves experiencing their analyst as if she were the part they feel to be missing in themselves, the part that they can no longer replace by food or concentration on it, or their body image. It is a stage in treatment when the defenses against engulfment or devastating separateness are threatened in the transference so that the patient fears that primitive terrors of unimaginable proportion are about to be unleashed. It is with this threat of impending and overwhelming disaster that the need for the "real thing," namely, the safe nurturing object (self object), is intensified. In my clinical illustrations I show how some patients at least are able to live through with their analyst–mother, what they imagined to be "an unsurvivable experience," and experience it as survivable.

An experience of adequate nurturing may be viewed as pleasurable to both child and mother, leading to the delineation of self and nonself, and ultimately to a sense of personal identity. This involves the child's capacity to accept and value her own feelings. In this connection I have found Margaret Mahler's (1961) concept of separation–individuation meaningful and helpful. Boris (1984) speaks of the failure of this process in terms of lack of transitional space for the anorexic and the lack of a "not me" and "not you" space. Birksted Breen postulates the possibility of a third term—the father who disrupts the fantasy of fusion—a point I will come back to later since I wonder whether the father's role in this illness may not at times be neglected.

I hope I have succeeded in emphasizing that the problem of the anorexic is not primarily oral, but is the terror of passionate longings and fears which the illness must obliterate by defenses such as projections, displacement, and reaction formations. In terms of intake, however, I suggest that the illness can be viewed as a compulsion to ingest while equally to avoid digesting. Thus the object can never be experienced as fully separate or satisfactorily internalized.

In this paper I hope to explore further the deprivation of "transitional space" in these patients—the causes, effects, and implications for treatment—and to develop the notion that the analytic process may recover and extend the safe experience of transitional space for the patient. I will further put forward the suggestion that in those cases where there has been an experience of both parents competing for a symbiotic relationship with their child, the achievement of a transitional space may be further threatened. Because individuation has never been achieved in relation to the mother, the child can only experience the father as fused into a joint internal image with the mother. In these cases overt suicide may appear as the only solution. To challenge death by starvation or suicide can mean to the patient that they are all-powerful and have no needs. They can at least achieve a separateness and an identity.

Over the last four years I have been struck by the almost religious fervor in the anorexic's need to develop a body so strong and self-sufficient that it can do without nurture. When one considers that food and touch (also sight and smell) are initially so closely related to the supplying object, it becomes meaningful that food, and often touch, must be denuded of value. Gradually all apparent interest in food and body contact may be removed in favor of the need to achieve the *lack of need*. But this solution can be seen to require further reinforcement when the patient is impelled to prove to herself that not only has she no needs but it is the others who are "needy." Thus she projects her needs onto those around her who experience an impulsion to feed, protect, and nurture *her*. In this connection I have found papers by Boris (1984) most helpful. He describes how the analyst can be caught in the countertransference trap of needing to nurture yet to remain apparently neutral. In the latter case, the analyst may become a superior sort of anorexic, strong and self-depriving, with even fewer needs than the patient, and therefore becomes an object of envy. But the "nurturing" analyst–mother is equally threatening since hidden behind these nurturing wishes is an enviable and tempting resource. A resource of which the analyst–mother must be denuded.

It is important to bear in mind that an experience of a disturbance in nurturing such as I am describing, colors, influences, and interacts with each phase of development and that the fact that the illness may first appear in adolescence is often misleading. However, adolescence with its new defense formation against body changes, identity conflicts, and loss of object, colludes with the illness.

CASE EXAMPLE

My patient, Ms. A. appeared to have warded off sexuality. She left her country of origin to "stand on her own feet." She was twenty when she came for treatment having been hospitalized at seventeen when her weight was under 70 pounds. Her menstruation ceased one year after it started and she was emphatic that she did not want her periods ever again. She had short dyed hair, a boyish gait, and her clothes were untidy. She was arrogant in manner, but could change into a warm friendly person with an open smile. The second youngest of a large family, with an eminent ambitious medical father around whom the entire family life centered, Ms. A. was seen as a docile, biddable, and exceptionally intelligent child. She felt that she was loved for her achievements which added to the family glory but that no one "caught on" to her personal gifts, longings, or interests. She believed her parents showed no pleasure in what she *was*. For a long time in treatment any sign of improvement was experienced as adding to my glory rather than to her well-being.

At school and later at a university, Ms. A. felt herself to exist only as her father's daughter and felt ashamed of her privileged background; but she felt equally ashamed of her family's puritanical attitude and the fact that she appeared poor and deprived of pocket money and other indulgences compared with her fellow students. She only felt happy when helping others and feeling needed. She left the university just before receiving a degree—ostensibly because she did not like "academia."

She came to see me reluctantly and angrily because treatment implied privilege and elitism. She complained of depression, panic states, feelings of unreality, and an inability to sustain relationships with roommates or other friends. She considered her overactivity and preoccupation with weight and diet normal and did not want it interfered with. She soon enacted her ambivalence by ceaseless talking, wanting me to make decisions for her, and complaining that she had no time for herself to exercise, jog, or swim, because she had to work to contribute towards her treatment. She never missed a session but averred that holidays were a period of freedom, and that she would drop her treatment at once if an interesting work opportunity occurred in another country. She complained and raged about her jobs. The happier and more valued she was in any job, the more she felt tied and suffocated by it so that she had no time for herself. Yet her need to be needed was such that she was always compelled to take on new commitments and fill up every moment of her time.

In spite of her regular attendance, for many months the feeling in the sessions was one of a lack of involvement and "inner absence." I believe she achieved this by projecting into me what she could not permit herself to feel. I found myself feeling that I was the needy greedy person who wanted to give her something to satisfy myself. At times I caught myself wanting to reach and comfort her and I feared her loss. Certainly she did not wish to *need* my analytic food. Boris (1984) sees this denuding of the analyst of nurturing value as based on envy of the mother's food, and greed for it. As with Ms. M. in my previous paper, Ms. A. described her mother as a denigrated figure whose prime role was feeding father and the family. When it became possible to speak of her need to deny that I might have something valuable and satisfying to give her and her possible envy of my good resources, her rage and fear of the commitments she felt impelled to take on outside the analysis increased. I spoke of her fear of commitment to me and of her longing to enjoy some of my comforting analytic food, and the dangers she felt this might lead to. Ms. A. now became terrified that I would fill her up, invade her, and take her over; then she wouldn't be able to think for herself or be separate. She became confused and for some days felt her thoughts to be out of control and that she must eat and vomit (vomit me out).

About this time Ms. A. brought her first song creation—"nice girls *cook and look* to satisfy men, but they have no lusts themselves." In the following session she commented that she had never brought a dream, while a friend who was not in therapy valued and wrote his dreams down. We agreed that if she kept her dreams hidden, they remained hers and I couldn't take them from her. Ms. A. was silent and then observed that she kept having an odd feeling that she had already left the room. She told me that this sense of panic and of having left the room was not new, that she had in fact, experienced it for some time in her sessions. I suggested that the panic had to do with a threat of dangerous closeness and that she was ensuring that there was a space between us and that she was "separate and able to leave the room and me behind." It was almost as if she felt split—both "here" and "not here." This conflict over terror of closeness and longing for it was associated with a sense of "nonexistence" (her term).

Ms. A. now described long hours of walking in the fields or by the sea alone. Sometimes she composed songs. One of these was "when will they discover me." I spoke of her feeling of nonexistence and her fear that she did not exist for me. That she longed to be close to me, part of me, the only person who existed for me. As her wish to be fused with me became clearer, Ms. A.'s sessions became more silent and anxious, although interspersed with rages about the nonsense I talked. At times she felt depersonalized. Ms. A. brought me a set of tapes with the words of songs she had composed in which she expressed her loneliness, longings, and primitive needs. The themes included "won't someone hear me," "listen, listen, listen," or the song of the dressmaker's dummy who was always there waiting patiently for her in the kitchen "because she is my friend and will stick by me whatever they say." We spoke about the implications of "the dummy," a nonintrusive mother–analyst who was both comforting and not actively threatening: separate and on her side. It was also like a child's dummy—not alive, yet something threatening to be alive but which she could spit out when she felt invaded.

Although opposed to academia and ambition, Ms. A. began to realize that without proper training she would remain dissatisfied. Three years after treatment commenced, she gained admission to a college specializing in her art form in which she uses her body as a medium of expression. At this point she brought her first dreams. Two are helpful to this discussion:

DREAM 1

Ms. A. was in a gym class where the instructor was demonstrating running and falling. He spoke of "release." She was loving it, falling down and then falling up. But the instructor shouted at her that it was all wrong. Ms. A. replied that she knew she wasn't as good at "falling up." The instructor shouted, "It isn't the rising—I want you to fall with a slam."

DREAM 2

This concerned a girl's "body popping" group. On the way to the performance there was an older girl, a little girl, and a boy who had run away. The police came. The older sister, whom Ms. A. thought was herself, had a gun. She told the children to run and hide. The little girl was crying, "I am hungry, I am hungry."

These dreams were central to our work for many months. Without going into details of our interpretive work, it contained the first acknowledgment of Ms. A.'s neediness, her envy of other people's resources and strengths, and her impulsion to hide from her rage and violence and from dependence and longing. The theme of risking trust was opened up and enabled her to recognize the need to abandon the delusion of self-sufficiency. Ms. A. told me that she had always experienced authority figures as "slamming her down." We spoke of whether I was the policeman threatening to take away her gun, her strength and self-protection, or whether I might really want to enable her to find release from her impulsions. This led to fears of hungry demands and thoughts of damaging me.

Ms. A. began to notice my other patients and admit to curiosity about them. We spoke of her personal separateness and mine and her fear that I could not value and enjoy her as a self, if she and I had lives of our own. Ms. A. risked missing a session without warning me "to see if she could do it." She had felt a bit like that when she had started eating increasingly less for each meal—the onset of her acute anorexia. But we now saw a further fear, namely that I might be able to survive as a separate person without her. The body popping group—a boy's province—referred to her determination to be strong both physically and mentally and able to bear any pain and deprivation. She told me that "in her anorexic days" her determination to be the strongest and best was such that she wouldn't have minded dying just as long as she could be the thinnest anorexic to die.

Ms. A. now began to show concern over her sexual disinterest and admitted to a brief sexual experience at the point of her hospitalization. She felt that something must be wrong since her friends moved on and were able to work in spite of partnerships with men. She observed that it was likely that I did so, too. It was at this point that her menstruation restarted and she admitted to being glad. She wondered whether her fear of closeness could be related to a wish to be like me—a working wife and mother. Only one of her sisters ever wanted children.

Ms. A. has recently started college so that we can only meet occasionally. She feels that there is hope for her since she is "more of 'a self' " and can make relationships and is so much happier. At one of her recent sessions she remarked, "I don't always know what I feel about you but there seems to be space in this room."

Ms. A.'s fantasy of being the thinnest anorexic to die emphasizes the anorexic's denial of emotional and bodily needs in an attempt at mastery over death. I do not think that death necessarily means the same to these patients as it does to us. I think they see it primarily as an escape from fusion. To risk death can mean having the strength to have no needs, to have an identity at last. In that sense it may mean having the space to live. Most anorexics challenge death by depriving themselves of food (representing the self object). Overt suicidal acts are not characteristic of anorexia, although I believe them to be more common in their obverse, the overeating patient. When overt suicidal attempts do take place, exploration may throw light on the unconscious dynamic of the illness in general.

It is in this connection that I wish to return to the role of the father in this illness. A common factor in all these cases appears to be the breakdown in emotional contact with the object so that the mother's containing capacity and pleasurable enjoyment in and with her child is interfered with. Birksted Breen (1985), in discussing fusion in terms of the lack of transitional space for the anorexic, suggests that one might speculate on the "lack of a third term" (the father who disrupts the fantasy of fusion). She is, I understand, suggesting that the patient is only able to experience the object in terms of part of the self—no third person can be allowed to disrupt the sense of symbiosis.

In my earlier communications I mention that several of my patients had fathers who were perceived as excessively seductive, collusive, or not available to either patient or mother. Two of my patients, one a bulimic and the other an anorexic were referred after making their first overt suicidal attempts. Both made subsequent suicidal attempts during treatment and I felt sure that not only was their father's pathology significant but that their suicidal attempts expressed a fantasy of killing the internalized father (myself in the transference) so that they could reach the mother.

Characteristic of both these patients was that from infancy onward they experienced their father as competing with the mother for symbiotic union with them. I hope to illustrate that in such cases, separation–individuation may not only be additionally impeded, but the father may be experienced as an extension or replacement of the "fusion object" (the mother). It is often difficult when working with these patients for the analyst to be clear who she represents in the transference at any one time and ultimately to enable the patient to disentangle the blurred mother–father image she represents. In neither of my patients did the transference reflect any evidence of paternal pleasure in the child's development of a "self," but only an external battle for possession.

In such cases, the process of adolescence intensifies the attempt to achieve a separate sense of identity and adds to an already paralyzing sense of confusion, longing, and terror of union. From the transference it appears that there seems to be no escape other than the delusion of strength and self-sufficiency by suicide; namely, by destroying the symbiotic father image in the hope of reaching a separate mother. Unless this is recognized and anticipated in time, the wish to identify with the analyst–mother may result in a period of hazard for the patient.

I hope I can illustrate this briefly by describing the terminations of these two patients. The first is Ms. M. whose treatment is described in my previous paper (1984).

Ms. M. was eighteen at the time of referral, had made a suicidal attempt at the age of eleven associated with her parents' separation, her mother's first boyfriend, and extreme conflict over her love–hate relationship with her father, whom she visited for weekends and holidays.

Gradually she felt compelled to run away from her father to mother. Yet, back with her mother, she felt no comfort either. She was unhappy in school, gorged and vomited many times a day, and had become acutely phobic. From the transference it could be seen that she had experienced her father as tyrannical in his overbearing adulation of her, and pathetic in his loneliness and dependence on animals, which he kept caged in his house. He had, she insisted, taken over her body care from infancy. She always felt that he saw her entirely in terms of what he wanted her to be: his slim, fragile extension who would travel the world with him and ultimately inherit and live in his house. She remembered parental rows over his indulgence of her. Her mother was experienced as a powerful yet tragic figure who attracted people to her as a spider draws flies into its web. By sapping their strength she made them dependent and masked her own dependence. Early in treatment Ms. M. said "Sometimes I think she is a witch from whom one can only escape by dying, as father did." She came into treatment still inconsolable over father's death six years before, feeling guilty that for many years visiting him had been unbearable.

In my 1984 paper, I described Ms. M.'s treatment at length; the many transference horrors of merging and loss of boundaries associated with fears of going mad while with me "as if there was no space between us" (her words). Ultimately, there were signs of progress: I seemed to become a less threatening mother in the transference. Ms. M. left home for an apartment of her own and found a college where her occasional phobic panics could be tolerated. She began to make men friends and then married a man with children. Their violent and tempestuous relationship repeated in many ways the pattern of her parents' marriage. Then the difficulties seemed to subside and there was a tranquil period. Ms. M. found her way back to her professional training while being the sort of mother to her stepchildren that she had longed for her mother to be. While food and body image no longer appeared to play such a significant part, both Ms. M. and her husband drank too much and their sex life was difficult. During a short holiday, while Ms. M. had my telephone number, she made another suicidal attempt following a violent row with her husband. She telephoned me from the hospital reporting that "mother is different now, she has changed, she is worried about me." Her next telephone call was despairing. It wasn't as she had thought. On her return she remained insistent that her suicidal attempt had nothing to do with my holidays, but she became furious and despairing that after so many years of treatment she should still want to damage herself. I had done her no good. I think that at the point of her attempted identification with me as the analyst–mother, I failed to catch on to the fragility of her identity and selfness or to anticipate the difficulty in differentiating between the fused mother–father image. I did not pay enough attention to the possibility that the disentanglement might still easily breakdown. I think this act was foreshadowed in the communication referring to mother as a witch from whom one could only escape by dying as father did. She separated from her husband and was determined to leave me, too. She broke off treatment abruptly by sending me a note saying that she would not be returning but would find a different form of therapy. Some months later she sent me a brief New Year's note saying that she and her husband were back together in a new house and that she was enjoying her work and home.

It is possible that my holiday had accentuated Ms. M.'s dependence upon her husband. On her return, she had complained that he stayed out late at night without warning her, showed little concern for her needs, and, in general, made no attempt to comfort and nurture her. Thus the discovery of his neediness and his inability to deal with her dependence and despair tempted her back into the symbiotic fusion with the internalized father–mother image. In her rage with her husband, she would be thrown back onto the mother–analyst in such a way as to experience her neediness and dependence as unbearable. She would be overwhelmingly threatened by the engulfing analyst–mother "with no space between us"—neither parent could help her. Suicide seemed the only answer.

Ms. D. weighed 238 pounds. She came into treatment because of a second suicide attempt at eighteen years of age associated with her inability to separate from a symbiotic relationship with her somewhat rigid Catholic father with whom she had lived since she was eighteen months old. He then finally took over the mothering role and the parents separated. Ms. D. was smelly and dirty, giggled stupidly, and insisted that she had to be fat so that she did not attract father into whose bed she still went. She demonstrated mad behavior by lying full length on the waiting room floor so that she would be found by the next patient, and she would eat from street garbage bins. She was pathetically unsightly, isolated, and friendless. She could not work and would lie in bed for days.

Her long and often painful analysis was characterized by

rage, destructive behavior, longing for and terror of merging, loss of boundaries, and madness. She insisted furiously that since we were born under the same astrological constellation, our life experiences and affects must be identical. This same patient flew into a paroxysm of anxiety and rage when I phrased an interpretation using her own words. She screamed "don't you know the difference, they are my words and thoughts and you used them as if you were me." It is possible that when I used her words she felt that she had got inside me and taken me over (or the reverse). Her demands for me "to be the real thing" were punctuated with suicidal threats and culminated in a third suicidal attempt. We worked on my fused father–mother role in the transference and how she felt invaded and over-whelmed by me. Gradually I became mother who first abandoned and failed to protect her, but equally failed to help her find a sense of transitional space.

This work led to Ms. D. achieving geographical separation from her father, an independent profession that required lengthy training, which she completed, and, after a period of alarming promiscuity, a partner whom she ultimately married. Her partner, although older was both dependent and needy. He suffered from an incipient addiction which Ms. D. took in hand.

Gradually our work brought about a changed juxtaposition. My patient found an easier relationship with her father and made contact with her mother. Food no longer played an important role in her life. She became pretty and dressed well. There came a point, however, when despite an increasing sense of selfness and achievement she became angry, depressed, and suicidal. She considered her husband not good enough for her and thought of leaving him (mother had left father). Much of her feeling was directed against me in the transference and the notion that I would not let her go. But she felt "too mad to manage without me." While working on the repetition of her relationship both to father and mother in the transference, and in particular on how her increasing selfness led to identification with a mother who denigrated and left her husband and children, Ms. D. made a fourth and serious suicide attempt which resulted in bringing father to her side.

We understood this as a transference repetition related to problems of terror which meant that a transitional space was as threatening as being invaded. As work proceeded we could see in the transference how her attempts to kill off the internalized self object, at times father and at times mother, left her at the mercy of the other parent. She could not visualize negotiating a safe identity of her own. While continuing to be angry and depressed, Ms. D. wanted to stop treatment, thereby frightening me and activating my nurturing feelings. We agreed that we would fix a termination date far enough ahead to work through the implications of her acting out and of where she felt I had failed to understand her need for space.

Work could now be done on how she could use the analyst and analysis to consolidate her own sense of selfness and gradually be able to experience me as a nonthreatening separate person. Thus she was able to acknowledge the fact that she had a personal identity that I could value. Her envy of my mothering qualities which had played a part latterly in her treatment and which she had threatened repeatedly to denude me of, could be explored again in her wish to have children. The sadness at separating (being abandoned and abandoning) was associated with the notion that she had no right to be happy without me. Before the end of treatment, Ms. D. and her husband bought a dog and she was able to express reparative and grateful feelings toward me by laughing references to herself as a feeding mother, "like you."

Ms. D. kissed me when she left. She kept contact over four years with brief six-month bulletins. Two years after treatment ended she brought her three-month-old baby to show me. The picture of her life was a contented one based on needing a partner to need her and to provide a backcloth for her as she did for father. This enabled her, I think, to identify with the analyst mother who is also the "fusion object"—the breadwinner father. Ms. D. has managed her affairs so that she can continue to work from home.

With patients such as Ms. A. and Ms. D., it is helpful to

bear in mind the anorexic's and bulimic's capacity to stimulate the analyst's omnipotent wish to nurture. The analyst has to come to terms with limited achievements which may include precipitate terminations or marriages in which either neediness or disturbance in the partner plays a significant role. The choice of a partner is frequently one on to whom the patient can externalize or project remaining aspects of her illness and thus feel free of them herself. Mostly the treatment outcome can only be judged in retrospect if one is lucky enough to keep contact.

Summary

I have tried to explore further the deprivation of "transitional space" in anorexic and bulimic patients—the causes, effects, and implications for threatment. I am suggesting that the analytic process may recover and extend the safe experience of a transitional space for the patient. I have further put forward the notion that in those cases where the child experiences the father's needs as leading him to compete symbiotically with the mother, the achievement of a transitional space may be further threatened since both internalized objects become fused into one blurred image. In these cases overt suicide may appear to be the only solution.

References

Birksted Breen, D. (1985), Working with an anorexic patient. *Bull. Brit. Psycho-Anal. Soc.*

Boris, H. (1984), The problem of anorexia nervosa. *Internat. J. Psycho-Anal.*, 65:315–322.

Hughes, A. (1985), Aspects of anorexia nervosa in the therapy of two adolescents. *J. Child Psychother.*, 2/1:17–32.

Mahler, M. (1961), On sadness and grief in infancy and childhood: Loss and restoration of the symbiotic love object. *The Psychoanalytic Study of the Child*, 16:332–351. New York: International Universities Press.

Sprince, M. (1978), Some observations on eating disturbances and their early infantile origins. Unpublished paper.

——— (1981), Early psychic disturbances in anorexic and bulimic patients as

reflected in the psychoanalytic process. Presented at the 32nd I.P.A. Congress, Helsinki, Finland.
———— (1984), Early psychic disturbances in anorexic and bulimic patients as reflected in the analytic process. *J. Child Psychother.*, 10/2:199–216.
Winnicott, D. (1974), Fear of breakdown. *Internat. Rev. Psycho-Anal*, 1/1–2:103–107.

Chapter 4

Torment of the Object: A Contribution to the Study of Bulimia

HAROLD N. BORIS

INTRODUCTION

As a freshman in college Ms. F. had developed a practice of writing and filling prescriptions for herself from a pad she took from a physician she consulted. By this means she acquired the laxatives and diuretics she felt she needed, but also, of course, as it was to turn out, no less significantly, she acquired the attributes of the physician—what the blanks, the signature, and the words symbolized.

At first she filled the prescriptions at a distance from the college and the physician, but presently she "got careless" and was caught by a pharmacist who knew the physician well enough to doubt he would prescribe what was written. The college furloughed Ms. F. with the prescription she see a psychiatrist.

The psychiatrist she saw was a younger colleague of mine, who at times, discussed his cases with me. Ms. F. turned out to be rather a recalcitrant patient. From the first appointment, when by a logistic snarl-up she couldn't have anticipated, she arrived a half-hour late, she continued to come late and, moreover, to behave in no uncertain terms as if the entire affair were an unjust punishment. By the time my colleague and I talked, he had felt that it was necessary to confront Ms. F. with the

89

notification that she could not be given a "clean bill of health" unless she did something more than "go through the motions."

It was concluded that further work one to one was untenable; that she could not be asked to "internalize" or swallow viewpoints she felt would ruin and incapacitate her; that the situation had to be reframed; that the most expeditious and possibly most all-around helpful way would be to start once more from the beginning; and that the beginning was the bosom of the family. I agreed to see the family, so that the individual work with my colleague might be possible in the future again.

Ms. F. took up the plan with enthusiasm, and within a week or two the F.'s were assembled in my consulting room.

INTRODUCTION TO THE IDEAS

Among the notions beginning to dawn upon me at the inception of this case was the idea of peripheries—boundaries and innards—and the traffic that flowed in and out. As with children who set up the play therapy room with spaces marked off from other spaces, so it was with Ms. F. From somewhere within her self reaching out to the furthest pharmacy, from the food which one minute was outside and then the next inside, to the cud, which was one moment inside and the next out, there was ceaseless, restless movement. Who was she? Where did she (spatially) begin and where did she end? Was she individuated, separate? Conjoined, fused? If one wanted to see her, where was she located?

The decision to see her as part of her family was not an attempt to do family therapy, for which I was then only marginally qualified. It was an attempt to take these questions seriously: Where is Ms. F.? Where is Ms. F.? Here she is! Here she is! Or so we hoped.

In the event, Lisa was to help throw light on those amazing sleights of mind by which people attempt to recreate a self and a world in which catastrophe is averted and possibility impregnated by the fairly simple devices of eating and purging, which, after all, any infant can manage.

The Family Sessions

By the chance of schedule, I could only see the family at tennis time. Mr. F. came from work, in a blue blazer, gray trousers and face. Mrs. F. and "the girls" came from the courts. In their tennis whites, they were like ripe flowers, pink patina upon dusky tan. Mrs. F. was more deeply tanned, like carved wood. Ms. F., too, wore tennis shoes and pom-pom socklets, and jeans, and emblazoned tee shirts, variously advertising rock groups, soft drinks, and causes. (In the end, I gave up trying to attach meaning to the messages, save that they were signifiers of being a normal teenager.) "The girls," who ranged from eleven to seventeen, sat on the three seats of the couch. Mother pulled the chair I had set away from the desk, back to the desk. She needed the desk for the documentation she brought in an Ivory soap carton. Father sat on an arm of the couch. Ms. F. sat in a chair that was neither here nor there. Mr. F. decided to abrogate the circle and Mrs. F. to break it.

The girls stared at me with the frank interest of children at a zoo. Mr. F. put on a cooperative face which looked rather more resigned than enthusiastic. Ms. F. looked down; her eyes were circled with anguish; her mouth was pinched; but she was not going to meet my eyes. Mrs. F. began unfurling documents. I could not help but feel interested, but I also wished I could be somewhere less lonely.

As events began to unfold, a fairly typical situation emerged. The girls didn't see why they had to be there. They volunteered nothing and took a certain shared pleasure in how uncommunicative each could be. Mr. F. would sometimes attempt to help me out by remonstrating with them, but since his role was to be futile, his attempts achieved what was intended. Mrs. F. impatiently awaited the denouement of our respective and collective uselessness and began to take charge. At this "the girls" rolled their eyes to one another, while Mr. F. impotently scolded them with hand gestures. Ms. F. had found the window and fixed her gaze at it like a prisoner will at patches of blue or green. At the halfway point of the hour-and-a-half session, I could tell two things: first, that Mrs. F. and I were to be left to it; and, second, that "it" was to get her into treatment. Anything else was going to be brought to a standstill.

Since by now Mrs. F. was unfolding her own Regent's scores from high school, which were indeed, as she said, in the 99th percentile, I could see that there might be a case for providing her with serious assistance. And I could see the power and force with which she was seeing to it that her daughters would complete what and where she left off. So I said:

> *Ms. F. is very ill.* And you may have to let her get well. But she can only get well if the rest of you accept your share of the sickness. Next time I am going to tell you what your share is—if there is a next time. There may not be a next time because Ms. F. will not want to come back. She is protecting you with her sickness and by not coming back she will remain ill and protect you. You will have to get her to come back with you. But you will have your own excuses for not coming back, and we will stay where and how we are now. If that is what you want, leave now. If you do not leave now, your job is to plan the next session. I have done all I can do—all I am prepared to do. *You are not my problem, you are yours.*

This rather pontifical statement met, of course, with the most spirited challenges. But I was adamant: I had set the fox among the chickens, and I was not to be drawn back in. I contented myself (and discontented them) with parenthetical remarks such as:

> To Mr. F.: Are you so ineffectual at your work as here, or is this something you work at?

> To "the girls": You are really giving your parents the business. If we knew why you do it and why they let you get away with it, we would know something.

> To Mrs. F.: You are only making matters worse. Why don't you develop a little curiosity?

To Ms. F.: You are counting on them failing. At the end
of the session, minus one, you will be free to keep your
family intact.

Sure enough, by the end minus one, they could not agree
why they were here, what this was supposed to accomplish, who
should return, if anyone, who could possibly be free when (there
were tennis competitions in particular), and so forth. Plainly if
something were to happen, I would have to do it—or else! But
of course in the mysterious fashion in which these matters de-
volve, a moment later we were all pledged for next week, same
time.

The next week I reiterated the salients of the previous
week, adding that I thought it impossible for Ms. F. to be other
than self-treating until people took on their own share of the
illness and were willing to work on it together. I further added
that while I doubted this could all be done in the present session
I anticipated the same difficulty about getting to a next session
and suggested that they work on that issue first. As I hoped,
this flushed out the various collaborating and reciprocating resistances and enabled me to draw attention to them.

None of the stories one tells one's self—the cover stories
one uses to represent and misrepresent what one experiences
and who one thinks one is—can survive except insofar as they
properly represent or properly misrepresent the stories held
dear by those to whom one is significant. In the F. family there
were three main stories, as it emerged.

First, there was the story that Mrs. F. wanted only the best
for everyone.

Second, there was the story that the best was at hand, if it
weren't for Ms. F.'s embarrassingly stupid behavior.

Third, there was the idea that the family could very well cope
without help if outsiders didn't meddle.

"The girls" were living proof (in dusky rose and tan) of this: could anyone doubt that not only were they flourishing, but flourishing (tennis tournaments were the objective criterion) *better than* the children of *other* families? I was continually assured that Ms. F. was the best player of the four girls. ("Is this so?" I asked Ms. F. "I don't know. It's been a year since I played and they have all improved." Mysteries and more mysteries!) In tandem with their ceding to Ms. F. this ambiguous superiority, was the admonition: "If you just started playing again, you wouldn't need those laxatives and stuff." It was recurrently plain: Ms. F. was not supposed to be "sick."

Indeed, whenever harkening to my insistence that Ms. F. wasn't able to play tennis anymore or pretend to normality more generally, or whenever Ms. F. would venture to talk of her binging or the like, there would be a silence so vast that it looked like a chasm. Then Mrs. F. (usually) or Mr. F. would begin to talk as if Ms. F. had said nothing. I would of course draw attention to this, and presently the family worked out a countering tactic:

"Darling, the doctor (sic) says you are sick. Why don't you see that nice psychiatrist, you know Dr. um, er . . .?"

"Leave us alone, Ms. F.!" I would interpret. "Do what you have to do, but get him out of our lives and leave us in peace. We don't believe you're sick, so it's just a matter of hitting against the backboard for a while, honey."

When I said such things, the family felt I was making fun of them; but I told them that though they did not like to think so, they were making fun of *me*.

The most powerful resistance, of course, was leveled against my insistence that the rest of the family "accept their share of the illness." Often none of the six of them could even remember a sentence of what I had said they were to do (except to come back, which they disposed of by making regular appointments). At these times they would drift off into chat and family gossip of the emptiest sort, to which Ms. F. contributed her share. The words *deadly dull* would recur to me: death by dullness. Only Mr. F. would convey an occasional sympathy with a raise of his eyebrow or a tilt of his head as if to say, "You see? I have to endure this, too."

After a while (mistakenly, I feel in retrospect) I asked him: "So why do you put up with it?" (I should have continued to interpret his complicity.) He said, "I don't, frankly, have the energy to stop them."

This break in the ranks, as it happened, turned on a terrific row. The gist of it was that *everyone* worked hard, not just he. Somewhere in the general acrimony I recall him saying to Mrs. F., "Yes, but when you go to the store, you get a quart, one single quart, of milk for them, for them!" This, of course, referred to "the girls" who plainly drank a quart each just for starters.

Mrs. F. was thunderstruck, partly by the bitterness with which the accusation was made, partly that it was made in front of me, and partly I thought because not only was it true, but it challenged an idea having to do with whether she should have to shop at all. She flung back at him how busy she was going from tournament to tournament and began to recite the schedule: "Isn't that right, girls?" It was true: Mr. F. didn't "have the energy." (This was when I saw that my earlier interpretation had been incorrect; now the question was, did I "have the energy?") For as Mr. F. retreated, the looks of discomfiture on the girls' faces and the frank anxiety on Ms. F.'s faded.

I said: "You have come together again. For a moment there was a serious question. It was, do you, Mrs. F., have the right not to shop or, if you have to shop, not to shop accurately. This was taken to mean, are you too busy. But that wasn't the whole question. The rest of it was about who should sacrifice what and for whom."

I managed, on and off, to keep that question in play until we reached some real talk about Mrs. F.'s premarital accomplishments and her famished ambition. We talked of what Mr. F. owed her for that and what her daughters did. Regarding Mr. F., there was his own view of Mrs. F. as the one "who wears the pants" and his own loneliness for his father. I remarked somewhere in this: "If only parents were allowed to change genders with one another!"

Finally the girls individuated enough to talk of the hardships in their lives and their fear of what would happen first to their mother, then to their parents' marriage if the family wasn't as it was. At this juncture, the youngest, Marita, said to me slyly, "Maybe Ms. F. isn't sick, like you keep saying. Maybe she's the only one of us who isn't crazy!"

This rather gave me pause. I wanted Marita's observation (sly as it was, not withstanding) to register. But I was equally aware that in all this time (we were by now in the sixth or seventh session—we were now meeting twice weekly because my vacation was coming up) Ms. F. hadn't really said anything. So I said: "Ask her!"

"Are you?" asked Marita.

"Honey!" said Mr. F.

"Let her answer," said Amanda, the sixteen-year-old.

"When, again, are you beginning your vacation?" asked Mrs. F.

"God, Mom!" said Beverly.

"Am I what? Normal? No. Crazy? I don't know. Out of control? Yes. Out of control so I'm not crazy? Maybe." To me: "What do you think?"

"I don't know—it's possible."

"Anyway this is what I started doing when I was fourteen . . ."

And so Ms. F. went public.[1]

---

[1] Unlike anorexia, (see Boris, 1984a,b) in which the public presentation of the thin body is of paramount importance, bulimia is a secret activity, amounting often to a vice. It is not uncommon for even close friends (certainly the family) of bulimics to be unaware for years of the gorging and disgorging. This secretiveness follows the bulimic into the therapeutic or more formal analytic situation and presents, therein, some rather special requirements for the development of the work.

The first of these was to do with how the treatment is framed. Of course no psychoanalytic treatment can be organized around symptomatic activity, since symptoms represent a profound achievement in compromise formation, and are at least ambivalently valued, often, indeed, valued deeply, if unconsciously. Bulimia is no exception to this general rule; it represents an intricate compromise worthy of (in geopolitical terms) a Metternich—interweaving strands of every sort and origin. Yet the patient often presents the symptom as the problem, inviting the analyst to join the ego in regarding the activity as alien. To accept this invitation, however, is as often as not a mistake. Egos have a way of changing their minds!

THE FAMILY DYNAMIC

When in meetings with a family like the F.'s, one is soon aware of the vastness of their indifference to one another. They know little and care less. They have settled one another some time ago. In the F.'s case, though I did not get to know them well, certain lines appeared like pentimenti beneath the regular American family they took themselves to be. Mrs. F. plainly felt that Mr. F.'s penis was wasted on him. Perhaps he thought so too, since it kept him from his lost but unmourned father, whom he replaced as best he could with Mrs. F. She, meanwhile, lived out her boyish ambitions for herself through her daughters. Were they meant to be boys? Was she a man in respect to them, too? Mr. F. was the foodgiver; that was important. "The girls" identified with one another, and at this time in their lives consolidated with one another's help a kind of identity that gave them a degree of imperviousness to their parents—and, as the chat session suggested, to other young people, competitors, and friends. But for all of this there is something at once chimerical and banal. One is dealing with mirrors and images, extensions and projections, falsities regarded as verities and truths agreed to be counterfeit. The banality lies in the answer to the question of where all the energy and intensity are. There were no particular vibrations—those radiations in the field of forces that arise when people are interested in each other. The F.'s relationship was with their inner objects. They had escaped one another's realities by an act of sheer sorcery. They had patiently reconstructed each other within and then serenely acted as if these reproductions were as real or realer than the real thing. Indeed, at those moments when my own efforts threatened to flood the chimeras with the unsparing light of reality, the family would together hastily assist in pulling the wool over one another's eyes.

THE WORLD OF INNER OBJECTS

There is an urgent need in mankind for an alternative to reality. Reality is simply too real. Its very realness torments, quite apart

from the qualities of pain or pleasure within the reality. People
need to dream as badly as they need to awaken. Dreaming
provides a certain immunity to reality, a degree of imperviousness, a spell of respite. Of course we are mainly mindful of
dreams when the lights are out and we can see them better.
Like the stars, they are hard to see in the full sun of consciousness. Yet like the stars, which are always "out," the world of
dreams is ever on. Some among us have so managed to attune
themselves to their dreams, night and day, that reality is but a
scrim requiring effort to penetrate, yet as permeable as gauze.
Others of us have to be quick as a cat to catch a glimpse of our
ongoing dream: continuous performance.

That ongoing quality, indeed, reveals a paradox. We are
in the position of the Sorcerer's Apprentice, who having set the
objects in motion, had not the magic and skill to stop them.
Having created an imaginative world to run sidereal to the
actual and thereby to give us an alternative, we need the real
world now to wake up into, for otherwise how to stop the world
of figments and dreams? Each world can be "too much with
us." Each persecutes by that, regardless of its contents. Yet the
only antidote to one is the other. But what if, like the Sorcerer's
Apprentice, we forget or fail to learn the spell? Never mind the
treasure each domain contains, the real treasure (as Barth had
it) is the key to the treasure.

At some point a child will accept a teddy bear or a Linus
blanket or a pacifier as an object with which to supplement what
actuality has to offer. Busy, tired mother thinks it good for baby
to have something with which to spell her; baby concurs. But
as Freud (1925) discovered while patiently retrieving his grandchild's spool of thread, baby has a different sort of spell in
mind. Freud, never one simply to retrieve the spool when he
could also follow the thread, got from there to the repetition
compulsion and the death instinct. That is, he saw or began to
see (depending on how far we wish to take the thread) that the
baby was magically controlling the stand-in for his mother, putting a spell on her. This was now no longer a supplement to
an absent mother, a toy to while away the time. It was a cere-

mony, a ritual designed omnipotently to take control of the spool-mother.

The hyphen in "spool-mother" is meant to be at once innocuous of meaning and open to further meaning. It is one kind of link, of which others are Spoolmother, Spool/mother, Spool-mother, *SPOOL* mother, and spool. The last no longer links spool with mother; mother is now gone. Only spool survives. Spool saves baby from mother; who will then save baby from spool? Similarly, internally speaking, how will Spoolmother get on, or especially SPOOL mother or even Spool/mother. In Ms. F.'s case these distractions and signifiers had a life of their own.

THREE MONTHS OF ANALYSIS

I was inclined to feel that only insofar as her family "came alive" for her would Ms. F. make use of analysis. Otherwise she would go on doing what I suspected she had been doing, which was to drain them of significance and replace their husks with cleverly crafted exact replicas—spools. Insofar as, in the transference, I, like my colleague, would be linked with the school authorities, the doctors, pharmacists, and so to the family, I would be drained not of food for thought, not of compassion or empathy, but of value, and thus denuded be left impotent and empty.

If I were to give the respectful consideration deserved by those who would prefer to make a case for tensions in Ms. F.'s relations with real objects, I would not get to writing my own adumbration of the matter. I do think Ms. F. had a difficult time of things in reality. I think the one-after-the-other of sisters deprived her of what little happy mothering Mrs. F. might have been able to offer; I think puberty undid some aspirations to be a boy (something that might have interested her mother and her father, if for different reasons). I think that as her sisters entered the competitive tennis arena, and her superior age could no longer award her an advantage, she was once again in danger of dispossession. And I think her separation from home at the advent of college came much too soon, given what good she could take with her (internally) and how much was left unhappy and unresolved. Given all of this, one would have expected to meet quite a sad, overwhelmed, young woman, uneasy about the Christmas box of help, but prepared to listen.

Rather one was to discover someone far more concerned about "being out of control." And that, it turned out, meant not of people, but of their effects on her. At her best, which was at her most symptomatic, she was able to achieve a total indifference to other people. There was a skin on her like a caul (some people get this from drugs like marijuana or drink) through which people were seen, felt, and experienced as through the proverbial glass darkly. Far more real, far more prepossessing, were matters of eating and weight, of emptiness and glut, of self-violation and rectification, of *imagining* what people thought or might say. No anorexic or bulimic patient I ever saw easily exchanges an existence in which they were at the mercy of the real world, in which people mattered; and there was so little, really, one could do for a world in which they *chose* what mattered and could, sometimes, do everything about it. Ms. F. was no exception to this pattern.

The family sessions served to allow Lisa to allow her family and me to matter a little—partly because they gave her reason to feel she mattered; partly because the hardship we went through assuaged her envy, partly because she got interested, briefly, in all of us. On this not very substantial basis, individual work began.

At the end of her confession, I told Ms. F. that she had been using her illness to buy her freedom and independence from "these people here. But also to deprive the lot of any wish they might have to matter—a wish obviously they all have. But they have won! You have not succeeded in making nothing matter. It is possible to make some things matter less by allowing other things to matter more, but you have forgotten how.

"I can help with this or Dr. A. (her former therapist) can."

"You," she said.

To the family, I said, "We will need you again, but you will have to figure out how to share in the responsibility."

At this time we interrupted for a vacation, after which we met for three hour-and-a-half sessions per week. The idea was that she would return to school for the second semester, but as it was to turn out she transferred to another school where she could live in another family and continue her analysis with a colleague in that other state.

For me there was a special problem in seeing Ms. F.: I knew too much about her and had continually to struggle to regain and preserve the sense of mystery necessary for encountering internal objects. For example, "knowing the family" I could get interested in "hearing the news" instead of wondering what telling me this or that was at one and the same time designed to do and offset.

Ms. F. began by remarking on how different it felt to "be here by myself." She then asked what she was to talk about. I said it would be helpful to find words in which to put what her experience of being in the room with me was like. For example, she had remarked on how different it felt.

In doing this I was putting myself forward as a force, a presence in her experience; I was suggesting she speak of that experience. I expected she would experience the conjunction of my presence and my absence as a torment. I thought she would feel that torment to be something I had a choice about—that I could make it otherwise and was deliberately set-ting out to impose torment upon her. In these respects she would not be unlike other patients I saw or was seeing. But I further felt that Ms. F. would not complain or get angry. Cer-tainly she would not resign herself to the difficulties or limi-tations of my methods—or the lack of adroitness with which I attempted to put my methods to use on her behalf. I felt, rather, that in no time at all Ms. F. would get busy with getting even.

I have since formulated the basis for these surmises in a formal communication (Boris, 1986). At that time I was still feeling my way toward answering the question of why Ms. F. was psychologically unable to find an appetite for such food for thought as I imagined I might in time be able to provide her. I certainly was interested in the answer; why wasn't she?

She wasn't, I thought, because she felt there was something better (what I was to later term the "other" breast) which she might miss out on if she took the one I offered her. But, all right, why not take that other, better something, because after all, there are better and worse in the world? The answer seemed to be because if she chose the alternative, she would miss out on what it was alternative to; she wanted to eat her cake and have it too. If that was the case, how would she manage the loss of me if she replaced me with a rival source of satisfaction? I thought that she thought she could not manage such a loss, that it would expose her to unendurable suffering. Therefore, she would have to do several things all at once. She would have to "split" herself (I am not ready to take the quotation marks off ' "split" '). Part of her (note how frequently we hear, even use, that turn of phrase!) would make use of me; part of her would not. The use could not be final; she could not use me up if she were to have me too. The third thing she would have to manage, therefore, would be a variety of relations with me, each of which would offset the other. Oh, what a tangled web!

Part of her would do one thing, another part another, and each of these would have to be reversible. Out of all that possibility, if only she could bear to simplify, to pare away, and, after weeping a little, make do. Perhaps she would be able to do so in time, or would there be time?

In saying what I did to her in the first minutes of the first session I was also saying something about this kind of simplification: she could simply continue to do what she started off doing and find words for what the experience of being in this time and this space with me was for her. It was this call to the fundamental rule that I anticipated would elicit a powerful impulse to get even.

There was a silence. After a bit Ms. F. repeated that she didn't know what to talk about. This can be said as a bit of information: it can be a shorthand way of saying, "My experience with you is such that I feel you want me to tell you more or other than what I am now saying and I cannot think what it is you want." Which itself may be a shorthand for "You haven't told me enough, blast you, and the frustration of it is such that I can't stand it—and this then makes me seek relief from experiencing my wants by beginning instead to think about *yours*; and now I know only that you want, but I don't know yet *what*. Indeed, should I know, I'm not at all sure what, if anything, I'm going to do for your wants—let you suffer, or try to assuage them. Much will depend on what you tell me."

Or, it can be said not at all informationally, but accusingly, vindicatively, plaintively, all sorts of ways which take the experience "you and I" and not only elaborate it but act upon the elaboration.

Now, I had thought I had said something fairly helpful and responsive, but evidently not. Ms. F.'s response was at once plaintive and accusatory. What I imagined I heard was, "Cut the crap, fella; you can do better and you know it. If you think I'm going to let you get away with this shit, you can forget it; you get nothing further from me."

Of course she may have intended nothing like this; of what the experience in the consulting room consists is ineffable. One can quote a patient, but are the patient's words the datum of psychoanalysis? On the other hand, if they are not, what is? If something else is the datum, are the words irrelevant?

Without attempting an answer to these questions (which would require an essay in itself), I can put forward only that where much is at stake, actions speak louder than words, and that insofar as words are used they are often used as actions; that is, for effect. Directly I felt Ms. F.'s silence and words were not merely informational. I began to take note of the effect they had on me. Is the reception therefore definitive of the transmission? I hope so! It is all I had (and have) to go on. In Ms. F.'s case, I felt "split." Part of me (!) felt I had made an affable and helpful statement and part of me felt that I had, very wrongly, fed Ms. F. a very bad portion, and that I could (and should!) do better than that, if I had my hopes of something coming of all of this. Part of me felt persecuted, as if what I had offered had been spat back in my face. And part of me felt attacked with some sort of splitting implement which took (or threatened to take) a feeling of being "together," "centered," or at one with myself and splintered it into contesting, conflictful smithereens.

To describe all this does not, I trust, reveal me to be suffering from delusions of reference. Instead I hope it puts forward something that requires interpretation. I have described an attack: why therefore such an attack? The why of it may not be clear, but it's toward it that the work of the session must progress. (Here is where I wanted to know less about Ms. F. than I did.) In the event, I had the choice of awaiting more understanding or using what little I had. I chose the latter course and said: "Your feeling that you are 'here by myself' is an expression of a view that I have more to offer you than I have done and that this view stimulates in you a feeling of terrible unfairness: I can get away with being me, while you can't quite get away with being you."

Ms. F.'s response to this interpretation was made manifest in a look of calm on the otherwise visually tense lineaments of face, shoulders, and hands. I had the impression that a decision had been taken: I had the idea that after the session she was going to have a binge. The rest of the session resembled the chat sessions I had become familiar with in the family sessions.

The binge divested the session of any moment; accordingly, I paid only perfunctory attention to what she said, and began to drift into imagining what the session would be without everything going into the binge. As I did so, I became aware that this binge had nothing to do with feeling starved or deprived—at least not of food. Rather I felt that I had become linked up with Mrs. F., a linking that stimulated a massive wish in Ms. F. *to be known*. I fancied that there was the most urgent wish imaginable to press, force, power her way into me-mother—to force out held ideas and replace them with the absolute, unvarnished, unalloyed truth: "Know me! Let me come alive in your view of me—*AS I AM!*"

Then I imagined a response to this lasering, this worming, this watercannoning and steam cleaning and sandblasting and jackhammering. It would have something in it about not jumping down one's throat, about one not having to swallow that, about getting off one's back—that sort of thing.

The binge, I thought, would be effected by Ms. F. dividing herself into two—subject and object. She, Ms. F. would force herself (food) into me-mother. The food would stand for who she is, her identity. It would be an identity projected into myself and her mother, a projective identification, as the jargon has it. The contents would be good; they would be expected to convey pleasure and interest. But there would be a fury there, too. The contents were not *not* to be refused. The pleasure would be *inflicted*. Imposed pleasure!

Then I imagined this all turning upside down and backside front. Now Ms. F. would switch her identification from the projector of food-cum-truth-pleasure into a fellow feeling with the recipient of this infliction. How awful to have to be forcefed —how helpless, how humiliating, like the victim of a rape. Where the precious identification was projective, now it was introjective: the plight of the victim would have entered Ms. F.'s sympathetic imagination, causing her to recoil with guilt and horror. How revulsive the deed, how gross! She would want to cleanse herself, to evacuate and disgorge.

Not that the contents are so horrible: Laing recounts the following experience. You or I draw for ourselves a glass of water fresh and clear from the source. Meanwhile, equally congenial to us, indeed utterly a part of us, is the saliva in our mouths. Good water; good saliva. But then (his story goes) we spit a globule of that self-same saliva into that glass of water, whereupon we contemplate drinking the glass down. Now suddenly we feel squeamish; somehow in crossing the boundary of self into notself, the saliva has become alien and repugnant. We don't quite relish drinking it down again. It is not me, now.

So, it is I think, with Ms. F.'s food. Suddenly it is no longer of her, but horribly in her, an alien contaminated and contaminating substance. Ping-pong, go the identifications, ping-pong. Where is Ms. F.? Where is Ms. F.? Here she is! Here she is! Nope. Wrong.

I now need to return to the session itself. The reader might feel that there was a lot of imagining going on; and so there was. Ms. F. had, so to speak, projected herself into my imagination, and I was identifying with her, as best I could. I don't think it matters so much whether I was accurate in what I imagined as that this was the action, ping-pong, of the session.

The "chat" was designed to be chaff rather than wheat. Ms. F. did not want to say, to tell. She wanted me-mother to *know*, to keep her from succumbing to the temptation of telling, which would have been degrading; she would have been found wanting. She took all the passion out of the session to (so I imagined) the binge to follow, leaving me a vacuum to fill with my imagination. Or leaving me with nothing at all. If I felt there was nothing at all, then I might have gone about wanting more from her, and I should have been the greedy pig.

Because I didn't feel that this entire maneuver was conscious, I could only think that she was as much at the mercy of her machinations as anyone. My job, accordingly, had to be to draw her attention to what was transpiring. Toward the end of the session, therefore, I said:

"I have been having quite a think about you, as I believe you needed me to do."

She said: "What did you think?"

I said: "It won't make very much sense. But I was thinking how badly you want to be known and how despairing you feel about it being possible."

She said: "Is that it?"

I said: "No, there's more but I can't find the words for it yet, not by myself, at least."

Ping-pong.

The next sessions brought a very anxious and tentative Ms. F. Every time I moved or went to say something, she would say, "What did you say?! I didn't hear you. What did you say?!" I felt she was now terribly afraid of having "returned" to her what she had "put" into me; as if it would be, like the saliva, alien and contaminating. But the anxiety and tension also seemed to mark a movement away from juggling the internal objects in the inner world, toward an occupation with what she and I were doing together.

PROJECTIVE AND INTROJECTIVE IDENTIFICATION

At this juncture I wish to return to the conceptual issues that I thought to be implicit in Ms. F. and her encounter with me.

As I mentioned, I felt that I must *imagine* Ms. F. She was projecting aspects of herself into me, not so as to rid herself of them, as in the process of projection itself, but to have me make them choate, sensible, coherent, and meaningful. This is projective identification, obviously a strong element in any psychoanalysis (indeed in any relationship), stronger still for bulimics, who force-feed one. So part of her was being forced into me.

This leaves a vacuum; and human nature, like nature itself, abhors a vacuum. So therefore part of me was then made part of her. This is introjective identification: the identity remains the same, the location is what changes. In this regard I was now imagined to be "part of her"; that is, an internal object. The her-space, more generally the self-space, consists of claimed and acknowledged characteristics, not-me or disclaimed and alien characteristics, and characteristics so valuable as to be too precious to be stored within the me, but rather put in the safety deposit box of the ego ideal. (These can also be projected into an other in a projective identification that results in an idealized self object.)

These claimed and disclaimed characters or characteristics move back and forth (without visa or passport formalities, like travelers in the common market countries or in the United States.) Now something is self, now not-self. Dreams, of course, dramatize this state of affairs.

When we speak of binging in bulimia, we naively speak as if the self stuffs the self. As Ms. F.'s case illustrates, Ms. F. was stuffing the "mother-in-her" or the "analyst-in-her." She was "jumping" not down her own throat but mine-in-conjunction-with-Mrs. F.'s throat.

This is, of course, a kind of sorcery. And, as in the story of the Sorcerer's Apprentice, it is not a very good brand of sorcery. For no sooner is the internal object fed, than it can dissolve its boundaries, like a pill capsule in the stomach, and become at one with (in the same identity as) the self. And, abruptly, the self is gorged, poisoned, ruined, and must be purged.

In Ms. F.'s case, the intent, the wish, was to make her way into her mother, Mrs. F., and there permeate Mrs. F.'s entire being. Ms. F. did not want to be one of many (a single pill capsule), but rather, fifth-column-like, stealthily to infiltrate and gain control of her mother. Invasion of the Body Snatchers; Invasion of the Mind Snatchers.

This proving impossible, she tried sorcery. Now taking her mother to be within herself, Ms. F. forced herself into the mother within. The means of doing so involved food; it might have involved drink, drugs, cutting, or even suicide. (One could see something about food from the exchange between Mr. and Mrs. F. in the family sessions and the material Mrs. F. "fed" me from the cartons.)

When the "scene switched"—to use dream language—and Mrs. F. dissolved into Ms. F., something had to be put in to put matters right. There is a song:

> I know an old lady
> who swallowed a fly.
> I don't know why
> she swallowed a fly.
> Perhaps she'll die.

> I know an old lady
> who swallowed a spider
> that wiggled and jiggled
> and tickled insider her.
> She swallowed the spider
> to catch the fly.
> I don't know why
> she swallowed a fly.
> Perhaps she'll die.

> I know an old lady
> who swallowed a bird. . . .

The spider and bird in Ms. F.'s case were the diuretics and laxatives, but, even more, the stolen prescriptions themselves—the daddy/doctor stuff, which would purge the decomposing, permeating mother and refill the vacuum with daddy/doctor things. The separation from her parents, exacerbating her helplessness by reason of distance, produced an efflorescence of her sorcery.

I am diagramming, then, a *reciprocal relationship* between projective and introjective identification, such that one "can't tell the players without a scorecard."

THE ANALYSIS (continued)

Whatever pain and helplessness Ms. F. experienced was not truly to be known by me. The analysis did not last long enough. When Ms. F. came to see that a surrogate mother in a substitute family might be more truly receptive, she (wisely, I think) went off to get herself a real-life corrective emotional experience, while continuing her treatment at the same time.

What I *was* able to learn with Ms. F. was that no frustration could be experienced by her as anything other than imposed, so that, reciprocally, no satisfaction could be experienced as anything other than inflicted. That is, there was no such thing as nothing; there was always something, good or bad, being done to her. So she had to do something back—helplessly, enviously, spitefully, repeatedly (see Boris, 1986).

As people who project a lot do, she felt as if she had no "skin," no secure boundary, no enclosed sense of self, no clear sense of other. She allowed me to show her that this was partly her doing, a function of her own quite desperate wish to get at and into others; to destroy the boundaries that kept them separate from her; to get into and under their skin; to make herself felt and known as someone to be conjoined with—sorcerer her.

With these realizations we could part. We had done a piece of work. We could identify in our sessions "who was doing what and with which and to whom." She understood her own sorcery, and felt less helpless, less furious, and less at the mercy of her own poor spell-making.

Still as she left the final session, her eyes lingered on a pad she had once mistaken for a prescription pad.

REFERENCES

Boris, H.N. (1984a), On the problem of anorexia nervosa. *Internat. J. Psycho-Anal.*, 65:315–322.
——— (1984b), On the treatment of anorexia nervosa. *Internat. J. Psycho-Anal.*, 65:435–442.
——— (1986), The "other" breast: Greed, envy, spite and revenge. *Contemp. Psychoanal.*, 22:45–49.
——— (1987), Tolerating nothing. *Contemp. Psychoanal.* 23:351–366.
Freud, S. (1925), Beyond the pleasure principle. *Standard Edition*, 18:1–64. London: Hogarth Press, 1955.

Chapter 5

Anorexia Nervosa and Bulimia: An Integrated Approach to Understanding and Treatment

MARTIN A. CEASER, M.D.

There are many approaches to the eating disorders, anorexia nervosa and bulimia. This chapter will emphasize the psychobiologic and intrapsychic. The frame of reference is Freud's (1920) concept of a complementary series: the contributions of heredity and early development to psychopathology will vary from case to case. For some, genetic biologic factors will be decisive whereas for others it may be environmental influences, or a combination of the two. The wisdom of Freud's outlook is that the decision of biology versus psychology or heredity versus environment is eliminated.

Clinically, anorexia nervosa and bulimia exist on a continuum from the food restricting anorexic at one extreme to the normal- or overweight binge eater at the other. From this viewpoint, eating disorders are not diseases; they are *syndromes* —clusters of symptoms varying in cause and function.

Biologically, the symptoms may be caused by hypothalamic tumor, by increased intracranial pressure (Krahn and Mitchell, 1984), or by "functional hypothalamic biochemical disturbances" (Mecklenburg, 1974). Psychologically, eating disorder symptoms may result from oral and rapprochement phase ego disturbance in the borderline patient, and from oedipal stage intrapsychic conflict in the neurotic. Despite this diversity in cause, function, and patient population, I believe there is an organizing concept in all eating disorders, namely oral incorporation fantasies, which bridge both the psychologic and biologic models. The anorexic's "morbid fear of fatness" (Russell, 1970) or what Bruch (1973) called the "relentless pursuit of thinness" is foremost an unconscious attempt to *deny* oral incorporation fantasies, whereas the bulimic's frenetic binge–purge is a *surrender* in displaced form to them.

In this chapter, oral incorporation can be defined as the actual physical ingestion of something, like food, for psychological reasons, or it can be the fantasies associated with thoughts of ingestion.

There is ample evidence for the central role of these fantasies in eating disorders. First, they may be inferred from the history of anorexic patients which often reveals actual episodes of increased orality—overeating, drinking, binging—just prior to the more overt second stage of self-starvation.

Second, patients in psychotherapy have described symptoms in which underlying oral incorporation fantasies are evident: A bulimic patient binged on mother's favorite Entenmann's cookies as a way of capturing and keeping her mental image. Anorexics have related the onset of their symptoms to disgust over the first kiss with a boy and to a physical assault where the attacker forced his tongue down the patient's throat.

Finally, the analyst can observe the function of oral incorporation fantasies as they relate to eating symptomatology. A bulimic man early in psychoanalysis became anxious in the hour when thinking how lying down was making him feel open and unable to "filter" what he could "allow in" of the male analyst's words. At that moment, to defend against unacceptable homosexual wishes, the patient turned his attention to food and suddenly became hungry.

This chapter will explore those biologic and psychologic factors that lead a patient to rely excessively on orality as a way of satisfying drives, as a form of defense, and as a response to a perceived loss. Reference will be made to the as-if quality of some patients and to depression, and how both may influence treatment. Finally, case material will illustrate central dynamic conflicts in one group of eating disorder patients for whom psychoanalysis is the treatment of choice.

We know the importance of oral phenomena in normal child development from Freud, Abraham, and others. The differentiation of the ego from the outer world is primarily through oral activities. According to Hoffer (1949), the nursing infant, using oral contact first with his own hands, eventually coordinated with vision, literally takes in the outside world under the pressure of oral drives, which gradually become transformed into an "ego activity" (Hoffer, 1952). A physical activity has become a prototype for a psychological function.

In this way, the early ego—a "body ego" (Freud, 1923)—forms around feelings associated with oral, tactile, and visual experiences, which are recorded in the infant's motor and sensory cortex.

Three factors influence oral drives in the emerging body ego. The first are hereditary influences. Eating disorders are associated with a high family incidence of alcoholism, affective disorders, and weight problems (Winokur, March, and Mendels, 1980), all of which have been traditionally recognized by psychoanalysts as involving oral traits.

The recent discovery of endorphins—the brain's own opiates—has increased our understanding of oral phenomena. In genetically obese rats and mice, the pituitary levels of endorphins are elevated at birth, and their blockade by naloxone, a narcotic antagonist, prevents subsequent obesity (Margules, Moisset, Lewis, Shibuya, and Pert, 1978). Bruch's (1973) observation that anorexic girls do not register internal pain in a normal way may correlate with Kaye, Pickar, Naber, and Ekert, (1982), who found elevated CSF endorphin metabolites in anorexics compared to controls. Theoretically, excessive orality may result from inborn differences in endorphins or other neuropeptides. This, in turn, may influence the infant's developing ego structure.

The second factor that influences orality in the infant is the effect of early experience on brain functioning. This is relevant because the overt symptoms of either anorexia nervosa or bulimia may ultimately reflect functional or even structural changes in the hypothalamus (Weiner, Hofer, and Stunkard, 1981).

Physiologists (Weiner et al., 1981) have shown the later life effects of maternal separation in infant animals. They have also studied how variations in the supply of milk alters subsequent hypothalamic regulation of their autonomic nervous system. Recently, the gut peptide cholecystokinin, which suppresses feeding, has also been found in the human brain where it acts as an opioid (endorphin) antagonist (Faris, McLaughlin, Bailc, Olrey, and Komisaruk, 1984). This suggests a possible way by which oral experiences may be linked to brain function and ego development. A most vivid example of the influence of early experience on brain function is the environmentally caused pituitary dwarfism in children, a conditioin reported to be accompanied by bulimia (Weiner et al., 1981), and which is correctable by a change to a more stable setting.

The third influence on orality is obviously the early mother–child relationship. Mothering that is excessive, inadequate, or inappropriate may impair the oral phase infant's ability to regulate his own internal needs (Lichtenberg, 1975). Hilde Bruch (1973) believed that anorexics have an acquired perceptual defect in their capacity to experience hunger, the result of the mother feeding the infant in response to her own rather than the child's internal cues. [Although some eating disorder patients have this ego defect, others do not. Bruch's theory overlooks the important role intrapsychic defense may also play in the apparent loss of hunger perception (Ceaser, 1979); for example, a bulimarexic stewardess was able to experience genuine hunger but only when traveling away from her parents.]

In eating disorders, the clearest example of oral phase disturbance is seen in those patients with as-if character pathology. Ms. S., a twenty-one-year-old woman with a history of promiscuity and severe family pathology, binge–purged for three years following her successful detoxification for alcoholism and polydrug abuse. She was what others wanted her to be, a "Zelig" who felt lost, bored, and in need of direction and energizing. She could only pretend to work in psychotherapy. However, she was helped by being in a drug program where, in large group sessions, she was exhorted and pressured to have the strength to resist evil in drugs and alcohol.

Helene Deutsch (1942), described the massive empathic failures of early mothering in these as-if patients. Annie Reich (1953), noted that in response to severe early narcissistic injury, they could neither separate from their mothers nor acknowledge the mother's limitations. This is observed clinically in patients who show either the pseudocompliance associated with a false self or the intense alternating clinging and rejecting behavior that Mahler, Pine, and Bergman (1975) called "ambitendency."

What the infant contributes by his own biologic variation and the mother by her failure to respond appropriately to her child's needs, combines to produce a "structural deficit" in the ego (Reich, 1953), or in the sense of self (Lichtenberg, 1975). In these patients with severe as-if pathology, the ego deficit is associated with faulty internalization of psychic structure; which is the cause and which the effect is unclear.

Oral incorporation in these more disturbed patients serves two functions: first, the fantasies represent the ego's compromise solution to conflict. Second, the process of oral incorporation, as in bulimia, is a primitive attempt to form a relationship in order to compensate for what is felt by the patient to be missing inside.

I do not think classical psychoanalysis is of value to these patients. The limiting factors are the patient's relative inability to appreciate the symbolic nature of their transference fantasies and the inevitable regression induced by the psychoanalytic situation. When serious self or ego pathology is present, treatments that function as an auxiliary ego for the patient are indicated, including structured, reality oriented behavioral and cognitive therapies. Kohut's self psychology model may be particularly helpful in providing a supportive treatment that allows for new identifications to occur.

An important practical issue often raised is when to focus on the treatment of symptoms in eating disorder patients. It is currently in vogue, especially in eating disorder programs, to aggressively address a patient's reluctance to eat, or her binge–purging. Commonly, patients are told "We can't deal with your underlying problems until your symptoms are controlled." This approach is unfortunate. Whether or not to focus on symptoms is a clinical decision based first on careful *diagnosis*, including assessment of each patient's ego functions and level of integration (Goldstein, 1985). It is simply a disservice to provide any of a patient's ego functions that she is capable of utilizing on her own. Whereas some patients definitely require nutritional counseling, and help in structuring their diet and their time, for others, such interventions by the therapist usurp the patient's autonomy and foster unnecessary dependence. Most important, the therapist may be colluding with the patient's conviction of her own limitations and helplessness rather than analyzing its origin in fantasy.

Part of a diagnostic workup also involves consultation with an internist to determine the need for blood and endocrine studies, nutritional replacement, and hospitalization. Then, the therapist can proceed with a range of possible treatment interventions that grow out of an analytic understanding of that patient.

Significant numbers of bulimic (Herzog, 1982) and some anorexic patients (Hudson, Pope, Jonas, and Yurgelon-Todd, 1983) are depressed. In a given patient, a distinction can be made between the presence of depressive affect (which like anxiety may act as a signal for defense) and depressive illness which may include atypical symptoms of hypersomnia, bulimia, and rejection sensitivity.

In 1932, the German psychoanalyst Wulf (1932) described the connection between periodic binging and melancholia as well as manic states. He reported that a number of patients who had unsuccessful love affairs became depressed, and then binged on sweets and pastries. This attempt, by oral incorporation, to restore a loss may also be a compensation for a physiologic deficit: Wurtman (1983) at MIT has demonstrated that ingestion of high carbohydrate foods, typical of bulimic patients, raises low brain serotonin levels found in some depressions.

Modern psychiatrists (Pope, Hudson, Jonas, and Yurgelon-

Todd, 1983) have rediscovered Wulf's findings linking major affective disorder (especially unipolar depression) to bulimia. This suggests an important role for antidepressant medication.

CASE EXAMPLE 1

In major affective disorders and in other selected cases, medication can significantly improve both the bulimia and, especially, depression. And for some depressed patients, antidepressants can facilitate or even make analytic psychotherapy possible. Ms. G. was a thirty-three-year-old single woman who was referred five years ago for analytic psychotherapy. She had a borderline personality organization, multiple obsessions, compulsions, and an eating disorder. She was already on antidepressants and in group therapy. Hospitalized in her early twenties for anorexia nervosa, she had gained weight, become bulimic, and then depressed. While her depression and vomiting ceased when she was placed on antidepressants, her binging continued unabated.

Initial attempts to decrease her antidepressant medication led to worsening of her depression with apathetic withdrawal and increased obsessive rumination. On tricyclic antidepressants, the patient is now productively in her fifth year of psychoanalytic psychotherapy three times per week.

Ms. G. had never dated men, insisting she was flawed by comparison and without a mind of her own. Gradually, aware of her fears of independent feelings, she began expressing anger that the therapist, like other men, "had it all." During the first two years of therapy, Ms. G. often experienced the therapist's comments as a hostile penetration. Because she confused her destructive thoughts with action, she had difficulty "taking in" his interpretations. By the third year of treatment, Ms. G. had stopped binging entirely and was clearer in distinguishing between thoughts, feelings, and action. These changes occurred, in large part, as she gradually understood the reasons behind her envious destructive wishes. She was still afraid of showing strength, competence, and independent thought. When she did so, she felt defective, envious, and afraid of being abandoned by her therapist-as-mother. On a few occasions, when allowing herself to have adult sexual feelings, she became frightened and felt debased and inferior. Her next thought was to castrate her therapist as a father and brother transference figure. In the fourth year, Ms. G. decreased her medication and left therapy to attend graduate school in a different city. She was unsuccessful and soon returned home to resume treatment. The question remains regarding her ability to ultimately achieve full separation. However, the combination of analytic psychotherapy and the mood stability provided by the antidepressants has helped this borderline woman to achieve greater autonomy from her family, to be able to pursue a graduate degree, to sustain friendships, and increasingly to tolerate fantasies of heterosexual intimacy.

The beneficial effects of antidepressant medication should be kept in perspective for they are not replacements for structural change. Some patients may develop symptom substitution on drug therapy. A chronically depressed bulimic woman refused medication and was unimproved after one year of insight oriented psychotherapy. She was referred for behavior therapy, but she continued her frequent binge–purge episodes. Finally, she agreed to take imipramine. After two weeks, the patient responded with a sustained elevation in mood, improved work performance, and a cessation of bulimia. However, alcoholic problems now recurred in the form of dangerous binge drinking episodes with amnesia and blackouts. Unresolved intrapsychic conflict remained despite significant symptomatic change.

There have been relatively few reports of psychoanalysis with eating disorder patients. Marmor (1953) successfully treated a depressed bulimic woman in 1953. More recently, Risen (1982) and Wilson, Hogan, and Mintz (1983) reported on the psychoanalysis of anorexic patients. Risen described the resolution of anorexia nervosa during the four-and-a-half year classical analysis of a fourteen-year-old girl. Her symptoms were a regressive response to unacceptable unconscious oedipal fantasies of impregnation by her father.

There is a different group of eating disorder patients for

whom classical psychoanalysis is the treatment of choice. They have a personality organization at the phallic narcissistic level of development. Edgcumbe and Burgner (1975) described this *preoedipal* phallic phase which is characterized by sexual and aggressive interests that are exhibitionistic and voyeuristic, and by relationships that tend to involve only one other person.

Greenspan's (1980), description of the ego functioning during this phase is typical of many eating disorder patients. It includes incomplete object constancy which affects the ego's organizing capacity, leading to impulsiveness, a tendency toward splitting, and a fear of excessive closeness.

These anorexic and bulimic patients become conflicted at the point of expressing active phallic strivings. They misperceive competitiveness, assertiveness, incisiveness, active use of the mind, and taking initiative as fundamentally masculine phallic attributes. They become overly concerned with their bodies as flawed, especially in comparison to some more perfect ideal; and they are conflicted over the *size* of everything from body parts to ideas and feelings.

An additional characteristic of this phase is a bisexual orientation. The anorexic's pursuit of thinness and fear of fatness express both phallic assertiveness as well as feminine receptiveness. Being thin can represent a wish for a nonthreatening frail femininity, but also at the same time represent an ideal of sinewy muscular strength. On the other hand, the fear of being full may be associated with a fantasy of being a powerful preoedipal (bisexual) earth mother or with fantasies of having a baby or a penis inside.

Bisexual conflicts are often expressed over exhibitionistic concerns. A fourteen-year-old girl became anorexic after feeling mortified when boys teased her that her developing breasts were "false." Many eating disorder patients express this fear of being exposed as a fraud. Consciously, they may feel childlike, pretending to be grown-up women, while unconsciously they fear the unmasking of competitive wishes to be more feminine. They may also have identified with phallic qualities of both parents and fear their being uncovered. This may be expressed clinically over conscious inhibitions about appearing to be too

"cocky" or of being accused of "wearing the pants in the family."
The conflicted wish is not over a repudiation of femininity for
masculinity, but rather over the wish for the "unlimited potential" (Fast, 1979) of being both.

CASE EXAMPLE 2

The following case history[1] is a portrait of a woman in conflict
over her active strivings, especially phallic ones, and illustrates
how such patients benefit from classical psychoanalysis. Ms. F.
was a single, twenty-four-year-old graduate student who began
psychoanalysis for anorexia nervosa. At that time, the 5 foot 3
inch woman weighed 99 pounds. Three years earlier, she had
lost weight from 145 to a low of 95 pounds. One year prior to
treatment, she recognized her thinness, became frightened, and
sought help. Her parents, both alcoholics, lived in a distant city,
but financed her treatment.

Ms. F. agreed to be followed by an endocrinologist to mon-
itor her weight and physical problems during the analysis.

She was particularly well suited for psychoanalysis: her
weight was low but stable; she was free of starvation induced
organic brain disease; she had an underlying neurotic character
structure with appropriate affect rather than being severely
depressed, withdrawn, or schizoid.

In her first analytic hour, Ms. F.'s associations suggested
ego fragmentation and narcissistic withdrawal. She feared "enveloping herself," felt in bits and pieces and like a "sieve." What
emerged, however, was a woman with highly intact ego functions.

As the transference unfolded, Ms. F. felt intruded upon
and violated by the analyst. She felt he was seeing into her and
using his words to "rip her open." In her associations, she was
observed, touched, and finally invaded. Gradually, Ms. F.'s passivity was understood as a protection against fears that *her* active

[1] I am grateful to my colleagues, Monroe Pray, M.D., Walter T. Davison, M.D.,
and Curtis Bristol, M.D., who helped me better understand an ego psychoanalytic
approach in treating this patient.

looking, touching, and use of *her* mouth were highly threatening, aggressive, and often phallic activities. She was afraid of retaliation for forbidden wishes to incorporate and take away the analyst's power, and to use that power destructively.

In the transference, the patient protected the analyst just as she had protected her alcoholic father. Like the emperor with no clothes, the illusion of the analyst's perfection had to be preserved. Rather than use her words to "pierce his authority," Ms. F. turned hostility inward, became self-critical, or fantasized herself as the object of his hostile scrutiny (Davison, Bristol, and Pray, 1986). This transference of defense repeats a child's adaptive response to the perceived vulnerability and narcissism of her parents (Pray, personal communication).

Initially, Ms. F. expressed fears of being abandoned by her analyst. She came to see how this was a way of warding off her active hostile aggression. When she had to take brief trips away from analysis, the patient felt she had seriously hurt and diminished the analyst–mother. In response, she would then identify with the victim, eat less, and become thinner.

Like other anorexics, Ms. F. had to diminish and deny her capabilities. In her case, this inhibition warded off castrative wishes: after becoming freer to use her mind and to observe herself and the analyst, Ms. F. became frightened he would see her as having "taken his tool and extending its use, leaving him behind . . . and having created a monster within her." In the next session she dreamt of seeing herself "all bloated" which she associated to being fat and pregnant as her mother had been, when carrying younger siblings.

Because of her destructive impulses, Ms. F. also was afraid of having feelings and of appearing greedy: "I don't have a right to feel, for then I'd want too much from you." At that point in the hour, she pictured the analyst as her mother yelling at her for having feelings. In this way, Ms. F. had provided external constraint over her threatening emotions and impulses with a male analyst. "I might do something to you I'd regret," she said. Then, identifying with the object of her own aggression, she suddenly "felt overwhelmed" and, with reference to her feelings, she had to "cut it off."

Through her physical wasting, the anorexic unconsciously makes literal her conflict over incorporating or creating anything big or valuable. This conflict pervades the content of the patient's thoughts, as well as limiting her capacity to think. Ms. F. feared being assertive in the analyst's presence lest she appeared "too big for her britches." At other times, she was afraid of imagining herself too successful and of "expanding without limits." If Ms. F. thought of closeness, she worried about her impact on the analyst, fearing she would "blow" the whole thing. In the next hour she felt "wooden and rigid." On one level this may have been a phallic identification to ward off the analyst's anger for her hostile (castrative) wishes. And on another level not accessible to analysis, feeling wooden and rigid may have also protected the patient against active receptive oedipal fantasies of a wish for father's baby.

After eighteen months of psychoanalysis, Ms. F. had access to her feelings, was more assertive, less frightened of feeling full, and, most important, she had begun to express excitement at the thought of "growing." She had gained 9 pounds although her menses had not yet returned.

After one-and-a-half years of analysis, Ms. F. was offered and accepted an important job in another city. At that time, it seemed extremely important to continue analyzing her transference fears of leaving the analyst. She had equated him with her parents, from whom she needed to separate. Recently, he heard from an analyst in another city that she was again entering treatment. She was reported to be thin but not anorexic, and seeking help because of a wish to resume menstruation.

In conclusion, case examples have illustrated the diversity of eating disorders. Oral incorporation fantasies are central to the syndromes of anorexia nervosa and bulimia. They serve the ego in multiple functions (Waelder, 1936): as a means of restoring a lost object, as a form of self-soothing, and as a compromise formation between the instinctual drives and the prohibitions against them.

Neurobiologic factors might join with early experience to shape ego development through the mechanism of oral incorporation. The associated fantasies are subsequently reactivated and modified to meet the needs of adolescent conflicts over autonomy and sexuality.

The choice of treatment for eating disorders will depend on diagnostic considerations, reality factors, and the training of the therapist. Along with medical management by an internist, treatment may include family therapy, antidepressants, reality oriented cognitive and behavioral training, and supportive and insight psychotherapy. In addition to patients with oedipal stage conflicts, psychoanalysis is also the treatment of choice for those with ego functioning at the dyadic phallic narcissistic phase. The latter are conflicted over active phallic impulses and undergo a partial drive regression. As a result the early developmental sequence involving looking, touching, and use of the oral cavity is reinstinctualized before becoming displaced onto food or inhibited and turned back on the self. The final result is that active strivings, especially oral-aggressive ones, are defensively turned into passive ones—the patient then becomes concerned with being the object of another's scrutiny, contact, intrusion, and abandonment.

The challenge for psychoanalytic treatment is to help appropriately selected patients become freer to reclaim their active strivings. In this way they may regain initiative, a sense of will, and ownership over their bodies through acceptance of their sexual and aggressive feelings.

References

Bruch, H. (1973), *Eating Disorders: Obesity, Anorexia Nervosa, and the Person Within.* New York: Basic Books.
Ceaser, M. (1979), Hunger in primary anorexia nervosa. *Amer. J. Psychiat.*, 136/7:979–980.
Davison, W. T., Bristol, C., & Pray, M. (1986), Turning aggression on the self: A study of psychoanalytic process. *Psychoanal. Quart.*, 55/2:273–279.
Deutsch, H. (1942), Some forms of emotional disturbance and their relationship to schizophrenia. *Psychoanal. Quart.*, 11:301–321.
Edgcumbe, R., & Burgner, M. (1975), The phallic narcissistic phase: A differentiation between preoedipal and oedipal aspects of phallic development. *The Psychoanalytic Study of the Child*, 31:161–179. New Haven, CT: Yale University Press.
Faris, P., McLaughlin, C., Bailc, C., Olrey, J., & Komisaruk, B., (1984), Mor-

phine analgesia potentiated but tolerance not affected by active immu-
nization against cholecystokinin. *Science*, 226/4679:1215–1217.

Fast, I. (1979), Developments in gender identity: Gender differentiation in
girls. *Internat. J. Psycho-Anal.*, 60:443–453.

Freud, S. (1920), The psychogenesis of a case of homosexuality in a woman.
Standard Edition, 18:145–175. London: Hogarth Press, 1955.

——— (1923), The ego and the id. *Standard Edition*, 19:3–66. London: Hogarth Press, 1961.

Goldstein, W. (1985), *An Introduction to the Borderline Conditions*. North Vale,
NJ: Jason Aronson.

Greenspan, S. (1980), Analysis of a five-and-a-half-year-old girl: Indications
for a dyadic-phallic phase of development. *J. Amer. Psychoanal. Assn.*,
28:575–605.

Herzog, D. B. (1982), Bulimia: The secretive syndrome. *Psychosom.*, 5:481–487.

Hoffer, W. (1949), Mouth, hand and ego integration. *The Psychoanalytic Study
of the Child*, 3/4:49–57. New York: International Universities Press.

——— (1952), Development of body ego. *The Psychoanalytic Study of the Child*,
5:18–24. New York: International Universities Press.

Hudson, J., Pope, H. G., Jonas, J. M., & Yurgelon-Todd, D. (1983), Phenomenologic relationship of eating disorders to major affective disorders.
Psychiat. Res., 9:345–354.

Kaye, W., Pickar, D., Naber, D., & Ekert, M. H. (1982), Cerebrospinal fluid
opioid activity in anorexia nervosa. *Amer. J. Psychiat.*, 139/5:643–645.

Krahn, D., & Mitchell, J. (1984), Case report of bulimia associated with increased intracranial pressure. *Amer. J. Psychiat.*, 141/9:1099–2000.

Lichtenberg, J. (1975), The development of the sense of self. *J. Amer. Psychoanal. Assn.*, 73:453–484.

Mahler, M., Pine, F., & Bergman, A. (1975), *The Psychological Birth of the
Human Infant*. New York: Basic Books.

Margules, D., Moisset, B., Lewis, M. Shibuya, & Pert, C. (1978), β-Endorphin
is associated with overeating in genetically obese mice and rats. *Science*,
202:23–25.

Marmor, J. (1953), Orality in the hysterical personality. *J. Amer. Psychoanal.
Assn.*, 1:657–671.

Mecklenberg, R. (1974), Hypothalamic dysfunction in patients with anorexia
nervosa. *Medicine*, 53/2:147–159.

Pope, H., Hudson, J., Jonas, J., & Yurgelon-Todd, D. (1983), Bulimia treated
with imipramine: A placebo-controlled, double blind study. *Amer. J. Psychiat.*, 140/5:554–558.

Reich, A. (1953), Narcissistic object choice in woman. *J. Amer. Psychoanal.
Assn.*, 1:22–44.

Risen, S. (1982), The psychoanalytic treatment of an adolescent with anorexia
nervosa. *The Psychoanalytic Study of the Child*, 37:433–459. New Haven,
CT: Yale University Press.

Russell, G. F. H. (1970), Anorexia nervosa: Its identity as an illness and its
treatment. In: *Modern Trends in Psychological Medicine*, Vol. 2, ed. J. H.
Price. London: Butterworth.

Waelder, R. (1936), The principle of multiple function: Observation and
overdetermination. *Psychoanal. Quart.*, 5:45–62.

Weiner, H., Hofer, J., & Stunkard, A. (1981), Brain, behavior and bodily disease. *Res. Pub./Assns. for Res. in Nerv. & Ment. Dis.*, 59:157–175.

Wilson, C. P., Hogan, C., & Mintz, I., Eds. (1983), *Fear of Being Fat: The Treatment of Anorexia Nervosa and Bulimia.* New York: Jason Aronson.

Winokur, A., March, V., & Mendels, J. (1980), Primary affective disorder in relatives of patients with anorexia nervosa. *Amer. J. Psychiat.*, 137:695–698.

Wulf, M. (1932), Uver einen interessanten oralca symptomen komplex und seine Beziehung sur Sucht. *Int. Zeitscrift Psa.*, 18:281–301.

Wurtman, R. J. (1983), Behavioral effects of nutrients. *Lancet*, 1:1145–1147.

Chapter 6

Self-Destructive Behavior in Anorexia and Bulimia

IRA L. MINTZ, M.D.

Anorexia and bulimia are both categorized as eating disorders. The clinical picture of both has been amply described (Thomä, 1967; Bruch, 1973a,b, 1978, 1982; Sours, 1974, 1979; Sperling, 1978; Wilson, 1986; Wilson, Hogan, and Mintz, 1983). Schwartz (1986) has provided an extensive and detailed review of dynamic and theoretical concepts of bulimia.

This chapter will focus upon the self-destructive aspects of both syndromes and will attempt to describe the clinical range and intensity of self-destructive behavior in anorexia and bulimia. It will also try to clarify the variations in expression of this self-destructive behavior and discuss the differences in ego structure between the two syndromes.

It is difficult to limit a discussion of self-destructive behavior to bulimia alone, if one considers that anorexia and bulimia represent alternate forms of the same illness (Wilson and Mintz, 1982). The clinical picture of anorexia and bulimia can exist in patients with different character structures ranging from neurotic to borderline to psychotic. It would be no surprise to recognize that those patients in the more severe range of pathology manifest the most severe self-destructive behavior.

DIFFERENCES IN EGO AND SUPEREGO STRUCTURE IN ANOREXIA AND BULIMIA

In order to clarify some differences between anorexia and bulimia, it is helpful to consider Wilson's little recognized but important contribution (Wilson et al., 1983). He stated that while the unconscious conflict in anorexia and bulimia is the same, the ego and superego controls are different. The starving anorexic who has unconscious impulses to gorge is usually able to refrain from doing so, because of the presence of more intact ego and superego controls. Although endlessly preoccupied with thoughts about food, often for as much as eight hours a day, the patient is able to suppress and repress giving in to the impulse most of the time. The mother of a ten-year-old anorexic boy whom I treated described his pathetic and poignant behavior (Mintz, 1985a).

> He would continuously spend hours in the kitchen watching us eat. He would look at every morsel that we swallowed. He would open and close the refrigerator 20 times a day without taking anything out. He opened and closed all the kitchen cabinets and looked longingly at the cookies that he used to enjoy. All the while, he ate four milkshakes at 7:00 AM and not a morsel of food nor a drop of water entered his mouth for the remaining hours of the day [p. 266].

There was never a loss of control, although it was obvious to her that he desperately wanted to eat. In some anorexics the controls are not that ironclad and they occasionally lose control, giving in to binges before the controls are reinstated. Additional evidence of the intact ego and superego control system is found in the repression of feelings of hunger, cold, fatigue, and weakness. Antecedent aspects of the long-standing concern about the issue of control over impulses are present in the premorbid obsessional character structure found in so many of these patients (Mintz, 1985b).

The bulimic patient, by contrast, has the urge to gorge which she cannot control because of impaired ego and superego control over impulses. The impairment in impulse control frequently extends beyond loss of control of eating. These patients often succumb to the impulse to lie, to steal, to drink, to take drugs, and to act out promiscuously or antisocially. The gorging, therefore, can be viewed as one aspect of a general loss of impulse control. Wilson also suggested that one factor contributing to the more intact ego and superego controls of the starver is related to her identification with parents whose ego and superego controls are more intact. In general, but not exclusively, these parents are more conservative in their attitudes and behavior, and are more organized and controlled in their life style. However, I have seen severe anorexics, whose parents are alcoholic and who gamble. Nevertheless, most parents of starvers do have a more rigid sense of morality, are interested in and are able to be responsive to suggestions that are helpful to the patient's well-being. The patient who gorges tends to identify with parents who have difficulty in controlling their own impulses. They tend to act out more. However, I have seen severe bulimic patients whose parents are very conservative, do not act out, and are quite cooperative about listening to suggestions that are helpful to their daughter's welfare. In general, however, the parents of bulimic patients have greater difficulty in adhering to suggestions about how to deal with their daughter's problem. It should be clarified that the parents in an ongoing counseling or treatment should be seen by a different therapist than the one treating the patient.

Untreated anorexic patients may eventually become bulimic when time and the repeated unconscious impulse to gorge eventually erode the defensive denial, suppression, and repression of the impulses to eat. Thus we see an anorexic patient change into a bulimic, or into a mixed form of bulimia followed by increased starving as the ego and superego controls reestablish themselves.

DIFFERENCES IN ANOREXIC AND BULIMIC SELF-DESTRUCTIVENESS

The manifestations of self-destructive behavior of the anorexic and the bulimic patients differ due to the presence or absence

of intact ego and superego controls. The starving anorexic patient is able to direct the preponderance of destructive and
sexual drives against the self. While the fantasy is not usually
that of starving to death, it is one of starving and starving and
getting thinner and thinner. Starving which results in death
usually occurs by error. Characterologically, the patient has
been markedly concerned, from early childhood, with how her
behavior affects others. Little concern is directed toward how
the behavior affects her own well-being and self-interest. I have
thought of it as behavior and attitudes affecting "the other."
There is little ego awareness of the impact upon the self. For
years, as a child, long before the development of anorexia, the
child made a point of doing and saying things to please "the
other" (the parent). The child unconsciously resented much of
her behavior and performed out of what she perceived was her
need to please and to avoid guilt. Unconscious resentment often
mounted with passing years. Finally, in adolescence, with burgeoning aggressive and sexual impulses and an unstable adolescent psychic structure to contain them, the patient shifted
the nature of her behavior. From doing everything to "please
the other," she shifted into doing certain things to "displease
the other." Eating was important, so she chose not to eat. Overdetermined and multidetermined factors coexisted, however.
The shift to control what she ate, how she ate, when she ate,
and what she weighed, although highly overdetermined by her
past history was currently determined by her relationship with
people. When she felt that she could not be in some control in
her relationship with external objects, and felt increasingly
overwhelmed, she regressed in psychosomatic fashion to controlling a function of her body—eating—and a part of her
body—her weight.

　　While starving, her unconscious fantasy almost invariably
present in the transference, reflected hostility toward the object
and the inordinate need to upset, frighten, and "displease the
other." Little or no attention is paid to the effect of the starving
upon the self. The patient becomes almost totally preoccupied
with the effect upon "the other" and to that end, starves and
starves. And she dies by mistake. In addition, unconscious am-

bivalent conflict over cannibalistically destroying the hated object results in directing hatred toward the internalized object which may be destroyed by cannibalism or by starvation. Increased starving then reflects an attack against the self and the internalized hated introject. In the process, from the aspect of the ego, the starving patient who cannot be stopped makes the parents and physician feel as helpless and as impotent in their current inability to control her as she has long felt in her inability to control aspects of her relationship with them. The starving is a reflection of a repetition compulsion in which the patient unconsciously identifies with what she perceives is the aggressor, while taking the self as the object of that aggression.

The bulimic patient, by contrast, gorges and vomits, or gorges and fasts. In either case, the degree of cachexia and threat of death from starvation is lessened. While the patient still suffers from feelings of guilt from the gorging, the degree of self-inflicted physical damage and threat of death is not as intense. With the continued presence of an untreated and unchanged punishing superego, that still requires its "pound of flesh," additional externally derived sources of pain and suffering appear necessary. This need for suffering in addition to thoughts and feelings of self-condemnation results in further self-destructive behavior. Clinically, this is almost always found in bulimic patients and presents in many aspects of their lives. Dynamically, repeated damage by external sources serves to punish them for their unconscious feelings of aggression toward others and also serves to attack the hated internalized introject; their aggression is also displaced to the food that they cannibalistically destroy. While the anorexic patient damages herself by excessive exercising, she does not actively search out and provoke punishment as much from the environment. One bulimic patient swallowed four large toothbrushes (seen in the stomach by X-ray) ostensibly by accident, as she used them to facilitate vomiting, but in part unconsciously directed toward intenstinal obstruction or perforation. Others scavenge through garbage cans to extract the greatest possible level of self-humiliation. Lying, stealing, and antisocial behavior are used to achieve impulse gratification, but also to provoke embarrassment, punishment, and humiliation. Drinking and drug usage serve the same purpose with use of dangerous drugs more serious and analogous to the starver's risk of death by cachexia. Most frequent are self-destructive relationships with people. They range from contact with unsavory characters and life-threatening incidents to severely masochistic relationships with marked physical, sexual, and psychological exploitation.

CASE EXAMPLE 1. ANOREXIA: MARGE

The patient was a nineteen-year-old girl beginning her second year of college, who was referred because of a 35-pound weight loss, a starvation type diet, and amenorrhea. The patient was 5 feet 3 inches, had previously weighed 115 and now weighed 85 pounds. Seen in consultation by a local psychiatrist, hospitalization was recommended, which the patient refused. The parents were uncertain of what course to follow and sought an additional opinion. The parents were seen first for two visits when they indicated that Marjory was reluctant to come and that they felt that she would not object to their coming in for a consultation.

Ordinarily, I prefer seeing a nineteen-year-old alone with little contact with the parents. In cases of anorexia, however, there is such a close tie between the child and the parents, that it is important for the parents to have at least some initial contact with the therapist in order for them to feel comfortable about the child's treatment, and turning her over to someone else for help. If the parents are openly resistant or markedly ambivalent to having the patient treated, the patient is often in so acquiescent a state that she will terminate the treatment or will identify with the parents' ambivalence and not become fully committed. This is a reflection of the anorexic patient's symbiotic attachment to the parent where the inability to separate contributes to the patient's "doing what is expected" without having to be asked. My colleagues and I (Wilson et al., 1983) have not found that reasonable initial contact with the parents has had an adverse effect upon the treatment. In addition, many of the starving, as well as a good number of the gorging anorexic patients, are reluctant to enter treatment and only do so under parental pressure. Finally, it has been found helpful and on occasion essential that the parents see a different therapist in order to help them more fully understand the nature of the illness, what to expect during the course of the treatment, and how to be helpful in facilitating their child's recovery.

The parents stated that Marjory seemed fine until the previous summer when they noticed a marked disinterest in eating, a finicky attitude toward food, and a preoccupation with losing weight. Reflecting back, they realized that she had slowly lost 10 pounds during the spring and that the increased dieting during the summer had resulted in a total weight loss of 35 pounds. She professed not to be hungry and to feel full, but never complained about feeling too fat, and on occasion had acknowledged that she was thin. Every morning she would get on the scale to check her weight, and then look at herself in the mirror. She began to drink nothing but diet soda, gave up all meat, and mainly ate lettuce, tomatoes, cottage cheese, and carrots. She ate so many carrots that the palms of her hands began to turn orange. They also noticed that while she always was a shy person, she had become increasingly withdrawn. Her period had stopped six months previously, and had also stopped during three months of the previous summer.

The parents were well educated, poised, and concerned about Marjory. The father was a minister who was thoughtful, reflective, and acknowledged that he enjoyed and was successful in his profession. The mother was a teacher who admitted that at times she was very firm and authoritative with the children. Marge was the second of three girls. The parents were unable to describe any unusual aspects to Marge's development. She was remembered as a normal child without separation or eating problems who played reasonably with other children. The family moved a good deal when the children were young because of the father's transfer to a number of different Presbyterian churches. However, in the last five years the family had lived in the same neighborhood and the children had all established substantial roots in the community. Menstrual history was not remarkable until six months ago when her periods stopped. Menarche began at thirteen. Periods were generally regular with occasional irregularities, but without depression, tension, or cramps of which the parents were aware. Marge was an excellent athlete, and excelled in swimming and volleyball. She was on both the swimming and the volleyball teams. Her swimming coach said that she had lost so much weight that he was thinking of benching her. She was upset by this and told us that she was trying to eat but she just felt full. She also admitted that she felt quite tired at times, and was no longer as well coordinated as she used to be.

The father stated that Marge had always been a thoughtful, considerate girl who, unlike her sisters, was rarely argumentative, even as a teenager. The parents always felt that she was the best adjusted of the three because she readily acquiesced to whatever was suggested without any argument or reluctance. He saw her as a perfectionist who expected a high performance from herself in everything and was distressed if it did not take place. She worked at three part-time jobs to save money for college, although she was told that it was not necessary. At times she worked fifty-five hours a week. She always needed to be busy. The mother interjected that Marge was always thoughtful. She would do things for people all the time. She would frequently clean the entire house without ever being asked. The mother acknowledged that the patient got along well with her two sisters, but did seem to have a grudge against the younger one, accusing the parents of favoring her. The youngest child was born with a congenital hip difficulty requiring a good deal of medical care, and the parents admitted that their concern for her may well have been viewed as favoritism.

THE FIRST INTERVIEW

The patient was a tall, thin, shy young woman who appeared ill at ease and reluctant to be in the office. In reply to my having asked her to tell me a little about what has been going on, she stated that she was there because her parents had forced her, that she had already seen a psychiatrist, and that nothing was wrong. With reasonably active questioning when necessary, she did tell a little about her anorexic symptoms and life experiences. She did not speak easily and there were many silences which required my active intervention. She repeated essentially what the parents had described, except for her view of when the anorexia began. She said that in the spring of her senior year in high school she was very conflicted over which of two colleges she should choose. Her parents chose the one with the lower tuition.

She decided that since they wanted her to go there, it really did not matter and it would make them happy. It was in that setting that the anorexia began. I commented that she must have felt that her wishes were not important and that she felt obligated to do what others wanted of her. She sat silently as the hour ended. When I suggested the second consultation hour, she stated that it would conflict with her earth science class, but that she would cut the class.

I felt tentatively optimistic at that point, though she stated that she was there against her will and needed a good deal of active participation on my part; but she did relate and did reveal her perceptions of how the anorexia began. There was some awareness that it was related to the conflict between her and her parents, her separation anxiety, her problems about aggression, and her defenses of passivity and helplessness. I chose to indicate in the first session that my feelings were on her side and that I felt that *her* wishes were important. This was essential since she had a life history of doing what others wanted of her, she was here because her parents wanted her here, and she feared that I would attempt to control her as she felt her parents did. Her positive response to my comment was not to use the conflicting science course as an obstacle, but to decide that she would cut it in favor of the next session. From the very first interview I was attempting to indicate that I would not try to control her, that I understood how she felt, and that I would be her ally in her dealing with her problems.

In the second session the patient had great difficulty in speaking and was often silent. I spoke of her difficulty in talking as a possible reflection of difficulty in asserting herself. She acknowledged that it was true and that she had been accustomed to doing what the parents wanted her to do and that she had rarely defied her parents. I interjected "except by not eating," and attemped to get across that I could understand that kind of defiance and was in no way critical of it.

In the third visit, with the silence persisting, I suggested that eating would result in her being able to speak more easily. Again silence as she watched me intently. I added that it might be difficult for her to trust someone that she did not know well. Silence. After a number of similar comments, I wondered if she had difficulty in trusting people because of broken promises. Surprisingly, she agreed and recounted in some detail that the father claimed never to have enough money for singing lessons for her, but always had enough money for his liquor. "I had to work to pay for my own singing lessons although he had promised to take care of it. When I reminded him of it, he told me to keep quiet." "That's why you feel assertion doesn't work," I added, and she agreed. At that point I asked if she had ever noticed that when she felt upset, she starved. She stated: "When I'm upset, if I starve I feel less upset, and if I eat, I feel more upset." I interjected that I understood that, and it was my impression that the upset feelings were absorbed by the starving, but then she had two sets of problems: the original ones, pushed away by the starving, and the new problems produced by the starving. I suggested that she had the opportunity to talk over the things that upset her and solve them, and then not need to starve. So ended the third session, which was an extra unscheduled session that she telephoned for because one of her classes was canceled.

It might be helpful even after three sessions to discuss the methods, technique, and early sought after goals. This was a patient already disillusioned with a previous therapist, who came for consultation in great part because of her passive acquiescence to parental demands, and whose silent, suspicious, withholding behavior was paramount in each of the three consultations and reflected indirectly hostile and uncooperative behavior. My early goal in speech, attitude, and behavior was an attempt to give her the feeling that there was no authoritarian cross-examination, criticism, or allying myself with parents or previous coercive medical attempts to get her to eat. My only comment about eating was related to pointing out that it would facilitate her ability to speak.

I attempted to indicate that there were reasons why she did not eat, rather than to coerce her into doing so, which was what she anticipated. Since not eating reflected defiance of authority, to pressure her to eat would encourage her defiance toward me, and undermine any possible cooperative attitude toward the treatment. Nevertheless, I was aware that I had limited time to obtain her cooperation and interest in treatment so that she would explore her motivations for starving, instead of starving. I tried to indicate that I knew that she felt that she was faced with overwhelming problems and that I might be able to help her deal with them without specifically saying so. In the first session I acknowledged *her* needs about school choice implying that I understood that she had felt overcontrolled and had been overly obedient. It was clear that I did not side with her father's condemnation of her choice of school. The relationship established in the first session contained enough positive elements to undo her previous negative attitude and to prompt her to suggest that she could cut one of the classes to make the second session. In the second session, along with a great deal of silence she further acknowledged her difficulties in self-assertion and that she rarely defied her parents. My pointing out the starving as a manifestation of defiance was a deliberate attempt to provide meaning to her symptoms and to undercut all the manifold rationalizations that patients provide to justify the starving. It was also done within the framework of her admitting her passive obedience and my indication that I could understand and accept her indirect defiance. In the third session, an attempt was made to further deal with her profound silence, suspicion, and fears of betrayal and criticism to which she responded by citing a conflict with her father and fearing that I might also betray any promises made. Her difficulty in talking was so profound that I chose to interject a question that pertained to almost every anorexic patient I have seen: namely that starving facilitated repression of conflict. She agreed. Her agreement was made more readily because we had not yet spelled out the specific nature of the conflicts. In essence she agreed to the form of the conflict, rather than to its content.

The patient was then seen in three times a week psychoanalytic psychotherapy, a consequence of limited finances.

The next few months of treatment were characterized by a gradual involvement in treatment. Initial ambivalence about being in treatment was gradually resolved. One of Marge's greatest difficulties was an inability to talk. She would sit quietly, watch me closely (often staring intently), and not utter a word. On many occasions this behavior would last for most of the session. Almost invariably there would be long periods of silence in the beginning of every session lasting at least fifteen minutes.

The silence permitted me to explain and clarify concepts that I thought were present. I pointed out that it was a reflection of her inability to express painful feelings and ideas; that not only was it difficult to discuss them, but they might also be difficult to think about. I suggested that when people felt that they could not cope with thoughts and feelings, they often pushed them away and thought about other things like eating and starving instead. I wondered aloud whether she had noticed that when she starved her anxieties and worries tended to subside: that it was one of the benefits of starving. I also pointed out that when patients felt out of control of their relationships with people and their lives in general, their need to control what they ate and what they weighed was an attempt to at least be in control of something: that it was a miniaturization of their world into a size over which they could exercise control. From that point of view, the starving was understandable and even momentarily beneficial, but that she paid a big price for that kind of solution. Perhaps there were better ways. I also indicated that since she had been so obedient and did what everyone wanted for so many years, not eating might also reflect an expression of independence, assertion, and defiance, that no one was going to make her eat. I agreed that assertiveness was helpful and even necesssary to regulate her life, but that she was doing it in a way that hurt her. I suggested that while others criticized her for it and pressured her to eat, that was not my purpose nor interest, but that I was interested in helping her solve the problems that caused the anorexia. Most of these interpretations were listened to carefully, but met with stony silence.

Infrequently a reply was forthcoming that was brief, often poignant, and filled with insight. "If I eat, something terrible will happen. . . . Terrible things will come out of me." I acknowledged that such a fear was not surprising. I wondered what made her think that she could not cope with it. This led to a discussion about her strict and punishing conscience which punished her for such thoughts, in part by starving. In response to other periods of silence, transference interpretations were made.

You described how obedient and thoughtful you were for so many years, often doing things before they were even asked. Maybe you have tired of that kind of behavior. Now at times you do the opposite of what is asked of you. If you feel that you are supposed to talk here, you remain silent. You know that it's a talking treatment so that being silent is being assertive and saying I won't do it. It may also be an expression of some of the defiance that you never expressed toward your parents in the past, and you are taking it out on me. . . . Should you take out on me the frustrations arising in relationships with others? It is certainly your right to assert yourself here by not talking, but it complicates your getting better. . . . Do you think that if you asserted yourself with other people, you might not have to be so silent here?

More silence and starving.

In addition to drive interpretations of transference, ego interpretations were made.

I suspect that you must have felt out of control for so long—even before you finally got anorexia. Are you aware of experiencing any sense of satisfaction in remaining silent

when you know that I think that it's better for you to
talk. . . . Does it give you a feeling of being more in control
here? . . . I could understand that it might make you feel
better. . . . It also occurred to me that when you felt out
of control, it must have made you feel helpless, or weak,
or pessimistic. When you sit there watching me wait for
you to talk and then you're silent, you may unconsciously
be trying to show me what it feels like to feel so helpless
and vulnerable.

I describe these kinds of interpretations because they ultimately facilitated Marge's ability to speak. There was so much
silence for over six months that it was necessary to make these
kinds of interpretations of the manifold meanings of her silence, rather than coercing, cajoling, or imploring her to speak.
Needless to say, for the therapist to remain silent, and match
the patient's silence, would be extremely inadvisable. It would
threaten the patient and make her feel that the therapist is
acting in an implicitly controlling or punitive fashion. It would
be viewed as a challenge and encourage the patient to continue
with increased silence. It would set off considerable guilt over
wasting time and money and encourage the patient to quit.
Finally, since the patient's silence is a manifestation of many
factors including unconscious drive and ego functions, the patient herself is unaware of all the manifold reasons for her
silence and cannot fully control it.

The attitude of the therapist during these times is crucial.
The patient does not only listen to what is said, but also the
manner and attitude in which it is said. Often she has felt criticized by important people in her life or experienced feelings
of aggression toward them. Reality and transference feelings
result in her anticipating coercion, control, frustration, impatience, insensitivity, and annoyance from the therapist. It is,
therefore, very important that none of that type of behavior
occurs. This means that the therapist should feel comfortable
experiencing the patient's aggression without retaliating, without withdrawing and leaving her feeling alienated, and without

treating it with such disdain that the patient feels that her anger has no impact.

During the three to six months when the silence was most pervasive, the patient's main behavior was related to increased starving and the silences in treatment. Very little of her other behavior was self-destructive. Areas of anxiety or trouble were avoided. Insecure in social situations, she remained withdrawn and alone. Invitations for dates and parties were turned down. She worked hard in school and managed to get along with her parents, teachers, and a few friends in spite of whatever reservations she had about them. Self-destructive behavior was mainly directed toward starving. She did not reach out for additional sources of pain and punishment.

CASE EXAMPLE 2. BULIMIA: MAUREEN

Maureen was a twenty-eight-year-old married woman, a computer executive, referred for consultation by her gynecologist because of gorging, vomiting, and bouts of weight loss. She was 5 feet tall and weighed 90 pounds; she was thin, but attractive, articulate, and very well dressed. In the first session she was quick to reveal her resistance.

> I don't feel that I belong here. I've had seven previous therapists in the past fourteen years and no one has helped me. Three gave me psychotherapy, two drugs, and two behavior modification. Nobody helped, so why should I see you. If I didn't trust my gynecologist, I wouldn't have come for the consultation. Besides, I don't have time for intensive treatment.

She stopped and stared. Other than greeting her, I had not had a chance to say anything.

In the very beginning of the first session, the patient had a need to inform me of how long she had been sick and how all kinds of treatment had failed. In addition, she spelled out that she was planning to be a difficult, provocative patient. Early transference attitudes illustrated one of her basic conflicts: self-destructive ways of dealing with aggressive conflict. She was attempting to provoke me into rejecting her before she had the opportunity to determine if she could be helped. In the service of ego mastery, she was attempting to make me feel overwhelmed, unable to cope with her, and induce in me a degree of the helplessness and pessimism that she experienced. She would be in control at the expense of ruining her treatment and remaining ill. She stoppped and stared, attempting to determine the impact of her self-destructive behavior upon me. It is important to recognize the purpose of her behavior and not to feel overwhelmed and threatened by her blandishments. These patients are very sensitive to the effect their behavior has upon others. If successful, she would redouble her self-destructive behavior in life and in the transference in an attempt to control and frighten the therapist. My comment asking her to tell me more, was an attempt to indicate to her, that rather than being overawed, I was interested in hearing more. The one positive element in the outburst was her reference to her gynecologist in whom her trust was strong enough to enable her to overcome a decision to ignore the referral.

> It's always been the same problem. I'm concerned about my weight and getting fat. It began when I was ten. I talk about it and talk about it until it gets boring. One of the therapists almost fell asleep. I guess I'm 88. I don't want to know what I weigh. . . . afraid to get on scales. I exercise for two hours a day, when I come home from work. The boys try and imitate me. My husband says it looks funny, but its really crazy . . . that I'm crazy and I'm going to get them crazy. I already got him crazy. Emil and Jimmy are hungry and want dinner, and I have to exercise. Most of the time, my husband has to make the dinner. . . . He's furious and keeps threatening to divorce me if I don't make dinner. I'm always on a diet. I eat as little as possible. Then I can't help it and I gorge and eat everything I can and end up feeling fat, and then I vomit. What bothers me is that I skip periods. I missed four periods in the last nine

months. I got my period the next day after calling you on the phone to make an appointment, but it was just chance. Every morning I check my bones in the mirror. I look at my hips, then my ribs, and then my stomach. If I think I'm fat, I'll be in a depression all day.

As the patient described her concern over her weight, exercising, and eating, she continued in the transference attempting to overpower the therapist. She would speak about unimportant subjects to interfere with his concentration and make him fall asleep like a previous therapist. She was crazy, able to get the family crazy, with threats to get him crazy. That she got her period the day after making the appointment was unconsciously perceived as a threat to her control which might have contributed to the intensity of her behavior in the initial hour. Her fragility was evident in the comment that if she thought she was fat, she'd be depressed all day.

I've always been a good child, a wonderful child, my parents said. I never gave them any trouble. I was so good because I felt too guilty to ever do anything they disapproved of. When I'm thin this way, I get attention . . . but it makes me feel miserable because my husband complains that I'm a bag of bones in bed. If I feel too fat, I don't want sex. . . . I don't trust you . . . can't trust people easily. When I was young, I always felt left out. Sometimes I just don't feel like being a mother to the boys. I am, but I constantly worry that I won't be a good mother to them. When Jimmy ran and tripped and cut his chin, I felt that I was a bad mother, that it was my fault, and I was depressed for two days.

During the first session, I had pointed out that she might be constantly preoccupied with thoughts about her weight in order to push away other thoughts.

In the beginning of the second session she volunteered that she looked at the mirror two to three times every hour while at work.

It must be over twenty times today. I did wonder if it was to push thoughts away, and I found that it was—good and bad thoughts. When I get upset, I realized that I thought, time to see what my body looks like, and the thoughts don't bother me as much when I think how fat I am. Sometimes I think I'm too fat and sometimes I think I'm too thin, in the same day.

In the remainder of the session she described her family. The patient was the youngest in a family of four, with three older brothers. Because her mother was forty-two when the patient was born, she felt that her mother was too old to take proper care of her. In addition, the mother weighed 250 pounds, with her weight limiting her mobility. The father was also obese, weighing about 260 pounds. He was vice president of a corporation "and loved to throw his weight around." The oldest brother, also obese, died of a cornonary at the age of forty-two. The other two brothers were married and living in the Midwest. The family saw them rarely. The middle brother suffered from repeated bouts of depression.

In the third session, a good deal of transference material emerged. The patient arrived feeling upset "that you and Dr. L., the gynecologist, decided that I had to see you in treatment." She added that she thought that I might prevent her from getting away with things—"not talking about what I should, avoiding things. . . . I used to do it with Dr. R. and he would let me." I pointed out that it was my impression that it was recommended that she call, but that she called of her own volition, and that no one was making her stay in treatment. I added that I would never attempt to control her, but that she had impulses to act self-destructively and wreck the treatment before it got started. If she insisted upon doing that, I certainly could not stop her and that she may have done that in some of her previous treatments.

The patient listened and then continued.

When I have a fight with my husband, I run to eat like a child whose friend drops her, or who falls and hurts herself and then needs a glass of warm milk to feel better. I had a big fight with my husband, he threatened to leave, and went home to his parents overnight. . . . Ten times he said that he'd leave. Then I go to the kitchen and stuff my face. The night he left I emptied the refrigerator. All the time I was eating I kept thinking that I'm fat, that I have to be on a diet . . . that I have to exercise . . . but my worry about my husband was less and I fell asleep.

The patient's associations to a fight with her husband to a child whose friend drops her, or who falls and hurts herself, is followed by the thought of taking a glass of warm milk. It suggests that distressing situations are mollified by drinking warm milk, an allusion to the early security found in sucking and drinking followed by sleep. This clear description of her awareness of the defensive meaning of her gorging was intermingled with denial about understanding it, and thoughts that she did not need treatment and should quit. At the end of the session, she volunteered her awareness that the displacement of conflict with people and the shifting of her preoccupation to gorging had taken place "hundreds of times."

I was thinking about what you said about eating being a cover-up and I realized that all weekend, whenever I got upset, I had a tremendous urge to eat vanilla ice cream. I remembered what you said and I didn't do it. I thought about what bothered me instead, and I suffered with the upsetting feelings. It was such an accomplishment that I wanted to tell you that I was better. I feel better than I have in fifteen years. I want to get rid of this problem.

While it is not unusual, by the fourth session the patient had become enough aware of the displacement of conflict from issues with people to food and was able to temporarily contain it. Many patients, even those with chronic illness, are able to achieve early recognition of this mechanism. Although it is a positive sign, it does not herald rapid progress nor a quick cure. In addition, one should not be misled by her hyperbolic enthusiastic description of her well-being. It can be evanescent and replaced by an equally exaggerated reaction in the opposite direction. With increasing awareness of the displacement, the patient may then self-destructively forget it completely, and regress into hopeless pessimism. In addition, awareness of some of her conflicts is not synonymous with resolution of them. An additional, positive feature was her early, strong tendency to identify with me, and to begin to think and behave as she thought I would. It was of particular value in a person with as many problems as she, a person with certain ego deficits and a long history of therapeutic failures. This identification became increasingly prominent with no attempt on my part to interfere with it. When a situation would begin to set off anxiety, or she would begin to act in a provocative or dangerous fashion, she would ask herself what I would do in that circumstance, and would I say that she's making trouble for herself. Except for periods of marked impulsivity or intense self-destructiveness, this identification would frequently facilitate a more rational resolution of the experience.

She continued:

> Since last week, I have become very angry with everyone and slapped Jimmy after he hit Eric with his shoe. I have "tons of anger" and I kept picking fights with my husband. I haven't felt this angry in ten years. I worry that it will wreck the marriage. My brother came over without calling first and I got mad at him and ended up screaming at him and crying like a child. He wanted to calm me down and I wanted to eat. I don't know why I'm so angry.

I suggested that she was using her mouth to talk instead of to eat. She said that she had "tons of anger" and that if she did not deal with it realistically, she feared putting on tons of weight. "Did I say that? . . . Something else occurred when I noticed that I could control the gorging. You said that I eat to avoid dealing with problems. I wondered, every time I eat, do I avoid problems? Then I thought, maybe I shouldn't eat at all, and I skipped two meals." I pointed out that she realized that there were reasons why she gorged, that if she dealt with the problems instead, she might be able to get better. However, she worried that she might not be able to cope with the tensions and anxieties that the problems caused, so she thought of starving instead. Unwittingly, instead of dealing with the anxiety by gorging, she would then deal with it by starving, exchanging bulimia for anorexia. In either case, she would push away the thoughts and feelings. If she felt that she could cope, she would not have to do this. Here one sees both her attempt to regulate her anxiety level by a different displacement as well as a self-destructive solution for it. Gorging and starving are opposite sides of the same coin, and illustrate that anorexia and bulimia are the same illness.

During the first ten sessions, endless self-punishing thoughts and behavior were described as an integral part of her past and current life experience. It was repeatedly pointed out that unconsciously getting herself in trouble was a desperate attempt to get people to care for and pay attention to her. On occasion it was also an expression of anger in an attempt to upset and aggravate them through hurting herself. She was punishing herself because her strict, rigid conscience required that she suffer; she did not deserve to have a good opinion of herself nor to achieve happiness and success in life. Pointing out the ego adaptive function of the thoughts and behavior, as well as punitive superego aspects, are well tolerated by patients from the very beginning of treatment, where a more active interpretive stance is required especially in the starving anorexic or in the markedly self-destructive bulimic. A good illustration of the consequences as well as the negative pitfalls emerged in the ninth session. She described feeling better in general and trying not to agitate her husband. She also noted better control over her binging. "I am attempting to think instead of just doing stupid things and getting myself in trouble or just getting anxious or depressed. It helps and it's a good *therapy technique.*" I wondered about the term. When she did not respond, I suggested that she might be thinking of it as a gimmick. "Yes, I think of it that way instead of realizing that most people grow up thinking logically. I never did. I think you're smart and can

help me. I used to waste time and talk about my weight and
other unimportant things . . . the others would let me . . . it
was self-destructive and you won't let me and it helps." I suggested that unconsciously, the unhealthy self-punishing part of
her personality might see that as a challenge to prove that I'm
not so smart and to wreck treatment. It was important for her
to remember that we could work together, but that I could not
cure her.

In viewing the past interchange, it is helpful for the reader
to know that I did not actively interfere with her discussions
about food, weight, and exercise. I interpreted their defensive
aspects and symbolic meanings when appropriate. The part of
her that wanted to get well and also recognized that she could
not contain her impulses to talk endlessly and wastefully about
food, ascribed the prohibiting qualities to me as her needed
source of external control. In addition, my interpretation of
her praise as possibly leading to trouble set off the following
associations.

> You know, I did something terrible. I never did it with any
> of the other therapists. I've been keeping quiet and not
> saying self-destructive things, but yesterday I did. I started
> provoking my husband, and he finally blew up at me and
> again threatened to leave. Later in the day, I started an
> argument with my boss after he insisted that I do something
> his way. I kept challenging him even though I thought he
> was right. I don't know why I did it.

I pointed out that she may have been challenging me and
the treatment. To lose her job, or her husband's commitment
to the treatment might put it in jeopardy. While the healthy
part of her wants to get well, the unhealthy part feels that fifteen
years of suffering is not enough and that she really does not
deserve to get well. The possibility of getting well is a threat to
her. She continued, "I almost acted suicidal. I drank the gravy
that was cooking in a hot oven and I burned my throat badly.
I almost felt my esophagus close up." I wondered if it was
related to feeling burned up inside and needing to choke off

talking. "I'm afraid that you're going to take away my identity. Worrying about my weight and how I look is a part of me. It helps me know who I am." I pointed out that she did not wish to see that she might be an intelligent and insightful person. 'I didn't hear that. What did you say?" And the session ended. While the interpretation of the reason for burning her mouth might be viewed by some as precipitous or even not fully substantiated, it was in keeping with the preceding material and her generalized, extensive self-punitive behavior in part related to her aggressive conflict. As described elsewhere (Mintz, 1983a), it is often necessary in dealing with the potential crises of starving anorexics or self-destructive bulimics to make inexact interpretations based upon past experience and the general understanding of the conflicts to attempt to head off a dangerous downhill direction.

The sessions continued, replete with endless self-destructive impulses and actions that required repeated interpretation. The self-punishing behavior and thinking would invariably intensify whenever she perceived that she was making progress. Her need to suffer became increasingly apparent as she reflected upon her worry at 9:00 A.M. that she was too fat and at 11:00 A.M. that she was too thin. The irrationality of her concern only became meaningful in the context of realizing that the unconscious goal was to feel upset and suffer, and that it did not matter what the vehicle was that produced it. The theme repeated itself a month later with the comment, "I will never give up my worry about my weight. . . . Now instead of twenty things to worry about, I only have five. . . . If I knew you wouldn't steal away my weight symptom, I could give up the other symptoms and just keep the weight worry." The patient increasingly recognized the self-destructive aspects of her behavior, especially related to gorging, and therefore found it increasingly difficult to gorge. She rarely gorged over a period of many months. She began to describe the increasing emergence and importance of phobias that absorbed her concern, caused her anxiety, and seemed to be replacing, at least temporarily, her previous self-destructive behavior and bulimia.

I've become increasingly afraid of fires happening in the house. It didn't used to bother me. I worry about the children. We have smoke alarms, but it doesn't reassure me. I pull electric plugs out of the wall all the time. Yesterday the worry got so bad that I had to take all the appliance cords and tie them together so that I knew none were mistakenly left in the socket. . . . I worry more about thunderstorms and windstorms, that they will blow down the trees next to the house and destroy the house when the children are home. . . . I also worry more about the children, I think of getting cancer. . . . I have started to check my breasts almost every day looking for lumps. It's very difficult for me to do because I have large cystic breasts. There is a family history, but I never worried about it before. I guess I had so many other things to worry about, I just never got the time.

It seemed reasonable to consider that since the discharge of aggression by gorging was no longer available to her, the repressed aggression was now projected out on to external symbolic objects. The underlying unresolved conflict was now expressed differently in the form of phobias. The ambivalently cathected, internalized object was now projected outward and became the feared symbolic object. Her rage and burning feelings, dealt with momentarily by burning her mouth, are more enduringly projected into the fear that the fires will burn her and her family. The thunder- and windstorms may represent projections of her uncontrollable impulses to scream thunderously in the violently exhaled air. The cancer phobia can relate to her ambivalent conflict over destructive eating, and being eaten from within by the feared and hated introjects.

CASE EXAMPLE 3. BULIMIA: ELAINE

Elaine was a sixteen-year-old girl, the oldest of four girls, who had developed bulimia at the age of twelve. Initial history by the parents revealed considerable family turmoil. The mother stated that she also had been bulimic for the past twenty years, initially, because she was a dancer. No treatment had helped her. Both her own parents were obese with her mother's weight averaging about 275 pounds and the father's about 300. As a consequence she was always terrified of getting fat. The father interjected that his own mother weighed over 200 pounds and was frequently suicidal, as well as very mean and punishing to him and his three sisters. His father was an alcoholic, who had been beaten by his own alcoholic father. The father also volunteered that he had been hospitalized twice for cocaine abuse and once for alcoholism, but that he had been off drugs for the past three years. The father had been in the steel business. During his drug and alcohol illness, he neglected his business and was forced into bankruptcy. At that time, he swindled funds from his customers' accounts and narrowly escaped jail, ending up on parole. He currently still goes to Alcoholics Anonymous four times a week.

With that introduction, the parents returned to their concern for Elaine. They acknowledged that Elaine had eaten and vomited for three years before they realized it. It was only over the past year that her weight had dropped from 126 to 96 pounds. She was 5 feet 4 inches. I later learned from the family doctor that it was he who was instrumental in pressuring the parents into seeking help. The patient's periods began at age twelve and were regular as far as she knew until six months ago when they ceased. While she still gorged and vomited, she tried to stick to health foods. Both parents were concerned over her taking food up to her room and hiding it. Once they found a tennis duffle bag filled with popcorn. The mother was especially distressed that Elaine had a lovely figure until a year ago and now looked skeletal. On occasion, the daughter would acknowledge that she was thin, but at other times she would look in the mirror and comment on how fat she was. The father stated that Elaine seemed to have to exercise. She ran for miles, bicycled regularly, and worked out at an exercise club. Both parents noted her considerable restlessness, which had abated somewhat. They also felt that she was often depressed and guilt ridden. She was preoccupied with "starving children all over the world" and would frequently contribute her entire allowance to charitable causes. They also acknowledged increased outbursts of resentment that had not been present earlier.

In the first interview, Elaine appeared as a thin, attractive, bright, articulate, and self-punishing girl.

> If I'm your patient, will you hospitalize me? The other doctor wanted to and had me on medication which helped just a little. . . . I eat a lot . . . but I don't keep it down. I hate myself when I gorge . . . then I hate myself when I vomit . . . then I hate myself when I don't eat proper food. . . . If I didn't vomit, I'd probably weigh 200 pounds. I don't see myself as skinny. . . . I still feel I'm fat. I used to think that if I was 100, I'd look good and have a boyfriend, but I don't.

I wondered aloud what made her think that. "When I was in the ninth grade I was happiest, and I weighed 115. By the tenth grade, I didn't like myself. I felt I was fat . . . and I decided to lose weight . . . and then I'd be happy. . . . I know that it's me. I don't like myself.

I asked why. "Well, I'm fat. I'll say that I'm stupid, but I know that I'm not, because I get all A's. . . . But I'm not as smart as some . . . and I'm not very nice." I interjected that it sounded as if she felt that she had to be perfect, or she criticized herself.

> I criticize others, too. I criticize my sister for not brushing her teeth and not showering enough. I tell her she doesn't know how to dress . . . that she has no style . . . that she wears her hair wrong. And she gets mad at me! . . . I have lists and lists of what's wrong with me. . . . I can't even eat meals like a normal person. I eat like an animal and can't stop. Even animals don't do that. I'm not good in physics. I didn't get 1400 on my PSATs. My skin is dry. . . . Last week I had a little pimple on my face. . . . It all sounds stupid. I'm mean to my other sister. I feel jealous when she gets more presents than I do. I resent all her friends when

I have so few. . . . I'm only third highest in my grade. It's
my duty to do well. I'm editor of the school paper, but I
don't want anyone to know that I want it for my college
transcript.

I commented that it was unfortunate that she gave herself
such a difficult time and made herself so sad. She looked tearful,
and began to cry. "Why am I crying?" I suggested that some
of her unhappy feelings might be coming to the surface and
that it might be related to her eating difficulty. "Eating is the
only thing I'm good at. It's an escape."

In the second session, she expanded further upon her
multiple self-critical thoughts and behavior, and described
many situations in which she found fault with herself. She volunteered that when she felt upset about not having a boyfriend,
she would begin gorging and thinking about eating, and the
worry would go away. She reported her mother's complaint
about how much her illness had cost the family thus far and
felt unhappy about being unhappy. She reiterated her inability
to consistently determine whether she was fat or thin in spite
of looking at her bones in the mirror.

The first two consultations revealed Elaine's overwhelming
preoccupations with self-criticism. She criticized almost all areas
of her functioning. There were almost no positive aspects to
her being that she could reveal. Her involvement with eating
and fear of being fat seemed to be related to worry about becoming like the grandparents, echoing both the mother's fear
as well as her method of coping with it. Her punitive superego
was in part increased by her mother's harsh condemnation of
her illness. Here we see a clear example of what Sperling (1949)
has described in the parent–child relationship: the mother displacing a hated part of herself onto the child in order to minimize self-condemnation. One can also anticipate the potential
ambivalence of the mother toward the child's getting well, since
the loss of her displaced object for aggressive discharge could
result in an increase in her own conflict, along with the typical
other sources of ambivalence described elsewhere (Sperling,
1949). Both parents clearly suffered from impulse disorders

related to their own upbringing and development. The mother's twenty-year history of bulimia was a negative factor in Elaine's prognosis because of the patient's identification with her, and the possibility of the mother's unconscious jealousy that Elaine could get well and that she still suffered. The severe impulse disorders of both parents, along with their self-destructive consequences were also negative prognostic factors. Finally the parents' markedly critical behavior reinforced Elaine's punitive superego functioning. It is not uncommon to find grandparents who suffer from many of the problems that are found in the grandchild, with their serving as a psychological conduit through the parents and on to the third generation. I have seen many such cases. These parents illustrate the point made by Wilson (1986) that the gorging patients, unable to control their impulses, identify with parents who have the same problem.

Illustrations of Elaine's perfectionistic strivings followed by disillusion abound. The attempted perfectionism reflects in part, obsessive–compulsive attempts at exercising control over aggressive and sexual impulses. Although most of her aggression was directed toward herself, part of it was directed outward against external objects as she treated them the way she perceived that she was treated. Interestingly, the patient herself provided part of the reason for the need to gorge, as she noted the displacement of concern and agitation from worry about not having a boyfriend to thinking about gorging. Thus, one sees that gorging also represents regressed dependency gratification. What she feels she cannot get from the other person, she gets from food in a regressed return to disappointed experiences of early mothering. This displacement, typical of obsessional defense, is almost invariably found in anorexic and bulimic patients. Some patients report that, as they became increasingly preoccupied with eating, they forget the original worry as the aggression is discharged by the gorging or the dependency strivings are gratified through the ingestion of food.

In the third session after the first two diagnostic evaluations when she spoke volubly, the patient had almost nothing to say. She stated that she could not think of a thing—that I should tell her what to talk about—that she's pushing thoughts away. "I know that when I eat and vomit, the worries go away." While some bulimic patients present difficulties in talking, it is usually minimal or temporarily present in self-punishing and provoking transference fashion. Since the difficulty in controlling impulses is so great, the silence can rarely be maintained for long, in contrast to that of the anorexic patient. She then associated to how difficult it was to get along with her father, with her solution to keep quiet, so he did not criticize her. The session revealed her difficulty in talking and facing her problems in the face of her habitual propensity to avoid them by eating and vomiting. The awareness that starving or gorging both tend to displace conflict to the preoccupation with food and the subsiding of the original problem, provides the therapist with the opportunity to emphasize the secondary gain provided by the symptom. Thus, one is not forced into the inadvisable position of attempting to encourage the patient to renounce the eating behavior, which only tends to set off defiance or the sense of being controlled. Instead, it is possible to point out that if the patient is willing to face and to deal effectively with the problems, the need to avoid them by starving or gorging will subside. Early discussion of the use of food as a substitute for frustrations in the world and to achieve security in a regressed manner is helpful and well tolerated by the patient. Discussing the primary destructive aspects of gorging should be postponed until some attempt is made to deal with the punitive aspects of the superego and ameliorate some of the intense self-critical behavior. Otherwise, one can get a paradoxical reaction to the precipitous interpretation of aggression with increase of the patient's feelings of guilt, resulting in accentuation of eating symptoms or in depression. The other major factors to be considered were her association to the fearful relationship to the father, her anxiety over being criticized, and her solution to it by remaining quiet, all emerging in the transference.

In the fourth and fifth sessions, Elaine revealed her capacity for insight and for progress. She spoke more about her need to be perfect and how it interfered with her functioning.

I am unable to study because I have to concentrate so intently and study for so long that I just avoid the whole thing. I tried to stop criticizing myself and decided I didn't have to be perfect, and sit for hours and hours without moving. It worked and I studied for an hour and was able to stop without feeling guilty. I also told myself that I was smart and nice and not a terrible person. I didn't have to go downstairs and gorge the way I usually do. I also just ate one bowl of cereal at breakfast this morning, but then I got depressed.

In the fifth session, she continued: "I'm thinking more and more about my problems and it's getting me upset, and I couldn't sleep well last night . . . and I'm depressed today, but I didn't gorge and vomit!" While the clinical data reveal her capacity for insight and progress, her need for self-punishment, her unconscious feeling that she did not deserve to be well and happy, and her difficulty in resolving these conflicts made the resolution of conflict a long way off. In addition, patients with such a punitive and primitive superego frequently regress in the face of potential progress, because they feel that they might be able to get well and do not deserve it. Her needs for immediate gratification and difficulty in tolerating the frustration associated with dealing with complex problems over a period of time also complicate the picture.

As the sessions continued to unfold, the degree of self-criticism was overwhelming. The need to be perfect continued except for minor moments of insight and relaxation. When she was unable to exaggerate one aspect of a situation in order to feel bad, she would think unrealistically in order to treat herself harshly. She continued to anticipate that I was going to treat her critically; that if I did not criticize openly, I thought it, but just did not say it. Waves of self-criticism and self-attack engulfed her. She was unable to think of anything good about herself or that anyone could possibly think well of her. She just did not trust anyone, not one single person. She even felt that her best friend was lying when she used to say positive things about her or indicated that she had a good time with her. Whatever anyone said was viewed as criticism. This distorted view-point was markedly aggravated by the thoughtless, inconsiderate, and insensitive behavior of both parents who actually did crit-icize her repeatedly in the most inappropriate fashion. Both had been in previous long-term and unsuccessful treatment and would not consider further help. Both were marginal in their adjustment except that the father was able to avoid returning to drugs and alcohol. The father's self-centeredness and in-ability to give was evident when, after a year of treatment, and very modest gains, he announced to the patient that he could not afford further treatment just after buying an expensive new car. The mother agreed, but relented when the patient cried and cried and said that she'd "shrivel up." She screamed at the father that he would rather pay for her in a hospital. Then he gave in.

Much of her self-punishing behavior described thus far related to her thinking. Elaine also acted in very provocative fashion attempting to alienate those friends who thought the most of her. She acted bored in their company and tended to avoid worthwhile relationships; she was frequently involved in contacts with girl friends who treated her thoughtlessly and boyfriends who exploited her emotionally and sexually. She would then complain that she was worthless because all the students in school thought of her as a whore. On occasion she would visit bars, get picked up by older men, go to their apart-ments and sleep with them. The next day she would be filled with guilt and become depressed. At home she would provoke her three sisters and then complain that their attacks upon her indicated that she was a terrible person. She would borrow their clothing and possessions without asking, and frequently lose them or damage them. She left one sister's radio out on the patio in the rain. After weeks of agitation that she would fail her driving examination, she passed it and then proceeded to drive 70 m.p.h. with virtually no driving experience. When she did slow down and cars would pass her, she felt terrible because she must have been going too slow and did not know how to drive. Careless when cooking, she set off two fires in the kitchen.

These kinds of self-punishing and provoking behavior

were also present in the transference. Elaine would skip appointments without calling, suggest canceling sessions for spurious reasons, and arrive late. Often she would not discuss issues that were important to her, would not pay attention when I spoke, and almost never looked at me. As a consequence, she would feel that I could not possibly be interested in her, that it proved that she was a bad person, that I only saw her because I was being paid and not out of genuine concern, that she was not making any progress, and that the treatment did not work.

DISCUSSION

The clinical picture of the young anorexic woman, Marge, illustrates that most of her self-destructive behavior is restricted to her starving and the consequences of that starving: emaciation and possible death. While the denial and repression are effective, the patient usually does not suffer from the sense of weakness, cold, fatigue, and hunger. With progress in treatment, accompanied by the erosion of these defenses, those symptoms reappear and are experienced as damaging and painful. Initial denial of body changes ultimately gives way to recognition of the cachectic, unhealthy, and unattractive physical appearance. Otherwise, little grief is heaped upon her from the external world. One does not see a consistent reaching out to the world in masochistic fashion in order to provoke additional sources of punishment, present in the behavior of so many bulimic patients. This does not mean that some anorexic patients do not act out in relation to other people. Lying is not unusual in anorexics. However, just as one does not consistently find anorexia in pure culture uncontaminated by bursts of bulimia, and vice versa, in general, masochistic object relationships appear restricted to a harmful relationship to one's own body. In similar fashion, the primitive, punitive superego requires endless psychological self-punishing and psychological attacks upon the body in the form of criticism suffering, and hopelessness. In essence, just as the anorexic patient does not lose control over her impulses, she does not lose control over the source and extent of her punishment. The bulimic patient by contrast, having lost control over her impulses, has also lost partial control over the source and degree of her punishment.

Frequently, the anorexic's starved, waiflike appearance evokes sympathy, understanding, and solicitude from friends, family, and total strangers, providing dependency gratificiation in a regressed manner requiring suffering. The bulimic patient who gives in to the impulse to eat derives dependency gratification, warmth, and security through regressed infantile sucking and eating. One cachectic anorexic patient used to report that the counterman at the local luncheonette would prepare unusually large portions of food for her in the hope that she would eat and look better. Once physically well, she bemoaned the loss of people's interest in her pathetic appearance.

One component of self-destructiveness in these starving patients, not directly related to the starving, was well illustrated by Marge. Not eating was accompanied by not talking. While the not talking was associated, in part, with a fear of using her mouth, one transference aspect of it was acting self-destructively. In a talking treatment, one needs to talk. Dynamically, there is often a reciprocal relationship between not eating and not talking. When a defiant element is playing a role in the starving, not infrequently the defiance is displaced in a transference attitude accompanied by not talking. While this can present temporary complications as illustrated by Marge's behavior, in certain crucial situations, it can have certain beneficial results. In the beginning of treatment when Marge's starving increased, with weight loss approaching a point when hospitalization was considered, not talking was viewed by the therapist as an alternative to further not eating.

The two bulimic patients by contrast, illustrate widespread self-punishing attitudes, thinking, and behavior as well as endless reaching out into the environment to provoke injury, humiliation, and punishment. Elaine, the sixteen-year-old girl, was almost totally preoccupied with a myriad of critical, self-condemnatory, insulting, and denigrating thoughts. She viewed herself as fat, ugly, stupid, mean, thoughtless, selfish, exploiting, worthless, and hopeless. Every positive achievement was twisted into something reprehensible. Intensely provocative behavior would evoke angry reactions from others that would substantiate her negative self-image. Elaine would take her siblings' possessions without asking and usually lose or destroy them. She was solicitous of those who exploited her in order to continue the relationship and ignored the acquaintances who treated her thoughtfully to abrogate the contact. Additional self-destructive behavior resulted in her being physically assaulted and sexually abused. Maureen, the married bulimic woman, held herself in the same low regard, and provoked her friends into verbally attacking her and her husband into physically assaulting her.

THE RECIPROCAL RELATIONSHIP BETWEEN GORGING AND SHOPPING

An interesting, associated behavior in some of the patients who gorge is the endless need to shop, often also present in their mothers. Here one sees at times almost frantic bursts of shopping for clothing analogous to the bursts of gorging of food. The mother who shops constantly puts endless clothing onto her body, while the patient who gorges repeatedly puts endless food into her body. In both cases, the individual attempts to satisfy the needs through use of the body, needs which are insatiable because the perceived past deprivation cannot be permanently resolved by current behavior as an alternative to insight. Further confirmation of the interrelationship is evident in the reciprocal relationship between gorging and shopping. A bulimic patient who reported this shopping requirement in her mother, noted that when the mother was not able to shop, she became very restless at home and ended up gorging until she "felt so full that she could not move." When the outside of the body is not gratified, the inside of the body requires it instead.

This mother also derived great satisfaction in shopping for her daughter and putting clothing on the daughter's back. The very close, unconscious relationship between them permitted the mother to enjoy clothing the daughter, while unconsciously also viewing it as clothing herself. In somewhat analogous fashion, the starving anorexic patient, who unconsciously wishes to gorge, is able to continue to starve herself and unconsciously starve her mother, but gives in to the urge to gorge herself by forcing food upon her self–mother. The close symbiotic tie to the mother facilitates an identification with the mother such that feeding the mother is unconsciously viewed as feeding the self. From the point of the ego, it is also controlling the mother's eating, including the type of food in the same manner that the patient has felt that the mother controlled her. Finally, it is an expression of aggression toward the mother by force-feeding her in the face of the mother's own fear of getting fat.

DYNAMIC CONSIDERATIONS

It is not surprising that the anorexic–bulimic patient uses the body to express conflict just like patients with psychosomatic diseases. The anorexic who starves, denies, and represses the impulse to eat, while the bulimic who gorges, cannot contain the impulse to eat. These eating disturbances are usually precipitated by an eruption of conflict, leaving the patient feeling that she has lost control over life's circumstances, especially over the external object. This is, in part, a loss of realistic control in dealing with people and in part a loss of unconsciously required, residual infantile needs for omnipotent control and immature gratification. This usually occurs when experiencing conflict over separation, with resulting feelings of abandonment, the inability to deal constructively with aggressive drives, so that the patients feel dominated, threatened, or humiliated by others, or in conflict over psychosexual development or sexual behavior. The regression that these unresolved conflicts liberate is symbolized by the eating disorder. The anorexic starver, who feels that she is not in control of her world, obsessively and compulsively miniaturizes her world and at least controls what she eats and what she weighs. The bulimic also feels out of control, with her out-of-control eating symbolizing it, not just that she is out of control of her world, but of her impulses. In both situations, there is displacement of conflict onto an eating disorder.

Feeling out of control under these circumstances and unable to use her mouth effectively to verbalize, define, and defend her legitimate self-interest, she regresses back to earlier stages of orality. This early feeding stage contains elements of drive satisfaction and frustration, and ego satisfaction and frustration. From the point of drive satisfaction, sucking and eating provide the earliest form of inner warmth, nourishment, and security. Early aggressive drives are also satisfied by sucking and biting. Viewed from the developing ego, satisfaction occurs through the early sense of mastery, by sucking and eating. Restless activity associated with signs of hunger is rewarded by the sensitive, nourishing mother by feeding with relief of tension. A response to the frustration experienced by the insensitivity and aloofness of the less empathetic mother can take the form of aggressive sucking and biting. Sucking and eating as a positive experience provide impulse gratification, ego mastery, and incorporation of the loved introject. Sucking, eating, and biting, as a negative experience, provide discharge of aggression and incorporation of the ambivalently cathected introject. Unconscious, cannibalistic fantasies in these patients tend to confirm the presence of these early experiences. While the cannibalistic fantasies are not always recovered, they seem to be more readily available in the younger anorexic patients (Mintz, 1983b).

THE AIR–MILK MOTHER

An additional component of the sucking is present during early infant development. The early importance of the unconscious meaning of air is derived from the infant's sucking, which contains an admixture of milk and air, with both having the potential for becoming incorporated as the unconscious fantasy of the early milk–air–mother (Mintz, in press a,b). This also provides the anlage for the close relationship between the respiratory and the gastrointestinal systems. This may be one factor that partially explains that dependency; aggressive and sexual preoedipal conflict is often expressed regressively through an admixture of depressive, asthmatic, and anorexic symptomatology (Mintz, in press a; Silverman, in press).

RELATIONSHIP TO OBJECTS

When the anorexic and bulimic patients feel that they cannot regulate their relationships with people, they displace the conflict with people onto food where the food unconsciously stands for the people. This displaced regression reactivates the early relationship with people where the sucking and eating provides nourishment physically, and incorporation of the mother psychologically. That the food of the anorexic stands for people is well illustrated by a patient of Schlossman's (1979) who reported that all her food was kept in the refrigerator in little containers with people's names on them. To gorge and destroy the food by eating symbolizes the destruction of and incorporation of the ambivalently cathected introject. The anorexic who starves represses the unconscious impulse to eat and destroy the ambivalently cathected object, or attempts to starve the already incorporated object. One anorexic woman revealed that her starving began at a point when she feared that she was pregnant (Mintz, 1983b). Symptoms of abdominal pain, cramps, discomfort, and constipation, and the desire for diuretics, laxatives, and diarrhea often reflect the unconscious attempt to eliminate the fecal introject through the bowel as feces. This is analogous to the asthmatic's attempt to expel the ambivalently cathected introject either in the expired air through the lung or through the bowel as flatus. This need contributes to the anal component of asthma described so frequently (Sperling, 1963; Greenacre, 1971; Mintz, in press; Wilson, in press b). Thus we see a physiological reaction in an attempt to lose weight, accompanied by a psychological reaction in an attempt to expel the hated introject.

The frequent coexistence of gorging and vomiting is reflective of conscious needs to deal with uncontrollable impulses to eat and to regulate weight. Unconsciously, additional requirements are satisfied. Gorging represents an overwhelming need to attempt to satisfy dependency longings and attempts to achieve security where the taking in of the food symbolizes the incorporation of mother and a wish for a symbiotic reunion with mother (Sugarman and Kurash, 1981). It also represents a sexual conflict about what goes into the mouth with unconscious fellatio fantasy, linked to thoughts about pregnancy and conflicts over psychosexual identification. Finally the prodigious and rapacious devouring of food reflects waves of uncontrollable aggression directed toward the food-person that becomes the ambivalently cathected introject, that can cause internal damage and usually must be ejected.

VOMITING

The typical vomiting which accompanies the gorging is also multidetermined. Moulton (1942) and Sperling (1983) point out that the use of the finger to induce vomiting can symbolize masturbatory behavior with associated fellatio and pregnancy fantasies, while Sugarman and Kurash (1981) describe it as an attempt at separation from or destruction of the mother. Hogan (1983a) reported patients who vomit in response to anal conflicts displaced upward as they experienced their mess. It can also be viewed in sexual terms as a rape fantasy and an orgiastic response to it. One young, bulimic woman described putting her finger into her throat with such violence that she cut her fingers on her teeth and also made her uvula bleed. She viewed it as a sexual assault, followed by bleeding, with the rhythmic, convulsive aspects of the vomiting reflecting the resulting orgasm (Mintz, 1985a). The vomiting also served to discharge aggression in a man, with bulimia before treatment, who decided with great effort and willpower, to renounce his vomiting. He had been running an average of 50 miles a week. When he stopped vomiting, he felt forced to run over 100 miles a week to compensate for the build-up of tension and unconsciously discharge the accumulated aggression.

The Liberation of the Introjects

Vomiting can also be viewed as an outpouring of aggression where the verbalization and expression of the anger is hidden in the vomitus. Concomitantly, the vomiting serves to facilitate the liberation of dangerous introjects in the vomitus. One bulimic man of twenty in analysis had a dream of "being at a large banquet. The tables were full of food. I began to eat and eat. Suddenly a rat hidden in the food jumped into my mouth. I grabbed it by the throat and pulled it out. Then I began to vomit up one rat after the other until I vomited up eight to ten of them. I felt disgusted." The party reminded the patient of a family party where his younger brother acted in his usual obnoxious manner. The rats reminded him of the pet hamsters he used to have as a child. He thought that they were rodents and used their teeth a great deal. "One got out and ate a hole in the cellar door. They had babies all the time and he used to worry that the babies would die. If I think of rats in my mouth, maybe that's why I brush my teeth so often." In the next session he spoke of his tank of tropical fish and the reassuring thought that he had as a child, that if the fish died, he always could get others.

In the rat dream, the meaning of the rats was multidetermined. From years earlier, they clearly represented his hated baby hamster-brothers into which he incorporated his cannibalistic conflicts and death wishes about them, and his identifying with the carnivorous all-consuming rats. The patient identifying with the carnivorous rat unconsciously viewed eating as incorporating the hated carnivorous brother–rat–person, who can destroy from within. Vomiting represented both ejection of the feared and hated introject as well as identifying with the hated violent introject and exploding out the destroyed brother-introjects. The vomiting also represented an attempt to reject that identification with the carnivorous animal. We see, therefore, a simultaneous, unconscious identification with the carnivorous animal and a rejection of that identification in the struggle about the conflict over aggression. These unconscious, primitive, destructive impulses are the source of the deeper levels of guilt and the subsequent needs for punishment through self-destructive behavior in these bulimic patients.

While the bulimic patient tends to utilize vomiting to consciously deal with weight gain, and unconsciously deal with conflict, the anorexic patient has the same conflict, usually dealt with without vomiting, because of the maintained control over impulsive gorging. However the fantasies are similar (Mintz, 1985b).

TREATMENT

A detailed description of the treatment and technical problems encountered is described by Thomä, (1967), Sours (1969, 1974, 1979), Bruch (1973a, 1978, 1982), Wilson (1974, 1986), Wilson et al. (1983), Selvini Palazzoli (1978), Hogan (1983a), Sperling (1983) and others.

I should like to focus only upon some specific aspects of the self-destructive behavior. Wilson (1986), Wilson et al. (1983), and Hogan's (1983a) focus upon the way in which the bulimic's loss of control over impulses sets the stage for self-destructive acting out. In addition, Hogan's (1983b) recognition of the tendency for restlessness and hyperactivity reflects the availability of the motor system for acting out.

PROGRESS: A STIMULUS FOR REGRESSION

Bulimic patients characteristically have a tendency to regress in response to progress or to anticipated progress. Regression may occur when the patient suddenly realizes that she might be able to get better because of a momentary insight. This can be followed by coming late to the next session, skipping it, or becoming preoccupied with bouts of pessimism. In the fact of actual major improvement, the regressive self-destructive behavior can be greater. Rudominer (1987) described a bulimic male patient in analysis who improved markedly and precipitously terminated treatment. This is not uncommon, has been described frequently, and does not take place in response to the patient's feeling of true well-being. A young woman patient of twenty-three in analysis for a nine-year history of severe bulimia gradually realized at the end of her second year of treatment that she no longer had to gorge and vomit. Prior to analysis she felt required to exercise five to six hours a day, while gorging and vomiting absorbed another two hours, making her virtually unemployable. With the subsiding of her exercise and eating and vomiting "a whole new world opened up. . . . I can get a job . . . and enjoy food normally without a fear of getting fat. . . . I can eat enough and stop. . . . [I can eat] foods I have been afraid of eating for five years." This feeling of optimism associated with her improvement was followed by a sudden cessation of treatment, a wandering about the country for ten weeks, during which time she behaved self-destructively and narrowly escaped severe physical injury during sexual encounters with a number of unsavory characters. Subsequently, she returned and continued her analysis. In addition, her need to reach out for external sources of punishment as a way of dealing with her aggression and in response to the criticisms of a primitive harsh conscience, a third factor emerged in this patient. With very controlling, obsessional parents, she had many obsessive–compulsive character traits of her own. In one session, a transference reaction emerged in which she behaved toward me as if I were her mother whom she had to please and resented it. Doing anything well was seen as pleasing her mother. This was followed by her prompt need to undo it. This undoing seemed to have taken place in the transference, where doing well in a constructive fashion in analysis was perceived by her as pleasing the mother–analyst, requiring prompt undoing with regressive self-destructive behavior. Having recognized anal components in other anorexia–bulimia patients, it may be worth considering that anal defensive undoing may play a role in understanding how success becomes a stimulus for regression.

SUMMARY

1. An attempt was made through the use of detailed clinical material to illustrate the manifold aspects of self-destructive behavior in anorexia and bulimia.
2. Differences in aspects of ego structure between anorexic and bulimic patients result in differences in the manner in which the self-destructive behavior is manifested.
3. The starving anorexic who feels out of control of her relationships with people, obsessionally miniaturizes and displaces the conflict onto food. With an intact ego structure, and a primitive superego, she controls food and weight the way she would like to control people, and inhibits her impulse to eat, as well as other impulses, in the service of repressing her destructive impulses toward people.
4. The gorging anorexic, feeling out of control of her relationships with people, also miniaturizes and displaces the conflict onto food. Unable to contain her impulses, however, she illustrates her out-of-control relationships with people by her out-of-control relationships with food and voraciously attacks the food the way she would like to attack people.
5. The restrictor anorexic with basically intact ego controls is able to direct the aggression against the self in the form of continuous starving leading to the possibility of death. This satisfies the needs of a primitive, punitive superego and mitigates against the necessity to reach out into the environment to encourage additional sources of suffering.
6. The bulimic anorexic by comparison, without an intact ego structure, is unable to contain impulses and attacks the food, symbolically gratifying aggressive, sexual, and dependency needs. The lack of substantial suffering demanded by a primitive, harsh superego requires additional self-punishing experience in the form of self-destructive relationships with people including physical injury, delinquent behavior, sexual promiscuity, lying and stealing, and the use of drugs and alcohol.
7. Turmoil and frustration in infancy, associated with sucking an admixture of air and milk during feeding, contributes to

later problems with aggression and dependency gratification. The unconscious fantasy of the early frustrating air –milk–mother results in the development of subsequent conflict involving the respiratory and/or gastrointestinal systems and is reflected in an interrelationship between asthmatic and anorexic symptomatology.

8. While the symbolic meaning of bulimic vomiting is multi-determined, the vomiting can represent both an ejection of the feared and hated introject as well as identifying with the violent, carnivorous introject. These unconscious, primitive, and destructive impulses are the source of the deeper levels of guilt and the subsequent needs for punishment through self-destructive behavior in these bulimic patients.

References

Bruch, H. (1973a), Anorexia nervosa. In: *American Handbook of Psychiatry*, Vol. 4, 2nd ed., ed. M. F. Reiser. New York: Basic Books.
——— (1973b), *Eating Disorders: Obesity, Anorexia Nervosa, and the Person Within.* New York: Basic Books.
——— (1978), *The Golden Cage.* Cambridge, MA: Harvard University Press.
——— (1982), Anorexia nervosa: Therapy and theory. *Amer. J. Psychiat.*, 139:1535–.
Greenacre, P. (1971), *Emotional Growth*, Vol. 1. New York: International Universities Press.
Hogan, C. (1983a), Psychodynamics. In: *The Fear of Being Fat: The Treatment of Anorexia Nervosa and Bulimia*, ed. C. P. Wilson, C. Hogan, & I. Mintz. New York: Jason Aronson, pp 115–128.
——— (1983b), Technical problems in psychoanalytic treatment. In: *The Fear of Being Fat: The Treatment of Anorexia Nervosa and Bulimia*, ed. C. P. Wilson, C. Hogan, & I. Mintz. New York: Jason Aronson, pp. 197–216.
Mintz, I., (1983a), Anorexia and bulimia in males. In: *The Fear of Being Fat: The Treatment of Anorexia Nervosa and Bulimia*, ed. C. P. Wilson, C. Hogan, & I. Mintz. New York: Jason Aronson, pp 263–304.
——— (1983b), Psychoanalytic psychotherapy of severe anorexia: The case of Jeanette. In: *The Fear of Being Fat: The Treatment of Anorexia Nervosa and Bulimia*, ed. C. P. Wilson, C. Hogan, & I. Mintz. New York: Jason Aronson, pp. 217–244.
——— (1985a), The fear of being fat: In normal, obese, starving and gorging individuals. Panel on Obesity and Related Phenomena, Fall Meeting, American Psychoanalytic Association, December 1985.
——— (1985b), The lizard phenomenon in male anorexic and bulimic patients. Psychiatric Meeting, Hackensack Medical Center, Hackensack, NJ, November 1985.

———— (in press a) The treatment of a case of severe asthma in childhood. In: *Early Psychic Stress: The Psychoanalytic Treatment of Psychosomatic Disease*, ed. C. P. Wilson & I. Mintz. New York: Jason Aronson.

———— (in press b), The unconscious meaning of air in asthmatic disease. In: *Early Psychic Stress: The Psychoanalytic Treatment of Psychosomatic Disease*, ed. C. P. Wilson & I. Mintz. New York: Jason Aronson.

Moulton, R. (1942), A psychosomatic study of anorexia nervosa including the use of vaginal smears. *Psychosom. Med.*, 4:62–74.

Rudominer, H. (1987), Panel Discussion. Transference in a male bulimic. Psychoanalytic Association of New York, Lenox Hill Hospital, New York, January 1987.

Schlossman, H. (1979), Psychiatric Meeting. Hackensack Medical Center, Hackensack, NJ.

Schwartz, H. (1986), Bulimia: Psychoanalytic perspectives. *J. Amer. Psychoanal. Assn.*, 34:439–461.

Selvini Palazzoli, M. (1978), *Self-Starvation: From Individual to Family Therapy in the Treatment of Anorexia Nervosa*. New York: Jason Aronson.

Silverman, M. (in press), Power, control and the threat to die in a case of bronchial asthma and anorexia nervosa. In: *Early Psychic Stress and the Psychoanalytic Treatment of Psychosomatic Disease*, ed. C. P. Wilson & I. Mintz. New York: Jason Aronson.

Sours, J. (1969) Anorexia nervosa: Nosology, diagnosis, developmental patterns, and power-control dynamics. In: *Adolescence: Psychosocial Perspectives*, ed. G. Caplan & S. Lebovici. New York: Basic Books, pp. 185–212.

———— (1974), The anorexia nervosa syndrome. *Internat. J. Psycho-Anal.*, 55:567–576.

———— (1979), The primary anorexia nervosa syndrome. In: *Basic Handbook of Child Psychiatry*, Vol. 2, ed. J. D. Noshpitz. New York: Basic Books, pp. 568–580.

Sperling, M., (1949), The role of the mother in psychosomatic disorders in children. *Psychsom. Med.*, 11:377–385

———— (1963), Psychoanalytic study of bronchial asthma in children. In: *The Asthmatic Child: Psychosomatic Approach to Problems and Treatment*, ed. H. Schneer. New York: Harper & Row, pp. 138–165

———— (1978), Anorexia nervosa (part 4). In: *Psychosomatic Disorders in Childhood*, ed. O. Sperling. New York: Jason Aronson, pp. 129–173.

———— (1983), A reevaluation of classification, concepts and treatment. In: *Fear of Being Fat: The Treatment of Anorexia Nervosa and Bulimia*, ed. C. P. Wilson, C. Hogan, & I. Mintz. New York: Jason Aronson, pp. 51–82.

Sugarman, A., & Kurash, C. (1981), The body as a transitional object in bulimia. *Internat. J. Eat. Disord.*, 4:57–66.

Thomä, H. (1967), *Anorexia Nervosa*. New York: International Universities Press.

Wilson, C. P., (1974), The psychoanalysis of an adolescent anorexic girl. Discussion Group on Late Adolescence, S. Ritzo, Chairman Fall Meetings, American Psychoanalytic Association, New York.

———— (1986), The psychoanalytic psychotherapy of bulimic anorexic nervosa. In: *Adolescent Psychiatry*, Vol. 13, ed. S. C. Feinstein. Chicago: University of Chicago Press, pp. 274–314.

—— (in press), Parental overstimulation in asthma. In: *Early Psychic Stress: The Psychoanalytic Treatment of Psychosomatic Disease,* ed. C. P. Wilson & I. Mintz. New York: Jason Aronson.

—— Hogan, C., & Mintz, I., eds. (1983), *The Fear of Being Fat: The Treatment of Anorexia Nervosa and Bulimia.* New York: Jason Aronson.

—— Mintz, I. (1982), Abstaining and bulimic anorexics: Two sides of the same coin. *Primary Care,* 9:459–472.

Chapter 7

Bulimia and Anorexia: Understanding Their Gender Specificity and Their Complex of Symptoms

CLIFFORD J. TABIN, PH.D.

JOHANNA KROUT TABIN, PH.D.

Bulimia and anorexia are two syndromes that are generally classified and discussed under the rubric of eating disorders. That view is understandable since the respective purging or denial of food is the most dramatic and life threatening symptom of each disease. However, it has been established that both bulimia and anorexia exist as definable collections of symptoms that are always present as inseparable complexes no matter what other disease entities may exist (from mild depression to schizophrenia), and no matter what other circumstances may exist in conjunction with them in a particular patient (Sours, 1974; Lowenkopf and Wallach, 1985). These complexes are summarized in Table 7.1 as established by Boskind-White and White (1983) for bulimia and by Sours (1980) for anorexia. It can be observed that from the standpoint of describing the archetypical syndrome, the eating disorder aspect of the diseases is no more fundamental than other, less traditionally emphasized symptoms such as amenorrhea (predating the eating disorder, not a trivial physiological consequence of it), denial of sexuality, splitting as a defense, hyperactivity, kleptomania, and so on. Thus a full understanding of the etiology of these diseases must encompass an explanation for the entirety of the complexes as

TABLE 7.1
Comparison of Bulimic with Anorexic Syndrome

Elements of the Bulimic Syndrome	Elements of the Anorexic Syndrome
Binge–purge compulsion	Rejection of food
Acutely difficult intrapsychic separation–individuation	Acutely difficult intrapsychic separation–individuation
Denial of need for help	Denial of problem
Amenorrhea predating bulimia	Amenorrhea predating anorexia
Collecting, but not wearing, feminine apparel	Collecting, but not wearing, feminine apparel
Avoidance of sexuality; extremely dependent relationships	Denial of sexuality
Bodily concerns: Uncertainty of identity image sensations control	Bodily concerns: Uncertainty of identity image sensations control
An as-if personality, the dominant behavioral mode during the prodromal period	An as-f personality, the dominant behavioral mode during the prodromal period
Helplessness	Helplessness
Passive repression (defense)	Passive repression (defense)
Preoccupation with the good–bad dichotomy	Preoccupation with the good–bad dichotomy
Splitting as a defense	Splitting as a defense
Anal preoccupation	Anal preoccupation
Oral–anal–genital admixture in fantasies	Oral–anal–genital admixture in fantasies
Suicidal ideation, re: control issues	Suicidal ideation, although unconnected with starvation
Secrecy of thought	Secrecy of thought
Kleptomania	Kleptomania
Hyperactivity	Hyperactivity
Narrow perception of space–time	Narrow perception of space–time

properly defined. More importantly, an optimally effective therapy can only be designed on the basis of such a perspective, which prior psychoanalytic theories have not provided.

There is, in addition, another indication that the current models of bulimia and anorexia are incomplete. Both diseases are found primarily in girls [nine times as frequently as in boys (Bruch, 1979)]. Moreover, when these diseases do appear in boys, there are important differences in the characteristics of the disease. In particular, male bulimics and anorexics take pride in their avoidance of food as opposed to the denial of the problem typical of their female counterparts (Garner and Garfinkel, 1979). Males also generally present with much more severe manifestations and more fragmented ego states than do the females (Sours, 1980). None of the models of the psychological etiology of these diseases provide explanations of the sex ratios and sex-specific manifestations of the disorders as one would hope might be provided by a complete theory.

The preceding discussion is not meant to say that previous models are all flawed, but merely that it is inevitable that they are incomplete. Therefore, to attempt to form a theoretical basis for understanding the complex of symptoms which coexist in bulimia and anorexia (without focusing extensively on one aspect and relegating the other symptoms to an ancillary status), and to attempt to conceptualize the basis for the gender-specific aspects of the diseases, we decided to take a fresh look at their genesis.

As discussed in the first chapter of this volume, prior work has traced the ontogeny of eating disorders to either times of infancy typified by the semisymbolic introjection–projection struggles and the separation–individuation period, or to times of formation of oedipal fantasies.

Following the supposition that previous studies, although incomplete, have identified important components of the dynamic, we will begin by focusing on the earlier of the two times previously identified in this context, a period roughly corresponding to the second year of life. It will be seen how the other suggested framework, that built around oedipal manifestations, naturally fits into the picture as well.

If one's goal is to understand the full array of normal or pathological attributes which relate to a particular stage of development, then one must take into account, as fully as possible, all of the psychological events which are of significance at that stage.

There is a vast literature dealing with different aspects of psychological development at age two. These writings have variously focused on the shift from oral to anal concerns (Abraham, 1934), dependence–autonomy issues, and the separation–individuation process (Mahler, 1965, Masterson, 1975), self –other identification (Kohut, 1971), and so on. Unfortunately, no psychological theory exists which adequately integrates all of the psychological tasks a two-year-old faces, along with mapping the interrelationships between those tasks into a single coherent picture. Yet, as discussed, only from such a unified coherent model could we hope to obtain a full understanding of the complex syndromes deriving from that period of life (i.e., if you want to understand all the diverse fallout from an age, you have to first understand all that is going on at that age). Therefore, our initial task is a reassessment of the dynamics of the two-year-old stage. Only then will one be in a position to reexamine the etiology of bulimia and anorexia.

There is general agreement that the second year of life is the time of organizing the first integrated ego, reflected in a sense of self. It has been well established that this is in part developed in relation to separation–individuation from the infant's mother (Mahler, 1965). During the same time of life, a child first develops an awareness of genital sensations (Kleeman, 1966; Galenson, Miller, and Roiphe, 1976). In part, through this awareness, the second year of life is also the time that gender identity is established (Stoller, 1968; Money and Ehrhardt, 1972); which is thus integrated from the start into the child's concept of self.

The nature of this first organized ego is influenced by a number of new capabilities a child first develops at this same time (Tabin, 1985). These include the ability to control the sphincters (giving a sense of inner control and of enough importance in and of itself that this phase of life can be discussed in terms of a shift from oral to anal concerns); expanded ability of locomotor potential; the first ability for object permanence (ability to hold objects fixed in the mind); the first development of language, which carries with it the first analytical cause and effect reasoning (added to the earlier prelinguistic associative reasoning); the capacity for categorical thought (at this early time in terms of dichotomous splitting: omnipresent–nonexistent, good–bad, etc.); the first basis for privacy of thought (allowing passive repression and denial); and the first concept of time. Finally, as a consequence of the development of a sense of self, there is the first capability to develop a sense of responsibility, and, therefore, to first sense shame and guilt. The dichotomous categorical thought of the age creates a harsh primitive super-ego, engendering extreme reactions to the newly perceived guilt feelings. The important point here is that all those things (ego formation, gender identity, awareness of sexual feelings, linguistic ability, sense of time, sphincter control, etc.), *all occur nearly simultaneously in development*. This fact sets up the complex dynamic we must attempt to understand. This simultaneous occurrence also means that the various elements form an associative network, which pattern the thought and behavior of an individual either at a two-year-old stage of development or later on when dealing with issues left over from that time.

It is important to bear in mind that these elements are only separate issues from the standpoint of adults trying to make sense of personality development and focusing for convenience on one or another aspect as an organizing principle in defining developmental stages and understanding pathology. For the infant, however, these factors are not distinct, but rather are aspects of a whole that the child must sort out and make sense of. All the new capabilities facilitate a greater exploration and understanding of the world and the child's place in it. Therefore, cataloging all the elements is not enough. We must create an initial theoretical framework that models the way those elements are handled in an interdependent manner by the toddler.

To accurately conceptualize the forces at play, such a framework must be built from the child's perspective. That is to say, it must be built around the task of sorting out who the child is. Previous names for this period of life have reflected an emphasis on processes that *contribute* to the establishment of an ego, such as, anal phase (Freud, 1905), separation–individuation phase and subphases (Mahler, 1965), and primary oedipal phase (Tabin, 1985). But all of these, and several other processes as well, are in reality different components of the complex dynamics the child must use for its first self definition.

Therefore, we will use the term *primary ego formation phase,* or *primary ego phase,* to connote the most basic task at hand when referring to this critical period of life.

Figure 7.1 gives a framework for viewing the way in which the interrelated psychological tasks of the primary ego phase contribute to self-definition and how they create conflicts which must be sorted out in the process.

The central task for the two-year-old is one of self-definition in its various manifestations. Thus, ego formation is at the hub of the diagram. It is based on a number of processes. One of these is that of separating the self from mother and self-individuation. As separation–individuation proceeds, the child feels a greater sense of self in relation to its world. (This is, of course, tied to such accomplishments as internal sphincter control and external physical control.) The child also gains an

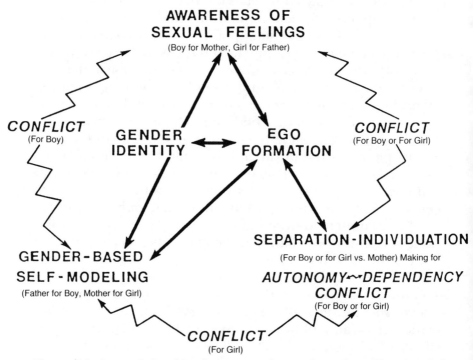

Figure 7.1. Interrelationships between various tasks and conflicts faced simultaneously by a young child.

awareness of self through an awareness of sexual feelings. The child additionally gains strength through self-modeling after the same-sex parent. Ego formation is further solidified through a child's growing awareness of its gender, identifying who it is in terms of an early dichotomous split between males and females. At the same time, the development of the ego allows the child further ability to develop each of these other tasks. Thus, a stronger ego allows the strength for greater separation and individuation, and ego growth reinforces the child's ability to define what it means to have a particular gender. A gender identity, in turn, creates a stronger basis for self-modeling on the same-sex parent. Also, a greater clarity of gender allows the focusing of sexual feelings toward the opposite sex parent. Thus, sexual feelings, self-modeling, and individuation are all reinforced and in turn lead to still greater ego growth; accordingly, the child's sense of self spirals to greater levels through a continued positive feedback network.

However, this ego growth is not an easy one; the process is fraught with dangers stemming from three interrelated conflicts. These conflicts have to be negotiated and eventually settled for the child to successfully move ahead. When these conflicts are not solved but rather compromises are created and defenses erected to mask them, then the child is left in an unstable state that can collapse into psychopathology later in life unless they are subsequently addressed and overcome. It will be seen that while the general form of the conflicts is parallel for a little boy and a little girl, the exact pattern is not truly symmetrical. The gender differences in the pattern will be seen to stem from the fact that both the boy and girl are separating from the mother. However, while the girl is attracted to her father (and is thus a primitive rival of her mother), the boy is attracted to the same mother he is separating from. Thus gender specific pathologies can potentially be generated by failure to resolve these two-year-old stage conflicts. This is apparent when considering the conflicts in detail as they occur for each sex.

A little girl is put into one conflict from the fact that ego formation depends on both gender-based self-modeling and the separation–individuation process. The separation from mother requires distance from her, and as the girl's ego growth continues, she will desire further individuality. At the same time, identification with her mother and hence further gender identification and ego formation requires closeness to her mother. Thus, knowing herself through her mother limits her individuality in a way that will not be true for a boy discovering himself. Conversely, gaining independence may mean denying femininity as modeled on mother in a way that independence does not threaten a boy's masculinity.

A second conflict for the girl comes from the fact that her awareness of her sexual excitement with her father makes her feel rivalrous toward her mother, from whom she is still attempting to define herself as a separate entity. The more autonomy she gains, the clearer her ego formation and gender identity, and, therefore, also the greater her ability to sense her sexual feelings. Thus, more independence leads to more rivalry and, hence, more danger. On the other hand, less separation and greater safety carries the burden of loss of sexuality.

The girl at the same time has one final source of conflict within the separation–individuation process itself. The comforts of dependency are opposed to the self-actualization of autonomy.

The little boy also has three interrelated areas of conflict in ego formation at age two. First there is a conflict between his awareness of his sexual feelings for his mother and his desire to separate from her. His excitement is increased in close contact with her, which supports his sense of self in gender-identity. Yet closeness to his mother threatens both his independence and his differentiating himself from her on the basis of gender. Therefore, closeness threatens a loss of self. Thus genital feeling and "closeness" seem at odds as one is tied to more, and the other to less of a sense of self.

A second conflict for the boy is that the growing sexual awarenesss he feels with the mother makes him a rival of the father on whom he simultaneously needs to model himself in establishing a sense of gender. Both sexual awareness and modeling based on stronger gender identity continue to grow with ego formation. Finally, the little boy also feels the conflicting desires for autonomy and dependence.

It is immediately clear that a subset of these conflicts foreshadows the form of later oedipal conflicts at four through six years of age. At the primary ego stage, the rivalries and sexual desires are not in as sharp focus as they will be at the oedipal stage (i.e., "I will kill Daddy and marry Mommy"). However, their psychological power is perhaps even greater at this earlier time. The two-year-old is considerably more helpless and dependent. The child has just barely established a sense of ego. There is not room to retreat out of fear of these conflicts without weakening that sense of ego to the point that it threatens a real loss of self-identity. At the oedipal stage, a child may fear a parent's wrath and physical annihilation, but at this earlier time there is the added tremendous threat of psychic annihilation. These fears gain more strength from the early thought patterns of a two-year-old, which is in terms of dichotomous thought and splitting into all or none, me or him, existence or annihilation, with no gray areas in between. Finally, the two-year-old conflicts are considerably more complex because those conflicts which foreshadow later oedipal conflict are intertwined with issues of individuation, gender identity, and core sense of self.

We have seen that sexuality and autonomy are completely intertwined at age two. At that age, they are not separate attributes but rather different aspects of a single nascent phenomenon. However, by the time of the oedipal stage, sexuality and autonomy, while still psychologically associated, are by definition distinct. They are distinct matters then because a sense of gender has already been developed along with a large degree of ego sense. By adolescence, sexuality and autonomy should be completely distinct. They never are totally so because there are always some remaining threads unwound from earlier times. But again, it is only at the primary ego phase that they are reduced to a single phenomenon. The degree to which sexuality and autonomy are still linked for an adolescent is the degree to which the person is still mired in the earliest phases of experience and is likely to resort to symptomatic behavior in dealing with basic issues.

While it may be apparent that as gender identity is forming, sexuality and individuation are linked and are dealt with in ways available to a two-year-old, it may be less obvious why they remain connected upon reactivation of a particular early issue—why such single issues need still evoke a whole complex of symptoms derived from the age and dealt with on a primitive basis. By adolescence, an individual has, after all, indeed formed a sense of his or her gender. One might expect that would obviate the need to tie all the early issues together. However, research on memory shows that when a "complex" of emotional tasks, such as those involved in ego formation, is worked through in development, an *associative network* is formed wherein emotions serve as memory units (Bower, 1980). Therefore, in later life the activation of any one of the elements of the complex can produce behavior associated with the entire emotional complex. Conversely, a therapeutic analysis can be based on one aspect of the complex with resultant alleviation of an array of symptoms without ever directly touching on other issues that make up the complex. Thus it is that clinical success has not required understanding all the interrelating conflicts that underlie pathologies dating to the second year.

The patterns for ego development and the various challenges they present to a child are universal. However, the way in which these challenges are met and their subsequent ramifications are greatly influenced by the physical state of the infant, familial dynamics, and cultural influences. Correlations have long been observed between such factors and the development of various psychopathologies. Why these have the particular influences that they do can be understood by investigating how the various conflicts a toddler faces are affected by particular family constellations. This will become clear as we now return to the specific problems of bulimia and anorexia and look at how the structure of the interrelated conflicts of the primary ego phase leads directly to the full array of symptoms associated in eating disorders and also leads to the gender specific nature of the diseases.

Since most bulimics and anorexics are female, we will start by looking at how those syndromes arise in girls. The general pattern of ego development for a girl is reviewed again in Figure 7.2A. To review, ego formation is based on awareness of gender identity, awareness of sexual feelings for father, self-modeling based on mother, and from the separation–individuation processes. The conflicts a primary ego phase girl faces include the autonomy–dependency conflict where ego growth requires separating from the one with whom closeness must be simultaneously maintained for the sake of security; a conflict of sexual desire creating a rivalry with the one still needed for support; and a conflict in that modeling on mother means ego growth accomplished by being like mother, but like mother paradoxically means less individuation and therefore less ego growth. The conflicts are more or less balanced and as all the contributing factors of ego formation increase, the conflicts are handled and the ego solidified.

Now in Figure 7.2B, we consider the outcome for a baby girl in an intensely emotional, close-knit family such as has been shown to be characteristic of those in which anorexic and bulimic children appear. In such a family, the close contact with father induces much stronger than normal sexual feelings at an earlier age than normal. At the same time, the unusually close emotional link the girl forms with her mother strengthens the bond of dependency. This combination heightens the conflict that she develops in her feelings of primitive sexual rivalry with her nurturing mother. Because this is occurring early in the time frame, she has little ego development to provide strength to handle the increased conflict. Therefore, she defuses the conflict by instituting an early form of repression. At the same time as she represses her sexual feelings, she reaffirms her loyalty to mother to atone for the sexual guilt feelings she has already generated. This means less separation from mother in an almost desperate drive for security. Since it is at the earliest time of the primary ego phase, oral matters still dominate. Mother is so connected with food in the child's mind that, in regard to issues that will later date back to this time, food will remain a metaphor for mother. Thus already we find sexual issues, autonomy issues, and eating intertwined.

In addition, the further development of her sense of self

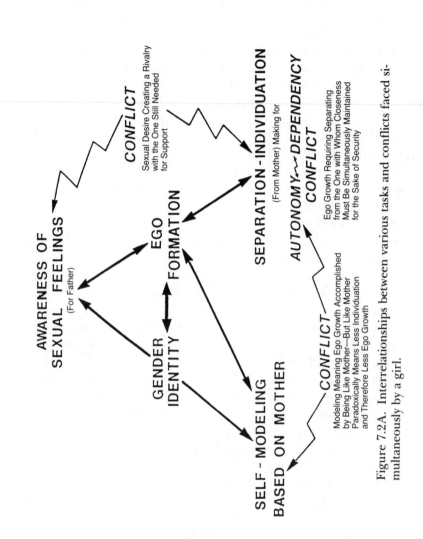

Figure 7.2A. Interrelationships between various tasks and conflicts faced simultaneously by a girl.

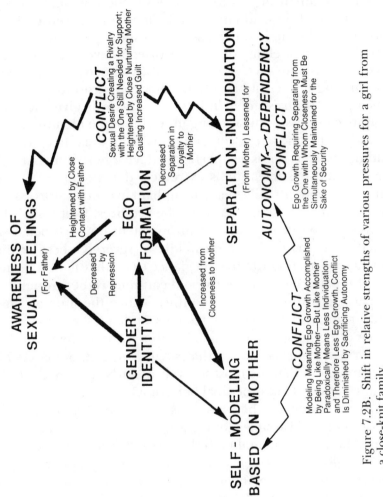

Figure 7.2B. Shift in relative strengths of various pressures for a girl from a close-knit family.

suffers greatly. By denying sexual feelings for father, she does
not have an awareness of sexuality to contribute to her sense
of gender and overall identity. In addition, by loyally staying
close to her nurturing mother, she loses the potential for ego
growth through individuation, and represses any sense of autonomy that she might otherwise gain as she explores her world.
Only the self-modeling component of ego development is not
weakened. It is, in fact, strengthened by closeness to mother.
Her clinging to security and hypermodeling lead to an aspect
of being a "Mama's good little girl." This can give the false
apearance of possessing a strong inner feminine identity. However, without concurrent contributions from the other two ego
building sources, this is a superficial effect. There is no real ego
consolidation possible. She is extremely dependent, an extension of her mother really, being compliant in every way to assure
that she will not lose the security she requires. Culturally, she
receives a good deal of adult reinforcement for such behavior
as well. The girl is also often mildly to severely obese at this
time, demonstrating further allegiance to mother in oral terms.

This pattern of behavior would continue right through the
oedipal age without signs of conflicts, since the little girl has
firmly repressed her sexual feelings and does not have the
degree of ego organization needed to approach the tasks that
are normally worked out in that stage. [Indeed, Sours (1974)
has pointed out that the most severely disturbed anorexics have
a history of no obvious oedipal behavior.]

At adolescence, when most cases of bulimia and anorexia
emerge, cultural variables come into play that help to determine
the psychodevelopmental path the girl will follow. As the physical changes of adolescence make her sexuality apparent, the
precarious balance begins to break down. In a culture where
some teenage female independence is expected, where sexuality
is pressured by the media and by her male and female peers,
and where thinness and dieting are emphasized, she never has
the chance to gradually develop her inner strength and freedom
that she might in a more sheltered, nurturing society. Issues of
sexuality and body form are raised too strongly. Yet she has

never achieved a real sense of self that would allow autonomy, nor has she ever gained inner permission for her own sexuality.

Her initial response to the intensified sexual impulses she feels is to follow her old pattern and try to deny them. That is why anorexics and bulimics typically develop amenorrhea months before they stop eating (Thomä, 1967), as opposed to the physiologically explainable order where amenorrhea would follow self-starvation. This pattern of denial then fails her as her sexuality is felt too overtly.

Finally, drawing on the resources of her primitive ego organization, the girl may react by becoming "anorexic": she gives up mother–food to gain a degree of autonomy. Desperately, as with constant activity, she strives to prove that she can survive without her mother. At the same time, by losing weight she minimizes her feminine form, denying her sexuality. Along with sexual repression, this appeases her mother by reaffirming her position as a nonrival. There is also the self-punitive aspect to it; feeling guilty over her sexual feelings and independence, she cuts herself off from the symbol of her mother's caretaking, rejecting food before her mother can withdraw it.

The girl will often engage in seemingly conflicting behavior. For example, she often buys very feminine clothing, then keeps it in a closet and only wears asexual apparel. This is because she is still attempting to gain ego strength from self-modeling on mother (the only route to ego growth she has formed), yet she needs to deny the possibility of presenting herself as a sexual being.

The bulimic develops from the same dynamic. This is clear because a single individual often goes from one eating disorder to the other. From the lists of elements of the bulimic and anorexic syndromes presented at the start of this chapter, it can be seen that there are two differences between them. One is the bulimic's binge–purge compulsion as opposed to the anorexic's rejection of food. The other is that the bulimic avoids sexuality, but focuses on having a man while the anorexic denies sexuality entirely. The bulimic may form extremely dependent relationships where she is so possessive that the man may reject her, or where he is the object of her extreme criticism so that he is unacceptable, but she does not have satisfying relationships. In other words, the bulimic is in the same dynamic outlined in Figure 7.2B. However, she has derepressed some sexual feelings, in keeping with a measure of autonomy compared with someone in the restrictive anorexic state. [Garner, Garfinkel, and O'Shaughnessy (1985) found bulimics to be significantly more impulsive (autonomous) and suicidal (conflicted) than patients in the restrictive anorexic state.] She feels compelled to atone for her sexual feelings by a loyalty act to mother, which is again represented by the oral metaphor of food dating to the early ego formation stage. Some bulimics feel humiliation and anger at this act because their lack of control is an act of dependency and of loss of ego differentiation.

Other bulimics report binging as a release. That is because they attain a symbolic fusion with mother by eating which releases them from responsibility for their sexual feelings. How a bulimic feels will depend on the degree to which her desires for autonomy are derepressed along with the derepressed awareness of sexual feelings. In either case, the bulimic then purges because having temporarily ameliorated her conflict over sexuality by eating, the girl or woman then feels her drive for independence which she has symbolically given up in eating. She, therefore, rejects the fusion with mother. [Garner et al., (1985) also found as a striking difference between bulimics and bulimarexics on the one hand and restrictive anorexics on the other that the former are significantly more able to think of themselves as mature.]

In addition, the bulimic often refers in fantasy to chewing as an aggressive destructive element which results in the swallowing up of food–body–mother. This mother–food is then inside as a dangerous enemy who must be gotten rid of (Milner, 1944). The reason the mother is seen as a dangerous enemy is, again, because the girl's sexual impulses make her a rival. On this symbolic level, the bulimic is trying to deal with the conflict by aggressively chewing the rival. But this fails, because in the act the mother becomes closer, the bulimic loses individuality and ego strength, and the symbolic mother is still there, now inside and must be gotten rid of. The internalized mother is also, to the bulimic, an enemy—a bad part of herself. She is symbolically fused to her mother after giving up autonomy by eating; yet her mother has bad, that is, sexual aspects. Thus, the fused mother is an enemy who represents the bulimic's own sexy thoughts and must be purged (Milner, 1944).

Bulimics also can associate their acts with primal scene fantasies enacted in oral terms (Schwartz, 1986) and with pregnancy–morning sickness fantasies. These are also explainable because of the oral matters typical of the primary ego stage when the child first develops awareness of genital impulses.

In examining the origins of the bulimic and anorexic patterns in girls, we have seen how they depend on the fact that primary ego stage girls equate sexuality with a rivalry with their mother on whom they depend. This is not true for boys at the same age. A review of the boy's ego formation is given in Figure 7.3A. Ego formation is again based upon awareness of gender identity, awareness of sexual feelings for mother, self-modeling based on father, and from the separation–individuation process. The conflicts a primary ego phase boy faces differ from those of a girl. These include the autonomy–dependency conflict where ego-growth requires separating from the one with whom closeness must be simultaneously maintained for the sake of security; the conflict of being the rival of the father who must simultaneously serve as a model, and the conflict from sexual attraction which brings a desire for closeness with the mother who must be simultaneously moved away from for individuation and ego growth.

Unlike a primary ego phase girl, a toddler boy's sexual feelings do not make him his mother's rival, so the bulimic and anorexic syndromes as defined above simply cannot occur. Another pair of pathologies can arise in boys which share the eating disorder traits described above. However, these are really distinct diseases with differences in symptoms (such as the degree of ego fragmentation required to produce them, and the lack of denial of hunger in boys) that are also intelligible in terms of the dynamics of the primary ego phase. The same time frame is involved in the etiology for the boy since the similarity

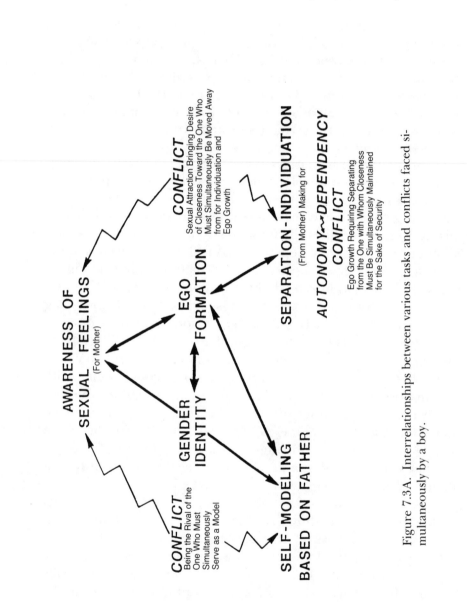

Figure 7.3A. Interrelationships between various tasks and conflicts faced simultaneously by a boy.

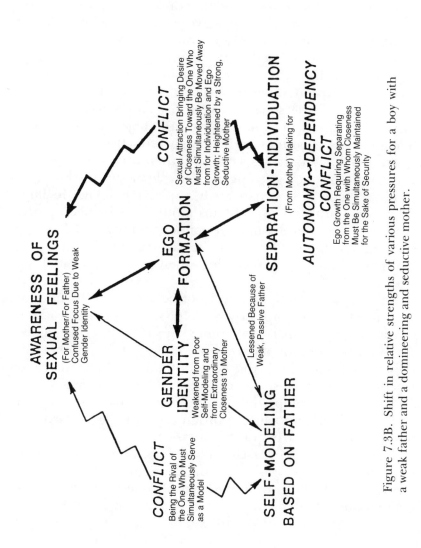

Figure 7.3B. Shift in relative strengths of various pressures for a boy with a weak father and a domineering and seductive mother.

in the pathologies reflects a similarity in the stage and issues at work.

The development of male eating disorders typically occurs in families with a father who is weak or otherwise makes it difficult for the boy to identify with him and a mother who is both domineering and seductive (Figure 7.3B); we have seen that a little boy has fears of engulfment by his mother and is threatened by fusion to her (which carries a loss of his gender). To overcome this he separates sexuality and autonomy from dependency, distancing himself from the object of his desire. When a mother is both overwhelmingly seductive and controlling, and the boy's father is weak and, therefore, does not provide a counterbalancing strong gender role model, the little boy may not be able to negotiate such a split. His sexual feelings will be overstimulated early by his mother's seductive nature, at a time of less developmental gender identity and less ego formation. As with the little girl, the early time frame also puts things in the time of oral concerns, when mother is symbolized by food.

The boy in such a state will not be able to overcome his sexual desires and strong early need for security to make a split that will distance him from mother. Since he has not gained enough autonomy nor moved close enough to his father for successful self-modeling, the boy continues to have a weakly formed ego and weak sense of gender. This is the reason that male anorexia develops only in the context of acute gender identity problems and why the prognosis for male anorexics in treatment is particularly grave (Sours, 1974).

The boy's only recourse to avoid engulfment can seem to him to be a denial of his need for his mother altogether. By denying food, the boy can simultaneously reject both his sexual attraction and his dependency urges toward his mother, and stave off the engulfment she threatens. This explains the fact that the boy feels the hunger and takes pride in resisting it, gaining ego strength in holding off mother, the engulfer. The girl, on the other hand, denies her hunger to herself to deny the fact that she has dependency feelings.

In turning his sexual urges from his mother the boy loses

the ability for further modeling his sense of gender and identity on his father; since he keeps his mother at a distance he cannot pattern after her fully either. The subsequent inability to take on a masculine role deprives him of support from his peer group and adults, and keeps him from enjoying the kind of acceptability the preanorexic mama's girl maintains for herself during latency. This explains the greater tendency for the male anorexic to become symptomatic even before adolescence (Falstein, Feinstein, and Judas, 1956; Sours, 1974).

The more severe ego crisis required for the development of a male anorexic pattern accounts for its relatively rarer occurrence.

In the foregoing analysis, we have seen how a number of the diverse symptoms of the bulimic–anorexic complex arise. Those have included the eating disorder, acute difficulty with intrapsychic separation–individuation, denial of the problem, amenorrhea (predating the eating disorders), collecting feminine clothing, and avoidance or denial of sexuality. The other symptoms arise because the bulimic or anorexic is functioning psychologically on a two-year-old level because her or his ego is at that state of development. The individual thus responds emotionally, and uses the defense mechanisms typical of the age. These symptoms, therefore, are general and would be expected to be found in any pathological state resulting from unresolved conflicts from the primary ego phase.

Table 7.2 repeats the lists of anorexic and bulimic symptoms, this time along with their primary ego cognates. We will explore just a few of them briefly here as all are fairly straightforward.

Passive repression is one of the defense mechanisms utilized by anorexics and bulimics. Davis and Marsh (1986) find that bulimics commonly display alexithymia, a lack of ability to "read" their own feelings. At the two-year-old level, object permanence and categorical thought are at their earliest stages of development. Therefore, that which is neither present nor labeled is not known to exist. By not labeling the disapproved of or conflicted, the child represses all thought of it.

Splitting is a second characteristic defense of patients with

TABLE 7.2
Comparison of Bulimic and Anorexic Syndromes with Primary Ego Level Behavior Patterns

Primary Ego Characteristics	Elements of the Bulimic Syndrome	Elements of the Anorexic Syndrome
Mother = food	Binge–purge compulsion	Rejection of food
Separation–individuation, a basic primary ego task	Acutely difficult intrapsychic separation–individuation	Acutely difficult intrapsychic separation–individuation
Denial–typical defense	Denial of need for help	Denial of problem
Confusion about gender	Amenorrhea predating bulimia	Amenorrhea predating anorexia
Self-modeling on mother focused on appearance	Collecting, but not wearing feminine apparel	Collecting, but not wearing feminine apparel
Repression—typical defense; repression of sexuality specifically observed when toddler opts to be "mama's good little girl"	Avoidance of sexuality; extremely dependent relationships	Denial of sexuality
Mapping out of bodily boundaries and sensations; newly developing systems of self-control	Bodily concerns: Uncertainty of identity image sensations control	Bodily concerns: Uncertainty of identity image sensations control
Ego just starting to integrate; assumed roles are experienced as real	An as-if personality, the dominant behavioral mode during the prodromal period	An as-if personality, the dominant behavioral mode during the prodromal period
Swings between helpless/all-powerful	Helplessness	Helplessness
First language: option of labeling or not labeling the conflicted or forbidden	Passive repression (defense)	Passive repression (defense)

TABLE 7.2 *continued*

Primary Ego Characteristics	Elements of the Bulimic Syndrome	Elements of the Anorexic Syndrome
Dichotomous thought patterns	Preoccupation with the good–bad dichotomy	Preoccupation with the good–bad dichotomy
Earliest time of categorical thinking and object permanence	Splitting as a defense	Splitting as a defense
Development of sphincter control	Anal preoccupation	Anal preoccupation
Sphincter competence concomitant with genital sensations and continued oral dependence	Oral–anal–genital admixture in fantasies	Oral–anal–genital admixture in fantasies
Violent oral–anal fantasy, all-or-none categorization	Suicidal ideation—re. control issues	Suicidal ideation— although unconnected with starvation
Control–ownership of thought an issue	Secrecy of thought	Secrecy of thought
Part-object, concrete symbolization	Kleptomania	Kleptomania
Locomotor maturation helps sense of self	Hyperactivity	Hyperactivity
Only "now"; space–time linked	Narrow perception of space–time	Narrow perception of space–time

eating disorders (Sours, 1974; Blum, 1978; Tabin, 1985). It is also typical of the toddler. The early capacity for categorical thought and passive repression which develop with the advent of language form the basis for splitting.

The bulimic's or anorexic's fantasies are characterized by an admixture of oral, anal, and genital elements. Moulton (1942), along with most others who describe the fantasies of bulimics and anorexics, makes the point that they confuse oral, anal, and genital material. In drawing attention to this phenomenon, Mintz (1983b) emphasizes fantasies about menstruation, control, and pregnancy that are wrapped into the material. As he points out, these are clearly relevant to the broader syndrome of the bulimic–anorexic. However, the general mixture of elements occurs because the time frame in these difficulties begins to develop when oral dependence is still in effect; this is the time when there is also a developing competence in sphincter control and awareness of genital sensations. The simultaneity of these developments along with their interrelated functioning in defining the sense of ego, leads to their concomitant representation in fantasy. Pure oral concerns predate this time frame. Focused anal concerns are only possible once initial issues of identity, including gender, have been dealt with sufficiently to give an ego platform from which to proceed developmentally. It is not until the classical oedipal period that a child establishes genital primacy.

Another characteristic of anorexics and bulimics is a preoccupation with secrecy of thought. A two-year-old's new linguistic abilities allow the child to maintain and hide thought. As this capacity first develops, the child is uncertain just how private the thoughts and feelings are. The two-year-old's lack of confidence in its privacy is fueled by the seeming omniscience of the adults who surround it. Moreover, the child is also just beginning to form a sense of self. Without an individual identity, there is a fusion with mother and hence no perceived capacity for secrecy.

Normally, concern over secrecy diminishes as one's sense of self becomes greater. And reciprocally, the ability to keep one's own thoughts, feelings, and actions to oneself is itself ego defining.

However, to the degree someone still operates on the primary ego level, especially at adolescence when sexual pressures suddenly intensify, she will be very concerned with secrecy of thought. Uncertain as to whether a bad (i.e., sexual) thought or feeling may also be known to others, especially mother or father, her feeling of danger in having unacceptable thought becomes more severe. This leads to a greater need for repression since the only solution is to make the feeling go away altogether. Since repression is never absolute, it also leads to a desperation for symbolically dealing with the feelings by bulimic-anorexic actions. The guilt and covert rituals that accompany binge–purge behavior thus come from the terrifying uncertainty of whether the actions and more importantly the feelings that compel them are in fact secret.

Kleptomania is another characteristic of these diseases (Thomä, 1967). As always when discussing kleptomania, the exact choice of stolen objects will be significant for their symbolic value as part objects. The essential thing here is that at the primary level of ego development (due to the degree of a two-year-old child's neurological maturation), part-objects and concrete symbols are interpreted as whole and real incarnations of the objects. The child still thinks in an all or nothing categorization. Thus, by association "part of" becomes "all of." Reality and fantasy boundaries are still vague and thus part-object usage substitutes for the reality. Stolen food is mother. Food in the gut is mother there inside. In the unconscious of a bulimic–anorexic, whose ego state reflects primary level ego formation, taking things is part of acting out her fantasies in direct terms.

Before moving on, we will tie one final characteristic of anorexic and bulimic syndromes to its origin in the primary ego phase. The knowledge of space and time are only possible with the advent of linguistic thought. As this is only beginning to develop during the second year of life, the toddler has a limited sense of space–time. This is reflected in the emotional response of individuals mired in issues from that age. Palazzoli (1974) and Székács (1985) mention and illustrate the toddlerlike way in which their bulimic patients operate as to time and space: limitation to perception of the immediate moment, emotional distance tied to physical distance.

We have now seen how, in addition to providing an explanation for the gender-related differences in the pathologies, the framework based upon the primary ego phase model provides a single, parsimonious explanation for the full range of bulimic–anorexic symptoms. However, parsimony is not an adequate rationale for accepting the correctness of this view. An alternative position that must be considered is that, as is often currently held in the field, some of the issues facing a bulimic –anorexic date to the toddler stage, such as separation–individuation problems, but others such as oedipal–sexual issues represent a regression to a different period of life—the classical oedipal stage, ages four through six. This view has been adopted because traditionally that is an age to which many sexual issues have been traced. However, that this is not the case for bulimics or anorexics is seen by the level on which sexual issues are handled. For example, the sexual aspects of the syndromes are expressed in fantasy. However, the form of the fantasy of a two-year-old differs from that of a five-year-old. In bulimic–anorexic fantasy, part-objects are utilized in a way typical of the two-year-old, but not expected by age five. Also, sexual fantasies and feelings are incorporated in a framework that is an equal admixture of anal and oral concerns, as opposed to the clearer genital primacy of the five-year-old. Good and bad labeling of sexual feelings are sharply maintained as strict dichotomies as opposed to the five-year-old's capacity to think in terms of gradations. We are not referring to separate symptoms here (such as splitting as a defense), but rather to the fact that the sexual issues themselves are dealt with on a primary ego phase level rather than on an oedipal phase level. The differences in the emotional complexes of the two periods are further compared in Table 7.3. Since sexual issues are handled by anorexics and bulimics in terms of the two-year-old's emotional and thought processes, it becomes inescapable that like the separation–individuation issues, they too are grounded at this earlier time.

Two other current views on the origins of eating disorders are worth briefly addressing before continuing. One set of explanations focus upon the food-intake related aspects. As we have discussed, this ignores the fact that starvation or binge–purge cycles are only a single, highly visible symptom that make up the syndrome. Thus, prior eating histories, cultural emphasis upon thinness, and so on, are incomplete explanations at best. The significance of early feeding histories of finicky eating and colic (Blum, 1978) has recently been thrown in doubt. Mitchell, Boutacoff, and Wilson (1986) studied the feeding histories of

TABLE 3
Contasting the First Two Organizational Stages of the Ego

	Two-Year Old	Five-Year Old
Thought Level	Primary process	Secondary process
Impulse Preocc.	Oral–anal–genital	Genital primacy
Attachments	Intense, uncommitted	Firm obj. constancy
Classif. Thought	Dichotomous	With gradations
Time Sense	Immediate moment	Future and past ego
Ego States	Fragmented, fast moods	Integrated
Gender Concept	Appearance	Role
Superego	Primitive, brutal	Able to compromise
Identifications	Imitative action *(Being* Daddy–Mommy)	Role concept *(Like* Daddy–Mommy)
Secret Thought	Repression	Confident lying
Ego Boundaries	Fluid	Fixed boundaries
Sense of Loss	Total, cataclysmic	Reparation possible
Sense of Place	Closeness = identif.	Closeness no threat
Choices	All or none	Accommodation poss.
Ego-def. & Power	Struggle	Cooperation
Gender Identity	In process of forming	Fixed
Guilt, Shame	Holistic, sweeping	Forgivable
Fantasy–Reality	Confused	Clear distinction
Auton.–Dependency	Fusion vs. abandonment	Closeness vs. discomfort
Resolution	With sense of personal identity	With sense of generationality

a group of bulimic patients by interviewing their parents and found that only 14 percent reported fussy or problematic eating in infancy or childhood of the patients. Thus, there is no consistent picture.

Societal pressures toward thinness and dieting are another matter. There is no question that the cultural milieu in which a girl finds herself strongly influences her psychological development. The young woman who has repressed her sexuality and limited her separation from her mother is confronted with an enormous psychological challenge at adolescence when internal and external pressure and expectations intensify. In a society where awareness of bodily form and sexuality are concurrently emphasized, the girl has less opportunity to build slowly on her primitive ego state. Moreover, the same two-year-old symbolic level that creates her later eating pattern from feelings about her mother makes it so that the cultural messages about thinness and sexuality which she receives will be symbolically interpreted by her in terms of her mother and oral dependency issues, in addition to the overt sexual issues. In this way, cultural emphasis is a very important constituent of the etiology of the disorder. However, what distinguishes the bulimic or the anorexic from the normal dieter is not the cultural setting, but the level of ego organization on which her actions are based. The bodily image distortions of the bulimic or anorexic are based on the primary ego processes which also form the basis for the rest of the syndrome. Thus, while bulimia often begins after a period of dieting (Mintz, 1983b), many girls diet. It is the inner promptings for it that differ in the preanorexic–bulimic, the same inner promptings which are subsequently responsible for the severe disorders.

The final class of explanation that we might consider is the view of bulimia as an affective disorder. That there exist physiological concomitants and even determinants on a certain level for depressed feelings is no more disputable than that there are such aspects to any other human behavior, including emotional expression. However, a causative relationship with genetically preset patterns is another matter. Hudson, Laffer, and Pope (1982), Hudson, Pope, Jonas, and Yurgelun-Todd (1983) felt that this was true. Stern, Dixon, Nemzer, Lake, Sansone, Meltzer, Lantz, and Schrier (1984) found no significant family patterns of affective disorders in their study of the situation, and Sabine, Yonace, Farrington, Barratt, and Wakeling (1983), who performed controlled placebo studies of treatment of bulimics with an antidepressant, also cast great doubt upon such a conclusion. Altschuler and Weiner (1985) echo this doubt after a scholarly review of the literature. Even if depression were a causative component of the story, that would not help us to understand the specific pathologies under consideration in this volume.

In contrast, we see how reevaluating the psychological tasks facing a two-year-old or primary ego phase child has allowed for a unified synthesis of the dynamics at that age. Applying that synthesis to the development of bulimia and anorexia (which are derived from issues dating to that time) has allowed fuller understanding of the pathologies, including an explanation for the full range of the symptoms making up the syndromes, and for their gender specificities. One would like to be able to apply these insights to provide more effective therapies. To do this one must first see the way in which the elements we have defined are displayed in actual cases.

We will start by reexamining cases already in the literature; for if the model presented here has validity, then it should be substantiated in reports gathered and written without a bias toward these concepts. The cases we select for review here we chose because the amount of clinical detail provided about them makes specific references possible. No cases in the literature that we could find of treatment of bulimia contradict the theory that we are examining.

There are two cases of anorexia–bulimia in young children reported in the literature in sufficient detail to permit us to see how the anorexic–bulimic syndrome reveals the operation of personality dynamics during the primary ego phase. One is a case of severe anorexia in a girl two years of age (Milner, 1944). The other is a case of severe anorexia and vomiting in a four-year-old girl (Sylvester, 1945), whose symptoms began when she was three and could easily be traced to her situation during the preceding period of her life.

CASE EXAMPLE 1

Rachel, the first case (Milner, 1944), we look at only briefly because she did not display bulimia. However, she still holds interest for us because as a two-and-a-half-year-old, she illustrates primary ego functioning in relation to the syndrome we recognize in both anorexics and bulimics. Her discovery during treatment that she could spit out what she did not want, is, in the context that she uses it, suggestive of a meaning of voluntary vomiting when bulimia does exist.

This case encourages us to concentrate upon the patient's inner dynamics. The little we learn of the family system hints at close involvement with Rachel on the part of both parents, as is typical between anorexic and/or bulimic girls and their parents. However, in keeping with Kramer's point (1974) that we pay attention to the intrapsychic factors in anorexia, Rachel was deeply involved in a particularly intense (and primary ego level) oedipal conflict, the dynamic in her illness. Milner underscores the fact in her discussion of the case.

Most preanorexics and prebulimics go successfully through childhood on the basis of an as-if personality (Deutsch, 1942; Winnicott, 1965), a compliant good eater (Blum, 1978; Bruch, 1979) who feels fused with mother. Rachel did display the symbiotic attachment to mother that is typical of bulimics and anorexics in which psychic fusion permits seemingly independent, energetic adultlike behavior.

For Rachel, this solution proved inadequate even during the primary ego phase. Rachel contracted the measles at eighteen months of age, upon which her parents abruptly moved her out of their bedroom. On the basis of material from her analysis, we may surmise that Rachel felt overwhelmed then by the combination of her physical misery and disruption off her fantasies of belonging with her parents during their intimacies (although they believed she was always asleep when they had intercourse).

Her anorexia started at this time and was severe enough by the time she was two years old that she became dehydrated. Leaving food around for her to eat at will soon failed because her sense of autonomy was too shaky; she survived by regressing to nonconflictual babyhood, eating only if on her mother's lap. Within a few months, she was brought to Milner for analysis.

A few of the primary ego level issues that are clear in Rachel's material, as indeed in that of older bulimics and anorexics, are

    1.   Ambivalence with an almost constant rhythm of shift-

ing from one psychological position to its opposite, and alternating in identifications;

2. Separation–individuation as a source of confusion played out in terms of whether her mother is to be with her or not and whether Rachel is herself or her mother;

3. Much anal material;

4. A constant power struggle, which is dramatic in the transference, Rachel constantly giving and withdrawing commands to her therapist;

5. Preoccupation with being bad or good;

6. Splits between being an as-if personality, a "good girl" whose behavior is all-conforming (but has an artificial quality that is clear to Milner), and a hidden "bad girl"; and also between being someone who is very intelligent and capable, in contrast to the tempestuous, helpless, infantile child within;

7. The oral apparatus being connected with oedipal concerns expressed in part-object concrete symbolization (as in oral impregnation fantasies and identification of her father with a voice, her mother with food).

When Rachel began treatment, she was in the throes of oedipal conflict as it is experienced on the level of the primary, primitive, and fragmented ego. We have postulated that oedipal and separation/individuation issues are at the root of anorexia and bulimia. In consonance with this idea we see that as Rachel began to be able to combine individuation with resolution of oedipal feelings, she no longer was subject to the primitive self-punishing symptoms of anorexia. An important step en route was her discovery that as part of allowing herself a separate identity from her (ingested dangerous, bad, sexy) mother, she had the power to eject her mother; not only by the processes of elimination, but through the consciously satisfying act of spitting her out.

We can see three ways in which Rachel's case illuminates the origins and meanings of bulimia. Granted that at her stage of development bodily processes are still confusing for a child and that mentation is still greatly based upon concrete symbolization and part-object identifications, we see first how

Rachel's perceptions equate eating–biting–disappearance. Second, we see how the mystery of what feces and urine are led to the fantasy that what one eats becomes dangerous when it gets inside. Milner learned from Rachel that this sense of the food–mother's danger to Rachel stemmed from the child's anger and jealousy because her mother would not let Rachel have her father; thus Rachel wanted to attack her mother. With separation–individuation not yet fixed, Rachel felt that her mother must know Rachel's feelings and thus be ready to retaliate. Third, we see how at Rachel's stage of thought development, the possibility seemed real to Rachel of protecting herself from the danger of food–body–mother, the "nasty lady" inside her who made her do bad things, by Rachel's utilizing her capacity to push contents out of her mouth, by spitting.

Spitting is not so self-punishing as is vomiting, but in Rachel's case the dynamics of it may offer clues to understanding bulimia as well. We notice that it was after Rachel had progressed toward self-differentiation that she thought of "Spit it out if you don't like it!" (Milner, 1944, p. 57) as a way of protecting herself against the food–body–mother.

In her spitting–oral rejection symptom, which developed as she achieved some sense of safety in separation–individuation, Rachel shows dynamics that differentiate bulimics from people in other phases of eating disorder. She could react after taking food into her mouth as if she had the power to differentiate herself from her mother instead of succumbing to fusion. Taking in food thus did not mean inevitable and total loss of self. This dynamic in Rachel, a clinical example of the theoretical suppositions above, perhaps explains why bulimics may appear to be more psychologically advanced than anorexics. Their greater degree of self-differentiation also permits them to feel that they can try to manage complete secrecy about their symptomatic behavior. Bulimia without anorexia is likely to appear among somewhat older individuals (Muuss, 1986), and they are more likely than restrictive anorexics to be able to talk about wishing for a good relationship with a man and even for sex, although they do not actually permit themselves these things (Boskind-White and White, 1983).

Bruch (1973) mentioned that the addition of bulimia to the anorexic picture is an expected development, establishing that one is dealing with "true anorexia." In accordance with the observation of bulimia (Swift, 1985; Muuss, 1986; Striegel-Moore, Silberstein, and Rodin, 1986), we may speculate that bulimia appears in cases when the anorexic feels she has accomplished a greater degree of self-differentiation through her anorexic behavior, although it cannot suffice (any more than it does for nonanorexic bulimics) to enable her to feel that she can permit herself age-appropriate autonomy, self-acceptance including her femininity, and happy living. The amount of self-differentiation displayed in bulimia is still limited to the primary ego level of ego development.

In the case that Sylvester (1945) treated, which we turn to next, vomiting was a prominent symptom. This provides an interesting comparison. Both children had enormous problems of separation–individuation, and both of them showed occasional ability to accept food as food rather than as extensions of mother, if they were being taken care of by someone other than the mother. However, Sylvester's bulimic and anorexic case in comparison to Rachel indicated greater clarity about her separateness from her mother–therapist.

Oral impregnation fantasies proved to be another important basis for her symptomatic behavior. She, like Lindner's case of Laura (1976), was influenced by witnessing her mother's morning sickness.

It is worthwhile to review Sylvester's case in a bit of detail also because it exemplifies this contrast: trying to handle the interrelationship of separation–individuation and sexual issues on the primary level of ego organization compared with trying to handle it during the classical oedipal phase.

These remarks anticipate the fortunate outcome of Sylvester's treatment. Although the child was four years old when treatment began, her intrapsychic condition, as well as the forms of her most dramatic symptoms (vomiting and anorexia), reflected the state of mind of the toddler age child:

She was confused about gender; preoccupied with good and bad, conceptualizing them in terms of extremes only; thought in terms of part-objects with concrete symbolization; oral, anal, and genital ideation were all intermixed.

Through her analysis, she came to possess definite gender identity; enjoy being herself without guilt and show her preferences for certain boys and men; could let her beloved good-mother-analyst know about her masturbation fantasies; and began to work on generational issues (allowing herself to learn from the good-mother-analyst about things that could eventually mean being an effective adult); and was no longer preoccupied with good versus bad—she no longer displayed anorexia or bulimia. These developmental changes came about in less than a year and proved to be stable. The child held her own, still thriving, according to a follow-up three years later, even though the rest of her family were locked into neurotic patterns.

When the child first came to Sylvester's attention, however, she was a four-year-old who had been so emaciated six months earlier from anorexia and bulimia that she weighed only 23 pounds and had to be hospitalized for tubal feeding. Many possible physical causes for her condition were investigated, but finally she was referred for inpatient psychoanalytic treatment, in the absence of any organic pathology.

Her recorded feeding history began at four months when her mother abruptly weaned her because of a new pregnancy. At that point, the child adapted by becoming a persistent thumb-sucker. Her mother was upset by this, but pleased that the little girl started to talk at seven months and was satisfactorily toilet trained by nine months. Her father at around this time was sent to jail for two years for having passed bad checks. The next significant event was at thirteen months, when upon her mother's return from giving birth to a little boy, the patient came down with a mild case of measles. She was slow to recover, and being difficult to feed, lost a great deal of weight, stopped walking, resumed soiling, and displayed temper tantrums. When she reached two years of age, however, she suddenly became oversolicitous of her younger brother, sharing her food with him, and generally gratifying her mother with her intelligence and helpfulness.

We might pause here to note that the child's reaction to her first large frustration was an adaptive one—thumb sucking—that was age appropriate and sufficient to allow for continued development. During her crisis at thirteen months, the tension between dependency wishes and her need to continue to individuate showed up in highly ambivalent and difficult behavior. This included angry behavior when her mother fed the baby, but also a lack of willingness to allow her mother to feed her. (Note: Gilbert, a brother older than the patient by three years and at the height of his classical oedipal period at this time in her life, was the family's oldest male in their father's absence. He may have played a significant role in the little girl's behavioral–eating crisis. If the behavioral–eating crisis had been due merely to sibling rivalry because of her mother's feeding the new baby, it is hard to understand why she would not have welcomed the times that her mother tried to feed her. The possibility of Gilbert affecting her development is suggested by the associations to him when the little patient played out her fellatio fantasies, as will be seen in the case material below.)

By two years of age, she settled into an as-if, adultlike continuation of her mother's personality (reminiscent of Rachel's adjustment at the same age, on the same basis). This state of affairs, comfortable for the mother, was disrupted when the father returned home. The child had been her mother's bed partner and refused to give up her place. Nonetheless, the mother became pregnant again. She developed toxemia with severe vomiting. The child's response was to develop pica, an apparent effort to share the impregnation with her mother, in keeping with an oral–anal interpretation of the process. When her mother was severe with her for this, vomiting ensued with great enough frequency and effect, coupled with anorexia, that the aforementioned hospitalization was required.

In the manner of many accounts of children in the earlier psychoanalytic literature, the father's role is hardly mentioned. However, in this child's first session with Sylvester, one of her few verbal communications was to ask to be called by the name of her older sister, supposedly the father's special favorite. It is interesting in this connection that the patient, according to the mother, was the child in the family who most resembled herself.

Subsequent material from the treatment gives insight into the intrapsychic meaning of the vomiting. In the first session, the father doll fed clay dolls to the whole family. The mother doll and the doll representing the patient both vomited. This play was repeated many times throughout the whole session, at the end of which she made her request as to her name. Daily repetition of these routines, now including genuine cuddling and feeding of candy by Sylvester, enabled the child to spare herself more vomiting for a week. Then her mother came to visit and announced the birth of a new sister. The child suffered severe vomiting attacks and in the next sessions tried to swallow plasticine and demand that Sylvester turn plasticine in little boxes into "babies," which the child then crushed and "fed" to the dolls.

During this period, play concerned sexless babies and mothers. The child did not vomit.

In the next phase, the play revealed awareness but confusion about sex differences. With great excitement she adorned girl dolls with penises on their upper bodies. The question of penis envy arises here, but it is difficult to be sure that the child's excitement was not on a libidinal basis. Again she vomited frequently. Sylvester points out that the oral-aggressive quality to the child's fantasies became clearer through the invention of a self object, Whoof. This little dog was at first lovable, but then devoured the whole family. He did not go without punishment: he became sick and vomited. Self-punishment for and denial of her destructive wishes were expressed through vomiting. The child was able to eat well without vomiting; Whoof, however, bit and had to vomit afterward.

She was next able to play out her fellatio fantasies through use of a boy doll with a golf club whom she named after her older brother, Gilbert. She broke his golf club and fed it to a girl–self doll on whose behalf she also exclaimed, "She gets all the candy from all the Gilberts."

Sylvester does not mention the vomiting during the account of this material, but she makes the point that the next phase was a regression to "sexless" babydom, during which, in contrast, there was no vomiting (Sylvester, 1945; Tabin, 1985). With the issue of sex eliminated, the hostile meaning in eating is eliminated and punishment is not called for. We might add that the separation–individuation issue is also not joined when the matter of gender is eliminated (so tied to the concept of self is the concept of gender).

There was only one more spate of vomiting on this little girl's part, while Sylvester was on vacation. During the analyst's two-week absence, the child sucked her fingers and became withdrawn and unapproachable on the ward. When Sylvester returned, she made rapid advance. She returned to exploration of her feelings about gender, but without the need to vomit. Eventually her progress permitted her to explore the masturbatory fantasies which she enjoyed while in her parents' bed until she was stricken for the activity, but even immersion in this material did not require reversion to the self-punishment of vomiting in order to protect her sense of self–autonomy –sexuality.

In the final portion of the analysis, Sylvester tells us that the child showed markedly increased ego integration; definite fantasies about her special choices of men on the hospital staff; a desire to identify with and learn from her mother–analyst; moderation of her superego which now permitted compromises and methods of reparation; and, above all, forgiveness, a sense of humor, insight, and creativity in her mental processes. In other words, she was treating the issues of identity, gender, and sexuality on a constructive basis in terms of the capacities of a five-year-old child.

Sylvester's case clearly illustrates how during the classical oedipal phase, the girl has fantasies about her relationships with father–adult males, but what she must deal with then is an acute competitiveness with her mother, not the very struggle for existence against her. In the happy outcome for Sylvester's case, she settled into concentrating on learning from her "good ice cream lady" (identification by role rather than by part-object) how to become an effective adult woman herself in the future.

A considerable difficulty in the diagnosis of such cases is that, in keeping with the relatively fragmented state of the ego during the two-year-old's stage of primary ego organization, "the child of the person" quickly switches from ego state to ego state (from fragment to fragment). This process is most persuasively seen in an older person who exhibits multiple personalities, still on a quick-switch basis. [Note: Study of multiple personalities (Ludwig, Brandson, Wilbur, Benfield, and Jameson, 1972) and hypnotic subjects (Hilgard, 1977), provides a model which helps us to comprehend how such a fragmented ego functions long after the natural quick switches of toddlerhood. We learn that there is always a core self that is aware of the rest of the ego, even when the other ego- or self-fragments are not aware of each other; but the core ego is not yet empowered to take over the executive functions of the total personality. This core self may be seen as the self that emerges triumphantly when freed up through successful therapy, although it may glint through at special times otherwise and shows up increasingly often as therapy progresses, until sufficient integration has taken place within the ego so that the core self can operate as being in charge most of the time.] Therefore, someone whose as-if adult personality operates very efficiently may display a primary ego level of behavior only when, pressed by unconscious conflicts, she "switches" into her symptomatic behavior, at which time the primary ego level of her symptoms can be identified.

A typical scenario for bulimia occurred in another case, whom one of us (JKT) saw in treatment, Ms. Y. Her material is illustrative of the regressive picture that bulimia presents.

CASE EXAMPLE 2

Ms. Y.'s binging, as with many bulimics, was on ice cream (Boskind-White and White, 1983). The meaning of this for her became plain in a dream with rampant penises on a school bus that took her to a "Dairy Queen" ice cream parlor, where she gorged herself in a fit of loyalty. *Dairy Queen* was thenceforth our euphemism for her mother: sweet and compelling, yet perceived as cold.

It is not difficult to understand that the ejection of what Ms. Y. consumed was likewise a statement about her mother. The point is that her sexual references were equally primitive: Sexual feelings were isolated, purely physical, and devoid of fantasy. Oral–anal–genital material swirled together. In relation to her symptoms, she displayed all of the mental operations that belong to the primary ego level of development: lack of whole-object relating; splitting, repression, and denial as chief defenses; concrete symbols as part-objects functioning as wholes; tenuous gender identity; tenuous boundaries of self and between reality and fantasy (the patient could not bear to look at either sexual or aggressive scenes in movies, angry feelings seemed totally destructive, and swear words could not be uttered; suicidal ideation started to diminish only as she got to the point of sending her mother knives for a birthday and could giggle about it); dichotomous thinking; time sense limited to the immediate moment (when depressed, she could not remember ever really feeling good—feeling bad was the worst she had ever felt and it was how she would always feel). The fragmentation of her ego, as with so many bulimics, revealed itself in the success she managed on an as-if basis where she could be active as a neuter. At the same time, she "knew" that she was garbage (not *like* garbage, *garbage*). If she had good feelings, she immediately suffered for them as they triggered her guilt about feeling sexual. We could trace this pattern only after several years of analysis, when Ms. Y. was able to let me know that she actually had sexual feelings.

The patient was the older of two children, the second child being a boy. Her father drank heavily during her early years and the parents fought over this constantly. However, her father was very warm and demonstrative, especially when drunk. Ms. Y.'s crib was in her parents' bedroom until she was two years old. We can infer the impulsivity she encountered in the adults around her from the very beginning.

From Ms. Y.'s memories of father's behavior with her when she was a teenager and the relief gained during analysis from reconstructions of seductive treatment of her when she was under two, it seems reasonable to believe that Ms. Y.'s early fantasies (arising from her sexual feelings) were confusing as well as guilt producing. The confusion came from the degree to which her father's excitement with her existed in fact and the problem of whom he belonged to. The guilt stemmed from her strong bond with mother. She was said to cry if her mother but frowned. Ms. Y.'s own thoughts were so dangerous to her that later, in school, she could not permit herself creative expression, but only to learn exactly what was prescribed and labeled good to know. No feeding difficulties were in her history. In fact, she was well rounded in all her early pictures.

When the patient was fifteen, she was invited for the first time to go out on a date. The boy, a senior in the high school she attended, asked her to go to the prom with him. She remembers her father's opposition on the grounds that her date was a "loser," and her mother's insistence that she was too fat. Her father's real reasons were exemplified when she attempted to date again when she was twenty-eight years old and he still opposed her doing so. However, a picture of Ms. Y. and her date on prom night shows that he was a very pleasant looking young man of her father's type and she did not appear to be overweight. (JKT has observed in another instance of eating disorder, where the mother treated her daughter as if she were fat when the child was well within normal limits, that this effectively told the girl how the mother expected the girl to remain unattractive to men, while overtly the mother was acting as if she wanted the child to diet in order to become attractive.) Ms. Y. recalled her first bulimic experience as beginning with the dinner during which she received the invitation to the prom. A particularly severe period of bulimia began the next year when Ms. Y. was on a bus with her classmates, returning from a two-day visit to the state capital. The physical temptations of that trip threw her into a panic.

As might be expected, the patient's relationship with her mother permitted her very little independence of thought—she constantly checked within herself for what mother would be thinking about anything that occurred to her. The first four years of analytic treatment transpired without the patient being able to sustain a single critical thought about mother. However, the bulimia subsided when she moved geographically away from her mother.

During this time she was unable to allow herself a relationship with a man. When she was willing to let me know that she even noticed men, both her dreams and her perceptions were focused on the crotch. However, she could not speak of sexual thoughts and denied that she ever had one. In her vigorous use of splitting, she could now admit to sexual feelings. This is consonant with the toddler's opportunity to repress dangerous thought in order not to contain in the mind anything which might bring on retaliation by the omniscient mother. Emotional feelings are repressed simply by not labeling them. Feelings in the body not connected to thought or emotion may escape the censor. Perhaps this mechanism helps us to understand why, especially in egos which remain highly fragmented after the usual primary ego phase, expression of the forbidden is accomplished with body codes; for example, psychosomatic symptoms.

At first Ms. Y. did not say more than that she had feelings, almost whispering, "They're so strong." When she allowed herself to describe them to me, it turned out that they involved her vagina. There was no mistaking her conflict over these sensations. She wept silently after mentioning them. For Ms. Y., sexual feelings were invariably followed by severe bouts of depression, until she had suffered enough to permit more sexual feelings, a constant cycle.

Eventually, Ms. Y.'s symptoms included acute colitis. This condition, the anal version of her bulimia, gradually responded to interpretation of her intense need to rid herself of the bad–mother–food inside of her. Disposing of food–body–mother by chewing her up and swallowing her was inadequate because of the problem of fusion this compulsion brought with it (which makes for feelings of humiliation in the binging). Once inside, the rivalrous and retaliative mother posed a danger which only vomiting or purging could save her from.

Colitic attacks during our sessions enabled the patient to pinpoint through the transference how desperately she needed to eliminate mother–me whenever either competitive thoughts about me or sexual feelings occurred to her. The first time she experienced intense cramping and the impulse to eliminate while we were together, Ms. Y. was in the process of telling me about her expertise with a computer. She surmised that I did not have her level of technical comprehension. Daring to feel superior to me required swift measures to ensure her safety. I responded with some appreciation for her audacity in ridding herself of excremental–dangerous–mother–me. Her urgency passed.

The separation–individuation achievement had its sexual side. Although it was a solitary activity, she found working at her computer to be exciting, bringing her into the world of men. This aspect of outwitting mother–me, including gender and sexual issues, added to her anxiety. It soon became apparent that colitis accompanied her sexual feelings, too. Again, the attacks ceased in acknowledging the necessity to save herself by expelling dangerous–mother–me.

As with Rachel and Sylvester's case, Ms. Y. demonstrates the contrast in symptomatology that develops in a bulimic patient as the level of ego integration increasingly reflects the achievement of a classical oedipal phase. Ms. Y. showed this development at the point when she ceased sensing her mother constantly in her thoughts. She began to have faith in her ability to discern the difference between fantasy and reality. She could tolerate aggression and sexuality on the television screen and even to be conscious of fantasies of her own. Her time sense expanded. When she felt depressed, she could tell herself that she was feeling good shortly before and that she would be feeling better again. Oral and anal concerns no longer preoccupied her. She began to talk of wanting to marry and have children and to feel that she could be a good mother. Relating to people as whole-objects, she could perceive good and bad in both sexes, and in herself as well. She began to enjoy her femininity. The slightest sign of her imperfection no longer seemed to betray badness–sexiness, no longer brought forth a death sentence. In the transference, I became a human being rather than someone with transcendental powers (for good or evil). While she was still highly competitive with me, and with other women, it was no longer a matter of lethal, only-one-to-survive intensity. In this emotional climate, while she still struggled over her right to succeed in the larger world and to form solid egalitarian relationships, symptoms such as bulimia and colitis faded out of her emotional vocabulary.

Case Example 3

Before turning again to the literature for examples, we offer one more unpublished case to show the manner in which bulimia can serve to express the primary ego level of someone's adolescent or adult experience. For Ms. Y. ice cream–mother was the exact identification of the food she used in her bulimic pattern. Such precision of food choice facilitated a fellatio fantasy in a twenty-two-year-old, Ms. B. She blushed dramatically when I (JKT) asked her what food she had binged on. It turned out to be bananas. Ms. B. reacted so strongly to my question because she took it for granted that "all-knowing mother–therapist" understood. Her reaction was as intense as if she had told me right out that she swallowed a penis (see Masserman, 1941, whose case of a woman vomiter avoided bananas on the same basis). At the primary ego level, when mother seems omniscient, part-object/whole-object/concrete-symbol are all the same.

The vomiting phase for Ms. B. was overdetermined. It relieved her in her conflict of loyalties because she could be both sexes at once as she enacted the primal scene. She also was preserving her father-fingers while ridding herself of dangerous–food–body–mother. For this orgastic pleasure, she suffered the misery of retching.

Ms. B.'s history was characteristic: Her observable as-if personality was her mother's adorable little doll whom her father could be close to only surreptitiously, while she felt inwardly that she was very bad (because of her sexual impulses that engendered rivalrous feelings toward her "noble" mother).

The swallowing of the banana–penis–father is not only a fellatio equivalent. The attachment of danger to sexuality because of mother's wrath can be compounded by the child's excited but fearful reaction to father's strength, with ambivalence born of confused loyalties. The question of penis envy in bulimic fantasies is a complicated one because penis envy is in itself a defensive maneuver (Horney, 1924; Tabin, 1985). For this reason, we will take note of penis envy for theoretical purposes here only to point out that real penises are not likely to be on the binger's menu. The use of a banana with such conviction identifies the mental operations involved in the symptom as being on the primary ego level of the patient's personality (e.g., banana = real penis = whole father). Automatically, concomitant emotional aspects involve her relationships to both her parents and her sense of her own body, intertwining her feelings about food–body–mother; father–nonmother (outside world)–excitement; intense, focused bodily pleasure (sexual feelings); and the good–bad dichotomy.

Greenacre (1948) gives significant reasons for recognizing the existence from the preverbal years of guilt-laden, isolated vaginal excitement (as in Ms. Y.'s case), which she discovered in patients of hers whose egos were particularly fragmented and regressed. This helps us to appreciate why primal scene fantasies may be played out by bulimics in the vomiting phase of their cycles (with their fingers as penis equivalents). Primal scene observation by a toddler girl could easily stimulate fusion of vaginal excitement with oral fantasy.

Many surveys of bulimic symptomatology refer to the connection between sexuality and bulimia. Indeed it is mentioned in nearly all published cases of treatment. Crisp (1977) and Schwartz (1986) make this connection central to their therapeutic approaches. However, most case reports in the literature are very brief and focus on the oral aspects of the material.

Masserman (1941), Leonard (1944), and Sperling (1968) wrote classic papers on treatment of young women with eating disorders and vomiting, describing the formative conflicts among female cases. We do not quote from them because the accounts do not detail the fantasies expressed by the vomiting. However, they are still useful in understanding the dynamics of such cases generally. In all three, the girls had been selected as a self object by their mothers. [This interesting, frequent aspect of the family dynamics was pointed out by Joanne Powers (1981) in personal communication.] The seductiveness of the fathers in two of the cases extended to lying with the patients even when they were adults, of fondling them, and masturbating in front of them. The bulimic–anorexic symptoms were precipitated in each when the girls were confronted with the possibility of becoming sexual. The form of the symptoms, the symptomatic syndrome, and specifically the oral–genital nature of their fantasies can be understood as manifestations of poorly resolved conflicts from the period of the primary organization of the ego.

Blum (1978) goes into considerable detail in describing a woman in her early thirties who became bulimic and depressed several years earlier. Blum includes the rest of the syndrome—her massive use of denial, splitting as a defense, intense struggles with dependency and autonomy, symbolic behavior, separation–individuation confused with matters of life and death, intense concern about good and bad, high level of activity, and, of course, oral and anal preoccupations. Oral impregnation fantasies were an important component of the symptomatology.

This patient began to exhibit severe bulimia during her first pregnancy, but only upon a separation from her husband during the last trimester. A fascinating sidelight about this timing is that the patient had a normal first trimester. She vomited then, too, only in conjunction with binging and it seems not very often. Apparently, she was able to manage whatever unconscious pressures which were difficult for her without disturbance of the physiology of her pregnancy until the threatened loss of her husband.

The account does not explain whether the separation from her husband was due to difficulties between her and her husband, or for how long it continued; but it fits the description

of her relationship with her mother to imagine that on a primary ego level, it was as if her omnipotent mother punished
her (by removal of the husband) for her hubris in creating a
child with her man. In any case, the vomiting that was stimulated by her husband's absence proved to be partly determined
by her memory of her mother's suffering during her mother's
pregnancy with the patient's younger brother (when the patient
was a toddler).

Blum tells of "symptoms, transference and dreams that
indicated the doing and undoing of her incestuous impregnation and masturbation" (p. 343). He also refers to "a deeper
level" of involvement with unresolved symbiotic wishes and cannibalistic fantasies, especially about mother–child relationships.
We can better understand the patient's predicament if we recognize that for her these are not separate issues. The bulimic
syndrome tells us that her impregnation fantasies are for-
warded from the same level of ego development as her sense
of her relationship with her mother: the stakes are at the level
of life or death, survival for only one. Mother is food, father
is excitement. In an oft-repeated fantasy, she saved herself from
dangerous conflict by dreaming of an orgasm which she controlled by a pulley at her vagina that pushed in or pulled out
a loaf of bread: sexual excitement with a mother–penis that
she, the patient, controlled. By the same token [as is typical
when bulimic patients are married), see Boskind-White and
White (1983)], she described her relationship with her husband
in terms of his maternal qualities. In this she reminds us, as did
Rachel and Sylvester's case, that symbiotic compulsions and cannibalistic fantasies can be ways of handling the anxieties from
primitive incestuous impregnation and masturbatory fantasies.

Another interesting piece of behavior was this patient's
need to binge before she could feed her own children. That
this was not simply a need to be fed first out of infantile greed
we know because she also had to vomit out the dangerous
mother, and the compelled gobbling up of food is, for the
bulimic, without taste or pleasure. The behavior is better understood as dramatically proving her loyalty to mother through
her own infantilism. Her rage at this humiliation can give her

no peace because the massacred mother–food remains inside her to take revenge. These "inner realities" make the split good–bad mother an ineffective creation in settling anxiety.

In Blum's case, as is commonly reported among bulimic women (Boskind-White and White, 1983), the good split mother transference was applied to her husband, terming him a mother figure. In this case, it may have been a "cover story." We learn that her memories of father before the age of two reveal him as warm, devoted, outgoing, and seductive in his play with her. She contrasts this somewhat with his treatment of her after her younger brother was born when she was two years old. The picture remains of him as being "an alternative source of supportive nurturance" (p. 355). The picture is most informatively confirmed when we learn that she enjoyed her husband's seductive play with their children (p. 345).

Competitiveness with her own mother is exemplified in her need to be a "supermom," validated by the achievements of her own children. Her mother's requirement that she be seen as a supermother by the patient is well documented in the material.

One of her split images of her mother was a " 'pure' mother/prostitute mother" (Blum, 1978, p. 344) constellation. The use of the split image to equate sexy with bad is an interesting use of primary ego level mentation in relation to the origins of bulimia, again reminiscent of the case of Rachel.

Blum discusses in depth the basis of his patient's illness in the complexities of the first two years of life, except for tracing to that stage the connection between orality and her relationships with her parents. When we trace the logic of her behavior to the way in which the separation–individuation issues intertwine with sexuality and loyalty issues, the whole of her condition becomes still easier to understand. At one point in her treatment, she produced many disguised dreams in which "she was pregnant with the food she gorged, having all the ice-cream cones, father's penis and baby, but also mother's breasts and love for herself" (p. 349). Here, indeed, the primary ego child's magical solution!

In describing this patient's transference neurosis, Blum distinguishes her case from that of a borderline personality.

However, we know that the bulimic syndrome can appear within the context of any diagnostic category (Sours, 1974). Bulimia can emanate from a fragment of the ego which still operates on the earliest level of ego organization, loose enough to permit ongoing structures that are relatively isolated from the rest of the personality. Thus, it is that bulimics in particular are some-times able to switch to primary level ego states in private while operating successfully without the knowledge of those around them, as if they were well-integrated adults.

Ego-fragmentation and other characteristics of the primary ego phase are discernible in male as well as in female bulimics. From his experience in treating anorexic and bulimic males, Sours (1980) notes that psychodynamic considerations primar-ily revolve around intense conflict over sexual feelings toward the perceived seductive mother. These features are apparent in a case that goes into the meanings of the vomiting.

Mintz (1983a) reports a case of male bulimarexia including material as to the role of the vomiting. Mintz tells of Henry, an adolescent. As he entered high school, Henry's mother noted that the boy became clingy with her. However, neither she nor his father observed Henry's vomiting after meals. Henry main-tained his secret practice all through high school. In keeping with general clinical observations of the male patient and the-oretical expectations from a boy's primary ego situation, Henry demonstrated his control. He modified his vomiting schedule to fit in with his running and bicycling schedules so that he would not be weak for those activities.

The parents were both overweight, as was Henry when he was younger, but Mintz did not find them to be as obviously controlling as families of bulimics and anorexics usually are. Nonetheless, the prospect of leaving home to go to college frightened Henry into revealing his bulimic pattern to his par-ents, who then brought him for treatment.

The self preservative aspect of vomiting was shown by Henry's reaction to the decision that he enter analysis. For the first time, Henry awakened at night to vomit spontaneously, twice, rather than needing to induce vomiting by inserting his finger down his throat. Mintz interpreted the behavior as unconscious assertiveness. This meaning in the vomiting was further confirmed later when Henry controlled the impulse to vomit, but felt impelled to exercise much more. From the perspective of primary ego theory, compulsive exercise is the locomotor expression of individuation, reminiscent of a major way in which body ego is established to begin with. Henry encompassed the rest of the bulimic syndrome in his need for secrecy, compulsive cleanliness, use of denial, and so on.

In Henry's material, food became the sum total of his relationships and he focused his energies entirely on controlling food–body–mother. He savored a routine of cutting up his food into very small bits before binging. The hostile element in his fantasies emerged through his desire to do away with his younger brother, leading to revelation of oral impregnation fantasies coupled with destruction of his own baby self. The archaic confusion of sexuality with oral fantasies of creation and destruction was clear.

Therapeutically, a turning point proved to be Henry's letting Mintz know that his eating pattern and monitoring of his body-shape had to do with expressing his confused gender identity. There was much material along these lines. At length, Mintz responded by informing Henry that he could eat for strength rather than feminization. This intervention by his strong–father–analyst combined with Henry's learning that he could express hostility without anyone being destroyed. The boy was able to utilize this encouragement by his good–father–analyst to develop a masculine identification. He began to eat normally.

Although the account gives only the earlier part of a three-year analysis, more in an effort to show that such cases are treatable than to explore the nature of bulimia in a deep way, the essential differences in the male and the female patterns are discernible.

Gender confusion was so significant in Henry's case that when he was able to use Mintz's help to know that he could eat without becoming a girl, he began to eat normally. It is obviously a different proposition, involving different conflicts, for a girl not to eat in order to avoid revealing that she is a girl.

In exemplifying the second major difference from the pattern in the female, Henry felt comfortable about his successful secret program of overeating and vomiting until he faced leaving home. He felt that he controlled every aspect of his eating even though he binged. He enjoyed his preoccupation with food. His libidinal use of food was followed by vomiting in order to prevent fusion, as an assertion of his individuality; however, he did not experience the humiliation that female bulimics so often report over their compulsions. It was his fear of not being able to continue this program that led him to tell his parents at last of his difficulties and then to allow himself to enter treatment (albeit with much reliance on denial) to experience the intense anxieties that were previously bound in his symptoms and gradually to free himself from them. We know from Mintz's introductory statement quoting Sours without contradiction (p. 265) that Henry's primitive struggles to maintain his individuality in the face of his mother's seductiveness caused this boy to develop the bulimic–anorexic syndrome when he reached adolescence.

It is not surprising that bulimia and anorexia are so difficult to treat when we appreciate that they reflect the rawest form of major human conflicts. The prognosis for a particular individual is more hopeful, depending upon how much ego development was possible for the person nonetheless.

The preceding cases demonstrate how the various emotional threads identifiable in bulimic and anorexic patients can be traced back to the two-year-old stage where the threads are interwoven into a single tapestry of ego definition. While any single thread can be traced back in therapy, a recognition of the full pattern allows more rapid insights as connections can be made between psychological phenomena which otherwise seem unrelated. The model presented here has explanative utility in understanding the range of symptoms and the gender specificities of eating disorders, but its true value lies in its allowing the designing of more effective therapies.

References

Abraham, K. (1934), A short study of the development of the libido, viewed in the light of mental disorders. In: *Selected Papers of Karl Abraham*, ed.

E. Jones. International Psycho-Analysis Library, no. 13. London: Hogarth Press, 1942, pp. 418–516.

Altshuler, K., and Weiner, M. (1985). Anorexia nervosa and depression: a dissenting view. *Amer. J. Psychiat.*, 142(3), 328–331.

Blum, H. P. (1978), Reconstruction in a case of post partum depression. The *Psychoanalytic Study of the Child*, 3:335–362. New York: International Universities Press.

Boskind-White, M., & White, W. C., Jr. (1983), *Bulimarexia*. New York: W. W. Norton.

Bower, G. H. (1981), Mood and memory. *Amer. Psychol.*, 36 2:129–148.

Bruch, H. (1973), *Eating Disorders: Obesity, Anorexia Nervosa, and the Person Within*. New York: Basic Books.

—— (1979), *The Golden Cage*. New York: Random House.

Crisp, A. H. (1977), The differential diagnosis of anorexia nervosa. *Proc. Roy. Soc. Med.*, 70:464–470.

Davis, M. S., & Marsh, L. (1986), Self love, self-control, and alexithymia: Narcissistic features of two bulimic adolescents. *Amer. J. Psychother.*, 40/2:224–232.

Deutsch, H. (1942), Some forms of emotional disturbances and their relationship to schizophrenia. *Psychoanal. Quart.*, 2:301–321.

Falstein, E. I., Feinstein, S. C., & Judas, I. (1956), Anorexia nervosa in the male child. *Amer. J. Orthopsychiat.*, 26:751–772.

Freud, S. (1905), Three essays on the theory of sexuality. *Standard Edition*, 5:135–243. London: Hogarth Press, 1953.

Galenson, E., Miller, R., & Roiphe, H. (1976), The choice of symbols. *J. Amer. Acad. Child Psychiat.*, 15 1:83–96.

Garner, D. M., & Garfinkel, P. E. (1979), The eating attitudes test: An index of the symptoms of anorexia. *Psychol. Med.*, 9:273–279.

—— —— O'Shaughnessy, M. (1985), The validity of the distinction between bulimia with and without anorexia nervosa. *Amer. J. Psychiat.*, 142 5:581–586.

Greenacre, P. (1948), Anatomical structure and superego development. In: *Trauma, Growth, and Personality*. New York: International Universities Press, 1952, pp. 149–164.

—— (1950), Special problems of early female sexual development. *The Psychoanalytic Study of the Child*, 5:122–138. New York: International Universities Press.

Hilgard, E. A. (1977), *Divided Consciousness*. New York: John Wiley.

Horney, K. (1924), On the genesis of the castration complex. *Internat. J. Psychoanal.*, 5:50–65.

Hudson, J., Laffer, P., & Pope, H. (1982), Bulimia related to affective disorder by family history and response to the dexamethasone suppression test. *Amer. J. Psychiat.*, 139:685–687.

—— Pope, H., Jonas, J., & Yurgelun-Todd, D. (1983), Phenomenologic relationships of eating disorders to major affective disorder. *Psychiat. Res.*, 9 4:345–354.

Kleeman, J. (1966), Genital self-discovery during a boy's second year. *The Psychoanalytic Study of the Child*, 21:358–392. New York: International Universities Press.

Kohut, H. (1971), *The Analysis of the Self.* New York: Basic Books.

Kramer, S. (1974), A discussion of the paper by John A. Sours on the anorexia nervosa syndrome. *Internat. J. Psycho-Anal.,* 55:577.

Leonard, C. (1944), An analysis of a case of functional vomiting and bulimia. *Psychoanal. Rev.,* 31:1–18.

Lindner, R. (1976), Laura. In: *The Fifty-Minute Hour.* New York: Bantam Books.

Lowenkopf, E. L., & Wallach, J. D. (1985), Bulimia. *J. Amer. Acad. Psychoanal.,* 13 4:489–503.

Ludwig, A. M., Brandson, J. M., Wilbur, C. B., Benfield, F., & Jameson, D. H. (1972), The objective study of a multiple personality. *Arch. Gen. Psychiat.,* 298–310.

Mahler, M. S. (1965), On the significance of the normal separation-individuation phase: With reference to research in symbiotic child psychosis. In: *Drives, Affects, Behavior,* ed. M. Schur. New York: International Universities Press, pp. 161–169.

Masserman, J. (1941), Psychodynamics in anorexia nervosa and neurotic vomiting. *Psychoanal. Quart.,* 10:211–242.

Masterson, J. F. (1975), *Psychotherapy of the Borderline Adult: A Developmental Approach.* New York: Brunner/Mazel.

Milner, M. (1944), A suicidal symptom in a child of three. *Internat. J. Psycho-Anal.,* 25:53–61.

Mintz, I. (1983a), Anorexia nervosa and bulimia in males. In: *The Fear of Being Fat: The Treatment of Anorexia Nervosa and Bulimia,* ed. C. P. Wilson, C. Hogan, & I. Mintz. New York: Jason Aronson, pp. 263–303.

———— (1983b), The relationship between self-starvation and amenorrhea. In: *The Fear of Being Fat: The Treatment of Anorexia Nervosa and Bulimia,* ed. C. P. Wilson, C. Hogan, & I. Mintz. New York: Jason Aronson, pp. 335–344.

Mitchell, J. E., Boutacoff, L., & Wilson, D. (1986), Absence of early feeding problems among bulimic women. *Amer. J. Orthopsychiat.,* 56/2:313–316.

Money, J., & Ehrhardt, A. A. (1972), *Man and Woman, Boy and Girl: The Differentiation and Dimorphism of Gender Identity from Conception to Maturity.* Baltimore: Johns Hopkins University Press.

Moulton, R. (1942), A psychosomatic study of anorexia nervosa including the use of vaginal smears. *Psychosom. Med.,* 4:62–74.

Muuss, R. E. (1986), Adolescent eating disorder: Bulimia. *Adolescence,* 21 82:258–267.

Palazzoli, M. (1974), *Self-Starvation: From Individual to Family Therapy in the Treatment of Anorexia Nervosa.* New York: Jason Aronson, 1978.

Sabine, E., Yonace, A., Farrington, A., Barratt, K., & Wakeling, A. (1983), Bulimia nervosa: A placebo-controlled double-blind therapeutic trial of mianseran. *Brit. J. Clin. Psychiat.,* 15:195–202.

Schwartz, H. J. (1986), Bulimia: Psychoanalytic perspectives. *J. Amer. Psychoanal. Assn.,* 34/2:439–463.

Sours, J. A. (1974), The anorexia nervosa syndrome. *Internat. J. Psycho-Anal.,* 35/4:567–576.

———— (1980), *Starving to Death in a Sea of Objects.* New York: Jason Aronson.

Sperling, M. (1968). Trichotillomania, trichophagy and cyclic vomiting. *Internat. J. Psycho-Anal.*, 49:682–690.

Stern, S., Dixon, K., Nemzer, E., Lake, M., Sansone, R., Meltzer, D., Lantz, S., & Schrier, S. (1984), Affective disorder in the families of women with normal weight bulimia. *Amer. J. Psychiat.*, 141:124–127.

Stoller, R. (1968), *Sex and Gender*, Vol. 1. New York: Science House.

Striegel-Moore, R. H., Silberstein, L. R., & Rodin, J. (1986), Toward an understanding of risk factors for bulimia. *Amer. Psychol.*, 41/3:246–263.

Swift, W. J. (1985), Assessment of the bulimic patient. *Amer. J. Orthopsychiat.*, 55/3:384–397.

Sylvester, E. (1945), Analysis of psychogenic anorexia and vomiting in a four-year-old child. *The Psychoanalytic Study of the Child*, 1:167–187. New York: International Universities Press.

Székács, J. (1985), Impaired spatial structures. *Internat. J. Psycho-Anal.*, 66:193–199.

Tabin, J. K. (1985), *On the Way to Self.* New York: Columbia University Press.

Thomä, H. (1967), *Anorexia Nervosa*. New York: International Universities Press.

Winnicott, D. W. (1965), *The Maturational Process and the Facilitating Environment*. New York: International Universities Press.

Chapter 8

Anal Components in Overeating

MARION MICHEL OLINER, PH.D.

An attitude toward food and eating typical for many overeaters has been relatively neglected: It concerns their tendency to consume a substance that will fill them, make them feel bad, and render them logy and insensitive to further needs or desires. Invariably, the patients mention that if the food is in the house, they are compelled to clean up; that is, eat until there is nothing left. Also, almost invariably, the food that is the object of such binges is described as junk or garbage, thus implicitly transforming the person who contains it into a receptacle for noxious products. Glenn (1974), a physician writing on the subject of weight problems, admonishes his readers that if they eat like a garbage can, they will look like one, which is something one of my patients, Ms. C., enacted in the following way: She would eat a big portion of a chocolate cake in one sitting, stop only when her stomach hurt so much that she could not eat any more, and throw the rest into the garbage can. One part of the cake was inside her and the other part with the garbage. In this way she transformed her body into the container for something hurtful and bad without consciously intending to. This is compulsive eating which must be distinguished from eating that is the expression of the oral drive. The two are clearly not synonymous; they are derived from different aspects of the personality, and I intend to concentrate on the compulsion and the anal drive derivatives of overeating, leaving aside all other components.

In order to illustrate compulsive eating, I shall describe one case in detail so as to couch the trait under scrutiny within the context of other personality characteristics rather than to present the eating problem in isolation. I hope to demonstrate that the patient's eating, like that of others who fall into the same category, did not so much tie the patient to the mother as it differentiated her from the latter. It enabled the patient to maintain an attitude of idealization at a distance, thus allowing further growth and independence which genuine oral dependency would not have done.

CASE EXAMPLE 1

Ms. M.'s weight became a problem very early in life. She thinks that she never knew what it was to be hungry as a child. She was taken to a doctor for weight reduction, and when she was successful, her mother rewarded her by taking her out for a piece of cake. The effort at weight reduction failed, and Ms. M. spent her early years being dressed and groomed by the mother to look like a doll. When she was older, she spent much time sitting on the couch eating potato chips and drinking soda and waiting for her parents, who worked late, to bring in the food that she ordered from their restaurant. In the meantime, the rest of the family ate dinner at the regular time, but she refused to eat with them. For about six years, from the time she was in college until her marriage while she was in analysis, she took diet pills which her mother helped her obtain. She considered herself addicted to them. Later, she ate and vomited, first as a result of gall bladder problems, and then, after her operation, as a weight control measure. This stopped after she met a masochistic man who treated her sadistically. She retaliated.

Her concerns about her weight were not the presenting problem, but they were often the focus of our attention. Nevertheless she made no progress in losing weight during her treatment. Only after terminating the analysis did she lose the excess weight.[1] This reinforced my conviction that she could not allow herself to be more slim and attractive because of an idealizing mother transference that did not yield to interpretations. When she returned for further treatment I feared that renewed contact with me might lead to her gaining weight, but it did not.

Ms. M., age twenty-three, entered treatment because of a depression following an abortion. The father of the child was a married man with whom she was having an affair, because the man to whom she was attached was homosexual. At the start, she described her parents as nice and her mother in addition as pretty. This naiveté was in keeping with her appearance, which was that of an overweight child. She wanted to be cooperative, but her cooperation was based on extreme submissiveness which slowly changed into an accusatory and demanding stance.

She approached the work of analysis with the following fantasy: she thought that she should be totally inactive, like a cow in the rodeo. If the cow is smart, she does not resist, allows herself to be tied up, lets the cowboy get the applause, and is released in the shortest span of time. When Ms. M. first reported this fantasy, it was totally ego syntonic. She could not imagine why this was not the most intelligent way of dealing with her situation: she cooperates, I do what I have to do, get recognition for my work, and she can leave cured. At a later date, this fantasy was superseded by the idea that the analyst should be like an abortionist. Her role again is passive in that all she does is spread her legs, and, once more, she was quite unaware of the cruelty of the event she imagined. She wanted the analyst to be the active one, herself to be passive, seemingly without will, which was a condition she was ready to accept.

As the treatment progressed and her tendency toward acting on impulse and fantasies needed to be analyzed, she ex-

---

[1] A number of other women patients whose weight problem received considerable attention during their treatment have reacted in the same way. One patient lost weight during my vacation, but kept it down only after terminating, and two other patients were successful in a weight reduction program after leaving treatment. In all cases, the conflicts which led to the overeating were analyzed, but it seemed as if the transference relationship made it impossible for them to lose weight during the treatment.

perienced my interventions as a scolding and herself as a bad patient, a situation that led to rebellion and antagonism. She lived the life of the sixties generation so that her acting out was rationalized by the norms of that culture with its condemnation of the white middle class and its idealization of the black and other third world cultures. In this way, she considered many of the analytic questions or challenges as expressions of personal preferences or biases that I tried to impose on her. It was at this point that she often treated the analyst as somewhat amusing and perhaps quaint, someone who has to be tolerated, while the patient was busy both professionally and romantically.

Until late in her treatment, when she began to choose partners with backgrounds similar to her own, the men in Ms. M.'s life came from other cultures. This led to acting out that slowed the treatment considerably.

When she was a teenager, she had accepted a ride with a stranger and involved herself in a potentially dangerous situation. During her treatment, she formed a relationship with a man who owned a gun and who robbed and then left her.

She invariably formed relationships during the analyst's vacation. This is how she married a man from a distant and very foreign culture; made temporary liaisons with married men when her husband was away; and after her separation and during my vacation, started a sadomasochistic relationship with one man who was devoted to her and whom she had difficulties giving up. At that point the treatment ground to a halt. The sessions were filled with complaints about him, but she did not think that anyone else would ever be there for her. Because of this stalemate, I suggested terminating the treatment within nine months. She experienced this as a rejection until she, too, realized that she was not ready to reach a decision with regard to her relationship to this man. When she came back into treatment three years later, she was determined to end that relationship, requested my help, and was indeed able to separate from him with great pain.

Even though she was at times disparaging, scornful, and patronizingly forgiving toward me, her main attitude was idealization. This idealization is best illustrated by the following incident: When she had overcome her desire for primitive living, torn covers on furniture, and the disorder that goes with "casualness" she bought herself an expensive rug. Her thoughts were immediately that she should not have it, but that I should be the one. She became very identified with this beautiful object, and she reacted badly when she was confronted with the fact that all along I had had a similar one which I had always intended to use in the office. I hesitated to bring the rug into the office after she bought the rug, but finally decided to risk her reaction, which was stronger even than what I had anticipated. When she saw the rug, she told me that now she felt totally useless, that this proved that I did not need her, that until then she had thought that she was bringing me her rug but that now she could see that I did not need her. She felt annihilated and worthless. We tried to analyze her inability to imagine that she still had value even if I had a similar rug. She became conscious of her difficulties in thinking that she could share some of her mother's attributes without disappearing, but this was not sufficiently resolved to help her give up the weight which gave her an identity, albeit negative, until after she terminated her treatment for the first time. It seemed as if anything worthwhile she and her mother had in common automatically would belong totally to the mother and she would remain empty.

BACKGROUND

Ms. M. was born a year or so after the death of an eighteen-month-old baby girl whose grave the family (and Ms. M.) visited regularly. After Ms. M.'s birth, the mother may have had one or more miscarriages, and when the patient was four or five years old, the mother gave birth to a baby boy who lived only a week. The patient remembers her father telling her about the birth and her mother coming home without the baby, but little else.

When treatment aroused her curiosity about this important event, she asked her mother, but was met only with "who can remember, it happened so long ago?" She knows that she went downtown with her mother, that her mother ate cheesecake, and that mother got sick. This is connected with the mother's going to the hospital and having the baby, but in a vague way that has never yielded a complete picture of the relationship between the two events. This notion, which is at least partly based on what the mother told her, is important because the birth is associated to eating bad food during an outing with Ms. M., therefore implicating her in the subsequent loss of the baby. She remembers her mother saying that her own birth was probably made possible by the mother's illness during pregnancy which meant that she had to take care of herself.

She was told that the dead children were with God: that they were so good that God wanted them. During her treatment, she voiced the fear that death was chasing her, and she made it clear that being good meant to her that she, too, might be taken.

After the loss of the little boy, the mother went to work probably to counteract a depression, which the patient does not remember, but which could be reconstructed during the analysis: One day she came to her session and saw me dressed in black. She became startled and frightened, said that someone died and that she would gladly go home and give up her session, that I did not have to see her that day. This was so real to her that no interpretation about her mother and the dead baby reached her. She gave vent to her fear of being put in a box, and associated to this fear the image of Flash Gordon on whom the walls close in leaving a hole for the blood. The interpretation that seeing me dressed in black recalled to her her mother's grief and depresssion at the death of the baby, and the possibility that she too might die was rejected in an almost mocking way, as if I were indulging in my own fantasies and her mother was never depressed. In reality, this mother, who only voiced a high opinion of herself, openly expressed her envy for women who had more than one child.

Ms. M. says that she felt as much manipulated as loved. Her mother dressed her like a doll, painted her toenails, and threatened to call the police when the child was uncooperative. They went downtown together and later went to shows and movies like two friends, but she did not consider this a genuine maternal love on her mother's part. In order to put this to the test, she "put marks on her face" which her mother noticed and for which she was taken to the doctor, and no one ever noticed that she had caused them herself.

She thought that the only good mother–daughter relationship she knew was that between her own mother and her grandmother. The mother came home from work and held the grandmother's hand when they were sitting together. Ms. M. felt that no one was ever committed to her, and her father and her mother going off to work together made her feel that she had no one. To this day she is struggling against the feeling that she is worthless, because her father did not choose her over another woman and because he thought so highly of her mother when she was alive. Only recently has she accepted the inappropriateness of the wish to be the equivalent of the father's mate.

The early years with her mother were happier than the later years with the grandmother and two aunts who worked, but many disturbing things were remembered as ongoing rather than following her own abandonment by the mother who spent long hours working with the father.

Actually, Ms. M. tends to consider the trauma in her life to be the move the family made when she was eight years old. I am inclined to believe that the move is a screen behind which lies the denial of the impact of the deaths of the other children. Ms. M. remembers feeling totally displaced by the move which was to another part of the country and took her from an ethnic urban environment to a "synthetic" culture. Ms. M. felt that she was fat and had the wrong hair. She says that she was a misfit.

Ms. M. reports that there was no privacy in her home. She never had a room of her own, but also never remembered seeing anything sexual despite the fact that she often slept in her parents' bedroom. She remembers her father taking care of a wound high up on her leg, and, when she was reticent, he told her that he was her father. Also there were many money transactions that made the issues of private property very unclear. The parents named the business after her which meant that while the mother was working there she was often called by the patient's name.

Interestingly enough, the failure to differentiate between mother and child was not true of food. The mother was fussy about the food she ate. On the rare occasions that the family ate together, she liked to call attention to the foods she was not eating. "My mother might, if she saw champagne, say that she only drinks Piper Heidsick." This did not prevent her from buying the "junk" which the patient ate, often while sitting on the couch and watching television. The father loudly disapproved of Ms. M.'s eating habits, chided mother and daughter for buying this type of food, but was unable to effect a change.

When Ms. M. started to menstruate, her mother told her to tell her father that she was a woman now. After that she bought sanitary napkins in school and hid them from her mother. She also pulled out her pubic hair.

The father admired the mother greatly, but the latter told Ms. M. that she, the daughter, was going to be much luckier in that she would not have to work like her mother and would eventually have a much better husband who would provide for her. This exclusion from the parents' fate backfired, and she identified with her unmarried aunts, the black men, the drug dealers, and even a criminal whom she befriended, acting out a Pygmalion-type fantasy which ended with her being robbed. (She thought of this man as someone who would transform himself: make something of himself in contrast to the white middle class toward whom she expressed nothing but contempt during that period.)

FANTASIES

Considering the extent of this patient's amnesia, including her experiences of the primal scene, many events had to be reconstructed from the fantasies the patient either told or acted out during the treatment. Neither were readily analyzable because she tended to rationalize her masochistic fantasies and had difficulties in treating some of her pronouncements as metaphors.

Thus she objected to a fee increase because she compared her entering treatment with going to Macy's to buy a couch: the store would never come to her a few years later and ask for more money.

Despite these difficulties, my persistent curiosity about how she thought, led her to question herself and ultimately become more reflective and genuinely introspective about herself. The fantasies she recounted, often without reflection, showed her inner world to be threatened and frightening.

She thought that her mother liked trophies and that the man she married, whose cultural background should have given the parents some difficulties, was received like a trophy. The patient did not want children because this would be another trophy for her mother.

She spoke about leaving home because she was the only high school graduate there, as if they could not have tolerated someone better than they, even their own child. In the same session she voiced fears that she would be pushed out of the nest in analysis. She had the fantasy that someone gave her a pill to make her smaller, and she is tucked away somewhere on my bookshelf. After this she reported eating again. She did not want to stop eating even though she thought that I would want her to. My success would be a paper in which I have my successful case, and she would be a person different from the one I am writing about, just as her mother has a daughter of whom she is very proud, but that daughter is not Ms. M. The real daughter sits on the couch, eating, watching television, and not relating to anyone, as she did during her teenage years. If she comes off the couch (here the couch at home and the analytic couch seem to become one), I take all her pleasures away so that she stays on the couch, resists my intrusions, and remains untouched. If I reached out to her, I would rob her and leave her bleeding.

Although she was considered spoiled by the family, she was convinced that to get something means enslavement. In the treatment situation, she assumed that I wanted her to change herself into someone mentally healthy (i.e., she would be a slave to my ideal). At a later time she expressed the idea of what she can receive in this way: she thinks of the Wizard of Oz who is a fake wizard because he only gives what the creatures already had; she thinks of me in this way too, not as someone giving her anything which she does not already have, but only perhaps helping her see where it is. While this represented progress in treatment, it was still linked with the unpleasant memory of her mother who gave her back as a gift something that she already had but that was supposedly taken away from her when she was being punished. She thought that she never got what she wanted, but everyone expected her to be grateful.

At one point, Ms. M. reported an incident that followed the pattern reported by Ms. C. who had to eat until her stomach hurt: Ms. M. said that she ate something, then she had to smoke dope in order to eat more. She really could not eat without smoking, because she did not feel like it, but once she was bad she was compelled to continue.

During her marriage, she was unable to eat the meat she was cooking because she saw it change from the raw to the cooked state so that she and her husband seldom ate together nor did they eat the same food. During that time also, she reported a dream in which a rat was gnawing at her dress which was native to her husband's country.

Once, she reported being full, that she is like a gas tank that is going to overflow, that she has a limited capacity, that the gas is going to overflow and cause a fire. Her middle name is Ethel (ethyl); this was always a joke and led her to think about the fact that she never gave her parents what they wanted.

Her marriage which was contracted without being analyzed was also described in terms of food: "I think of it as an apple with a black spot and a worm." This turned into the baby that I, as the abortionist who could have killed her, will take from her. My question as to what I would do with the rotten apple was answered without hesitation: enlarge my ego. The danger is that she will become me, and she is afraid that she will turn into the devil in order not to become me. As a child she was told by her grandmother that she was bad; she was so ugly and angry always telling people what she thought of them, always being nasty (foul mouth). But being bad also made her different

from her mother and those dead children whom God wanted
for himself.

Being good meant to Ms. M. being someone's possession
or not to exist. Otherwise she might feel so good about herself
that she would steal another woman's husband. That is why she
had to eat: Feeling bad keeps her restrained.

After about four years of treatment, Ms. M. developed gall
bladder problems for which she consulted a doctor and a surgeon. I urged her to speak about this, but she treated the issue
as if it did not concern analysis, and she reacted as if I were
competing with the doctors whom she was consulting. She tried
to convince me that her gall bladder was ill, and, since these
men confirmed the need for surgery, she interpreted any involvement on my part as an unnecessary interference. It was
as if I were saying either that there was nothing wrong with her
gall bladder or that the decision was mine to make. It would
have been foolhardy for me to enter into what she considered
a dispute over her need for an operation. But it was fortunate
that I had another avenue which led her to think about the
issues involved: When she came back to a session after a meal
in a Mexican restaurant, I was able to point out that she wanted
to be in charge of her gall bladder, that she fought with me
over it, but that she also wanted to be free to deny any difficulties
when it pleased her. Subsequently she was operated on, and
she returned triumphant, reiterating that the doctor said that
the operation was essential.

The operation had a totally unexpected by-product: the
patient who up to then had only menstruated twice a year, now
had regular periods. What was the nature of this diseased organ
that was removed? Was it the gall bladder of psychosomatic
medicine that has no meaning other than as an indication of
stress for which there were insufficient affects? Was it a symbol
for the feces over which mother and child fought, and father
came to the rescue? (She had no memory of her toilet training.)
Was it an imaginary penis which she surrendered in a symbolic
castration after which she allowed herself to become a woman,
in an act that Kestenberg (1956) describes as a castration wish?

Or was it a fecal baby that was being eliminated by an abortionist?

These questions could never be answered in a satisfactory way except to conclude that the meaning of the gall bladder operation was condensed. Since it was inflamed, it was first and foremost unsymbolic and needed to be taken out. But it also became symbolic for the idea repeatedly voiced by the patient that she possessed within her body a bad thing: food, an organ, an explosive, an anal penis, and an unwanted baby which she could have removed while she was passive. She controlled it totally, surrendered it to a man, and then became a full-fledged woman.

Attached to the diseased gall bladder were a number of fantasies that also concerned the food she consumed when she overate: both created for the patient the sense that she had a bad thing inside that she has to control and cling to in order to be an individual. (She also mentioned that her husband's penis reminded her of shit.)

On the other hand, her beautiful possession, her rug, was only of value to her as long as she considered it unique. When it was not, it became devalued and useless like all the other objects which become anal by virtue of not being unique.[2]

DISCUSSION

The case of Ms. M. was presented as an illustration for the dynamics I have observed regularly in patients who overeat (Oliner, 1982):

> The inhibition against the outward direction of the need
> to control, to master, and to dominate, as well as the often

---

[2]Bela Grunberger and Janine Chasseguet-Smirgel have studied extensively the process of idealization among anally fixated subjects. In their work, they have demonstrated repeatedly how easily devaluation takes place because of the anal nature of the individual's ego. Thus purity or uniqueness can be the attributes that lift an object, a person, or a creative effort out of anality, but because of the precarious underpinnings on which the idealization rests, it is easily threatened.

prevalent regression to orality make it sometimes difficult to assess the role of the anal component instincts in the study of case material. . . . Thus the types of eating, already mentioned by Lewin, which must be considered as being coprophagic, have often been confused with purely oral derivatives. They constitute the reincorporation of an anal product rather than a feeding substitute, and we must continuously be aware of the considerable overlap between the psychosexual phases where possibly a sharp differentiation can be made only at the cost of artificiality. Thus the wish to fill the digestive track in order to have an internal object to manipulate, to mitigate against loss, emptiness, and penetration, and to create pressure to calm the excitations emanating from the genitals is not primarily a wish to be nourished. It creates a feeling of fullness which negates the loss and penetrability; at worst it gives the girl a bad inside which the mother would not want anyway and therefore gives her some sense of possession and separates her securely from the mother. Often the quality of the eating suggests its dominant aim, and patients talk about stuffing themselves with junk food and report that the enjoyment is not in the eating; as a matter of fact, they do not taste the food. Yet it cannot be accidental that food is often brown" [p. 51].

It remains now to enlarge upon these points and place them in the context of the case material and the theoretical formulations that seem pertinent:

1. There is the Inhibition Against Outwardly Directed Aggression, Most Specifically Aimed at Controlling the Mother. The rage Shirley experienced could only be expressed by "bad" behavior which gave her the reputation of being a spoiled child. Time and again, there is evidence in her case that her naughtiness was ineffectual, self-damaging, and on the order of a temper tantrum. It never seemed to reach the mother in a way that compelled the latter to control the child effectively. Punishment consisted of a threat to call the police, or else the taking of one of her toys which was followed with its being returned to her as a gift. Ms. M. was a discontented child, yet basically submissive, because the anger never led to an open struggle for control between the mother and her. This failure in the mother's response led to an increase in the child's need for provocations, and thus started a pattern that was partially controlled by the overeating.

This control is derived from anal sadism that has undergone one of the vicissitudes described by Freud (1915). It has been turned on the subject's own self which constitutes a mode of defense against the instinct in that it spares the external object. It re-creates the relationship between the fecal mass and the intestines. In this case, overeating is differentiated from pure orality by a number of factors prominent among which is the nature of the food: the food is not linked to the mother (in Shirley's case it was generally food that the mother did not eat herself). The mother did not cook for the family, the father did so at the restaurant. The food is considered bad and filling, but not nourishing and, after eating it, it remains an internal lump, is frequently regurgitated, and the patient suffers from remorse.

Nevertheless, it is important to note that the patients whom I have observed had no history of coprophagia, whereas the one patient, Mrs. W., who remembers being photographed or seeing a picture of herself eating her feces or holding them in her hand, has no serious overeating problem. Perhaps the fact that Mrs. W.'s mother, an otherwise very troubled woman, was concerned about feeding her family and stored food against the eventuality of a shortage, made greater erogenization of the anal zone possible. The mother's concern about feeding her family also made overeating unsuitable for an assertion of separateness. In this case, as in others like it, overeating would mean submission.

The anal erotic investment provided Mrs. W. with a source of body pleasure lacking for the overeating patients. This is in keeping with Fliess's observation (1956) that, "The relation of the thought to the particular 'affectivity' (Freud) here concerned, i.e., to the erogeneity of the anal zone, is . . . variable;

in compulsive and in paranoid thought it is close, in manic and phobic thought it is distant if it exists at all" (p. 143). Overeating creates a state reminiscent of mania, but without the excitement.

In the present cases, unlike the cases of coprophagia, the erogeneity of the anal zone is not immediately apparent. Nevertheless, the overeating should be interpreted as an acting out of an unconscious anal fantasy; this, despite the involvement of the mouth, rather than the anal zone, which makes the strong anal drive component less apparent. The aim of overeating is control, independence, and the abolition of pleasure. Instead of being in the service of pleasure (Ms. C. said that she does not taste the food when she is overeating), the eating aims at obliterating both erotism and aggression, except feelings of self-loathing which these patients invariably report.

Shengold says that:

> [T]he establishment of the ego, the 'I,' is—to paraphrase Freud—in the first place [vor Allem] the happy establishment of the body ego; and a gigantic step forward in the differentiation between self and other, between being controlled and controlling, is the mastery of the anal sphincter. The "happy" attainment of mastery implies the ability to contain and neutralize aggression and rage." [Fliess (1956, p. 124) conceives of the anal sphincter as being "charged with the mastery of regressive and archaic affect"] [1982, p. 336].

The anality I am referring to is of this nature, not the investment of anal erogeneity as much as the desire for mastery by means of control of the inside of the body. As Fliess said (1956), "It is often . . . as though the ego chose anal–erotic elaboration upon instinctual strivings of whatever nature as the most reliable means of preserving its organization" (p. 124).

These patients are obsessed with food, meaning that they have "thoughts which the subject feels himself obliged to have—by which he feels literally besieged" (Laplanche and Pontalis, 1973, p. 77). This assertion was substantiated by the fact that Ms. C. was compelled to eat until her stomach hurt, and

Ms. M. reported that she once had to drug herself in order to continue eating past the point at which she wanted to stop. Furthermore, none of these patients could tolerate having tempting food in the house without being compelled to clean it up (i.e., eat it or throw it into the trash).

This compulsive behavior must be distinguished from impulsive behavior. In compulsions, there is a coercive factor, a dictate from a prestage of the superego, which, when disobeyed, leads to anxiety. The anxiety is generated by the aggressive impulses against which overeating defends.

The complex relationship between aggression and eating has been touched upon by Abraham's monumental 1924 article on the difference between melancholia and obsessive–compulsive neurosis. He postulates that the lost object in melancholia has been reincorporated as feces. He thinks that the melancholic experiences the lost object as having been expelled and, therefore, its reincorporation is the equivalent to the taking in of feces.

> My own observations on a number of cases have always shown that the patient makes his love-object the target of certain impulses which correspond to the lower level of his anal-sadistic libidinal development. These are the impulses of expelling (in an anal sense) and destroying (murdering). The product of such a murder—the dead body—becomes identified with the product of expulsion—with excrement. We can now understand that the patient's desire to eat excrement is a cannibalistic impulse to devour the love-object which he has killed [Abraham, 1924, p. 444].

"In his unconscious he identifies the love-object he has lost and abandoned with the most important product of bodily evacuation—with his faeces—and re-incorporates it in his ego by means of the process we have called introjection" (1924, p. 481).

Abraham contrasts this with obsessive–compulsive neurosis in which "the conserving tendencies—those of retaining and controlling his object—are the more powerful, this conflict around the love-object will call forth phenomena of psychological compulsion" (1924, pp. 430–431). The eating behavior of the patients under consideration comprises aspects of both dynamics, the coprophagic–cannibalistic as well as retaining-compulsive aspects, a compromise that might be expressed as controlling the object from within. It constitutes the expression of anal sadism, but saves the object from attack by turning the impulse inside. It differs from normal anality in that it attacks food as if it had already undergone the digestive process in which the good has been assimilated and is part of the subject. In this way the ingested food forms an entity inside that is experienced like a foreign body—like a bridge between subject and object—in other words, like feces.

Whether or not it is warranted to equate the food with the mother, or more accurately with the bad part of the mother that has been split off and taken in, is a matter of choice of explanatory models. In Ms. M.'s case, there were unconscious cannibalistic fantasies as evidenced by her inability to eat the meat she cooked for her husband and the image of the rat in her dreams. Shengold (1967) thinks that the cannibalism inherent in the rat image has anal components because he considers the image of a rat gnawing to be related to the idea of anal penetration. In 1971, he said, "It is particularly linked with anal erogeneity because of its association with dirt and disease" (p. 280). Another patient, Ms. L., who also had a problem with overeating, rushed out of the toilet as a child in order to avoid the mice coming out of the flushing toilet. According to Shengold, the patients concerned with rats and mice identify with these rodents because of the cannibalism as well as the connection to dirt. Thus the fear of rodents expresses the fear of biting and being bitten in an anal mode.

Nevertheless, it seems to me to be a matter of personal style rather than a question of scientific validity whether to interpret the overeating as an introjection of the bad part of the mother or stress the observable phenomena, which are that the food is bad, is generally not associated with the mother and what she herself would eat, relieves loneliness, and inhibits the expression of hostility. The fact that these patients ate secretly when they were alone and might have felt abandoned suggests that the food compensates for a loss; thus their obsession with eating overshadowed all other affects that might have been generated under those circumstances. They swallow their anger and with it the awareness that they are disappointed. In this respect overeating represents a return to narcissism and self-sufficiency.

That there is a greater prevalence of eating disorders in women than in men[3] which is in keeping with the observation that, developmentally, girls tend to control outward directed aggression earlier than boys who tend to be more mobile and exercise less self-control.

2. Denial of the Object's Bad Qualities. The symptomatic behavior, overeating, leads to submissiveness and inhibits the power struggle and the competition between the daughters and their mothers. The daughters disappear into stupor or withdrawal rather than engage in active competition. In this latter respect they share important characteristics with the "submissive daughters" described by Chasseguet-Smirgel (1986). The women described in her study showed remarkable passivity and endangered themselves by not exercising sufficient judgment when facing truly dangerous men. This is also true of Ms. M. who lived through at least two episodes during which she failed to appreciate the danger she was facing. Even after being robbed, it was difficult for her to give up the denial of the potential danger in seeking revenge or pursuing the relationship with this man in order to refute his accusations which rationalized his criminal behavior toward her.

The study of such submissive daughters led Chasseguet-Smirgel (1986) to cite, as an example of passivity, President Schreber who identified his own body with a rotting and putrified corpse that can be manipulated. Chasseguet-Smirgel attributes this tendency to the lack of distinction between good and bad, so that the bad aspects of the mother and subsequent objects had to be denied.

The passivity described by Chasseguet-Smirgel is evident

[3]Statistics gathered by the Metropolitan Life Insurance Company as well as a statement by Ritvo (1977) concerning complaints about eating disturbances among college students support this assertion.

in Ms. M.'s attitude toward these dangerous men who she thought would change. (It can also be seen in many aspects of her fantasies of her own body and its contents, reminiscent of Schreber's fantasies.) Recognizing the criminal for who he was meant giving up the fantasy of his transformation (i.e., someone who is finally "making something of himself" under her influence). Transformation is implicit in the fate of anal erotism as described by Freud (1917). This transformation fantasy blurs the distinction between good, bad, feces, baby, and penis, which was acted out when she overate, and thus provided the groundwork for denial.

Overeating achieves passivity in a better, less destructive way than the submission to violence-prone men. Overeating may relieve the necessity for such dangerous acting out because of its narcississtically gratifying nature leading to greater independence. In this way, the regressive gratification reduces the aggression and provides an outlet for sadism by turning it against the inside of the body and the self. In addition, it provides a form of self-punishment.

Thus, overeating enables the patient to separate from the object, to identify the body with a stool, to remain passive, and to maintain a sense of badness and worthlessness. Since this enhances narcissism, it allows for greater autonomy and, thereby, lessens the need for more object-dependent and dangerous submissiveness.

3. The Return to Body Narcissism. In this context, narcissism refers to independence and self-sufficiency. It does not suggest self-esteem. On the contrary, the body image achieved through overeating is almost totally negative, its asset lies in the fact that everything is controlled. I have compared overeating to other symptomatic behavior patterns stemming from similar defenses and have concluded that genuine coprophagia involves greater erogenization of the body, especially the lower bowels, whereas submission to dangerous men suggests greater object dependency. Thus, overeating, being more narcissistic (also in the sense of being further removed from autoerotism), allows for

greater autonomy which fits Shengold's description (1985) of
a return to body narcissism.

> A regression toward any kind of "body-ego narcissism"
> brings with it a reactivation of old dangers, but also of old
> ways of mastery. Return to domination by the "anal-
> sadistic organization" provides a kind of haven which I am
> calling anal narcissism; this haven promises the predictable
> and the orderly, but it contains its own perils of anal de-
> structiveness. This danger of destroying and, therefore, of
> losing much-needed others (like parents) diminishes as
> narcissism is regressively increased and, at least delusion-
> ally, no other is needed. But this regressive, narcissistically
> enhanced anal defensiveness provides an unhealthy im-
> balance with scales tipped toward the elimination of affect
> and of object-related emotional achievements consolidated
> subsequent to the anal stage. Anal narcissism involves a
> regressive reduction of ego to body-ego dominated by the
> "sadistic anal organization . . ." [p. 59].

Shengold thinks that anality must be experienced in order
to be transcended, in this way it can help to attain perspective
and wisdom. "I believe that anal defensiveness (sphincter defensiveness is an alternate term but it leaves out the associated
anal phenomena) is the most important part of 'body-ego' defensive functioning. If it is denied and it prevails we remain
mired in compulsive 'thing-ness' living in our own cloaca even
though we pretend to be in a palace" (1985, p. 52). Once the
anal-sadistic need for control has been set in motion, the object,
inside or out, becomes, by that fact alone, fecal in nature (see
Grunberger, 1960). And, as the case material clearly shows, the
whole body was identified with it.

Throughout the first years of treatment from which the
case material is taken, the patient's wish to be immobile and
almost inanimate is apparent. The immobility in the tied cow
fantasy concerns the whole body. Such a thinglike existence was
achieved through overeating which converts a conscious subject
living in a body endowed with sensations into an amorphous

and passive entity. One might say that the patient becomes one with her pressured stomach, and that she had achieved a sense of solidity that made her invulnerable to other sensations, especially anger at the mother. In Ms. M.'s terms, it was another way of becoming the tied cow.

Francis Pasche (1982), a prominent French psychoanalyst, has addressed the issue of the inanimate:

> Material reality can be felt, and it is felt undoubtedly from the beginning, as an inanimate reality, dead and fecalized. The awareness of the body producing such a strictly material reality: the feces, is an important step in this process. In any case, this reality brings forth disgrace, and, in certain respects, the advantage of not being credited with any intention toward the subject, it is *thing*. If it moves, it is because of the universal mechanism or the activity of another psychic reality, and not a wish or a will that belongs to it (the subject) [p. 986].

The case material demonstrates that the whole body, not only the feces, can attain the image of a thing which proves innocence and passivity in the spheres of sexuality as well as aggression.

Ms. M. thought that if she were more attractive, she would seduce men who belonged to other women, foremost among whom was, of course, her father whom she had never really given up as an unsuitable object. Instead she harbored the fantasy that she could not have him because she was ugly or because her mother was powerful and possessive. This was the lesson she learned from her mother's painting her toenails, curling her hair, and rewarding her with cake after she lost weight. She had to remain fat, put marks on her face in order to draw attention to herself, and think of herself as ugly in order to be separate and not be a threat to her mother. They enjoyed each other's company when they were alone and "did the town" together like sisters, otherwise she was living proof that her mother had no equal.

4. The Presence Inside the Body of an Essentially Fecal Substance

Controlled and Manipulated Bordering on the Idea of an Anal Phallus or Baby. The return to body narcissism, in which the anal-sadistic fantasies concern the total body portrayed as a thing to be manipulated, does not tell the whole story. There are other fantasies involving the control and manipulation of part-objects such as those of the analysis as an abortion, in which the object is not identified with the total self. For despite the fact that the fetus also represents a worthless self, and the abortion undoes her own birth, it is still an object in a container—the container being the whole body. (The patient consciously identifies with the pregnant woman.) The same is true of the gall bladder that lent itself to an acting out of the fantasy that she is the container of an undesirable substance of limited dimension. It is the most striking, even though it is only indirectly related to overeating by means of eating food that irritates the diseased organ. More directly linked to intake is the fantasy of containing an explosive, ethyl, and blowing up.

Kestenberg (1956) suggests that the vagueness of vaginal sensations cause girls to mistake genital excitement with hunger. In this case the food functions like an introjected penis calming internal excitations. Yet its undesirability suggests that it is mainly fecal in nature, recalling the concept of the anal penis introduced mainly by Grunberger (1979) and Kestenberg's (1956) description of the anal baby—the precursor of the real baby. The anal nature of this internal substance is further corroborated by the fact that neither the analysis-as-abortion fantasy nor the actual gall bladder operation carried with it any notion of regret or mourning, which was remarkable considering that this patient was quite afraid of doctors and hospitals. It would suggest that the operation was the equivalent of a bowel movement which she was going to have at her convenience and without any interference. But there was more than that: she allowed a man to cut her, violate her, and make a woman of her. The sexual connotation is unmistakable; it is an anal-sadistic interpretation of intercourse—with the doctor in control, she is passive, and the other woman, the analyst, is excluded.

There are here the beginnings of condensation, the precursors of real wishes for a baby, but because of the defenses against the fantasies concerning the death of her siblings, these were still expressed in the anal-expulsive mode.

Schwartz (1986) pointed to the "introjection of and identification with the external source of self-regard—the paternal penis-baby" (p. 452), in patients who overeat. This provides the motive for Ms. M.'s eating to be big like her husband. Her not eating with him and her not eating the same food constitutes the defense against these cannibalistic fantasies.

Schwartz also linked this with a marked fondness for horses, which applied to Ms. C., who loved horses, thus giving expression to her masculine identification. (She also masturbated using a carrot or a sausage and, in a more regressed mode, enjoyed that her kitchen and toilet were not separated by a door so that the smells could mingle.) Ms. F.'s mother bought "crap" for her overweight husband which she did not want the daughter to eat. The daughter, who was my patient, said: "You have heard of penis envy, now you hear of crap envy." In each case, the multiple determinants of the food are evident and its phallic characteristics unmistakable. However, even though the meaning of the substance inside the body can be a condensation of various layers of psychosexual development, the dominant aim was anal-sadistic, thus denying it value.

The need to find a regressive solution through incorporation, eventually leads to anality, even if the introject in question has certain features of a baby or a penis. So that despite the evidence for the food's multiple determination, its essentially anal nature is compelling. This view is based on assessment of the amount of control its introjection achieves and the narcissistic gain inherent in its being inside. It is the border between "I am it" and "I have it." Here then is a phallic or a feminine identification achieved on an anal-sadistic mode.

As Grunberger and Shengold have pointed out, the fact that the anal-sadistic mode is available, that it gives the illusion of mastery over difficult issues in life, makes the object (internal or external) toward whom it is directed relatively unimportant. The fact that it is introjected by mouth, that it is still a substitute rather than a genuine wish to have a baby or a penis, all point to the regression involved, as does the wish for domination and mastery, leading to fecalization. Overeating, either because of the nature or the quantity of the food, leads to an undesirable inside, no matter what this inside is fantasized to be.

It is evident from the case material that there was an evolution in Ms. M.'s thinking and that her identification with the fecal object became less total as treatment progressed. Later, she did not resort to overeating as a solution to problems, and she now states that she does not need to go on binges. However, food plays an important part in her life, especially because of her recent very gratifying involvement with a man whose orientation is strongly oral.

CONCLUSION

This patient's present pleasure in eating and her interest in food and cooking should not be confused with the overeating that was the focus of this work. In the latter, there is a regression to the use of the mouth, compulsive eating, in which the object was abolished and placed inside where it could be controlled, manipulated, and possibly expelled. Genuine orality aims at assimilation of the food into the subject. It also allows the subject to spit out what is bad or in excess. Once taken in, the good part of the food ceases to exist, and the bad undergoes degradation and is eliminated because it is unusable.

There is strong evidence from the material described that the subjects were unable to refuse the food that was there when they were alone, that after overeating there is no such healthy assimilation as provided by the normal digestive process. The food, which is often vomited, is there to be manipulated and to be an object within the subject, albeit a bad one. This food–object undergoes the control and manipulation, retention or expulsion usually directed at the fecal mass in the rectum.

The meanings attributed to this object are multiple and displacements as to the body zone and the meaning of the food abound. This is the reason for the lack of precision in some of the formulations. I believe that greater clarity can only be obtained at the cost of validity, as the case material demonstrates. Interpretations based on body ego do not lend themselves to simple formulations because the responses stem from the earliest development and are highly condensed. As a matter of fact, it is precisely this wish for simplicity on the part of these patients acting as if they were following the dictum "take it all in, make yourself independent, and master it from the inside" which makes the anal mode so attractive since it creates homogeneity; that is, it does not require differential treatment for an imaginary baby or a penis, good food or bad food.

The overeating constitutes a regression in the face of erotic and aggressive wishes involving an object. It abolishes the need for an object and satisfies the prohibition against competing with the mother. It exhibits innocence through the repudiation of the wish to be attractive and the demonstration of ugliness (anal exhibitionism). It provides an outlet for aggression but on a regressed level, which also contains the inhibition of aggression directed against the object as well as the punishment for the pleasure. Because of the drive gratification, the punishment in the aggression turned against the self and the narcissistic completeness it affords, overeating is the difficult problem we know it to be.

The difficulties that arose in the treatment of the patient whose case was used as an example of overeating are evident from the material I presented. Years of interpretation were required to render the patient's passivity less ego syntonic, and to enable her to appreciate that her clinging to a sadistic object revealed her underlying negative self-image, so often hidden by rationalizations based on ideology or gratification obtained from quick love affairs or overeating. She lost all the excess weight after the termination of the first phase of treatment, but clearly as a result of it, a result which has been retained despite the resumption of the treatment.

Summary

This work dealt with one aspect of overeating that is generally neglected—the derivative of the anal drive. It has been shown to be an important component in the cases that were used to illustrate some typical fantasies of women who think of themselves as being containers for a bad substance that they must control and manipulate.

It was postulated that this component of overeating enables the patients to reverse the flow of the anal sadism from the object to themselves, thereby freeing themselves from the object, discharging the impulse, and punishing themselves as well. In the process, they tend to see themselves as separate but as possessing a bad or undesirable body.

The food that is the object of such overeating is generally considered bad, which leads to the patient's multiple fantasies being a container for substances ranging from garbage to an anal, rotten baby or penis. It is treated as such and leads to frequent vomiting, or fantasies of containing or controlling the noxious substance from within.

Typical fantasies were presented as illustration for the presence of the anal drive derivative in overeating, and treatment issues were discussed.

It is my conviction that seeing overeating only as an oral problem ties it up too closely with dependency and the feeding mother. This is erroneous in the light of the evidence for the existence of powerful aggressive motives in overeating and for seeing the mothers of some overeaters as more frustrating than gratifying. Thus, overeating should not invariably be reduced to a fixation on a previously gratifying situation. It can be that, but most of the time it is a great deal more complex by the time a neurotic patient enters into treatment.

REFERENCES

Abraham, K. (1924), A short study of the development of the libido, viewed in the light of mental disorders. In: *Selected Papers on Psychoanalysis*. London: Hogarth Press, 1968, pp. 418–501.
Chasseguet-Smirgel, J. (1986), Submissive daughters: Hypotheses on primary passivity and its effects on thought mechanisms. In: *Sexuality and Mind*. New York: New York University Press, pp. 45–49.
Fliess, R. (1956), *Erogeneity and Libido*. New York: International Universities Press.

Freud, S. (1915), Instincts and their vicissitudes. *Standard Edition*, 14:111–140. London: Hogarth Press, 1957.
—— (1917), On transformations of instinct as exemplified in anal erotism. *Standard Edition*, 17:125–134. London: Hogarth Press, 1955.
Glenn, M. B. (1974), *But I Don't Eat That Much*. New York: E. P. Dutton, 1980.
Grunberger, B. (1960), Study of anal object relations. In: *Narcissism*. New York: International Universities Press, 1979, pp. 143–164.
—— (1979), *Narcissism*. New York: International Universities Press.
Kestenberg, J. (1956), On the development of maternal feelings in early childhood: Observations and reflections. *The Psychoanalytic Study of the Child*, 11:257–291. New York: International Universities Press.
Laplanche, J., Pontalis, J. -B. (1973), *The Language of Psychoanalysis*. New York: W. W. Norton.
Oliner, M. M. (1982). The anal phase. In: *Early Female Development: Current Psychoanalytic Views*, ed. D. Mendell. New York: SP Medical and Scientific Books, pp. 25–60.
Pasche, F. (1982), Cure type et realité. *Revue Française de Psychanalyse*, 46:981–1001.
Ritvo, S. (1977), Adolescent to woman. In: *Female Psychology*, ed. H. P. Blum. New York: International Universities Press, pp. 127–138.
Schwartz, H. J. (1986), Bulimia: Psychoanalytic perspectives. *J. Amer. Psychoanal. Assn.*, 34:439–461.
Shengold, L. (1967), The effects of overstimulation: Rat people. *Internat. J. Psycho-Anal.*, 48:403–415.
—— (1971), More about rats and rat people. *Internat. J. Psycho-Anal.*, 52:277–288.
—— (1982), Anal erogeneity: The goose and the rat. *Internat. J. Psycho-Anal.*, 63:331–345.
—— (1985), Defensive anality and anal narcissism. *Internat. J. Psycho-Anal.*, 66:47–73.

Chapter 9

Bulimia and the Mouth–Vagina Equation: The Phallic Compromise

HARVEY J. SCHWARTZ, M.D.

The universality and symmetry of the mouth–vagina equation has long been recognized by analytic investigators (Greenacre, 1950, 1952; Fraiberg, 1972; Sperling, 1973). A fluidity of cathexes between these inner loci of sensation serves both maturational and defensive purposes. Displacements in both directions are used by the ego in its efforts to maintain a consciousness free from anxiety and in search of a solution for phallic disappointment and guilt-ridden arousal.

In the higher functioning patient with bulimia, masochistic receptive fantasies are regressively transformed into active expelling urges, and passive genital ideation is defended by phallic identification. The binge–purge eating disorder is a compromise effort entailing a narcissistic condensation on one's own body of the original object-directed incestuous wishes of the oedipal period. Defensively, narcissistic body-phallic grandeur is turned to in an effort to deny the feminine longings of the positive oedipal period.

A patient is presented whose severe binging and purging was resolved through understanding its function as a phallic defense against passive feminine arousal associated with primal scene overstimulation. Discussion focuses on the centrality of the phallic period as a stimulus for the development of a feminine body image and sense of self. This developmental phase is later reawakened under the new genitality of adolescence. There, phallic-bisexuality is transiently hypercathected as a function of the phase-specific turning away from the idealized parents and as part of the intensified narcissism of that period. Ordinarily this gives way to the unconscious acknowledgment of object-directed incestuous wishes which in turn are mourned in the context of a genitally polarized sexual identity. This encourages under superego sanction, a gradual shift to nonincestuous love objects. The development of a sense of adulthood that includes a right to possess one's own mature genital is seen as fundamental to the resolution of the adolescent phase of the universal dilemmas of the oedipal period and as the central challenge that is failed by patients with eating disorders.

CLINICAL MATERIAL

Ms. L., a single, European-born woman in her mid-twenties of average weight, suffered from bulimia for five years. Her symptoms consisted of uncontrollable and frantic binging of large quantities of food followed by forcing her *right* index finger down her throat to induce vomiting. The frequency of this compulsion varied from one to eight times daily and resulted in her consuming up to $75 a day in additional food costs, which was provided by her father. The violence of her finger thrusting not infrequently led to bleeding from the back of her throat. Her longest asymptomatic period was two-and-a-half weeks. A central feature of the vomiting ritual was her preoccupation with being overheard through the walls of her bathroom by her apartment neighbors. Consciously she feared exposure and shame lest she be "caught" at her self-stimulated vomiting. She would turn on the shower and turn up the radio to mask the sounds of her repetitive regurgitation. Between binges the patient was overwhelmed with obsessive thoughts about eating, starving, and her body. She could only briefly concentrate on other subjects before images of food intruded into her consciousness. "Food," she noted, "is something to grasp."

The patient was not consciously aware of the precipitants to her binging and vomiting and was desperate to achieve perfect control—"like a man"—over her bodily functions and desires. Her symptoms began after she was painfully disappointed by being rejected by an older male neighbor of her family with whom she was engaged in an unconsummated sexual relationship. Immediately thereafter she began a passion-filled "secret" affair with an older married man during which time her binging became worse, especially when she was separated from him. This relationship ended abruptly when the patient saw her lover with his wife. In a rage born of vengeance and defeat, she left him.

Ms. L. presented herself in an attractive, engaging, but suffering manner. She described her distant physician father as a shadowy, powerful figure who preferred her athletic older and younger brothers despite her best efforts to be "one of the boys." Her quite close relationship with her architect mother was portrayed in near religious imagery—"I live my life for mother"—and she felt they could read each other's thoughts. She, of all her siblings, was closest to her mother and felt a special responsibility to heal her mother's intermittent depressions with an ever responsive availability. Her central concern with any new boyfriend was whether mother would approve of him. In response to being told that mother and father got along poorly when she was home with them, she felt increased self-disgust, renewed her dedication to mother's well-being, and more ferociously binged and vomited. She was tortured by feelings of being a "home-wrecker."

Initially the patient manifested massive repression of sexual fantasy and genital imagery. Despite an active, though mostly inorgasmic, sexual past, the presence of sexual fantasy was suggested only by the totality of its repression. Scoptophilic–exhibitionistic impulses and compensatory body–phallus fantasies—"to be as thin as a carrot"—seemed particularly pressing in her endless quest to possess the "perfect" body and in her work in ballet. Masturbatory activity was frequent, frenetic, and without any conscious fantasy. Masturbation was strictly limited to clitoral rubbing with her *left* hand.

Through the consistent interpretation of the defensive aspects of her pregenital homosexual regressions and through focused superego analysis, the patient slowly and with great anguish began to become conscious of her sexual thoughts. Gradually we joined forces in the process of discovering what was beneath her obsessive ruminations of food. Binging, we learned, followed heterosexual fantasy and arousal. After extensive work around her inhibition in reporting masturbatory activity and fantasy, she described that for the first time in memory she masturbated with her right hand, the hand reserved for her mouth, and inserted her right index finger into her vagina. At that moment she was overcome with uncontrollable shuddering, became frightened, and stopped short of orgasm. She then began stuffing food down her throat and went to sleep. When asked, she was unable to clearly describe her ideation during the shuddering because of the food ruminations, but had vague feelings of wanting to be with a man though she felt frustrated they never gave her what she wanted. She described great warmth in touching her vagina, "It makes me feel more sexual," and associated to feeling upset that a man she had previously seduced spurned her for a rival woman. She also recalled early childhood experiences of guiltily "finger-fucking" with her right hand.

This woman went on to describe, like Fraiberg's (1972) nine-year-old patient, the similarity of tactile sensation between putting her fingers into her vagina and in her mouth—"both are warm, wet and channels." With this beginning return of cathexis she began to become conscious of and remember her *genital* hunger—"my aching empty vagina." At the same time, her defensive intimacy with mother evolved into tentatively being able to recognize and protest against mother's disparaging attitudes toward her and her supposed "incompleteness," as well as mother's view of her as a selfless appendage whose autonomy is hurtful and abandoning. These evolving discoveries enabled the patient to begin to acknowledge the deferential gratification contained in her sickly "oral" presentation, and its regressive function of soothing mother's emptiness and self-disdain. She began to carve a separateness from mother out of the derepressed anger of her phallic disappointment—"I hate her ugly haircut!"—and rivalry. Her father, who had always been seen as at fault in family arguments was now becoming consciously recognized as the preferred parent of great kindness and warmth. He increasingly became the object of her intense and severely guilt-ridden competitive wishes to be possessed and loved by him exclusively. The patient's distorted body image similarly proved to be a defensive construction. The binge-induced "obese" abdomen she had railed against became the pregnant fullness she craved—"The only thing growing is on the outside, it's empty inside!" The imagined "bulges" of fat on her thighs that had disgusted her became the "bulges" in men's pants that she wished to consume with her eyes, mouth, and genitals. She also remembered that as a child she often walked around with her stomach distended and always slept with a pillow on top of her abdomen.

The piecemeal analysis of her displaced self-stimulation and the slow to emerge accompanying masturbatory fantasy, and the tentative acknowledgment of her previously denied vaginal receptivity, gradually reinitiated progression, though by no means linear, from the negative to positive oedipal position. This enabled her to begin to recognize her disdain for her perceived castrated state, her vengeful castrating impulses, as well as her reflex "solution" of becoming phallic herself. Ostensibly "oral" wishes proved to be a reflection of these underlying phallic concerns, "I want my body to be held and enveloped by you—like a man grasps and holds his penis." Indeed, her (and her mother's) insistence that she only speak to me about her "oral" problem was unconsciously designed to hide and reveal her (and her mother's) underlying secret shame in being a woman. The defect she in fact sought cure for was her "castration." (The patient would later comment, "My mother's problem is just like mine—she also denies that she wants a penis.")

Through the continuous analysis of the mouth–vagina displacement[1]—"forcing an ice-cream cone up my vagina"—we uncovered her searching curiosity about and wish to explore her genitals with her fingers, and underlying that, the wish for a man to do to her what she does to herself. At the same time derivative primal scene imagery arose, early and frequent exposure to which has been noted to intensify the mouth–vagina equation (Greenacre, 1950). Multiple dreams detailing open and shut doors and her parents killing each other, acted-out derivative scoptophilic impulses, and a depersonalization experience outside the closed door of my office, led to screen images and memories of repeated aural and visual primal scene exposure, with particular infuriating feelings associated with being an ignored outsider. Additionally, her vocation involved the meticulous and repetitive staging of "scenes" that she would alternately observe and then participate in, with others looking on. In response to the later evolved transference frustration over sexual exclusion, this defensive reversal would be briefly acted out with the transference figure being cast in the helpless position of the excited but rejected and disappointed voyeur. This revenge-filled reversal of her primal scene exclusion was also at the core of her early masturbatory fantasy. This consisted of her picturing herself in a forced humiliating sexual encounter with a faceless man in the center of a large crowd of highly aroused and frustrated onlookers. She identified alternately

---

[1] The mouth, while seemingly representing a simple upward displacement of the receptive genital, in fact, by virtue of being an orifice common to both male and female, serves as a phallic repudiation of the vagina. Sprince (1984) documents with clinical data the bulimic's common experience of denying the existence of the vagina and instead using the mouth as a source of sexual gratification. She notes as well these patients' tendency to invest the uvula with phallic meaning.

It is reasonable to consider furthermore that the extreme secrecy with which female bulimic patients cloak their "oral" binge–purging stimulation reveals not only its masturbatory equivalence and reaction to exhibitionistic wishes, but more specifically may reflect the persistence of the mystery, shame, and guilt that surrounded the earlier discovery of the "secret" vagina. Ritvo (1977) has noted the common reaction of concealment in response to menarche and indeed the patient being reported here described her vomiting as "the flow from my mouth."

In males with bulimia, this genital–oral equation is an effort at a protective upward displacement and derives from the intense castration fears that stimulate the regressions to negative oedipal sexuality that one regularly encounters in these maternally identified men.

with all the characters in the fantasy, as well as with the man's ejaculating (urinating) organ.

It appeared at this time that the stereotyped ritual of gorging and violently forcing her finger down her throat to induce regurgitation was, in part, a regressive acting out on her own body—a "narcissistic condensation" (Gero and Rubinfine, 1955)—of the sadomasochistic primal scene that so unconsciously preoccupied her. In simultaneously identifying with both parental partners—she both inflicted and suffered penetration—it seemed she was attempting to undo her humiliating exclusion and "castration," narcissistically desexualize her object-directed libidinal wishes, and thereby, most importantly, defend against and reverse her passive oedipal impregnation fantasies. What was gradually becoming evident to the patient at this time was her intensive concerns and conflicts over impregnation, stated early on as, "I must vomit up every last bit of food in me, if I leave any in there it will grow." Indeed, when wearing her maternitylike dresses, she was often assumed by others to be pregnant.[2]

With the progression of her symptom into the transference neurosis (in the second year of treatment, thrice weekly on the couch), a rather compelling one at that, her obsession became the sadomasochistic relation with the ambivalently awed transference object, with particular focus on fellatio and oral–ocular introjection imagery. Regressive episodes, increasingly short-lived and focused around her sessions, consisting of solitary binging, vomiting, and hypersomnia were precipitated by emerging latent erotic (and maternal rivalrous) transference fantasies with their massive regression-inducing guilt, self–other vindicative rage, and narcissistic retreat, as well as disguised gratification.[3] The discovered hidden pleasure in gorging re-

[2]There is a noteworthy similarity between the fantasies resulting from primal scene overstimulation and exclusion that underly this patient's uncontrollable binging and vomiting and those reported in a seven-year-old girl with compulsive masturbation (see Geleerd, 1943).

[3]We would later learn that underlying this apparent oral regressive sleepiness was a guilt-filled transference wish to be sexually awakened by father, as well as an acting out of the lazy languor associated with the subsequent condition of pregnancy.

vealed the forbidden transference wish for genital "filling"—"I binge on food outside of here instead of allowing myself to want to take you on in here, to binge on you, to feel like an attractive sexual woman." We learned that what she was unconsciously fearful of being "caught" for, by her "mind-reading mother," was "losing control" of her murderously competitive sexual (masturbatory) wishes for father. "I want to consume him—I never realized I had such strong loving feelings for my father"; "I'd rather binge and vomit and feel sick than feel sexy"; "When I feel strong and sexy, I feel sexier than my mother—she would die"; "I want to be his favorite so badly—but then there's always Mom—it's like stabbing her in the back."

Despite a propensity for at times quite considerable action (as well as dramatic "acting") and superego resistances, the patient was intermittently able to develop the ability to tolerate and recognize as a signal her now materialized severe anxiety, as well as her previously disavowed and projected drive-fantasies.[4] This grew from the steady analysis of her acting in, her narcissistic withdrawal, and most centrally her self-punitive (defensive) submissiveness to mother and her various surrogates. This led to a gradual awareness of the underlying wishes for sexual triumph and of "someone's wife dying." She now on occasion allowed herself to ride horseback faster than her mother. The tendency remained, however, that every brief foray into feminine transference fantasies involving her father—conceived of as "getting my foot in the door"—was followed by a massive retreat into self-punitive phallic competitiveness and hostility. Dressing fashionably one day was followed by appearing as a disheveled boy the next.[5]

---

[4]The intertwining of action resistances and conversion, in Rangell's (1959) broadened meaning, has long been noted as reflecting a superego induced underdeveloped capacity for the recognition and tolerance of anxiety on a signal level. The regularity with which patients with eating symptomatology also utilize both postural and motoric acting in evidences the continuity between action and somatic expressions of unconscious fantasy. Felix Deutsch has commented that "acting in could be construed as a 'precurser' of conversion hysteria" (Zelig, 1957).

[5]An interesting and, for a time, confusing expression of the patient's autopunitive regressiveness was her intermittently feigning, unconsciously, an inability to distinguish between the experiencing and observing aspects of her ego. This resulted in *the appearance* of an insoluble erotized transference. With repeated scrutiny of the fantasies

An intensely cathected childhood memory became an equally resisted transference wish to put her head on her mother's lap for stroking and soothing. In the mother transference this was an effort to secure consolation and gender affirmation and be reassured that her "wound" will be healed and "everything will be okay when I wake up." This came to include fantasies of hungrily sucking at her mother's breast. This parallel experience of deprivation—later often turned to when faced with frustrated paternal transference wishes—served as prototype to, became intertwined with, but ultimately proved to be a screen for her deeper (i.e., more repressed) wishes to take in father's penis through her mouth. "When I feel sick I want to put my head *on* your lap—when I feel like a woman and dress nicely I want to put my head *in* your lap—that makes me uncomfortable and I sit up and giggle and enjoy the feeling for a few hours and then I go vomit—to vomit I have to eat first—I so want a baby—I want to feel full inside—to attract a man is all of my self-worth."

In time, the patient became able to identify a particular experience of "panic" to which she automatically responded with binging and purging. Significantly, this anxiety also often initiated simultaneous binges of "desperate and ferocious" clitoral masturbation. The meaning of these parallel enactments was revealed by the fantasies that regularly accompanied them. At these times the patient imagined herself a homosexual woman who had her own penis and alternately as a seductress who teasingly aroused and hurt men. These guilt-free phallic images, we learned, served as a defense against another entirely different form of profoundly guilt-filled masturbation—involving exploration of her vagina—that was associated with inner sexual longings to be gently loved by a single kindly man. These frightening and eventually masochistically endowed underlying fem-

---

that propelled these apparent ego regressions, this transference resistance was revealed to be a manifestation of her guilt-derived inhibition in exercising her full capabilities and maturity (as well as serving to gratify her masochism). Acknowledging her growing ability to both experience *and* analyze her fantasies in an abstinent arena that was generally tolerable was equated with being a healthy adult woman and associated with surpassing her mother.

inine wishes were associated with the forbidden masturbatory excitement linked to overhearing the noises of her parents' sexual activity and of seeing her father's genitals. These fiercely resisted, though ultimately in part transferentially relived fantasies were screened by her retreat to phallic masturbation and identification with the phallus.

Fundamentally, the patient's genital wishes toward father were *displaced upward,* but the resultant genitalization of the passive oral experience required further disguise which was achieved by *reversal* of the passive wish into activity through vomiting and *identifying with the penis* through the body–phallus equation. "I desire father's baby" became "I am his penis."

Accordingly, during periods of heightened resistance, the patient would defiantly bring into sessions a cup of coffee that she had been drinking. Significantly, in contrast to this defensive posture of narcissistic self-sufficiency, she would avoid at practically all costs bringing into the office any groceries she had been carrying as these appeared to be associated with the guilt-filled object-directed wish to share a full meal with me.

The interpretive undoing of the defensive competitive and castrating urges that served as a resistance to the underlying transference that was filled with bloody masochistic impregnation–parturition fantasies—initially screened by a narcissistically condensed image of violently cutting herself—was accomplished slowly and against considerable compensatory and retaliatory transference acting out and dissociative resistances. Her turn from a phallic self-image to a feminine one was initially agonizing and evoked a profound sorrow and depression. An aspect of this shift of cathexis involved episodes of profuse weeping that had previously been screened by her vomiting. This too was a defensive displacement upward that represented an active (phallic) defense against her passive genital excitement. It also reflected her melancholy (and rage) at her "pitiful state" remaining unrelieved as well as serving as a supplication for abusive attention (see Greenacre, 1945).

A particularly difficult but interesting resistance to the emergence of her oral–genital receptive transference fantasies was her periodic demands for antidepressant medication. Reinforced by her mother's insistence that she defer to her wishes and ingest these pills, the patient used this issue to regressively present herself as sick and helpless as well as to resist her fellatio–impregnation fantasies. Later, becoming able to allow herself to enjoy the sensual and femininity affirming pleasures of oral and genital sexuality, the patient had the fantasy of now proudly asserting to her mother that she in fact had found her own antidepressant—her boyfriend's penis. With that, the patient admitted to feeling appreciated and strengthened by my unwavering commitment to considering her prior pleas for pills only as a retreat from the analytic task at hand.

This transition from wishing to consume a pill to wishing to consume her boyfriend's penis, while reflecting awareness of less derivative imagery, nevertheless continued to reveal that the patient's self-esteem remained attached to a current concrete external object which kept her longings outside the infantile fantasy realm of the transference neurosis. Fears of losing the boyfriend as a safe object of displacement led to renewed states of agitation and "action symptoms" (McDougall, 1985), which included jumping off the couch, pacing the floor, and, on occasion, running from the office. Though these physically centered dramas would be recognized by her as defensive reactions to transference stimulated preconscious ideas and feeling states—initially related to "closeness" and "submission" —their diffuse, narcissistic, and *actual* quality occasionally left one with the impression that one was dealing with unstructured psychically emptying (i.e., psychosomatic) defenses against primitive preverbal affects and memories.

The dawning interpretive awareness though of the defensive basis of her tendency for immediate discharge of tension gradually led to its diminution—the employment of trial action in thought and fantasy with occasional humorous self-observations on her motoric responses to anxiety—and its replacement by a more clearly neurotic compromise resistance. The defense of hyperemotionality with dramatic affect storms rose to center stage from its prior supporting role. This was a less disruptive and destructive resistance that nevertheless similarly served to placate her harsh maternal superego through its di-

vestment of erotic–oedipal content, all the while allowing gratification through the displaced sexualized excitement. Discovering
its exhibitionistic and provoking defensive function led to the
reestablishment of a joint analyzing mode. This made way for
the coherent emergence of underlying masochistic transference
fantasies which were crystallized around a lifelong primal scene
derived rape fantasy consisting of being operated upon by her
physician father in order to heal her perceived genital "wound,"
the origin of which, it would later be indicated, was blamed on
her mother.

A similar progression of understanding took place in relation to another aspect of the patient's acting out—her telephone calling. Periodically over the course of treatment the
patient would call me between our sessions in an effort, she
said, to avoid binging. She felt that if she spoke to me while in
the erupting phase of a binge urge she would be able to avoid
it, though she did not know why. Occasionally she would call
after purging and inform me of her failure either to call me
early enough or of her overall restraint. These calls, which were
never to my increasingly fantasied-about home, had a desperate
out-of-control and suffering quality to them, though they were
never revealing of specific content nor associated with any childhood experiences. My initial impression that she was calling in
an effort to be soothed by hearing my voice seemed at first
confirmed as she later developed the practice of silently calling
my office answering machine late at night, often around a binge.
Again this behavior did not appear connected to current transference material and its increasingly frantic nature was of concern to me.

Late one Friday afternoon, after a morning session and
before the weekend break, the patient called feeling desperate
and overwhelmed by an unnamed inner feeling associated with
what she characterized as an unfillable neediness for me. She,
as usual, complained of being unsure if she could continue in
treatment in particular as she was now assuming greater finan-
cial responsibility for it. Suddenly, in the midst of a lengthy and
confused outburst of verbal and affective pleas for help, the
patient abruptly fell silent and then said in a new somewhat

coquettish tone of voice that a strange thought had just crossed her mind that she did not want to tell me. With a dramatic clearing of her frenetic neediness, she "confessed" that as we spoke she imagined that my wife was in the office and was helplessly watching and waiting while she, the patient, was stealing me from her by possessing me on the telephone. This sudden affective recognition of her apparently ever-present latent fantasy, which was directly related to current transference material and infantile memories, brought to her awareness the defensive elements in her helplessness and was a piece in her growing voluntary control over her increasingly conscious instinctual impulses. It also ended the phone calling.

The continuing analysis of the patient's regressive retreats from her receptive oedipal yearnings led to the evolution of the parallel distortions in her body image. Throughout the prolonged opening phase of treatment, relentless rageful attacks on her "fat body" were syntonic. Men's obvious interest in her attractive figure were not registered, though fiercely competitive fantasies with other women's bodies were frequent and uniformly led to submissive self-disdain. With her slowly developing ability to observe the defensive anxiety-relieving intent of her obsessions about unattractiveness and misery, the association between the warded off pleasure in her sensuality and its related guilt-filled seduction fantasies became meaningful to her. Specifically, the stimulus for attacking her "ugly body," which at times included punitively tearing at her cuticles—for the "sins of the flesh"—became centered on jealously comparing herself to other women with idealized figures. With the maturation of her symbolizing capabilities, this "other woman" became the image that stared back at her when she examined herself naked in the mirror. She "saw" her mother's less attractive body in the mirror and in defensively identifying with it needed to remain destructively preoccupied with dieting, criticizing her figure, and deferring to mother's style of dressing. "It's *her* body that I see in the mirror and it's *hers* that's too fat!" This near depersonalized disavowal of her more youthful and attractive body was a continuation of her lifelong defensive efforts to try to convince mother to buy more stylish clothes.

This was in service of undoing her own anxiety-filled wish to be more desirable to father and of being secretly more loved by him. "When I feel that my body is attractive, I must immediately take that away." With repeated working through in the transference, the patient began to be able to take pleasure in her figure, tolerate the associated transference incestuous fantasies, and appropriately enjoy her optional seductiveness. "I'm finally becoming able to feel my body and realize how important it is to me." "I hope I can make up for all the years I lost when I was binging and vomiting."

The patient's frantic urges to consume were eventually brought directly into the transference (i.e., "The only way I know how to deal with you is by throwing up"). Their analysis, along with the accompanying insistent demands for transference gratification, were central to her eventual affective recognition of the underlying sexual fantasies. Oral hunger became identified as a screen for genital arousal, and out-of-control binging began to be experienced as a regressive manifestation of the guilt-filled intent of her genital masturbatory urges and fantasies. In turn, the receptive vaginal ideation and sensations became more defined, containable (not requiring immediate masturbatory discharge), and consciously object directed. Along with considerable repression and conscious suppression, transference acting out and acting in served as a resistance to recognizing the original longings for the older brother and father of her positive Oedipus. This turn to father brought with it an intense and profoundly guilt-filled cathexis of him and a deep inner arousal and wish to permanently fill her "empty cavity" with his "huge" phallus and bear his child. "When I'm not binging I become so aware of my vagina"; "I can fill my stomach by myself—to fill my womb I need a man—but they always pull out leaving me with nothing. I can't stand that emptiness." Reflecting on this emerging ability to undo her defensive upward displacement, "When I think of my father, I want to vomit," and acknowledge her genital cathexis of father, she commented, "Around him I wish I could forget that I have a hole between my legs." Indeed, at times she experienced episodes of amnesia for her feminine transference urges, as she had initially for much of her early relationship with father.

These wishes emerged affectively as she became able to acknowledge her deeply repressed, though ultimately transferentially evoked (alternately me as prohibiting mother, and my wife), maternal rivalrous hostility. Intense destructive wishes toward mother emerged in the competition to be given precious gifts by the father and eventually in the primal scene rivalry. This permitted her to recognize the defensive elements in her identification with her perceived depressed, bitter, and unfulfilled mother, and the inhibiting fear of losing her love as she began to feel like a more healthy, vibrant, and sensual woman. It also confronted her with her overwhelming disappointment and castrating (and symptom-evoking) rage at her failure to win father.

This rejection by father, which was of both her fantasied oedipal strivings and age appropriate needs for feminine validation, was interpreted by her as confirmation of her defectiveness. This was an additional narcissistic blow to her feminine esteem, already damaged by her masochistic identification with her undervalued mother, and considerably reinforced her retreat to a compensatory phallic stance.

The analysis of the patient's early masochistic *behavior* into masochistic *fantasy* was overall the process that set in motion developmental maturation and symptom alleviation. The identification, affective draining, and canalization of her unconscious masochistic masturbatory fantasies from a syntonic acting–living out mode via the transference neurosis into observable dystonic infantile sexual imagery provided relief from her symptoms and characterologic inhibitions.

The patient's adolescence and early years of treatment were marked by a behavioral and compulsive reactivity to a wide range of inner stimuli which were, however, uniformly identified by her as originating from outside of herself. Superego prohibitions and resistances interfered with the development of the capacity for awareness of fantasy—libidinal and aggressive—all the while utilizing their energies to exact considerable suffering on their account. Binging and purging, along with

the parallel characterologic compromises, was the final masochistic common pathway that expressed the multiple components of her infantile sexuality safely hidden in syntonic activity.

The introduction of the transference figure into her repetitive, action-dominated psychic script served as the nidus for
the unfolding of the underlying object-directed fantasies, and
the narcissistic resistances to them, that drove the masochistic
enactments. In time, the patient began to repeatedly initiate
each session with dramatic detailed descriptions of her continuing misery and brutal self-abuse, which included "*ravaging* my
face." When it was possible to bring this behavior to her attention in a meaningful fashion, she too began to wonder about
its meaning and intent. A full range of sadistic and masochistic
transference fantasies were found to be contained in this resistance that was gradually replacing the prior autoerotic and
autopunitive symptomatic behavior.

Wishes to professsionally castrate me, in a phallic competitive triumph, by demonstrating by her continued sickness the
impotence of my therapeutic power emerged early. Her further
awareness of this self-punitive mechanism of disavowal of her
own vengeful rage introduced the question to her of what it
was that was provoking her anger toward me. This led to her
deepening affective experience, intermittently defended by
brief anxiety-provoked retreats into eating preoccupations, of
the painful frustration of her genital longings. Her masochistic
proclamations became recognized as a supplication, "Look what
your refusal is doing to me!" That is, it was an effort to get me
to act out with and on her while she maintained a safe defeated
stance as a nonsexual and noncompetitive woman. She could
not present herself overtly as a happy or sexy woman as this
entailed for her in fantasy the rivalrous defeat of her perceived
depressed and disaffected mother.

Ultimately, the masochistic ideation, by now almost entirely
contained in the fantasy realm, began to be experienced as an
expression of her libidinal wishes to be raped (i.e., "This is what
I want you to do to me!") and were demonstrated, from the
side of the drives, to be the etiologic regression-inducing stimulus for her violent binge–purge behavior. The growing aware-

ness of her sadomasochistic perception of primal sexuality allowed for the return of cathexes downward and the uncovering of the fantasies underlying her characterologic rigidity and, for the first time, her persisting and problematic inorgasmia. Childhood memories of frequently being the object of peer abuse emerged for the first time and as a screen allowed for the recognition of increasingly clear primal scene related affects. This led to the undoing of her insistent denial of—and therefore acted out (on herself)—parental sexual activity allowing for the fuller exploration of her murderous and masochistic primal scene fantasies. The manifest binging and purging behavior was beginning to be recognized and transferentially experienced as a compromise representation of her infantile theories of sexuality; that is, of her exciting wish to be beaten–impregnated by her powerful father just as he did to mother. This affective exploration of her masochistically colored libidinal wishes was intermittently resisted, particularly at times of disappointment (i.e., vacations), by heightened states of narcissistic pseudoindependence and aggressiveness: "I'm not going to let you get to me!" These increasingly brief regressive retreats into phallic self-sufficiency were revealed, from the side of the defenses, to be the precipitant to the symptomatic outbursts and served to ward off her positive oedipal longings, "Fighting those feelings of opening up to you is what I do when I binge and vomit." As these wishes became identified and tolerated in the transference, they became less in need of regressive disguise. This permitted the cautious emergence of her enjoyable feminine receptivity and the ability to pleasurably entertain the fantasies of being overpowered by the nonidealized, but clearly phallic man.

Through the analysis of a brief sore throat of psychic origin, and in the context of a deepening transference experience of incorporative wishes which included multiple dreams of our sharing lunch and of her being distended with food, the patient became aware of her heightened attention to her swallowing wishes. This identified oral incorporative urge emerged in conjunction with awareness of an anxiety-provoked upward displacement involving thoughts about her "wet hair." This led to

fantasies of genital wetness and receptivity which were linked
to clear images of first oral then genital impregnation.

It was through her experiential awareness of the masochistically colored genital fantasies—represented by both their
defense and wish in her repeatedly placing the couch pillow on
her abdomen and between her legs—of her wish for me to do
to her what, through displacement and narcissistic condensation, she acted out on herself, that her symptoms gradually
resolved. The compulsive vomiting was the first aspect of her
symptomatology to fall away. She had become able to become
conscious of and tolerate her forbidden desire for the exclusive
incorporative possession of father's phallus and love, and the
murderous rage borne of its frustration, and no longer needed
to defensively undo it. With the further working through of
the multiple characterologic and symptomatic compromises
formed from her infantile wishes for the death of her mother
and oedipal possession of her father, her binging behavior similarly continued to resolve. Her phallic defense of "stiffening"
while in the fantasied sexual embrace of her father gave way
to the wish to femininely open herself to him, more attractively
than mother, and take in his powerful penis.

The diffusing of the instinctual pressure from these infantile incestuous fantasies, by their entrance into consciousness,
created for her for the first time the capacity to *have a choice* as
to whether she would binge and purge. Similarly, greater desexualized and appropriate closeness with father became possible and even pursuable as a result of the diminuation of the
guilt associated with the formerly latent sexual fantasies and
their concomitant murderous intentions toward mother, who,
it is significant to note, quite independently was not without
her own considerable rivalrous feelings toward the patient.

The acknowledgment of the patient's positive oedipal strivings developed in parallel with a delicate process of self-discovery of her inner feminine longings and strengths. This
aspect of her self that had earlier been entirely denied initially
came to be conceptualized as existing only through the structuring presence of the transference object's phallic power and
excitement. This began to mature into the ability to recognize

her womanhood as a nonvisible but nevertheless clearly defined, worthwhile, and creative inner experience.

With the repeated experiencing of the pain and rage over the frustration of her transference demands for gratification, and through it the slow emergence of memories of the early wishes toward father, the patient developed the capacity to observe and hence modify her need for her original oedipal objects, or their very close derivative, and to move beyond what had been her ceaseless, albeit unconscious, quest to wait for and ultimately possess father in an all-or-nothing fashion. This initiated for the first time the late adolescent process of mourning for her lost oedipal objects. She became able to both value and attach herself to nonincestuous objects, which were now respected, at least partially, in their own right. She at first experimented with and eventually discovered the ability to open herself to an appropriate lover whom she could allow, relatively comfortably, to satisfy her sexual longings. "I have every right to date men and be happy. After all, no one is hurt by it, except my mother. I'm tired of holding myself back."

With the working through, in the third year of treatment, of the self-disdain, envy, and guilt that had inhibited the flowering of her feminine pleasures, the patient gradually ended her long self-imposed estrangement from men and began a loving relationship with an appropriate man who enjoyed her femininity and whose masculinity was pleasingly acknowledged as complimentary—"With him I feel that he's the man and I'm the woman and that feels good"; "It's a lot more fun to have sex than it is to make myself throw up." The "desperate" infantile longings that initially flowed to this new object, in particular her inhibited and inhibiting masochistic wishes, were intermittently able to be redirected back into the transference neurosis allowing for greater reality-based flexibility in her new and first "give and take" relationship with a lover. At the same time she was developing access to inner wellsprings of creativity and confidence, associated with greater conscious access to increasingly dystonic unconscious fantasy, that allowed her professional work to blossom. Competitive wishes toward women were recognized and tolerated, and urges to seduce married men, when present, were discovered to be containable as fantasy.[6]

For this patient, an exhibitionistic body-phallus identification had persisted as a component of her phallic phase with its phallic "pre-puberty ego-ideal" (Hendrick, 1964). "I want to be an extension of a man, to be his penis, to be him"; "I want to be impressive and famous with him." Men were "gods," the embodiment of phallic perfection, as well as being the objects of deeply repressed sadistic castrating impulses. For her (and apparently, her mother as well), the only solution for "castration" was body–phallic grandeur. The analysis of the phallic exhibitionistic fantasies surrounding her adolescent horse-riding championships, a dream of a penis rising up and being transformed into a stunning naked woman on display, and her own impulsive (and quite overdetermined) standing up in sessions contributed to our recognizing that initially for her, her beauty served as (ideal) phallus; her secret power to induce awe and arousal in men. This was an effort to "stand-out," to reverse her own early scoptophilic mortification and excitement, and to act as compensation (and distraction) for the privation associated with her "castration." Similarly, her homosexual fantasies consisted of her possessing a penis and thereby being able to cure mother's depression as well as finally win her love and admiration. As the now active man she also imagined, and briefly acted out, that "I could do to the woman [herself/mother] what I want a man to do to me."

It was the realization that these efforts to be a man, acted out in her phallic binging and vomiting, were a defense against

---

[6]In follow-up, after three years of treatment, the patient's required transfer to another city for professional reasons led to a premature termination leaving much accomplished and much yet unworked through in the transference neurosis. Faced by the loss of the transference object—the potential provider of the still-hoped-for baby—the patient's reawakened sense of castration led to, in compensation, an increase in the ambivalent infantile attachment to her boyfriend whose absence she would not be facing. This contributed to the contamination of that fundamentally loving relationship with feelings of bitterness displaced from her transference frustrations. At this point the patient is increasingly orgasmic, capable of heterosexual intimacy, and able to commit herself to a career independent of her mother's. The pain over her oedipal defeat, however, remains a not always observable experience.

her inner feminine longings to be loved and penetrated by the forbidden man that ultimately led to the process of resolution of her symptoms. To narcissistically possess a grand man of mother's choosing for display in order to be loved by her as her sons were, emerged as a defense against the rivalrous desire to femininely open herself to object related intimacies with a loving man of her own liking. Her continuous transferential impulsivity to vengefully arouse and seduce married men emerged similarly as an active and sadistic defense against her own guilt-filled genital arousal and masochistic longings to be "healed" by father's phallus and filled with his baby. The specifically superficial, guilt free, and somewhat demeaning sexual liaisons the patient frequently engaged in early on with disrespected men, were a product of phallic conflict in that they arose from the guilt she felt over her competitive castrating impulses and were an effort to appease the potential avenger through offering herself sexually to him. Her agonizing oedipal disappointment, lived out repeatedly, had led to the regressive compromises characteristic of the phallic phase—identifying with the phallus and seeking triumphant revenge on men. As painful and unsatisfying as this solution was, it served to avoid her profoundly guilt-filled incestuous feminine longings and frustrations that were initially displaced, reversed, projected, and acted out, but increasingly recognized as her own. With this shift from exhibitionistic–phallic to inner-vaginal awareness there emerged a parallel progression from food binging to pleasurably eating a full satisfying meal, initially associated transferentially with father and then with an appropriate lover.

For Ms. L., the continued concretization and externalization of early phallic ego ideal percursors characteristic of the phallic phase interfered with the depersonification and abstraction of the illusory penis fantasy into the maturing feminine ego ideal that initiates and accompanies the positive oedipal phase. The ongoing depreciation by mother and daughter of a "scarred" femininity, and in turn a view of oneself as a failed man, ultimately led to an inability to establish an enduring self-respectful maternal identification. As with many women who binge and purge, this patient had defensively regressed to the phallic position where an active identification with the phallus persisted as the primary regulator of her self-esteem (Jacobson, 1954; Blos, 1974). Her underlying feminine receptive fantasies had become infiltrated with a frightening masochism that was both born from guilt, and as gratifier of disguised libidinal wishes, was itself an initiator of further guilt and regression. Ultimately her acted out self-destructiveness was demonstrated to derive from an identification with the masochistic partner in a deeply repressed, masturbatory, primal scene beating (spanking) fantasy. This violent dimension to her impregnation fantasies had remained in the acting out sphere and as such led to an unsuccessful negotiation of her oedipal phase.

DISCUSSION

Psychopathology traceable to the narcissistic conflicts in phallic phase development has long been recognized as playing a central role in male and female sexual identity formation and eventual consolidation. The recognition of the differences between the sexes leads to a host of progressive and regressive methods of adaptation. In the young phallic-phase girl, the emergence of the compensatory fantasy that she possesses the organ to which she and perhaps those around her have attached such great importance is a common transient development. Its persistence, however, can interfere with the eventual acceptance of and pleasure in her feminine destiny. The turn from this fantasy of the phallic clitoris to the acknowledgment of her receptive organ is a fragile phase of development, disturbances in which can lead to the later symptomatology of eating disorders and their associated body-image distortions.

This delicate shift from a masculine–bisexual to a feminine self-concept entails as well a turn in desire, never completed, from mother to father. A continuing clingy attachment to mother, while easily mistaken for earlier oral dependency on her, is often revealed on closer examination of ancillary ego development and cathexis of triangular relationships to be a manifestation of regressive phallic closeness (Nagera, 1975). In general, it is the conflicts around these phallic fantasies, and not those of orality, that are the point of regression in the hysterical character (Krohn, 1978; Sandler quoted in Lapanche, 1974).

The continuity, usually as a regressive defense, of this masculinity complex has ramifications in the spheres of body–image development, the proportion of libidinal energy available for object relations (i.e., bisexual autoerotic vs. heterosexual alloerotic), and the capacity to acknowledge, mourn, and neutralize the anger and disappointment at the loss of the oedipal parent. These are the crucial conflictual issues for many of the higher functioning patients with eating disorders. The two major periods of life, as will be discussed, where these major shifts of developments take place are the phallic–oedipal years and puberty–adolescence. The unconscious fantasy life, and consequent behavior, of the parents usually plays a critical role in either aiding or inhibiting the child's progress through these precarious straits of psychosexual development.

Freud (1925, 1931) discovered that in response to the discovery of the anatomical differences between the sexes, the young girl's narcissism is badly damaged. Drawing upon the all or nothing greed of her earlier development, the awareness of the lack of an external, visible, and touchable genital leaves her feeling damaged, worthless, and unloved. The coping response of the young girl, and those around her, to this observation of the genital differences determines to a large extent her future relationship with her body. One of the common resultant fantasies to this perceived traumatic situation is the unconscious belief that it isn't so; that is, that she too is in possession of that valued organ. Assuming the child's ego does not respond with a gross disturbance in recognizing reality, the location of this phallus may take many forms in accordance with its now illusory properties. The development of a penetrating mind, grand ideals, or, as in the case of Ms. L., awesome beauty, may all serve as a compromise fantasy representing the compensatory phallus.

The ubiquitous body-image distortions of patients with eating disorders quite regularly can be traced to this persistent quest to have their body represent the illusory phallus. The endless and rageful demand, including tortuous exercising, that their body be "perfect," the brutal disdain for the feminine identified fullness and roundness, and the insistent regressive retreat from a feminine self-image that would express the otherwise disavowed rivalrous wishes toward mother are all easily recognizable derivatives of this body–phallus equation.

Closer examination of the patient with this fantasy reveals though more subtle qualities that demonstrate the essentially phallic nature of their body image. The idealized beauty these patients seek is in the service of attaining a narcissistic goal. As such, the superficiality in this wish to be admired defines the character of the beauty sought (Edgcumbe and Burgner, 1975). There is an emphasis on the concrete external–peripheral aspects of the body—an exteriorized organization—that derives from the exhibitionistic qualities of the phallus they unconsciously are seeking to emulate. This is evident in both the ubiquitous histories of phallic displaying activities entailing muscular hypermotility (i.e., dance, horseback riding, solo athletics), as well as in the accentuated physicality of their postured demeanor. Subtle, warm, and inner derived notions of beauty have no meaning or value to these patients as they are associated with the femininity they so disdain—in themselves and others—and seek to avoid. This is in contrast to a matured erotogeneity of the entire body that contains gracefulness, receptive openness, and object related resonance. This more developed sense of self unconsciously acknowledges the sexual differences and consequently transforms envy and awe into a sublimated exhibitionism and prideful complimentarity with the phallic oedipal father, displacing the inner vaginal cathexis onto the entire body.

The fulfillment, if it were possible, of this narcissistic wish to attain the "perfect" phallic body accordingly never leads to the hope of thereby capturing a desirable mate. In the intrapsychic world of the eating disorder patient, the existence of potential objects of desire are kept safely hidden under the repression barrier. The libidinal object related elements in this self-destructive compromise quest for narcissistic perfection are further disguised by the transformation of "love-desire into hate-desire" (Kaplan, 1984, p. 264). Accordingly, attaining phallic perfection is used to seek revenge on men—a common wish now defensively emphasized—in accordance with her unconscious belief that she has been unfairly denied a penis. These retaliatory wishes often included the intent to induce in men, by her intelligence, beauty, and so on, the same mortifying awe the girl felt toward father's perceived grandiose phallus. While teasingly parading a narcissistic self-sufficiency and sexual or intellectual rapaciousness may fulfill the revenge fantasies of some, blatantly castrating fantasies and activities of stealing are resorted to by others in an effort to "even the score" and bisexually complete a sense of self. This accounts for the common occurrence of kleptomania and its derivative clothes and shoes shopping compulsion in patients with eating disorders. This persistent instinctualization of and failure to successfully neutralize and master the phallic active facets of their character, furthermore, eliminates the possibility of their transformation into sublimated activities (i.e., work) that could further assist and strengthen the establishment of a balanced feminine sense of self.

These different types of body images, phallic or feminine, reflect the quality and balance of narcissistic versus object related energies and accordingly autoerotic versus heterosexual wishes. The defensive inclination to retroflexively turn object directed impulses on the self, so common in the binge–purge patient, includes the transformation of libidinal wishes into narcissistic preoccupations and aggressive fantasies into self-abuse. The failure to turn from the narcissistic fantasy of possessing a penis to the expectant wish to receive a baby from father results in a continuation of bisexual fantasies that underly a "defiant persistence" in clitoral masturbation (Freud, 1931), as well as "hysterical attacks in which the patient simultaneously plays both parts in the underlying sexual fantasy" (Freud, 1908, p. 166). This defensive simultaneous masculine and feminine sexual identification marks "the highest degree of complexity to which the determination of a hysterical symptom can attain, and one may therefore only expect to find it in *a neurosis which*

this regressive position of narcissistic nonrelatedness, masturbatory self-sufficiency, and divalent bisexual identification.

As one might expect the internal and external forces that encourage retreat from the positive to the negative oedipal constellation are many. In patients with eating disorders, one regularly encounters this giving up of the receptive wishes toward father with their parallel rivalrous intentions toward mother for the phallic disavowal of one's femaleness and a clingy attachment to mother. The consequent difficulties in separating from mother at this stage do not, as mentioned, represent oral level fixations, but are instead the defensive expression of the intense competitive conflicts with the oedipal mother (Nagera, 1975; Krohn, 1978). The back pressure from these regression-inducing rivalrous impulses may be augmented by earlier pregenital conflicts. Excessive residual anal level ambivalence with mother, for example, makes the move toward father more frightening by synergistically adding its earlier hostility to the destructiveness of the oedipal rivalry. In very severe cases, though, the early unbound aggression that keeps part-objects split so infuses the later oedipal images with sadism and urgency as to have them be recognizable in caricature only (penis = breast). However, most often the struggles of the oedipal triangle, with their formalized use of repression and regressive disguises, so synthesize and progressively amalgamate earlier dyadic conflicts as to take, in the treatment setting, interpretive precedence.

The underlying fantasy of the unconscious paradigms that regularly become activated with the girl's psychological entrance into a stage of erotic receptivity toward father, and the frequent stimulus for regression, often entails masochistic ideation. Through an instinctualized cognitive perception of coitus, organized around the emerging cavity erotism of her receptive genital, the girl child assumes it to be a hurtful and damaging encounter. The mastery of the sadomasochistic fantasies associated with parental sexuality will determine, to a large extent, the child's capacity to remain in and move forward from the father-directed positive oedipal position. Retreating from these stimulating and guilt-provoking rape fantasies through action defenses, which include narcissistically condensing them and acting them out on one's own body (Gero and Rubinfine, 1955; Mintz, 1983), spares the child anxiety in the short run, but sets the stage, as we shall see, for a problematic adolescence and heterosexual adaptation.

The masochistic aspects of the incestuous fantasies, whose presence is revealed in the disguise of symptomatic self-abuse and ancillary acted out provocations, are often attributed to the self-punitive guilt over the forbidden rivalrous and erotic wishes, as well as from the fantasied expectation of genital injury from father's frightening phallus. To this should be added in particular the turned on self castrating impulses directed toward the frustrating father. However, notwithstanding the recent trends toward deemphasizing the libidinal aspects of masochism, the centrality and ubiquity of the unconscious wish to be overpowered by father cannot be ignored. The exciting image of being sexually beaten by father remains a common, though fiercely defended, unconscious fantasy of most oedipal and pubertal girls (Freud, 1919; Deutsch, 1930). It normally can constitute the transition to object finding and can serve to awaken the awareness of the inner genital. It acts as a final compromise expression for the multiple drive organized fantasies stimulated by the incestuous wish though may pathologically serve to secretly maintain the oedipal tie in regressive disguise. As revealed routinely in dreams and analyses, and as Anna Freud (1923) convincingly demonstrated in a latency age child, even in situations where affectionate and romantic daydreams serve as the manifest heterosexual wish, underlying and frequently conflicted unconscious fantasies of being beaten often form the gratifying substrate. This split between the romantic and the masochistic object relation continues, as we shall see, in the woman who later develops an eating disorder. At that time it often takes the form of an overt active identification with the phallic father which conceals by reversal the covert masochistic erotic relation with him. The neutralization of these masochistic fantasies into an active pleasurable receptivity often hinges on the availability of a competent and individuated feminine mother and her genitality for identification.

The unconscious fantasy life of the parents of the oedipal child contains the same irrational fears, wishes, and distortions as their four-year-old and plays a key role in either assisting or interfering with their daughter's developmental maturation. The importance of each parent's relatively unambivalent acceptance of and pleasure in, on an unconscious level, their distinctive sexual identities cannot be overemphasized as a powerful influence on the young child's psychosexual development. Ideally, the mother takes pride in her feminine self and recognizes as worthy of respect her complimentarity with her phallic mate. This allows her to accept her daughter's developmental disappointment in her with its turn to father while remaining available, as needed, as a strengthening presence. Her mothering capacity and her anatomically modeled psychological intimacy with her husband is available for identification by the daughter and is sufficiently unconflicted as to permit the father to enjoy his daughter's flowering femininity. The father, in his more rather than less successful cathexis of his wife as a postoedipal nonincestuous object, is secure in the intactness of his genital claim on fatherhood and is therefore not in need of the pseudoreassurances of exhibitionistic phallic grandiosity or identificatory mimicry. Accordingly, he comfortably values his wife's femaleness as unique and can enjoy and affirm his daughter's receptive wishes to him with minimal anxiety-initiated abandonment or overstimulation. This affirmation as well includes reinforcement of the sublimated aspects of the daughter's phallic strivings.

While this scenario perhaps represents something of an ideal, the parents of patients who develop eating disorders usually are grossly unable to establish a nurturant climate within which their daughters can successfully claim an inner derived object related feminine self. Behaviorally, there is often a failure to protect the young child from overstimulating parental nudity and primal scene exposure, or derivative physical violence, which can reinforce the intrapsychically derived sadomasochistic primal scene fantasies as well as phallic awe (Greenacre, 1953). In addition, the fathers of these patients-to-be often express their affection toward the daughter in a regressive teasing and abusive mode that at once defends against the erotized intimacy as well as acts out the joint sadomasochistic fantasy.

Equally important is the frequently encountered maternal disdain of her own and her daughter's femininity, as well as her unresolved rivalrous wishes, which unconsciously discourages the daughter's individuating turn to her father and covertly encourages the continuity of a subservient phallic self designed to serve mother as a narcissistic extension. Mother's investment of daughter with narcissistic as opposed to object libido—varying considerably from a negative oedipal denial of her emerging sexuality to a preindividuation disavowal of her separate existence—serves to bypass for both parties the meaning of the sexual differences and hence conflicts over sexual identity and oedipal object wishes.

Father's fearful avoidance of fully cathecting his wife with his incestuous desires often leads him to turn to his oedipal daughter for the missed intimacy and genital acknowledgment. This can lead to seductive overstimulation or its opposite—denial of the daughter's emerging sexuality and a defensive reinforcement of his preference for a boy. The instinctualized failure by the father to establish generational boundaries denies the daughter the all-important opportunity to have her feminine wishes and nascent sublimations acknowledged, enjoyed, and affectively contained by him. Appropriately recognizing the power of the daughter's newly organized positive oedipal wishes creates the possibility that they will be able to be transiently desexualized in latency and tolerably disappointed and redirected in adolescence.

ADOLESCENCE

The period of transformation of the family-focused passions of the oedipal phase into the peer-directed sublimations of latency serves as a template for the later period of transition from adolescence to adulthood. Puberty–adolescence brings with it a reemergence of the oedipal desires in the context of an ego that has been enriched by the latency experience of desexualization. Thus one measure of the difference between the first five years of life and their recapitulation in the second decade is the availability of object displacements to help organize the turn away from the family toward peers and the world at large. On the side of the instincts, the adolescent stages of infantile sexuality are passed through on a different plane than earlier, based as they are ultimately on differing premises of resolution. It is the existence of physically matured and functioning genitals in adolescence that requires a new resolution for incestuous wishes that takes into account the now real capability of their being acted out and the need for sanctioned redirection outside the family unit. This phase-specific process of displacement is more precisely described as a uniquely irreversible mechanism of "object removal" (Katan, 1951). It is the successful transition from child within the family to genitally matured adult within the social world that defines the stages of adolescent development and characterizes the point of failure of future eating disorder patients. While the seeds for eating difficulties are planted in childhood, they only come to fruition with the adolescent's confrontation with the sexual and moral dilemmas brought about by their physical maturation.[7]

The turning away from infantile objects in adolescence to a search for new sexual objects does not take place without a major reorganization of self concept and, in particular, a new

[7]The emphasis on adolescence as a reworking of earlier infantile schemata is not to suggest a linear process of recapitulation. The suggestion by some that adolescence is a simple repetition of an earlier separation–individuation phase, "as though [adolescents] were larger, more sexually active infants who need once again to 'separate' from their parents" (Kaplan, 1984, p. 16), in my view does a disservice to the complex web of phase specific passions, strivings, and potentialities that at times so entangle the maturing young adult. Theoretically and clinically denying the genitality of the adolescent may often be a sign of counterresistance in the therapist and has been noted to arise from feelings of stimulation toward and envy of youth's erotic vitality. As Kaplan notes, the eating disorder patient "is not an infant struggling with issues of separation–individuation, but an adolescent trying to come to terms with genitality" (1984, pp. 259, 81–100). Similarly, Behn-Eschenburg (1935) concludes that it is in those young women who appear only to be struggling with a mother-fixation, that more careful study reveals that an early oedipal constellation is present and impacting the apparent dyadic relationship. [For a detailed discussion of eating disorder patients' use of dyadic separation issues to screen triadic sexual conflicts, see Tabin (1985, pp. 183–277.)]

relationship with one's body. The idealization of parents must give way to a transient hypercathesis of one's self that includes an acknowledgment of the new genital capacities. Accordingly, a period of heightened narcissism sets in that, when unobstructed, sets the stage for future object relatedness that contains both positive self-regard and the capacity for loving heterosexuality.

This period of narcissistic self-cathexis acts as a protective withdrawal from the earlier power and influence of the idealized parents and serves as a focal point for maturation of all the psychic structures. When buoyed by earlier successful developmental transitions and unencumbered by either external trauma or parental regressive influences, this period of self-involvement creates the capacity to canalize infantile narcissism, use fantasy as a bridge to object relatedness, and sufficiently neutralize instinctual demands as to be able to tolerate the anxiety of intrapsychic conflict. Accordingly, from the side of the ego, this period of intensified narcissism can serve progressive forces, and includes the discovery of the use of metaphor to safely transform body-derived instinctual pressures into postrepression ideation and creativity. Rigid asceticism needs to mature into comfortably ambivalent inspiration. These capacities, lacking in many eating disorder patients, depend as Hartmann noted (1950), on the availability of relatively neutralized, as opposed to still sexualized and aggressivized, energy as a source of "fuel" for this period of narcissistic nurturance and incubating autonomy. In addition, superego prohibitions must yield and recoalesce around accepting the adolescent's turning away from and mourning the idealized parents (i.e., fantasied parricide) and the lifting of repression sufficiently to permit the acting out of sexual wishes with objects recognized as nonincestuous. The evolving superego of the adolescent must come to be imbued with "clemency and tenderness" (Harley, 1961) that derives from its increasing independence from its instinctual origins and which permits the marshaling of the emerging aggressive and masochistic energies into ego expansion and enrichment and the organization of diffuse genital pressures into a coherent orgastic capacity.

In parallel with superego development, ego ideal maturation also characterizes the adolescent process. Accordingly, through the late adolescent girl's desexualization of the homoerotic aspects of her preliminary bisexuality, early concrete, personified, and quite regularly pallocentric ideals give way to aspirations that are abstracted, gender affirming, and link the young adult to the realistically valued and historically bound ethos of the tolerably imperfect community at large. The adolescent ego ideal that is initially phallic develops into one that is feminine, transforming the early imitative idealizations of the phallus into sublimated paternal identifications that can become available for the ego itself.

From the perspective of libidinal development, the narcissistic withdrawal from the mental representation of the parents leads to a reencounter with the bisexuality reminiscent of the earlier phallic phase of development. It is well known that in the young adolescent boy this increase in self-involvement leads to narcissistic object choices based on a wish to possess the idealized aspects of himself that he identifies in the other. Less recognized is the parallel development in the adolescent girl where this crucial stage of heightened narcissism leads to "a perseverance in the bisexual position with an attending overvaluation of the phallic component" (Blos, 1962, p. 89). This is the period, in my view crucial to the adolescent manifestation of an eating disorder, where the

> [I]llusory penis is maintained as a psychic reality in order to protect the girl against narcissistic depletion; and equality with boys is still a question of life and death. Bisexual representation with more or less vague perception of the body finds an expression in all sorts of activities, interests, preoccupations, and daydreams. This condition continues to exist until the girl deflects onto her whole body that part of narcissistic libido which was attached to the bisexual body image, and seeks completion not within herself, but in heterosexual love [Blos, 1962, p. 86].

The pathological continuity of the regressive narcissism of

the bisexual illusory penis fantasy inhibits the full development of and acts as a point of regression from an object-seeking, inner genital cathexis that perceives the entire body as a source for complimentary heterosexual pleasure giving and receiving. In the patient destined to develop an eating disorder, this prolongation of adolescence becomes libidinized and fiercely maintained. Progression into full positive oedipal ideation is avoided, in deference to the perceived retaliatory mother, and the body is regressively turned to in a concretized mode in an effort to deny the existence of the mature genital and its development into a potential receptacle for father's penis. Defensively, the binge–purge patient transforms sexual excitement and its imagery into obsessional thinking insistently focused on manifestly oral concerns and a regressive narcissistic pursuit of externalized perfection. This in essence serves to "save the vagina for father." Progressive turning to peer relations is reversed as the eating disorder patient retreats from burgeoning sexuality to a childlike (specifically early latency) overinvolvement with the functioning of the body and with the family. With the arrested maturation of the adolescent's psychic structure, there is a failure to develop a harmonious "intensification of inner life" (Deutsch, 1944, p. 277) as a result of a persistent turn to narcissism to protect against the emergence of intolerable masochistic fantasy.[8]

On a clinical level one regularly encounters the loss of a boyfriend activating binging and purging behavior. This typically does not derive from restimulated failed mourning for the oedipal father. With many patients, the missing boyfriend signifies the absence of the narcissistically possessed idealized penis—castration in the bisexual fantasy—and precipitates depression and a literal return to a body-phallus identification in a desperate rageful quest for narcissistic compensation (i.e., the ego ideal of *being* the penis). Regressively, loss of love equals

---

[8]The young woman's assumption of a phallic self may serve not only as a defensive retreat from the receptive feminine longings of the positive oedipal engagement. In the more disturbed patient, a masculine self-concept also may act as a progressive psychic stabilizing repudiation of a passivity that is linked to an engulfing symbiosis with a perceived malignant preoedipal mother.

castration, a tension state for which there is no tolerance. This possession of the boyfriend for exhibitionistic purposes reenacts the patient's own partly soothing past of being a parental appendage and is an aspect of their ongoing effort to spare themselves the mortification associated with experiencing the sexual differences. This leads to the necessity to deny the boyfriend as a separate phallic object which would in turn evoke castrating and masochistic impulses. It also avoids endowing him with oedipal cathexes which would unconsciously signal triumph and provoke the rivalrous wrath of the oedipal mother.

In these cases the early adolescent narcissistic investment in the body fails to act as a nidus for the progressive elaboration of a finalized object-related sexual identity and instead:

> [T]here is an unconscious rejection of the sexual body and an accompanying feeling of being passive in the face of demands coming from one's own body, with the result that one's genitals are ignored or disowned or, in the more severe cases, the feeling that they are different from what one wanted them to be. It is a breakdown in the process of integrating the physically mature body image into the representation of oneself [Laufer and Laufer, 1984, p. 22].

Accordingly, the common tendency in eating disorder patients to concentrate their concerns about their body into a preoccupation with a localized ounce of fat serves to bypass awareness of the underlying difficulty in accepting their femininity. As Blos noted (1941), the conflict involving the differences between the sexes becomes condensed and concretized in this ostensibly controllable "defect." Under the insisted upon belief that all that is needed is greater control over one's eating, the expectation is supported that an external physical change will solve the underlying conflict in gender identification.

Metaphoric fantasy formation which ordinarily serves as a bridge from auto- to alloerotism and bisexual undifferentiated to polarized heterosexual body image is developed, in part, from the practiced transformation of trial actions into mental ideation. Adolescent masturbation, through the vehicle of the masturbatory fantasy, ideally serves as a synthesizer of earlier pregenital impulses and a facilitator of genitally organized fantasies and wishes. It serves to integrate the mental image of permissible derivatives of the oedipal objects with the associated drives thereby establishing the primacy of genital fantasy in the context of heterosexual object relatedness. Through this trial shifting of mental images and their cathexis in the setting of tolerable masturbatory excitement, adolescent masturbation paves the way for the all-important centrifugal turn from narcissistic self-sufficiency to object related expectancy. It also helps form the capacity to contain in fantasy the derivative instinctual and self-punitive wishes that enjoy an adolescent phase specific tendency to be acted out.

In the eating disorder patient, in contrast, based on the earlier failure of phallic-oedipal differentiation, there is an inability to use masturbation and the accompanying fantasies to integrate a distinctive sexual identification. The repetitive displacement of the masturbatory activity upward taking food as its object signals not just a phobic avoidance of the genitals, though it is that as well, but a wholesale retreat from the acknowledgment of sexual excitement and fantasy. The desperately wished for control over hunger in the bulimic patient is an effort to tame the emergent inner erotic sensations that link her to her masturbatory fantasies of primal scene sexuality and her associated unconscious fantasies of being penetrated by father. In its stead, she defensively turns to her own body as if it were an "object from which satisfaction flows toward the self" (Spiegal, 1959, p. 101).

Spiegal's patient, like Ms. L., would have a burst of compulsive masturbatory activity as a form of tension regulation whenever passive feminine fantasies came to the fore. In her self-described effort at those times to make herself into a penis, she was not substituting masturbation for intercourse, but under superego pressure was replacing the object with her genital as a source of satisfaction. Accordingly, a more precise understanding of the commonly identified masturbatory equivalence of binge–purge activity is that it represents a displacement of compulsive clitoral–phallic (bisexual) masturbation, where the individual is simultaneously subject and object, active and passive, male and female, and which is itself a protest and defense against receptive vaginal object cathexes and ideation. In the eating disorder patient, masturbatory behavior and fantasies organized around the intrapsychic meaning of the vagina are fiercely resisted in an effort to deny their relation with the internal oedipal objects from which they are derived. Inner desire is defensively deflected outward and upward culminating in a phallic identification. The only orifice permitted a receptive erotic cathexis is the mouth; hence the ubiquitous sexual/orgasmic dysfunctions. The anatomical distinction implied between types of masturbation derives not at all from the unabstracted question of clitoral versus vaginal orgasm. What is at issue is the unconscious sexual self-concept of the individual as it emerges from the acknowledgment, or lack thereof, of fully matured and fantasy endowed heterosexually polarized genitals.

The failure to mentally integrate the vagina and uterus with the clitoris into an inner sexual center of gravity leaves no receptacle to metaphorically contain the wished-for baby from father. Without the experience of this object orienting frustration and emptiness, there is little capacity to unconsciously coalesce impregnation fantasies into a feminine identity and little motivation to seek out nonincestuous objects. The eating disorder patient is not unique for the presence of incestuous impregnation wishes; indeed, they are ubiquitous and a part of normal development. What characterizes these patients and leads these fantasies to become concretized in their disguise and expressed motorically is their inability to unconsciously integrate them in the fertile container of a receptive genitality which would form the basis for a postoedipal identification with an individuated feminine mother. Precluded as well is the neutralizable experience of taking father inside which can provide an inner locus for mature paternal identifications and an active relatedness to the outside world. What is truly missing is a fully developed capacity for masturbatory fantasy which would allow the incestuous impregnation wish to be unconsciously acknowledged and syntonic and thereby orient the late adolescent toward femininity and oedipal displacements.

This turn to the surface of the body to somatically manifest drive organized fantasies more properly belonging to an inner located metaphoricized terrain leads to an inability to tolerate instinctual tension and a tendency toward action. Clinically, the emergence of even distant derivatives of a positive oedipal transference, including sensations of closeness, submission, and disappointment, regularly activate action resistances that include reversing the drive and taking the body as its object. This subjects the transference wish to the same defensive narcissistic condensation as the original longings for father. Not only does this keep erotic masochistic and maternal rivalrous wishes out of awareness, and outside of treatment, but a process is created that permanently bypasses acknowledgment of the oedipal defeat. The defensive autoerotic bisexual identification of the bulimic patient short-cuts coming to terms with the object related frustration of the reality principle (Freud, 1911), which includes the reality of primal scene exclusion, and thereby fails to liberate the anger of disappointment that would serve to stimulate the capacity for sublimation and a turn toward nonincestuous objects.

In eating disorder patients the unconscious persistence of the attachment to the oedipal father occurs through the relationship with the erotized sadistic superego. In addition, as Sachs noted (1929), the girl often denies the genital loss of father by regressively turning to him with her oral longings, as in compulsive eating, in an effort to incorporatively make him part of herself. This paternal imitation, originating as it does in the phallic phase, serves to blur the dichotomy of the oedipal object and subject, interferes with the integration of libidinal masochistic object wishes, and leaves her indefinitely at the mercy of a perceived retaliatory rivalrous mother.

Without some measure of acknowledged disappointment at the failure to unconsciously possess father over mother with at least a partial renunciation of the oedipal bond, there is no possibility for autonomy, self-responsibility, and a life free from inexhaustible punishment (Loewald, 1979). The adolescent reencounter with the Oedipus complex must, if a final sexual organization is to be reached, entail the unconscious recognition of the wish for and failure to achieve the incestuous relation in the context of a clearly defined genitally polarized sexual identity. The failure to achieve supremacy in the universal incest dilemma entails a gradual process of vacillating and painful detachment as opposed to the less finalizing, preemptive and abrupt withdrawal often leading to a reactive narcissism, which is ubiquitously observed in eating disorder patients. The loss of father must be slowly mourned and the attachment neutralized and directed outward toward a new nonincestuous object with whom one ideally finds a reincarnated love born from the earlier period of passion.

Similarly, unconscious matricidal wishes must be freed from their self-destructive inverted oedipal clinginess to become integrated into an identification with a respected fully genital mother. The regressive quest for narcissistic phallic "perfection" must give way, ideally under the guidance of a nondepressed and nonenvious mother, to a sense of heterosexual competence based on a right to possess her own mature genital. Late adolescence, if an eating disorder is to be avoided, must lead the daughter to the "full realization of the vagina as an organ of pleasure—an exchange of the desire for a penis for the real and equally valuable possession of a vagina" (Deutsch, 1925, p. 405). The hard fought for cathexis of this valued inner genital—the "whole ego in miniature"—serves as a protective nucleus against external and internal forces that would symptomatically and characterologically distort the woman's psychogenetic heritage of unconscious fantasies and deny her access to the richness of her femininity.

The growing numbers of young women with eating disorders who manifest the failure to successfully integrate their genitality into postincestuous object relatedness has led many to look for recent cultural influences that may be contributing to what some see as an "epidemic." In light of the proposed neurosogenic mechanism involving the regression to a conflicted phallic-narcissistic body image, it is worth noting that in 1933, in describing this very condition, Reich reported that at that time this condition was rarely found in women, though mostly in "productive women" (p. 219). In the clinical material presented, this patient's initial rejection of her vagina and child-bearing urges was associated with perceived cultural demands to be an "important modern woman," that is, to be phallic. It is conceivable that recent increased social obligations on women to succeed at traditionally defined male tasks may, as an unfortunate side effect, have a tendency to reinforce the intrapsychic back pressure on positive oedipal wishes to phallic strivings.

This formulation provides the intrapsychic mechanism by which the cultural influences reported by phenomenologic investigators (Garner, Garfinkel, and Olmstead, 1983; Silverstein, Perdue, and Peterson, 1986) may contribute to individual psychopathology. These researchers suggest that the decreasing specificity of sex role definitions in recent years has led to the availability of a wider and less polarized range of identifications for the adolescent girl. While liberating for those who do not require strict social guidelines, for the predisposed fragile adolescent who is in need of persistent external sex specific strictures for her femininity, that is, in the young woman who remains defensively mired in her earlier unconscious bisexuality, this lack of cultural rigidity may contribute to a developmental crisis where the body becomes the focal point for the struggle with conflicting gender identifications.

While social forces cannot in and of themselves cause a neurosis, they can through the medium of unconscious family assumptions and consequent child-rearing practices subtly reinforce one or more otherwise fluid facets of psychosexual development leading to a distorted final feminine adaptation. The apparently increasing continuity into adult life of the infantile paradigms of the phallic phase is demonstrated by the recent behavioral psychology research that finds that a woman with a curvaceous figure is perceived by other women as being less intelligent and less competent (Silverstein et. al., 1986). This current cultural idealization of the phallic woman makes the developmental transition from the masculine–bisexual to the feminine—already "the hardest task in the libidinal development of the woman" (Deutsch, 1925)—an even more difficult developmental step and may be contributing to the widespread occurrence of eating disorders in young women today. The self-respecting and object-relating woman with an autonomous superego, strong and effective ego, and vibrant feminine ego ideal, who can work productively and has an expansive sexuality—the "female 'vaginal' character" (Jacobson, 1937)—is only beginning to prevail.

REFERENCES

Behn-Eschenburg, H. (1935), The antecedents of the Oedipus complex. *Internat. J. Psycho-Anal.*, 16:175–185.
Blos, P. (1941), *The Adolescent Personality*. New York: D. Appleton-Century.
——— (1962), *On Adolescence*. New York: Macmillan.
——— (1974), The genealogy of the ego ideal. *The Psychoanalytic Study of the Child*, 29:43–88. New Haven, CT: Yale University Press.
Deutsch, H. (1925), The psychology of woman in relation to the functions of reproduction. *Internat. J. Psycho-Anal.*, 6:405–418.
——— (1930), The significance of masochism in the mental life of women. *Internat. J. Psycho-Anal.*, 11:48–60.
——— (1944), *Psychology of Women*, Vol. 1. New York: Grune & Stratton.
Edgcumbe, R., & Burgner, M. (1975), The phallic-narcissistic phase. *The Psychoanalytic Study of the Child*, 30:161–180. New Haven, CT: Yale University Press.
Fraiberg, S. (1972), Some characteristics of genital arousal and discharge in latency girls. *The Psychoanalytic Study of the Child*, 27:439–475. New Haven, CT: Yale University Press.
Freud, A. (1923), The relation of beating-phantasies to a day dream. *Internat. J. Psycho-Anal.*, 4:89–102.
Freud, S. (1908), Hysterical fantasies and their relation to bisexuality. *Standard Edition*, 9:159–166. London: Hogarth Press, 1959.
——— (1911), Two principles of mental functioning. *Standard Edition*, 12:218–226. London: Hogarth Press, 1958.
——— (1919), A child is being beaten. *Standard Edition*, 17:179–204. London: Hogarth Press, 1955.
——— (1925), Some psychical consequences of the anatomical distinction between the sexes. *Standard Edition*, 19:248–258. London: Hogarth Press, 1961.
——— (1931), Female sexuality. *Standard Edition*, 21:225–243. London: Hogarth Press, 1961.
Garner, D., Garfinkel, P., & Olmstead, M. (1983), An overview of sociocultural factors in the development of anorexia nervosa. In: *Anorexia Nervosa: Recent Developments in Research*, ed. P. Darby, P. E. Garfinkel, D. M. Garner, & D. V. Coscina. New York: Alan R. Liss, pp. 65–82.

Geleerd, E. (1943), The analysis of a case of compulsive masturbation in a child. *Psychoanal. Quart.*, 12:520–540.

Gero, G., & Rubinfine, D. (1955), On obsessive thoughts. *J. Amer. Psychoanal. Assn.*, 3:222–243.

Greenacre, P. (1945), Pathological weeping. *Psychoanal. Quart.*, 14:62–75.

—— (1950), Special problems of early female sexual development. *The Psychoanalytic Study of the Child*, 5:122–138. New York: International Universities Press.

—— (1952), Anatomical structure and superego development. In: *Trauma, Growth and Personality*. New York: International Universities Press, pp. 149–164.

—— (1953), Penis awe and its relation to penis envy. In: *Emotional Growth*, Vol. 1. New York: International Universities Press, pp. 31–49.

Harley, M. (1961), Some observations on the relationship between genitality and structural development at adolescence. *J. Amer. Psychoanal. Assn.*, 9:434–460.

Hartmann, H. (1950), Comments on the psychoanalytic theory of the ego. *The Psychoanalytic Study of the Child*, 5:74–96. New York: International Universities Press.

Hendrick, I. (1964), Narcissism and the prepuberty ego ideal. *J. Amer. Psychoanal. Assn.*, 12:522–528.

Horney, K. (1926), The flight from womanhood: The masculinity complex in women, as viewed by men and women. *Internat. J. Psycho-Anal.*, 7:324–339.

Jacobson, E. (1937), Ways of female superego formation and the female castration concept. *Psychoanal. Quart.*, 45:525–538, 1976.

—— (1954), The self and the object world. *The Psychoanalytic Study of the Child*, 9:75–127. New York: International Universities Press.

Kaplan, L. (1984), *Adolescence—The Farewell to Childhood*. New York: Simon & Schuster.

Katan, A. (1951), The role of displacement in agoraphobia. *Internat. J. Psycho-Anal.*, 32:41–50.

Kohon, G. (1984), Reflections on Dora: The case of hysteria. *Internat. J. Psycho-Anal.*, 65:73–84.

Krohn, A. (1978), *Hysteria: The Elusive Neurosis*. New York: International Universities Press.

LaPlanche, J. (1974), Panel on "Hysteria Today." *Internat. J. Psycho-Anal.*, 55:459–469.

Laufer, M., & Laufer, M. E. (1984), *Adolescence and Development Breakdown*. New Haven, CT: Yale University Press.

Loewald, H. (1979), The waning of the Oedipus complex. *J. Amer. Psychoanal. Assn.*, 27:751–775.

McDougall, J. (1985), *Theaters of the Mind: Illusion and Truth on the Psychoanalytic Stage*. New York: Basic Books.

Mintz, I. (1983), Psychoanalytic description: The clinical picture of anorexia nervosa and bulimia. In: *The Fear of Being Fat: The Treatment of Anorexia Nervosa and Bulimia*, ed. C. P. Wilson, C. Hogan, & I. Mintz. New York: Jason Aronson, pp. 83–114.

Nagera, H. (1975), *Female Sexuality and the Oedipus Complex*. New York: Jason Aronson.
Rangell, L. (1959), The nature of conversion. *J. Amer. Psychoanal. Assn.*, 7:632–662.
Reich, W. (1933), *Character Analysis*. New York: Simon & Schuster.
Ritvo, S. (1977), Adolescent to woman. In: *Female Psychology—Contempory Psychoanalytic Views*, ed. H. Blum. New York: International Universities Press, pp. 127–137.
Sachs, H. (1929), One of the motive factors in the formation of the superego in women. *Internat. J. Psychiat.*, 10:39–50.
Silverstein, B., Perdue, L., & Peterson, B. (1986), Possible causes of the thin standard to bodily attractiveness for women. *Internat. J. Eat. Disord.*, 5 5:907–916.
Sperling, M. (1973), Conversion hysteria and conversion symptoms: A revision of classification and concepts. *J. Amer. Psychoanal. Assn.*, 21:745–771.
Spiegal, L. (1959), The self, the sense of self and perception. *The Psychoanalytic Study of the Child*, 14:81–109. New York: International Universities Press.
Sprince, M. (1984), Early psychic disturbances in anorexic and bulimic patients as reflected in the psychoanalytic process. *J. Child Psychother.*, 10 2:199–215.
Tabin, J. (1985), *On the Way to Self—Ego and Early Oedipal Development*. New York: Columbia University Press.
Zelig, M. (1957), Acting in. A contribution to the meaning of some postural attitudes observed during analysis. *J. Amer. Psychoanal. Assn.*, 5:685–706.

Chapter 10

A Psychoanalytic Study of Bulimia and Pregnancy

DANIEL B. GESENSWAY, M.D.

[I]t is impossible to eat with disgust and pleasure at the same time (p. 89).

vomiting [is] a substitute for moral and physical disgust (p. 131).   Freud (1895)

INTRODUCTION

Before Freud formulated the technique and theory of psychoanalysis, he discovered that the key to an understanding of a symptom lay in the elucidation of an unconscious conflict. In his detailed case study of Frau Emmy von N., Freud (1895) wrote that anorexia, a form of inhibition, "depends on the presence of affectively-toned and unresolved associations which are opposed to linking up with other associations, and particularly with any that are incompatible with them." Emmy ate so little food "because she did not like the taste, and she could not enjoy the taste because the act of eating had from the earliest times been connected with memories of disgust whose sum of affect had never been to any degree diminished. . . ." (p. 89).

When Freud (1895) wrote that symptoms are "memories of pains" (p. 90), he had not yet uncovered other important cornerstones of psychoanalysis: infantile mental life, psycho-

299

sexual development, and the theory of unconscious wishes. All of these concepts were to become important in elucidating the complexities of the incompatible ideas that occur in the eating disorders.

In the case of Mrs. H., from which I am reporting, her disgust at eating occurred in the familiar bulimic pattern of binging and vomiting. The feeling of disgust associated with her vomiting was separated by a time interval from the feeling of pleasure derived from stuffing herself. Freud's preanalytic observation appears to have stood the test of time: incompatible unconscious associations lie at the heart of the riddle of disturbed eating patterns that are not organically based. Mrs. H.'s chronic pattern of secret binging and vomiting was interrupted by a pregnancy that effectively cured the patient of the symptom, only to have the pattern of behavior return when it became necessary to wean her infant. I shall trace some of the "incompatible associations" that contributed to this problem.

GENERAL CONSIDERATIONS OF DIAGNOSIS

The syndrome of bulimia consists in episodes of binge eating followed by purging, usually by induced vomiting. It occurs predominantly in well-educated, middle- and upper-class women who rarely show significant deviations from normal weight even though their minds are obsessed with food, diets, exercise, and weight. Bulimics are above average in scholastic and occupational achievement and bulimia is common among nurses, dietitians, social workers, and female doctors (Kalucy, Gilcrist, McFarlane, and McFarlane, 1985). The binge–vomiting behavior may be carried out for years, often in complete secrecy, with little apparent physical harm. Nearly all investigators agree with the view articulated by Bruch (1985) that the syndrome of bulimia is not basically a disturbance of the eating function, but reflects underlying personality disturbances. Difficulty in interpersonal relationships, drug abuse, stealing, and promiscuity are frequently associated problems.

Many different terms have been introduced in the contemporary literature on bulimia. *Bulimia nervosa* (Russell, 1979), *bulimarexia* (Boskind-Lodahl and White, 1978), and *dysorexia* (Guiora, 1967) all describe variations of the same clinical picture. Many typical cases do not clearly conform to either anorexia or bulimia. Anorexia occurs in a younger population, and bulimia may, in some cases, be preceded by a period of anorexia. Bulimics are more sexually active than anorexics, and they are often married. Depression is more often reported with bulimia, but, unlike anorexia, suicide and death from complications are not characteristic of bulimics.

There does not appear to be good reason to distinguish rigorously between the syndromes of bulimia and anorexia on the basis of psychodynamic evidence. While the symptom picture in these two syndromes can be strikingly different, and *The Diagnostic and Statistical Manual* (1980) of the American Psychiatric Association (DSM-III) gives specific criteria for the diagnosis of each, anorexia and bulimia may simply represent two sides of the same coin. There is no consensus in the literature that these clinical syndromes are separate illnesses, and the dynamic picture so far suggests a continuum (Fenichel, 1945; Guiora, 1967; Sours, 1974; Kalucy, Crisp, Lacey, and Harding, 1977). Some authors emphasize that eating disturbances are only symptom pictures and as such may occur in a wide spectrum of diagnoses (Fenichel, 1945; Risen, 1982). Bruch (1985) challenges the concept of bulimia as a diagnostic category at all, and Rich (1978) claims to have been unable to find any reported cases that conformed to the then newly proposed diagnostic category of bulimia in DSM-III.

Fenichel (1945) is one of the few who links the eating disorders with the rituals of normal mental life. He has observed, for example, that bulimia is "institutionalized in the form of funeral repasts, reminiscent of the totem festivals of savages. . . ." This "comes within the limits of normal grief," and "unconsciously means the idea of eating the dead person. . . ." (p. 349). The refusal of food, which also occurs in normal mourning, means the rejection of this idea.

THE BULIMIC EPIDEMIC

Many investigators, such as Bruch (1985), are impressed with the great increase in the number of reported cases of anorexia since 1960. In more recent years, the statistical evidence points to an epidemic of bulimia among young women. Rosen and Leitenberg (1985) estimate that between 5 and 10 percent of college women in the United States are binging and vomiting regularly. In a survey of college students by Halmi, Falk, and Schwartz (1981), using DSM-III criteria, 13 percent of a normal college population was found to have experienced all the major symptoms of bulimia. Of this group, 87 percent was female, a figure consistent with most other reports.

The epidemic idea is probably exaggerated. The apparent spectacular increase in the incidence of anorexia and bulimia is more likely to be the result of new diagnostic considerations as well as changes in social and cultural attitudes and alterations in life-styles that have followed advances in health and medicine. Bulimia and anorexia can hardly be regarded as new phenomena; both were described in sixteenth century medical literature. The morbid, canine hunger of bulimia was, even then, associated with the mentally ill, but the word *bulimia* was also used when referring to any piggish, or doglike, appetite.

Eating disturbances are important signs and symptoms in a great many medical conditions. In the preantibiotic era, infectious diseases, especially tuberculosis and syphilis, wasted the body of the patient as his appetite and resistance to disease diminished. Undoubtedly, many cases of anorexia nervosa were not diagnosed earlier in this century because they were indistinguishable from infectious diseases, diabetes, endocrine disorders, pernicious anemia, and vitamin deficiencies. Death by *cachexia,* a term commonly used to describe general poor health, with weakness and malnutrition, was common. *Chlorosis,* a kind of iron deficiency anemia usually affecting girls at puberty and giving the skin a greenish pallor, "vividly described by careful observers before 1900 . . . has mysteriously disappeared" (Brown, 1979). The mystery can be explained away by the dramatic improvements in diet that have occurred in this century, notably, iron-enriched bread and vitamin D-enriched milk. Many of the clinical findings of iron deficiency anemia are to be found in cases of psychoneuroses: fatigue, breathlessness, headache, irritability, palpitations, dizziness, and "multiple gastrointestinal complaints such as anorexia, pyrosis, flatulence, nausea, eructation, and constipation are common. . . ." (p. 1748). It seems most likely that cases of anemia and neurosis were often indistinguishable in the not-too-distant past.

The apparent increase in bulimia may reflect modern ideas about weight and nutrition as well as the increasing public awareness of matters pertaining to health. The term *bulimia* does not appear in standard textbooks of medicine until 1985 when Russell used it in an article. Until the middle of this century, thinness was evidence of poverty, not success; and to be poor meant increased morbidity from disease, especially the infectious ones. The signs of a happy and affluent man in the nineteenth century were his paunch, his fat wife, and his chubby children. Freud (1900) describes a woman whose vomiting was an unconscious way of making herself unattractive (p. 570), quite the reverse of today's woman who "fears fat" (Wilson, 1982).

FOOD, HUNGER, AND FAT

It must be remembered that food fads and diet rituals, as well as concerns over body shape, body hair, complexion, and bowel functions are part of the normal and usual behavior in all human beings. The anorexic and bulimic simply borrow on these commonly held attitudes and beliefs. Food, for them, is a vehicle for the expression of unconscious impulses and attitudes.

Food, and hunger for food, is either unconsciously hated and rejected because it symbolizes things dirty, painful, or evil (mother's poisonous milk, feces, penis), or it is a threat because it is too desirable (Fenichel, 1945; Boris, 1984a,b). Most patients have observed in themselves that the urge to overeat differs from the sensations of true hunger. One patient aptly described it: "It is not hunger. Hunger is a feeling of a gap inside you.

You eat something small to stop that feeling. I go on eating after I've satisfied that hunger. I want to keep on eating until I feel full—it's the final limit—you can then eat no more" (Russell, 1979, pp. 436–437).

By extension, all of the attitudes about food become manifest in ideas about fat. For the adolescent girl special meanings are attributed to fat in relation to the bodily changes and emotions occurring with each menstrual cycle. The bulimic woman may be repeating in her purging the experience of her menstrual period when the menstrual flow from the body brought relief from feelings of bloating and tension. "The fat-making dirt is pouring out; now I am slim again, and will be a good girl and not eat too much" (Fenichel, 1945; see also Sperling, 1968). Hatred of their mothers expressed by bulimic women is often specifically directed at mother's fat, her breasts, and her special role as the bearer of babies. All things feminine are associated with a disagreeable inner tension that demands and rejects food at the same time.

An adolescent patient in a study by Strober and Yager (1985) said, "I can't stand the way I look; how can you sit there and tell me I'm not fat? You're supposed to help me, not torture me" (p. 367). Such vignettes are common. The patient sees herself as fat, not the therapist or others. One of Russell's patients (1979) said, "If I can see my ribs it makes me feel happier" (p. 440). *Fat* is a metaphor for something wrong with herself; it is self-directed, not a general espousal of thinness for everyone. This is consistent with the finding that the majority of bulimics are within a normal range of weight.

The Female Predominance

There are very few attempts, especially in the nonpsychoanalytic literature, to account for the single most striking fact about bulimia and anorexia. Namely, that it is overwhelmingly a disease of women. Most of the causal theories proposed apply equally to both males and females. Bruch (1985), for example, cites the absence of consistent need fulfillment in infancy as the cause that "deprives the developing child of the essential groundwork for 'body identity'. . . ." (p. 13). Wilson's conclusion (1982) seems not very helpful when he writes, "This prevalence . . . in women . . . is caused by developmental differences in the female superego and maternal ego ideal. . . ," and then says that "anorexia nervosa is caused primarily by the female's unique superego structure" (p. 253). Guiora (1967) suggests that the little girl must identify with her mother for successful development, while boys can weather early maternal deprivation through identification with the father. He believes that maternal deprivations lead to defects in the girl's ego structure that later arrest her feminine development in adolescence, evoking the oral fixations seen in anorexia and bulimia.

Such formulations, while simple and appealing, fail to distinguish between the actual experiences of the child and their intrapsychic representations in the developing mind of the child. Not all severely orally deprived girls become anorexic or bulimic, and it is notable how many of these patients come from families that have been anything but deprived, at least materially. Though there is no question that emotional scarring and pregenital fixations are prominent in these patients, little boys are just as susceptible to maternal deprivations, yet only about 10 percent of cases occur in males.

It appears that the dynamic factors that lead to the eating disorders in women are not simple at all, but exceedingly varied and complex, and that they touch on nearly every aspect of the special functions and roles that define womanhood. The striking impact of pregnancy on the clinical picture observed in the case of Mrs. H., reported here, is an example.

Most reports in the literature share the view that anorexia and bulimia represent aspects of self-hatred and rejection of femininity, especially rejection of the role of woman as mother. Feminist therapists see some exceptions to this view. Boskind-Lodahl and White (1978), for example, state that the college women they studied "overwhelmingly rated themselves as being quite satisfied with their gender." But they then note that this "population . . . exhibits distorted body image . . . [and] complains of low self-esteem, feelings of inadequacy, helplessness, and despair. Often isolated, she fears men, distrusts women, and expresses great shame regarding [her] behavior" (p. 85).

The breasts for these patients often stand as symbols for the worst aspects of their injured feminine narcissism. Like Risen's (1982) young anorexic, many patients with anorexia or bulimia express pleasure when their breasts shrink with dieting. Risen's patient feared being raped and dreamed of being tortured by Nazis. In the masochistic masturbation fantasies of Mrs. H., her breasts were cut off. This was a highly ambivalent image for Mrs. H., since it was her breasts and the milk they produced for her baby that gave her great pleasure, even when her prolonged nursing was obviously harmful to her child. Sperling's (1968) patient declared breasts unimportant because men did not have them. They stood for the penis which she expected to grow: In her fantasy: "breasts were first inside and then penetrated the chest and grew outside [as did] penis and . . . hair" (p. 683). Any absence of regular menstrual cycles is not usually complained of unless the woman is trying to become pregnant.

PREGNANCY AND THE EATING DISORDERS

There are only a few references to pregnancy in the literature on bulimia or anorexia (Russell, 1979; Mogul, 1980; Lacey, 1985; Anderson, 1985; Kalucy et. al., 1985), and in none of these papers is there any attempt to separate the reality of pregnancy from its representation as a narcissistic, infantile, incorporative fantasy, although the brief case material cited often suggests this. Since the early psychoanalytic literature frequently mentioned oral-impregnation fantasies (Freud, 1899, 1900; Fenichel, 1945), this is somewhat surprising. In any discussion, the fact of pregnancy should clearly be distinguished from its representation as a fantasy.

Anderson, in a study of pregnancy and fertility (1985), has summarized the usual findings that anorexics are generally younger and physically sicker than bulimics, and, therefore, have more problems conceiving and mothering. Pregnancies, when they do occur, are not often seriously affected by the symptoms. He saw several patients who began their practice of inducing vomiting during a pregnancy because they felt nauseated. In Anderson's experience, bulimic women with good premorbid personalities, who are strongly motivated to be mothers, did not have trouble with pregnancy or its aftermath. He cautions, however, that the narcissistic needs of the bulimic mother may make it difficult for her to attend to the needs of her children. One of the cases reported by Anderson, a thirty-year-old, married, bulimic woman, felt that her own needs were not being met adequately because of the care her child required. There is a strong narcissistic investment for a woman to be able to conceive and to be a good mother, even when the responsibilities of motherhood are unwanted and resented.

Lacey (1985) reports that many of his bulimic patients wished to be pregnant but were fearful of damaging the fetus with binging and vomiting. In Lacey's study, no one who became pregnant had hyperemesis and all had normal deliveries. He concluded that "dietary abuse does not return after the puerperium . . . [and that] patients apparently cope without difficulty [with] . . . the increased caloric demands of lactation" (p. 449). Kalucy et al. (1985) reported on two anorexics in their study who had a decrease in symptoms on becoming pregnant. The pregnancies were uneventful and experienced positively. "One patient, however, had a great deal of trouble in giving up breast feeding, continuing it until the child was three years old, in a way that suggested that she had difficulty in letting the child separate from her . . ." (p. 475). In both cases, the mothers became depressed when the children reached the age of approximately nine months.

Russell, in his study (1979), points out the presence of surprisingly good sexual adjustment in bulimics, including the desire for children. This contrasts with the commonly expressed disgust at sex met with in anorexics (Anderson, 1985). Attitudes in the group of patients Russell studied seemed to cover the spectrum that might be found in any group of women, and there were no findings consistently related to bulimia. He does not report on the postpartum experiences of those who had children, and he makes no comments about any psychological factors operating in bulimics who become pregnant.

Beumont, Abraham, and Simson (1981) found that a majority of the thirty-one anorexic or bulimic women they studied believed that a sexual challenge had precipitated their illness. Although five of the women referred to ongoing sexual problems as factors that maintained their anorexic behavior, the majority expressed the desire to marry eventually. Eleven expressed negative attitudes about pregnancy, citing fear of the pain of childbirth or of changes in their body shape during pregnancy. "One of the patients who expressed a positive attitude felt pregnancy would absolve her from the need to maintain a perfect figure. Another said she would get gratification from feeling that 'the load was gone' after she had delivered" (p. 134).

The linking of the symptoms of hysterical vomiting with the fantasy of pregnancy was reported by Freud in *The Interpretation of Dreams* (1900). He wrote:

> In one of my women patients, then, hysterical vomiting turned out to be on the one hand the fulfillment of an unconscious phantasy dating from her puberty—of a wish, that is, that she might be continuously pregnant and have innumerable children, with a further wish, added later, that she might have them by as many men as possible. A powerful defensive impulse had sprung up against this unbridled wish. And, since that patient might lose her figure and her good looks as a result of her vomiting, and so might cease to be attractive to anyone, the symptom was acceptable to the primitive train of thought as well; and since it was permitted by both sides it could become a reality [p. 570].

The discovery of oral sexuality came many years later and shed light on the important world of infantile fantasies and the mental mechanisms by which a pregnancy can occur, magically, by incorporation. *Oral incorporation,* a broad concept, sometimes refers to oral impregnation—as is often dramatized in the symptoms of hysterical neurosis—but frequently the term refers to much more regressive phenomena. There may be, for example, in the unconscious fantasies of the anorexic or bulimic the confused symbolic incorporation of one's own mother as baby, or of the identification of oneself with an incorporated penis or baby.

If one accepts the fantasies that are expressed by the words and the symptoms of these patients—a basic psychoanalytic tenet—then there is indeed strong confirmation of the significance of unconscious pregnancy fantasies. Several psychoanalysts have reported on pregnancy fantasies in cases of anorexia (Risen, 1982), but none from cases of bulimia.

ANALYSIS OF A CASE OF BULIMIA

Mrs. H., age twenty-five was a 5 foot, 6 inch, 115 pound, attractive and intelligent woman, married to a medical student and working as a secretary. She sought help for self-induced vomiting, a practice that she had been carrying out in secret for six years. Because of her desire to become pregnant and her concern about the effects of her vomiting on the well-being of the fetus, she finally confessed her problem to her husband, agreeing to a psychiatric evaluation. She recognized that her problems were neurotic, but felt no particular need to stop her behavior for the sake of her own health. Her primary concern—almost a shame—was her eating binges, described as "overeating," often the result of an intense craving for sweets.

She had no particular complaints about her marriage of one-and-a-half years except that she saw her husband as too much of a boy and not in any hurry to start a family. He planned to follow in his father's specialty and to join him in practice. Mrs. H. described herself as perfectionistic and highly critical of others and herself. Since her adolescence she had been depressed and irritable for inexplicable reasons. She had a spider phobia, which she is certain was inherited from her mother and grandmother because they shared similar fears. (Although skeptical, she averred that the women in the family also had psychic powers.) She also noted that she always seemed to be cutting herself in trivial accidents in the kitchen.

She seemed sufficiently motivated for treatment, having taken the difficult step of bringing her problem to light and, with a prospect of at least three years until her husband's graduation, psychoanalysis was recommended. There was no evidence of any psychotic thought processes, although her insistence that she had an "eating problem" despite her trim figure, suggested the operation of primitive splitting fantasies. There was much data in the first few interviews that suggested that oedipal neurotic factors were present and analyzable. There was no history of any life-threatening behavior. Because of her limited funds she was seen at a greatly reduced fee.

Her analysis lasted a year-and-a-half, four sessions per week, interrupted by her during her second trimester of pregnancy. She had a complete remission of her symptoms at that time, although she acknowledged that she was already thinking of resuming her analysis later if necessary.

She returned to treatment when her daughter was nine months old. At that time, Mrs. H. was having difficulty weaning her daughter from the breast; she seemed to be encouraging her child to remain an infant. There had been a return of bouts of anxiety and she had begun to induce vomiting after eating. Since she now knew that they would be moving in three months to another city, arrangements were made for her to see another analyst there. We explored her current problems in weekly therapy sessions until she moved.

She decided not to take my recommendation to resume her analysis. But when her attention was attracted to some publicity about research on endorphins and bulimia, she began therapy once a week with the author of the research. She wrote to me of her enthusiasm and of her optimism for the success of this new treatment, which prescribed a plan of exercise, time away from her baby, and the meticulous recording of everything she ate. She was also given small doses of lorazepam. At the time she wrote to me she had been in this therapy for a month, and she had been once again able to stop the vomiting. She admitted that she was, however, still obsessed with her weight and foods. How long she continued with this regime, and its results, were never made known to me.

Her mother was born and raised until adolescence in England, and Mrs. H. felt strong ties to all things British. A sense of naive innocence and her identification with romantic and helpless women, such as Thomas Hardy's portrayal of Tess in *Tess of the D'Urbervilles*, were significant character resistances. During the analysis these characteristic poses served to keep in check her sense of inferiority at having been created a girl—made inferior—and to temper her aggressive outrage evoked by frustrations. All aspects of her instinctual drives were either consciously suppressed or were out of her awareness. Her hobby was fencing, but she had a flawed technique—she could not thrust home.

DEVELOPMENTAL HISTORY

Mrs. H. is the second of five children born in a closely knit, upper middle-class family. All of the children were encouraged to be successful and were given the best of educational opportunities. Her older brother, two years her senior, is an engineer. When Mrs. H. was twelve or thirteen years old, she and this brother engaged in mutual sex play for a period of time. When she was seventeen months old, her next brother was born, and when she was four-and-a-half years old, her only sister was born. She remembered that she believed that babies were made by kissing. This brother and sister were both in college at the time of her analysis. Her sister was reported to be grossly overweight and had been enuretic until her early adolescence. Mrs. H. recalled a strong feeling of wanting to hurt babies by pinching their toes when she was seven or eight: "I guess I was jealous." She was not sure whether she ever acted on the impulse.

Her youngest brother was born when Mrs. H. was sixteen years old. She felt intense envy of her mother during the pregnancy. She also felt contempt for her mother, who had become depressed, commenting, "She acted like she had cancer." (She had been told that her mother was depressed after Mrs. H.'s birth as well, and that her grandmother had been depressed after the birth of Mrs. H.'s mother.) Her resentment of her father only barely concealed her frank wish for her father's baby. She recalled thinking that she could have been a better wife to her father than her mother was, and when her brother was born she attempted to take over his care, pretending that he was hers. This complex of feelings resurfaced when she was twenty-two years old and had become pregnant accidentally, unable to know for sure which of two men was the father. A therapeutic abortion was performed at seven to ten weeks gestation.

Her father was a successful investment counselor whom she described as hard. She had occasional dreams of being chased by her father—in one he was a *Tyrannosaurus rex*—and she had always felt him to be harsh and lacking in understanding. He used to tease her as a child because she was so little, called her "wasp-waist" and "thimble-belly." Her paternal grandfather had been paralyzed most of his life by multiple sclerosis and died before his son's marriage. The paternal grandmother was described as very intolerant as, for example, in her attitudes toward homosexuals. Mrs. H. regarded herself as liberal in her views and respectful of the rights of others.

Teased for being a picky eater as a child, she was indulged as well. Her grandmother used to put a single corn flake in a bowl for her to eat because she usually refused to eat breakfast. (Mrs. H. describes her current difficulty as "overeating.")

Sometime before the age of four she had a birthmark removed surgically from her vulva, an area she described as "between my legs." She was toilet trained late, wearing diapers until she was four.

About the age of seven, she saw a sock containing rosin hanging in her father's workshop that looked to her like a man's testicles. That made her think that she might have been born a boy and had had her genitals cut off. She had been told that her parents had wanted her to be a girl. Her mother told her that she herself never had any wish for a penis, but had wished that she could compete in sports like a boy during her adolescence. Mrs. H.'s erotic fantasy of having her breasts cut off began, she believed, about the age of six.

She remembered being dreadfully afraid of being left alone or abandoned by her parents, and she didn't accept baby-sitters. Parental arguments were unsettling for her. She once attempted to stop one of their arguments by running into the house announcing that a snake had bitten her knee. She had a birthmark on her knee that she pointed to as evidence. She also recalled trying to wash this mole off in the bathtub.

She had many fears as a child (in addition to spiders) and there was a long chain of things that made her feel squeamish: childhood horror stories—especially of being buried alive —touching kidneys when making kidney pie, gutting a fish, and looking at illustrations of cadavers or diseases in her husband's medical books. Her brothers teased her by calling her "the black widow," after the spider who is said to devour her mate after copulation.

She discovered her vagina at age eight when she put something small into it and told her mother; her mother only admonished her not to put anything into her vagina. There were no unpleasant affects associated with this screen memory, which seems out of keeping with her mother's extreme prudery over sex. She was frequently reminded by her mother of the proper behavior for a lady. Once she was chided for sitting in her father's lap at a family picnic.

Mrs. H. always hated school, ostensibly because of her fear of being called upon to say something, even though she was a good student. Her mother took her to school on the first day of each term until the seventh grade. She was especially afraid of a teacher in the fourth grade, but could not remember the reason for her fear. Her associations, however, linked her fear of this teacher with a "queasy feeling in the stomach" that came over her when she happened upon a centipede in the school yard.

Adolescence was a time of unhappiness and tears, of feeling unattractive, and of not having boyfriends. "I felt my father didn't love me." She cried a great deal and her mother would come into her room to comfort her. "But," she reflected, "nothing terrible ever happened to me; not like many of my friends who are seeing psychiatrists."

She had no difficulty in leaving home for college and spent her third year abroad studying in London. She weighed 130 pounds at that time, her heaviest, and was introduced to the practice of vomiting after meals by fellow students. She shared the British desire for sweets.

She worked in her home city after graduation doing secretarial and editorial work. She had met her husband while in college, but did not develop a serious interest in him until a few years later. She became pregnant during her first year out of college, about the time she began seeing her future husband regularly, and had her therapeutic abortion. Always in good health, her only other surgery was a bunionectomy at age twenty-three. Her husband had pushed her to it for cosmetic reasons, a decision she later regretted because of the prolonged and painful recovery.

THE COURSE OF THE ANALYSIS

Many aspects of Mrs. H.'s analysis dealt with neurotic formations and character distortions that were only peripherally related to her pregnancy and her bulimia. In what follows I shall highlight those aspects of her analysis that linked her bulimia with her pregnancy.

In her first communications from the couch she recounted her troubled relationship with her father, only to have any further associations to her father vanish from her conscious thoughts in the analytic hours for six months. She stated that she did not dream much, but she reported many dreams in the course of her analysis. In her dreams she was often able to approach ideas that were too embarrassing for her to discuss openly at first. She used intellectualizing defenses and obsessional mechanisms to ward off affect-laden fantasies. She showed a consistent pattern of intellectual reserve, of being the proper lady: nice girls only say nice things. After a month she said, "It seems to me the only thing I haven't talked about is sex—and I don't want to—but I don't think there's anything significant there to talk about." She once described a nonsexy, flannel nightgown as "wholesome."

She repeorted having headaches after particularly resistant and unproductive sessions. She had anxiety dreams occasionally, and in the frightening one in which she was pursued by her father, who was portrayed as a dangerous flesh-eating dinosaur, she turned into an egg for protection. In her first dream after beginning analysis, although not reported until a few weeks later, she was making coffee for her boss and spilled the grounds. These dreams, and others, typically dealt with the interplay of her dangerous instinctual wishes on the one hand, and her protective defenses, on the other.

During her first week in analysis she stopped the binging–vomiting pattern and felt very pleased with herself, but then reported a relapse over the weekend break that left her feeling depressed and discouraged (she had spilled the grounds). She had many associations that proclaimed her wish for babies, a wish that was to be expressed repeatedly in words, and symbolized in dreams and symptoms. When a friend became pregnant she grew intensely envious, and it brought to mind her sadistic childhood wishes to do harm to babies, to pinch their toes. She closely followed her friend's progress, dutifully reporting in her analytic sessions such facts as, "She's at three-and-a-half months and hasn't gained any weight," associating such ideas with her binging and vomiting. To become pregnant was viewed as a competition, a race to motherhood, and she was angry for her husband for not getting on with it. She once joked that she hoped to win the "Russian mother-of-the-year award" for her fecundity. She was ashamed of herself for her secret wishes that her friend abort.

Despite her longing for pregnancy, she said that the appearance of her "stomach" bulging distressed her; it was the *feeling* of distention, however, not her actual appearance that impelled her to vomit. She must sleep on her side or on her belly, positions contrived to prevent the unpleasant sense of pressure on her "stomach." She didn't like her abdomen touched whenever she felt that it protruded.

She reported an intense craving for sweets, but was reluctant to reveal the heart of her problem—the secret binging. She spoke "about it" and around it for a long time before she felt able to confess it and openly discuss her actions and feelings. A month into her analysis she commented that she was down to overeating three times a week; that is, "being good" most of the time. It soon became clear that she forgot (repressed) the craving for the sweet food almost immediately after vomiting, and she never felt the craving during her sessions, which were usually in the midafternoon. She arranged her binges so as not to interfere with analysis, just as she had kept them from her husband.

Her pattern for years was to buy boxes of cupcakes and similar sweets, storing them in the back of the refrigerator or pantry. The binging was a ritual that started by "finding" the goodies, as if by accident, and quickly ingesting them. Vomiting, initiated by putting her fingers down her throat, followed soon after.

Her associations to binging were linked to her impatient wish for pregnancy, to her feeling of shame and moral self-condemnation at having become pregnant before marriage, and to her disgust with her mother for becoming pregnant during Mrs. H.'s adolescence. Her mother's pregnancy and her own were condensed into one: she felt strongly that some wrong had occurred in each case. She kept forgetting, and then reminding herself, that she would never know if her husband had been the father of her earlier aborted pregnancy. I pointed out that her forgetting suggested that, for her, it didn't really matter who was the father, that her old adolescent wish for her father's baby was unconsciously predominant. She gave further associations that joined her fear of her father's condemnation with her binging and vomiting. He often teased her about her skinniness, and in her mind to be thin meant to be despised by him; unconsciously, this meant he rejected her for not being pregnant by him. Many themes in her analysis led to the same conclusions: binging with food made her feel distended and pregnant and guilty; vomiting made her feel, "I'm good," but depressed and longing for her father's baby.

She related a "funny" dream: "I am having a diaphragm fitted, but the doctor does a tubal ligation, sewing up the scar on my abdomen with black thread, making the contraception irreversible." In reality, plans to have a diaphragm fitted had stirred up in her a fear that she had destroyed her fertility by using the pill, because it had, in fact, greatly altered her menstrual cycle. Her fear pointed to infertility as a form of punishment, a moral judgment upon her, first, for her wishes for a baby, and second, for her abortion. Black thread was a reference to the "horrible stitches" she had to endure with her bunionectomy, which, like the abortion, was an "unnecessary" operation.

Analysis was a spilling of her guts, and like vomiting, evidence of her shame and guilt. She hurried to become pregnant, it seemed, to make her analysis into another unnecessary operation.

Her spider phobia and her fear of suddenly coming upon a picture of a disease in a textbook related to her childhood impression of the nature of her own genital organs. Having been "made" by her parents into a girl she regarded her own vulva as a shameful wound: slimy, wet, and creepy, yet the source from which babies came. Babies, like spiders, emerge and crawl, having been buried alive, and, like her baby siblings, were objects of her destructive aggression. Babies were at first like cancers, slimy, wet, and creepy, growing inside, making the belly distend.

A series of three dreams led to a revelation of her wishes, in the transference, for her analyst–father's baby. The first dream: "I am taking a shower, but in a restaurant, behind a curtain, feeling embarrassed. I emerge from the shower, with only a T-shirt on. I try to punch in the nose of a man who is eating and looking at me, but I can't reach him." The dream was difficult for her to relate and to analyze because of her embarrassment at the overt sexuality expressed in it. The dream reminded her of her embarrassment a few days earlier in an analytic session when I had discussed her sexual life with her. She regarded me as the lascivious diner, eating her with my eyes, and someone who, like her fencing opponent, couldn't be reached. In her words, "I never quite make the connection," a multiply determined idea that referred not only to fencing and to making analytic connections, but to her secret sexual longings as well. (The phallic implications, her wish for the penis, portrayed so well in her dream, was obvious, but will not be discussed here.) The man dining in her dream resembled a fat man in one of the pictures in her wedding album, and, by a series of connections, also stood for herself, fat and pregnant.

This dream and its analysis shook her demeanor and a wave of resistance took over. For the next two weeks there were long periods of silence, and she complained of headaches. She then revealed a dream that had occurred several days before: "I am at an analytic session. You [the analyst] are not behind me, but sitting in a chair across the room. I ask you if I can lie on my side, as I do at home when my back hurts. Then I am baby-sitting in your house; you have a small child." Her associations to the dream had to do with "being nice," and how defensive she is because, "nice girls don't say un-nice things." A transference theme took the form, "If you were a nice man, you wouldn't look at me exposing myself." She then pointed out that the dream was associated with feelings of sexual attraction for the analyst, and her need to ward them off by her niceness. The condensed symbolism (lying down—back pain—baby-sitting) in the dream that pointed to conceiving, bearing, and tending the analyst's baby was at first skimmed over by her.

A third dream came a week later: "I am jogging with a man named Dan, who is in my fencing class. Then we are in bed together. I feel ashamed and guilty for betraying my husband." Her efforts at analyzing the dream revealed that she had completely repressed the fact that Dan was the analyst's name as well. The associations to the dream, however, reconfirmed the presence of active unconscious wishes for the baby that she felt was rightly hers: the baby that father gave to mother. Jogging and fencing related to her vomiting, activities aimed at reducing the size of her belly, whose meaning was the undoing of the "not nice," wished-for pregnancy.

She became increasingly aware of the danger implicit in her sexual wishes and her defenses against them. She was afraid to go to a company Christmas party, an ended her indecision by staying home, desirous of binging, but able to hold off knowing that she would be coming to her analytic session later in the day. She had made the analyst into a policeman, an externalized conscience. She continued to eat and vomit several times a week, and she read everything she could find that seemed to offer alternate routes to solving her problem. Her discomfort in analyzing reminded her of her chronic fear of being called upon in school.

Her chosen solution was to become pregnant, which in fact she did about six months later. During this time the analytic data all pertained to the struggle that she was going through to free herself from the infantile sense of guilt and shame associated with her desire for babies. One aspect of her struggle, the idea that a baby is compensation for having been castrated, followed from a "funny dream": "I pull on a front tooth and it comes out—leaves a big hole—part of my palate comes out, too. I'm worried that I can't get it back in." Her associations linked the guilt of masturbation with the guilt of pregnancy and abortion. The palate referred to her injured genital, to the baby she wanted, and to the diaphragm that she didn't want to use. Angry thoughts directed at her husband (and her father) followed from her associations to *funny;* it was funny for her to recall that her husband had had similar dreams of a tooth coming out, which he related to his occasional fear of impotency. She had tearful spells in which she voiced her fear that she would never solve her problem, and she fervently hoped that she was pregnant.

An interpretation was offered that a major determinant of her vomiting was the wish to magically reject her mother's pregnancy. This concept also helped to explain her willingness to believe in the psychic powers of the women in the family, a belief that went against her own reason. These psychic powers were supposedly demonstrated when, without prior knowledge, one woman in the family would experience distress at exactly the moment that another woman in the family was delivered of a baby. Further confirmation of the interpretation came from the analysis of a dream in which she stabbed a woman and tried to hide the body, "like in Poe." This turned out to be a reference to the fears of her oedipal phase, when she dreaded being abandoned or buried alive; now, it seemed, in retaliation for her murderous wishes to mother and siblings, especially siblings unborn (buried alive).

Her continued struggle over conceiving was revealed in a dream in which she looked into a mirror and saw herself pregnant, but "the fatness is all in the upper part of my body, my chin, neck, and breasts." She felt snappish with her husband and picked arguments with him. She could not assimilate the idea that the pleasure and fun of sex can be related to the wish for a baby. Her masturbatory masochistic fantasy of having her breasts cut off was recalled by the image of her enlarged breasts in the dream. About the time she conceived, she dreamt of being a vampire and of bearing a defective child. In yet another of many dreams she was chased by a 185-pound bear. The weight, 185 pounds, referred to her father, and the defective baby turned out to be herself; that is, a distorted and condensed image of herself with a defective penis. This dream association derived from her knowledge that her husband had been born with an undescended testicle and was "defective." That the baby she longed for was to be a replacement for her imaginary, damaged penis was also portrayed in an ecstatic dream of flying. Flying, a common dream experience for many, associated with erotic feelings, stood for her penis that could rise against gravity.

Fifteen months after starting her analysis, she reported a positive pregnancy test. She was overjoyed at the news; there was a dramatic change in her demeanor, and her binging and vomiting ceased entirely. The character of the analytic material changed as well. There were many veiled associations to getting rid of, or no longer needing, a husband, just like the black widow of her childhood fantasy. In one of her dreams she lost her engagement ring. She had many fantasies of giving birth to a defective child, and she was bothered by an uncanny sense of doubt as to who was the father of her baby. (There was no real uncertainty with this pregnancy.) She interrupted her analysis early in her second trimester.

RETURN TO THERAPY

When she returned to therapy, her daughter was nine months old, and Mrs. H. had just resumed her former practice of inducing vomiting. She now weighed 125 pounds and looked and felt well. She reported that she had experienced some anxiety about her weight only during the last two weeks of her pregnancy. She was still breast-feeding every three hours. Her daughter had yet to sleep through the night, and despite urging by the pediatrician had not yet been given solid food. Mrs. H. had not resumed sexual intercourse. Her only comment at this time was, "I know this is all connected to my feelings about pregnancy, but I'm not clear how it's connected." She did seem to understand that she was not actually *overeating*, although that was her word. It was clearly the *idea* of overeating that troubled her. After the purging by vomiting, she always had a pleasant sensation of being clean.

While she was pregnant she had felt completely attached to someone and very happy. As long as her new infant remained orally dependent upon her, Mrs. H. felt blissfully contented; all cravings for sweets abated. When the pediatrician insisted that she begin to offer the cup instead of the breast to her baby, her intolerable frustration returned and she began the pattern of secret gorging and vomiting. She kept herself in ignorance of her resentment and hostility toward her own baby, totally denying the potential damage she might be doing to her child through forced infantilization. In the guise of being a good mother, who gives food and love, she actually became the bad mother she did not want to be.

THE PSYCHOANALYTIC POINT OF VIEW

The therapeutic method and general psychology that is called psychoanalysis was discovered by Sigmund Freud and elaborated by him and others over the first third of this century. The essential component of psychoanalysis that distinguishes it from other psychological approaches and methods is the attention that is paid to that province of the mind called the unconscious. Slips of the tongue, double meanings, symbolic expressions of inner thought, and dream interpretation are all aspects of the unconscious that have become familiar parts of everyday thinking for twentieth-century man. That most of the important mental activity of the mind occurs outside of awareness is a bedrock concept for the psychoanalyst and has led to the special technical procedure that aims at the understanding of unconscious mental processes through the analysis of resistance and defense. Symptoms are analyzed for meaning in exactly the same way that dreams and other activities of the normal mind are investigated. The technique utilizes free association, interpretation, and reconstruction pursued as far as possible, and attempts to minimize subjective interferences, most notably those projections called transferences, by analyzing them as well.

UNCONSCIOUS FANTASY

The unconscious is a storehouse of memories of all kinds—real experiences and feelings that start in early childhood, as well as distorted versions of those experiences, and gross fabrications and misrepresentations of reality in the form of myths and beliefs. These memories form layers in the mind that are continuously overlayed by new memories. The old layers persist, however, and form the substance of much of our mature character, our attitudes, and our choice of symptoms when we fall ill with a neurosis.

These buried memories are organized according to the pleasure-unpleasure principle whereby human beings are unconsciously motivated to seek compromises in life that increase pleasure and that, at the same time, minimize displeasure. That this is not always possible leads to conflict and frequently to unsatisfactory compromise solutions. The entire spectrum of pleasure-seeking activities and compromises, in the broadest sense, is referred to by psychoanalysts as sexual.

The psychoanalytic approach to understanding a symptom complex such as bulimia is based on the assumption that each aspect of the symptom is a compromise formation, formed by the special store of unconscious memories that are unique for that individual. The compromise is formed from a powerful defensive impulse that is erected against an equally powerful unbridled wish (Freud, 1900). The symptom picture often can be understood by the elucidation of a central core fantasy—the unbridled wish—from which spring many of the secondary symptoms and modifications of character. The Oedipus complex is the most important of the core fantasies in the psychoneuroses; while in conditions that are found more toward the psychotic end of the diagnostic spectrum, contributions from earlier stages of development (oral, anal, and phallic) overlay the oedipal conflicts and assume prominence.

PSYCHOSEXUAL STAGES OF DEVELOPMENT

The conflicts that lead to eating disturbances, including anorexia and bulimia, derive from all stages of development and can be traced back to eating disturbances in childhood. Typically, anorexics show more pathologic regression than bulimics, and phallic- and oedipal-stage fantasies are more common in bulimics. But oral-stage modes of expression can be utilized at any later stage, so that phallic conflicts, for example, may be represented by oral pregnancy fantasies based on eating, or sadistically biting off the man's penis, with reactions in the form of disgust that are displaced onto food. Anal conflicts can be unconscious prohibitions against taking feces or dirt into the mouth or expressions of stubborn determination: "I will not let myself be controlled; I eat when and what I like. . . ." (Fenichel, 1945, p. 176). Risen's (1982) young anorexic patient had oedipal conflicts but complained of constant diarrhea and told her doctor that "she liked to feel she could empty her insides out and not feel bloated" (p. 436). Although she was an accomplished cook and baker, she felt disgust with food and never ate what she made for others.

Phallic aspects of eating disturbances are the basis of the commonly associated symptoms of pathologic lying and kleptomania. They are disguised denials of castration, as if to declare, "I do possess a penis" (Abraham, 1924). A patient of Abraham's revealed that, "telling these imaginary facts gave her strong sexual excitement and a sensation as if something was growing and swelling out of her abdomen. This sensation was connected with a feeling of physical strength and activity; and in the same way the act of lying made her feel mentally powerful and superior to others" (p. 484).

A case of bulimia in a twenty-eight-year-old, unmarried woman (Leonard, 1944) demonstrates phallic dynamics that were derived from infantile penis envy and superego elements of self-condemnation. She concealed her vomiting from the analyst at first since it represented punishment for the gratification of her forbidden wishes. She could not eat with a man unless she paid for her own food, and even then, if she felt any sexual stimulation from being with him, she vomited. Relationships were attempted only with married men, who were, therefore, unavailable for her. Intercourse was for her a sinful, oral incorporation, a wish to devour a penis, like eating candy. She was jealous of pregnant women, as was Mrs. H., and like her, had a hatred of bugs. Bugs, which she sometimes searched out to kill, were nuisances like children who ate too much.

The conflicts of early childhood that form the basis of disturbances later in life may take on a very altered dynamic significance. The yearning for sexual fulfillment in a hysteric may have sprung from childhood feelings of not being given enough food and love.

Fenichel (1945) cites a paper by Wulff that describes an oral symptom complex, much like bulimia, in which episodes of eating and sleeping alternate with periods of abstemiousness and insomnia.

Wulff has described a psychoneurosis, not infrequent in women, which is related to hysteria, cyclothymia and addiction. This neurosis is characterized by the person's fight against her sexuality which, through previous repression, has become especially greedy and insatiable. This sexuality is pregenitally oriented, and sexual satisfaction is perceived of as a "dirty meal." Periods of depression in which the patients stuff themselves (or drink) and feel "fat," "bloated," "dirty," "untidy," or "pregnant" and leave their surroundings untidy, too, alternate with "good" periods in which they behave ascetically, feel slim, and conduct themselves either normally or with some elation [p. 241].

Mrs. H. often started her analytic hour with the comment, "I've been good," meaning she had not induced vomiting since her last analytic hour. Fenichel continues:

The body feeling in the "fat" periods turns out to be a repetition of the way the girl felt at puberty before her first menstruation, and the spells often actually coincide with the premenstrual period. The menstrual flow then usually brings a feeling of relief: "The fat-making dirt is pouring out; now I am slim again, and will be a good girl and not eat too much." The alternating feelings of ugliness and beauty connected with these periods show that exhibitionistic conflicts also are of basic importance in this syndrome. Psychoanalysis discloses that the unconscious content of this syndrome is a preoedipal mother conflict, which may be covered by an oral-sadistic Oedipus complex. The patients have an intense unconscious hatred against their mothers and against femininity. To them being fat means getting breasts, being uncontrolled, incontinent, or even pregnant. The urge to eat has the unconscious aim of incorporating something that may relax the disagreeable inner "feminine" tension, eating meaning reincorporation of an object, whose loss has caused the patient to feel hungry, constipated, castrated, feminine, fat; that is, the food means milk, penis, child, and narcissistic supplies which soothe anxieties. The exhibitionistic behavior signifies a tendency to compel the receipt of these supplies and the fear of not getting them because of repulsive ugliness. The depression signifies the recurrent failure of the tendency to regain the lost stability, a failure that occurs because of the forbidden oral-sadistic means by which this re-establishment is attempted. The ascetic periods, by pacifying the superego, achieve a greater degree of relaxation [p. 241].

ORAL IMPREGNATION FANTASY

The prominent role of the mother in the lives of anorexics and bulimics derives from the importance of oral symbolism in the unconscious, and is epitomized as an oral incorporation (impregnation) fantasy. All forms of physical nurture become symbols for emotional nurture throughout life: mother, breast, food, eating, and fat are most typical. They become linked inextricably in the mind of the orally fixated individual so that all later expressions of incorporation, such as making a baby, have the confused meaning of taking in food or love. Whenever love is unacceptable, then food also becomes unacceptable. This is the psychoanalytic meaning of "oral impregnation fantasy" that is so prominent in the literature on eating disturbances and yet is so frequently misused. Some authors (Bruch, 1985; Goodsitt, 1985) flatly state that they do not find oral impregnation fantasies in their patients. They seem to be referring to the absence of consciously verbalized wishes for impregnation in conjunction with an eating disturbance. Goodsitt, while rejecting the concept of "oral incorporative fantasy," nevertheless gives some clinical examples that are consistent with the psychoanalytic view. He writes, "an anorexic frequently stops eating when her mother or anyone else is pleased by her eating" (p. 77), and, "Often she feels she is a special or precious child, born to fill an emptiness or the needs of a parent" (p. 79). Goodsitt prefers to call these "vestiges of infantile, archaic grandiosity." Orbach (1985), who describes herself as a feminist psychoanalyst, emphasizes the point that anorexics have been deprived as infants of sufficient oral incorporative gratification. She sees this as a cultural problem, especially the bad cultural effects of mothers on daughters, and she has no interest in the Oedipus complex.

Boris (1984a,b) supports the idea of the importance of orality for the anorexic, but he narrows the problem to envy of the symbolic breast, writing in a manner that flows back and forth from reality to metaphor. He writes (1984a):

[T]he anorectic does not wish to want; she wishes to be the object of other's wants . . . a greed akin to gluttony . . . greed for the breast is metamorphosed into gluttony for punishment, yearning into abstinence, retention into elimination (in bulimia) via each and every alimentary orifice, indeed, by exercise and sweating, through the very pores themselves" [p. 317].

He goes on to say later in the same work: "Food, as part object, necessarily also excites desire and envy. The envy is devoted to food's ability to penetrate the of-me boundary and reach into the very marrow of being. This once was an intention the anorectic experienced in respect to the body and soul of her mother" (1984b, pp. 437–438). Hughes (1984) describes a similar theme stressing the use in these patients of projective identification with the powerful mother.

The oral impregnation fantasy is a reconstruction of a hypothetical infantile mental construct that is unconscious. Risen (1982) bases the entire understanding of his case of anorexia on defenses against oral impregnation fantasies. Sperling (1968) treated a sixteen-year-old anorexic with cyclic vomiting who pulled her hair and ingested it. Hair, for the patient, had the symbolic meaning of mother; as a child she pulled wool from her blanket. In her fantasy, hair pulled from her head stood for her mother's genital hair, and the ball of hair in her stomach "was like her mother's face with hair on it. I have my mother jumping around in my stomach" (p. 683). The hair ball also meant father's and brother's genitals, and an act of sexual intercourse was dramatized by the hair going into her mouth, which made her swollen stomach a forbidden pregnancy. She was afraid that bugs, ants, or other insects would fly into her mouth, and live in her stomach. Her stomach was conceived of in infantile terms: as a bag; a place for food, baby, and her period. Hair represented the pregnant mother cannibalistically incorporated.

THE OEDIPUS COMPLEX AND THE SUPEREGO

The superego, that structure of the mind that fulfills the role of conscience and the setting up of ideals, is the product of the Oedipus complex. The oedipal desires of the little girl for her father's baby normally are resolved by the establishment of unconscious ideals that direct the maturing girl toward eventual motherhood or other mature choices.

In bulimia the superego is shaped by oedipal taboos that are presented in regressive, preoedipal terms. "Eating is carnal . . . eating is whoring; to eat is to sin," declared one patient (Guiora, 1967). Eating a favorite food, even when ingested in small amounts, is referred to as "overeating" because it represents forbidden pleasure that leads, in turn, to guilt and the need for self-punishment and atonement. Fenichel (1945) writes that the superego in the eating disturbances is based on the idea that you are not supposed to eat what is good, but rather what is good for you. Being good comes to mean rejecting the goodies, the bad food. Vomiting is rarely described as pleasurable in itself, but is commonly described as a gratifying relief of tension. Fat becomes the stigma of guilt, unconsciously standing for an oedipal (or preoedipal) pregnancy. Secret eating has all the affective qualities of masturbation. For the bulimic the ritualized shopping for the forbidden foods, with its attendent excitement and anxiety, described by Russell (1979), is much like the compulsive search for pornography by some in their quest for forbidden and elusive sexual fulfillment. Just as much of the pornography that is purchased is soon discarded, bulimics frequently throw away food they have bought without eating it. Shoplifting is frequent in both situations and for the same reasons.

Even a nonpsychoanalytic researcher such as Russell (1979)

is impressed by the remarkable intractability of bulimic symptoms: "remarkable in view of the patients' deep sense of shame and common awareness of their harmful effects" (p. 432). Russell favors a biologic theory to explain bulimia, yet his patients made clear to him that favorite foods were symbols of taboo pleasures.

Risen's (1982) successful treatment of a case of anorexia was based on an oedipal wish for her stepfather's baby. "The misconception of her body image terminated the day she discovered that her fear of getting fat was related to her wish for her stepfather's baby" (pp. 457–458). She felt that she could be a better wife to her own father. (Mrs. H. expressed the same idea.) "I know I can surpass her. . . . It's like killing her, stabbing her, destroying her" (p. 449). "I wanted to have a baby—my stepfather's baby. . . ." (p. 450).

Many authors (Boris, 1984b; Kalucy, Crisp, and Harding, 1977) have pointed out that the vomiting and the excessive use of exercise by the bulimic is not solely to evacuate calories but to disgorge the oedipal guilt as well. Weight control is equated with well-being, self-control, and "rightness." Anorexics express even harsher superego attitudes. Strober and Yager (1985) worked with a patient who declared that she had to have her therapist in charge of her weight because she felt unable to deal with "the guilt of eating." One patient of Russell's (1979) explained, "If I can see my ribs it makes me feel happier," and when another patient reached 55 kilograms, she said that her stomach constantly felt too fat. For another patient "to be thin means I feel more attractive and cleaner. I have more energy and I feel happy; if I gain weight, I feel ashamed" (p. 440).

Ego Defenses

Anorexia and bulimia, like all symptom complexes, are always in the service of unconscious problem solving, regardless of how maladaptive they may appear on the surface. Mogul (1980) has made an important contribution by pointing out that anorexia may achieve some real positive goals in adolescent development; it may assist in the "struggle against the real excesses of out-of-control hedonism" that is very dangerous. The ego of the bulimic is generally in better control, but the same observations apply. "Self-discipline, frequently extending to ascetic discomfort and self-denial, is a vital adaptive resource . . . in establishing the capacity to survive independently and in mastering the requirements and skills for life. . . ." (p. 173). This ego-adaptive aspect is generally overlooked in the varieties of therapeutic programs described in the literature. Nearly all therapies, except psychoanalysis, aim only at removing or attenuating symptoms, often with disastrous consequences to the developing ego.

Johnson and Larson (1982) quantify the affects of guilt and anger and the ego functions of alertness and control throughout the bulimic cycle. During the binge phase they found that there is a rise in the feelings of guilt, which increase even further during the purge phase, subsiding afterward. Feelings of anger tend to decrease slightly while binging, but drop to their lowest level while purging. Alertness is obtunded slightly during the binge phase, but while purging the woman becomes most alert, followed by a precipitous drop. The sense of control stays fairly level throughout the bulimic cycle with some decrease only while binging.

Many authors, such as Guiora (1967), have suggested that oral fixations, based on severe early maternal deprivations lead to permanent ego structure defects that make the adolescent passage to mature feminine development impossible. This very popular theme that implicates the mother as the prime cause of anorexia or bulimia in the daughter is especially prevalent in the nonpsychoanalytic literature. But, for the psychoanalyst, such dynamic formulations appear simplistic, and unfair as well, because they do not consider the multidetermined possibilities that contribute to the complexities of human behavior. It is a striking fact that anorexics and bulimics often show admirable ego qualities of the highest sort and come from families that have provided good environments. Oedipal conflicts may trigger regression to the oral- and anal-phase fixations that entirely mask a woman's finer character.

OTHER CLINICAL MANIFESTATIONS
OF THE BULIMIC SYNDROME

In the course of analyzing Mrs. H.'s bulimia, several related problems surfaced that are regularly noted in the literature on bulimia. Spider and bug phobias, poor control of aggression including self-injurious actions, depression, poor body image, painfully distorted views of femininity, and disturbed sexual relations are all frequently associated with the obsessional concerns over all aspects of food, fat, and weight.

Stealing and compulsive lying did not appear among Mrs. H.'s patterns; they may in fact have occurred and been withheld by her from treatment. Her discomfort at revealing emotionally charged material and her eagerness to leave analysis in order to be spared embarrassment was striking. The phallic–aggressive implications of her fencing hobby and her flawed fencing technique were not deeply analyzed by her. Stealing and lying occur prominently in cases in which there are significant phallic fixations. The stolen, or lied-about, symbolic penis stands for power, prestige, and perfection. Vomiting in these patients represents a reaction, a disgorging of the stolen penis (Abraham, 1924; Leonard, 1944). Stealing, especially food, is reported to be very common in bulimics, and along with lying, represents an act of aggression toward others. The act of eating the stolen food itself is often described by patients in very aggressive terms. The fantasy behind stealing takes the form, "If mother fed me, I wouldn't have to steal." Guiora (1967) quotes one patient who said, "I was angry, furious, almost exploded, then opened the icebox and bolted down all that was there. . . . I starve myself to anger my husband and my parents, to make them worry" (p. 392). The rigid control of weight stands for self-control and moral strength and provides a general sense of well-being.

That bugs, spiders, and vermin of all kinds can symbolize various aspects of sexuality, and reaction formations against it, is well documented in the psychodynamic literature. In dreams, as well as in the eating disorders, bugs and spiders represent the impregnating agent (penis, vulva), the impregnating sub-

stances (semen, dirt, things that make one sick), and the products of impregnation (fetus, baby). Mrs. H. dreaded spiders
because they represented her forbidden wishes for her father's
penis–baby as well as her oral aggression (the black widow)
against her mother and mother's babies. The fantasy of a bug
flying into the mouth and living in the stomach is very common
(Sperling, 1968). Sperling (1971) believes that spider phobias
are of special diagnostic and prognostic significance, but "are
not readily disclosed because they relate to the patient's most
guarded and feared impulses" (p. 487).

Suppression of the libidinal side of life, frequently leads
to increased acts of aggression directed toward oneself. Mrs. H.
was aware that there was some inner need to hurt herself evidenced by her frequent, accidentally self-inflicted cuts in the
kitchen. Many patients sublimate masochistic expressions into
puritanical moralizing, ascetic behavior, or excessive exercising
(Mogul, 1980; Boris, 1984a). Consciously experienced positive
feelings of pleasure accompanying purging is rare, although it
has been reported as giving perverse sexualized pleasure in
certain male anorexics (Sours, 1974).

Some patients may become disabled physically, socially, and
psychologically as a result of their eating disorder, but decom-
pensation to the point of suicide does not appear to be common.
In an excellent study of therapeutic problems, Kalucy et al.
(1985), found in a group of chronic anorexics that forcing them
to gain weight led to psychological deterioration of a severe
degree, and could "precipitate not only severe psychiatric disorders, but also a very painful awareness of all that has been
missed in life" (p. 477). Some did commit suicide. These authors
have pointed out that recovered cases frequently lead to profound disturbances in the family—especially in the parents.
Two suicides, one by a mother, one by a father, were reported.

There are very few papers that deal with the problems of
self-mutilation in bulimics (French and Nelson, 1972; Simpson,
1973). Genital mutilation is probably rare, but displaced and
disguised self-injury, as occurred in Mrs. H.'s case, is a neglected
topic.

THE NONPSYCHOANALYTIC VIEW

In general, the nonpsychoanalytic approaches to the problem of bulimia stress the treating of symptoms instead of the searching for meanings. Nonanalytic discussions of bulimia attempt to be pragmatic, and nonanalytic therapists frequently express much greater therapeutic optimism than the psychoanalyst. Patterns of dieting and eating, mechanisms of hunger, and consciously expressed attitudes regarding fat and weight, are dealt with directly and treated as problems in themselves, especially by those who advise behavioral methods (Kalucy et al., 1977; Boskind-Lodahl and White, 1978; Rosen and Leitenberg, 1985). Causes, when considered at all, are generally attributed to instances of actual historical events in the life of the patient, such as physical deprivations and poor mothering, or to social, familial, and cultural pressures, or various combinations of several factors (Guiora, 1967; Wilson, 1982; Bruch, 1985; Orbach, 1985; Wooley and Wooley, 1985).

The nonpsychoanalytic literature, in general, does not distinguish between the reality of actual relationships in the life of a patient and the fantasies—conscious and unconscious—that are held by that same patient. They seem to assume that the patient's report about his life correctly presents a documentary without contradiction. For the psychoanalyst, of course, the so-called *real* experiences, for example, the *real* mother who was good or bad, is not nearly so important as the internalized representations of that mother and the experiences with her. The thoughtful review of the literature on normal-weight bulimics by Mitchell and Pyle (1982) tends to support the psychoanalytic view. They point out that the issues of weight, food, and hunger are attached to fantasies, and that bulimics do not show any greater vulnerability to food stimuli, a finding also confirmed by Wilson (1976).

Some workers in the field—notably Bruch—have utilized both analytic and nonanalytic approaches at various times. Behavior modification, group and family therapy, chemotherapy, hospitalization, and supportive psychotherapy are widely used with varying degrees of success reported. Since bulimia occurs in an older group of women who have often moved away from their parents, family therapy is less often used.

Only a few researchers stress biologic origins of the eating disorders. Friedman (1972) confirmed a hypothesis in eight obese subjects that spontaneous oral activity waxes and wanes in cycles similar to the REM cycle in sleep. He found a relationship between states of tension (intellectual restlessness) and shorter oral activity cycles. He offers the speculation that the shortened oral drive cycle relates to instinctual regression, an early and regressive response to stress, since babies and young children are known to have shorter REM cycles.

Wooley and Wooley (1985) put forth a provocative idea based on the concept of the phantom limb in relation to body image. "It is interesting to speculate," they write, "whether tissue lost in starvation may have a continuous representation, which may account for persistent and irrational feelings of fatness. . . . The preoccupation with the stomach, and the often inexplicable perception of bloat and distension, may be attempts of the brain to represent the missing functions and sensations normally associated with eating" (p. 398).

Russell (1979), who introduced the term bulimia nervosa, believes that the condition is most likely based on a failure of the satiety mechanism, postulating the operation of an undiscovered hypothalamic pathway. He admits, however, that "overeating could at times be interpreted as meeting an unfulfilled emotional need" (p. 443).

Nearly everyone has agreed that symptoms of depression are common concomitants to bulimia, but much remains to be learned about the relationship of these two conditions. Rich (1978) advises treatment of the underlying depression, even questioning whether bulimia is a valid diagnostic category. Russell (1979) acknowledges the frequent presence of depression, for which he advises treatment, but points out that bulimic symptoms are unaffected by alleviation of the depression.

Bruch (1985), a major investigator in the field for decades, downgrades the influence of the "cultural emphasis on increasing slenderness" as a major factor in these disorders. But she upgrades the demands of "the changing status of women" and of the expectations placed on them. Boskind-Lodahl and White (1978), however, report that the common fantasy among college women with eating disorders in their study was that "their lives would be successful only if they were thin and pretty . . ." (p. 85). For Bruch, "the basic illness is not a disturbance of the eating function . . . [but due] to underlying disturbances in the development of the personality." She says that patients feel helpless and ineffective; "the severe discipline over their bodies represents a desperate effort to ward off panic about being completely powerless. . . . of not having a core personality of their own, of being powerless and ineffective when they 'give in' " (pp. 9–10).

Bruch's psychoanalytic approach, following that of her teacher, H. S. Sullivan, does not pay heed to the Oedipus complex or to sexual factors. She writes that there has been a change in thinking over the years and that "instead of searching for definite underlying unconscious conflicts, the focus [is now upon] . . . reconstruction of what had really happened during patients' early development or on how they recalled the past" (p. 17). Her approach is in sympathy with the recent trends in self-psychology proposed by Kohut and others.

The self psychology technique described by Goodsitt (1985) calls for "filling in the deficit" in the self that is assumed to have occurred in early development. This is accomplished, in his opinion, when, for example, "the therapist takes over responsibility for feeding the patient," force-feeding when necessary (p. 73).

Sexual factors in the eating disorders are not often considered in the nonpsychoanalytic literature and, for the most part, are played down in importance. The broad-based concept of sexuality that is intrinsic to psychoanalytic theory is usually narrowed by nonanalytic researchers to include only adult aspects of sexual behavior and attitudes. In a study by Beumont et al. (1981), for example, of the sexual attitudes of young women with anorexia nervosa, the authors found that many of their patients saw sexual problems as "major precipitants" of their illness. But the authors arrive at the puzzling conclusion that since "no one type of psychosexual history is common to all . . . it would seem unlikely that sexual factors have a specific role in the etiology of the condition, although in some individual patients there may be a direct relationship between the onset of eating difficulties and concurrent sexual problems" (p. 138). It is also true that some psychoanalytic workers diminish the importance of sexual factors in anorexia and bulimia (Mushatt 1982; Wilson, 1982).

THE BULIMIC FANTASY

The strongest evidence supporting the importance of unconscious pregnancy fantasies in anorexia and bulimia derives from an examination of the actual words, attitudes, and convictions of these patients. Obsessively held ideas, which seem so bizarre at first and which are regularly enacted in the symptoms of these patients, take on a clear and consistent meaning. All of the functions relating to sexual reproduction are displaced to functions of alimentation. The prominent patterns of anorexia and bulimia are only two of the many symptom complexes that give expression to a woman's sexual anxiety. The fact that these syndromes occur predominantly in women lends support to this approach. Those cases that occur in men probably represent examples of identification with the woman's reproductive capacity.

The fantasy that something special exists within the body of the woman is an important theme. Sperling (1971) has analyzed cases of ulcerative colitis in women (some had anorexia as well) who imagined that little people were in the colon. A patient, described by Bruch (1978), verbalized a familiar theme in anorexics: "I feel [my mother] is in me—even if she isn't there" (p. 53). Sometimes the thing within her body is described as a monster (Rizzuto, 1985); or sometimes as a nondescript, insatiable void or "empty aloneness" (Russell, 1979). The thing within her body is sometimes attacked by the bulimic "in an all-destroying rage" (Guiora, 1967).

The work of nonanalytic investigators, such as Rosen and Leitenberg (1985), who use behavioral techniques in the treatment of bulimia, is especially noteworthy for the psychoanalyst. Behavioral models of the mind try to understand the symptoms in terms of misconceptions and as expressions of habits set up as reactions to stress. Behaviorists who study bulimia have carefully elucidated these misconceptions and errors of perception, which, for the psychoanalyst, provide a rich source of data about the fantasy life of the bulimic. These fantasies can nearly always be understood as infantile—and therefore distorted—aspects of impregnation, now symbolized in habits and displaced to nonsexual areas.

A morbid fear of weight gain along with binging and a plan to vomit, occur in almost every case and are untouched by logical argument or rational persuasion. Fat and weight stand for a pregnancy; vomiting, for its termination. Even a normal intake of food is feared as if a large weight gain will follow, and the exaggerated concern about nutrition is often completely at odds with accepted facts. One of its milder forms is demonstrated by the group of bulimic college women cited previously who expressed the conviction that for their lives to be successful they must be thin and pretty (Boskind-Lodahl and White, 1978).

Vomiting is believed by the bulimic to rid her of the entire intake of food, even after a lapse of time. This irrational conviction makes sense if one accepts the premise implicit in the bulimic's belief that the effect of eating (fat, weight) is an all-or-none reaction, like conception. If forbidden pregnancy is unconsciously at the roots of the bulimic binge, then the fact that vomiting so often effectively relieves guilt is explained. The following convictions were all expressed by normal-weight bulimics (Rosen and Leitenberg, 1985) in the course of behavioral therapy. They are completely consistent with the data of psychoanalysis:

—If I eat normally, but do not vomit, I will gain an enormous amount of weight.
—Slight weight variations are noticeable.
—Losing weight will alter other physical characteristics of my body.

—Only certain foods add weight (irrespective of caloric content).

—Some foods cause immediate weight gain.

—Vomiting, even after a long delay, will prevent food already eaten from being digested. (As an abortion undoes a pregnancy.)

—If I gain a pound, it might as well be a hundred. (One is never only a little bit pregnant. Food is spoken of as if it were a contaminant.)

—One's personality and worth as a person depends upon whether one has lost or gained a few pounds.

—The sensation of fullness after eating, a most unpleasant sensation, will not go away (be digested), so I must vomit.

These fantasies can be nicely explained as aspects of distorted (infantile) pregnancy fantasies. Food is analogous to the impregnating substance—the semen—a little bit of semen makes a woman *very* pregnant. Vomiting on the model of abortion is an evacuation of the incorporated pregnancy. Altering the physical characteristics of one's body is like the hiding of a guilt-ridden pregnancy. Slight weight fluctuations are noticeable just as an unwanted pregnancy will surely be noticed in the inevitable, at first, slight, physical alterations in a woman's body when she conceives. Only certain foods are believed to be capable, and are assigned the unconscious role of impregnation in the woman's fantasy. An anorexic patient said, "I always had the feeling that if I had the tiniest bit of rice, I'd blow up and be huge" (Risen, 1982, p. 451). The characteristics of the food in this regard are usually highly specific, and texture, smell, and taste are idiosyncratic for each woman (see, for example, the case reported by Leonard, 1944). Food is categorized as good or bad, or as allowed or forbidden. Sweets, bread, and red meat are commonly among the bad foods, while diet foods are good.

Behavioral treatment seeks to modify irrational beliefs and, foremost, to relieve the anxiety and depression that is provoked by eating, rejecting the notion of deeper psychologic causes. Psychoanalytic therapy aims at analyzing these irrational fears and to make them conscious for the patient. The relief of anxiety and depression are side effects of ego growth. Analysis, as in the case of Mrs. H., led to the discovery of some of her unconscious, infantile, oral-incorporative, pregnancy fantasies that served to defend against the Oedipus complex.

THE BULIMIC FANTASY IN FICTION

At some point nearly every case of anorexia or bulimia reveals underlying fantasies that have the quality of psychosis. It is always striking when an intelligent, productive, sometimes vibrant young woman begins to show signs of splitting and denial of reality. Therapy is arduous in the best of cases and is often filled with doubts and frustration for the therapist. It is difficult to reproduce in reports, the emotional intensity of the work. Several great writers, however, have caught the emotional turmoil and the sense of intellectual paralysis that so often characterize the work with anorexics and bulimics. Literary fictional creations reveal truths because they have their roots of origin in everyone's private daydreams and secret fantasies, and, like actual symptoms, are derived from unconscious fantasies embodying basic childhood wishes and forbidden impulses—aggressive, sexual, and grandiose in nature—that give rise to intrapsychic conflict (Arlow, 1986).

Franz Kafka's story, "A Hunger Artist" (1938), captures the uncanny mixture of horror, ecstasy, and misunderstanding aroused by observing self-imposed starvation. Obsessive determination, victory in resignation, indifference to the onlooking world around, and a willingness to die, if necessary, for a cause are all wrapped up in a rationalized package. The hunger artist (a man in Kafka's story) starves himself periodically in public displays in order to make his living, a paradox that lies at the core of many a case of anorexia. (The bulimic also feels starved, but she performs her rites of starvation in a disguised cyclical pattern.) Kafka's hunger artist, with his dying breath, makes sure that his observers understand that he craves food like anyone else. "I couldn't find the food I liked," he says. "If I had found it, believe me, I should have made no fuss and stuffed myself like you or anyone else" (p. 277). Selvini, an Italian researcher, asserts that "hunger often persists in starving patients until the terminal phase" (Sours, 1974, p. 569).

The obsessional victory in self-starvation is reminiscent of another amazing character from fiction. Herman Melville's Bartleby, the scrivener (1856), puts his face to the wall in prison and dies, curled in a fetal position, victoriously defiant toward those who wished for him to eat and to live. In his obsessional refusal to comply with any demands made upon him he is like the anorexic who cannot accept any intrusion into her body or mind in the form of food or thought.

When the anorexic dies it seems that it is always a victory, a victory that no one other than the patient can appreciate. The hunger artist felt that "the world was cheating him of his reward" through its failure to understand, through its indifference and its malice. Kafka concludes the story of the puzzle of the hunger artist, whose insatiable hunger leads to death, with a brilliant, explanatory metaphor. After the dead man is cleared out of his cage and buried, "straw and all," the cage is filled with a young panther, leaping, hungry, free, and full of the joy of life. The anorexic, surprisingly, is usually superficially full of life, even as she approaches death.

In a short story by Isaac B. Singer, "One Night in Brazil" (1978), a woman, Lena, is possessed by a dybbuk, the spirit of her dead former lover. She feels his head inside her belly, tormenting her, sometimes pressing up into her throat choking her. The possession occurred after her current husband became impotent. In her quest for love, she attempts to seduce the narrator of the story who is a guest for the night, a man she had met in her youth. "Sometimes I want the dybbuk to go up to my throat and finish me off. . . . I'm ripe for death, but I lack the courage to act. Don't laugh at me, but I still dream of love." Before he took up a position in her belly, she felt her former lover tickling her, pinching, pushing, and choking her. "All of a sudden, I got up one morning with a huge swelling there. It's actually a head, his head. . . ." The doctors diagnose neurosis, which she dismisses with contempt: "When an X-ray shows nothing, it doesn't exist. But a head has settled inside my stomach. I can feel his nose, his brow, his skull." In the attempted seduction in an Edenlike setting, Lena and her guest fall from a hammock into a slimy marsh and are attacked by mosquitoes. She regards the fall as a punishment for the wish to sin. The man is washed and tended to and is then wrapped naked in a sheet, "like a corpse in a shroud." This symbolic birth and swaddling of a baby shows that her dybbuk is unconsciously an incorporated pregnancy, and the former lover is a magically incorporated baby. The flat belly represents the nonpregnant state. Singer's dybbuk-possessed woman says, "I've always done calisthenics and I had a flat belly, almost like a man's," a declaration of her innocence and a defense against the transgressions against the oedipal mother.

CONCLUSION

The symbolic pregnancy is a frequent dynamic factor in anorexia and bulimia. Mrs. H., a married woman without children, was obsessed with the wish to become a mother. Her bulimia was an unconscious rejection of pregnancy that was based on, and linked up with, incompatible associations that began in childhood. Food ingested in secret binges was the unconscious fulfillment of a forbidden wish—to have her father's baby. The clash of impossible contradictions in her competing wishes brought her to treatment.

Whenever Mrs. H. ate "too much," she felt very uncomfortable, especially in bed, because of the sensation of a bulge in her stomach. It was clear from her description that she was protecting an imaginary fetus in her belly. A flat stomach represented her nonpregnant state, a physical declaration of her innocence, even as she longed to conceive.

Mrs. H. was envious of her mother's pregnancies and, by means of the mental act of oral incorporation, took her mother and her mother's baby into her own belly. She never felt better than when she was actually pregnant, and the head in her belly was real.

Many of the cases in the literature on eating disorders demonstrate the same phenomena. In the case of anorexia investigated by Sperling (1968), an adolescent girl with anorexia pulled and ate her own hair. The hair pulled from her head represented her mother's genital hair, and the ball of hair that formed in her stomach "was like her mother's face with hair on it. . . ." (p. 683). Bruch's patient (1978) spoke of feeling full of her mother, "I feel she is in me—even if she isn't there" (p. 53).

As long as Mrs. H.'s new infant remained orally dependent upon her she remained blissfully contented; all of her cravings for sweets abated. It was as if the child was still inside her. When the pediatrician insisted that she begin to offer the cup instead of the breast to her baby, her intolerable frustration returned and she began the pattern of secret gorging and vomiting. She kept herself in ignorance of her resentment and hostility to her own baby, totally denying the potential damage she might be doing to her child through her forced infantilization of her.

Oral incorporation is both a loving taking in and a hostile devouring of a love object. In the guise of being a good mother who gives food and love, she actually became a bad mother.

REFERENCES

Abraham, K. (1924), A short study of the development of the libido, viewed in the light of mental disorders. In: *Selected Papers on Psycho-analysis.* London: Hogarth Press, 1949.

American Psychiatric Association (1980), *Diagnostic and Statistical Manual of Mental Disorders,* 3rd ed. (DSM-III). Washington, DC: American Psychiatric Press.

Anderson, A. E. (1985), Pregnancy and fertility in patients with anorexia nervosa or bulimia. In: *Practical Comprehensive Treatment of Anorexia Nervosa and Bulimia.* Baltimore: Johns Hopkins University Press, pp. 160–164.

Arlow, J. (1986), The poet as prophet: A psychoanalytic perspective. *Psychoanal. Quart.,* 55:53–68.

Beumont, P. J. V., Abraham, S. F., & Simson, K. G. (1981), The psychosexual histories of adolescent girls and young women with anorexia nervosa. *Psychological Med.,* 11:131–140.

Boris, H. N. (1984a), The problem of anorexia nervosa. *Internat. J. Psycho-Anal.,* 65:315–322.

——— (1984b), On the treatment of anorexia nervosa. *Internat. J. Psycho-Anal.,* 65:435–442.

Boskind-Lodahl, M., & White, W. C. (1978), The definition and treatment of bulimarexia in college women: A pilot study. *J. Amer. College Health Assn.*, 27:84–86, 97.

Brown, E. B. (1979), Hypochromic anemias. In: *Cecil, Textbook of Medicine*, 15th ed., ed. P. B. Beeson, W. McDermott, & J. B. Wyngaarden. Philadelphia: Saunders, pp. 1743–1751.

Bruch, H. (1978), *The Golden Cage*. Cambridge, MA: Harvard University Press.

——— (1985), Four decades of eating disorders. In: *Handbook of Psychotherapy for Anorexia Nervosa and Bulimia*, ed. D. M. Garner & P. E. Garfinkel. New York: Guilford Press, pp. 7–18.

Fenichel, O. (1945), *Psychoanalytic Theory of the Neuroses*. New York: W. W. Norton.

French, A. P., & Nelson, H. L. (1972), Genital self-mutilation in women. *Arch. Gen. Psychiat.*, 27:618–620.

Freud, S. (1895), Studies on Hysteria. *Standard Edition*, 2. London: Hogarth Press, 1955.

——— (1900), The Interpretation of Dreams. *Standard Edition*, 5. London: Hogarth Press, 1953.

Friedman, S. (1972), On the presence of a variant form of instinctual regression: Oral drive cycles in obesity-bulimia. *Psychoanal. Quart.*, 41:364–383.

Garner, D. M., & Garfinkel, P. E., Eds. (1985), *Handbook of Psychotherapy for Anorexia Nervosa and Bulimia*. New York: Guilford Press.

Goodsitt, A. (1985), Self psychology and the treatment of anorexia nervosa. In: *Handbook of Psychotherapy for Anorexia Nervosa and Bulimia*, ed. D. M. Garner & P. E. Garfinkel. New York: Guilford Press, pp. 55–82.

Guiora, A. Z. (1967), Dysorexia: A psychopathological study of anorexia nervosa and bulimia. *Amer. J. Psychiat.*, 124:391–393.

Halmi, K. A., Falk, J. R., & Schwartz, E. (1981), Binge-eating and vomiting: A survey of a college population. *Psycholog. Med.*, 11:697–706.

Hughes, A. (1984), Book review. *Fear of Being Fat: The Treatment of Anorexia Nervosa and Bulimia*, ed. C. P. Wilson, C. Hogan, & I. Mintz. New York: Jason Aronson, 1983. *Internat. J. Psycho-Anal*, 65:497–498.

Johnson, C. (1985), Initial consultation for patients with bulimia and anorexia nervosa. In: *Handbook of Psychotherapy for Anorexia Nervosa and Bulimia*, ed. D. M. Garner & P. E. Garfinkel. New York: Guilford Press, pp. 19–54.

——— Larson, R. (1982), Bulimia: An analysis of moods and behavior. *Psychosom. Med.*, 44:341–351.

Kafka, F. (1938), A hunger artist. In: *The Complete Stories*, ed. N. N. Glatzer. New York: Schocken Books, 1971, pp. 268–277.

Kalucy, R. S., Crisp, A. H., & Harding, B. (1977), A study of 56 families with anorexia nervosa. *Brit. J. Psychol.*, 50:381–395.

——— Lacey, J. H., & Harding, B. (1977), Prevalence and prognosis in anorexia nervosa. *Austral. & N.Z. J. Psychiat.*, 11:251–257.

——— Gilcrist, P. N., McFarlane, C. M., & McFarlane, A. C. (1985), Evolution of a multi-therapy orientation. In: *Handbook of Psychotherapy for Anorexia Nervosa and Bulimia*, ed. D. M. Garner & P. E. Garfinkel. New York: Guilford Press, pp. 458–490.

Lacey, J. H. (1985), Time-limited individual and group treatment for bulimia.

344 DANIEL B. GESENSWAY

In: *Handbook of Psychotherapy for Anorexia Nervosa and Bulimia*, ed. D. M.
Garner & P. E. Garfinkel. New York: Guilford Press, pp. 431–457.
Leonard, C. E. (1944), An analysis of a case of functional vomiting and
bulimia. *Psychoanal. Rev.*, 31:1–18.
Melville, H. (1856), Bartleby the scrivenor. In: *Four Short Novels*. New York:
Bantam Books, 1959.
Mitchell, J. E., & Pyle, R. L. (1982), The bulimic syndrome in normal weight
individuals: A review. *Internat. J. Eat. Disord.*, 1:61–73.
Mogul, S.L. (1980), Asceticism in adolescence and anorexia nervosa. *The Psychoanalytic Study of the Child*, 35:155–175. New Haven, CT: Yale University
Press.
Mushatt, C. (1982), Anorexia nervosa: A psychoanalytic commentary. *Internat.
J. Psychoanal. Psychother.*, 9:257–265.
Orbach, S. (1985), Accepting the symptom: A feminist psychoanalytic treatment of anorexia nervosa. In: *Handbook of Psychotherapy for Anorexia Nervosa and Bulimia*, ed. D. M. Garner & P. E. Garfinkel. New York: Guilford
Press, pp. 83–107.
Rich, C. L. (1978). Self-induced vomiting. *J. Amer. Med. Assn.*, 239:2688–2689.
Risen, S. E. (1982), The psychoanalytic treatment of an adolescent with anorexia nervosa. *The Psychoanalytic Study of the Child*, 37:433–459. New
Haven, CT: Yale University Press.
Rizzuto, A. (1985), Eating and monsters: A psychodynamic view of bulimarexia. In: *Theory and Treatment of Anorexia Nervosa and Bulimia*, ed. S. W.
Emmett. New York: Brunner/Mazel.
Rosen, J. C., & Leitenberg, H. (1985), Exposure plus response prevention
treatment of bulimia. In: *Handbook of Psychotherapy for Anorexia Nervosa
and Bulimia*, ed. D. M. Garner & P. E. Garfinkel. New York: Guilford
Press, pp. 193–212.
Russell, G. (1979), Bulimia nervosa: An ominous variant of anorexia nervosa.
Psycholog. Med., 9:429–448.
——— (1985), Anorexia nervosa. In: *Cecil, Textbook of Medicine*, 17th ed., ed.
J. B. Wyngaarden & L. H. Smith. Philadelphia: Saunders, pp. 1188–1191.
Simpson, M. A. (1973), Female genital self-mutilation. *Arch. Gen. Psychiat.*,
29:808–809.
Singer, I. B. (1978), One night in Brazil. *The New Yorker*, April 3:34–40.
Sours, J. A. (1974), The anorexia nervosa syndrome. *Internat. J. Psycho-Anal.*,
55:567–576.
Sperling, M. (1968), Trichotillomania, trichophagy, and cyclic vomiting: A
contribution to the psychopathology of female sexuality. *Internat. J. Psycho-Anal.*, 49:682–690.
——— (1971), Spider phobias and spider fantasies: A clinical contribution to
the study of symbol and symptom choice. *J. Amer. Psychoanal. Assn.*,
19:472–498.
Strober, M., & Yager, J. (1985), Developmental perspective on the treatment
of anorexia nervosa in adolescents. In: *Handbook of Psychotherapy for Anorexia Nervosa and Bulimia*, ed. D. M. Garner & P. E. Garfinkel. New York:
Guilford Press, pp. 363–390.
Wilson, C. P. (1982), The fear of being fat and anorexia nervosa. *Internat. J.
Psychoanal. Psychother.*, 9:233–255.

Wilson, G. T. (1976), Obesity, binge eating, and behavior therapy: Some clinical observations. *Behav. Ther.*, 7:700–701.

Wooley, S. C., & Wooley, O. W. (1985), Intensive outpatient and residential treatment for bulimia. In: *Handbook of Psychotherapy for Anorexia Nervosa and Bulimia*, ed. D. M. Garner & P. E. Garfinkel. New York: Guilford Press, pp. 391–430.

Chapter 11

On Eating Disorders and Work Inhibition

MARIA V. BERGMANN

In my work with several patients, both eating disorders and work inhibition occurred, alerting me to the possibility that a connection between the two syndromes might exist. Eating has to do with taking in and eliminating, and working requires taking in (by learning) and putting out (a product). Were there similarities in the psychic structure and object relationship pathology underlying these phenomena?

It appears that disorders in both food intake and elimination may lead to subsequent disturbances in the capacity to work, particularly when working by oneself or when producing an original piece of work. Both eating and working disturbances may have their inception in the earliest infant–mother interaction.

There is a maturational time at which oral and anal experiences take on more than the fulfillment of life-sustaining functions. In the child, they become instinctually cathected, and care-giving objects transmit affects and internal conflicts as they interact with infants. The vulnerability or solidity of the child's internal structure will depend on constitutional factors, the mother's behavior as a care giver, and auxiliary figures in the child's environment who may facilitate or disturb the child's adaptive processes. It is not easy to explain why in some children minor disturbances emanating from care givers markedly affect their affective disposition, structure, and character. The mother's attitudes are central and Stern (1980) has observed and re-

ported on a number of early object and infant interactions that
have an almost immediate impact on modes of internalization
while the psychic structure is being formed.

The child who enjoys self-feeding and expresses pleasure
in filling a spoon with food and putting it into the mother's
mouth is learning what gives pleasure to the body, and how to
obtain pleasure by imitation and identification with a care giver.
The mother's manner of handling the child's body and the
concomitant affect is her earliest communication and the child
will either feel loved and also wish to "do it" to and with the
mother, or, when there is no object love, it will feel discomfort,
anxiety, and even a sense of being abandoned.

The child who is fed and taught to eliminate within the
framework of a developing object relationship will love its own
body, experience pleasure, and wish for mastery and self-feeding. A capacity for identification with the care giver will establish
a mutuality wherein the activity or the product are experienced
together as pleasurable, and this, in turn, may become a paradigm for a later capacity to create something on one's own and
to derive pleasure from it.

If object representations become internalized without excessive conflict, fantasy, an increased scope for affective self-
expression, and greater cognitive and symbolizing capacities,
all promote further differentiation of self and object. The child
will experience a growing sense of an internal core-self, which
is essential for play, learning, and the capacity to thrive. Ac-
quiring the capacity to work and become independently creative
depends on its earliest expression of the mother's approval of
the child's first productions and achievements *away from her*. A
balance of feeling dependent, yet loved, and, at the same time,
increasingly autonomous and receiving narcissistic gratification
from experiences of mastery will promote a wish to work. Successful separation strengthens symbolic processes and motivation for learning. Individuation enhances enjoyment of learning
and promotes a capacity to thrive in social situations.

The initial experience of food intake and elimination may be
thought of in the terms of Hanna Segal's (1957) "symbolic
equations," wherein the symbol substitute is felt *to be* the original

object and the substitute's own properties are not recognized or differentiated from it. Such symbolic equations belong to the earliest stages of development, and the child, with only presymbolic capacity, does not differentiate the mother and her milk or the body products as belonging to either infant or mother, and these are therefore neither internal nor external.

Toward the end of the first year of life, internal representations increasingly assume a transitional quality of "me and not me" (Winnicott, 1953) and differentiation is further developed during the practicing subphases (Mahler, Bergman, and Pine, 1975). Sugarman and Kurash (1982), in discussing addicted adolescents maintain that the incapacity to take the maturational step from symbolic equation to symbol formation proper, that is, from the differentiation of the actual mother to her maternal representation, "leaves the infant arrested at the stage of symbolic equation" (p. 531). I believe that a regressive pull for the need of an immediately soothing product or activity may occur in nonaddicts as well, particularly when the early object interactions were experienced under stressful or traumatic conditions. Ensuing character formation will likely include an addictive predisposition.

When object relatedness has been substituted by the giving of concrete things to the child, the child is deprived of the capacity to libidinally cathect its interactions with primary objects and its body with pleasure. A child who misses object love will yearn for immediate substitute gratification and, in extreme cases, will never master waiting; it then cannot develop a realistic sense of time.

Children feel loved while being fed and physically cared for, but if the child never experiences the mother beyond being a feeder or a dispenser of need gratification on an archaic level, the child's capacity for symbol formation will remain arrested: the psychic representation of feeder and food may remain insufficiently differentiated. This may be observed in patients who as children had been subjected either to an unpredictable oscillation between frustration and oral gratification or to excessive indulgence. As long as feeder and product remain equated, differentiation of self and object will also become arrested; the capacity for anticipation will be short-circuited and self constancy and development of autonomy will be curtailed.

The experiences of intake and elimination probably influence the character of many later internalization and externalization processes. Incorporation may not allow for a separate inner space for an object, so that the object becomes part of the inner world of the child without maintaining its function as an object per se. In introjection, on the other hand, there is intermittent separateness from the object. In identification, the *quality* of the object is differentiated and preserved, and, thus, the object can be experienced as having an autonomous existence. The degree to which this separateness has been achieved is crucial for the level of internalization and capacity for symbolization that will develop.

Krystal (1982) has observed that "Drug dependence may be used as a process of taking in and using the drug rather than . . . having it" (p. 582). The drug-dependent person attempts to introject a benign maternal object, yet his ambivalence toward this object causes the individual to reexternalize the substance as quickly as possible (p. 283). This seems to me to be a significant statement, because, while internalization *does* take place, it is lost because the object cannot be counted on and object constancy remains underdeveloped. Excessive hostility toward the object does not permit an addiction-prone individual to hold on to a good feeling toward an actual or emotional feeder for any length of time: internalization may be achieved and lost again. I believe this tendency is found not only in real addicts, but also in *charcterological* addicts and in bulimic–anorexic disturbances, as I shall describe in the case vignettes that follow.

The need for a "quick fix" will be established when the child cannot sustain the intolerable gap of anxious waiting for gratification from the object, because waiting is equated with object loss. If the mother is an unpredictable feeder and care giver, she will interfere with separation processes and with what Mahler (1971) called the mother's need to relinquish the child's body as her own possession. When the mother uses the child's body without sufficient attunement to the child's needs, but rather as an instrument to quiet her own anxieties or conflicts, she promotes conflict in the child because she remains too important as "external mother" and as a result interferes with the child's ability to build an internalized representation or symbolization of her care-giving activities. When the external mother is too controlling, the child's needs oscillate between separation and closeness during the rapprochement subphase and this will interfere with its developmental spurt toward separation.

EATING DISORDERS, LEARNING, AND WORKING

Minimal frustration tolerance and incapacity to wait for results produce difficulties in learning. The need to master something new may be experienced as a burden; a feeling of helplessness may ensue and the child may respond with rage and a fantasy that the task was imposed by a frustrating object who is withholding, forcing, and demanding. The child then wishes for the mother to do it, rather than to be taught *how* to do it. If the mother continues to do things for the child, she is experienced as a good feeding object and as a need-gratifier. A precedent is set for an object relationship where need-gratification has been substituted for mastery of new tasks. In its adaptation to new tasks, the child will continue to feel helpless, anxious, or enraged, and the mother's lack of readiness to continue to help may be experienced as abandonment. The development of ego functions as well as independent feeding and toilet functions may be slowed by this conflict.

As these early pathological interactions involve the child's body, it may become a battleground between parent and child. The child may use the body as an instrument for punishing the feeding object, who has been experienced as depriving, and who has not permitted independent mastery and has not shared in the joy of achieving it.

Overeating, vomiting, and self-starvation may become expressions of archaic revenge fantasies. The stage has been set for anorectic or bulimic behavior. In bulimia and anorexia, the tendencies toward destruction of self and object seem always to be present. There are pervasive mechanisms of self-punishment; the self is punished by the superego for its battle against introjected objects, but continues to behave punitively toward the internalized object representations. Feeling states engendered in interactions between self and object may resurface with their full traumatic impact and may create a conflict representing a struggle between life and death. In both bulimia and anorexia, the individual unconsciously needs to destroy the object or the self in lieu of it. In eating disturbances, symptom formation includes fantasies about the body as an instrument of hostile communication between parent and child. This hostility may be so intense that it may cause disturbances in levels of self-cathexis; there may be states of depersonalization, unleashed by an estranged body whose functions have been put into the service of defense. The child's externalization of conflict is used to avoid anxiety, yet the body remains the battleground. In treatment, internal conflict is not initially verbalized, only the discomfort accompanying it. There is a tendency to attempt to master internally perceived states of neediness through activity in the external world. There is never a sense of satiety. In concretizing the conflict, the bulimic or anorectic patient severs the connection between internal conflicts and ongoing external activities. The object continues to be experienced as ungiving, but at the same time neediness toward the object continues. Continued despair may lead to addictive forms of eating disorders in an attempt to refind the good object through substitute gratifications which allow a temporary "high."

Masturbation as an expression of a need for solace or discharge of rage often accompanies "characterological" addictive tendencies. Masturbation guilt based on forbidden fantasies may cause displacement of an inhibition into the cognitive or creative areas.

Freud recognized this in 1938 when he remarked:

The ultimate ground of all intellectual inhibitions and all inhibitions of work seems to be the inhibition of masturbation in childhood. But perhaps it goes deeper; perhaps it is not its inhibition by external influences but its unsatisfying nature in itself. There is always something lacking for complete discharge and satisfaction . . . [p. 300].

In these cases, masturbation, infantile perversions, or addictive behavior may temporarily substitute for the difficulty of refinding the good object, but inhibit self-expression in other areas.

WORK INHIBITION

When reality becomes intolerable, fantasy will be substituted for reality and accrue to the object representation to permit adaptation and to assure survival (Bergmann, 1980, 1982a,b). Rebellion against eating, toilet training, and other forms of learning may start very early. Negativism and rage may be an attempt to communicate internal distress. Having to "do it" alone arouses discomfort, anxiety, rage, and a feeling of being abandoned. Learning is not accompanied by pleasure. It becomes something the child is not sure it can master. A sense of incompetence and rage may extend into other areas and inhibit ego functions and the capacity for sublimation. Even when the child initiates an independent effort, it may experience its actions as imposed by a frustrating external object.

Just as a young child with eating disturbances fails to thrive, the work-inhibited child in an analogous way fails to thrive in social situations, particularly from latency onward. Some children can only play, some can only work, and there are some who can do neither. The sudden awareness of gender differences may cause cognitive and affective disturbances, inhibit independent efforts already in the second year of life, and create intellectual and learning inhibitions (Roiphe and Galenson, 1981).

Parental overindulgence promotes pathological narcissism, magical thinking, and passivity which interfere with reality testing and with self-confidence in achievement. Patients with work inhibition rarely remember having been praised by parents or teachers for what they produced as children. Failure to thrive in school leads to social alienation, estrangement, and anxieties connected with independent work. Intrapsychically, the object representation remains forever depriving and critical about the child's work activity and product. Narcissistic problems and superego pressure become active against success, although both child and adult usually attribute learning or work difficulties to concrete situations in the outside world.

While in eating disorders, direct attacks are lived out against the subject's body, with body-image distortions and a need to punish the body, in work inhibition, the *product* is attacked or must never be given birth to. In both types of disturbance, hostility caused a tendency toward depression and a melancholic and masochistic stance in which the wrath toward the object "falls upon the ego" (to paraphrase Freud, 1917).

I wish to advance the possibility that work inhibition re-creates a traumatic interaction from the past. A dialogue with an important past object is relived. My case studies suggest that some work inhibitions can be traced to the earliest conflicts related to eating and elimination. A major psychic conflict is expressed while "getting ready to work" or while obstacles toward working are being created. This conflict is grafted upon the external work in delays and activities, often ritualistic in nature, which represent the early conflict. Work-inhibited patients repeat certain rituals over and over. These rituals unconsciously represent or connect to the original trauma. Unconscious fantasy resulting from early trauma makes it impossible to work. Under these conditions, symbolic capacity is impaired and the arena of conflict shifts into the real world—to action. Children who were not praised and achieved little independent mastery do not have a firm internal representation of themselves as independent workers in adulthood. When they attempt to work, a traumatic feeling state of being ignored, in spite of great efforts, may be revived. It is as if the patient must make restitution and create peace with a critical internalized parental object before work can be attempted on an autonomous level and in an adult manner. It is as if earlier failures have to be undone symbolically to create self-confidence. Staving off the return of the traumatic feeling state that led to rage and frustration is necessary as it interferes with working. A major psychic conflict may be expressed while getting ready to work or while seeming to attempt to remove obstacles that are in the way of working.

Compulsive masturbation and fantasies or activities of a perverse nature may be the outcome of failures in work and creativity. The internal object representation who is experienced as critical and hostile is frequently the same as the nonfeeding object of early childhood, unempathic, not helpful, and thereby a direct inhibitor of autonomous activity.

As long as work is not possible, the need to work intermittently becomes "unreal" or meaningless in the nonworking state. In this state, a good self-feeling is achieved through "giving oneself something" in the form of food, masturbation, perverse activities or fantasies, or other forms of flight from reality in order to obtain relief from intense frustration, rage, and from superego pressures. As soon as these good feelings cease, superego punishment returns. Superego pressure is also experienced as stemming from oedipal objects who represent authority and toward whom the nonworker experiences rebellion and a wish for revenge. As the oedipal parent has to be punished, success cannot be achieved.

I found it necessary to separate rituals that work-inhibited people undertake before they work from their frustrations from the work itself, which often represents a traumatic reliving from the past. Psychic conflict is reenacted in the preparation preceding work. At the same time, restitution may be made symbolically for a traumatic object relationship so that work may commence.

CASE EXAMPLE 1

Ms. L., who had done original work in sculpture, entered analysis in her forties. She came to treatment because she was "stuck." She was able to complete short projects on her own, quickly, almost furtively, but a current project was of larger proportions and promised recognition in her field. This frightened her.

When Ms. L. came to treatment she was overweight, a chain smoker, a heavy coffee drinker, and often consumed alcohol to the point of stupor. She was easily aroused sexually, but did not experience orgasm after marriage. She often suffered from a sense that she lacked self-continuity so that she would "forget her work" and catch herself believing what she pretended to others, namely, that she had in fact completed a work of art. In a feeling state of greater continuity, she asked, "Where have I been all this time?"

Ms. L. came from a close-knit family and in her first consultation brought photographs of family members. She could not present herself alone. She could not be alone and was phobic about traveling far away from home; when she did so, she packed enormous amounts "to feel safe." Following adolescence, she had lost both parents—her father after a brief but severe illness, and the mother suddenly, under traumatic circumstances. When the patient tried to work, she had to be away from home and close to other artists. It took her a long time to get ready; she had to lie down, take a nap, eat, drink, or make telephone calls. She could go through several boxes of cookies in a short time. When these were not available, she went looking for the "junk food" of her childhood. Her colleagues who worked nearby told her that, as she always arrived so late, they were tempted to raid her drawers for her food and that they knew they could always have a meal.

She thought that these activities lessened her anxiety. Her attention span at work would last from three to twenty minutes until she was able to work with concentration as a result of treatment. But initially work was also delayed because she felt compelled to disassemble the pieces of her work and start all over again or use new parts to integrate already existing shapes in a new way. After doing so, she thought she would never able to make her sculpture whole again.

In childhood, she was allowed to do her homework after dinner, sometimes late into the night. Her mother brought sandwiches, cakes, and candy, and stayed up late to type the children's school papers. The family atmosphere was one of overgratification via food. Services were given instead of personal closeness and love, and the patient remembered being forever hungry and yearning, and feeling starved unless she could find new foods or new activities. Stuffing herself had the function of making herself whole, particularly when she was enraged and had death fantasies against members of her family.

From an early age, Ms. L. took care of a cranky and demanding younger brother whom the mother could not handle. The little boy cried a great deal and the father could not stand to see his son needing or wanting. Ms. L. was the only person who could handle the boy and was frequently called on to do so, not without feeling annoyed. No one ever thanked or praised her for all her efforts or for restoring peace in the family.

During latency, Ms. L. had serious surgery for which she endured a long hospitalization. Her father, who came daily and brought her the funnies, remained in the doorway of her room. He never entered to kiss or touch her, although she was not contagious. We reconstructed that he was unable to do so because he had a germ phobia. But the patient thought that her father did not come into her room because of her wounds, which he considered ugly. As her hostility toward her father was unleashed, she believed her rage was created by his inability to touch her when she was so very ill and that this ultimately accounted for her feeling ugly. However, a more important injury was hidden beneath this screen memory: mother stayed in an adjoining room throughout the illness and father spent many hours in that room. Ms. L.'s injured self-esteem came from the realization that, in spite of her illness and pain, her father continued his intimacies with her mother, but never entered her room to be close to her.

When she returned home, she was emaciated, and the family rallied to "fatten her up." She began to eat compulsively "to have a little extra" so she would not die if she became ill again. She also began to masturbate compulsively, and developed a masturbation fantasy in which she was spreading germs and infecting everyone, particularly her father, who was afraid of infection. She equated spreading germs with impregnation and semen, fantasized producing an infected or defective baby for her father. Both masturbation and overeating had a death-revenge theme against the oedipal father. Ms. L. also needed to fend off her attraction and cannibalistic wishes toward mother, to whose body and excessive weight she felt drawn. She had repetitive dreams in which she both wished and feared that her mother's layers of fat would engulf her. She sometimes fantasized that her mother was alive inside of her or that she was carrying her as a dead baby. At the same time the patient continuously competed with the analyst in regard to appearance and weight. When Ms. L. succeeded very much later to shed excess weight, she felt ugly for other reasons. She began to feel ugly and unfeminine, and thought that this came from her masturbation. She grew heavy, and her mother, who was an extremely heavy woman, had clothes made for the patient that concealed her heaviness. After a shopping trip, mother and daughter usually celebrated with an ice cream soda.

She remembered being physically awkward and a wall-flower at dances in adolescence. Her father appreciated her wit, intellect, and artistic talent, but he admired women who were thin and were showgirls and film stars. The only woman he loved, whose heaviness he even encouraged, was her mother, which enraged Laura. Her father did not appreciate Ms. L.'s attempts to make herself beautiful when she reached adolescence. She lost self-confidence as a girl at that time and never regained it. She had an unsuccessful marriage in her twenties and was divorced after she had several children. Subsequently, she developed a strong need to fail and a tendency toward depression.

The father's behavior seems to have been an important unconscious motivational force for her self-devaluation and her need to destroy achievements. Overeating had become a masturbatory equivalent in addition to her compulsive masturbation, which she needed particularly when she felt rejected.

During treatment, the patient gradually lost her excess weight and gave up smoking, coffee, and alcohol, but continued to nibble on nonfattening foods, particularly when she worked.

In fact, she had to nibble all day long. Her feelings of being injured were revived as soon as she attempted to work creatively. She said, "My sculpture represents a child's deformed body and, therefore, I cannot complete it." When creating a form in sculpture, there was a reenactment of her surgery in fantasy and a restitution of a diseased body. The thought of completing her work increased her fear of death: she expressed the idea that she would kill her little brother or both of her parents by becoming successful.

Almost daily Ms. L. reenacted reviving her parents. At the beginning of her day she did those things for herself that her mother would have done were she still alive and then proceeded to make herself beautiful or "hide her ugliness" from her father. Only after these ritualistic traumatic reenactments did she feel ready to start her work, but as a rule, it was late in the day or evening by that time, too late to get started.

At a certain point in treatment, the patient wrote about her difficulty in working instead of saving her thoughts for her hour and working in her studio instead.

I begin every day with convictions and end in doubts—coffee, cigarettes, vodka, and wastebaskets filled with the day's fresh start. These line up in my studio like the sentinels of a beheading. Everyday I murder a few hours before I start my work and then run from it in guilt, only to return the next day to retrieve what I had lost, thereupon doubling my losses. The third triples them and the fourth quadruples, and so on into the following day's loss. What is strange is that like a true gambler, I return each time with a fresh hope that I have found some winning combination. My fantasy is that the work accomplished will arrive whole, magically out of one sitting. It is a childish, passive fantasy.

Luck or nature or God or hired hands will do the work for me. My role is only to conjure up something for their benefit. The passive fantasy makes me lazy about serious work. I use it more for the sense of the perception of pleasure than as a tool for survival. I never navigate, I drift. Most of mankind is made up of drifters, I suppose there is nothing morally wrong about being one myself. I feel I belong nowhere, everything blocks my path like weeds and vines. I cannot get to my destination nor can I go back to where I started. I'm lost and my time is running out. I use ideas for my entertainment, to be *consumed* [emphasis added] by me, not to be understood, certainly not to be put into some framework which will help me navigate from here to there. In my fantasies I think that success could kill me, a heart attack or cancer. Meanwhile, I'm eating up my savings. Worse, I'm eating up my heart. Who wants to die like that? In my fantasy, it's better to die with a little posthumous work, and if you'll forgive the pun, it could be inscribed on my tombstone, I met my last deadline. The biggest risk you take is that it may be said of you that your little operation was a success and wasn't it too bad that the patient died?

In the patient's description of her work inhibition what stands out are her murderous thoughts—she murders time instead of a person, she also attacks her treatment and would like to be helped magically (hired hands). She is concerned with "eating up my savings" and "eating up my heart." Her statements are replete with oral aggression and fear of starvation. She is afraid to lose her body products, and working produces a feeling of starvation. The work product represents a child whom she cannot nourish; if she did, she would starve. The "child" is also the patient, ugly from surgical wounds, rejected by her father, and having death wishes against him. Her revenge fantasies make her reach her oedipal feelings in content, but not in structure. Extensive hostility engendered in childhood traumatization interfered with oedipal strivings, and oedipal guilt made it difficult for her to complete her work. Guilt feelings stand out in Ms. L.'s conflict formation in reliving her traumatic losses from childhood and early adulthood. Attempting to ward off a traumatic repetition of childhood injuries and losses, she has the psychology of a survivor, but her ritualistic activities, designed to avoid recurrence of trauma, led to severe disruptions of self-continuity. In states of diminished self constancy, she found herself "faking" working and "faking" in her analysis and in certain aspects of her object relations was reminiscent of perverts and impostors.

The patient's work inhibition represented a traumatic reenactment of her childhood illness from which she almost died and which had brought forth a pervasive feeling of ugliness and rejection by her father, primal scene envy, and envy of her little brother. Phallic-narcissistic competitive strivings and narcissistic and sexual problems via-à-vis men had their inception at that time.

As Ms. L. attempted to master her traumata, she was able to turn to life as "more real" and accept its finiteness. She realized that she turned her rage masochistically against herself when she refused to do her creative work. As the cohesiveness of her self representation increased, Laura became less phobic and better able to separate from her fantasy parents, whom she had daily re-created in order to kill them again instead of doing her work. Her improvement was interrupted by long periods when she lived in fantasy and could not work. During such periods she lost touch with her internalized objects and certain aspects of her self-representation. These feeling states appeared akin to a mourning process. In the ensuing period, she would be able to create again and increasingly experience her work as her own.

CASE EXAMPLE 2

Ms. A. came to analysis in her late twenties. She was the oldest of three children, a musician and performer of popular songs. When I met her, she had moved far away from home, putting almost the entire width of the United States between herself and her family. Since her separation from home, she had been extremely upset, lonely, and afraid to perform her songs. Her artistic work had become sporadic, and she had developed a tendency to spoil opportunities to perform. She impressed me as a fragile little bird, highly intelligent, erratic, probably talented, and painfully thin. Her motions were anxious and her speech clipped, as if she was uncertain whether I would help or hurt her.

During the patient's childhood, her mother had little time to spend with her children. She had been a performer in a related field. Ms. A. had the impression that her mother had been competitive with her. The mother also planned and arranged everything for her children, instead of giving them the opportunity to consider what they wished to do. The patient felt that she grew up in a straitjacket.

The mother was very concerned with Ms. A.'s toilet functions when she was two to three years old. She had been constipated and had spent long periods on the toilet, reading as soon as she was able to. When she did not produce stools, the mother forced her to have an enema, a practice that continued well into the oedipal phase. Later, reading adult books came to represent forbidden pleasures and during analysis the patient realized she had always feared that she would be punished for seeking independent knowledge. During the phallic and oedipal phases, the enema ritual became sexualized; while mother administered the enema, Anita had the fantasy that she was united with both her mother and father. As she was lying on her belly receiving the enema, her clitoris was apparently stimulated and she developed a masturbation fantasy in which she became an indispensable link responsible for the happiness of her parents. This fantasy produced feelings of omnipotence and probably contributed to her ability to tolerate the pain and rage caused by the procedure itself. She was also force-fed from early on and usually allowed her food to get cold. If she ate it all, she frequently vomited afterward. She survived by stealing food from the icebox and devouring it furtively in what constituted an astonishingly nourishing combination of edible items.

Throughout her growing years, Ms. A. was periodically anorexic and was sent for psychotherapy for brief periods. As soon as she improved, the parents interrupted her treatment. During the sixties and early seventies, she became a very poor student, abused drugs, and hung out with friends who offended her parents' social status. Ms. A. had felt force-fed all her life.

She developed food fads, continued to be constipated, and went to a myriad of "healers" and nutritionists who tried, not very successfully, to deal with her many allergies and physical aches and pains. The physical intrusions into her body from early childhood on had physically overstimulated and frightened her. She could consult a regular physician and have her body examined only after she trusted me. In adulthood working became equated with being forced. She worked sporadically and again her parents paid for her treatment, but she lived in great poverty, eating one meal a day.

After the analysis had progressed toward greater individuation and a less passive, masochistic, and self-destructive stance related to her forcing mother and indifferent father, the patient was less frightened, fell in love, and after some analytic work was able to enter an excellent marriage. She began to cook and enjoy food for the first time in her life. She gained a great deal of weight, which she had difficulty taking off again. As her body-image improved and became less an object to be intruded upon and beaten down and was gradually experienced as belonging to her, she became less fragile, her allergies lessened, and her hysterical reactions decreased. In short, while the physical symptoms abated, the work inhibition remained. It belonged to a deeper, traumatic layer of early childhood and was uncovered later in analysis.

Ms. A. continued to fear exposing her talent in public. She likened performing to exposing herself naked. A paranoidal fantasy of being exposed and having to avoid having her products forcibly removed interfered with her work and creativity. She did not believe that her talent belonged to her. Differentiation from her parents had remained partial. Unconsciously, the narcissistically protected, sexualized body products had remained the joint property of herself and her parents. Only as long as she could keep her work secret could she believe that it belonged to her.

During this period, Ms. A. was presented with an opportunity to produce a musical composition of potentially great importance to her career. At first it was difficult to know what aspects of her traumatic childhood experiences most paralyzed her creativity. Her composition demanded that she establish an organized hierarchic structure within the music which followed a certain logical sequence. However, her notations showed inconsistency and both compositional structure and sequence were confused. She was incapable of synthesizing her work. She felt powerless and driven. A thinking disorder had become manifest, and, paralyzed with anxiety, she considered giving up the project.

Ms. A. then decided to bring her work to her analytic sessions. The first clue revealed that when she attempted to establish a sequential order in her composition, it felt as though everything was "rushing in on me simultaneously." She remembered how her body felt when the water from the enema bag rushed into her and she was so frightened that she could not hold it inside herself long enough. As long as everything rushed in at the same time, she could not synthesize or structure it. It remained in "bits and pieces." Her work had to be messy. What was messy belonged to her and what was orderly belonged to mother. Separation from the mother had initially been achieved by a regression from cleanliness to being messy. It had appeared to her that all that was clean had to be given up to mother. Secondary process thinking equaled the good product and represented closeness to father, from whom she felt barred. Such thinking Ms. A. felt had to be handed over to mother. Thus her real productions, like her eating during childhood, had to remain secret. After this connection was worked through, her sense of autonomy improved and she was able to produce an original piece of work without having to hide it. She gradually overcame her cognitive inhibition and thinking disorder. Subsequently, she resumed performing in public.

The patient's thinking confusion, which had created her work inhibition, was based on reliving a traumatic state from the oral and anal periods which surfaced when she attempted to work. Her mother's forcing had become sexualized and had made it impossible for her as an adult to claim her work products as her own. After the patient had achieved autonomy over her thinking, a spurt in oedipal development followed. Ms. A.'s success helped her to separate from her forcing mother and give up the fantasy of being a part of her parents' sexual union via her enema fantasy. Subsequently, her adult love life in her marriage improved as well.

CASE EXAMPLE 3

Mr. M. was a middle-aged businessman who had been in treatment several times before I met him. He complained of a discrepancy between his intelligence and his capacities and his much lower level of performance. He consistently created situations which made things go wrong after he and I had worked to improve his life. He came from a large, poor family where education ranked high. He loved learning, but he could not integrate his efforts because he erotized his professional activities. He engaged in certain perversions, predominantly a type of pedophilia, and he was bulimic. The perversion and bulimia compelled him to interrupt his work and then to live in terror of discovery.

This behavior had its roots in his earliest history, of which only *one* aspect can be reported here. He was told that he almost died shortly after birth because of a milk allergy. He had an organizing screen memory in which he was two-and-a-half to three years old. His mother had put him on top of a bedroom dresser. He was fat, had round cheeks and they smiled at each other. She was feeding him. They were both laughing and were happy together.

In actuality, his mother force-fed him as long as he could remember. He had a weight problem and found her force-feeding increasingly intrusive, but he shared mother's fantasy that he might die if he did not eat everything she served him. Because of his lifelong anxiety that he might die, he could not fend her off.

During analysis, this theme was relived—initially by a bout of insomnia during which he raided the icebox, gained several pounds overnight, and jogged them off within the next twenty-four hours. He always enumerated what he had eaten, and when it included entire cakes and quarts of ice cream, I became concerned.

After several years of work, during which the patient accused me of not helping him and of interpreting things he already knew, he developed nightmares. They were wordless, but he felt in terror and totally alone. He asked to sit up. He did so and held his head in his hands, feeling unable to look at me. He complained about the light in the room and I realized he had developed a photophobia. I had to draw the shades and close them tightly. We worked this way for months, often sitting in silence.

When he began to talk, the patient said he could not bear to be touched. I told him that I thought he reacted like a person who was beginning to remember having been overstimulated intolerably to the point of feeling that if it continued, he would perish. Working on this theme helped him to connect his fear of the light in the room with the fear of being intrusively force-fed by mother and with his fear of death. Certain aspects of the pedophilia could also be understood: he became the mother who "force-fed" a child by penetrating its body. His genital stood for the force-feeding spoon and the little girl represented himself. But a theme of merging with mother and excluding father was also most prominent (Freud, 1905, 1920, 1922; Kestenberg, 1971; Schwartz, 1986).

In his perverse activities as well as in his bulimic behavior, the patient unconsciously shared a fantasy with his mother that unless he compulsively overate or intruded sexually upon a young person's body (who then would feel overfed), he would perish. Both eating and pedophilia staved off death and were based on sexualized and destructive unconscious needs and wishes, including death wishes against mother. Excessive guilt was associated with the destructive aspects of the bulimia and pedophilia and a constant fear of being caught.

The influence of the mother had been so predominant in this case because the father disappeared from Mr. M.'s life when he was still a very young child. His siblings were no protection against his menacing mother.

The photophobia had represented a displaced wish of shutting out his intrusive mother, who was represented by the incoming light. As memories from childhood appeared, the nightmares became less frequent and the patient gradually gained autonomy over his eating habits and impulse control over his perversion. As he struggled to gain autonomy and to separate from mother, his phallic and oedipal needs emerged in treatment. Conflicts preventing productive work gradually moved to the area of intrapsychic conflict and could be analyzed. He gradually became the arbiter of his own destiny.

This case deals with the wordless reliving of early traumatization at a time when the mother was almost his only object, and with the re-creation of a traumatic feeling state in his nightmares, which emerged in the transference. Both the bulimia and the perversions were represented in the photophobia, which was an iatrogenic symptom that appeared and disappeared during treatment. The addictive aspect of bulimia and perversion represented a shared fantasy with his force-feeding mother. Mr. M. had made a pseudophallic adjustment, but in fantasy the bulimia and pedophilia were the magic that would keep him alive. The bulimia had been experienced as a compliance with the trauma-causing mother, who was unconsciously experienced as phallic, while he felt castrated. The patient had relived feeling states close to the original trauma in the analysis by displacement from the mouth to the eyes. In the transient photophobia, I became, in transference, the overwhelming mother. As long as the patient engaged in pedophilic activities, he forever remained a child, more girl than boy, and death could not touch him. He had been too frightened to be an adult and thus denied the adult's necessity to work in order to survive.

DISCUSSION

In the three cases discussed, anxious care givers had a tendency to libidinally starve their children by substituting overgratification for attunement, or their behavior expressed conflict in which they used their children's bodies to combat their own anxieties. The three patients discussed here had suffered from severe libidinal deprivation since early childhood. A traumatic core appeared both in patients with eating disorders and in those who suffered from work inhibitions. A direct relationship between eating and elimination patterns established early in life was traced to a later work inhibition. With Ms. L., the addictive characterological atmosphere of food and services given to satisfy frustration began early in life; traumatic body intrusion only in latency. Both determined her later work inhibition.

The traumatic core centered on intrusion into the child's body which influenced the earliest object relationships to care givers and undermined the development of autonomy. It undermined the wish to feed oneself; enjoy other body functions, including elimination; and get pleasure from the body as a whole, later from body products, and, ultimately, from products created independently as an expression of sublimation. When independent ego functions become arrested early, individuation is postponed. The body may become an instrument of pathological communication between parent and child. In the cases presented, therapeutic problems were looked upon in terms of external events and concrete acts. The patient as a child experienced himself or herself as forced and victimized, and needed to remain attached to an object who was experienced as preventing autonomous development. Oedipal triangulation was frequently displaced to a battle raging in another arena which overshadowed oedipal conflicts. This was apparent in each of the presented cases. As long as only partial separation between self and object exists, there is a tendency to turn hostility directed toward the bad introjected object against the self: the patient behaves as if the self were the punishing object by punishing itself. In bulimia and anorexia, as well as in work inhibition, where the incapacity to work is based on an unconscious wish to destroy one's talent and means of livelihood, a life and death struggle takes place. The body, or fantasies and activities derivative of traumatic body intrusions, constitute the battleground.

Maturity of the ego depends on how fantasy and symbolization will be structured. In these cases, various symptoms could symbolically stand for each other. For instance, mistreatment of one's own body by overeating created self-hatred in Ms. L.'s case, which led to masturbation and narcissistic injury. In Mr. M.'s case the perverse actions and fantasies represented a conflict of wishing to merge and at the same time free himself from mother. In view of the involvement of the body and its affective derivatives which came from psychosomatic problems, compromise formations are structured differently in some cases: where problems are expressed with the body as a focus, this focus becomes the neurotic vehicle of self-expression and initially obscures the intrapsychic conflict.

If possible, the therapist has to engage the patient into finding a way that leads away from the body and its products to the arena of parent–child conflicts and to the underlying intrapsychic struggle. I believe this is not possible unless or until a patient has reached an internal state of wishing to differentiate and separate from internalized objects. Such a turning point is of critical importance because it is not enough to explore why one is the way one is. Early external disturbances leading to intrusiveness into the body and learning inhibitions are not directly transformable into therapeutic technique or improvement in the patient. Children acquiesce masochistically to mistreatment or regress in their body or ego functions, but these events are reachable in treatment only in their present-day derivatives, in reconstructions, and in the transference neurosis, provided the patient is capable of turning toward intrapsychic conflict.

The neutralization of hostility toward parents is of pivotal importance in promoting the forging of the patient's identity, capacity to work, and ability to sublimate. When these conflicts become the subject of treatment, work inhibition frequently enters the analysis. When the patient is helped to work in treatment, without being forced, a precedent for a new internal experience may be created which furthers insight into the work inhibition. This was the case with Mr. M.

Once the treatment has reached the intrapsychic level, oedipal problems may surface separated from early traumatic reliving. Schwartz (1986), quoting Brenner (1974), has noted that oral symptoms represent oral aspects of the genital phase and the oral Oedipus (p. 445). The patients discussed here were overly attached to care-giving objects who were unconsciously perceived as phallic and on whom the patients felt totally dependent. Without this object of dependency, the patient fears he or she will die. Conversely, as long as this tie is in force, the patient may remain attached forever and fear of death is denied. Because the parental object is seen as all-powerful, fusion with it makes everything possible and every wish gratifiable. This leads to what I have called a characterologically addictive feeling state or an aspect of addictive character formation. This defensive operation creates an escape hatch to counteract superego pressures, at least intermittently. A temporary flight from the pressures of life tasks and from the superego may lead to a tendency of faking or impostership to keep the demands of the external world at bay. This was so in the cases of both Ms. L. and Mr. M.

In view of the early inception of these disorders, it appears that the theory of pathogenesis described here overemphasizes the role of the bad object and the child as a victim. I want to make clear that while the focus of this material lends itself to such a view, I believe with Kernberg (1987) that:

[I]nternalized object relations [are not reflected in] actual object relations from the past. Rather, they reflect a combination of realistic and fantasied—and often highly distorted—internalizations of such past object relations and defenses against them under the effects of activation and projection of instinctual drive derivatives. In other words, there is a dynamic tension between the here-and-now . . . and the there-and-then unconscious genetic determinants derived from the "actual" past, the patient's developmental history [p. 201].

The presentation of these cases clarifies an inherent connection between anorexia and bulimia on the one hand, and independent work and creativity on the other. The bulimic–anorectic patient cannot take in food; in transference the difficulty is transmuted into an inability to take in interpretations—except when he replicates the good mother–child relationship in the form of "advice" or empathy—or what is perceived as such.

The difficulty in taking in is reencountered when the analysand has to produce and create from within his own storehouse of knowledge and creativity. These patients have great difficulty in transforming what they have taken in into a new and creative output. At times, a model for such intake can be created in the transference by identification with the analyst who "takes in" what the patient presents. This, together with the analysis of his psychic conflict regarding intake and output, may make it possible for a patient to hold in and retain what was assimilated without feeling forced and, subsequently, to use it autonomously.

I have postulated some theoretical assumptions which may form a foundation for later character and symptom formation and internalization processes. I have assumed that the earliest infant–object experiences related to the body may form a basis for early fantasies of incorporation and for affective expressions experienced by the child in relation to the body. In the treament of adults, a shift from the body and the inhibiting forces created by traumatic intrusiveness to the intrapsychic arena may make it possible to analytically treat and improve the psychic derivatives of body problems and the inhibitions which related to the "body of work," the body product, and creativity.

REFERENCES

Bergmann, M. V. (1980), On the genesis of narcissistic and phobic character development in an adult patient: A developmental view. *Internat. J. Psycho-Anal.*, 61:535–546.

——— (1982a), The female Oedipus complex: Its antecedents and evaluation. In: *Early Female Development*, ed. D. Mendell. New York: Spectrum, pp. 175–201.

——— (1982b), Thoughts on superego pathology of survivors and their children. In: *Generations of the Holocaust*, ed. M. S. Bergmann & M. E. Jucovy. New York: Basic Books.

Brenner, C. (1974), Depression, anxiety, and affect theory. *Internat. J. Psycho-Anal.*, 55:25–32.

Freud, A. (1946), The psychoanalytic study of infantile feeding disturbances.

The Writings of Anna Freud 4:39–59. New York: International Universities Press.

Freud, S. (1905), Three essays on the theory of sexuality. *Standard Edition*, 7:125–244. London: Hogarth Press, 1953.

———(1917), Mourning and melancholia. *Standard Edition*, 14:237–243. London: Hogarth Press, 1957.

——— (1920), Psychogenesis of a case of homosexuality in a woman. *Standard Edition*, 18:145–172. London: Hogarth Press, 1955.

——— (1922), Some neurotic mechanisms in jealousy, paranoia and homosexuality. *Standard Edition*, 18:221–232. London: Hogarth Press, 1955.

——— (1938), Findings, ideas, problems. *Standard Edition*, 23:299–300. London: Hogarth Press, 1964.

Kernberg, O. (1987), An ego psychology-object relations theory approach to the transference. *Psychoanal. Quart.*, 56:197–221.

Kestenberg, J. (1971), From organ-object imagery to self and object representations. In: *Separation-Individuation: Essays in Honor of Margaret Mahler*, ed. J. B. McDevitt & C. Settlage. New York: International Universities Press, pp. 75–100.

Krystal, H. (1982), Adolescence and the tendencies to develop substance dependence. *Psychoanal. Inq.*, 2/4:551–617.

Mahler, M. (1971), A study of the separation–individuation process. *The Psychoanalytic Study of the Child*, 26:403–424. New York: Quadrangle Books.

——— Bergman, A., & Pine, F. (1975), *The Psychological Birth of the Human Infant*. New York: Basic Books.

Meissner, W. W. (1981), *Internalization in Psychoanalysis*. New York: International Universities Press.

Roiphe, H., & Galenson, E. (1981), *Infantile Origins of Sexual Identity*. New York: International Universities Press.

Schwartz, H. (1986), Bulimia: Psychoanalytic perspectives. *J. Amer. Psychoanal. Assn.*, 34:439–461.

Segal, H. (1957), Notes on symbol formation. *Internat. J. Psycho-Anal.*, 38:391–397.

——— (1978), On symbolism. *Internat. J. Psycho-Anal.* 59:315–319.

Stern, D. (1980), *The Interpersonal World of the Infant*. New York: Basic Books.

Sugarman, A., & Kurash, C. (1982), Marijuana abuse, transitional experience, and the borderline adolescent. *Psychoanal. Inq.*, 2/4:519–538. (Hillsdale, NJ: The Analytic Press).

Thomä, H. (1967), *Anorexia Nervosa*. New York: International Universities Press.

Wilson, C. P., Hogan, C. G., Mintz, I. L., Eds. (1983), *Fear of Being Fat: The Treatment of Anorexia Nervosa and Bulimia*. New York: Jason Aronson.

Winnicott, D. W. (1953), Transitional objects and transitional phenomena. In: *Collected Papers*. New York: Basic Books, 1958.

Chapter 12

Love, Work and Bulimia

LYNN WHISNANT REISER, M.D.

INTRODUCTION

Eating disorders have become increasingly prevalent in our culture. This suggests that psychosocial as well as biological and intrapsychic factors must be playing a large contributing role in pathogenesis of these conditions. Numerous articles in both lay and medical literature discuss such dimensions.

The form of neurosis changes with social change (Fenichel, 1945; Rangell, 1959; Brumberg, 1982). For example, "classic" conversion hysteria appears to be less prevalent than in years gone by (Krohn, 1978; Satow, 1979), but the previously rare case of bulimia is now common, particularly among women. Bulimia was recognized as an official diagnosis only in 1980 (American Psychiatric Association, 1980; but of course this "new" syndrome is not itself new. What has changed is the widespread incidence of bulimia (Casper, 1983; Halmi, 1983).

Striegel-Moore, Silberstein, and Rodin (1986) asked: "Why women? Which women in particular? Why now?" They summarized the conclusions of studies by researchers who had addressed these questions using large populations of woman as subjects. Like a clinical microscope on low power, they have scanned a wide field. In this chapter, the observation is of a much smaller field, but at a higher degree of resolution. The case material complements and supplements survey research. It focuses on the circumstances of an episode of bulimia in one

373

individual. Risk factors identified in population studies are illustrated in this case; but the clinical material also suggests how
examination of a single case enriches such observations, clarifies
some of the reasons why a particular individual became symptomatically bulimic, highlights the overdetermination of the
syndrome, and thus adds depth to the information available
from survey methods.

CASE EXAMPLE

DESCRIPTION OF THE PATIENT

When she began treatment, Ms. Y. was twenty-five years old.
She was tall, of medium build, an attractive freckle-faced, hazel-
eyed, redhead from a middle-class Jewish family. She appeared
confident and self-assured. She dressed neatly in severely tai-
lored business suits. She was the oldest of three daughters (one
sister three years younger, another four years younger), her
father was a businessman, her mother a full-time homemaker.

Ms. Y. had majored in art history in college, but in her
senior year decided to change direction and to devote the extra
time needed to get a degree in mathematics and then a master's
degree in engineering. Having done this, she found an excellent
job in a large construction company where her fellow employees
were predominately male. Shortly after beginning work, she
sought treatment to deal with difficulties in a relationship with
a boyfriend. At her initial evaluation for psychotherapy she had
explicitly denied symptoms of anorexia nervosa or bulimia.

BULIMIC BEHAVIOR

From time to time in treatment, Ms. Y. had complained about
feeling overweight, particularly when she exercised with her
peers in a health club located near the building where she
worked. She also had mentioned feeling self-conscious—both
about what she should say and what she should eat—while at
lunch with her co-workers. However, she did not complain
about having an eating disorder.

Her first clear description of an eating disorder took the form of an embarrassed remark that her eating had become "out of control" and that she had become preoccupied with eating. In the afternoon at work she would fantasize about food. She struggled to resist her hunger and excited cravings by bargaining with herself; for example, she told herself she would bake chocolate chip cookies, but only eat one or two, and then mail the rest to her youngest sister in college. Later, at home, having prepared the batter, but before making it into cookies, she sampled it. She found herself taking another bite, then another, and another—gulping more and more rapidly, not even tasting what she was eating. She felt compelled to finish the whole batch "in order to end the temptation." Stuffed, distended, nauseated, guilty, and somewhat numb, she fell into an uncomfortable, stuporous sleep.

This behavior developed into a regular pattern. After her workday ended, she would go to a convenience store and choose food on which to gorge; or, if at a friend's home, although feeling guilty and afraid of being caught, she would secretly raid the refrigerator. She would then sleep fitfully and awake each morning feeling "hung over"—nauseated, headachy, and ashamed of her behavior the previous night. She desired little or no food at breakfast and lunch. Despite her resolve not to repeat the overeating, hunger and thoughts about food returned in midafternoon and increased toward evening. She began to gain weight rapidly. Her clothes pulled at the seams. She felt humiliated to think that someone would notice that in order to ease the tightness of her skirt she had it unzipped under her jacket.

Because she felt so desperate, it was at this point in therapy that she confessed her binging. She then revealed that this pattern of behavior had intermittently occurred at other times; but because she felt deeply ashamed of her actions, to herself she had attributed them euphemistically to "difficulty with dieting."

Ms. Y.'s pattern of binging fits the DSM-III criteria for bulimia.

PATIENT'S LIFE SITUATION

Initially, Ms. Y. did not connect her binging behavior with her feelings about events which had occurred in her life at the time. Two months before, she had broken up with her boyfriend. Feeling alone, she had begun desperately to work harder, being very assertive about getting a long desired job change. Her efforts had been successful. The week before her eating went out of control, she had been promoted to project manager in a division that had just been reorganized. She was the first woman to hold this position. Excited, she wanted everyone to know about it, but at the same time she also felt frightened. She thought that she looked, acted, and was "too young for the position." She expected to be resented, especially by her women friends. Feeling the need to assure everyone that she would not be promoted again so fast, she even lied to acquaintances at parties and implied she still had a windowless cubicle, not admitting her new office had a window, a status symbol in her company.

Her sense of competition was also evident in her expectation that her business associates who exercised at the same health club were watching her more carefully and evaluating her physical shape and skill. She became even more self-conscious when she displayed her body in her workout clothes, because she thought "all eyes would be on me." To hide her body, she had kept her underwear on and took "splash baths," instead of showers. She changed her bra in a corner, all the time feeling humiliated about behaving in a way she regarded as peculiar.

Ms. Y.'s recent weight gain did not help: it made her feel unattractive and unfeminine. She was proud of working out aerobically "like the other men" [her words] while her female peers did "Jane Fonda exercises," but she was acutely sensitive about sweating. She was firmly convinced that men sweat and women do not.

Ms. Y. also felt stressed by the structure of her new job which gave her authority over an older man who had held his same job for a long time. She felt anxious that the older man would be hostile and depressed about her having been promoted over his head. At the same time, she considered him "pitiful." She found herself unable to be comfortable instructing or managing the "old man," and procrastinated about doing the part of her job that involved authority over him. Her new manager had worked with the older man for years and the two men liked to joke together. She felt excluded. She wished her new boss had spent more time with her explaining how to do her job, but had been embarrassed to ask.

Ms. Y. had mixed feelings about how her parents would respond to her promotion. She had already been hurt by her (now ex-) boyfriend's response. He had told her he was sure it was not the job for her, that she was "too nice a woman." (Ms. Y. interpreted this to mean that she was unambitious and not assertive enough.)

She and her former boyfriend had been in graduate school together and they had often discussed their careers—a relationship similar to the one Ms. Y. had with her father who had been interested in her decision to get an engineering degree. Mr. Y. had helped his daughter prepare a résumé after college and had discussed job possibilities with her, sharing his expertise. He was a taciturn man and this had been a special kind of interaction with him. Now she found herself afraid to tell her father about her promotion. She anticipated that he, like her former boyfriend, would think she was too inexperienced and did not deserve such a position. When she finally told her father about her promotion, characteristically he made no comment.

Ms. Y. had been apprehensive that her parents would decide that she would no longer need money from them to subsidize her psychotherapy since she had received a pay raise with the promotion. Her fear of being left to take care of herself was further evidenced in her relationship to her therapist, who she also feared would conclude that she was doing so well she could stop treatment.

PREOCCUPATIONS: NURSERY RHYMES, MARCHING SONGS, AND LULLABIES

We now had information about Ms. Y.'s symptomatic binging and her current life situation. How might these be related?

Additional material from her psychotherapy hours provided some clues.

In a session soon after her promotion, Ms. Y. mentioned that she was puzzled by fragments of four childhood rhymes and tunes that kept running through her head: First, "This old man, he played two, he played knickknack on my shoe . . . he played seven on the way to heaven"; second, "The grandfather clock that stopped ticking when the old man died"; third, a marching song, "The ants go marching up the hill"; and fourth, a lullaby, "Too ra lu ra lu ra." Associations to these provided a link between Ms. Y.'s current situation and her past—particularly early adolescence—and offered more insight into the exacerbation of her eating disorder.

The first two lyrics were about *old men*. Since childhood Ms. Y. had been particularly touched by the sight of lonely old men ("with no woman to care for them"). Recently she had volunteered to be a "telephone pal" in a geriatrics program. She associated "the old man" in the rhyme with the old man she felt she had displaced by her promotion. The patient then realized that she felt she was like the "young rascals" who came into her father's firm after a reorganization, displacing her father, an action which had forced her family to move to another city. (Significantly, this had been around the same time she changed majors in college and career paths.) She "hated to realize" that she associated her father with the "old man," the co-worker over whom she had been promoted and for whom she felt both compassion and contempt.

In examining her apprehension about telling her father about her promotion into a "man's" job and her feelings about his response, she began to focus on his long history of feeling chronically pessimistic, mistreated, and defeated. Since childhood she had been critical of her mother for not being more understanding and supportive of her father and his plans. At the time, she had blamed her mother for her father's failures. Now, she began to realize how hollow and grandiose many of her father's plans and ambitions had been, but how much she had wanted to believe in him in spite of his shortcomings. She noticed, too, that she had experienced the same conflicted feelings toward her boyfriend when he had been unable to find a job after graduation.

She also began to be more aware of her fear of her own competitiveness with men. The rhymes about the old man dying expressed these problems: by competing successfully she would harm her beloved but rival father.

The first two rhymes clarified some of Ms. Y.'s distress at being promoted. The second two related this more clearly to her feelings about her body and her choice of symptoms.

The third song, the marching song, was one she had learned at camp in sixth grade. This had been a very stressful time for her. Ms. Y. vividly remembered how she had been excluded by two popular girls from a group around a campfire. She overheard one saying "We don't want any old age here" (she thought that they were referring to her, given that "age" rhymed with her name). She felt humiliated, connecting their comment with her feelings of being different because of her physical maturity. A year earlier, at age ten, she had reached menarche. She had been the first girl in her class to experience this. She had felt self-conscious, deeply ashamed, and secretive about it. She had told only her mother and her best friend. She remembered the night of her first period, lying in bed wearing an uncomfortable, bulky, binding sanitary napkin, and feeling despair, that "it would be like this the rest of my life."

Ms. Y. came from a "very private" family where sex was not discussed. She believed her mother disapproved of sex, and had imagined that her mother would not condone her having sexual thoughts (or acting upon them). Her mother's lack of communication in words about caring for Ms. Y.'s maturing body became evident when the patient got her first bra. Receiving no instructions from her mother, Ms. Y. had thought that she had to wear the bra all the time. Later she had been embarrassed when she realized that it was not customary to wear a bra at night. It was around this time that her mother had given her dress shields to wear to protect her clothes from sweat. These also had been uncomfortable and binding (none of the other girls she knew wore dress shields).

Her feelings of being "out of step" (in the march) with her

peers in the sixth grade resonated with her feelings of being
too young for such a "mature" job and her fear that her peers,
especially two other women at work would begin to exclude
her.

The fourth song Ms. Y. hummed was a *lullaby*. Her associations took us a step further in understanding the meaning
of her binging. The song was one of her mother's favorites and
Ms. Y. had also sung it at camp. The lullaby recalled her counselor at the camp in sixth grade who "like a mom" had helped
her put up her tent, rather than just "telling me to do it myself
so I'd learn." (The latter was her complaint about her new boss.)

While the junior counselors had been chronologically
older, physically Ms. Y. was more like them than she was like
her peers. She remembered yearning to be close to her counselor, like a favorite daughter, as she perceived the older junior
counselors were. Ms. Y. wanted both to be given responsibility
and to be nurtured.

In thinking about her wish to be cared for and the tune
of her mother's lullaby, her further association had been to the
other side of her mother. Her mother would hold a grudge
when angry, and without explaining why, refused to speak to
Ms. Y. and/or her sisters for hours or even days. Ms. Y. recounted that during a recent visit to her parents in their new
home, her mother had sulked. Ms. Y. finally had confronted
her directly for the first time: "Say what's wrong, stop behaving
like this." Ms. Y. had felt frightened by her experiment. Immediately afterward, she had run out of the house into the new
strange neighborhood. No one had pursued her. She had felt
like a frightened, lost, little girl who might be killed without
anyone, particularly her mother, even noticing, or caring.

OTHER MATERIAL FROM THE TREATMENT:
THE IMPORTANCE OF FOOD, SHOPPING,
EXPRESSION OF EMOTION, LOVE, AND WORK

The circumstances and some of the meanings of the onset of
one episode of binging have now been described. During the

course of Ms. Y.'s treatment several other significant aspects of her bulimia became clarified: the importance of food in her family, the expression of binging in other kinds of behavior, such as shopping; the use of all kinds of binging in the management and expression of feelings; and the connection of the vicissitudes of her relationships with men, female friends, and performance at work with periods of binging and dieting.

Preparing, sharing, and eating food was an important way of communication in Ms. Y.'s family. Her mother was reserved and liked to express her affectionate feelings through carefully selected messages in greeting cards and in presents, especially food. She baked cookies and cakes, and gave candies as presents on each holiday. A batch of fresh chocolate chip cookies was always ready for the patient when she came home for a visit. Ms. Y. felt obliged to eat them, not wishing to make her mother feel rejected. This was in keeping with a family custom: when angry at a relative, family members did not open the presents they had offered. Thus, since childhood, Ms. Y. had connected being given food with being loved and eating with accepting love.

Ms. Y. enjoyed eating with friends and at family get-togethers where a festive meal was often the center of activity. She was an excellent cook and an expert on where to get the best cookies, ice cream, and ethnic food. Ms. Y. laughed when she described how, shortly after her job change, she shared a pizza with a woman friend while they lamented together about being overweight and talked about diets. Ms. Y. had planned the dinner to let her friend know that, although she had been promoted, they could still be close.

Most of the women in her mother's family were heavy. However, being overweight was conflicted for Ms. Y. On the one hand, Ms. Y. longed to be "thin and popular," on the other, she recalled an early wish (recorded in her diary) that she would "grow up to be a mom—so that I can eat all I want." Her thin, younger sister was "the pretty one." Ms. Y. had been a chubby child. "Coincidentally," she first remembered beginning to feel self-conscious about her weight at age ten. She felt heavy mainly in her hips, thighs, and buttocks (like her mother) and had

begun the first of a long series of diets. Her father teased Ms.
Y. in a hostile fashion when she snacked between meals.

Her envy of other women (and the therapist in the transference) was evident in her belief that they were not only thin
without effort, but were provided with all the things that Ms.
Y. wanted: material possessions (car, house, clothing), success
in business, and all the sex and food they desired. She perceived
these other women as both able to care for themselves *and* as
being cared for by nurturant men. She was concerned that she
alone had to take care of herself, and that she was both too little
to care for herself and too big for others to care for her.

Often a period of success and added responsibility at work
ended in disappointment and terror that she now "had to take
care of herself." (This, too, had been evident after her promotion.) She would then stop concentrating and begin to procrastinate at work hoping to get attention from her boss both
to be reprimanded (which would dampen down her own sense
of triumph and excitement) and to be noticed and helped.

This kind of behavior was also evident in the transference.
For example, procrastinating and being late had been habitual
ways she infuriated her father who was organized, always on
time, and disliked waiting. Being late for her sessions reflected
her wish to be given something extra in the treatment. She
repeatedly hoped that, if she were late, the therapist would
extend the time and could also use her disappointment about
this as a way to express her anger and sense of being mistreated.

Fenichel (1954) stressed the plasticity of binging behavior
and its ability to be expressed in other modalities besides food.
Ms. Y.'s concern with her clothing and shopping behavior is an
example of this. She was as concerned about her clothing as she
was about her weight. Quite self-conscious about her appearance, she wished to seem older and more professional at work,
and younger and more beautiful in her social hours. Her attitude toward her clothing, like her feelings about food, was
only at times "conflict free." Then she felt in control and able
to enjoy both food and clothing. However, she sometimes "lost
control" of food intake and clothing purchases.

Later in the treatment, Ms. Y. revealed that during times

of particular stress on her way home from her psychotherapy session (which followed her work day), she would stop at a convenience store to select food for a binge, or at other times skip eating altogether and go to the shopping mall to purchase clothing. There she would excitedly choose many items and charge them, oblivious to her usual worry about spending too much money. She complained about the limitations of her clothing budget as she did about her diet and was overdrawn on her charge cards and overweight on her scales. Her sporadic craving for new clothing, her feeling of having transgressed, and her guilty resolve to control her spending after a shopping spree, closely paralleled her behavior and emotion about binging. Although Ms. Y. did not purge after a food binge, she did "undo" her clothing shopping sprees, often returning most of what she had bought.

She was embarrassed when she shopped with a friend and bought a dress she thought the friend would think was too extravagant or which made her look thinner than her friend. (This echoed her self-consciousness about what foods she chose to eat at work with friends watching.) A shopping binge seemed able to substitute for an eating binge. Either could take on symbolic conflicted meanings.

Ms. Y. used binging both to express and to control overwhelming feelings. For example, Ms. Y. had become filled with anxiety and sexual excitement after she had resisted the urge to invite a man to whom she had been attracted to her apartment. After she had hastily said goodnight, she rushed out to a fast food restaurant and binged. Likewise, when she had been furious about a brief telephone message from her mother (whom she felt should be more attentive to her) Ms. Y. began to eat compulsively. This was similar to her response to the powerful, conflicted feelings about her promotion. As Ms. Y. began to express feelings more directly in words, and was able to be aware of distinct and vivid emotions, this use of action to contain and express feelings diminished.

Ms. Y.'s weight and body shape symbolized how she felt about herself and those close to her. During the treatment, several patterns emerged which connected Ms. Y.'s feelings about her body and eating with her performance at work and her relationships to women and to men.

Ms. Y. had begun dating in her last years of high school and first began having sexual relationships immediately after leaving home. During her first two years in college, she was involved in a series of impulsive, casual sexual encounters. After that she had several longer term relationships with men. Two of the men had been interested in marriage, but she did not feel ready to commit herself. In these relationships, she had enjoyed sex, and for a time felt good about her body. However, she felt very dependent on the man's admiration. Her most recent boyfriend had been critical of her figure and this "made her feel terrible."

When she found a man she was interested in, she was able to control her appetite, diet, lose weight, and feel attractive (her weight fluctuated over 20 pounds). She became distracted at work and began to concentrate on her social life. At these times, she felt competitive with other women and afraid of their envy. She compared her body with theirs, but was embarrassed when another woman commented about her weight loss and she would deny it. She became obsessed by what she perceived as an exclusive, close relationship between two other women —sometimes women at her office, sometimes her sisters or her mother and one of her sisters—and suffered from feeling left out of the relationship between these women. This was reminiscent of the two girls in the sixth grade, her sisters and mother during adolescence, and a series of pairs of women friends throughout high school and college. At those times, she began to be increasingly needy and helpless, and clung to her boyfriend, quite unlike her initial self-assured independent stance. This escalated, and often ended in feeling guilty about sexual activity. She then felt ashamed, damaged, and exploited. Convinced that the man had disappointed her, she withdrew. Her eating would "go out of control" and she would begin to gain weight. Ms. Y. would seek out women friends with a resurgence of determination to pull herself together and to take care of herself.

As mentioned in the example of her promotion, when suc-

has persisted for a long time and within which a great deal of organization has taken place" (Freud, 1908, p. 165; emphasis added).

The compulsive, frenetic, and defensively fantasyless binging and purging attacks represent this persistent masturbatory turn to one's own body upon which is acted out the double identifications of the hysteric's failed attempt to fully cathect the father of the positive Oedipus with her feminine self. Genital receptive fantasies toward father are displaced to their oral counterpart and further defended by the disavowal of their receptive ideation. The patient is now both phallic aggressor and castrated victim. Receptive and expulsive object related wishes, defensively drained of their fantasy content, overlap and intertwine revealing the patient's

> wandering between one object and the other, paralyzed between the two, unable to choose between them, frozen in a gesture of apparent resolution. . . . The two situations combine, but never quite mix, nor are they resolved . . . [She] cannot define herself as a man or as a woman because she cannot finally choose between her father or her mother. [She] will always remain in the middle, moving constantly between one and other, without getting close to either one: petrified half-way, she postulates the impossible [Kohon, 1984, p. 81].

This "divalent" position (Kohon, 1984)—neither and both female and male—results from an inability to accept femininity which is perceived by her as castrated and worthless. Significantly though, more disturbing than the perceived shame of her genitals is the guilt from the associated unconscious object related fantasies. The elements of compromise in the binge–purge syndrome demonstrate the presence of the fully heterosexual wishes the anxiety over which requires their disguise. Accordingly, as Horney noted (1926, p. 335), this "flight from womanhood," from the wish "to avoid the realization of libidinal wishes and phantasies in connection with the father," leads to cessful at work, she became self-conscious about both men and women looking at her, feeling they evaluated her sexual attractiveness. She was afraid to look anyone in the eye for fear the person would assume she was sexually attracted to them. She had conflicted fantasies of triumphing over co-workers, but feared envy and retaliation.

When she felt anxious about success at work, she sought closeness and reassurance from other women. She had several close long-lasting friendships with women and at times wondered if she might be homosexual since she was more consistent in relationships with women than with men. She would then have fantasies of never marrying, but of living with girl friends and doing without men. She would also begin to eat and gain weight, that is, become "more like mother," whom she felt was overweight, hence not "feminine" from a sexual perspective. Ms. Y.'s times of success at "men's" work were followed by feeling that her eating was out of control, the gaining of weight, and feeling herself to be a neuter. Several times she had become distressed enough to develop a clinical depression.

Ms. Y.'s cycle of alternating success at love and success at work was repeated several times during the course of her treatment. She gained increasing self-awareness each successive time. Gradually she began to understand, then to modulate and control her behavior with consequent improvement in her relationships with men and women, her work, and her control of binging.

A DREAM

Several years into her treatment, Ms. Y. recounted a dream. It expressed in condensed form many of her concerns described above. Ms. Y.'s dream and her associations to it suggest the complexity of the material available (in contrast to the simplified summary in the preceding section). It is included here to give an example of the process of beginning to understand the way such material emerges, and is elaborated and clarified in the psychotherapeutic work.

Ms. Y. felt this dream was especially significant. Waking up from it, Ms. Y. had the thought that she had been "following in her father's footsteps" and that she had identified with his career choice, successes, and self-defeating ways. She had discussed this already in her treatment, but had never realized it so clearly. Ms. Y. had dreamed: "I was a little girl, about five or six years old. I looked up at a large woman and complained that my father had been making me drag a bucket of dirty earrings behind me." Ms. Y.'s associations to the dream follow: The large woman was like her mother. "Bucket" sounded like buttocks, like her mother's fat buttocks—the part of her own body she was most self-conscious about, dragging behind her. The bucket reminded her of a pail of dirty water. This was both like scrubbing the floor, which is womens' work; and her feeling of her body (and its fluids, menstrual blood, sweat) being dirty (sexual). The image of the dirty water connected the bucket and the "earrings" with another thought: when she felt depressed, she would leave the ring in the bathtub and then feel burdened by having to scrub it out for herself later, the familiar theme of having to care for herself when she wished her mother would take care of her.

Earrings had feminine meanings. The day before the dream she had been feeling good about herself and had bought a pair of fancy dangling earrings which "caught the eye" and attracted attention—these were like the pretty earrings that her very feminine, thin sister wore. (This sister had married at a young age, following their mother's example.) Earrings also reminded her of being cared for by her mother. When she was in high school, her mother had gone with her to a doctor to get her ears pierced; and once for Hanukkah her mother had given her "real gold" earrings. This in turn brought back a memory of feeling "dirty": Years later she had lost one of these earrings when hurriedly leaving a man's room, she felt angry at him, humiliated and guilty after sex, and unworthy of her mother's gift. Significantly, she had decided to go out with the man on impulse after her mother, in order to be at a recital with her youngest sister, had called to cancel an event that she and Ms. Y. were to have attended together and that Ms. Y. had looked forward to as special. The thought of forgetting this earring brought up another recent memory. She had left her very plain, everyday earrings at her married sister's house after a particularly difficult visit which had followed a long period of not speaking to each other. Her sister had invited her to come to celebrate her birthday and had baked Ms. Y. a cake. The food was not enough. She had still felt excluded from her sister's confidences and compared her life and career with her married sister's more conventional female life-style.

The earrings, especially the fancy ones, were to show off and be delighted with; gifts from her mother, both evidence of her mother's caring and suggesting that her mother had accepted her wish to be attractive in a sexual way. (Her loss of the earrings reflected her guilt about this and anger both at her mother's disapproval and her wish to be cared for, not only in symbolic ways.) Pierced earrings were part of her clothing (body), yet did not really belong to her. They could be lost (like weight), but also seemed dirty and shameful because of their connection with sexuality and her wish to attract attention. The dream repeated many of the themes already discussed —particularly Ms. Y.'s mixed feelings about being a woman and what kind of woman to be.

DISCUSSION—WHY THIS PARTICULAR WOMAN AT THIS TIME?

Symptoms of bulimia (like hysteric conversion symptoms) are not indicative of a particular underlying character, and may be present in patients with neurotic, borderline, or psychotic personalities with varying severity of psychopathology, just as bulimia may be present in extreme thin, emaciated patients, or normal weight or obese individuals. The case is one typical presentation of bulimia; however, it does not represent an extreme example of this syndrome.

As noted in survey studies, the widespread prevalence of normal weight bulimia in women like Ms. Y., belies the poor prognosis for bulimia when associated with anorexia nervosa cited by Halmi (1983). The manifestations of Ms. Y.'s eating disorder were not dangerous to her health. Her change in weight, although troublesome to her, was not enough that her peers would remark upon her figure as either especially thin or fat. Except for her decision to seek treatment for other reasons, it might never have been evident to Ms. Y. that she suffered from bulimia, and indeed she was well into her treatment before she revealed this problem.

Ms. Y.'s developmental and social history falls within the normal range. For example, her menarche at age ten was early, but not abnormally so (Jones and Mussen, 1958). Both in adolescence and adult life, Ms. Y. had close friends even when she felt most isolated. Her parents continued in an intact marriage and although they had often been unhappy and at times depressed, neither had severe enough disorders to disrupt their employment or to require hospitalization. Ms. Y. was quite successfully employed and her performance at work was sometimes outstanding and always adequate, although it varied in both quantity and quality. She appeared to be a representative member of her age group of women in this time and culture.

So let us return to the questions posed by Striegel-Moore, Silberstein, and Rodin in 1986. "Why women? Which women in particular? Why now?" and consider them in regard to this individual.

The question at this degree of magnification becomes: *Why this particular woman now?* In any individual, social, familial, biological (both constitutional and current), and psychodynamic factors interact. The meaning of a symptom and the circumstances of its occurrence are extremely complex and overdetermined. However, when Ms. Y.'s history is reviewed it seems clear that she was fated to develop bulimia. As Freud (1920) pointed out:

> So long as we trace the development from its final outcome backwards, the chain of events appears continuous, and we feel we have gained an insight which is completely satisfactory or even exhaustive. But if we proceed the reverse way, if we start from the premises inferred from the analysis and try to follow these up to the final result, then we

no longer get the impression of an inevitable sequence of events which could not have been otherwise determined. We notice at once that there might have been another result, and that we might have been just as well able to understand and explain the latter. The synthesis is thus not so satisfactory as the analysis; in other words, from a knowledge of the premises we could not have foretold the nature of the result.

It is very easy to account for this disturbing state of affairs. Even supposing that we have a complete knowledge of the aetiological factors that decide a given result, nevertheless what we know about them is only their quality, and not their relative strength. Some of them are suppressed by others because they are too weak, and they therefore do not affect the final result. But we never know beforehand which of the determining factors will prove the weaker or the stronger. We only say at the end that those which succeeded must have been the stronger [pp. 167–168].

Keeping this in mind, let us review the particular aspects of Ms. Y.'s presentation, focusing on how psychodynamic issues and developmental history interacted with social and biological risk factors. In discussion of a single case, these dimensions cannot be presented separately, all intertwine to produce a unique clinical picture.

Biologically, Ms. Y. had a family history of affective disorder. Several studies have suggested that both affective disorders and substance abuse may be more common in relatives of patients with eating disorders (Herzog and Copeland, 1985). The history of affective disorder in Ms. Y.'s family was strong, thus Ms. Y. may have had a biological predisposition to become depressed. Ms. Y.'s clinical depression is also shared by one subgroup of bulimic women (Herzog, 1984).

The family history of affective disorder was more than just biologically important. Ms. Y.'s longing to be cared for and fear of being abandoned if she asserted herself seemed to be related to her very early childhood experiences. Her mother had told her that when she was three years old, following the birth of her next younger sister, she (mother) had had a severe post-partum depression. (Her father had been traveling on business frequently around that time.) It seems likely that this unavail-ability of her mother and father at a vulnerable developmental stage, that of separation–individuation when she was around two years old, followed quickly by the birth of another baby, must have contributed to Ms. Y.'s sense of having to care for herself when she still felt too young to do so. She must have developed ways of coping beyond what she felt were her ca-pacities, leaving her yearning to be nurtured. Her feelings about her younger sisters—both loving and resenting them—may have repeated the theme of fearing punishment (the withdrawal of caring) for wishing to triumph over helpless, incompetent, loved, and hated rivals. Binging contained for her both sides of this dilemma—being indulged and being punished as she stuffed herself with food beyond pleasure to the point of dis-comfort. This theme then reappeared in her anxiety about her promotion, focused on her relationship to her neglectful boss (her mother), and the "old man" (her father and younger sis-ters). Her memory of her mother singing lullabies to her younger sisters and her fascination with her boss joking with the "old man," instead of helping her, must also be related to her expectation of being punished for being successful. There the very early roots of Ms. Y.'s distress were suggested in her wish both to compete with men and to be close to women.

There were other characteristics of her family which also predisposed Ms. Y. to bulimia. Schwartz (1986) suggested that women from families where food is especially valued are more prone to develop eating disorders. This was clearly true of Ms. Y. For example, her choice of chocolate chip cookie batter to binge on may be related to her mother frequently giving her that particular cookie.

Her mother could be remote and cold, or nurturing, in-dulgent, and comforting, particularly with food. Steiner-Adair (1986) stresses the connection of conflict about the wish for attachment to the development of eating disorders. The un-availability of her mother in early childhood may have left Ms. Y. deficient in modulating and containing emotion. Ms. Y. was not bulimic except during times when she felt under particular stress. She then turned to a familiar but unsatisfactory way of comfort. Ms. Y. managed any strong feelings—anger, sexuality, despair, or triumph—by binging. For Ms. Y., the binge represented both a symptom of distress and an attempt to deal with painful feelings.

As an adult, Ms. Y. lived alone. She spent most of her waking hours working hard in an environment where self-sufficiency was valued. She came home after work to continue working at homemaking tasks. She took care of no one but herself and no one cared for her except herself. The possibility of achieving an altered state of consciousness through eating (Reiser, 1987), as well as the connection of being fed with being mothered, made food a form of self-medication. The processes which began in early childhood continued as Ms. Y. grew up.

At puberty, early conflicts are reawakened and dealt with afresh (Freud, 1905). Oedipal as well as preoedipal issues were apparent in this case. Ms. Y. deeply wished to please her father and be his favorite, and manifested oedipal wishes again and again in adult relationships.

Ms. Y. remembered "the old man who played knickknack on *my* shoe" as well as "he played seven on the way to heaven." This might be thought of as reflecting her wish to play with her father—his games. This meant to be close to him by sharing his work, to be able to ask him for help and advice, and for him to be proud of her accomplishments. She believed that her father had wanted a son, and that he valued her more when she was successful at work. She had been close to her father when she was a young girl—a very active tomboy. Her attitude to her first job, as a gas station attendant, was very evocative of her later career choices. It had been especially significant for Ms. Y. that her new job was a "man's job" which she was the first woman to have. Later she had realized it reminded her of her favorite job in high school when she had been the first female gas station attendant in her town.

Both as an adolescent and an adult, she did not wish to relinquish her femininity, but sought the specialness of being a girl in a boy's job. Success at men's work seemed to provide closeness to her father, both through identification with him and in expressing her wish to be the son he always wanted. She wished, like Helene Deutsch, "to be simultaneously my father's prettiest daughter and cleverest son" (Deutsch, 1973).

This patient clearly illuminates the importance of the particular circumstances of early adolescence in contributing to the choice and meaning of symptoms. Ms. Y. dated her concerns with weight, body shape, and eating to puberty. She first revealed the details of her eating disorder along with memories of early adolescence, particularly her accelerated physical development.

Developmental history has been cited as a risk factor for bulimia. Striegel-Moore et al. (1986) mentioned the significance of the timing of puberty, citing Neugarten (1972) who found it a stressor to be out of step with peers. For Ms. Y., this seemed especially significant. Survey research has found that early developing girls are reported to be "less popular with female peers, to experience greater emotional distress, to perceive themselves as less attractive, and to hold a lower self-concept than their peers" (Jones and Mussen, 1958; Peskin, 1973; Simmons, Blyth, and McKinney, 1983). They have been found to be particularly unhappy with their weight and tend to be fatter than their peers and remain so (Simmons et al., 1983; Tobin-Richards, Boxer, and Petersen, 1983). They may also be perceived as sexual, enjoy greater popularity with male peers (Simmons et al., 1983), and be treated with more protectiveness by their parents (Hamburg, 1974). The strict sexual morals in her family had caused Ms. Y. to experience early maturation and emerging sexuality as shameful rather than as a welcome chance to be "more popular with boys."

Bruch (1981) suggested that there might be a connection between early menarche and the development of eating disorders. Ms. Y.'s memories and associations help to elucidate how these might have been connected for her. The affective sense of her body being "out of control" was intensified at puberty along with her shame and mystification at the hygienic aspects of growing up. For example, although the circumstances of her experience of her menarche was unremarkable (Whisnant and Zegans, 1975), the extent of her inhibition was suggested by her hesitation about using tampons, which was delayed until after she had begun having sexual intercourse. This might be seen as reflecting her effort to keep a distance from her sexually mature body—particularly her internal feminine genital (Shopper, 1979; Whisnant, Brett, and Zegans, 1979).

Her feelings about her body—that her peers would be more curious about it and would stare at her in the exercise room—paralleled experiences in early adolescence. The "splash baths" she took at the health club were like the ones girls at school who had their periods had taken after her junior high school gym class. (Her conviction that other women do not sweat might also have been connected to the era when she had begun to produce apocrine [odoriferous] sweat earlier than her peers and her perception of this difference.) Even Ms. Y.'s complaint about her skirts—too tight and binding after she gained weight—echoed the adolescent theme, and expressed in the binding sanitary napkin, bra, and dress shields which constricted and confined her body.

Around the time of menarche, girls gain weight. A high percentage of this weight gain is fat, and the shape of the body changes from the long-legged, thin-hipped, prepubertal silhouette to a more rounded, mature figure. (This may have been exacerbated in Ms. Y. who early on developed large hips and buttocks "like her mother.") For Ms. Y., the desire to begin dieting in young adulthood and her feelings about the physical changes of puberty seemed to be unconsciously connected. Her rapid gain of 20 pounds after her promotion echoed the pubertal growth spurt.

The theme of being "too old" and "too young" which began in an earlier childhood experience was reinforced at puberty. Certainly in early adolescence, Ms. Y. again felt too old (physically) and too young (emotionally) for the independence expected of her (later her promotion again stirred up these feelings).

Ninety percent of bulimics are women (Striegel-Moore et al., 1986). Rodin, Silberstein, and Striegel-Moore (1984), de-

clare that dieting, concern with weight, and the wish to be thin
have become normative with women in this culture and that
the stigmatization of obesity, the importance of being attractive,
thinness as a measure of attractiveness, and the female stereotype which prescribes preoccupation with and pursuit of
beauty are some of the ways in which society instructs women
to alter their bodies in order to achieve beauty. Ms. Y. was
biologically predisposed (heir to the genes of her mother's family) to deposit fat in a set pattern over her hips and buttocks.
Such distribution of fat is considered to be particularly undesirable in the present culture (Beck, Ward-Hull, and McLear,
1976); any weight Ms. Y. gained seemed especially objection-
able. Her father's teasing about eating, and the marital discord
she observed made it hard for her to identify positively with
her own mother's shape. Here social, biological, and psychological factors converged to reinforce Ms. Y.'s discomfort with
her weight.

At this time in this culture she had the opportunity to work
with men at "men's jobs." She felt most attractive when working
closely with a man who admired her. Overt sexual activity
plunged her quickly into remorse and guilt, and led to eating
as a way of both changing her state of mind by concentrating
on thoughts about food and changing the shape of her body
to be more like her mother's body—maternal, nonsexual. She
consciously wanted to be a wife and mother, but was very dog-
matic and rigid about the idea that she must not marry a divorced man. (Again reflecting conflict about oedipal wishes;
her need to deny and defend herself against her attachment
to father and her early fantasies that she would know how to
make him happier than her mother could.) She retreated from
sexuality to her mother, both through eating and offering food
(her mother's way of expressing love) and through getting fat,
like her mother, and thus feeling neuter and unattractive to
men. She repeated this in her relationships with her women
friends. Like a patient discussed by Ritvo (1984), Ms. Y. "turned
to men as a substitute for women, but as a consequence felt she
had lost the women. In that situation eating was a substitute for
losing the women and for the lack of satisfaction with men"

(p. 461). Ritvo's statement about his patient that, "Eating could serve in place of getting sexual fulfillment from men and enable her to keep her mother as well" is also applicable to Ms. Y.

Striegel-Moore et al. (1986) report speculation that although thinness represents the antithesis of the ample female body associated with woman as wife and mother (Beck et al., 1976), that it has become linked with femininity. They advance the notion that thinness may be viewed as an accomplishment in itself. These authors point out that women now compete not only for academic or work success with men *and* women, but also with other women for the achievement of a beautiful (i.e., thin) body. They stress the concurrence in our society of a need to look feminine with the pursuit of ambition and power, noting that women who have achieved occupational success continue to worry about thinness. Socially, Ms. Y. fits the stereotype of the bulimic woman: successful, competitive with both men and women, and concerned with being competent, beautiful, and thin. She was conscious of competing with women (peers, mother, sisters) about weight and attractiveness (as well as homemaking skills) and with both men (and women) about athletic prowess, and success in business.

Striegel-Moore et al. (1986) also pointed out the importance of current culture as contributing strongly to the increased incidence of eating disorders. Relevant to Ms. Y. is the shift toward an increasingly thin standard, the effect of media attention on dieting and fitness, and shifting sex roles, and in particular the career choice, advancement possibilities, and living situations open to women. The observation of Steiner-Adair's (1986) survey of adolescent girls' self-images is striking: "Girls who saw the 'super woman' as consonant with their own goals had elevated eating pathology scores" (p. 257). In Ms. Y.'s efforts to be successful in all spheres of her life, this statement rings true.

CONCLUSION

This chapter reviews aspects of the history of a single individual—an attractive, successful, young professional woman

—whose eating went out of control immediately after she received a significant career promotion. This clinical material has been presented to illustrate how detailed information from a particular case may supplement data from survey research. The case also portrays the way in which focus on the individual psychodynamics of a representative patient may elicit information that resonates with and adds clinical relevance to principles derived from survey studies of large populations.

REFERENCES

American Psychiatric Association (1980), *Diagnostic and Statistical Manual of Mental Disorders*, 3rd ed. (DSM-III). Washington, DC: American Psychiatric Press.
Beck, J. B., Ward-Hull, C. J., & McLear, P. M. (1976), Variables related to women's somatic preferences of the male and female body. *J. Pers. & Soc. Psychol.*, 34:1200–1210.
Brumberg, J. (1982), Chlorotic girls, 1870–1920: A historical perspective on female adolescence. *Child Develop.*, 53:1468–1477.
Bruch, H. (1981), Developmental considerations of anorexia nervosa and obesity. *Can. J. Psychiat.*, 26:212–217.
Casper, R. C. (1983), On the emergence of bulimia nervosa as a syndrome: A historical view. *Internat. J. Eat. Disord.*, 2:3–16.
Deutsch, H. (1973), *Confrontations with Myself.* New York: W. W. Norton.
Fenichel, O. (1945), *The Psychoanalytic Theory of Neurosis.* New York: W. W. Norton.
——— (1954), Anorexia. In: *Collected Papers of Otto Fenichel*, ed. H. Fenichel & D. Rapaport. 2nd series. New York: W. W. Norton, pp. 288–292.
Freud, S. (1905), Three essays on the theory of sexuality. *Standard Edition*, 7:135–243. London: Hogarth Press, 1953.
——— (1920), A case of homosexuality in a woman. *Standard Edition*, 18:167–168. London: Hogarth Press, 1955.
Halmi, K. (1983), Anorexia nervosa and bulimia. *Psychosom.*, 24:111–129.
Hamburg, B. (1974), Early adolescence: A specific and stressful stage of the life cycle. In: *Coping and Adaptation*, ed. G. Coelho, D. A. Hamburg, & J. E. Adams. New York: Basic Books, pp. 101–126.
Herzog, D., & Copeland, P. (1985), Eating disorders. *New Eng. J. Med.*, 313:295–303.
Herzog, D. B. (1984), Are anorexic and bulimic patients depressed? *Amer. J. Psychiat.*, 141:1594–1597.
Jones, M., & Mussen, P. H. (1958), Self conceptions, motivations and interpersonal attitudes of early and late maturing girls. *Child Develop.*, 29:491–501.
Krohn, A. (1978), Hysteria: The Elusive Neurosis. *Psychological Issues*, 45/46. New York: International Universities Press.

Neugarten, B. I. (1972), Personality and aging process. *Gerontolog.* 12:9–25.

Peskin, H. (1973), Influence of the developmental schedule of puberty on learning and ego functioning. *J. Youth & Adol.*, 2:273–290.

Rangell, L. (1959), The nature of conversion. *J. Amer. Psychoanal. Assn.*, 7:632–662.

Reiser, L. W. (1987), The oral triad in bulimia. Presented at the Fall meeting, American Psychoanalytic Association, New York.

Ritvo, S. (1984), The image and use of the body in psychic conflict. *The Psychoanalytic Study of the Child*, 39:449–469. New Haven, CT: Yale University Press.

Rodin, J., Silberstein, L. & Striegel-Moore, R. (1984), Women and weight: A normative discontent. In: *Psychology and Gender. Nebraska Symposium on Motivation.* Lincoln, NE: University of Nebraska Press, pp. 267–307.

Satow, R. (1979), Where has all the hysteria gone? *Psychoanal. Rev.*, 66:463–478.

Schwartz, H. (1986), Bulimia: Psychoanalytic perspectives. *J. Amer. Psychoanal. Assn.*, 34:439–462.

Shopper, M. (1979), The (re)discovery of the vagina and the importance of the menstrual tampon. In: *Female Adolescent Development*, ed. M. Sugar. New York: Brunner/Mazel pp. 214–233.

Simmons, R. G., Blyth, D. A., & McKinney, K. I. (1983), The social and psychological effects of puberty on white females. In: *Girls at Puberty*, ed. J. Brooks-Gunn & A. C. Petersen. New York: Plenum Press, pp. 229–278.

Steiner-Adair, K. (1986), The body politic: Normal female adolescent development and the development of eating disorders. *J. Amer. Acad. Psychoanal.*, 14:95–114.

Striegel-Moore, R., Silberstein, L., & Rodin, J. (1986), Toward an understanding of risk factors for bulimia. *Amer. Psychol.*, March:246–263.

Tobin-Richards, M. H., Boxer, A. M., & Petersen, A. C. (1983), The psychological significance of pubertal change. Sex differences in perceptions of self during early adolescence. In: *Girls at Puberty*, ed. J. Brooks-Gunn & A. C. Petersen. New York: Plenum Press, pp. 127–154.

Whisnant, L., Brett, E., & Zegans, L. (1979), Adolescent girls and menstruation. *Adol. Psychiat.*, 7:157–171.

———— Zegans, L. (1975), A study of attitudes toward menarche in white middle class American adolescent girls. *Amer. J. Psychiat.*, 132:809–814.

Chapter 13

Bulimia and Adolescence: Individual Psychoanalytic Treatment

REMI G. GONZALEZ, M.D.

Bulimia as a symptom or in association with anorexia nervosa has been described by various authors (Gull, 1873; MacKenzie, 1888; Osler, 1892; Soltman, 1894; Abraham, 1916; Stunkard, Grace, and Woff, 1955; Bruch, 1962; Thomä, 1967; Sperling, 1978; Casper, Eckert, Halmi, Goldberg, and Davis, 1980; Wilson, 1982). Gull (1873), who first coined the term *anorexia nervosa*, reported overeating followed by vomiting in one of his patients. Abraham (1916) described "attacks of ravenous hunger" which the patient recognized as being different from normal hunger. He suggested that such conditions were associated with repressed libido, citing the "great frequency of these hunger attacks in frigid women." He also noted that the behavior of these patients was "extraordinarily similar" to that of individuals suffering with addictions. Stunkard et al. (1955), described bulimic behavior in obese patients which he labeled "the night eating syndrome." These patients consumed large amounts of food during the evening and night and suffered with sleep disturbances, impulsive behavior, and cravings resembling addictions. Clinical symptoms of bulimia have since been described by several clinicians, but they were regarded as part of a neurotic symptom complex and not a separate entity. The recognition of bulimia as a distinct syndrome occurred when it became evident that binge eating and vomiting behavior could be found in individuals who did not have histories of weight disorders such as obesity and anorexia nervosa (Boskind-Lodhal and White, 1978; Strangler and Prinz, 1980). Several analysts, amongst them, Thomä (1967), Sperling (1978), and Wilson (1983), include bulimia under the diagnostic category of anorexia nervosa. This idea was shared by Boskind-Lodhal (1976) who coined the term *bulimarexia* to describe a condition characterized by alternating episodes of eating and rigid dieting pointing to different manifestations of the same syndrome. Bulimia as a separate entity is defined in *The Diagnostic and Statistical Manual of Mental Disorders* [(DSM-III) American Psychiatric Association, 1980] as a condition characterized by repeated episodes of rapid ingestion of large amounts of food in a discrete period of time, usually less than two hours. These individuals are aware that their eating pattern is abnormal, but fear being unable to stop eating voluntarily. They also experience depressed moods and self-deprecatory thoughts following the eating binges. Additional characteristics include: weight fluctuations of greater than 10 pounds; consumption of high-caloric, easily ingested food; and the termination of such eating episodes by abdominal pain, sleep, and self-induced vomiting. They are also prone to the use of severely restrictive diets, laxatives, and diuretics in order to effect weight control. Since DSM-III stipulates that the bulimic episodes should not be due to anorexia nervosa, a true bulimic should be at or above normal weight. This has prompted research in this area with some evidence that there is a group of women with no history of weight disorder suffering from the condition. The studies thus far have been, for the most part, limited to college students. (Hawkins and Clement, 1980; Halmi, Falk, and Schwartz, 1981). The prevalence, according to these studies, ranges from 4.1 to 13 percent. Johnson, Lewis, Love, Lewis, and Stuckey (1984) found an incidence of 4.9 percent in a study of 1,268 high school students who met the criteria for bulimia. It should be noted that these studies were not rigidly controlled, relying on self-reporting questionnaire answering which, due to the fact that these patients tend to lie, make the results suspect. There is no question, however, that the condition is prevalent in this population regardless of the difficulty in assessing its frequency accurately.

Although the condition frequently first manifests during adolescence, the typical bulimia patient is a single, white female in her early twenties who is well educated and of average weight (Johnson et al., 1984). These individuals are frequently impulsive, moody, complain of both anxiety and depression, engage in obsessive–compulsive behavior, have poor self-esteem, feel confused about their sex-role identity, and are severely preoccupied with food, weight, and thinness. These studies have also attempted to deal with the issue of whether there is sufficient data to support the creation of a separate diagnostic entity or whether, as previously believed and still held by some, bulimia is one of the manifestations of anorexia nervosa.

With this in mind, some researchers have embarked on a search for a clearer delineation of the similarities and differences between these conditions. Thus, the term *bulimia nervosa* (Russell, 1979) has been suggested for those patients with anorexia nervosa who also manifest bulimic behavior. These patients are said to have an older age of onset, have a higher incidence of premorbid obesity, and appear to have a more chronic outcome (Beaumont, George, and Smart, 1976; Garfinkel, Moldofsky, and Garner, 1980; Strober, Salkin, Burroughs, and Morrell, 1982). They also, like normal-weight bulimics, manifest a greater incidence of depression, anxiety, impulsive behavior, body image distortion, and a more extensive family conflict pattern (Katzman and Wolchick, 1984). These findings seem to point to the fact that bulimic anorectics behave more like normal-weight bulimics than restrictor anorectics.

It would appear that the majority of patients diagnosed bulimic are suffering with bulimia nervosa. This fact is frequently uncovered during analytic work once the defensive structure is penetrated and the rage and denial manifests in the transference. Early on in treatment there is a need to present a distorted picture as a way of dealing with the internalized bad self. They fear being rejected and abandoned if exposed and have to adhere tenaciously to their initial presenting story.

When it can no longer be sustained, their anxiety level rises dramatically; and they are prone to acting out destructively, frequently missing sessions, and threatening to discontinue treatment, or contemplating it.

The recent apparent increase in the incidence of bulimia has generated much interest in the elucidation of possible etiologies, but the body of knowledge thus far generated is limited. Biological factors, particularly endocrine disturbances, have been studied with no significant etiological findings having resulted. The possibility that bulimia may be related to unipolar or bipolar illness has been postulated (Pyle, Mitchell, and Eckert, 1981; Johnson and Larson, 1982; Glassman and Walsh, 1983) but thus far no conclusive evidence exists that points to a definite connection, though dexamethasone suppression tests and the thyroid releasing hormone stimulating test appear to be positive in bulimics with the same frequency as in patients with major depressions (Hudson, Laffer, and Pope, 1982; Gwirtsman, Roy-Byrne, and Yager, 1983). Reports that antidepressants, both tricyclics and MAO-inhibitors, appear to have a salutory effect on bulimic symptoms (Jonas, Pope, and Hudson, 1983; Brotman, Herzog, and Woods, 1984) is thought to support the depression hypothesis. It is also equally possible that there is no relationship and that the depression is common to both conditions.

Another area of investigation has been the family environment among bulimic patients. Studies comparing normal-weight bulimic families with families of anorexics who binged and families of restrictor anorexics (Strober et al., 1982; Garner, Garfinkel, and Olmsted, 1983), as well as families of bulimics, bulimic anorexics, and normals, point to similarities amongst the bulimics and the bulimic anorexics as compared with restrictor and normal subjects. Garner et al. (1983) found normal-weight bulimics' families were strikingly similar to the anorexic–bulimics' families on six of eight measures of family interaction style used in their studies. The degree of pathology in affective expression, affective involvement communication, control, values and norms, and social desirability was not only considered pathological, as compared with normals, but also well above that of families of restricting anorexics. So that in many respects, the families of bulimics and bulimic–anorexic families appeared to manifest similar distresses.

The question of what characterizes bulimic families has been posed. Studies so far suggest that the bulimics' families appear to be disengaged, highly conflicted, have a high degree of life distress, and tend to use less direct, frequently contradictory, communication patterns. Thus, at times such families appear chaotic, less intellectual, and yet have high achievement expectations. There is an inability to express negative feelings openly and directly. The parents give negative, more contradictory (double-bind) messages to their daughters, especially when issues of control versus autonomy are at stake. Marital distress also manifests in the lack of emotional intimacy, depression, and sometimes alcohol abuse. The parents themselves may manifest affective disorders which may prove to be transgenerational (Goodsitt, 1983; Hudson, Pope, Jonas, and Yurgelum-Todd, 1983). Parents also, although well intentioned and interested in the well-being of their children, may have difficulties in nurturing because of their own experiences in earlier life. Typically they are concerned with food and encourage "dieting" for everyone in the family. At the same time, as previously mentioned, there is evidence of loss of control in that obesity and alcohol abuse are not infrequent (Pyle et al., 1981). Exhibitionistic parental behavior is another feature, found at times together with seductive sexual behavior by the fathers.

The result is a general environment where control issues relating to separation–individuation are constantly at play and oral conflicts in the form of binging–vomiting syndrome manifest concretely as expressions introjection–projection struggles of early infancy and childhood.

PSYCHODYNAMICS

The psychodynamics of eating disorders have been formulated by numerous authors. Psychoanalytic observers favor the idea of a regression from adult sexuality, as these conditions frequently manifest in adolescence, accompanied by a regression to preoedipal oral–anal modes of drive discharge and ego function (Waller, Kaufman, and Deutsch, 1940; Masserman, 1941; Moulton, 1942; Lorand, 1943; Fenichel, 1945; Sperling, 1953, 1968, 1978; Thomä, 1967; Sours, 1974; Volkan, 1976; Risen, 1982; Wilson, 1983; Gero, 1984). Sperling (1978) states that "unresolved preoedipal fixation to the mother contributes to the difficulties in psychosexual development and to the intensity of the oedipal conflict in these girls" (p. 166). In her opinion, these patients displace "sexual and masturbatory conflicts from the genitals to the mouth, and food and eating become equated with forbidden sexual objects and sexual activities" (p. 166).

She also believes that "the unresolved preoedipal fixation of the mother contributes to the difficulties in psychosexual development and to the intensity of the oedipal conflict" (p. 166) in these patients. The reason for symptom manifestation during adolescence is due to the demands for proper sexual identification, the establishing of peer and heterosexual relationships, and the necessity to separate from primary love objects. All of these elements are the essential tasks of adolescence. As part of the defensive deemphasis of the instinctual drives, these patients tend to deny sexual and masturbatory conflicts at a genital level displacing them to the mouth, so that food and eating become equated with forbidden sexual objects and activities. The degree of manifest pathology is dependent upon the degree of regression and fixation; the more orally fixated, the poorer the prognosis. As is the case with all pregenitally fixated character disorders, which retain a high degree of narcissism and omnipotence, their ability for object cathexis and for reality testing is impaired to varying degrees.

It is clear in the analysis of normal-weight bulimics that oedipal conflicts are present. Accordingly, the pathology is not only the result of preoedipal fixation, but also the result of regression from oedipal strivings.

Sperling (1949) did an exhaustive study of the unconscious bond that exists between the mother and the child and the resulting pathology that results when the mother is incapable of allowing the normal psychological separation. She frequently views the child as a narcissistic projection of her own self, symbolically her wished-for-penis. The maternal overcontrol interferes with ego differentiation between mother and child (Bird, 1957), so that the mother's ego continues to be dominant and thus prevents the child's from functioning autonomously, working out conflicts between ego and id.

This would speak for fixation and arrest in development of the autonomous ego functions. When the pathology is viewed from a structural perspective, however, the emphasis is on defensive regression and displacement from genital wishes. This would appear to be conflictive, yet perhaps both views have a degree of truth, for as Brenner (1974) pointed out, oral and anal wishes do not disappear with the advent of the oedipal period. Also, the concept of arrest and fixation allows for certain functions of the ego to develop in what appears to be a normal fashion (e.g., cognitive functions), while other aspects of the ego may be impaired to varying degrees. The result is the well-known ego splitting which is not only characteristic of this disorder, but is also present in other conditions exhibiting significant preoedipal unresolved conflict. This would give one explanation for the bulimic's impulsivity, disobedience, and rebellion (both at home and in school), antisocial behavior, promiscuity, and addiction tendencies. Of course, all of these behaviors are not always found in every case.

Conflicts of separation–individuation are denied by the parents (Wilson, 1986) who have a tendency to be perfectionistic and infantilizing, thus depriving the child from developing the capacity for decision making.

More recently dynamic formulations have emphasized one of the ego functions, namely object relations. Theorists interested in this important function of the ego (Spitz and Wolf, 1946; Winnicott, 1951; Klein, 1959; Mahler, 1963; Mahler and Furer, 1963; Jacobsen, 1964, Bowlby, 1969) have studied the earliest dyadic relationship in childhood, that between the child and the mother. One of the reasons for this focus is perhaps the fact that direct observation of the interaction can be done, thus providing a measure of objectivity to the process. Unfortunately, as Kramer (1974) points out, description of the manifest behavior between mother and child "tells us nothing about the mother's intrapsychic processes, and sheds little light on the mother–child psychopathology" (p. 578). The most frequently used point of reference is Mahler's (1967) concepts regarding psychological developmental unfolding with particular emphasis on the separation–individuation phase. The rapprochement subphase is generally considered most critical in the pathological development of the bulimic. According to this view, the conflict between the mother and the child occurs primarily during this subphase (Sours, 1974) resulting in severe difficulties later when the child reaches adolescence and instinctual drives as well as environmental and maturational influences push toward separation from parental figures. Others (Sugarman and Kurash, 1981) are convinced that the damage occurs earlier and results in developmental arrest at the level of the practicing subphase of the separation–individuation period, causing difficulties in "self-other boundary differentiation, individuation, and capacity for symbolization" (p. 58).

It is frequently difficult, if not impossible, to pinpoint the genetic origin of the pathology in the developmental continuum. Historical facts provided by the parents often describe what could be considered an ideal developmental state with pregnancy, birth, and early infancy being within normal limits. Feeding during infancy and eating behavior during early childhood are usually reported as ideal with nothing out of the ordinary being recalled by the mother. Some inferences may be made during analysis as to the nature of the interaction between the mother and child, but I do not believe we can specifically pinpoint the exact time. From a practical point of view, this may not be crucial, for one must deal with the pathological manifestations as they surface in the analytic situation, noting first manifest behavior, followed by the defense analysis, and later, if possible, drive and genetic interpretation.

The conflict between the bulimic patient and the parents, especially the mother, has been described in numerous publications. The bulimic presents as the victim of a domineering mother who forces the child into submission, allowing practically no overt aggression to manifest. Thus the child is described as generally compliant, though not affectionate. The child's contributions to the pathological situation are much more difficult to assess and only when significant analytic work is accomplished can some insight into the conflict be gained. The complexities of the interaction between mother and the child have been delineated by Mahler (1967), who also emphasized the fact that the child with reasonably good endowment will draw sufficient mothering to prevent severe pathology. It is difficult to attribute the strength of the drives, the capacity for fantasy formation, and the degree of ambivalence and aggression, solely to the dyadic interaction between the mother and the child. We know that a significant contribution is inherent in each individual as part of the genetic endowment.

Additionally, there are the individual experiences such as major illnesses in the child or in a significant person in the family, the birth of a sibling, separations relating to school attendance or the mother's work, hospitalizations, and other situations that may impinge upon the child's experience. These facts would account for the wide spectrum of psychopathology frequently found in these patients.

TREATMENT METHODS

The recommended treatment methods range from the use of medication to the employment of psychoanalytic psychotherapy. The treatment utilized in the present communication is psychoanalytic. This type of treatment is not suitable for all cases, for instance when the patient presents with serious suicidal impulses and hospitalization is necessary. Most present with various degrees of what could best be described as borderline or narcissistic disorders in which the bulimia is but one of the symptoms and treatment has to be directed at the underlying psychopathology as a whole rather than the presenting symptom.

Due to the nature of the psychopathology, these patients present with pregenital pathological formations, particularly early in treatment. The symptom constellation is the result of both pregenital developmental arrests and regressions from triadic oedipal positions. There is evidence of sadomasochistic oral-phase conflicts resulting in an ambivalent relationship with primary objects and difficulty in psychosexual development at an oedipal level. These facts must be kept in mind throughout treatment in order to understand the nature of the resistances and the development of the transference and countertransference.

Since the majority of these patients come into treatment at the insistence of parents, they are, for the most part, negativistic and resistant to their treatment, feeling that their parents are once more forcing and controlling them. Under these circumstances, the analyst is viewed as an agent of the parents and therefore held suspect. Since the main conflict is with the mother, she is initially blamed for orchestrating the moves while the father, though also an object of anger for cooperating, is seen as more understanding and somewhat of a victim of the mother, who after all, controls everything. The analyst is soon viewed ambivalently. On the one hand, he is the agent of the parents and therefore suspect; while on the other hand, the patient's observing ego is aware of the pain and conflict involved in the bulimic episodes, particularly the fear resulting from their inability to control their impulsive binging and the depressive moods resulting thereafter, and ambivalently hopes for help. These circumstances militate against the development of a therapeutic alliance and the emergence of a positive transference. This is not particularly different from the general situation frequently found in considering the issue of analyzability in adolescence where the capacity for object relations, the synthetic and integrative functions of the ego, and the ability for working through the complex relationship necessary in the analytic situation have been questioned. The fact that adolescent fantasies and verbalizations are present oriented with severe amnesia for the past and a seemingly lack of capacity for regression, as well as their tendency to respond to the analyst as a real object, tend to support the idea that a transference neurosis is slow in developing. This fact may be most frustrating for the analyst who then has to deal with his own countertransference reactions, such as the wish to reject and abandon the resistant, acting out patient.

As Adatto (1972) states, the adolescent has little interest in cathecting the analyst, he is preoccupied with his own narcissistic interests and thus lacks a sustained capacity to work with the transference. This does not mean, however, that transference manifestations are absent; they are present, but need to be defensively devalued. This is particularly true of middle adolescence, but since many of these patients are in late adolescence, there is a greater capacity for object stability and a diminution of narcissistic interests resulting in a certain degree of stabilization of the psychic apparatus.

This apparent lack of commitment to treatment where the patient is not very communicative—in fact is frequently silent, claims he has no fantasies, cannot remember dreams, and challenges the analyst to make him well—makes treatment problematic. It becomes necessary to guard against the demands, particularly of the parents, but also nonverbally from the patient, that interpretation be dispensed with and the analyst enter into management. This is particularly tempting when the patient acts out and limit setting seems appropriate. This should be kept to a minimum, for it invariably reinforces the resistance by placing the analyst in the position of being the controlling parent. At the same time, there is a need to convey to the patient the fact that the analyst is genuinely interested in his well-being. This empathy can best be transmitted by the analyst's presence and willingness to continue to analyze and survive the attacks and complaints on the part of the patient. The patients' lament for instance that they are wasting their time, their missing of appointments, and their devaluing of the analyst and the analysis in general can be most distressing for the analyst.

Normally the middle phase of adolescence has to do with unresolved conflicts with primary object relationships, separation from them, and the formation of new attachments. When separation–individuation has been incomplete, this disengaging becomes problematic and severe regression is apparent, making the analysis more difficult. This is the case with bulimics who are engaged in a sadomasochistic relationship with the primary objects.

While countertransference, just like transference, is ubiquitous to every analysis, it is necessary to be especially alert for its manifestations in the treatment of these patients for it is frequently strong and can disrupt the course of analysis.

These patients frequently present with intense, rapidly fluctuating transferences characteristic of severe character disorders and borderline conditions. This tends to evoke strong countertransference reactions in the analyst who may then engage in interpretations designed to give himself relief rather than giving the patient insight about his mental processes. The problems are very similar to those described by Boyer (1979) in treating severely regressed patients and Thomä (1967) who describes the countertransference conflicts aroused in the analyst by the prolonged negative transference in anorexic patients. Bulimics, though quite controlling, are more expressive and have a tendency to act out more often; thus providing the analyst with greater opportunity to interpret their projection of the archaic superego introject onto the analyst and other significant objects, most frequently the parents. In this regard, it is important to keep in mind the role played by projective identification in their defensive structure, realizing, of course, that the behaviors represent reenactments symbolic of past activities and conflicts (Ekstein, 1976; Boyer, 1979). These, as with any patient, are nonverbal communications which are crucial to the analysis. They appear more crucial in these cases, however, since a great deal of communication, particularly in the beginning phase, is nonverbal, with the patient in a state of negative transference. They have "nothing to say," but obviously want to be "heard."

As Sperling (1967) clearly described in treatment of patients with psychosomatic disorders, the analyst must withstand the patient's constant testing, be alert to changes in transference feelings, and resist the patient's attempts to turn the analyst into the image of the omnipotent, controlling mother. It is also necessary for him to be aware of the patient's nuances as demonstrated in facial expressions, tone of voice, posture, movements, just as the patient is aware of the analyst. This mutual scrutiny is constant, and at times crucial, especially when the patient prefers to conduct the session face to face, which is not an unusual occurrence.

A most prominent feature in the analysis is the degree of hostility which manifests, particularly early in the analysis when negativism toward treatment and contempt for the analyst is rampant, as the therapist is perceived as an agent or extension of the parents, possessing at this juncture all the negative attributes. It is imperative under the circumstances that insofar as possible, the analyst constantly strives toward the identification of the sources of the hostility and interprets it rather than responding to it. For to respond to it re-creates the power struggle so familiar to the patient.

This confrontational behavior, manifesting in the form of stubbornness and lack of cooperation, is designed to force the analyst into arbitrary impulsive decisions, like those of the mother. This pregenital manipulative behavior has provoked anxiety, hopelessness, and retaliatory behavior in the mother, and it must not repeat in the analytic situation. The analyst has to interpret rather than react. This is not done without some trepidation at times, for there is a constant need to assess the state of ego integration of the patient at all times in order to titrate the dosage of interpretation.

Addressing technique more specifically, I do not think that there is a need for a great deal of modification or the introduction of unusual parameters. It is well known that in the analysis of adolescents some modifications are necessary, especially in early and middle adolescence. Late adolescence is very similar to the situation with adults where the patient uses the couch, can usually free associate, analyze dreams, and develop a perceptible transference neurosis. These features are present in the analysis of early and middle adolescents to varying degrees, depending on the degree of pathology, character structure, and the degree to which the individual has been able to negotiate growth and psychic restructuring. Since these patients present with many features common to borderline conditions, techniques such as the one proposed by Kernberg

(1975) have been recommended. In this approach, the pre-dominantly negative transference is systematically interpreted in the present avoiding full genetic interpretations.

Later, in some cases, a more complete interpretational approach is possible. Because of the propensity for acting out, limit setting is tempting, but should be kept to a minimum for it tends to promote power struggles which may in turn interfere with the development of a therapeutic alliance.

Since these patients frequently have little to say, the analyst may find himself being more active, particularly in dealing with primitive idealizations reflecting splitting of good and bad objects, an approach well described by Boyer and Giovacchini (1980). Again, the degree of activity is dictated by the patient and the style of the analyst. Style here refers to a multitude of attributes involving both verbal and nonverbal communications. These patients, as a rule, do not free associate, especially early in the analysis. They report dreams, but have few associations, and have a difficult time connecting both the manifest and latent content to past events or day residue. Therefore, an understanding of the meaning cannot be fully achieved even though the analyst, based on his understanding of the patient's psychodynamics, may gain some insight into the meaning of the dreams. The frequent forgetting and minimizing of the dream's importance is consistent with their fear of losing control. Masochistic behavior associated with their archaic superego has to be interpreted prior to the interpretation of defense against aggressive impulses. There is a need to persist in interpreting the punitive aspects of the superego at the same time as the analyst provides auxiliary ego strength and a more rational superego (Boyer and Giovacchini, 1980; Wilson, 1986).

The need for immediate gratification manifested by the impulse disorder, and the masochistic and the aggressive aspects of the behavior, as well as the suicidal and homicidal impulses, have to be repeatedly interpreted. As these interpretations begin to take, the bulimic behavior subsides and dreams are recalled and reported, but the acting out in the form of poor school performance, drinking, and sexual promiscuity may persist. Better control of the drives and its derivatives is not achieved until ego strength improves and the superego gains a certain degree of flexibility.

CLINICAL MATERIAL

CASE EXAMPLE 1

June, a sixteen-year-old adolescent was referred for treatment by her pediatrician. He had tried to counsel the family and the patient for four months prior to referring her for treatment at a center where behavior modification and group therapy was used. June was resistant, and although she went to the center and superficially was cooperative, she admitted lying and thinking that she was not going to be helped. At the end of nine months of treatment the family felt that the situation was unchanged and the pediatrician then suggested the possibility of intensive psychotherapy. The patient was not thrilled by the prospect of seeing another psychiatrist, but felt she had no choice, though she admitted that she hoped that something could be done because she "felt miserable." She stated that she had been gorging since she was twelve, but denied vomiting until she was fourteen, when she discovered that her friend, who was also bulimic, vomited. When she was nine, she was seen for about a year by a child psychiatrist because of stomachaches for which no physiological reason was found by the pediatrician. "It was psychosomatic." She had been overweight since she was a little girl and had few friends. She disliked the psychiatrist because he wanted her to "play silly games" and tell him what she thought, and she would not do that. The symptoms subsided, however, and she discontinued treatment.

When she was eleven, she went to camp, lost 20 pounds, and felt great. This was considered slightly below the ideal weight and she was criticized by the family, especially her mother. She could not understand it, because before she had been criticized for being fat. For years her mother had prohibited her from raiding the refrigerator and at one time a lock was used to help her control her food intake. She felt great after losing the weight because she thought that for the first time that her "thighs and legs were normal." Mother's criticism was devastating. "She was never satisfied, she complained no matter what. She is fat herself; same for Dad. I had knocked myself out just to please them."

Prior to that time she "ate a lot," but she did not think she actually binged. After that she started to binge, especially at night. "I would get up in the middle of the night and eat a lot of whatever was available. Sometimes it was hard to go back to sleep, but I would not say anything. I started to think about food all the time and mother continued to be mean." During the day she would not eat or else had "salads and lots of tea." During her binging, she would consume enormous amounts of ice cream, soda, cakes, and chocolate. When her favorite things were not available, she would just "pig-out on anything" she could find and then feel terribly guilty. She was convinced that she was a horrible person. The only good thing she could do was to study. She would learn everything and the teachers liked her, except for a couple who were like her mother: "impossible to satisfy; they were mean and hateful. I tried hard to please them . . . made me cry, because it was impossible."

When she "discovered" vomiting, she could eat more without gaining weight. But she continued to feel that she was ugly and fat, though people did not think of her as being overweight. She felt she was overweight and so did her mother who at the same time "kept buying all kinds of food." She hated her two sisters and her brother who were younger. They did not have her troubles. She would sometimes eat some of their food, especially sweets, and hit them if they told on her. This, too, made her feel bad. She was better than they were in one respect, she made better grades.

To my surprise, June was voluble in her first few sessions, describing her behavior, her previous treatment, and her shame for not being able to control herself. She cried several times and apologized for doing so, insisting that she knew it was her problem. If only her parents were not "so mean." She admitted to death wishes for her mother when she was so angry, as well as suicidal thoughts, but no actual plans. Her father was a professional, but spent a great deal of time with the family and was nicer to her than the mother, but she was afraid of him because she perceived him as seductive and at times exhibitionistic. He was also constantly dieting and exercising and, like her mother, was preoccupied with food and appearance. Her sisters were coping better, they were able to speak out. Her brother had friends, was interested in sports, and was an average student who had no major problems.

The psychoanalytic process was explained to June, including the use of dreams in the analysis, the frequency of four times per week, and the role of the analyst. This is no different from the usual explanation given to other adolescent patients at the beginning of an analysis. It is designed not only to explain the process, but also to deal with the resistance to engaging in treatment. June said she understood, and explained what happened during her two previous experiences with treatment during which she "had a horrible time."

The parents were seen after the first session. They described the problem as being of longstanding, first because of her tendency to be slightly overweight and more recently due to her bulimia. They had also been afraid of her becoming anorexic. They were not aware of her vomiting until recently as she had kept it a secret.

June was very bright, her IQ being in the superior range. The parents felt that she was liked by her peer group, but June felt rejected and did not date. She made some efforts to reach out to friends, but felt like she did not belong. This was true of both boys and girls, but especially boys.

June's parents described her as a very bright, sensitive adolescent who as a young child was prone to mood swings, felt easily rejected, and tended to isolate herself. At the same time, she aimed to please and tried hard to be part of the group. She felt ill at ease in her peer group and had few friends. She clearly resented the birth of a sister, three years her junior, and became more clinging and demanding as a result. This was repeated, but to a lesser degree, when her next two siblings, a second sister and a younger brother, were born. Being a good, conscientious student was important to her, particularly in grade

school. Recently she had become increasingly defiant and her
grades, though still very acceptable, were not as good. She
tended to procrastinate in doing her schoolwork, and would
stay up for hours completing work long overdue. When confronted with such behavior, she would get extremely angry and
upset, but would still fail to complete it. The parents had been
basically healthy except for the father's cardiac phobia which
contributed to his obsession with his weight and exercise. The
patient had no major problems during the first three years of
life. She was bottle-fed and took solid food without problems.
Toilet training was accomplished by twenty-six-and-a-half months
without problem. She was clingy and reluctant to stay in nursery
school, but there was no evidence of severe separation anxiety.
The mother admitted being concerned about her being fat and
not getting a good balanced diet. She had to watch her own diet
carefully and did not want June to develop similar problems.

It was clear that these were concerned parents who needed
to exercise a great deal of control over the patient and her
younger siblings. They were in agreement about the need to
help June with her problems, but beyond that there was little
they could agree upon. They were both quite preoccupied with
their own narcissistic needs and could give little in terms of
warm human understanding. They argued and were verbally
abusive with each other and the children. Conflicts were fought
out in the open with inconsistencies being quite apparent. Both
parents drank to excess at times and appeared to have some
defects in both their ego and superego structures. There was
no consistent model that the children could emulate. The parents were blind to this reality despite the fact that both had had
the benefit of some treatment themselves; this did benefit the
analysis, for at least intellectually they were supportive of treatment.

The next few sessions were devoted to more history. This
was presented in the form of complaints, particularly about her
mother whom she viewed as critical, unsympathetic, manipulative, controlling, and cruel. A good example was her mother's
failure to tell her about her menses, which started when June
was twelve. She was frightened and was happy when they failed

to appear again for another four months. Now she had been amenorrheic for over a year and before that she was irregular. "The doctor says there is nothing physically the matter." She had been tested. "It's a relief not to have them, but also a worry." She also complained about the fact that her parents worried about her eating and yet "they eat a lot themselves." She also indicated that her parents encouraged her to date, but feared that she would act out sexually. She was afraid of that, also, although she claimed she had done nothing wrong. Her fears had to do with her concern about losing control like she does with her eating. "So I set rules, strict ones." After running through all these events and concerns, she became less verbally productive, but did not miss appointments. She preferred to sit face to face at first, but could not look the analyst in the eye. After some three months of analysis, when it was clear that this avoidance of eye contact was most prominent when highly charged material was being dealt with, I wondered if she would consider the use of the couch. She admitted being embarrassed and said she would think about lying down which she did several sessions later with obvious relief. This did not immediately increase her free association, but did serve to recall dreams which up to this point had been reported infrequently. She knew she had them, but could not remember them by the time she came to session. She was trying to be compliant as she had been with her parents, particularly her mother, fully expecting to be controlled and deceived. These transference manifestations were clear in her treatment behavior where she was cooperative yet suspicious and incapable of fully trusting the analyst. There were inklings at times of resentment and hostility, which she denied being aware of when the possibility was presented. She needed to keep the work of the analysis at a conscious level where she could feel in control. Gradually the need for this defensive position was interpreted. She would, for instance, concentrate on daily events and avoid fantasy and associations to issues which were highly charged emotionally. When this was carefully pointed out she would at times acknowledge it; at others she would become silent.

The silences, we soon discovered, duplicated her behavior

with her parents, particularly her mother, when she felt accused and afraid of expressing herself for fear of retaliation. These periods of silence were at times prolonged and even when they were interrupted by my asking for her thoughts, a frequent answer was, "nothing." There was also the fantasy that I knew what she was thinking about. When this thought was strong she would ask if it was time to leave or if she could leave. When I would point out that perhaps something disturbing was happening, she would venture some small piece of information designed to pacify me. Eventually she was able to share some of the thoughts which frequently had to do with binging, feelings of worthlessness, aggressive fantasies, and sexual preoccupations. The latter were particularly "embarrassing" because they showed that she was bad. She had discovered masturbation around the age of eight, she thought, and "knew it was bad," but could not help herself; she had to do it, just like binging. She had no control. It was possible then to understand the stomachaches for which she was sent to the psychiatrist when she was nine. The stomach pain was not unlike the pain she would experience now after excessive eating. Over a period of time, the connection between masturbation, pregnancy fantasies and fears, menstruation, amenorrhea, flat chest, fat thighs, and her feelings of general ugliness began to make sense. The material produced in each session varied. There were times when she had "nothing to say" and would say "I am wasting your time and mine," and could not understand why I wanted to see her. The controlling aspects of silence were interpreted with her responding with a great deal of anger and hostility, something that she had been unable to express before. She felt that I was intrusive and, like her parents, would not respect her right to be an individual. At the same time, it was clear that she could not feel like a separate individual, she was "stuck." Then she would feel extremely guilty. Once she left the session quite angry, missed the next session, and when she came next, said she just did not want to come; she had cried for a long time after her last session thinking that there was no way for her to "get straightened out." As the need for controlling emotion was presented, she again became sad and the pain of being "depressed most of the time" was voiced. The meaning of her depression, the suicidal thoughts, and the fear of losing control and acting out her aggression, not only against herself, but also toward others was the subject of analysis for some time to come. Included in this was her guilt about masturbation and her concern about acting out sexually, getting pregnant, and making "a mess of things." She was also "doing some drinking" which meant she was getting drunk, but was avoiding drugs for fear of "going nuts." She was being invited to some parties, but would not wear makeup and did not really want to go to the parties. Her friends did not like to be social either. She was bothered with sexual fantasies now, and hated for boys to smile at her "in a sexual way." She knew some people who were promiscuous. She did not want to dress attractively (femininely), would not wear makeup, and would not wear a bra in order to avoid showing her breasts.

She hated to be like that: "why can't I be normal like other people." As she was asked for elaboration, she admitted that she had taken laxatives in the past, "not often, but some, and that was crazy." The situation at home would not come up for long periods of time, even when on one occasion the parents called saying they might need to come in because things were going badly. The appointment was never made because June became less confrontational at home and kept up with her schoolwork better. She also agreed to buy some clothes that were more appropriate. In the past she had tried to remain a little girl and would wear "things that were not right." But her mother "did not help," she would buy her clothing that she liked and "forced" her to wear it.

After one-and-a-half years of analysis, she admitted feeling better, but still dissatisfied. Her weight, according to her, would fluctuate as much as 15 to 20 pounds, but it was hard to tell because her way of dressing was designed to avoid showing body shape. During one session, based on the surfacing material, it appeared as if she might be menstruating. I commented on the fact that it made me think of that, and she almost reluctantly admitted that she had had four consecutive periods—the first two skimpy, the last two normal.

I wondered about the fact that it had not surfaced before. She could not explain it, but began to recall dreams that she had forgotten to report. They had to do with eating a great deal of food and getting very fat, "like when a person is pregnant." This led to the exploration of her fears of being pregnant, "looking pregnant." It was silly, she thought, because she had not been sexually active and she knew that masturbating did not make a person pregnant, though when she was younger she had thought it possible. Then there was the "crazy fantasy" that she could get pregnant by something she ate. This was "stupid and embarrassing," adding "maybe I still do." Soon after that she reported "another silly dream" in which she was in the kitchen and was getting ready to eat a large meal consisting of chocolate, a cheeseburger, chicken, and spaghetti with meatballs. Just as she was about to start eating, with a feeling of happy anticipation, she noticed that there were worms in the food. She became nauseated and disgusted, and did not eat it. She was not sure, but she thought she felt so sick that she had to vomit.

At first she had no ideas about the dreams. She liked all that food. It was something her mother fixed, especially the spaghetti and meatballs, the chicken was what her father prepared sometimes. He fancies himself as a chef. On second thought, she said she had been controlling her eating better, fewer binges, though she thought her appearance was much the same. The complaints about her mother and her father's wishing to have "talks" with her was changing. They were less critical. I suggested that perhaps that was an important dream, one that might be of help in understanding a number of her feelings.

The themes she began to explore dealt with her attachment to her mother—the controls, the anger, the ambivalence. She had tried so hard to please her, do what she demanded. She always felt guilty because she could not please her; she was incapable of disagreeing with her. At times she had to lie as a means to avoid conflict and then there was conflict anyway. "She is always criticizing me . . . makes me so mad . . . doesn't respect my feelings. It's like I am always wrong; sometimes I feel like hitting her, but I just get out, leave the house." We discussed her tremendous rage at her mother, connecting it to her devouring feelings when she binged and her vomiting being like spitting mother out, destroying her. She thought it was terrible, but "as crazy as it sounds," she said, "I felt better when I went home after realizing those things." She came to realize how angry she was at her mother for always wanting to know what she was doing, where she was, and trying to guess what she was thinking. She could not be a separate person. She began to realize that she had to please everybody—her friends, her teachers, the analyst. She could get along better with her father. They could talk and at times she knew that her father liked her better and that felt good, but at times it also felt strange. "I can talk to him and don't feel strange, I don't think." Her mother seemed jealous and they would get into an argument. I suggested that perhaps she was competing with her mother (e.g., she could have made a better wife), and that this might have something to do with her conflict about her own sexuality. She then admitted that she had experienced some wishes and fantasies, but they had made her feel guilty. I suggested that perhaps her wish to be flat chested, not wearing a bra, avoiding makeup, and her way of dressing had something to do with such feelings. She did not protest; instead she said she had been thinking of buying a pretty dress to go to a party at school and thought of wearing a bra. The problem was that bras really "felt uncomfortable."

This led back to the pregnancy fantasies and the thoughts about food. She did not know how it worked, she said, but she was feeling better. The worms in the food dream was recalled. She remembered playing in the neighborhood with her group of friends, boys and girls: "some kind of sexual games, like showing each other off, and being very excited, but also scared. We got out of there (the hiding place) quickly and went to my friend's house and ate some stuff, I think it was chocolates." There was no conscious memory of any connection between the sexual activity and excitement and the eating, but I believe the recall is confirmatory of such a possibility. She was not sure of the age when this occurred, but she thought it was when she was in the first grade or earlier.

She continued to work, her memories obviously connected with oedipal issues—her wish to be with her father and her enjoyment of their talks. He would put her to bed when she was eight and younger, and sometimes would fall asleep in her bed on top of the covers. She had fantasies that maybe he would get under the covers when she was asleep. I suggested that maybe it was as if he preferred her to her mother. She admitted to having had such wishes for a long time and the wish that she would have a baby. Now we could look at the stomach aches again for they "happened around that time." After she went to see the psychiatrist, her father did not put her to bed anymore. Then she was fat and her father also wanted her to eat less, "but he was nice to her." She missed his not putting her to bed, but was also happy that it stopped because it made her "nervous." She explored her oedipal strivings for some time, expressing some surprise at the idea that maybe all these things were connected. She would not contradict the interpretations at first, choosing to be quiet and reflective, later she was more outspoken and would offer some thoughts of her own.

She now began to report a change at home. "Things were not perfect," but they were leaving her alone and she was beginning to go out. No dates, but with a group of boys and girls. She also went to a school dance and participated actively. To her surprise, she was chosen by her classmates to be in the homecoming court. She was not sure she looked "all that good," but "had a good time." She was still "eating too much," but she was not "really binging." She would still think of vomiting, but would not, and the laxatives had long been abandoned. Her periods were still irregular, but her pediatrician told her that this was not abnormal, and she felt like "things were really better" and began to think about college. She had by now been in analysis close to three years. She had some worries about going away to college, and thought maybe she should go to college in town. Her parents had a similar concern. She had a good school record despite her uneven performance and several colleges had expressed interest in her.

After much deliberation on her part, she decided to proceed with applying to several colleges away from home, planning to terminate treatment during the summer. We continued to work for the next six months during which she consolidated her gains and worked well through the termination phase. She kept in touch by telephone while home on holiday for the first year of college. She was doing well socially, academically, and personally, without symptom recurrence. She had several serious relationships, the last one culminating in marriage after she graduated from school.

CASE EXAMPLE 2

This seventeen-and-a-half-year-old, high school senior was referred by another psychiatrist who had treated her for several months with antidepressants and individual psychotherapy. The patient was seen once or twice a week, the frequency being dependent on the patient's needs. The patient had agreed to one session per week, but would call the psychiatrist in a panic after one of her binges, crying and depressed, and unable to attend school. After several such episodes, she was placed on medication. She was initially relieved by the expectation that the medication would cure her but was erratic in taking it. Also, not infrequently she would manage to vomit soon after its ingestion, thus neutralizing its potential benefits. Her parents, particularly her mother, were soon involved in her taking of the antidepressant so that the taking of medication became an issue similar to food intake, and power struggles for control ensued. What began to concern the therapist was the fact that she began to "binge" on the medication; that is, she would avoid taking it for some time and then take several at one time. As he expressed his displeasure about this type of behavior, she became angry and refused to continue in treatment, for she immediately associated the therapist's attempt at setting limits with the parental controls. "You are just like my mother," she claimed angrily, "and I won't take that shit from you."

Alice came to see me under duress for she was given an

ultimatum, either she continued to see her previous psychiatrist or she came to see me. Another alternative was to go to the hospital, which she did not want to do.

According to the parents, Alice began to gain weight in the second grade. Prior to that, she was described as a "delightful child." The parents could not remember any difficulties before that time. She had a broken arm at age three and was hospitalized briefly, but the mother stayed with her and she appeared to cope well, though "she has never forgotten it." She presented no problems with feeding or toilet training and was a very happy child until her sister, three-and-a-half years her junior, was born. At that time she regressed, becoming angry and demanding, expressing obvious displeasure at the new arrival, while claiming that she loved her. The parents, however, did not find this unusual. No thought was given to the coincidence of the broken arm occurring during the mother's pregnancy, which provided her with attention that she never forgot. She adjusted well to school and was liked by the teachers because she was a good student. While in the second grade, following the birth of a second sister, she started to gain weight and the power struggle with her parents, particularly her mother, began.

According to the parents, a concentrated effort was made to help her reduce, which was without results. She continued to eat, and though she was not considered obese, she was overweight by the pediatrician's and the parents' standards. The parents, as well as the rest of the family, were "big eaters" and Alice felt deprived, criticized, and diminished, especially by her mother who felt guilty and responsible for Alice's behavior. The father was overweight himself and would periodically start exercise programs. The mother was better controlled, and for the most part was able to maintain a normal weight; however, she suffered with depressions and was in need of antidepressants for long periods of time. There were frequent arguments in the family, principally between the parents about the most minor issues.

When the patient reached her fourteenth birthday, she became "depressed" about her appearance. She was convinced that she was ugly, obese, and disliked by everybody, especially her peer group. In reality, she was an attractive adolescent who was slightly overweight but was liked by others, both male and female. She dressed seductively and appeared to be fairly outgoing. It was at this juncture, however, that she decided that she had to lose weight and began a strict diet, managing to lose 40 pounds. The family was at first pleased and then worried about the possibility of her endangering her health. Actually she was at the lower end of normal weight for her size, but appeared to be very thin in comparison to her previous appearance. She was also involved in an exercise program, but was erratic about it. She was very manipulative and prided herself on being able to "get her way" most of the time, particularly with her father. What prompted the push into treatment was the discovery by her parents that she was gorging and vomiting, and her teeth, according to the dentist, were deteriorating. She was very angry at their demand that she should be treated, and became quite depressed and despondent, claiming that they had no right to control her life. Once her behavior was in the open, she would openly binge and make it a point to vomit at the most inappropriate times. There were many hysterical features in her character structure. She was now much more outgoing and made friends easily, though there was an air of superficiality to most of the relationships. She was inconsistent in her studies, making "dumb" mistakes. There was a childlike quality to her whole demeanor with much denial, omnipotent thinking, and magic belief. There was a world of fantasy where everything would be beautiful and conflict free, including her relationship with her parents. There was a great deal of sibling rivalry with her sisters, which she would also deny. Her relationship with her boyfriend was also idyllic; they would eventually marry and have a wonderful life together, she thought.

She admitted that she had been binging and vomiting since she was fifteen and did not think it was a problem, except for the fact that she was unhappy about her teeth deteriorating and her boyfriend thinking that her behavior was abnormal. As for her depression, she admitted that she was moody, but she had been that way as far back as she could remember. She did not want to take any medication and agreed to four times a week sessions reluctantly. She had been amenorrheic for nine months, but blamed it on the fact that she had been on the pill prior to its onset. She was placed on the pill supposedly because of her acne condition.

She was quite talkative, filling the sessions with details about daily living intermixed with complaints about her mother who was "stupid and controlling." She was sure that part of the problem was due to the fact that she was her father's favorite and her mother was jealous. There was considerable seductiveness involved in her dealings with her father, something the father did not discourage. Her stealing of small items of clothing from stores was minimized, particularly since the two occasions she was caught she "talked her way out of it." She also admitted to lying in order to avoid conflict and to impress others. All of these behaviors were minimized and characterized as "silly pranks" done by other people as well. The primitive defenses of denial and splitting together with projection were prominent. There was a constant denial of feeling so that she could not be hurt since she did not care. There was also a constant need to split affect from experience thus avoiding resolution of conflict. Her conflict about aggression, for instance, was totally repressed.

Though she was keeping her appointments, the nature of the therapeutic alliance was tenuous so that behavior and defense were interpreted over a considerable period of time. It was clear that once the conflicts were re-created in the transference she would feel threatened and her impulse would be to leave the analysis. The first six months of treatment were characterized by the continuation of her gorging and vomiting, with some actual weight gain. She was testy and demanding, wishing to be told what was right, thus trying to get the analyst to be partisan to her constant conflict in all areas of her life. As this was interpreted, her repressed anger began to surface. She would stop on her way to the sessions and eat two or three hamburgers, fries, malts, and other similar foods, and vomit in my bathroom just prior to the beginning of her session. This was not unlike her getting up from the table at home to do the same thing. I was aware of my own anger at her for doing this to me. One of the issues in the treatment of these patients involves their ability to evoke strong negative countertransference feelings where the analyst, if not aware of his reactions, can act out and in effect gratify the patient's wishes for rejection and punishment by encouraging their flight from treatment.

This type of behavior would vary in frequency dependent upon her capability to analyze rather than act out the tremendous amount of rage. She would frequently claim that she was sorry, but could not help it. She would appear regressed and pathetic like a helpless child who is desperately seeking love and acceptance. On occasion she could relate the behavior to her anger at her mother, but could not see the re-creation of the struggle in the analytic situation. I should "understand" for I was the doctor. This would be followed by sadness or hostile comments about my failing to understand "just like everybody else." She would miss sessions, but would claim that she could not come because she was ill. There was a great deal of somatization and she was afraid of developing all kinds of diseases. The exploration of the meaning of all these concerns would often result in more anger surfacing; she was "misunderstood, rejected, and abused" by the analyst; she should stop coming. After some of her gorging episodes, she had to vomit because her stomach "looked like a watermelon, like being pregnant" and that was "terribly embarrassing." This concept led to her being able to explore some of her fantasies about pregnancy and her masturbatory guilt. These were present prior to her vomiting, when she used to just overeat and was chubby. She was afraid of masturbating after excessive eating; she might get pregnant. She "kind of knew it was silly," but it was bothersome. She could not make a connection between gorging, masturbation, and vomiting, insisting that she vomited to maintain her weight. This is not unusual. Patients, particularly adolescents, frequently have to deny connections during one session and subsequently show that they have incorporated the insight. There was much evidence of preoedipal conflict, but also evidence of oedipal strivings. The pregnancy fantasies were not all primitive in nature; there were signs of conflict having to do with her seductiveness toward men (father–analyst), and the fear of retaliation by mother, who thought she was sleeping "with everybody."

By now her amenorrhea had subsided. She was now having "almost normal periods," by which she meant the flow was light, and she wanted them to be like her friends' periods.

One-and-a-half years into the analysis, she had graduated from high school and was in college. Her performance in school was uneven, but she was passing. She would miss class frequently, as she would sessions, always for superficially logical reasons. Her binging was not as frequent, and she had discontinued her eating prior to coming to session and vomiting in my bathroom. She was happy about not having to face mother since she lived in the dormitory, but when she visited home she still got into power struggles. Her involvement with her boyfriend was also more stable. She was remembering dreams, but her associations were limited, though she was not as opposed to exploring them—"perhaps there is something to be learned."

The therapeutic alliance was now much stronger and transference manifestations were clearly present. She could understand how her mind worked. There was a developing observing ego and a more forgiving superego. At the end of the second year of analysis, she reported a dream that she could remember in its entirety. She was pleased with it, although "it did not make sense." In the dream, she was at a fast food restaurant with a number of her friends. They were eating hamburgers, fries, and salads. There were waiters, however, who were serving regular food, which was strange. She was eating chicken, which she dislikes. Though they were her friends, she could not really recognize any of them, but they were nice. She could not understand her eating chicken because she prefers hamburgers and the kind of food the others were eating. She also liked salads although it reminded her of her diets, especially when she had lost the 40 pounds. That was not pleasant. There were, as usual, many meanings to the dream, but one aspect of it had to do with her ability to control her eating, being selective. She had food preferences, but when her preferred food was not available, she ate anything in the refrigerator. Now she was still overeating, she thought, but her binging was infrequent and the vomiting was very rare. Her weight was basically unchanged, and she was unhappy about that, for she wanted to "lose some pounds." She was dressing in a similar style to other college students, though she still had a flair for the unusual. She was interested in art, but perhaps she would study merchandising and become a buyer.

There was evidence of structural change. She continued in treatment until her junior year and then decided that she would like to stop. She was coping well, and while not all of her neurotic conflicts were thoroughly analyzed, she had no further motivation to continue. Her binging and vomiting were no longer present, her self-image was improved and her social life was satisfying. She had joined a sorority and was an active member. She had a new boyfriend whom she found less critical than the one she had in the beginning of treatment. She still wished she was thinner, but she had no need to go on "any more superduper diets." The parents were pleased and were also in favor of her stopping. There was a termination period of three months, with her stopping at the end of the spring semester. She wanted to have a "free summer." She had plans for visiting her friends and enjoying herself. It seemed an appropriate decision. She was aware that she might be in need of further treatment in the future, but for now she was satisfied. I saw no reason to force the issue.

CASE EXAMPLE 3

Sara, an eighteen-year-old college student came for treatment upon the recommendation of her internist who had performed a complete physical examination at the insistence of her parents. She was pronounced physically fit, but he was in agreement with her parents that she should seek professional help for her bulimia. Sara was angry at her mother for insisting on the physical and the treatment, but consented to come because she had kept her bulimia a secret from her boyfriend, and as the relationship was quite serious, she was afraid that he would abandon her if the facts were known. Both she and her boyfriend, who was two years older, were taking a premedical curriculum. She was of normal weight for her body build and claimed that she had never been obese or anorexic. She had been amenorrheic for several months earlier, but was now having her menses, though the flow was usually limited. She admitted to binging, vomiting, and the use of laxatives. She would also on occasion take some of her mother's diuretics. She hated to take the diuretics because they made her feel particularly bad. She had been bulimic since age fifteen, but had managed to keep it a secret from her family until approximately the age of sixteen-and-a-half. She had been in constant conflict with her mother all her life, but when her bulimic behavior came to light, the conflict escalated to major proportions. There was no civility left; they would either scream at each other or avoided speaking altogether. She felt that the only time her mother addressed her was to be critical and controlling. I never met her parents, having had one telephone contact from her mother who wished to know if she was really coming to her sessions. She wanted to know because Sara would not talk to her and also because she had a tendency to lie. Her mother was slightly overweight, and had to be on constant alert in "order to maintain her figure." The father was fat and concerned about his weight, but did nothing to reduce. He was a businessman and was away from home most of the time. The parents had slept in separate bedrooms for several years and it seemed like every time they spoke, it ended in an argument. It had always been like that. When her mother was not present, however, she felt she could talk with her father and that they could communicate well. She described herself as an obsessive who did a lot of worrying and procrastinating. She had always been a good student, though she would miss classes and delay her studying so that prior to exams she had to spend long hours studying, missing sleep.

She was quite hostile, but agreed to come four times per week with a great deal of trepidation. She was worried about the consequences of her bulimia, but did not think she was

mentally ill and associated the frequency of sessions with severity of illness.

It was evident that she immediately established a power
struggle with the analyst where in the transference he either
represented the controlling mother or the rejecting father who
did not wish to be bothered. As these possibilities were offered,
she would become rageful and question the whole premise. At
the same time, she would be superficially cooperative and would
try consciously to be pleasant. Her mother made insulting remarks, and would remind her that unless she stopped her gorging and vomiting, she would lose her boyfriend, for he was
bound to find out that she was ill. The food at home was practically measured ounce by ounce in addition to the fact that it
was always low calorie. She had a constant feeling that she was
being starved, and would have her binge episodes in the middle
of the night; but even then she was in constant fear that her
mother would awaken to check on her.

She had read a great deal about bulimia and anorexia, and
had tried to control herself in various ways without results. She
was totally unaware of her tremendous rage toward her parents,
principally her mother. She was aware of her depressive moods,
but could not connect them to anything specific. She soon began
to realize that when she was upset or depressed, she would eat.
She also realized that eating was used to cover up anxiety. As
the analysis progressed, it also became clear that she was very
attached to her parents. She hated to live at home and yet, when
she had the opportunity to be away for college, she returned
after one semester. She was totally dominated and could not
assert herself. She now realized that she harbored a great deal
of resentment toward her parents. This pent-up anger was expressed indirectly by her eating behavior. She claimed that she
had a good relationship with her boyfriend, but as she began
to gain some insight into her coping mechanisms, she realized
that she was quite controlling and capable of alienating him.
This was a frightening thought.

As she gained insight into the meaning of her symptoms,
her bulimia ameliorated. She still felt that her mother was demanding and infantilizing, but she would avoid the power strug-

gles. There were many issues that were unresolved, but claiming much improvement, she began to miss sessions.

The resistance was interpreted with practically no change in her determination to stop. She had been in analysis now for one year. She had managed to keep treatment a secret from her boyfriend, as she had her bulimia, and, though she agreed that there were many unresolved conflicts, she would not deviate from her determination to discontinue. She was controlling her binging and vomiting, was not depressed, though she would admit that she was not a happy person, and could not bear the idea of losing the only person she had ever been in love with. She was convinced that she could now continue to work on her own utilizing the gained insight, if not, she would return to analysis. She never did. She did finish college and went on to graduate school, but the degree to which she was able to maintain her gains, I do not know.

CASE EXAMPLE 4

Jane, a fourteen-year-old student, was referred by her pediatrician. Jane was a very attractive, intelligent girl who was quite unhappy. She stated that she had been gorging and vomiting for one-and-a-half years. She was 5 feet 3 inches and weighed 109 pounds, but had previously weighed as much as 140 pounds. She had been overweight since she was a young child and had been constantly preoccupied with her weight. Finally she had succeeded in losing 28 pounds and had felt very happy, but eventually she began to regain them. She would manage to avoid eating breakfast, but then would overeat at lunchtime and binge in the evening. This would be followed by vomiting, terrible feelings of depression and anger, and then sleep. She was aware that she used sleep as a means of trying to control her eating, but that brought her little satisfaction. She felt that she was a terrible person who was constantly preoccupied with food. When she was supposed to be doing her schoolwork, she would eat, get angry, and postpone her work. Consequently, she was behind in school and felt under constant pressure to do better. She was also aware that she used eating as a way of avoiding things she did not wish to do. This too made her angry.

She would try to diet, but that would not work because of her binges, so that the only way to control her weight, she thought, was to vomit and exercise. She did not take laxatives because she felt that was stupid. She was involved in school athletics although she did not enjoy them and, in fact, had to force herself to participate. She was only a fair athlete because she was so conflicted about her participating. Jane's mother had a weight problem herself and had tried in the past to diet with Jane, but without much success. The father came from a "family of big eaters," but he was of normal weight. He would exercise and felt that everyone in the family should do likewise. Jane's brother, two years her senior, was a good athlete and did not have a weight problem. He had little contact with the family, devoting a great deal of his energy to athletics.

Jane readily agreed to entering analysis because she was very unhappy and wished to feel better. She was concerned about losing some of her friends because she was feeling more and more isolated. Her periods were irregular and she admitted missing an occasional one, but she claimed not to be disturbed by it. She had headaches which she noted followed her numerous arguments with her mother. Her father she could talk with for the most part. She felt fat and unattractive. There was no aspect of herself that she considered undamaged. It became clear during treatment that there was a relationship between the emotional state and her binges; they occurred when she was upset, and the feeling seemed to disappear during the bulimic episode. As she gained insight into her anger toward both parents, but especially toward her mother, her ability to control the impulsive gorging and vomiting improved. She hated herself for her eating pattern and her vomiting. She was also aware of hating her mother, feeling guilty, vomiting, and then feeling relieved. Vomiting had multiple functions, such as expressing anger and punishment as well as having an expiatory function.

She also noted that her family was in constant turmoil and that there was a lack of warmth in their daily interaction as far back as she could remember. This realization resulted in the surfacing of much sadness and anger; she would cry quietly at times during the session. It now became possible to understand her resistance to the emergence of affectual feelings toward the analyst. It was dangerous to allow feeling to break through for fear of rejection, ridicule, and even abandonment. As the conflict behind this fear became conscious through careful, systematic interpretation of the defensive aspects of her behavior in the analysis, she was able to experience some aspects of the positive idealized transference. This, in turn, provided an opportunity to clarify distortions in early object relations resulting from primitive ego states. The degree of psychic pain evident during this phase of treatment may evoke countertransference issues having to do with the analyst's wish to rescue the patient from such misery by means of interpretations which may really be disguised supportive statements designed to "correct" previous injury. This must be avoided for it might come across as infantilizing comments not unlike mother's, or as seductive moves on the part of the analyst. In the first instance, the result is anger, while in the second, it may result in the gratification of an unconscious oedipal wish with its inherent traumatic results, and the patient may leave the analysis if it is not dealt with properly. Another aspect of this state of affairs may be the analyst's unconscious gratification of the patient's wish for the omnipotent preoedipal mother whom the patient can control.

These issues were evident during Jane's analysis, but as she gradually gained insight into the meaning of these defensive maneuvers, she was able to explore not only the present reality, but also her fantasy life. She was especially surprised by the fact that sexual thoughts became prominent and she then remembered having had such preoccupations. A number of these had to do with primitive erotic fantasies and wishes, as well as masturbatory memories and pregnancy fantasies. This was "embarrassing." Her capacity to deal with such issues was the result of the working through of early conflicts and the restructuring of both ego and superego elements. This occurred over a protracted period of time requiring many hours of scrutiny. She was persistent, however, and her parents were able to allow her to work with relatively little interference. This was particularly difficult for her mother who would at times threaten to call the analyst about seemingly trivial issues.

The headaches had ameliorated soon after analysis began and her menses became normal in flow and regularity toward the end of the first year of analysis. Her dieting behavior gradually changed, with periods of good control and relative satisfaction with herself followed by regression with binging and vomiting, usually precipitated by what appeared to be minor stressors. During such times, the control issues with her parents, especially her mother, would exacerbate and much of her symptomatology, including her mood swings, would return.

She was now dating and appeared to have a fair relationship with her peer group, though she was not always satisfied with her coping abilities in social situations. She was not entirely happy with her appearance either, though her dressing was conforming in style with her peer group and she was actively seeking dates. Her weight had been stable for two years and she was no longer preoccupied with dieting nor feared getting fat again. The vomiting had stopped prior to her attaining relatively good control of the binging. School performance was quite good; she could maintain a good grade average with relatively little effort, particularly since she kept up with her studies fairly regularly. The home situation "was not great" but they "left her alone" and she expected ultimate liberation when she left for college. She had been asymptomatic now for a considerable period of time and significant structural change had been achieved so that she was coping reasonably well with the adolescent tasks normal for her age.

Jane remained in treatment throughout the fall semester of her junior year. She had by then been able to work out her problems to the point where she felt strong enough to try it on her own. Two years later as a freshman in college she was still coping well with no signs of symptom recurrence.

DISCUSSION

Various modalities have been advocated in the treatment of bulimia. The approach used here is psychoanalytic. In contrast

to the starving, emaciated anorexics whose eating behavior may
be life-threatening and may require hospitalization in order to
prevent loss of life, normal-weight bulimics are very suitable
for analytic work. Since the three primary eating disorders
(obesity, bulimia, and anorexia nervosa) exist in a continuum,
some of these patients have at times had symptoms consistent
with one of the other conditions, with obesity or some degree
of being overweight being common. So that bulimia may coexist
with obesity or anorexia nervosa, or it may manifest as a distinct
entity in the form of the so-called normal-weight bulimia. The
cases presented were at the time of their treatment of normal
weight, though three had a history of having been heavy earlier.
All had a family history of excessive interest in food and dieting,
with parental weight problems. Sara insisted that she had been
of normal weight all her life. Since the family was not seen, this
assertion could not be corroborated. As a rule, there is an earlier
history of obesity which is the result of their inability to contain
their impulse to gorge. Again consistent with most histories,
these patients had been gorging and vomiting for some time
prior to seeking treatment, and when they did come into treatment, they did not engage in therapy of their own volition but
rather were forced to do so by the parents. This is no different
from the way most adolescents enter analytic treatment, but it
does contribute to the resistance, particularly early in treatment,
for it lends itself to the power struggle, the controlling battles,
and the general state of resistance frequently encountered in
the treatment of this age group.

In psychodynamic terms, the manifest pathology is attributed by some to arrests in development at presymbolic oral-
separation levels. This fixation, with its accompanying fears of
loss of object, is thought to be caused by parental overcontrol
with the mother being the principal culprit. In this view, the
emphasis on food and control transforms eating into a symbol
of love. The incomplete resolution of this phase then has dire
consequences in subsequent phases, both anal and oedipal. This
dynamic is undoubtedly present in these cases, most clearly seen
in June's situation. I emphasized incomplete resolution because,
in my view, fixation and arrest refer to relative situations.

There has to be a certain degree of resolution which I believe is inherent in the genetic substrate so that, independent of the environmental circumstances, progress is made. What clouds the issue is that there is no accurate way to measure retrospectively the degree of regression present in each case. In all cases, there is sufficient evidence to demonstrate arrests at the anal level which manifests later on in obsessive–compulsive behavior. The poor impulse control common to all these patients attests to this. Then there are oedipal issues which in these patients, as Brenner (1974) indicates, manifest in part as oral conflicts. Alice's behavior perhaps best illustrates this situation. There was a clear oedipal triangle in her dynamic constellation. This situation is not as clear in the other cases, but the elements are equally present. One of the masks covering this aspect is the initially presenting primitive defenses of denial, projection, and splitting characteristic in these patients, though not as glaring in bulimics as they are in anorexics. So, although there is no question that preoedipal conflict is prominent, oedipal manifestations are also present and though the analysis is geared toward the resolution of these preoedipal conflicts in order to progress toward the resolution of the Oedipus, we are not dealing solely with fixations at earlier levels, but with both fixations and regressions from advances in development reached much earlier. The genitalization of the oral cavity is a good example.

The role of food as an object of conflict as well as the mothering medium (Schwartz, 1986) is clear in all these patients. They all felt deprived and controlled by the mother through its symbolic deprivation.

None of these patients were able to make much use of their dreams. June's dream concerning the worms in the food marked the beginning of her control over the binging and vomiting, and perhaps had something to do with her incestuous oedipal strivings, but her associations were not sufficient to warrant the interpretation of such possibilities. This denigration of the importance of dreams is not uncommon in the analysis of adolescents, who defensively tend to fear what they might reveal about their unconscious.

438 REMI G. GONZALEZ

Separation–individuation issues are clearly present in all analysis, but they can perhaps best be viewed as part of the overall problems inherent in ego restructuring, and not as an all-encompassing aspect of the work of the analysis. Obviously a multitude of processes are taking place at the same time as the rapprochement phase is in progress.

The underlying psychopathology in these patients is relatively severe and the exploration of the inherent conflicts is intense and painstaking. If the goal is that of bringing about significant structural change, rather than pure symptomatic relief, psychoanalytic exploration is not only indicated but necessary.

Abraham, K. (1916), The first pregenital stage of the libido. In: *Selected Papers of Karl Abraham*. New York: Basic Books, 1954, pp. 248–279.

Adatto, C. (1972), The relationship between developmental characteristics of adolescence and analyzability. *J. Amer. Psychoanal. Assn.*, 20:134–144.

American Psychiatric Association (1980), *Diagnostic and Statistical Manual of Mental Disorders*, 3rd ed. (DSM-III). Washington, DC: American Psychiatric Association.

Beaumont, P. J., George, G. C., & Smart, D. E. (1976), Dieters and vomiters and purgers in anorexia nervosa. *Psycholog. Med.*, 6:617–622.

Bird, B. (1957), A specific peculiarity of acting out. *J. Amer. Psychoanal. Assn.*, 5:630–647.

Boskind-Lodahl, M. (1976), Cinderella's stepsister: A feminist perspective on anorexia and bulimia. *Sign: J. Women in Cult. & Soc.*, 2:342–356.

—— White, W. C. (1978), The definition and treatment of bulimarexia in college women—A pilot study. *J. Amer. Coll. Health Assn.*, 27:84–86.

Bowlby, J. (1969), *Attachment and Loss*, Vol. 1. New York: Basic Books.

Boyer, L. B. (1979), Countertransference with severely regressed patients. In: *Countertransference: The Therapist's Contribution to the Therapeutic Situation*, ed. L. Epstein & A. H. Feiner. New York: Jason Aronson, pp. 347–374.

—— Giovacchini, P. L. (1980), *Psychoanalytic Treatment of Schizophrenic, Borderline and Characterological Disorders*, 2nd rev. ed. New York: Jason Aronson.

Brenner, C. (1974), The concept of phenomenology of depression, with special reference to the aged. *J. Geriat. Psychiat.*, 7:6–20.

Brotman, A., Herzog, P., & Woods, S. (1984), Antidepressant treatment of bulimia; the relationship between binging and depressive symptomatology. *J. Clin. Psychiat.*, 45:7–9.

Bruch, H. (1962), Perceptual and conceptual disturbances in anorexia nervosa. *Psychosom. Med.*, 24:187–194.

Casper, R. C., Eckert, E. D., Halmi, K. A., Goldberg, S. C., & Davis, J. M. (1980), Bulimia: Its incidence and clinical significance in patients with anorexia nervosa. *Arch. Gen. Psychiat.*, 37:1030–1035.

Ekstein, R. (1976), General treatment philosophy of acting out. In: *Acting Out*, 2nd ed., ed. L. E. Abr & S. L. Weissman. New York: Jason Aronson, pp. 162–171.

Fenichel, O. (1945), *The Psychoanalytic Theory of the Neurosis.* New York: W. W. Norton.

Garfinkel, P. E., Moldofsky, H., & Garner, D. M. (1980), The heterogeneity of anorexia nervosa: Bulimia as a distinct subgroup. *Arch. Gen. Psychiat.*, 37:1036–1040.

Garner, D. M., Garfinkel, P. E., & Olmsted, M. (1983), An overview of sociocultural factors in the development of anorexia nervosa. In: *Anorexia Nervosa: Recent Developments in Research.* New York: Alan Liss, pp. 65–82.

——— O'Shaughnessy, M. (1983), Clinical and psychometric comparisons between bulimia and anorexia nervosa and bulimia in normalweight women. In: *Understanding Anorexia and Bulimia*, Report of the 4th Ross Conference on Medical Research. Columbus, OH, Ross Laboratories, pp. 6–13.

Gero, G. (1984), Book review of J. Sours: *Starving to Death in a Sea of Objects: The Anorexia.Nervosa Syndrome. J. Amer. Psychoanal. Assn.*, 32:187–191.

Glassman, A. H., & Walsh, B. T. (1983), Link between bulimia and depression unclear. *J. Clin. Psychopharmacol.*, 3:203.

Goodsitt, A. (1983), Self-regulatory disturbances in eating disorders. *Internat. J. Eat. Disord.*, 2:51–60.

Gull, W. W. (1873), Anorexia hysterica (apepsia hysterica). *Brit. Med. J.*, 2:527.

Gwirtsman, H. E., Roy-Byrne, H. E., & Yager, J. (1983), Neuroendocrine abnormalities in bulimia. *Amer. J. Psychiat.*, 140:559–563.

Halmi, K. A., Falk, J. R., & Schwartz, E. (1981), Binge-eating and vomiting: A survey of a college population. *Psycholog. Med.*, 11:697–706.

Hawkins, R. C., & Clement, P. F. (1980), Development and construct validation of a self-report measure of binge-eating and tendencies. *Addict. Behav.*, 5:219–226.

Hudson, J. I., Laffer, P. W., & Pope, H. G., Jr. (1982), Bulimia related to affective disorder by family and response to dexamethosone suppression test. *Amer. J. Psychiat.*, 139:685–687.

——— Pope, H. G., Jonas, J. M., & Yurgelum-Todd, D. (1983), Family history study of anorexia nervosa and bulimia. *Brit. J. Psychiat.*, 142:133–138.

Jacobsen, E. (1964), *The Self and the Object World.* New York: International Universities Press.

Johnson, C., & Larson, R. (1982), Bulimia: An analysis of moods and behavior. *Psychosom. Med.*, 44:333–345.

——— Lewis, C., Love, S., Lewis, L., & Stuckey, M. (1984), Incidence and correlates of bulimic behavior in a female high school population. *J. Youth & Adol.*, 13:15–26.

Jonas, J. M., Pope, H. G., Jr., & Hudson, J. I. (1983). Treatment of bulimia with MAO inhibitors. *J. Clin. Psychopharmacol.*, 3:59–60.

Katzman, M. A., & Wolchik, S. A. (1984), Bulimia and binge eating in college women: A comparison of personality and behavioral characteristics. *J. Consult. & Clin. Psychol.*, 52/3:423–428.

Kernberg, O. F. (1975), *Borderline Conditions and Pathological Narcissism*. New York: Jason Aronson.

Klein, M. (1959), *The Psychoanalysis of Children*. London: Hogarth Press.

Kramer, S. (1974), A discussion of Sours' paper on "The anorexia nervosa syndrome." *Internat. J. Psycho-Anal.*, 55:577–579.

Lorand, S. (1943), Anorexia nervosa: Report of a case. *Psychosom. Med.*, 5:282–292.

MacKenzie, S. (1888), Anorexia nervosa vel hysterica. *Lancet*, 1:613–614.

Mahler, M. (1963), Thoughts on development of the individual. *The Psychoanalytic Study of the Child*, 18:307–324. New York: International Universities Press.

—— (1967), On human symbiosis and the vicissitudes of individuation. *J. Amer. Psychoanal. Assn.*, 25:740–763.

—— Furer, M. (1963), Certain aspects of the separation–individuation phase. *Psychoanal. Quart.*, 32:1–14.

—— —— (1968), *On Human Symbiosis and the Vicissitudes of Individuation*. New York: International Universities Press.

—— La Perriere, K. (1965), Mother–child interaction during separation–individuation. *Psychoanal. Quart.*, 34:483–493.

Masserman, J. H. (1941), Psychodynamics in anorexia nervosa and neurotic vomiting. *Psychoanal. Quart.*, 10:211–242.

Moulton, R. (1942), Psychosomatic study of anorexia nervosa including the use of vaginal smears. *Psychosomat. Med.*, 4:62–72.

Nugelberg, D. B., Hale, S. L., & Ware, S. L. (1984), The assessment of bulimic symptoms and personality correlates in female college students. *J. Clin. Psychiat.*, 40:440–445.

Osler, W. (1892), *Principles of Practice of Medicine*. New York: Appleton.

Pyle, R. L., Mitchell, J. E., & Eckert, E. D. (1981), Bulimia: A report of 34 cases. *J. Clin. Psychiat.*, 42:60–64.

Risen, S. E. (1982), The psychoanalytic treatment of an adolescent with anorexia nervosa. *The Psychoanalytic Study of the Child*, 37:433–459. New Haven, CT: Yale University Press.

Russell, G. F. M. (1979), Bulimia nervosa: An ominous variant of anorexia nervosa. *Psycholog. Med.*, 9:429–448.

Schwartz, H. J. (1986), Bulimia: Psychoanalytic perspectives. *J. Amer. Psychoanal. Assn.*, 34:439–462.

Soltman, O. (1894), Anorexia celebralis un centrale nutrititione nervose. *Jahrbach der Kinderheilklinik*, 8:1–13.

Sours, J. A. (1974), The anorexia nervosa syndrome. *Internat. J. Psycho-Anal.*, 55:567–572.

Sperling, M. (1949), Neurotic sleep disorders in children. *Nervous Child*, 8:28–46.

—— (1953), Food allergies and conversion hysteria. *Psychoanal. Quart.*, 22:525–538.

—— (1967), Transference neurosis in patients with psychosomatic disorders. *Psychoanal. Quart.*, 36:342–355.

——— (1968), Trichotillomania, trichophagy, and cyclic vomiting: A contribution to the psychopathology of female sexuality. *Internat. J. Psycho-Anal.*, 49:682–690.

——— (1978), *Psychosomatic Disorders in Children.* New York: Jason Aronson.

Spitz, R., & Wolf, K. (1946), Anaclitic depression: An inquiry into the genesis of psychiatric conditions in early childhood. *The Psychoanalytic Study of the Child,* 2:313–342. New York: International Universities Press.

Strangler, R. S., & Prinz, A. M. (1980), DSM-III: Psychiatric diagnosis in a university population. *Amer. J. Psychiat.*, 137:937–940.

Strober, M., Salkin, B., Burroughs, G., & Morrell, W. (1982), Validity of the bulimia-restrictor distinction in anorexia nervosa and parental personality characteristics and family psychiatric morbidity. *J. Nerv. & Ment. Dis.*, 170:345–351.

Stunkard, A. J., Grace, W. J., & Woff, H. G. (1955), The night eating syndrome: A pattern of food intake among certain obese patients. *Amer. J. Med.*, 19:78–86.

Sugarman, A., & Kurash, C. (1981), The body as a transitional object in bulimia. *Internat. J. Eat. Disord.*, 1:57–66.

Thomä, H. (1967), *Anorexia Nervosa.* New York: International Universities Press.

Volkan, V. D. (1976), *Primitive Internalized Object Relations: A Clinical Study of Schizophrenic, Borderline and Narcissistic Patients.* New York: International Universities Press.

Waller, J. V., Kaufman, M. R., & Deutsch, F. (1940), Anorexia nervosa: A psychosomatic entity. *Psychosom. Med.*, 2:3–16.

Wilson, C. P. (1982), The fear of being fat and anorexia nervosa. *Internat. J. Psychoanal. Psychother.*, 9:233–255.

——— (1983), Psychodynamic and/or psychopharmacologic treatment of bulimic anorexia nervosa. In: *Fear of Being Fat: The Treatment of Anorexia Nervosa and Bulimia,* ed. C. P. Wilson, C. Hogan, & I. Mintz. New York: Jason Aronson, pp. 155–213.

——— (1986), The psychoanalytic psychotherapy of bulimic anorexia nervosa. *Adol. Psychiat.*, 13:274–314.

Winnicott, D. (1951), Transitional objects and transitional phenomena. In: *Through Paediatrics to Psycho-Analysis.* 46:81–87.

Chapter 14

Psychoanalytic Family Therapy Approaches to the Adolescent Bulimic

There is relatively little research or clinical literature on bulimic families. Only since 1980 has bulimia been distinguished from anorexia nervosa. The extensive literature on eating disorders focuses primarily on anorexia, which often has a late onset bulimic phase. Although it is possible that an increase in the incidence of normal weight bulimia accounts for its recent recognition, a more probable explanation is that bulimics and their families have decided to "come out of the closet" because of a change in medical and social attitudes around this characteristically secretive and embarrassing problem.

Family therapy has been recommended for the treatment of eating disorders by researchers and clinicians (Bruch, 1973; Crisp, Harding, and McGuiness, 1974; Minuchin, 1974; Minuchin, Rosman, and Baker, 1978; Garner, Garfinkel, and Bemis, 1982). Focusing on dysfunctional family systems, Minuchin et al. (1978) and Selvini Palazzoli (1978) have pointed out that psychosomatic families avoid familial and marital conflict through symptomatic behaviors of one or more family members, including eating disorders. Selvini Palazzoli notes that the symptomatic member serves a homeostatic function for the family, with anorexic behavior masking the conflict in the parental relationship and precluding change. Characteristics of anorexic families noted by Minuchin (1974) and Minuchin et

443

al. (1978) are enmeshment, rigidity, overprotectiveness, and lack of conflict resolution skills, with the symptomatic child caught in the parental subsystem through either triangulation, scapegoating, or parent–child coalitions. Until the covert function of psychosomatic or eating disorder behavior is removed, conservative homeostatic forces in the family will maintain the problems. As structural family therapists using a systems approach, their assessment and intervention techniques are active and directive.

Compared to anorexia, there is only scant literature on bulimic families (Madanes, 1981; Schwartz, 1982; Saba, Barrett, and Schwartz, 1983). The first family typology for the bulimic family was offered by Schwartz, Barrett, and Saba (1984), adding three characteristics (isolation, consciousness of appearance, and a special meaning attached to food and eating) to Minuchin's original five anorexic family characteristics mentioned above.

Root, Fallon, and Friedrich (1986) feel that bulimia represents a more advanced maturational state in which the adolescent and family have difficulty negotiating movement from adolescence into young adulthood and independence as they and their family attempt to negotiate the stage of emancipation and launching. They observe that all bulimic families have individual and subsystem boundary problems, with weight and appearance being important factors, along with an inequitable distribution of power reinforced by a sexist cultural system. Because the father usually holds the power, the bulimic patient finds herself caught between a more distant, often critical father and an overprotective, powerless mother.

Root et al., (1986) describe three different family types in which a member is likely to develop bulimia in order to maintain personal and family homeostasis: the *perfect family*, the *overprotective family*, and the *chaotic family*. Often with a prior history of anorexia in the late adolescent bulimic member, the *perfect family* is characterized by the overt appearance of appropriate coping, while underneath there are rigid expectations about achievement and appearance, deep concerns about family identity and reputation, and subordination of individual identity.

Deviation from these expectations mobilizes demands for conformity and harmony. Reflecting the patient's attempt to individuate, bulimia secretly releases "unacceptable feelings," and maintains the perfect veneer of the family.

Similar to bulimics in the treatment literature, the *overprotective family*, like Minuchin's (1974) observations of psychosomatic families, is enmeshed and overprotective, lacks conflict resolution skills and involves children in marital conflict. In addition, they lack confidence in the bulimic's competence, have inadequate rules for age-appropriate behavior, and suffer from the impact of unresolved family-of-origin issues, often involving chaos or victimization in the mother's family.

Similar to families of substance abusers, the *chaotic family*, while sometimes enmeshed and lacking conflict resolution skills, is typified by the unavailability of one or both parents; the victimization experiences of family members; the chaotic organization and rules; the inappropriate and often violent expression of anger; and substance abuse. Bulimia becomes a response of the member to the abuse and chaos. Root et al. (1986) caution that families rarely fit these pure types, and that the selection of the symptom of bulimia is multidetermined, involving predisposing factors such as sociocultural pressures, victimization experiences (as child or adult), individual body frame and weight set points, as well as family dynamics.

PSYCHOANALYTIC FAMILY THERAPY AND BULIMIA

Currently, there are no references from the psychoanalytic family therapy school on bulimia. As with other systems of family therapy, there is a growing theoretical and clinical literature on this school itself. Probably the single most useful reference, with bibliography, is *Object Relations Family Therapy* (Scharff and Scharff, 1987). As a technique, psychoanalytic family therapy can be used as both a clinical and research tool in the investigation of disordered families. Because there are still so many unresolved theoretical and clinical questions about bulimia, this chapter will focus on the contribution of psychoanalytic family therapy to certain clinical research questions. The usefulness of this powerful approach in the treatment and resolution of bulimia will have to be discussed at some other point.

Incorporating many aspects of pure systems approaches, psychoanalytic family therapy uniquely emphasizes the intrapsychic, the unconscious, the past, individual marital and family development, transference and countertransference, and insight. It is an active uncovering approach, not a directive controlling one. Conceptually, the major bridge between the intrapsychic and interpersonal levels within the family is object relations theory, providing the theoretical underpinning for psychoanalytic family therapy. A brief review of object relations theory will now be presented, relying heavily on Scharff and Scharff (1987). Only those aspects relevant to bulimia will be emphasized.

OBJECT RELATIONS THEORY

Object relations theory holds that the human infant is capable of relating actively from birth. The baby is seen as an active partner seeking to develop a relationship with its mother, responding to and modifying her ways of relating. Infant research now supports this view (Brazelton, Koslowski, and Main, 1974; Stern, 1977, 1985). The baby's "ego" (that part of self that copes with reality) is capable of attaching and relating to an "external object" (mother or caretaker) from birth. Experience with this object is internalized within the mind as an "inner object" in close connection to the ego partly in consciousness and partly repressed into unconsciousness. Subsequent development in the two-person preoedipal or three-person oedipal situation rests on this foundation. Balint (1968) observed in certain individuals suffering from an inner emptiness an early fundamental flaw, a "basic fault," and hypothesized a failure of fit between mother and baby leading to an insecurity in future object relations. Winnicott (1956) noted that infants, when not receiving "good enough mothering," suppress a "true self" and develop a "false self" due to a split in personality. Empathic mothering organizes the baby's internal world, leading to a "psychosomatic partnership" (Winnicott, 1971).

Fairbairn (1954), seeing libido as object-seeking and aggression as a response to frustration, proposed a model for psychic development. Noting that real objects are inevitably unsatisfying, he concluded that the ego defends itself against such frustration by internalizing the unsatisfying object as a defensive mental structure called an internal object. The ego further defends itself against this painful internal object by splitting it into two parts, its intolerably frustrating aspects called the rejected object and the need-exciting aspects called the exciting object. The ego splits off and represses two analogous aspects of itself that invest in these rejecting and exciting aspects of the rejected object, namely the antilibidinal ego and the libidinal ego, along with their intolerable affects of rage and longing respectively. This leaves the more rational conscious area of the ego called the central ego in relation to the ideal object. Fairbairn felt that splitting and repression are part of the same mechanism. The vicissitudes of later object relations determined the level and degree of their persistence or modification in favor of ambivalence.

The conscious, adaptable, central ego system maintains its freedom by repressing the libidinal and antilibidinal systems. Unless repression is severely maintained, the unconscious antilibidinal system (characterized by repressed affects of rage and contempt), and the unconscious libidinal system (characterized by repressed affects of intolerable longing and excitement) constantly threaten to reinvade the central ego functioning. Because of their repression, the rejecting and exciting objects remain unmodified by further experience, and the libidinal and antilibidinal egos do not develop more mature ways of relating to such objects. The better the mothering, the less the ego is sequestered in unconscious relationship to internal objects. Although the infant's temperament influences outcome, the quality of mothering is a large determinant of internal object relations and splitting.

Klein (Segal, 1973) hypothesized that the infant during the first year of life organizes experience by primitive mental processes of splitting, projection, and introjection. She then formulated the "paranoid-schizoid position" for this initial developmental phase. When the mother is experienced as frustrating, the angry infant projects his rage and experiences her as persecutory. He defends himself by reintrojecting her as an inner "persecutory object." The infant, imagining the mother as an external "ideal object" (source of all goodness) and feeling painfully isolated from her, may feel like greedily devouring her or may envy her power, in either case leading to destruction of the desired object with a confused sense of disintegration inside the self.

The reason an infant projects aggressive and loving feelings onto the external object is to protect the good experience from destruction within the chaotic, destructive self. The reason the infant reintrojects the aggressive feelings is to protect the object from destruction. The good feelings are reintrojected to counter the bad feelings inside and to give a sense of possessing the ideal object inside. For our purposes, it is important to note that reintrojection occurs as a fantasy fueled by the oral incorporative drive. Both the ideal and persecutory objects are part-objects, since the very young infant is incapable of ambivalent awareness of the mother as a whole person.

The infant begins to recognize its mother as a whole person about whom ambivalence is felt at about eight months of age. The persecutory aspects are not split off and as a result she is not so idealized. Now vulnerable ideal parts are temporarily mourned and persecutory aspects tolerated. The emergence of mourning and guilt mark the development of the "depressive position." Subsequent developmental challenges involve a regression to first the paranoid–schizoid and then the depressive position as they are worked through. A persistent tendency toward splitting, an incapacity for mourning, and a depressive affect signify a particular vulnerability toward the paranoid–schizoid position.

Introjective and projective identification (Segal, 1973) are two other Kleinian mechanisms useful in understanding marital and family interaction. Introjective identification results when the object is introjected into the ego which then identifies with some or all of its characteristics. Conversely, projective identification results from projection of parts of the self into an object with which the self identifies. Various defensive aims may be served by projective identification: to avoid separation from the ideal object; to gain control of the source of danger in the bad object; to get rid of bad parts of the self by putting them into the object and then attacking it; to put the good self outside to protect it from the badness in the self; or "to improve the external object through a kind of primitive projective reparation" (pp. 14–15).

Introjective and projective identification are mutual processes going on between mother and baby, between spouses, parent and child, siblings, and also between the family group and the therapist (Scharff and Scharff, 1987). The configuration of object relations that develop between individual family members is initially largely determined by the nature of the marital relationship, echoing the earlier dyads and triads of each parent during his or her childhood. As children are born and develop, this balance shifts in reciprocal ways. In family therapy, since experience with past generations is internalized and reenacted through present relationships, the family therapist can discover these interlocking sets of object relations. The range and severity of need-exciting and need-rejecting object experiences, and the variations in the developmental lines along which they appear account for the wide variety of family and individual normality and pathology.

In object relations family therapy (Scharff and Scharff, 1987), several concepts are important: centered relating, centered holding, and contextual holding. Centered relating refers to the direct, eye-to-eye mutual mirroring situation between mother and baby in which they are directly and centrally relating. Centered holding refers to the mother's ability to provide the space and material for centered relating through her physical handling of and mental preoccupation with her baby. Contextual holding is the environmental extension of the mother's presence and maternal preoccupation, providing the special envelope of space within which centered holding and relating occur. The father contributes to mother's centered holding by supporting her and contributing to her contextual holding. At first, the father is not directly involved in centered relating and holding, only later making his own contribution to dyadic and triadic relationships with the infant.

Centered holding and contextual holding provide the conceptual basis for the modifications in family therapy technique when doing psychoanalytic individual, couples, and family work. By engaging the family through providing centered and contextual holding, the family therapist attempts to expand the family's capacity to perform the holding functions for its members and their capacity to offer holding of each other. The therapist observes not only the network of interlocking direct or centered transferences, but also observes individual and group transferences within the family and to the therapist and his holding environment. This represents the family's shared contextual transference. Through attention to transference and countertransference, and the use of clarification and interpretation, the family therapist helps the family analyze defenses and work through resistance on both the intrapsychic and interpersonal levels. Analysis and working through of the shifting contextual transference in couples and family work provides a major therapeutic basis for fundamental family change. Through the discovery and resolution of pathological projective identification fueled by unhealthy internalized object relations from past generations, the family therapist helps the family to free itself and to find mutual development and healthy functioning in the present.

BULIMIA

In reviewing the individual and family literature on bulimia, I have found myself asking a number of questions. Granted there is virtually a teenage epidemic of vomiting as a method of weight control given the American madness for feminine thinness, but why does the bulimic behavior become a true primary symptom for only certain individuals and their families? Why does this syndrome usually develop in mid- to late-

adolescent females? What is the core intrapsychic and interpersonal pathology of this symptom? Are there structural precursors of this compulsive, ego defect-based, impulse disorder?
And finally, what are its developmental roots? Through the use
of the psychoanalytic object relations family therapy concepts
and approaches, I have traced in my clinical work the individual
and familial developmental vicissitudes of this disorder in several families with the hope of answering some of these questions.

Of crucial importance, however, is defining just what type
of bulimic is being discussed, because of the problems of com-
parability. I have decided to present a particular bulimic case,
selected from many, that I feel is prototypical of the normal-
weight, single impulse disordered, female adolescent bulimic.
I have chosen to focus in depth on a single case because I feel
this provides the kind of rich, multilevel developmental data
that allows us to make new formulations with greater confidence. Although every case has unique elements, in my experience this case is sufficiently characteristic to assure a valid
basis for an initial object relations formulation of bulimia in
general. I will be focusing on etiology and developmental dynamics primarily, with only a postscript about the treatment
and outcome of this particular case.

A PROTOTYPICAL CASE OF BULIMIA

When Ms. P.'s mother heard her vomiting at age seventeen and
realized what was going on, she was frightened, and also feared
her husband would take the patient to task. His reaction when
he came home was disgust and anger at Ms. P. for not controlling herself. As time went on he became more furious, distant, and rejecting. He felt she should just get a hold of herself
and stop it. Mother sought help over his initial objections. Initially, I saw mother and daughter together, and then apart
during the first session, and then indicated I would continue
seeing Ms. P. but would want to see them all together, as well
as the parents separately. I wanted to see all levels of interaction.

Ms. P., a pretty, tall, large-boned young woman, of normal weight and attractive figure, was scared and anxious, fearing her father's wrath and worrying about her mother's tearful overconcern. She touched briefly on the fights between her mother and father and the various conflicts between her and her parents, rushing on quickly to her frenetic, tension-filled life at school. She revealed that her secret binging and vomiting had been going on for over two years, ranging from once to several times a day depending on how tense she felt. She thought it began when she got involved with a boy and then lost him. Only later did we reconstruct that she also lost her very close, love–hate relationship with her fifteen-year-old brother who left for boarding school at that time.

Like her mother, father, and most of her friends, she was deeply preoccupied with being thin and attractive, but had sudden strong cravings to fill herself up with sweets to relieve her emptiness and anxiety. She confided that 20 percent of the girls in her class induced vomiting for weight control, but when her binging and vomiting got out of control, she became embarrassed and secretive about it. As I heard all this I found myself filled with varying feelings of being flooded, wanting to control and criticize her, and wanting to hold and calm her. She gave early indirect indications of fearing that I, too, would be critical and disapproving like father or intrusive and worried like mother. She was relieved when I wondered out loud about such possible concerns, and went on to give me more information about each of her parents.

As I sat in the initial parent sessions, I was struck by how large her parents were. Her mother was neatly coiffed, fadingly attractive, and large. Her father was imposing, rumpled, and dumpy. The room was filled with tension. Mother, with tears soon streaming down her face, felt guilty about failing and undercutting her daughter. She said, "My daughter needs more from me than I have to give—I can't fill her void, never could." Father exuded cutting impatience and contempt, furious at his daughter's embarrassing loss of control and the family seeing a psychiatrist. He blamed both mother and daughter for the problem. Mother interjected that she had been trying for all these years to keep them together as a family, not to get a divorce despite their grave differences, but this situation was scaring her.

At one point, in exasperation, she said her husband would "step on the fingers of drowning nonswimmers." Early in the couple's work I felt a tense knot in my stomach as I sensed their anguish and anger, and found I dreaded the idea of wading in between them. I had an inkling that I knew why their daughter rushed off to school, omnivorously looking for supplies. I finally dared to suggest that things seemed a little too damp and dangerous between them for a psychiatrist to help them navigate, and yet I sensed they both wanted that for their child and themselves given this painful and embarrassing impasse. To my surprise and relief, they both cracked a smile, relaxed a little, and became more reflective. Nevertheless, the marital tension persisted for months until I recognized my overconcern about Ms. P.'s father's vulnerability and my inhibited anger at him. My countertransference had kept me from interpreting his fragile, stifling competitiveness with me—and his wife. When I mentioned this, father, a brilliant hard-driving lobbyist, recalled the time when his old firm was splitting up. He developed the shakes and panic attacks, and saw a psychiatrist for a while. Although painful and humiliating at first, it had helped. Mother also saw someone during that period, continuing much longer than father.

In the family sessions, father was initially impatient and critical, blaming and exhorting Ms. P. about her disgusting loss of control. Mother was alternately deferential and critical of father, protecting the patient. Ms. P. seemed to absorb all this, sinking further into herself at first. Each of her attempts at offering explanations was met with suppressive comments from father, and then brief skirmishes between her parents as mother tried to protect her. Tears began to stream down mother's face, which appeared to torment Ms. P. There seemed to be no space for her to expose her true feelings. Finally, when I asked why she was grimacing at her mother, she said she could not stand her mother's tears, it made her feel so guilty and distant. When I noted that she did not say anything about her father, she looked apprehensive, then with tearfulness said she felt crushed and helpless.

As the family sessions progressed, it became clear to what degree father dominated the women with scary bluster, while they disarmed him with "helpless tears." While Ms. P. was clearly caught in a displaced parental cross fire, it slowly emerged that they all shared a basic, though ambivalently held, assumption of deep dependent loyalty to the family and the untrustability of outsiders. Blaming and shaming were used extensively to keep people in line. Later, we generalized Ms. P.'s fearfulness about separating to a family discussion of their mutual sensitivity to loss, independence, and the riskiness of being out there with others on one's own. This led to family discussion of father's firm splitting up and later to associations about fears that the family and extended family might split up. Affectively charged history discovered through a similar psychoanalytic treatment approach will now be presented in more narrative form.

Everyone's confidence had been shaken around father's crisis in his firm, which was not too long before Ms. P. turned twelve. As a child and preadolescent, she had been chubby, on the social sidelines, and receiving school criticism about her self-centeredness and mercurial temper. As she turned twelve, they took a summer safari to Africa where she became deathly ill with severe vomiting, not eating for two weeks and losing a great deal of weight. She returned to school in seventh grade and, to everyone's amazement, was trim and temperate, becoming a popular, active social butterfly. From that time on, she seemed both selfless and totally absorbed in her world of peers. As we reviewed other family experiences during this period, they realized father's father had died about the same time, further precipitating his midlife crisis. Each of these reminiscences led the parents on different but important tracks in subsequent parent sessions.

Mother became tearful again, remembering her sense of loss and rejection when Ms. P. became more successful with peers. Mother was hurt and jealous. It reminded her of aspects of Ms. P.'s early years and other losses. When she was born, she reportedly cried for twenty-two of twenty-four hours and rarely slept. Mother's milk could not satisfy or soothe her, both because she did not have enough, and the milk was "bad" ("black milk"). Mother followed a pediatrician-prescribed "two-hour demand schedule." After two weeks there was no weight gain, and after four weeks a loss. Her husband had to be away for several weeks. During this period mother felt utterly overwhelmed and alone. She felt she "had no real help" despite the fact that her mother came before her husband left. She had always felt criticized and deprived by her mother, who only supported achievement, leaving a reservoir of hidden craving and resentment. Consequently, she constantly sought her approval and acceptance, giving her mother complete outward respect. Her father, though subtly seductive, was usually distant and quite critical, noticing her only for ideas and academic achievement. Her parents had a formal, intellectualized, seemingly asexual relationship covering many disappointments and hostilities which occasionally erupted toward each other or her. At such times, her mother would withdraw tearfully and father would become verbally abusive of her. Secretly she welcomed the intensity of his feeling and attention.

Eventually, with a change in pediatrician and an unrestricted formula schedule, the baby began to thrive, becoming a butterball. Even so, she remained high-strung, irritable, with mother feeling she was a demanding, all-consuming "bottomless pit." A sense of being a misfit prevailed, with Ms. P. being pictured as insatiable and unsatisfied. There was some question of "congenital hyperactivity and nervous system immaturity." Father apparently got some sadistic enjoyment out of clapping and setting off her Moro startle reflex. Worried that she was basically at fault for not giving her enough, mother never limited Ms. P., spoiling her completely for years, yet underneath hating herself and Ms. P. for it. From the beginning, she felt something was wrong with the baby, too. When she was one year old, mother saw early signs of her being "very social, going off with anyone—she had no sense of family, I felt so rejected, abandoned." For fear of not being a good mother and of being restricting and ungiving like her own mother, she never limited

or denied Ms. P. food or social license, fearing anger and rejection. Yet she found herself hurt, and secretly angered, by
her independence and separateness. She found she constantly
had to suppress the negative side of her ambivalence about her
daughter. Later, she recognized that she also envied what her
daughter was getting from her that she had never gotten from
her mother.

Early in the process of childrearing, father's mother got
deeply involved when she visited and had a "tremendous effect
on Ms. P., enveloping her like an octopus, and I let her do
whatever she wanted." When Ms. P. was around age two, her
brother was born, and, at age four, the paternal grandparents
actually moved to the same city. Mother allowed the paternal
grandmother's pervasive influence because "there were such
profound differences between my husband's family and mine,
between him and me, that I gave in to her, gave my daughter
over to her completely, so as not to risk further divisiveness and
loss." Father's mother was an extremely phobic, dependent,
smothering woman, who shaped her empty days around her
granddaughter, catering to her, and protecting her from imagined inner and outer fears. Mother wanted to deal with nightmares and night fears, and turn off the night lights, but mother-
in-law urgently said no and prevailed. Redoubling her effort
in the face of this competition, mother devoted herself even
more to her daughter, wearing herself out and resenting her
own mother and mother-in-law even more.

The context for this focus on Ms. P. was a bitter family
disagreement suffered by the paternal grandparents in their
previous city resulting in the paternal grandfather never talking
to his own brother again, and followed by the move. They were
an extremely dependent, devoted couple, and mother "could
not be so unkind and impolite as to assert myself, differ with
them, and push her out." "I despised her all-encompassing need
to have a relationship with my daughter, but I tolerated it."
Sadly, this same disruptive fraternal pattern was reenacted between father and his own brother shortly thereafter, with his
brother becoming so envious of father's career that they
stopped talking and both families quit seeing each other, though

living in the same city. The paternal grandparents were caught in the middle. A year later, mother suffered a placenta previa, lost her uterus with the child, further precipitating her midlife crisis. She confessed she has "never gotten over it—and my daughter must have suffered terribly because I needed that child so much—our marriage was so rocky and father wanted ten children." Ms. P., five years old at the time, could not come in and see her mother, so she cut off a lock of her hair in desperation and sent it in to mother.

Perhaps as a reaction to these family impasses, father refused to let his daughter or her younger brother go to camp, insisting that the family always be together on vacations. Mother observed once, "We were dominated by his wishes in all things, and were never separated as a family. He was domineering and intimidating about everything. He also drank too much, but then so did I. We both had an alcohol problem. My family gave me my head, respected my opinions, while my husband sat on my head, never respects anything I think." So mother, fearing her husband's anger, sharp tongue, and aggressive outbursts, swallowed her opinions and differences to keep the peace.

For years, until age twelve, Ms. P. was supported by mother in thinking just of herself, covertly supporting her expression of negative opinions, and asserting herself. Mother observed, "I guess I allowed her to be negative and opinionated due to my completely positive attitude and suppression of myself. I never said 'no' and was the opposite of my negative cynical husband; I felt so used and exploited, so I encouraged my daughter not to be used and exploited. It was my fault that she was so self-centered, opinionated, and hot-tempered. That's why she alienated peers, had no friends, and got in trouble in grade school. As a result, we were closest friends though we actually fought a lot."

She went on to say:

I also found it much easier to criticize her, compared to my lovable son. He could make me laugh, but with my daughter, some of her anger and aggressiveness reminds me of my husband. I was ambivalent about her rebelliousness. She dared to do things I never did. When she began to skip classes and lie about her activities and homework in the last few years, I wondered if I was at fault. She has always had an impulsive, defiant side, though most of the fire went underground when she was twelve. With my son, it wasn't so perfect either, he is dyslexic, had self-image problems, was hyperactive, and was failing courses despite his motivation and determination. He was getting into a negative, self-defeating cycle with school and friends. My husband couldn't stand that and I found our ideal relationship was going sour. We felt he needed a fresh start with more structure away from us. So when he was thirteen and my daughter fifteen, we decided to send him to boarding school. We had not anticipated how different it would feel around here without him. We all missed him and felt sad, but his sister seemed to miss him the most. She used to tell him everything, and vice versa.

Ms. P., incidentally, was enuretic until age twelve. In the context of brother leaving for school, mother surprised and upset father and daughter by arranging to go back to school herself, "to become a landscape architect so I can have something meaningful of my own to do and become more financially independent."

Individual, Couples, and Family Development

The Marital Couple

Ms. P.'s mother characterized her relationship with her parents as one in which she felt superficially valued for good products and performance while personally criticized and deprived. As a result, she developed a "false self," suppressing her negative thoughts and feelings in favor of pleasing and appeasing, while harboring deep dependent cravings and bitter resentment. Hoping to escape her parents and satisfy her longings, she married a man with seeming strength, brilliance, and independence, only to discover that he was critical and distant—like her father. He resented her dependency and uncertainty because of his own counterdependent and counterphobic tendencies. Because his own parents, especially his mother, were so dependent, phobic, and smothering, he sought a woman who would not challenge his dominance and independence. Prior to their daughter's birth, they felt trapped in a sadomasochistic struggle fueled by mutual patterns of projections based on original familial conflicts. Mother hoped that having a baby would save the marriage while father was dubious about the encumbrance.

The "Psychosomatic Partnership"

When the baby was born, her strong appetite and irritability collided with mother's anxiety and inadequate milk supply and resulted in a sleepless, insatiable, inconsolable infant. Already deeply ambivalent about nurturing because of her own maternal experience, Ms. P.'s mother found herself in exactly the position she most dreaded—failing to satisfy her child and instead becoming the seeming object of her ravenous child's tormented fury. In addition, her husband was abandoning her rather than giving her more love and support and her mother was witness to her failure to perform well as a mother. She felt overwhelmed by loss and rejection from everyone, but especially by her daughter. Characteristically she attempted to suppress her disappointment and rage, and began to deplete herself by limitless giving.

The resultant failure in bonding between mother and child—mother's failure to provide an adequate holding environment for her infant—began a very bad, even catastrophic experience for both of them. In terms of mother's internal object world, through role reversal and projective identification, the baby became mother's "bad, demanding, libidinal" self and she became her "bad, rejecting, antilibidinal" mother. As a result, she found herself attacked from without by her persecutory little baby and sabotaged from within by her harsh critical self. Attempting to ward off these pernicious perceptions, she enacted with her baby her wish to become her fantasied self-sacrificing, all-loving, all-giving, ideal mother. This combination of repression and splitting, suppression, and projective identification, exacerbated by the baby's temperament, caused serious distortion in the formation of their "psychosomatic partnership" from this point on. Because of mother's inner conflicts and projective identifications, she found it virtually impossible to know where she stopped and her child began. Due to the distortions in her centered holding and relating, she did not create a growth-sustaining holding environment nor function as a nurturing regulating self object. She failed to provide, or assist child in the development of self-regulation (Box, 1981). At first the infant exhibited a "failure to thrive" pattern.

Recovering somewhat from her rage and regression, with time, defensive reconstitution, and a change to a more flexible pediatrician, mother and baby moved from a more rigid demand schedule to "ad lib" feeding. Baby became a "butterball" with mother unable or fearing to limit her in any way. Early in this process, father began his characteristic sadomasochistic, overstimulating intrusions with Ms. P., enjoying startling her into her Moro reflex. Basically, however, mother felt she was at fault, spoiling Ms. P. yet failing to give her enough, experiencing her as a demanding "bottomless pit who ran her ragged." Her feeling of something being wrong with child, with herself, with "them," persisted.

CENTERED AND CONTEXTUAL HOLDING

In addition, father proved unable to protect and nurture mother, contributing significantly to her difficulties. Uncomfortable as he was with passivity and dependency as a result of his maternal experience, he remained aloof and critical of mother's troubled efforts, contemptuous of her spoiling Ms. P. and her inability to control the bothersome child. This psychological failure on father's part was continuous, though sometimes subtle. At the heart of his difficulty was his internalized yet still continuing conflicts with his mother and father. As a result of his upbringing by his phobic, overprotective mother, he now defended against his similar conflicts by his dominating abusing style, sadistically criticizing everyone else for their fearful helplessness.

A striking example of his and their shared difficulty in creating an appropriate centered and contextual holding for Ms. P. involved the paternal grandmother. Despite their shared awareness that his mother wanted to "swallow Ms. P. up, overprotect, and smother her like an octopus," they allowed the grandmother, each for differing reasons, to become overly involved on her visits, overriding mother and monopolizing Ms. P. Father seemed relieved to have his overwhelming mother focus on mothering his daughter instead of him. Mother, because of her internal doubts and ambivalence about mothering, surrendered her child to her mother-in-law in order to save her marriage and preserve extended family harmony. She sensed her mother-in-law's narcissistic sensitivity to criticism and loss, her voracious need to control everyone and everything. This was heightened by their family losses in their old hometown and move to this city, making them more dependent on Ms. P.'s parents.

The focus on Ms. P. became even more intense because of the competition between her father and his brother for the affection of the newly arrived grandparents (a repetition of what grandfather had just been through). Mother sensed that her husband did not want to lose his parents to his brother, despite all his counterdependent claims, and Ms. P. became the vehicle for capturing them. Father's brother became jealously enraged and cut him off, with the grandparents and Ms. P. the only go-betweens. She became the sacrificial object as mother and father colluded in avoiding personal, marital, and extended family conflict. As the extended family worked out its conflicts around dependency, greed, envy, and paranoia, and enacted its tendency toward persecution and splitting off, they revealed a shared incapacity for mourning, ambivalence, and compromise.

As a result, Ms. P.'s parents were not able to provide sufficiently firm generational boundaries, as mother and father
reenacted their pathology and allowed his mother a primary
caretaking role. Mother's stifled rage at her mother, daughter,
and mother-in-law, fueled by her deep sense of inadequacy and
guilt, led her to surrender to all her daughter's urges, and to
everyone else's wishes. This lack of limit-setting, failure in mod-
ulation and regulation (Box, 1981), and surrender of appropriate boundaries, all created an amorphous, ill-defined centered
and contextual holding environment for Ms. P. At the same
time, this holding environment was suffused with often intense,
conflicted, confused feelings and interactions between Ms. P.
and her caretakers because of their individual and collective
unexpressed and unresolved conflicts. These early repetitive
experiences had a profound effect on her process of internalization of her primary objects and the development of identity
formation, self-regulation, and self-control around affects and
impulses. This distorted family structure and functioning, with
its boundary violations and intolerable affects, provided the
extended family context for all that Ms. P. was internalizing.

Triadic Relationships and Oedipal Issues

For her parents and the extended family, the birth of her
brother, when she was two, proved a contrasting relief for everyone—for a while. Early on, Ms. P. was fascinated by him. They
became close and played endlessly. Mother marveled at the fact
that she never felt inadequate or enraged with him. He seemed
easygoing and easily satisfied. Later, instead of characteristic
escalating angry interactions with her daughter, she found her
son somehow got her to smile and relax, breaking the tension.
As a result, she felt good about herself and him. They developed
an intense, positive "mutual admiration society" with each
other. Even though he proved to have learning disabilities, she
felt he was somehow always more self-contained and self-
sufficient, leaving her fulfilled rather than enslaved and
drained. This obvious splitting between her daughter and son

set the stage for mother's intense oedipal involvement with him, as well as her later envy of her daughter's relationship as a teenager with her brother, given the marital impasse.

Two years later, the marriage was still in precarious shape and mother hoped, with her next pregnancy when Ms. P. was five, that she could please father and satisfy his "deep need for ten children." The loss of not only this pregnancy (a male child), but also her childbearing capacity, plunged mother into deep despair about herself and her marriage, just as her daughter was dealing with triadic phallic–oedipal issues. Death and disappointment plunged both parents farther into their own mid-life crises. Mother's postpartum and reactive depression (incorporated into her reservoir of unresolved losses) and father's disappointed, angry withdrawal into business left his daughter relatively abandoned and deeply unsatisfied. To the degree her own unresolved earlier issues allowed her to make an oedipal bid for father during this period, family recollection reveals it was fickle and frenetic. Father would alternately displace his marital desires and frustrations onto his "hot-tempered little darling," igniting a love–hate sequence, only to withdraw entirely for periods. This established him further as a tantalizing and tormenting inner object for her.

LATENCY

Ms. P., from age six to twelve, emerged as a self-centered, opinionated, hot-tempered girl. Because of her impulsiveness and splitting, peers and teachers tended either to like her a great deal or not much at all. With a style so different from mother's self-sacrificing masochism, she identified much more with father (identification with the aggressor), though also expressing mother's suppressed rebellious side. When she and father were not keeping their distance, she engaged in heated struggles with him unlike her more acquiescing mother. This same sadomasochistic pattern was also evident in her battles with her brother. Her libidinal interests, displaced in part from her father, were much more overt with him. She relished beating and being beaten, and then making up, with her parents too much the distant but fascinated spectators. Everyone enjoyed the drama.

Despite parental looseness about boundaries within the extended family, father's absolute insistence that they spend all vacations and summers together cut Ms. P. and the family off from peer and camp experience in later years. In fact, both mother and father held a deep shared assumption that to go off too far with others outside the family was disloyal, danger-ous, and threatening—almost a phobic paranoid stance. Both parents projected bad aspects of themselves onto outsiders. As a result, the age-appropriate process of separation and object removal was partially blocked for Ms. P. Forced family vacations stemming from this overly rigid aspect of the family holding environment also contributed to a relatively unmetabolizable affective "hothouse effect" in this family. Because they imbued outsiders with so much harshness and danger, and inadver-tently set them up as external family social control agents, family members found themselves much more painfully regulated by shame than by guilt. Internal regulation through identification with parental values and prohibitions—through the formation of conscience and ego ideals—was deficient. The agency and actions of self-control were defensively projected onto outsiders because parental experiences and internalizations were too painful. For the most part, the locus of control for this family was outside, and shame was the motive.

Parental problems around impulse control and self-regu-lation were evident in other ways also. Excessive drinking and overeating were a constant preoccupation in the family, with the parents swinging back and forth between periods of greedy self-indulgence and embarrassed self-denial. Both bordered on obesity and alcoholism at times. During latency and early pre-adolescence, Ms. P. was somewhat impulsive or incontinent in several ways also. She was both pudgy and enuretic, as well as opinionated and mercurial.

ADOLESCENCE

As Ms. P. approached prepubescence and preadolescence, sev-eral things conspired to alter both her outer and inner world, and to shift her dynamics. Shortly before this time, as we have heard, father's firm experienced a hostile takeover attempt from within and he decided to split off from it. He found himself so narcissistically injured and threatened that he regressed. Losing his confidence, he became physically shaky and shifted into a phobic, dependent state, something he suppressed at the office but showed at home. Injured, beaten temporarily, and depressed, he recovered over six months with psychotherapy and medication. Getting help for her reaction to his collapse, mother had to temporarily assume more independence and leadership at home. Acting the hero at work, father set up his own firm, suppressing his shameful rage and humiliation. At home, he was threatened by his wife's friendly "takeover from within," becoming more anxious, rigid, and critical of his "defiant, impulsive wife and uppity daughter." Not too long after this, father's father also died, adding to his depressed, hostile state.

Somewhat tomboyish, Ms. P.'s major identification with her father had a significant defensive aspect to it, based on identification with the aggressor and mother's suppressed resentment. This dramatic turn of events and the relative shifts in mother's and father's positions were not lost on her. She found herself with a seemingly new and then harshly reaffirmed family reality at the same time she was experiencing an upsurge of sexual and aggressive urges. In addition, she was becoming interested in boys and worried about her looks and chubbiness. Just as her father seemed to be softening up—only to come down on her harder—her pediatrician, usually warm and permissive, made some seemingly critical remarks about her weight problem. Mother had put him up to this to control her daughter. Unfortunately, this echoed not only mother's new weight campaign, but also teasing by body-conscious preteen classmates. Underneath, mother was feeling challenged by daughter's budding seductiveness with father and upsurge in critical defiance of mother. In effect, mother joined father in coming down on their daughter to protect herself and displace her own feelings.

That summer, in the context of the "fun family safari to

Africa," which proved to be more of a forced march by father, she experienced her "vomiting sickness" and lost a great deal of weight. She had become frightened of rejection by her mother and father for her new adolescent independence and experimentation within the family. Because she felt so excruciatingly sensitive, threatened, and shamed by her parents, pediatrician, and peers, she internalized a harsh, rigid reinforcement of her antilibidinal internal objects. She experienced a consolidation of her false self, repressing further the upsurge of her sexual and assertive yearnings for her parents and peers. To everyone's surprise, she came out of Africa a changed young woman, her primitive, threatening internal objects repressed, and her central self overly civilized and constricted. No longer as self-centered, defiant, and impulsive, she swallowed her real desires and became a selfless appeaser, representing an identification with her subjugated mother. Both mother and father felt, in retrospect, that she seemed to lose her fiery, firm directness, becoming in father's terms, an "air-brained social butterfly, with no personal depth or direction—like her mother."

In fact, Ms. P. became consumed not only by her pursuit of thinness, but of "being in on everything, never on the outs with anybody." She became particularly self-conscious about her weight, appearance, and style, wanting to be pleasing and palatable to everyone. Losing her center, she became an "as if" personality (Deutsch, 1942). She projected everything good outside herself into peers and teachers, while sensing in them the potential for harsh criticism and humiliation. She felt no basic trust or sense of constancy within herself or with others, making every new social interaction tantalizingly precarious should she make a false move and not do the imagined "right thing in their eyes." She repressed, or felt compelled to suppress, any feelings or actions she suspected might trigger such catastrophic reactions. Because her defenses were fragile, she was prone to microprojection and misperception. As a result, she was excruciatingly sensitive to even subtle differences or separateness, which she experienced as criticism or rejection. Usually she drove herself crazy trying to keep her whole social world positive and ideal. But occasionally, when she experienced such inevitable "rejection" she could no longer contain her anger. The person would become suddenly all bad, revealing her propensity for splitting. The relationship would turn sour and spoil. She would experience herself as rotten, becoming frightened and disgusted with herself as she hid in shame from the other person. No longer identified with the aggressor, she suffered masochistically as the victim.

THE ONSET OF BULIMIA

The frequent onset of bulimia during midadolescence, in a general sense, is related to both personal psychological and family developmental tasks (Stierlin and Ravenscroft, 1972; Ravenscroft, 1974). The implications of the impending second order structural change for the family when the adolescent is preparing to leave home, as well as the special challenges for the adolescent female and marital couple at this juncture, are often cited as the reasons for the onset of bulimia in midadolescent females. The unusual number of losses found in bulimic families is also often cited. It is likely that their unusual shared sensitivity to, and incapacity for dealing with, losses is involved here.

MIDADOLESCENCE

For Ms. P. and her family, the loss of her brother to boarding school just as she and her family were beginning to anticipate college created the overdetermined circumstances for actual onset of her bulimia. Within the "hothouse" of the family adolescent issues were germinating. Unfortunately, her parents did not provide an appropriate developmental holding environment and were not directly available for the progressive developmental tasks of adolescence within the family. Mother and father were sufficiently anxious about separation–individuation and oedipal–heterosexual issues that their anxiety and defensiveness interfered with their daughter's reworking of these issues. Yet they also interfered with her moving fully or for very long into the peer group. As a result, both Ms. P., and her younger teenage brother, entered into a highly charged sexual and aggressive relationship, tinged with and reenacting the same regressive anal sadomasochistic struggles seen with their parents. Because of their marital, and in particular, their sexual impasses, the parents alternately fueled and criticized this hot brother–sister relationship. In this context, Ms. P. was noted to oscillate back and forth between her peer group and her brother as she experimented abortively with separation and heterosexuality. Her parents, although nominally for her growth, regularly managed to criticize and limit her peer group forays, citing poor judgment and shameful behavior, but implying family disloyalty and their own marital anxiety.

During this period, as brother began to have increasing scholastic difficulty, mother nevertheless idealized and adored him while father became disappointed over the embarrassing struggles of his son. He felt his wife babied him, but also secretly resented their erotic intimacy, as well as his son's intimacy with his daughter. This oedipal challenge was too threatening. For this mix of reasons, he partially rejected his son. By sending him out of the family, father broke the unwritten family rule of loyal enmeshment. Unresolved oedipal issues for the parents had been displaced onto son and daughter leading to their splitting them up as a sibling couple and sending the son away. Father's problems around competition, envy, and shame in male relationships, in and outside his family, were now being reenacted with his son (Levi, Stierlin, and Savard, 1971).

When the parents sent their son to boarding school, they lost their tension-relieving oedipal displacement, and Ms. P. lost her safe in-house romance. His departure, besides facing everyone with partial loss and their shared incapacity to grieve, also brought home the possibility of Ms. P. leaving, too, and the parents' prospect of an empty nest and barren marriage. The result for everyone was powerful intensification of conflict, regression, and somewhat uncharacteristic personal and family defensive maneuvers. Fueling this were their separate midlife crises. Because of marital anxiety, father became more distant and critical. At first, mother became characteristically more dependent and tearful. Father engaged his daughter in more hot but critical encounters. Mother attempted to envelop and control her. Soon, however, mother herself broke covert family rules and assumptions as she reacted to her son's expulsion. Her assertive and defiant decision to go back to school was unspeakably threatening to her daughter and husband, implying rejection and loss. Ms. P. had just moved tentatively into her first romance, possibly in anticipation of her brother leaving, but then under the inner and outer onslaught of his actual departure and mother's major independent move, she retreated from this outside relationship, collapsing loyally back into the family, while becoming secretly but defiantly bulimic. She could not escape, yet could not stomach what was going on in the family.

THE BULIMIC EPISODE: A COMPOSITE DESCRIPTION

Let me offer a picture of one of Ms. P.'s characteristic bulimic episodes, using a composite of her own words:

> I was at school, sleepless and homework unfinished. So many people had called me the night before to gossip or get help. I had wanted to really do a terrific job on my homework for once and really please the teacher, but I couldn't say no to them, they needed me so much. But then I didn't have any time for myself or my homework. At school things were buzzing socially and I couldn't stand to be left out of anything. It was exciting and overwhelming. I was flying around talking to everybody. I was a regular social butterfly trying to please everyone, just like my mother felt I should and my father hated. I was into so many activities that I was way overextended. Yet there were so many more things I wanted to do, be part of.
>
> Once I sat down in class I had to slow down. I began to feel empty and lonely, left out, cut off and distant. I found myself fretting about all the things I hadn't done for

people, worried I had told secrets or said some mean things, about people not liking me, not approving of me. I also tormented myself over what I was missing out on. At the same time, I couldn't help but worry I would be called on, not having my homework done, not know my stuff. I became more anxious and lonely, began to have a knot, a gnawing in the pit of my stomach, thinking the teacher wouldn't like me, approve of me—something I longed for. I even began to think of my father, how contemptuous he'd be of my embarrassing performance. I felt so ashamed and small, so misunderstood and abandoned. I also felt angry at them, wanting to break away and be free of them. I was filled with feeling anxious, empty, and hungry.

There was only one way to relieve the way I felt. I was disgusted with myself for giving in to the impulse—though as I slipped into that delicious frame of mind, I could almost taste the relief. I began getting excited, sometimes it almost feels sexual. At class break, I slipped into a private bathroom and gorged on my secret supply of Twinkies, chocolates, and Reese's Pieces. I'm embarrassed to tell you how many. As I filled up, I began to feel relief at first, relishing swallowing the forbidden rich, fattening stuff despite my own and my family's dislike of fatness. I felt so relieved and satisfied, so free and together—a real high. I felt in my own special private world. You know, separate and in complete control just for a passing moment, doing my secret thing. Once I even masturbated a little. I never told you that before. Anyway, I couldn't stop myself. I kept going, and as I did so my mood and my feeling about what I was doing, about myself and the food, began to change fast, just like it always does.

I began to feel the food turn rotten, bad, disgusting, as if it were turning in my stomach, attacking me. It no longer gave me absolute relief and pleasure. It always spoils the perfection. I began to think about the outside world again. I began to hate myself because I couldn't stop, because I had given in, because I was gluttonous and the food would make me fat. I had to get it out of me, get away from it, control it, and control my urges. Giving in had gotten out of control. What was so completely good turned so completely bad I had to get away from it or everything would be ruined. I'd be caught or collapse. Somehow I felt I had to punish it and myself. So I stuck my fingers down my throat repeatedly and vomited it all up—got rid of it—to protect myself from becoming fat, disgusting, embarrassing.

I began worrying about someone having heard me, catching me at it. I desperately wanted to prevent the other kids, my Mom and Dad, from knowing, criticizing, making fun of me, though I hated myself enough for the vomiting. Actually, though, there is such relief, almost a rush, from vomiting, that even that feels special and good. It's such a physical feeling, yet such a relief to get rid of the bad stuff, almost as if it was taking me over, threatening to make me sick from within. I had to get away from it, get it out of me. That's the good part of vomiting—the relief despite being ashamed. I guess it is almost like masturbating.

After I come out of it, the tension is all gone, though I'm left with a strange hangover in my body and feelings. I know it won't build up again, at least for a while. I want to get away from the scene of the crime. I almost feel like someone else took me over, someone else did it. Yet it's so special, it's all mine, it's private, and I haven't wanted anyone to know about it—or take it away. It's my baby. And yet its such a shameful burden, I'm so out of control, I know it's wrong and dangerous. Maybe that's why I got myself caught. Anyway, when I leave the bathroom, it takes a while for me to feel myself again. For a while I feel people know somehow I've been doing it, like they can see through me, smell it, or something. I feel fuzzy like they can read my mind. I have to be extra careful and good. I'm so tired from it, feel so transparent and ashamed, that I like to keep my physical distance, get away and rest. That's impossible at school, so I bury myself in a book or stay out of social things. After a while I feel normal again.

What Ms. P. made repeatedly clear was that she went through similar repetitive cycles every day, with the prodromal buildup of very specific psychodynamic tensions with familiar content, followed by the impulse to binge and then purge. The triggers or precipitants proved to be both inner conflicts and outer events. Always involved were object-related, object-directed fantasies about herself and others with familiar but varied psychodynamic content. As the impulse to binge gathered strength, she would first fight it, then feel compelled and even eager to binge. As the urge to binge reached an obligatory phase in some safe secret place, she underwent a regression to a different psychological state—a special private world—with altered personality, reality testing, and ego functioning. Within this state she experienced a very specific cycle with two characteristic phases: a binge phase and a purge phase. A very interesting question, in addition to those about restrictors versus eliminators, concerns the personality differences among bulimics who use dieting, diuretics, laxatives, and vomiting as their means to purge. For this discussion, I am limiting myself to the predominant type of bulimic, the classic normal-weight vomiter.

OBJECT RELATIONS AND DYNAMICS

I have found most psychodynamic explanations of bulimia unsatisfying because they usually do not make a sufficient clinical and conceptual distinction between structure and content. As a result, I find myself expecting to find *the* psychodynamic explanation of bulimia and come away with the impression that *any* psychodynamics might be involved including a smorgasbord of psychosexual levels. In addition, there is a tendency to get lost in confounding secondary psychophysiologic effects of both the binge–vomiting physiology and the guilt-, hunger-, and endorphin-related anorexia and starvation after a binge–purge cycle. Also, there are the confounding psychological secondary, subsequent, and stratified causes within the bulimic individual and the family. Many clinicians, understandably, have been led to the conclusion that bulimia can arise from any developmental level and that almost any type of personality, and dynamic pathology can underly the condition. This unsatisfactory conclusion overlooks certain important clinical observations and leads us to seek an answer at a different level.

Sophisticated clinicians point to the obvious impulse disorder involved in bulimia and conclude rightly that a structural defect in the ego must be present. Since the predominant difficulty seems to be at the oral level and involves defensive maneuvers of "taking in" (binging) and "eliminating" (purging), the defenses of incorporation and projection must be involved. Discussions elsewhere in this book cover these areas thoroughly. Pathological as well as healthy defenses can give form to varied dynamic and psychosexual content, accounting in part for the discrepancies and confusion reviewed above.

Much of psychoanalytic thinking is predominantly drive oriented, dealing with the vicissitudes of libidinal and aggressive drives in terms of internal structural relationships. Object relations theory, and, especially, object relations family theory, on the other hand, make the important theoretical and clinical distinction, as I have pointed out earlier, that libidinal and aggressive drives are all directed at objects, resulting not in the incorporation or projection of disembodied drives in relation to reified "mental structures," but rather the incorporation or projection of personified drives involving the personal self in relationship to other real significant people, as part or whole objects, mediated through internalized object relations.

PREMORBID PERSONALITY CHARACTERISTICS

With these theoretical and clinical considerations in mind, I worked with Ms. P.'s family individually, as a couple, and as a family group using active receptive uncovering techniques to discover their here-and-now pattern of interlocking transferences—their reciprocal projective identifications—and to uncover their inner world of internal object relations. The resulting detailed clinical observations on all these levels gives additional insights into the intrapsychic and interpersonal as-

pects of the bulimic in her family, and into the bulimic episode
itself.

As we have discovered, Ms. P. felt ashamed or fearful about
much of her private internal world, constantly obsessing about
her feelings and thoughts about people. Like many teenagers,
she spent much of her day rehearsing and sorting out her ideas
and feelings, constantly imagining everyone's reactions, and
then modifying her responses. For her this was more dangerous
and draining because of her deep cravings, impulsiveness, and
sense of impending disaster. Because she experienced so much
of what she was as unacceptable, she felt she needed to hide
most of her self. Not only did she have a false self and repressed
true self, but a sizable conscious to preconscious *hidden self* in
relation to *hidden others*. This constituted a seething cauldron
of consciously doubted or feared parts of herself leading to her
sense of shame and urgent need for secrecy. As a result, she
often felt quite isolated. In Kleinian terms, she had a tendency,
when anxious, to operate from a predominantly paranoid–
schizoid position, trying urgently to relieve her sense of isolation
and separateness, yet fearing both "internal sabotage" and "external assassination."

From a personal and family developmental point of view,
impasses around dyadic separation–individuation and triadic
oedipal issues, made it difficult for her to move beyond mid-
adolescence. Her deep analytic dependency, intrapsychic and
interpersonal boundary problems, severe identity confusion,
and immobilizing projections left her psychologically unable to
move out of the family solidly into her peer group. Her failure
in identity formation and midadolescent identity consolidation
has been traced from her maternal dyadic "psychosomatic partnership," through each stage of development, to midadolescence. In effect, she suffered from severe difficulties in identity
formation stemming from early dyadic and triadic experiences,
unresolved and even further distorted by later developmental
experiences. Because of the lack of a constant maternal object,
the lack of provision of an integral constant dyadic "psychosomatic partnership," and the lack of appropriate triadic
boundaries and relationships, she has serious structural and

functional deficits in her ego, her available defensive operations, and her identity.

Because of the pathological content, form, and interrelationships of her real and internal object relationships, the usual
healthy process of identity formation through depersonification
and integration of internal objects into a true coherent personal
self did not occur. Thus, the conscious and unconscious aspects
of her identity did not develop appropriately. Unable to take
in (swallow), metabolize, and incorporate her self in relation to
her parents and extended family, she has been, for the most
part, left with powerful, threatening, unconscious internal object relations, and with partially conscious, personified introjects
rather than healthy identifications. What she could not take in
entirely because of her pathological centered holding and relating with her mother, she now holds in preconscious limbo
within herself, threatening to destroy her inner and outer
boundaries. In essence, she now suffers constantly from partially digested unstable "rattling introjects," giving rise to her
fragile fluid identity and brittle defenses, and her proneness
toward projective identification and splitting.

Put another way, she has, in fact, taken in the fragile, in-
constant, and shifting pathological boundaries, dynamics and
content of her family in bits and pieces through a process of
projective and introjective identification—and her internal
identity, structure, and function reflect this experience. Like
other defense mechanisms, projective identification normally
serves a constructive developmental purpose in the process of
personality and identity development. Projective identification
in conjunction with Winnicott's good enough mothering, usually contributes to healthy development of the central self, allowing the true self to flourish. Similarly, a conscious sense of
the ideal object develops. Because of the pathology in this family, and in particular in the "psychosomatic partnership," there
is a preponderance of pathological projective identification and
a failure of central self development, a failure of normal identity
formation. Instead, pathological repression and splitting occur,
and a "false self" predominates, leading to Ms. P.'s unstable
"as if" personality. In addition, there is a hypertrophy of the

conscious and preconscious ideal object due to her urgent projections of the good parts of herself onto her mother, split off
from the bad, amplified by mother's unrealistic limitless enactment of herself as all-gratifying and unfrustrating. The conscious and unconscious fit of mother's and daughter's projective
systems left an idealized infantile *cornucopia fantasy* residing in
mother and the environment (the central and contextual holding environment) while retaining the badness within the daughter or her unconscious, giving rise to her proneness to projections
of tantalizing plenty into those around her while always tinged
with harsh foreboding.

For the midadolescent and her family, the major developmental challenge is to promote the final formation of a coherent integrated identity or "shell" (Scharff and Scharff,
1987), so the adolescent can be "hatched" out of the family—a
whole, separate, self-regulating individual ready for emancipation and launching. Ms. P., like most female adolescent bulimics, found the disparate aspects of her family, internal object
world, and potential identity impossible to swallow (incorporate), metabolize, and integrate. To become a person like her
parents, to become a female like her mother, to enter into a
heterosexual couple's relationship like her parents, to leave a
family such as hers, to enter a world such as they project—all
was too much to incorporate or "package" for her and her
family. In addition, she feared that if she left there would be
both a real life catastrophe (a parental divorce) of her external
objects and an internal catastrophe within her precarious internal object world.

OBJECT RELATIONS AND THE BULIMIC EPISODE

From Ms. P.'s composite narrative of her bulimic episode, we
can sense the buildup of intense craving, frustration, and anger
as she seeks to satisfy her omnivorous appetites with the people
in her life. Prior to the binge proper, she uses a combination
of repression and splitting, suppression, and projective identification to distribute in a characteristic pattern the intolerably

good and bad aspects of her self and others, fueled by the powerful interplay between her internal objects and her peers and teachers. She represses and splits off her gluttonous, devouring, libidinal and aggressive self and her tantalizing, tormenting, exciting other. She also represses and splits off her angry, critical, antilibidinal self and rejecting other. These major intolerable aspects of her self and her objects become repressed as her internal bad self and bad objects.

As a result, she experiences her central self as depleted and empty. Devoid of sufficient self-organizing appetites and assertive directedness, she becomes selflessly outer directed. At the same time, she projects onto others around her the good idealized aspects of herself, experiencing herself surrounded by people filled with everything good and exciting which she so hungrily craves. She then feels compelled to seek and incorporate these libidinal supplies on all psychosexual levels, giving the various oral, anal, and oedipal tinges to her interactions with her objects. In addition, because she suffers from preconscious suppressed introjects of her mother, father, paternal grandmother, and others, she constantly experiences a sense of paranoid foreboding as her cravings raise these ghosts toward consciousness. Because they so frequently frustrated her, stirring intolerable rage, current needful interactions with them and others occasion considerable anxiety. She is threatened in her strivings by both the return of the repressed and the resurrection of introjects—hence, her particular structural fragility and affective–impulsive lability—like that of every bulimic.

This internal and projected distribution of good and bad aspects of herself and others is maintained both to protect herself and others, and to protect these good and bad aspects of herself and others from coming into contact with each other, thus avoiding the catastrophic risk of spoiling and destroying each other. Such catastrophic risks and failures, we will recall, were part of Ms. P.'s damaging early "psychosomatic partnership." Because of her ego defects and faulty identity formation, she maintains this fragile and precarious distribution with great difficulty.

REGRESSION AND BINGE PHASE

As she approaches a bulimic episode, her mounting voracious hunger, sense of deprivation, and rage over projected criticism and rejection become intolerable. She reports not just thinking about her peers, teachers, and parents at such times, but actually sensing and hearing people acting and sounding like them. As internal tension mounts, she can no longer tolerate the internal and projected tyranny over her appetites by her rejecting bad objects and antilibidinal self. A loosening of boundaries, de-repression, and activation of introjects occurs—due to increasing desire, anxiety, and shifting defenses. Eventually, she feels compelled to give in to her impulses and defy this tyranny. Regression to another state of consciousness occurs when she finds a safe setting for her impulsive binge.

In a sense, the bulimic episode is a manic, even orgiastic, feast on all the denied and projected good parts of the self and others, past and present, internal and external. It is also a manic triumph over the tyranny of harsh forbidding and foreboding part and whole objects, whether parents, peers, or authorities. In an orgy of libidinal and aggressive incorporation, she devours omnivorously everything she desires—the forbidden ideal mother, her breast, her milk, the food, the soft relinquished feces, her father's penis, everything about them and her peers she envies. All the derivatives and sublimations of her appetitive goals and objects undergo regression and condense into the archaic dream substance of the forbidden rich food she craves and engulfs voraciously.

She also destroys with biting oral rage those tyrannical aspects of herself and others that have been oppressing and tormenting her—internal saboteurs and external assassins alike —swallowing them whole or barely chewing them up. In this orgiastic regressive collapse of self and other, inside and outside, unconscious and conscious, the manic wish for undifferentiated reunion with everything ideal and good, including all later developmental derivatives, is acted out symbolically through the literal oral incorporation of her part and whole objects. Her fragile false self; faulty identity; and defective personality structure, ego, and defenses have collapsed under the onslaught of libidinal and aggressive impulses. Instead of suffering masochistically as the victim, she has become the gluttonous saboteur and assassin herself. Massive self-indulgence in every sphere of deprivation leads to gluttony, biting, smearing, and messing, fleeting fantasies of matricide and patricide, and even to masturbation and orgasm.

TRANSITION AND PURGE PHASE

Typically, this impulsive yielding to urges, this collapse and shift of defenses, this manic implosion of usually separated aspects of the self, results in a very transient, unstable personality configuration and mental state. For all the same internal reasons that these intolerable aspects of self and other were kept apart and out of consciousness, they now begin to collide and create an intolerable, chaotic, destructive internal state. As the reality of actual fullness and satiation sets in and the manic phase reaches its climax, she rapidly begins to experience a sense of the good food spoiling and turning rotten—the bad ruining the good, the hate destroying the love. She senses her destruction of her parents and their rules coming back to haunt her. She fears discovery, criticism, and catastrophe. She feels as if she is losing herself, being taken over by what she has consumed, being attacked by what she attacked.

On a literal level, her eyes were bigger than her stomach and she was in pain. She must do something to relieve her physical discomfort and relieve a new intolerable internal tension. In another sense, she has been omnivorously gluttonous, violating every internal and external rule, and must pay. As a developmental experience growing up, it was intolerable to incorporate, hold, metabolize, and integrate her object-directed impulses and relationships. She never was held by her parents in a way that allowed her to take them in as a self-holding structure (Box, 1981) that would allow her to become internally tolerant, coherent, and whole. As a result, she never developed the defensive personality structure to deal with these impulses and relationships inside her conscious central self. Now that she has given way to her impulses and swallowed them all into her conscious self, a microcosm of the same internal and interpersonal catastrophe is occurring that she has so long avoided by her fragile combination of repression and splitting, suppression and projection.

Purging becomes an urgent and deeply desired escape route from this intolerable physical and psychological state. In fact, since she has regressed back to the level of the "psychosomatic partnership," both mind–body and self–other boundaries have dissolved. Because of this unity, the infant is essentially a body–ego. One's self includes the other, body and soul, as a self object. Unfortunately, the ideal reunion with the perfectly satisfying mother rapidly dissolves. With no compartmentalization psychically or physically, the overwhelming signal anxiety of this impending implosive catastrophe—this collision of internal objects—is experienced as body tension and action impulse. Annihilation anxiety is rapidly approaching, the explosive fragmentation of self. The earliest and worst aspects of her faulty psychosomatic partnership experience are re-emerging. This reflects the painful interplay between constitutional, temperamental, psychological, and social factors leading to a physical zonal fixation and a powerful tendency toward the oral incorporative mode for defensive purposes.

In essence, urgent purging is an emergency maneuver, mentally and physically, to explosively expel, redistribute, and compartmentalize these incompatible internal aspects of self and other. First, the completely regressed bulimic automatically uses expulsive elimination as an emergency maneuver—a psychosomatic defensive operation. I am tempted to call this "projective" vomiting since vomiting is one of the earliest psychosomatic anlage or prototypes for projection. Other forms of elimination, such as cathartics and diuretics, probably represent a variant on these structural and dynamic considerations since they use different body parts and functions, have different meaning, and have a different time frame.

Postpurge Transition and Reconstitution

During the purging, the bulimic rapidly emerges from her regressed state. Impelled by near annihilation anxiety, she uses repression, splitting, and projection to reestablish her central self (false self) in relation to her unconscious, and to her real objects. During this transition back to her normal self, she suffers from loose boundaries, having trouble knowing where she stops and her body, her unconscious, and others begin. She also suffers from activated, but receding introjects and proneness to reality distortion. Derealization and depersonalization can occur. For these reasons, as well as cathartic–orgiastic exhaustion, a bulimic likes to go off and be alone, feeling the need to protect and nurture her fluid reemerging self-structure. She feels fragile, transparent, and vulnerable. After a while, she gets back to feeling her old self, only to discover in time she is in precisely the same internal and interpersonal predicament she was in in the first place. Thus the cycle begins again. It is of particular importance to note that the dynamics of the binge–purge cycle are a microcosm of the dynamics of her underlying personality structure. While bulimics can seem on the surface to have a range of personality styles, at their core this deep structure and dynamics are present, similar to structures described by Deutsch (1942), Kohut (1971, 1977), and Kernberg (1975, 1977).

Conclusion

It is important to differentiate epidemic peer group fad binge–purging on the one hand, and postanorexic binge–purging on the other, from true normal weight bulimia. Most fad bingers do not go on to develop true bulimia despite the exposure to and use of vomiting as a weight control technique for the maintenance of an ideal figure. Only certain anorexics proceed to bulimia, perhaps as a result of treatment or growth in some instances. Why do certain midadolescent females, whether through self-discovery of vomiting or through similar peer ex-

posure to the technique of vomiting, eventually develop the full
syndrome? Clinical experience developed through psychoanalytic family therapy approaches suggests it is a function of their
family and personal development, their structure and function,
and in particular their object relations, both internal and external. Clear antecedents and a particular vulnerability were
there prior to self-discovery of, or peer group exposure to,
vomiting, accounting for the onset of bulimia in adolescence.

Normal-weight bulimia, with its onset predominantly in
midadolescent females, is an eating disorder caused by specific
interrelated personality and family pathology. Characteristically, the mother is in a relatively hostile–dependent, masochistic relationship with her husband, while deeply ambivalent,
guilty, and overindulgent with her daughter. Typically, the
father is somewhat counterdependent, counterphobic, and sadistic with his wife, while overstimulating and rejecting with his
daughter. In my experience, sometimes, though rarely, these
roles can be reversed. Because of interlocking pathological familial and parent–child patterns of projective identification,
there is a characteristic failure of the "psychosomatic partnership" during early childhood. Often notable, contributing, constitutional factors are present such as feeding difficulties,
intense orality, and increased aggressiveness. As a result the
prebulimic child, with a strong tendency toward a defensive use
of oral incorporation and projective identification, develops a
false self, fragile identity, and a vulnerability toward regression
to the paranoid–schizoid position. She also comes to suffer from
introjects reflecting the faulty and incomplete process of internalization and identity formation due to her pernicious object
relationships.

Both child and parents share, to a varying degree, an underlying assumption of deep familial dependency and paranoid
distrust of outsiders. They also share an intolerance of loss,
mourning, and ambivalence, based on structural ego defects
leading to the characteristic excessive defensive operations of
repression, splitting, suppression, and pathological projective
identification. Because of the mutual fit of the projective systems of mother, father, and daughter, the prebulimic child

retains an excessive, unmodified infantile cornucopia fantasy about the ideal mother. She comes to feel basically that all the ideal oral supplies she craves reside outside of her, while her experience of her central self is one of emptiness and deprivation. Each subsequent individual, marital, and familial developmental phase is distorted in reciprocal fashion by the family's disordered central and contextual holding capacity, as well as by their distorted direct relationships. Because of difficulties around boundary regulation on all levels within the family, the prebulimic child comes to share the familial difficulty around self-holding and self-regulation. The vicissitudes of the related ego defects, identity formation, and impulse regulation can be traced developmentally, revealing that the bulimic's ultimate impulsive eating disorder has clear developmental precursors and parallels in the family.

Given the bulimic's pathological process of internalization, structural defects, and particular set of internal objects, she and her family are particularly vulnerable to difficulty specifically around the familial and personal developmental tasks of mid-adolescence. Facing the necessity of "hatching" and "launching" their adolescent female, the parents, themselves in their midlife crisis, must face the prospect of an empty next and their marital impasse. At some point in this process, a crisis occurs in such families—especially around and within the female mid-adolescent as she moves toward heterosexual peer relations. Usually this is in the context of either mother or father, though sometimes a sibling, making a major attempt at separation. This move violates the basic assumptions or rules of the family around dependency, loyalty, and aggression, and threatens their shared defensive posture. This precipitates a regressive realignment in the family and in the adolescent. She collapses loyally back into the family while secretly and defiantly developing bulimia.

Her bulimic episodes represent a biphasic regression in which she first gives way to an impulsive oral incorporation of her infantile ideal part and whole objects, followed immediately by an internal implosive catastrophe necessitating emergency projective elimination and redistribution of these objects to protect self and others. The bulimic episode also represents a microcosm of personal and family life. While there are many primary and secondary physiologic concomitants to the binge–purge cycle in bulimics, as well as secondary gain and subsequent causation on the individual, family, and peer group level, the predisposition for this syndrome is based, fundamentally, on the powerful interplay between inner and outer family object relations.

POSTSCRIPT

With approximately one-and-a-half years for treatment before Ms. P. would be leaving home for college, I felt the family was faced with the several individual and collective developmental impasses already outlined. My hope was to help them resolve these impasses which I felt were intimately related to the resolution of her bulimia. Initially, I met with Ms. P. weekly and alternated the family and couple's sessions biweekly. Whenever the son was home from boarding school, he attended the family sessions, and upon occasion saw me alone at his request. As we explored family experiences together and the history presented above emerged in a meaningful way around affect-laden themes and conflicts, shared family assumptions emerged around compulsive loyalty and dependency on the one hand, and shame and envy around outsiders on the other. As anxiety mounted around exposure and intimacy, especially in father, the family, under his intimidating sway coalesced against me as an embarrassing outsider. At first I felt hurt, angry, and inclined to counterattack until I identified their shared projections, expressed mainly by father, which were kindling my countertransference. I then shared with them my sense that they were filling me with enviable things and a harsh conscience, making it hard to feel safe with me and share their intimate problems. I sensed they felt ashamed and wanted to hide them. Later, I wondered if their seeing me as critical had something to do with their own shared fear that being separate and different from each other, and being angry or disappointed with each other felt too disloyal and aggressive, so they dealt with these feelings by banding together and uniting against me as the divisive threatening outsider. Working through their conflicts, splitting, and projections helped them reach increasing levels of intimacy while tolerating their negative affects and impulses progressively.

As these shared, basic assumptions became less rigid and intense, the family holding environment allowed the parents to work on their sadomasochistic relationship, exploring how they handled their tensions around intimacy, sexuality, and competition by putting their feared aspects of themselves into each other, or by splitting and projecting them, putting them differentially into their children—their daughter receiving most of the feared or undesirable aspects of each of them which they then had to manage, control, or suppress. Couple and family work facilitated this process of working through, as did the individual work. As they came to recognize that what they projected onto the outsiders, onto me, and onto Ms. P. represented aspects of themselves, they began to work more on their own relationship, mourning lost time to some degree, and accepting their differences partially. They also began dealing for the first time with their own midlife crises with more tolerance for each other, while preparing for letting their daughter grow and go.

In the individual work, Ms. P. first feared that I would be critical like father or smothering like mother and kept her distance. As we worked through these transferences, she developed a very dependent, somewhat idealizing and eventually very sexualized transference with me. Our major focus was not on the bulimia, at least at first, but rather on what she brought in, which was centered on her empty drivenness to pursue what she envied in everyone else—fearing their disapproval and rejection. As we worked through each microprojection around her peers and around her parents—and noted the similarities—we also began to analyze her self-depleting and -denigrating experience with me as she idealized me. As she became more assertive and comfortable expressing her differences and accomplishments, no longer fearing my envy and competition so much, she came to trust me and herself enough to feel romantically inclined. This began to have more of an adolescent feel to me, indicating sufficient progression and integration that she was more developmentally on track. She was dating again by now but not too seriously. During the course of this work, she realized what had been going on with her brother and how she had longed to be cherished and safe with her father. For his part, he was much less contemptuous of her, opening his arms and heart to some degree. Mother was less jealous. By this time the summer before college and Ms. P.'s separation from home and me were approaching.

Periodically throughout our work, she would refocus on her bulimia, and more of its meaning would emerge. Slowly, we forged the linkages between her bulimic episodes, her daily life, and her inner object world. It would then drop out of sight. Finally, for long periods, the binging and vomiting had abated as she felt more whole, full, and together. Couple and family work had long since stopped because her parents had reached an accord and level satisfactory to them, and were no longer interfering with her development interpesonally.

With the approach of termination and leaving home, the bulimia returned. At first I found myself becoming alarmed and acting more like an overconcerned parent, until I realized this represented a termination regression. In fact, there was a couple and family regression going on too, with familiar old assumptions and projections reactivating. We mutually agreed to add some family and couple sessions to address these issues and rework them yet again in the face of the family's intolerance for loss and mourning. By the time for summer vacation and our parting, Ms. P. was more self-contained and at peace, sad and ready—with some remaining urges to binge and purge, and occasional slippages. These imperfections did not panic her, as we reflected on the fact that our "termination" was really a forced "interruption" of her still incomplete personal growth. I recommended that when she got to college, after taking a break from treatment and settling in, that she consider further work, which I would help her arrange. She did just that, finding it very hard not to hang on to me by telephone from college as she faced the anxiety of college and a new therapist stirring familiar old fears. Yet she made the transition from home and me to college and another therapist without any major upheaval or return of her binging. In the process, she found a boyfriend rather rapidly, suggesting some degree of substitution for me and unresolved positive transference, as well as defense against the new male therapist. Beyond this I have no further follow-up.

REFERENCES

Balint, M. (1968), *The Basic Fault: Therapeutic Aspects of Regression*. London: Tavistock.

Box, S. (1981), Introduction: Space for thinking in families. In: *Psychotherapy with Families: An Analytic Approach*, ed. S. Box, B. Copley, J. Magagna, & E. Moustaki. London: Routledge and Kegan Paul, pp. 1–8.

Brazelton, T. B., Koslowski, B., & Main, M. (1974), The origins of reciprocity: The early mother–infant interaction. In: *The Effect of the Infant on its Caregiver*, ed. M. Lewis & L. Rosenblum. New York: Wiley-Interscience, pp. 49–76.

Bruch, H. (1973), *Eating Disorders: Obesity, Anorexia Nervosa, and the Person Within*. New York: Basic Books.

Crisp, A. H., Harding, B., & McGuiness, B. (1974), The starving hoarder and voracious spender: Stealing in anorexia nervosa. *J. Psychosom. Res.*, 245:225–231.

Deutsch, H. (1942), Some forms of emotional disturbance and their relationship to schizophrenia. *Psychoanal. Quart.*, 11:301–321.

Fairbairn, W. R. D. (1954), Observations on the nature of hysterical states. *Brit. J. Med. Psychol.*, 27/3:105–125.

Garner, D. M., Garfinkel, P. E., & Bemis, K. M. (1982), A multidimensional psychotherapy for anorexia nervosa. *Internat. J. Eat. Disord.*, 1:3–46.

Jacques, E. (1965), Death and the mid-life crisis. *Internat. J. Psycho-Anal.*, 46/4:502–514.

Kernberg, O. (1975), *Borderline Conditions and Pathological Narcissism*. New York: Jason Aronson.

———— (1977), Structural diagnosis of borderline personality organization. In: *Borderline Personality Disorders*, ed. P. Hartocollis. New York: International Universities Press, pp. 87–121.

Kohut, H. (1971), *The Analysis of the Self*. New York: International Universities Press.

———— (1977), *The Restoration of the Self*. New York: International Universities Press.

Levi, L. D., Stierlin, H., & Savard, R. J. (1971), Fathers and sons: The interlocking crises of integrity and identity. *Psychiat.*, 35:48–56.

Madanes, C. (1981), *Strategic Family Therapy*. San Francisco: Jossey-Bass.

Minuchin, S. (1974), *Families and Family Therapy*. Cambridge, MA: Harvard University Press.

———— Rosman, B. L., & Baker, L. (1978), *Psychosomatic Families*. Cambridge, MA: Harvard University Press.

Ravenscroft, K. (1974), Normal family regression at adolescence. *Amer. J. Psychiat.*, 131:1

Root, M. P. P., Fallon, P., & Friedrich, W. N. (1986), *Bulimia: A Systems Approach to Treatment*. New York: W. W. Norton.

Saba, G., Barrett, M. J., & Schwartz, R. (1983), All or nothing: The bulimia epidemic. *Fam. Ther. Networker*, 7:43–44.

Scharff, D. E., & Scharff, J. S. (1987), *Object Relations Family Therapy*. New York: Jason Aronson.

Schwartz, D. M., Barrett, M. J., & Saba, G. (1984), Family therapy for bulimia. In: *Handbook of Psychotherapy for Anorexia and Bulimia*, ed. D. Garner & P. Garfinkel. New York: Guilford Press, pp. 280–310.

Schwartz, R. (1982), Bulimia and family therapy: A case study. *Internat. J. Eat. Disord.*, 2:75–82.

Segal, H. (1973), *Introduction to the Work of Melanie Klein*. London: Heinemann.

Selvini Palazzoli, M. (1978), *Self-Starvation*. New York: Jason Aronson.

Stern, D. N. (1977), *The First Relationship: Infant and Mother*. Cambridge, MA: Harvard University Press.

———— (1985), *The Interpersonal World of the Infant: A View from Psychoanalysis and Developmental Psychology*. New York: Basic Books.

Stierlin, H., & Ravenscroft, K. (1972), Varieties of adolescent "separation conflicts." *Brit. J. Med. Psychol.*, 45:299–313.

Winnicott, D. W. (1956), Primary maternal preoccupation. In: *The Maturational Processes and the Facilitating Environment*. New York: International Universities Press, pp. 45–59.

———— (1971), The location of cultural experience. In: *Playing and Reality*. New York: Basic Books.

Chapter 15

Bulimic Equivalents

C. PHILIP WILSON, M.D.

Psychoanalysis or analytic psychotherapy represent the most comprehensive approach to the treatment of bulimic anorexia nervosa because their central focus is on the resolution of the underlying personality disorder. Precipitous relief of bulimic symptoms by treatments such as behavior modification or antidepressant medication may be dangerous to the patients' mental functioning or even to their life. If symptoms are cleared before there has been sufficient change in the underlying neurosis and the object relations, the bulimic ego functioning may be replaced by bulimic equivalents (Wilson, 1982; Wilson, Hogan, and Mintz, 1983; Wilson, 1986a,b,c). These symptom equivalents, which may alternate with or replace bulimia, include:

1. Self-destructive acting out (Sperling, 1968; Wilson, 1968; Wilson et al., 1983; Schwartz, 1986; Wilson, 1986a);
2. Another addictive disorder such as obesity, alcoholism, or drug addiction;
3. Another psychosomatic symptom formation such as a stiff neck (Wilson et al., 1983), ulcerative colitis (Sperling, 1983), migraine (Hogan, 1983), and asthma (Mintz, 1983);
4. Neurotic symptom formation;
5. Severe regressive symptom formation (Mintz, 1983).

BULIMIC EGO FUNCTIONING

In order to delineate the ego functioning of the bulimic patient it is necessary to present my research on the classification (Wilson, 1983), etiology (Wilson, 1973, 1974, 1977, 1978, 1980a, 1982, 1983, 1986a,b,c, in press), and psychodynamics of bulimia.

During the past thirty years there has been increasing evidence that *anorexia nervosa*, a generic term that I use to include both the bulimic and restrictor syndromes, is a psychosomatic disorder (Thomä, 1967; Bruch, 1978; Sperling, 1978; Sours, 1980; Wilson et al., 1983; Schwartz, 1986). Specifically, the bulimic patient has strict but ineffective ego controls that are unable to regulate the impulse to eat (Wilson, 1982, 1983). This defect in self-control is so threatening to the patient that the slightest gain in weight may produce panic, excessive exercising, starving, and vomiting. The bulimic patient, unable to control eating, is also unable to control other impulses, so that one sees sexual promiscuity, delinquency, stealing, lying, and running away more frequently than in the starving anorexic patient. This defect in ego controls arises in part from identifying with parents who frequently argue, fight, and act out destructively more often than parents of starving anorexics (Wilson, 1986a).

Restrictor and bulimic anorexia nervosa are symptom complexes that occur in a variety of character disorders: hysterical, obsessive–compulsive, borderline, and, in some cases, conditions close to psychosis. However, even in the most disturbed cases, there are areas of relatively intact ego functioning and a capacity for a transference relationship.

For the diagnosis of bulimic anorexia nervosa, gorging and vomiting as well as amenorrhea are usually necessary. Some cases begin with a restrictor anorexic syndrome and then develop bulimia. Other patients are predominantly restrictive in their eating behavior, with infrequent episodes of bulimia. Many bulimics can keep their weight at a near normal range by balancing their starving, gorging, vomiting, and laxative use.

I concur with Thomä's (1967) delineation of anorexia nervosa, which includes both the restrictors and the bulimics:

(1) the age of onset is usually puberty; (2) the patients are predominantly female [although male cases have been reported by Falstein, Feinstein, and Judas (1956); Mintz (1983); and Sours (1980)]; (3) the reduction in nutritional intake is psychically determined; (4) when spontaneous or self-induced vomiting occurs, the diagnosis of bulimia is made; (5) amenorrhea (which is psychically caused) generally appears either before or, more rarely, after the beginning of the weight loss; (6) constipation, sometimes an excuse for excessive consumption of laxatives, speeds up weight loss; (7) the physical effects of undernourishment are present and in severe cases death may ensue [7 to 15 percent die (Sours, 1969)]. Hogan (1983) added three further observations: (1) there is commonly a tendency toward hyperactivity, which may be extreme; (2) in females there is often a disproportionate loss of breast tissue early in the disease; and (3) the symptom complex is often accompanied by or alternates with other psychosomatic symptoms (or psychogenic equivalents such as depressions, phobias, or periods of self-destructive acting out that may include impulsive sexual behavior, stealing, or accident-prone behavior). With successful psychodynamic treatment, we (Wilson et al., 1983) have found that all the physical signs and symptoms of bulimic anorexia nervosa return to normal except for irreversible tooth and gum damage caused by gorging and vomiting. However, menstruation may not resume, even though the patient's weight returns to normal limits, if significant psychosexual conflicts have not been resolved.

I recently (1980a, 1982, 1983; Wilson et al., 1983) presented hypotheses about the diagnosis, etiology, psychodynamics, and technique of treatment of anorexia nervosa. My research indicates that *fat phobia* should replace *anorexia* as a diagnostic term. These patients do not suffer from lack of hunger but from the opposite—a fear of insatiable hunger as well as of impulses of many other kinds (Thomä, 1967; Sperling, 1978; Sours, 1980; Wilson et al., 1983). Psychodynamic work with these restrictor and bulimic anorexics focused on the various components of their overdetermined, unconscious fear-of-being-fat-complex, which are etiologic in causing their conscious fat phobia, and associated conscious fear-of-being-fat body image disturbance. Neurotic analysands also evidenced less intensely cathected, but clear-cut, fear-of-being-fat obsessions and body image disturbances. These findings, coupled with nonanalytic research, lead to the conclusion that in our culture most women and certain men, those with unresolved feminine identifications, have a fear of being fat. Normal women readily admit to the fear. No matter how "perfect" a woman's figure may be, if she is told she is fat she will have an emotional reaction out of all proportion to reality. On the other hand, if she is told she looks thin or has lost weight, she will be inordinately pleased.

It is a central hypothesis of my research that restrictor and bulimic anorexia symptoms are caused by an overwhelming terror of being fat that has been primarily caused by an identification with a parent or parents who have a similar fear of being fat, and that anorexia (fat phobia) is secondarily reinforced by the general, irrational fear of being fat on the part of most other women and many men in our culture. Ceaser (1977) noted the role of maternal identification in three bulimics and one restrictor anorexic.

The Family Psychological Profile and Its Therapeutic Implications

Psychodynamic research with the families of one hundred anorexia nervosa patients (Wilson, 1986a) revealed a parental psychological profile that appears to be etiologic in establishing a personality disorder in their children that later manifests itself as anorexia nervosa. Sperling's (1978) analysis of anorexic children and their mothers laid the groundwork for this research with her findings that the predisposition for anorexia nervosa is established in early childhood by a disturbance in the mother–child symbiosis. Four of the six features of the psychological profile correlate with parental attitudes and behavior described by Bruch (1978) in fifty cases and by Minuchin, Rosman, and Baker (1978) in fifty-three cases. Sours (personal communication) confirms these features in his family research. The last two features of the following profile are usually only uncovered in the course of psychoanalysis. While there are exceptions to the profile (Wilson, 1986a), the great majority confirm the profile. A useful acronym for the profile is PRIDES: P = perfectionism; R = repression of emotion; I = infantilizing decision-making; D = dieting and fears of being fat; E = sexual and toilet exhibitionism; S = the unconscious emotional selection of a child for the development of bulimic anorexia nervosa.

1. All the families showed perfectionism. The parents of restrictor anorexics were overconscientious and emphasized good behavior and social conformity in their children. Most were successful people who gave time to civic, religious, and charitable activities. Many were physicians, educators, business executives, or religious leaders (i.e., pillars of society). The parents of bulimic anorexics, although they are perfectionistic, seem to have a greater incidence of neurosis, marital conflict, divorce, and addiction than the parents of restrictors. In other respects this psychological profile with variations that are noted applies to both groups. For example, the mothers of two bulimics were addicts (one to alcohol, the other to morphine), but their addictions were family secrets and both women were compulsive, perfectionistic college professors who tried to be perfect mothers. Their addictions expressed a rebellion against their hypermoral character structure.

2. Repression of emotions was found in every family group; it was caused by the hypermorality of the parents. In several cases, parents kept such strict control over their emotions that they never quarreled in front of the children. The loss of temper, quarreling, and conflict that was characteristic of the bulimic's parents was ego alien. Aggressive behavior in the children was not permitted, and aggression in general was denied (e.g., one father's volunteer military service was disdained by his family). Most families laughed at the father's assertive male behavior and saw him as the "spoiler" in the sexual relationship; the mother was the superior moral figure. The father's authority was diminished further by his busy schedule, which left him little time for his children.

3. The overconscientious perfectionism of the parents in these families resulted in infantilizing decision making and overcontrol of the children. In some of the families, fun for fun's sake was not allowed. Everything had to have a noble purpose, the major parental home activity was intellectual discussion and scholarly reading. It was no surprise that the anorexic daughter hated the long hours of study she felt compelled to do. In therapy, it was difficult for them to become independent and mature, and to get rid of the humiliating feeling that they were puppets whose strings were pulled by mother and father.

4. Parental overconcern with fears of being fat and dieting was apparent in every case. The mother and/or the father and other relatives were afraid of being fat and dieted. In some families there was a predominance of the father's fear-of-being-fat complex.

The research of my colleagues and myself (Wilson, Hogan, and Mintz; 1983) has confirmed Sperling's (1978) obserations that specific conflicts and attitudes of the mother and/or father predispose a child for the development of psychosomatic symptoms (e.g., a mother's overconcern with bowel functions may predispose a child for ulcerative colitis). The specific etiological factor in anorexia is the parental preoccupation with dieting and the fear of being fat, which is transmitted to the daughter by identification. The other features of this profile are also found in the parents of patients suffering from psychosomatic symptoms such as asthma, migraine headaches, and colitis. The last two features of the profile are usually uncovered only by psychoanalysis.

5. Exhibitionistic parental sexual and toilet behavior, whose significance was completely denied, was found in every family. Doors in these homes were not locked, and bedroom and toilet doors often were left open, which facilitated the curious child's viewing of sexual relations and toilet functions. The children frequently witnessed parental sexual intercourse. Such experiences, coupled with parental hypermorality and prudishness, caused an inhibition in normal psychosexual development in

the anorexic daughters. Many were virginal, sexually repressed girls who feared boys.

Sours (1980) confirmed the anorexic family psychological profile, but did not observe as much exhibitionistic behavior in families of self-starving young anorexics. However, he notes exhibitionistic parental behavior in families of gorging, vomiting anorexics, including frequent seductive sexual behavior by the fathers.

6. In these families, there was an emotional selection of one child by the parents for the development of anorexia. This child was treated differently than the other children. Such a choice may result from: 1) the carryover of an unresolved emotional conflict from the parents' childhood (e.g., the infant may represent an unconsciously hated parent, brother, or sister); 2) an intense need to control the child, so that the child is treated almost as a part of the body of one parent; 3) a particular psychological situation and emotional state of the parent(s) at the time of the child's birth which seriously damaged the parent–child relationship (e.g., the child may be infantilized because he or she is the last baby or may be overcathected by a parent who has suffered a recent loss).

EXCEPTIONS TO THE FAMILY PSYCHOLOGICAL PROFILE

Hogan (1983), although confirming the difference in character structure of the restrictor and the bulimic, questions any validity to a family psychological profile. He notes a restrictor anorexic who grew up with alcoholic parents. Sperling detailed the analysis of a restrictor anorexic whose mother was psychotic (Wilson, 1983). I have also seen exceptions to this profile. One restrictor anorexic came from a family where the father, mother, and siblings were all obese. Another restrictor's family included a father who was an alcoholic gambler. I realize that the number of cases we have seen is limited and the complexities of early development are multiple. Moreover, in some families one child may be a restrictor, another bulimic. Nevertheless, in the great majority of cases the family psychological profile is applicable.

In many adolescent cases, conjoint or individual therapy of the
bulimic parents which focuses on aspects of the family psychological profile is absolutely necessary for therapeutic success.

PSYCHODYNAMICS OF BULIMIC ANOREXIA NERVOSA

In psychodynamic terms, bulimic fat phobia is rooted in unresolved sadomasochistic oral-phase conflicts that result in an
ambivalent relationship with the mother. Fixation to this phase
of development, with its accompanying fears of object loss, is
caused by maternal and/or paternal overcontrol and overemphasis on food and eating functions as symbols of love. This
unresolved conflict influences each subsequent maturational
phase so that anal, oedipal, and later developmental conflicts
remain unresolved.

The unresolved preoedipal fixation on the mother contributes to the difficulty in psychosexual development and the
intensity of the oedipal development. Bulimic anorexia nervosa,
that is, fat phobia, can be considered a specific pathological
outcome of unresolved oedipal conflicts in a child whose preoedipal relationship to the mother has predisposed her to this
particular reaction under precipitating circumstances.

The genetic influences on this complex are parental conflicts about weight and food specifically, and about aggressive
and libidinal expression generally. In addition, the neurotic
and/or addictive parents are perfectionistic, significantly denying the impact on the developing child of their exhibitionistic
toilet, bedroom, and other behavior. Other genetic factors are
cultural, societal, and general medical influences, as well as
secondary identification with women and/or men who share the
fear-of-being-fat complex. From an economic point of view, the
unremitting pressure of repressed, unsublimated aggressive
and libidinal drives, conflicts, and fantasies is a central issue for
these inhibited patients. The terror of loss of control (i.e., of
becoming fat) comprises the conscious fear of overeating and
the unconscious fear of incorporating body parts, smearing or

eating feces, bleeding to death, mutilating and/or becoming nymphomaniacal, which could result in orgastic pleasure.

All these feared drive eruptions are held in check by the terror of retaliatory punishment from the archaic superego. These conflicts are displaced onto and condensed into the fear of being fat. The defective bulimic ego is unable to contain impulses to gorge; there is a giving in to voraciousness, and then an attempt at self-punishment and undoing by vomiting and/or the use of laxatives. In the bulimic there are also parallel attempts by the ego to suppress and repress libidinal and aggressive fantasies, drives, and impulses; a surrender to these impulses and masochistic behavior which also expresses self-punishment and undoing.

From a structural point of view, ego considerations are central. In the preoedipal years, the ego of the bulimic anorexia-prone (fat phobic) child becomes split. One part develops in a pseudonormal fashion: cognitive functions, the self-observing part of the ego, adaptive capacities, and other ego functions appear to operate normally. While the restrictor anorexics in childhood are most often described as "perfect" and have excellent records in school, the bulimic anorexics have more evidence of disobedience and rebellion at home and school. In adolescence, there is more antisocial behavior, sexual promiscuity, and addiction. The ego represses, denies, displaces, externalizes, and projects conflicts onto the fear-of-being-fat complex. In many cases, conflicts are displaced onto habits such as thumb sucking, enuresis, encopresis, nail biting, head banging, and hair pulling. In other cases, there is a concomitant displacement and projection of conflict onto actual phobic objects in some patients, bulimia anorexia alternates with other psychosomatic disease syndromes. This split in the ego manifests itself in the intense, psychoticlike denial of the displaced wishes, conflicts, and fantasies. In other words, the split-off neurotic part of the personality is denied in the fear-of-being-fat complex.

From an adaptive point of view, conflicts at each maturational and libidinal phase are denied, displaced, and projected onto the fear of being fat. Conflicts in separation–individuation are paramount and are denied by the parents and developing child (Mushatt, 1975, 1982). Normal adaptive conflict is avoided and denied. Many parents of bulimics raise them in an unreal, overprotected world. Perfectionistic parents impair the ego's decision-making functions with their infantilizing intrusions into every aspect of their child's life. In each case, a focus of therapy is on the pregenital object relations that have been caused by the unresolved parental relationships and conflicts in separation–individuation.

Unlike Sperling (1978), I, along with Hogan (1983) and Mintz (1983), include males under the diagnostic category of anorexia nervosa. Mintz (1983) and Welch (1983) have shown that male bulimic anorexics have oedipal and preoedipal fixations and unresolved problems in separation–individuation, severe latent homosexual conflicts, a feminine identification, and the same fear-of-being-fat complex seen in the females, caused by an identification with the mother and/or the father's fear of being fat.

BULIMIC DEPRESSION AND ITS CAUSES

As the conflicts underlying bulimic symptoms are analyzed, a variety of affects emerge, particularly those of depression (Wilson et al., 1983). It is the analysis of affects, particularly depressive affects, that is crucial to therapeutic success. However, as these affects emerge various psychic shifts occur which result in bulimia being replaced by other symptoms.

The components of bulimic depression are overdetermined and are caused by unresolved oedipal and preoedipal conflicts. Among the important determinants are:

1. Unhappiness because of failure to achieve the perfectionistic goals required by the archaic superego.
2. Unhappiness because of neurotic guilt inflicted by the archaic superego, which legislates against the expression of libidinal or aggressive impulses and fantasies.

3. Unhappiness because of failure to achieve mature object relations.
4. Unhappiness and anger because of a failure to actualize magical narcissistic fantasies.
5. Unhappiness at adaptive failures.
6. Unhappiness because of failure to achieve normal separation–individuation from parents or parent surrogates.

CLINICAL MATERIAL

The following clinical material from two patients illustrates the (1) replacement of bulimic symptoms by a psychosomatic symptom, asthma, and (2) the replacement of bulimic symptoms by structural changes in the underlying personality disorder.

CASE EXAMPLE 1

A twenty-five-year-old lawyer, Ms. A., came to analysis for symptoms of chronic bulimic anorexia nervosa. An intelligent young woman, she dated the onset of her symptoms to her first year away at college when she felt homesick and depressed. She initially went on a diet and lost 30 pounds over a two-month period. However, she could not maintain the diet and began gorging, vomiting, and taking large quantities of laxatives (Ducolax). Her bulimic episodes were three to five times daily.

Developmental. The patient was born and brought up in Los Angeles; she had an amnesia for large periods of her childhood development. She recalled nightmares at the time of her second brother's birth when she was four years old and school phobia during the first grade at age six. She had a habit of nail biting which cleared up "more or less" in adolescence. She was, on the surface, a very well-behaved little girl. She had two younger brothers, one who was born when she was one year old and another when she was four. She knew that her mother was sick during the pregnancies, with symptoms of nausea and vomiting.

When she was twelve, her parents divorced. The divorce was a shock to the patient as the parents had kept their many years of quarreling from the children. As in many anorexic homes, the mother, a hypermoral, religious woman, whose only "vice" was smoking, was the dominant force. The father smoked cigarettes, had a boisterous sense of humor, and enjoyed social drinking. He was looked down on and seen as "the spoiler." His considerable success in the insurance business was also deprecated. After the divorce, the father remarried within a year's time, moving into a house two blocks from the patient's home. She saw a lot of father, his new wife (a divorcée) and their little girl, who was five years younger than the patient.

The parents' behavior correlated with the bulimic–anorexic psychological profile (Wilson, 1980a, 1983, 1985a 1986a; Wilson et al., 1983): perfectionism, repression of emotions, infantilizing decision making for the child, parental dieting and fears of being fat, sexual and toilet exhibitionism that was denied (the father wore boxer shorts at home and the patient had many memories of seeing his genital half-revealed).

The patient had been unconsciously chosen by the mother for the development of anorexia. Contributing to this choice was the fact that the patient was the first child and the only female. The patient knew that her mother had felt guilty about her sons' births, though she felt they were favored as males. "Mother felt she had to atone to me because I was no longer the only child."

Psychosexual Development. The patient did not "know much about sexual matters." The mother was a strict Catholic, the father a "lapsed Baptist," and the patient went to church and confession until adolescence, when she came to the conclusion that religion made no sense and became an agnostic. She was not prepared for pubertal changes and menstrual periods, which were late, at fourteen years of age. She did not date until the third year of college. Her boyfriend, a classmate, was Jewish, and in their senior year she moved in with him. They talked of marriage, but she was afraid of her parents' objections to the difference in religious background.

At the time of referral, the patient was functioning in a law firm with great difficulty. She was depressed and tried to relieve the depression by prodigious eating, which set in motion self-induced vomiting to expiate, and the taking of laxatives, up to 100 Ducolax a day. She had been on antidepressant medication and in group therapy and individual psychotherapy one or two times a week for many years. She gained some insight into her conflicts, but no improvement in her symptoms. She came for consultation through a friend of hers who had resolved her neurosis and eating disorder by analysis. My evaluation at this time was of a mixed neurosis. She began four-times-a-week analytic therapy.

Course of Therapy. For the first year she was seen vis-à-vis. I interpreted her defenses against admitting to her anger toward and mistrust of her previous therapy, other doctors she had seen, and me. For a time she called me on weekends, depressed and crying, and I interpreted the primitive preoedipal need to totally control me, to have my exclusive love and attention in the context of dreams and associative material. The calls decreased and stopped after six months of treatment. At this phase of therapy, her masochism was interpreted in the context of the harsh demands of her archaic superego and the guilt she experienced over admitting to any conflict. Next, defenses against aggressive conflicts and impulses were interpreted.

Asthma as a Bulimic Equivalent. Six months into the third year of analysis, the patient evidenced a "flight into health." Her episodes of bulimia stopped, she curtailed her use of Ducolax to one or two a day. She reported improvements in her sexual relations with her boyfriend. At her job, she received a promotion, was assigned to work on an important case with a senior lawyer, and her salary was doubled. She began an exercise program. Most significant of all, her periods returned, although they were irregular. To the patient and external world, these healthy changes seemed remarkable; however, she began to develop increasingly severe episodes of bronchial

asthma. She had had minimal asthma in early adolescence; tests
showed her to be allergic to dust and molds. The following
material documents the replacement of bulimic symptoms by
asthma.

The patient began a session reporting that she awoke with
asthmatic wheezing after the following dream:

> I made a serious factual mistake in a letter to a client.
> There was a bulimic woman who went out of control and
> began ravenously eating a box of chocolates. My mother
> and a policewoman came into the room and began scream-
> ing at the woman to stop gorging. Then I was walking
> down a deserted waterfront area, crying and feeling lonely.
> Next I was talking to a priest about how lonely I was. The
> priest was confused with my analyst.

> Associations: When I first began to gorge and vomit,
> my mother once caught me doing it and yelled at me. The
> bulimic woman in the dream must be part of me that would
> like to gorge and vomit again, the way I used to do when
> anyone left me or anything bothered me. Last night I felt
> depressed and cried. I have been crying on and off in
> recent days and have not told you about it. Last night I was
> angry about the time analysis takes and the money I pay
> you. When I used to go to confession, the priest would
> absolve me of guilt if I confessed; you don't do that. You
> confront me with my problems and my conflicts in asserting
> myself. I guess I saw mother and sometimes must see you
> like a policewoman. I know you aren't and you tell me
> about my strict, perfectionistic conscience. I guess that may
> be the policewoman inside me. Sometimes I can't believe
> the things that analysis uncovers; that it is healthy to assert
> myself. The mistake in the letter to the client is my obs-
> ession with being perfect, that I have to endlessly check
> and recheck my work. The senior partner the other day
> told me I worry too much, that people make mistakes, and
> we are only human. It is not that I just recheck my work,
> I have a law clerk working for me and I do her work for
> her. I even make her reprints of law opinions she should

look up for herself. She has not learned to use our law library yet because I baby her so much. She teases me and calls me "Mamma X.," for always taking care of her.

My interpretation to the patient was to remind her that I had told her that I was not going to see her for sessions the following week and that she had not mentioned her feelings about separation; that she wished I was a priest (mother), who would always be there for her; that I would have no one else to love except her, and that I would have no self-interest, not cancel sessions, and not charge her. The patient confirmed the interpretation, saying, "It is funny, I forgot about the canceled sessions. I must be angry with you and want to go on vacation myself. I am sick and tired working the way I do."

Two weeks later the patient reported a dream in which she was a little girl in bed with her mother. She began to choke as gas filled the room. She thought someone left the oven gas jets on. She was afraid of dying.

Associations: She awoke from the dream wheezing from an asthma attack. She thought of the previous evening when she and her boyfriend went to a dinner party at her mother's; that evening mother was "full of gas"—she never stops talking about herself and her wonderful work as an interior decorator. There was one thing which had always really bothered the patient about mother—her cigarette smoking. "Mother was so hypermoral; she had no vices except her smoking. Mother had a perfect figure and often said that if she stopped smoking she would gain weight." When the patient was fourteen years old, she tried smoking secretly in her room, but mother caught her and screamed at her to stop; that it was bad enough that she, mother, had the habit. After that, the patient went on a diet—it was the beginning of her eating disorder. More thoughts about the dream were that smokers gas people, make nonsmokers ill, by smoking. "Mother must know this; how could she smoke like that at her own dinner party?" Once when the patient was young, a baby-sitter who made herself a cup of coffee left the gas on and the patient, who was asleep, woke up choking on the gas that leaked into her room. She remembered the sitter rushing into the room and frantically opening the windows. Her final thought was that the gas in the dream was mother's cigarette smoke, that she must have choked on the smoke as a little girl. Mother's fingers were always yellow with nicotine stains. An interpretation was made that the patient was choked to death by asthma as a punishment for her anger at her mother and that there was a talion wish to poison mother with gas (smoke) as she felt poisoned by mother.

The analysis of the sadomasochistic conflicts that were repressed and internalized in the psychosomatic symptoms resulted in a clearing of the patient's asthma. Space does not permit detailing the analysis of the underlying personality disorder in this patient. Analytic technique in such cases has been described by my colleagues and myself (Karol, 1980; Mintz, 1980; Wilson, 1980a; Wilson and Mintz, in press).

CASE EXAMPLE 2

Structural Shift in the Pesonality Disorder Replacing Bulimic Symptoms. A thirty-eight-year-old married woman, Ms. R., came for consultations because of marital conflicts. She felt that she was in some way provoking her husband. He complained that she was bitchy. Ms. R. had been born and brought up in a suburb of Chicago. In childhood, she was enuretic and a thumb sucker until nine years of age. Her mother was the perfect "chicken soup mother," who did everything for her children. The patient was the youngest of three children. A two-years-older sister was married and had two children. Her brother, four years older, was also married with one child. Ms. R. had been the baby, a Jewish-American princess, a role that she was teased about, but that she not so secretly enjoyed. Ms. R. was a very well-behaved girl and did well in school. Beginning in her early years, she took ballet and the family thought she would become a ballet star, but in adolescence she broke her ankle practicing ballet steps and gave up formal ballet although she continued with daily exercise, jogging, and aerobics. She was inhibited about sexual matters, and upset and shy at the development of precocious puberty at nine years of age. She thought that her first menstrual bleeding was a hemorrhage, and was ashamed of the development of her breasts. She achieved excellent marks in high school and college.

She married the first man who really dated her, a medical student at a university near the women's college she attended. Shortly after marriage she developed symptoms of bulimic anorexia nervosa and after four years of hiding her symptoms from her husband, a successful surgeon, she came to me for consultation. I referred her to a colleague for analysis. She was in analysis for four years and her bulimic symptoms cleared; however, she terminated analysis prematurely against the advice of the analyst who told her that she had not worked through her resentment and anger with men. For a time following termination, she did well. She had a child, a healthy little boy, and she was promoted to senior editor in a publishing firm. However, she had increasingly severe and painful quarrels with her husband. She was completely free of her bulimic symptoms but her fear of being fat and obsession with a thin body image, although less intense, still preoccupied her. The following clinical material illustrates the structural shift that replaced the bulimic symptoms in this patient.

In the second week of therapy the patient reported a dream of an operation in which some flesh was removed. Her associations were to a fight that she had had with her husband after she bought a book entitled *How to Take 20 Pounds Off Your Man.* (Simon & Schuster, 1985) Her thoughts were that her husband was 20 pounds overweight and did not exercise regularly. He became angry when she brought up the book and suggested that he join a health club. She thought of how much she enjoyed her aerobics class. She realized her husband worked long hours in the hospital and knew that she should not nag him about his weight, but she could not help it. She knew that her nagging had something to do with their not having had sex for two weeks. Her association to the dream was the thought that surgeons should be able to remove fat from people's bodies by operations. The interpretation was made that the patient still had the process in her that demanded instant perfection of

herself and her husband, and that it would be in her best interests not to pressure her husband about losing weight because
she had not fully analyzed her fear-of-being-fat complex. Her
reply was that she knew I was right, that her husband repeatedly
told her that he was not that much overweight, that she had a
thing about weight, and that she turned him off by talking
about weight.

Two weeks later, the patient reported another dream of
a woman's body with a weird sort of penis attached to it. The
patient's associations were to missing her husband who was away
at a medical convention. She knew her husband was faithful to
her, but she was jealous of the women doctors he would be with
at the meeting. She recalled how angry her mother used to be
with father when he came back from business trips. Father
"confessed" to mother that he was unfaithful to her. As a little
girl, the patient knew that father and mother quarreled behind
closed doors, but she could never think of her parents divorcing
even though when she got older, her mother told her of their
quarrels. She remembered father in the bathroom urinating,
his genitals looked so strange. She could not recall whether she
saw his testicles or not. The patient ruefully said about the
dream, "I must want my husband to be a female with a penis."

The interpretation was made that the patient unconsciously
confused her husband with her father and that she was expressing anger (castrating him) that she could not express to
father as a child. The patient burst into tears and said that on
the weekend she had been depressed and missed her mother.
A further interpretation was made of her wanting me and her
husband to mother her.

It is not possible here to go further into this woman's analysis; of course, her dreams had many other meanings. Her
unresolved penis envy and problems in separation–individuation
were central themes. The one dynamic I want to emphasize is
the defense of identification with the aggressor. An emerging
identification with her father's strict superego enabled her to
master her bulimic symptoms (her acting-out impulses). As she
talked of her "bitchy," controlling loss of temper with her husband and me in the transference, many memories emerged of

her father's rigid, perfectionistic, moralistic demands and his outbursts of righteous anger. At meals, for example, he would snap at her about her overeating and table manners, just as she did with her husband.

This case illustrates another problem with these patients, that just when major changes occur in symptom resolution, the patients may terminate abruptly before working through their conflicts. In this case, as the patient came to understand the conflicts underlying her neurosis and was able to analyze them in the transference neurosis, the marital quarrels decreased in frequency, and a healthy sexual relationship developed with the husband.

DISCUSSION OF CLINICAL CASES

In Ms. A.'s clinical material we can see that her bulimic behavior, which is represented in the dream as the bulimic female who gorges and vomits, has become ego alien. When a patient dreams of a symptom, they are on the way to giving it up. Likewise, the patient was becoming aware of her identification with masochistic aspects of her mother's behavior. Ms. A.'s developing insight into her archaic, punishing superego is expressed in the appearance of the policewoman in the dream and particularly the wish that the analyst was a priest. All these and other conflicts were lines of interpretation that had been repeatedly interpreted in analysis. The point must be reemphasized, however, that insight and structural change can lead to sudden internalization, and the alternate psychosomatic symptom that emerges should be analyzed like any other symptom formation in the course of analysis. The follow-up dream of being gassed shows that further sadomasochistic impulses and fantasies, which are recurrent conflicts in asthma (Wilson, 1980b), were being worked through in the analysis.

In the second case, we can see what developed when Ms. R. terminated her first analysis prematurely because her bulimic symptoms had cleared. In her bulimic phase, she had been submissive to her husband; she recalled, for example, that one time when she was angry at her husband's being out to play golf, leaving her on a Saturday, she ate a whole box of chocolate cookies, vomited into the cardboard container they came in, which she put in a drawer and "forgot." Her husband found the "smelly" box a week later and "almost lost his temper with her." Now when her husband left her for male activities, instead of gorging and vomiting, she became bitchy and critical. For a time she was flooded with narcissistic fantasies that her husband should be able to work long hours as a physician, but also make the beds, do the dishes, and baby-sit with their child while she went out and did what she wanted. She wanted to resume every premarital pleasure that she had enjoyed: ballet lessons, horseback riding, and travel. Her dream of the woman with the penis reflected her magical wishes of her husband, that he be a magical mother with a breast–phallus. They also reflected her wishes for a penis herself.

DISCUSSION OF BULIMIC EQUIVALENTS

Because of the ineffective and inconsistent ego functioning of the bulimic anorexic (who basically suffers from an impulse disorder), abrupt changes in behavior (acting out), neurotic symptoms, or different manifestations of psychosomatic disease can be caused by changes in the level of stress or in patterns of defense, in shifting intensity of drives, and in alternating levels of ego integration and regression as well as changes in object relations (Sperling, 1968; Wilson, 1968, 1980b; Mintz, 1980; Wilson et al., 1983). At different times, for reasons that are overdetermined, the conflicts that compose the underlying bulimic personality disorder can be expressed in different illnesses. Depression, anxiety, neurosis, or other psychosomatic symptoms may precede the development of bulimia or may appear after bulimic symptoms subside.

More than thirty years ago, Gero (1953) described anorexia as a depressive equivalent, and Sperling (1959) emphasized that psychosomatic symptoms in general were depressive equivalents. Bulimia has been reported as alternating with stiff neck

(Wilson et al., 1983), ulcerative colitis (Tucker, 1952; Sperling, 1983), migraine (Hogan, 1983), asthma (Mintz, 1983), celiac disease (Ferrara and Fontana, 1966), and masturbation (Levin, 1985).

Bulimic equivalents are an aspect of the more general problem of psychosomatic equivalents (Wilson and Mintz, in press). I have seen psoriaris replaced by asthma (Wilson, 1968), migraine by ulcerative colitis and then by migraine, obesity by hypertension, and ulcer by globus hystericus (Wilson, 1981). A patient of Mintz's (1980) developed in sequence ulcerative colitis, asthma, depression, self-destructive acting out, migraine, noninfectious monoarthular arthritis of the knee, angioneurotic edema, eczema, and nasorhinitis.

I regard bulimic fat phobia (anorexia nervosa) as an impulse disorder and the first phase of analysis involves the interpretation of such defenses as denial, rationalization, withholding, lying, projection, and projective identification so that the patient can become aware of the split-off narcissistic aspects of their personality disorder, particularly in the dyadic transference. As this part of the patient's behavior is analyzed, acting out, of which gorging and vomiting are manifestations, becomes ego alien and abrupt processes of *internalization* can occur.

INTERNALIZATION AND SUPEREGO FORMATION

My research confirms Blum's (1985) observations

> that the superego is never fully independent of the original objects throughout childhood and adolescence, and the child continues to interact with the postoedipal parents (as well as with peers). The individual, his original objects, and surroundings are all different from what they were in childhood. To my mind, the superego has a far greater legacy than as "heir to the Oedipus complex." In addition to the preoedipal roots of the superego, the internalization and consolidation of parental relationships, their authority, at-

titudes, and values continue beyond the oedipal phase through preadult life.

Cognitively, the child can gradually make more subtle moral discriminations and more abstract moral judgments, distinguishing his own moral code from that of the parents and others. The parents are at first idealized, as are their standards and values. The child's first "morality" is conformity and blind obedience to the parents' authority and appraisal.

Initially, externalized authority and global introjections give way to more selective, enduring identifications. [p. 891]

Anna Freud (1936) stated, "True morality begins when the internalized criticism, now embodied in the standard exacted by the superego, coincides with the ego's perception of its own fault" [p. 119].

The Healing of the Split in the Ego and Its Transference Manifestations

When bulimic symptoms subside in analysis, the split in the ego (Wilson et al., 1983) has been partially resolved and the abrupt processes of internalization occur in the context of the development of the superego. No matter what the age of the bulimic anorexic, a delayed adolescent maturational process occurs in analysis. However, as Ms. A.'s dream so graphically illustrated: revived archaic superego introjects emerge, coexisting with new superego developmental elements. The dream images of the mother, policewoman, and priest, and the confusion of the analyst with the priest, illustrate the working through of superego conflicts in the analysis. In this situation, the patient can abruptly project the archaic superego introject onto the analyst (projective identification).

I described the appearance of asthma de novo in analysis (1968, 1980b) as a manifestation of processes of abrupt internalization and superego formation in a patient with a severe impulse disorder. The dynamics involved in the development of asthma in this case shed light on similar processes that occur in the analysis of bulimics when asthma and other symptoms develop.

CASE EXAMPLE 3

In 1968, I reported on a patient who, with no previous history of asthma, developed symptoms of bronchial asthma in the terminal phase of her analysis. The asthmatic attacks, some seventeen in all, responded to analysis; the patient terminated treatment successfully, free of asthma.

The patient, a twenty-five-year-old woman, came to analysis with intense oral conflicts. An alcoholic who drank herself into a stupor every evening after work, she was severely depressed and suicidal. She lost one job after another. Behind a facade of helpless, childlike behavior was overwhelming oral greed. Denial and exhibitionism characterized her neurotic parents' behavior as she grew up. The wealthy socialite mother was an alcoholic whose drinking was denied completely by the family. The father, a very successful businessman, insisted that the family was poor and they lived in a rent-controlled building in an impoverished area. A compulsive man, he did daily exercises in the nude in a ritualistic fashion in front of his wife, son, and daughter. These exercises, which were preceded by a large glass of water and followed by a copious urination, dated from the time of the patient's earliest memory. He also kept binoculars on the living room windowsill so that he could look at certain exhibitionistic women in nearby apartments. A second analysis confirmed my 1968 hypothesis that transference caused by a precipitous superego formation played a significant role in the asthma de novo. Also clearly demonstrated was the pathological effect that perverse sexual and toilet behavior had upon the patient's psychosexual development.

The patient's asthma developed in the analysis as the expression of a final wish to control and defeat me by being sick and forcing a termination of treatment. As the patient later admitted, she wanted to marry her big lover because on the surface he looked healthy, but she knew that she could control him. She wanted to defeat me as I had come to stand for the end of her acting out.

In the working through of unresolved oedipal conflicts in the transference neurosis, the most regressive narcissistic drives struggled for expression. A new and strict superego forced an internalization of incorporative impulses that had formerly been externalized in her acting out. Displacement upwards had already been established in the symptom of stream weeping. This weeping had expressed a wish to get sympathy and pity; however, as Greenacre (1945) points out, the tears are crocodile tears and they mask intense oral-sadistic incorporative drives. This patient wanted to devour with the eyes. The tears also variously symbolized urine, semen, and saliva. This symptom had been successfully interpreted many times in the analysis. At the time of the development of asthma, there had been marked improvement in the patient's ability to let herself cry and to tolerate affects. All her oral sadism was internalized and expressed by way of respiratory incorporation. Many times previously in analysis, she had expressed wishes to kill, bite, and devour me; and at other times, to kill herself in order to placate her primitive superego.

The patient's psoriasis which had expressed preoedipal exhibitionistic drives cleared up prior to the development of the asthma, which was now the last somatic outlet for this neurotic exhibitionism. A physical illness, pneumonia, which occurred at the height of the oedipal period, provided a channel (somatic compliance) for the expression of symptoms when oedipal conflicts were revived and worked through in analysis.

Unanalyzed transference played a crucial role in the precipitation of the asthma. What took me by surprise was the precipitous superego formation. Many different conflicts were interpreted during the two years that she had asthma, but I would like to emphasize the interpretation of the overly strict superego. An example of such an interpretation occurred at the time of her third asthmatic attack. The patient reported that she had been walking to work and had the thought that

I (the analyst) was really trying to help her; then she suddenly got asthma. In the session, I pointed out to her that if she admits to my doing anything for her, she has to do everything to please me, she has to be perfect; her only recourse is to be sick and asthmatic.

I would like to contrast the dynamics in these cases with those I observed in the analysis of another case. A male patient had been enuretic up to the age of five years, at which time (following a tonsillectomy), the enuresis cleared but he developed severe bronchial asthma. The asthma did not subside until he left his home (mother) to go to college. In this case, the development of asthma represented clearly an identification with the father, who had been an asthmatic for many years. Urinary fantasies were prominent in this case. The patient always utilized condoms in his sexual affairs. Analysis revealed that following intercourse, which was usually effected with a partially full bladder, he would urinate into the condom, ostensibly to find out if there were any leaks in the rubber. Unconsciously, urine and ejaculation were equated, and his repressed wish was to drown (impregnate) the woman with urine. The man's asthmatic attacks were a talion punishment for this sadistic infantile wish: he was drowned for wanting to drown. In this man's case, as in the first patient, an overly strict superego was present while the patient had asthma. Polymorphous perverse impulses emerged as analysis progressed and acting out became a serious problem. The course of analysis was the reverse of the asthma de novo case in that he started with the strict superego and asthma, which she developed in termination.

Space does not permit further detailing of the case of Ms. A. Her allergies to dust and molds had anal meanings. The analysis of her laxative habit revealed sadomasochistic anal fantasies and conflicts. In the majority of analyzed cases of asthma, the primary fixations are at the anal level (Sperling, 1963; Wilson, 1982). However, the fantasies repressed and internalized in asthma are specific for the individual case, but not for asthma in general. Oral fixations and fantasies appear in every case; for example, the asthma de novo case dreamt of me (the analyst) as hamburger meat that she was eating. In a significant number of cases, urinary fantasies and fixations predominate (Fink and Schneer, 1963; Knapp, 1963; Wilson, 1968; 1980b).

BULIMIC EQUIVALENTS AND THE
USE OF ANTIDEPRESSANT MEDICATIONS

An examination of the recent use of antidepressants to relieve the depression of bulimics highlights the psychodynamics of bulimic equivalents.

Because of the increasing number of reports of the use of antidepressants in the treatment of bulimic anorexics (Walsh, Stewart, and Wright, 1982; Brotman, Herzog, and Woods, 1984; Pope and Hudson, 1984; Walsh, Stewart, Roose, Gladis, and Glassman, 1984; Wilson, Hogan, and Mintz, 1983), I recently (1982a,b,c) explored the psychodynamics and etiology of the bulimic anorexic's depression; outlined our psychoanalytic technique with bulimics and documented the psychoanalytic resolution of depressed affects in the course of treatment; and described in detail the dangers, risks, and consequences of the use of medication.

The rationale for the use of antidepressant medications is that in some cases they achieve dramatic resolution of symptoms which seem related to the finding of affective disorder in the family (Pope and Hudson, 1984). On the other hand, Altshuler and Weiner (1985) seriously question the research methodology that links restrictor and bulimic anorexia nervosa to a family history of major depression. Whatever genetic, constitutional factors there are in bulimic anorexics (Pope and Hudson, 1984), they do not preclude psychoanalytic treatment. Some of our cases would have been diagnosed as "endogenous depression"; however, they were analyzable. The parallel may be with asthmatics, some of whom have a constitutional genetic allergic predisposition. Such asthmatic patients can be successfully analyzed. After analysis they may still test positively for allergies, but they no longer experience asthmatic attacks in conflictual situations (Sperling, 1978).

The treatment of bulimics has to be guided by the psycho-dynamic diagnosis of the individual case and the presenting clinical situation (Wilson, Hogan, and Mintz, 1983). The presenting situation can be one of alcoholism, drug addiction, and/or a suicidal crisis. Obviously, if the patient is acutely suicidal, his life must be preserved; and if an antidepressant drug can alter the patient's behavior, it, like other medication and total parenteral nutrition, may have to be used. However, if analytic psychotherapy or analysis is feasible, the patient will have to be weaned from the drug to which they may have developed a psychological addiction. Bulimic depression is caused by multiple preoedipal and oedipal conflicts. A crucial goal of the psychotherapy of bulimia is to strengthen the patient's ego so that they can face and tolerate both realistic and neurotic depression. Like the restrictor, the bulimic anorexic is obsessed with fantasies of remaining young forever and being free of any conflict, realistic or neurotic. They do not want to grow up (Wilson et al., 1983). They deny the conflicts they manifest; for example, their dependency on their parents or parent surrogates. They vehemently deny the masochistic nature of their symptoms and their character structure. It is the aim of a psychodynamic treatment to analyze their defenses against experiencing painful emotions, particularly depressed feelings. It is an advance in therapy when they become depressed and cry. To relieve depression by medication prevents the analysis of this most important aspect of their neurosis. Moreover bulimic anorexics experience hyperactive states. In these anxiety conditions they gorge and vomit endlessly, and will also disobey monoamine oxidase dietary restrictions inducing dangerous side effects and may ingest dangerous amounts of prescribed medication. Supervised cases attempted suicide with aspirin, acetaminophen, ipecac, imipramine, and amitriptyline. A colleague's case experienced a resolution of bulimic symptoms following the administration of phenelzine, but developed a toxic manic psychosis, became noncommunicative, and acted out sexually. Dangerous overdosage with laxatives is a manifestation of the either/or nature of their ego functioning (Sperling, 1978; Wilson et al., 1983). Bulimics, for example, resort to extremes of exercise to relieve anxiety and take off weight. Only a psychodynamic approach can change this neurotic behavior. Because of unresolved oral conflicts, the bulimic patient believes in magical solutions to problems, is intolerant of delay, and is ambivalent about such a lengthy learning process as analytic therapy. The temporary removal of symptoms can eventuate in premature termination of treatment.

The crucial therapeutic force is the transference neurosis. Patients must reexperience in the transference the dyadic relationship with the mother and understand the depression and rage at not being able to control the therapist as they did the mother. Likewise, later in therapy, the triadic Oedipus complex emerges and can be analyzed in the transference neurosis. If they are on medication, the transference loses its intensity and the therapist's interpretations become diluted and intellectual. From the ego and psychodynamic point of view, a paradox emerges. Only those bulimics who are well motivated and less regressed can be medicated without the risk of alternate symptom development or acting out; however, it is just such healthier patients who have the most favorable psychotherapeutic prognosis.

In those situations where the use of medication (particularly antidepressants) is necessary, i.e., medical crises, when patients cannot be motivated for psychotherapy, in treatment stalemates, or where cost and therapist availability are problems, the use of drugs is a trade-off with potentially disadvantageous consequences. Therapeutic stalemates can occur in cases of chronic bulimia where there has been a long-term resistance to insight and change in analytic therapy.

While medication in some intractable cases may facilitate therapy, we have found that even in severely regressed states knowledgeable interpretations have resolved the impasses. Mintz's (1983) detailing of the analysis of such a severely regressed hospitalized bulimic and my (1983) analysis of an emaciated bulimic's repeated provocative, brinksmanshiplike, and suicidal use of laxatives document the effectiveness of our technique in these crisis situations. Before resorting to medication, consultation and/or supervision are advisable. In cases seen in consultation and supervision, and in cases presented to the psychosomatic study groups of the Psychoanalytic Association of New York and the American Psychoanalytic Association, such therapeutic impasses have been resolved by a deeper psychodynamic understanding, a review of the countertransference conflicts of the therapist, and an exploration of the often subtle treatment sabotage on the part of the parents, who frequently are unable to accept self-assertive behavior by the enmeshed bulimic anorexic. It must be kept in mind that at best medication may make the patient more amenable to dynamic therapy, but it cannot change the underlying impulsive, masochistic personality disorder.

ANALYTIC CURE, BODY IMAGE, AND BULIMIC EQUIVALENTS

Unless the bulimic anorexic's pathological fear-of-being-fat body image is resolved, one cannot say that there has been a "cure" (Wilson, 1982; Wilson et al., 1983). The conscious fear of being fat masks unconscious preoedipal and oedipal conflicts. In the first case, during the times that she was asthmatic, there was a decathexis of the conscious fear of being fat and obsession with being thin, but the unconscious fear-of-being-fat complex and distorted body image were not basically changed.

In the second case, although Ms. R.'s bulimic symptoms had been cleared in the first analysis, there was still a disturbed body image. She was no longer intensely fat phobic, but was still afraid of being fat and wanted to keep her figure on the thin side; not thin to a skeletal level, but thin in the sense that she wanted to have a muscular body with no fat or "flab." Although she was no longer extremely compulsive about exercise, she was still overly preoccupied with it; she jogged, did isometric exercises, and went to a health club as often as she could. Body–phallus conflicts still had to be analyzed.

During the alcoholic phase of her analysis, the asthma de novo case had a very disturbed body image. She consciously hated her obese body and her psoriatic lesions that were even on her breasts. When she developed impulse control and a functioning superego, she was able to give up her addictions to food, cigarettes, and alcohol. However, she *developed a fear-of-being-fat body image*. She exercised regularly and was very careful about her figure, keeping her weight 4 or 5 pounds under normal. Further analysis was needed to resolve this body image pathology.

All three of these women secretly controlled the frequency, intensity, and quality of their sexual relationships by controlling their weight. When they took off a few pounds, their lovers would unconsciously react to the castrating meaning of this behavior and become upset or angry. These women avoided being curvaceous, zoftig, and sexy, which they knew would arouse a man. The deepest fear of the bulimic anorexic is of losing control. Likewise, antidepressant drugs may clear bulimic symptoms, but they do not resolve the underlying body image pathology.

Summary

If bulimic symptoms clear before there has been sufficient change in the underlying neurosis and the object relations, bulimic equivalents emerge which include self-destructive acting out; an alternate addictive disorder such as obesity, alcoholism, or drug addiction; alternate psychosomatic symptom formation; neurotic symptom formation; or severe regressive symptom formation. Clinical material was presented to document in one patient the replacement of bulimia by psychosomatic asthma and in another patient the replacement of bulimia by a neurotic character development, epitomized by "bitchy" behavior.

Anorexia nervosa is a generic term that includes both the restrictor and bulimic syndromes. The term *anorexia nervosa* is a medical misnomer, a historical artifact, as these patients do not suffer from a lack of appetite, but the opposite—a fear of being overwhelmed by impulses from every developmental level, including voracious hunger. Both groups of patients have a fear-of-being-fat complex caused by similar unconscious conflicts. Fat phobic symptoms and the underlying personality disorder are caused by an identification with certain parental conflicts and attitudes which are described as a parental psychological profile. Restrictor anorexics (fat phobics), part of whose ego structure resembles that of the compulsive neurotic, overcontrol both the impulse to gorge and other impulse gratifications. Bulimics have the same fear of being fat and obsession with being thin, but because of deficient ego controls they give in to gorging and other impulse gratifications. Because of guilt inflicted by their harsh superego, they try to undo and expiate by vomiting and/or the use of laxatives. Bulimic equivalents (acting out, etc.) may develop when drugs are used to relieve symptoms.

REFERENCES

Altshuler, K. A., & Weiner, M. F. (1985), Anorexia nervosa and depression: A dissenting view. *Amer. J. Psychiat.*, 3:328–332.

Blum, H. (1985), Superego formation, adolescent transformation, and the adult neurosis. *J. Amer. Psychoanal. Assn.*, 33:887–909.

Brotman, A. W., Herzog, D. C., & Woods, S. W. (1984), Antidepressant treatment of bulimia: The relationship between binging and depressive symptomatology. *J. Clin. Psychiat.*, 45:7–9.

Bruch, H. (1978), *The Golden Cage: The Enigma of Anorexia Nervosa*. Cambridge, MA: Harvard University Press.

Ceaser, M. (1977), The role of maternal identification in four cases of anorexia nervosa. *Bull. Menn. Clin.*, 41/5:475–486.

Falstein, E. I., Feinstein, S. C., & Judas, I. (1956), Anorexia nervosa in the male child. *Amer. J. Orthopsychiat.*, 26:751–772.

Ferrara, A., & Fontana, V. J. (1966). Celiac disease and anorexia nervosa. *NY State J. Med.*, 66:1000–1009.

Fink, G., & Schneer, J. (1963), Psychiatric evaluation of adolescent asthmatics. In: *The Asthmatic Child: Psychosomatic Approach to Problems and Treatment*, ed. E. Schneer. New York: Harper & Row, pp. 205–223.

Freud, A. (1936), The Ego and the Mechanisms of Defense. *Writings*, Vol. 2. New York: International Universities Press.

Gero, G. (1953), An equivalent of depression: Anorexia. In: *Affective Disorders: Psychoanalytic Contributions to their Study*, ed. P. Greenacre. New York: International Universities Press, pp. 117–189.

Greenacre, P. (1945), Pathological weeping. *Psychoanal. Quart.*, 3:359–367.

Hogan, C. (1983), Psychodynamics. In: *Fear of Being Fat: The Treatment of Anorexia Nervosa and Bulimia*, rev. ed., ed. C. Wilson, C. Hogan, & I. Mintz. New York: Jason Aronson, 1985, pp. 115–128.

Knapp, P. (1963), The asthmatic child and the psychosomatic problem of asthma: Toward a general theory. In: *The Asthmatic Child: Psychosomatic Approach to Problems and Treatment*, ed. H. Schneer. New York: Harper & Row, pp. 234–255.

Karol, C. (1980), The role of primal scene and masochism in asthma. *Internat. J. Psychoanal. Psychother.*, 8:577–592.

Levin, E. (1985), Bulimia as a masturbatory equivalent. *Jefferson J. Psychiat.*, 3:24–35.

Mintz, I. (1980), Multideterminism in asthmatic disease. *Internat. J. Psychoanal. Psychother.*, 8:593–600.

——— (1983), Anorexia nervosa and bulimia in males. In: *Fear of Being Fat: The Treatment of Anorexia Nervosa and Bulimia*, rev. ed., ed. C. Wilson, C. Hogan, & I. Mintz. New York: Jason Aronson, 1985, pp 263–304.

——— (1985a), Psychoanalytic therapy of severe anorexia: The case of Jeanette. In: *Fear of Being Fat: The Treatment of Anorexia Nervosa and Bulimia*, rev. ed., ed. C. Wilson, C. Hogan, & I Mintz. New York: Jason Aronson, pp. 217–244.

——— (1985b), An analytic approach to hospital and nursing care. In: *Fear of Being Fat: The Treatment of Anorexia Nervosa and Bulimia*, rev. ed., ed. C. Wilson, C. Hogan, & I. Mintz. New York: Jason Aronson.

Minuchin, S., Rosman, B. L., & Baker, L. (1978), *Psychosomatic Families: Anorexia Nervosa in Context*. Cambridge, MA: Harvard University Press.

Mushatt, C. (1975), Mind-body environment: Toward understanding the impact of loss on psyche and soma. *Psychoanal. Quart.*, 44:81–106.

——— (1982), Anorexia nervosa: A psychoanalytic commentary. *Internat. J. Psychoanal. Psychother.*, 9:257–265.

Pope, H. G., Jr., & Hudson, J. I. (1984), *New Hope for Binge-Eaters: Advances in the Understanding and Treatment of Bulimia*. New York: Harper & Row.

Schwartz, H. J. (1986), Bulimia: Psychoanalytic perspectives. *J. Amer. Psychoanal. Assn.*, 34:439–462.

Sours, J. A. (1969), Anorexia nervosa: Nosology, diagnosis, developmental patterns, and power-control dynamics. In: *Adolescence: Psychosocial Perspectives*, ed. G. Caplan & S. Lebovici. New York: Basic Books, pp. 185–212.

——— (1980), *Starving to Death in a Sea of Objects: The Anorexia Nervosa Syndrome*. New York: Jason Aronson.

Sperling, M. (1959), Equivalents of depression in children. *J. Hillside Hosp.*, 8:138–148.

——— (1963), Psychoanalytic study of bronchial asthma in children. In: *The Asthmatic Child: Psychoanalytic Approach to Problems and Treatment*, ed. H. Schneer. New York: Harper & Row, pp. 138–155.

——— (1968), Acting out behavior and psychosomatic symptoms: Clinical and theoretical aspects. *Internat. J. Psycho-Anal.*, 49:250–253.

——— (1978), *Psychosomatic Disorders in Childhood*, ed. O. Sperling. New York: Jason Aronson.

——— (1983), A reevaluation of classification concepts and treatment. In: *Fear of Being Fat: The Treatment of Anorexia Nervosa and Bulimia*, rev. ed., ed. C. Wilson, C. Hogan, & I. Mintz. New York: Jason Aronson, 1985, pp. 51–82.

Thomä, H. (1967), *Anorexia Nervosa*, trans. G. Brydone. New York: International Universities Press.

Tucker, W. I. (1952), Lobotomy case histories: Ulcerative colitis and anorexia nervosa. In: *Anorexia Nervosa*, ed. J. E. Meyer & H. Feldman. Stuttgart: Georg Thieme, pp. 51–59.

Walsh, B. T., Stewart, J., & Wright, L. (1982), Treatment of bulimia with monoamine oxidase inhibitors. *American J. Psychiat.*, 139:1629–1630.

—— Roose, S. P., Gladis, M., & Glassman, A. H. (1984), Treatment of bulimia with phenalzine: A double blind placebo controlled study. *Arch. Gen. Psychiat.*, 41:1105–1109.

Welch, H. (1983), Psychoanalytic therapy: The case of Martin. In: *Fear of Being Fat: The Treatment of Anorexia Nervosa and Bulimia*, rev. ed., ed. C. Wilson, C. Hogan, & I. Mintz. New York: Jason Aronson, 1985, pp. 305–314.

Wilson, C. P. (1968), Psychosomatic asthma and acting out: A case of bronchial asthma that developed *de novo* in the terminal phase of analysis. *Internat. J. Psycho-Anal.*, 49:330–335.

—— (1973), The psychoanalytic treatment of hospitalized anorexia nervosa patients. Paper presented at Psychoanalytic Association of New York meeting, November 19.

—— (1974), The psychoanalysis of an adolescent anorexic girl. Discussion group on "Late Adolescence," S. Ritvo, Chairman. Meeting of the American Psychoanalytic Association, December 12.

—— (1977), Group discussion on "The Parent–Child Relationship in Anorexia Nervosa." Regional Psychoanalytic Meeting, Grossinger's Hotel, October 20.

—— (1978), The psychoanalytic treatment of hospitalized anorexia nervosa patients. Panel discussion on "Anorexia Nervosa." *Bull. Psychoanal. Assn. NY*, 15:5–7.

—— (1980a), The family psychological profile of anorexia nervosa patients. *J. Med. Soc. NJ*, 77:341–344.

—— (1980b), Parental overstimulation in asthma. *Internat. J. Psychoanal. Psychother.*, 8:601–621.

—— (1981), Sand symbolism: The primary dream representation of the Isakower phenomenon and of smoking addictions. In: *Clinical Psychoanalysis*, ed. S. Orgel & B. D. Fine. New York: Jason Aronson, pp. 45–55.

—— (1982), The fear of being fat and anorexia nervosa. *Internat. J. Psychoanal. Psychother.*, 9:233–255.

—— (1983), Fat phobia as a diagnostic term to replace a medical misnomer: Anorexia nervosa. Meeting of the American Academy of Child Psychiatry, October, San Francisco, California. Tapes 96 and 97 by Instant Replay, 760 S. 23rd Street, Arlington, VA 22202.

—— (1985a), Obesity: Personality structure and psychoanalytic treatment. Panel on "Compulsive Eating: Obesity and Related Phenomena." Pietro Castelnuovo-Tedesco, Chairman. Winter Meeting of the American Psychoanalytic Association, December 11, 1985, New York. Tapes obtainable from Teach Em, Inc., Pluribus Press, 160 East Illinois St., Chicago, IL 60611.

—— (1985b), The psychoanalytic treatment of anorexia nervosa and bulimia. Panel on "Anorexia Nervosa and Bulimia." Pietro Castelnuovo-Tedesco, Chairman, Spring Meeting of the American Psychoanalytic Association, Denver, Colorado, May 19. Tapes obtainable from Teach Em, Inc., Pluribus Press, Inc., 160 East Illinois Street, Chicago, IL 60611.

———— (1985c), The treatment of bulimic depression. Paper presented at Grand Rounds, Department of Psychiatry, St. Luke's–Roosevelt Hospital Center, New York, March 6.

———— (1985d), Psychodynamic and/or psychopharmacologic treatment of bulimic anorexia nervosa. In: *Fear of Being Fat: The Treatment of Anorexia Nervosa and Bulimia*, rev. ed., ed. C. P. Wilson, C. G. Hogan, & I. L. Mintz. New York: Jason Aronson.

———— (1986a), The psychoanalytic psychotherapy of bulimic anorexia nervosa. In: *Adolescent Psychiatry*, ed. S. Feinstein. Chicago: University of Chicago Press, pp. 274–314.

———— (1986b), A discussion of E. Levin's paper: Bulimia as a masturbatory equivalent. *Jefferson J. Psychiat.*, 3:24–35.

———— (1986c), Letter in response to J. M. Jonas's paper: The biological basis and treatment of bulimia. *Jefferson J. Psychiat.*, 4:78–82, 83–85.

———— (in press), Psychoanalytic treatment of anorexia nervosa and bulimia. In: *The Eating Disorders*, ed. B. J. Blinder, B. F. Chaitin, & R. Goldstein. Jamaica, NY: S. P. Medical and Scientific Books.

———— Hogan, C. G., & Mintz, I. L., Eds. (1983), *Fear of Being Fat: The Treatment of Anorexia Nervosa and Bulimia*, rev. ed. New York: Jason Aronson, 1985.

———— Mintz, I. L. (in press), *Early Psychic Stress and Somatization*. Riverside NJ: Jason Aronson.

Chapter 16

Bulimia and Kleptomania: Psychodynamics of Compulsive Eating and Stealing*

H. U. ZIOLKO, M.D.

This chapter reports on oral symptomatology in the form of bulimia (compulsive eating) along with kleptomanic behavior (compulsive stealing) in a patient undergoing psychoanalytic treatment. In addition to the bulimia, the kleptomania closely related to it and the insight into its psychogenetic determinants appear to be of interest.

The patient was a twenty-two-year-old female student with unremarkable physical, neurological, and EEG findings at the beginning of treatment. The biographic and anamnestic data showed that the patient was born by cesarean section, nursed for three months, and toilet trained at barely one year old. She was an only child. In addition to the usual childhood illnesses, she had an appendectomy at twelve and a tonsillectomy at sixteen. At eleven, she sustained a concussion when tobogganing. At thirteen, she evidently had poliomyelitis with temporary paralysis of both legs, but no permanent residua. Menarche occurred at thïrteen.

She graduated from high school after an uncomplicated school career, and went on to college. Because of events at the

*This chapter is a translation of Zur Psychodynamik der Ess-und Stehlsucht (Hyperorexie und Kleptomanie). *Psychother. Psychosom.*, 14:226–236 (1966), trans. Joseph Steg, M.D. Reprinted with permission.

college, residence restrictions were imposed and she left. She then worked at a hospital, a children's home, and, lastly, at a publishing house.

FAMILY MEMBERS

Father, who was self-employed, was experienced by her as weak with a tendency to eccentricity. Because of a long-standing illness, he had to walk with a cane and was bent over. The patient recalled that she felt very drawn to him, in fact, "flew at him." Yet she was also shy toward him, reticent and timid, and felt he was not tender enough, even though he spoiled her a great deal. At age eight she would deny any resemblance to her father, saying she would never want to look like him. She was afraid of becoming crippled and sick like him. Particularly when she had polio, she feared that she would be paralyzed and handicapped like her father. Most recently, her father was unhappy because the patient did not let him participate in her life and had a boyfriend whom he disapproved of strongly.

Her mother, though younger than her father, was thirty-six when she was born. The patient experienced her as cold, insensitive, and domineering. She was self-righteous and intolerant, yet complained constantly that no one had time for her; she made limitless claims on the rest of the family. She demanded gratitude and asserted that only parental love is unselfish and that her daughter (the patient) belonged to her (the mother). Thus, she read the patient's mail and turned off the light at a regular time every evening.

The patient found childhood pictures of herself meaningful; whereas she cuddled up to her father, her outstretched arms are always between her and her mother. She felt herself vulnerable to mother's demands and defended herself against these by denying her own dependent needs, often with heightened aggression. She firmly rejected empathy.

Countless experiences of disappointment determined her vengeful impulses and activated her aggression. For example, as a very young child she had found several cans of a chocolate soda which she gorged herself on and then was quite excited and tremulous. Father pumped out her stomach while mother held her. She was profoundly disappointed and angry; she felt herself "overpowered," "something had been done to her." This theme and her reactions to it came up over and over again.

The hateful attitude toward her mother came up repeatedly. She expressed it directly: "I know that I wanted to annihilate my mother, annihilate her completely." This occurred to her when talking about her mother in association to a dream.

Dream 117. She goes swimming in a deeply wooded area. She has a harpoon. She is in the water; there is a crocodile on top of her which she shoots the harpoon at. Behind her is a more frightful crocodile which "tears her leg off." She can barely escape by going up a tree.

This highly aggressive type of interaction with her environment appeared very early in her development. She remembered her own hatefulness toward other children; when she was four to five years old she enjoyed ruining their toys and making them cry. Later, her mother had to bring her to school and then back home, otherwise she would beat up other children on the way. She also gloried in being superior to boys in school, but particularly when other children were physically hurt. It was her goal to hurt others. Furthermore, those who were superior to her had to be brought down. She could not tolerate losing at games; if she didn't win, all hell broke loose.

Her pleasure in destructiveness showed itself periodically in actions such as breaking dishes, ruining things, breaking old bottles, tearing paper, and so on. She rationalized the destructive relationship with her environment in terms of her vengeful impulses. She was getting even for not having that which she was missing, and to which she felt entitled.

The persistence of her vengeful aggressive affects can be seen in relation to a teacher who, in her early school years, once took her sweater off because she was playing with it. She was surprised by this kind of punishment and indignant because of her exposure. She had been overpowered again, something had been done to her. She received no support from her mother for her protests and anger against this teacher. A few years ago when the patient read the obituary of this teacher, she experienced this as a gratifying vindication.

As a child she readily identified with martyrs and heroes, for instance with Brunnhilde, who avenged the shame inflicted on her. When, at age eight, she heard the tale of the king who locked his wife in a cage because of her infidelity, she had the thought that this could never have happened to her. She would have spread the bars of the cage apart and put the king in it.

With regard to her libidinal development, we have to say that experiences of early childhood were mostly subject to infantile amnesia. At age eleven she was fascinated by illustrations of Greek statues of Apollo and Venus, spent her allowance on such books, and thought about studying archaeology or medicine in the future. At age thirteen, she looked for sexually suggestive passages in the *Bible*. At sixteen she was able to defend herself against attempted seduction by a lesbian maid, but reacted to it with increased anxiety and agitation.

The attitude of her parents, especially that of her mother, is notable for its hostility toward sexual drives. For example, when they learned that the children told dirty jokes in a summer camp where the patient stayed at age ten, they took the patient out of the camp. At twelve, the patient saw a newborn baby and asked about the male genital; mother told her indignantly that she shouldn't ask about such things. At this time, mother also condemned sharply any masturbatory activity that she observed. Even at age twenty-one, when she first had intercourse with her boyfriend, mother forbade this form of sexual drive satisfaction also and exacted a promise from the patient that she would not do it again.

Concurrently, patient was preoccupied with sadistic sexual ideation, such as the following dream: The (female) dog is loose, she ran away, a male dog chased her. Then the body of the female dog is brought to the patient. She is criticized because she did not keep her on a leash. She adds, in association, that she was told once that sex would kill her dog.

Dependent wishes were inhibited by fear of being ridiculed and devalued. This reminded her of the ridicule she received from her mother when, in childhood, she once reported proudly that her bones had grown overnight.

Thus she required constant defensive measures to avoid possible inferiority. She inhibited expression of feelings, since she equated this with vulnerability, giving in, and weakness. In this way her real needs, wishes, and claims to deeper tenderness, which she even experienced consciously, were subjected to strict repression and denial.

She experienced menarche in the hospital at age thirteen. She barely remembered that she was totally disconcerted. In this traumatic situation of helplessness she saw herself confronted with the glaring fact that she was a girl. In this role, she felt herself to be worthless. In the same way as the parental condemnation of sexuality as dirty and forbidden motivated her to commit "amoral" acts (of theft), thus using this form of protest to refute her parents, the passive feminine role imposed on her which she did not accept led to an unconscious motivation to retaliate against her parents by active, forbidden, pleasurable behavior.

Her problem about sexual identity becomes clearer when we learn that her parents would have preferred to have a boy, and her mother was disappointed at the time of her birth that she was a girl. When the patient learned this later, she felt betrayed, particularly upon hearing that her father fainted of fright at the news that he had a daughter. Thus she considered therapy, a genital injury at age five, and her menarche as being similarly intolerable and shameful situations. She manifested her resistance in many forms. When separations came up, she would reactivate her oral symptomatology and, through her regressive behavior, attempt again to demonstrate her triumphant superiority. This is shown in her dream: She is lying in a large white bed. She is to undergo an exchange transfusion by the therapists. A large cannula is driven into her larynx; the blood flows out, rises into a container, and is exchanged. She is nauseated and has a bitter taste in her mouth. Bright red blood comes out of her mouth and she spurts it into the therapist's face.

She rebelled and felt betrayed, something was being done

to her again. She associated the larynx to the disgust she felt as a child toward men's Adam's apples including her father's. She also remembered observing the same up-and-down movement at age ten in the genital of a male boxer which attempted to mount her dog as she was taking her for a walk. She beat off this male dog angrily, but with fascination.

Besides the eating disturbances—which will be detailed further—and the kleptomania, numerous anxiety symptoms were present. She remembered that at five she was afraid of the devil, at nine she was afraid of being at home alone, thunderstorms, the Last Judgment, riding by car on highways. She was afraid of swimming, injections, electric appliances, and also examinations in school. Her anxiety would increase if there was a political crisis.

Compulsive symptoms also appeared. In childhood she always had to wash her hands when she lied. This compulsion also occurred after the kleptomanic acts to be detailed below. For some time she slept compulsively on her stomach because she was afraid her appendix would be removed at night.

Family history revealed one ne'er-do-well who also stole from his parents and drank a great deal. Another one ran away from home. A great-grandmother was said to have been interested only in eating and drinking and was unrestrained in her impulses and behavior. An aunt had what was evidently anorexia nervosa following puberty during World War I. She refused to eat more food than the poorest people were able to eat, then died at age twenty-four of tuberculosis. Her brother, the patient's father, witnessed this "hunger period."

In the patient's case, a kind of compulsive eating appeared at about age sixteen during a sea voyage. She kept eating more and more to prevent seasickness; she fed herself as if it were a form of sedation. This led to her being happy only when she could gorge herself. She related this intensified drive to eat to a diffuse feeling of her own incompleteness which she had at the time.

Her greedy demand always to get the biggest piece had already shown itself in childhood. Oral envy also appeared in the form of fear that something would be taken away from her or that she would have too little. Other oral symptoms appeared in childhood in the form of oral protest—she refused to eat bread with rancid butter and stayed hungry until she succeeded in getting something else to eat from mother.

Her bulimic impulses showed themselves more clearly at age nineteen. At the same time there was also significant thirst, which she met with increased drinking (fruit juice, later alcohol). She ate a lot and eagerly, stuffed herself, and saw herself as "senselessly gorged." She experienced this overeating as ego-syntonic and justified, and did it for the most part secretly. Her insatiability was also contributed to by vomiting after meals. This happened or she did it, from her standpoint, in order to be able to eat again, since she was hungry again. Furthermore, it avoided weight gain.

In addition to the vomiting, other self-denying and penance behavior (long walks, compulsive washing) were needed. She also attempted to defend against the overeating by starving herself, albeit her anorexic efforts were minor. She found that the impulse, against which she rebelled in vain, was always there again. Thus overeating was followed by vomiting and renewed hunger, and this, in turn, by overeating. Yet she enjoyed the stress of this drive to eat, through which she felt whole and superior. Thus she would not need to give in to other drives and desires; she gained a feeling of self-sufficiency and independence from others and from the demands of other drives. By eating a lot, she can also get rid of anything that frightens her.

The secret removal of food from dining room or refrigerator, most recently also involving items belonging to her mother, was tantamount to theft. Likewise, the stolen money was used for food. Thus eating and stealing are specifically related to each other.

The symptomatic stealing also had precursors. First, at about age seven, she stole sweets at the market together with a classmate. At one of her childhood birthday parties, she generously handed out candy and other items, then observed that she didn't have any left for herself. She felt cheated and was ready to take back everything she had handed out.

Within six weeks, at age twenty-two, she committed about twenty thefts of money under very similar circumstances. She stole the purses from the pocketbooks which her fellow students had put down in the anteroom of the ladies' room. About a year later, during treatment, there was a relapse. She stole money from nurses in the hospital where she worked, eight times. She spent this almost entirely on food, except for minor gifts to acquaintances, either to gain their sympathy or to relieve herself of guilt feeling.

If she did not consider this behavior reprehensible, but rather that it was justified and that she had the right to commit these thefts, this still represented only an attempted defense against guilt feelings. At least she experienced a feeling of guilt for bringing difficulties and disappointment to her parents. It would appear that she also needed her criminal (symptomatic) actions as defense against guilt feelings over her bulimia, the stealing of food at home, and the unconscious implications of these acts. She remembers restitution fantasies as early as age six; when she grew up, she would give a beggar a significant amount of money. Even when she stole, she thought she was taking something away from somebody who would then be hungry. She even regretted that the victim would then suffer hunger. Here the feelings attributed to the victim coincide with those of the perpetrator.

As with bulimia, the kleptomanic behavior had an intoxicating and sedating quality. This was connected with the tension and the libidinized danger and permitted a discharge through action.

When she succeeded (in her stealing), she felt superior and independent. A kind of triumphant feeling of omnipotence was associated with seeing how easily she could harm others. She found that her destructive tendency was related to stealing. She experienced stealing as a kind of revenge for that diffuse feeling of being damaged.

The particular aggressive (castrating) quality of oral incorporation and manual grasping discharged itself in the kleptomanic act. Oral–nutritive elements are mixed with oral–phallic ones (Stekel, 1922). This coupling with kleptomania which frequently occurs in anorexic patients also is elucidated in Lore Berger's autobiographical description: "Now I learned the joys of kleptomania; the heart-stopping excitement, the satisfied desire, and the contempt for the victim. This grasping and wish to take is something basic like eating, loving, killing" (Berger, 1944).

In our patient, the deeper oral incorporative wishes expressed themselves also in fellatio fantasies related to her childhood experiences of being overpowered by father and having to swallow the tube. They recur in several dreams in which her manual-destructive impulses also appear:

She is in a crib, her hands tied to the sides. A toy crane runs around the crib, increases in size in a threatening manner, while she is shrinking. It wants to stuff something into her face, into her mouth. She resists, gets her right hand free, and is able to break the crane, which gets smaller again. Its jaws fall apart, and disgusting worms come out.

Both symptoms, kleptomania and bulimia, have a clearly impulsive quality, that of an inner irrational compelling need, which always gains satisfaction in the same self-damaging and usually forbidden way (Matussek, 1959).

Alexander and Staub (1929) distinguished more autoplastic neurotic symptoms from more alloplastic behavior directed against the external world, which allows the relief of drive tension through the acting out of a substitute gratification unknown to the ego. In the symptomatic act—as in this case of kleptomania—the relationship between ego and id favors the latter, as compared to neurotic symptoms where the activity of the id is less direct.

Other factors are also involved; maybe the inability of the ego ideal to offer real and adaptive wish fulfillment, so that renewed deprivations determine further regression to more primitive omnipotence fantasies. These pleasurable fantasies are retained to compensate for the unpleasure experienced in contact with the environment (Wittels, 1929; Lampl de Groot, 1963–1964).

Sexual substitute gratification is seen in both the kleptomania and the bulimia. In the past, Stekel (1922) showed this
sexual meaning in kleptomania (see also Deutsch, 1932; Fenichel, 1945; Aggernaes, 1961). The stolen objects often represent an erotic substitute. Further, the intensified wish to grasp
possession of objects indicates that these things signify strength
and power (Fenichel, 1945). This is clearly related to the deepest
experience of incompleteness, as in our patient. Van der Sterren (1946) was able to show this relationship of genital damage
to the impulse to steal in the cases of two young men.

The aggressive interactions are of extraordinary importance. The pathogenic determinants can be pursued back to
childhood. This applies similarly to the observations of Aggernaes (1961), who emphasizes in all cases the prominence of
aggressive conflicts in the mother–daughter and father–son
relationships.

In our patient, the obvious revenge motive in the act of
stealing cannot be overlooked. Abraham (1924) documented
these aggressive impulses directed toward the penis in kleptomanic women of the "revenge type"; another example (Bychowsky, 1932) also hints at this in a simpler manner.

In our patient the conflict was worked out mainly on the
oral level in relation to her mother; this was further confirmed
by her bulimia. Oral-erotic and oral-aggressive impulses were
dominant, as in a similar observation by Barag (1953).

In her actions, her intense wish for object relationships was
also expressed. To be sure, her behavior was directed exclusively against women, corresponding to her manifest hateful
protest which was determined by disappointment. Yet in this
way an otherwise inhibited relationship can come to realistic
expression. Thus she was always looking, full of curiosity,
through the stolen property for personal items such as notes,
photographs, family pictures. Stealing gave her the pretext and
the possibility for relating to others, also for expressing her
demand for attention and love.

We should also note that in other observations of kleptomania, the acts are considered simply as incomprehensible "foreign bodies in an otherwise unremarkable and harmonious

personality," or are related to an "organic restructuring" in response to a stress (Bychowsky, 1932). Otherwise it is emphasized that there is nothing to analyze, since an occurrence is involved that the techniques of psychoanalysis cannot reach, let alone explain. In one patient, the compulsion to steal was said to be caused by menstruation; when, after castration by radium, the kleptomania did not return, this was considered as proof that the cause had been menstruation (Hirschmann, 1953).

In the case of our patient, against whom criminal charges had been brought on account of her acts, other experts in court dismissed the use of the stolen money for food as an attempt at legal defense, and simply negated any relationship to her bulimic impulses. This occurred despite our attempt to prove the presence of unconscious motives as far as was possible, a requirement also pointed out by Solms (1955). In any case, the existence of relevant unconscious determinants did not mean that the accused could not be found guilty.

In this connection, a similar observation is of interest. A patient, in whom eating disturbances appeared alternately as bulimia and as anorexia, also had kleptomania, which was directed toward food, but also toward useless objects. In her case, too, the expert witness could not bring the thefts into any comprehensible connection with her oral symptoms. Nonetheless the court acquitted this patient. Then she lost her life crossing the street. She was run over by a car as she was greedily swallowing a sausage which she had just begged from someone.

REFERENCES

Abraham, K. (1924), Versuch einer Entwicklungsgeschichte der Libido. Leipzig/Wien/Zürich: Internat. Psychoanal. Verlag. A study of the development of the libido viewed in the light of mental disorders. In: *Selected Papers on Psycho-Analysis*. London: Hogarth Press, 1965, pp. 418–501.
Aggernaes, M. (1961), A study of kleptomania with illustrative cases. *Acta Psychiat. Neurol. Scand.*, 36:1–46.
Alexander, F., & Staub, H. (1929), Der Verbrecher und seine Richter. Wien: Internat. Psychoanal. Verlag. *The Criminal, the Judge, and the Public*. London: Allen & Unwin, 1931.
Barag, G. (1953), Clinical notes on kleptomania. *Samiksa*, 7:203–215. Cited in J. Frosch & N. Ross (1953), *Ann. Surv. Psychoanal.*, 4:239–240.

Berger, L. (1944), *Der barmherzige Hugel.* Zurich: Buchergilde Gutenberg.

Bychowsky, G. (1932). Uber Encephalose mit kleptomanen Impulsen. *Nervenarzt,* 5:82.

Deutsch, L. (1932), Zur Frage der Kleptomanie. *A. ges. Neurol. Psychiat.,* 152:208.

Fenichel, O. (1945), *The Psychoanalytic Theory of Neurosis.* New York: W. W. Norton.

Hirschmann, J. (1953), Periodische Kleptomanie im Rahmen von Zwischenhirnstorungen. In: *Kriminal biologische Gegenwartsfragen. Mitt. kriminal biol. Ges.,* Stuttgart:

Lampl de Groot, J. (1963–1964), Ich-Ideal und Uber-Ich. *Psych,* 17:321.

Matussek, P. (1959), Suchtige Fehlhaltungen. In: *Hdb. d. Neurosenlehre und Psychotherapie,* Vol. 2. Munchen/Berlin: Urban u. Schwarzenberg.

Solms, W. (1955), Zur Frage der Monomanien. *Wien. Z. Nervenheilk,* 11:165.

Stekel, W. (1922), *Impulshandlungen.* Wien: Urban u. Schwarzenberg.

Thomä, H. (1967), *Anorexia Nervosa.* New York: International Universities Press.

van der Sterren, H. A. (1946), Onbewust drijfveren bij het stlen. *Ned. T. Geneesk.,* 90:289.

Wittels, F. (1929), Some remarks on kleptomania. *J. Nerv. Ment. Dis.,* 69:241–251.

Ziolko, H. U. (1966), Hyperphagic und Anorexic. Nervenarzt (im Druck).—Anorexia nervosa. *Fortschr. Neurol.,* 34:353.

Name Index

535

Subject Index